GC Gunther Carstensen

Soundlab-Series

Udo Weyers

The Complete
Cubase
Handbook

Soundlab-Series

Copyright © 1992
by GC Gunther Carstensen Verlag, Munich
First published in 1992
Translated by T. Green, Gunther Carstensen
Front cover photograph by Niki Zander
Printed in Germany by
Anthofer's Satz + Druck Organisation
ISBN 3-910098-02-9
This book was designed and produced by
GC Gunther Carstensen Verlag,
Hansastraße 181,
8000 München 70,
Germany

All rights reserved. No part of this publication may be reproduced,
stored in a retrieval system, or transmitted, in any form or by any means,
mechanical, electronic, photocopying, recording, or otherwise,
without prior permisssion in writing from GC Gunther Carstensen Verlag.

Contents

Foreword by Manfred Rürup — 15

Introduction — 17

Chapter	1	**Installing the System**	19
	1.1	Versions	19
	1.2	Installation	19
	1.3	Setting up the computer	19
	1.3.1	The dongle	19
	1.3.2	Disks	20
	1.3.3	Hard disks	20
	1.4	Cable connections	21
	1.5	Power up!	24
	1.6	Initial settings	26
	1.7	The classic stumbling block: MIDI Thru	28
	1.8	Control: mouse v keyboard	29

Chapter	2	**The Basic Functions**	31
	2.1	Your first recording	35
	2.2	Important! Entering values	35
	2.3	Back to the song	35
	2.4	Changes	36
	2.5	The tempo	39
	2.6	The count-in	39
	2.7	New Tracks - the MIDI channels	40
	2.8	Mute and Solo	41
	2.9	Recording mutes	42
	2.10	Naming Tracks and MIDI channels	42
	2.11	Personalizing your Cubase	43
	2.12	Track handling	43
	2.12.1	Deleting Tracks	44
	2.12.2	The Undo function	44
	2.12.3	Moving Tracks	44
	2.12.4	Copying Tracks	44
	2.12.5	Overdub/Replace	44
	2.12.6	Manual Punch In/Out	45
	2.12.7	The locators/automatic punching	45

Contents

	2.12.8	Options	46
	2.12.9	Target practice	47
	2.12.10	Back to the locators	48
	2.12.11	Cue points	48
	2.12.12	You've got the power - Snap!	49
	2.12.13	Saving the work so far	49

Chapter	**3**	**The Parts**	**51**
	3.1	Let's go	51
	3.2	The Cycle	52
	3.3	The Cycle modes	52
	3.4	More on cycling	53
	3.5	Useful items	54
	3.6	Let's get started	55
	3.7	The first Verse	56
	3.8	Programming the locators	56
	3.9	The second Verse	56
	3.9.1	Selecting Parts	59
	3.10	Repeating Parts	60
	3.11	Deleting Parts	60
	3.12	Merging Parts	60
	3.13	The Toolbox	61
	3.13.1	The Eraser	62
	3.13.2	The Magnifying Glass	63
	3.13.3	The Part Mute	64
	3.13.4	Pencil, Scissors, Glue and a little relaxation	64
	3.14	Summary and useful tips	65

Chapter	**4**	**Additional Arrange Functions**	**67**
	4.1	The Inspector	67
	4.2	The Inspector's functions	68
	4.2.1	PRG Change and Volume	68
	4.2.2	Transpose	68
	4.2.3	Velocity and Compression	68
	4.2.4	Length	69
	4.2.5	Delay	69
	4.2.6	Exercise	69
	4.2.7	Ghost Parts	69
	4.2.8	Part Info	70
	4.2.9	The realtime aspect	70
	4.2.10	The Clipboard	71
	4.3	More Arrange functions	71
	4.4	Group Tracks	72
	4.4.1	Creating and editing Groups	72
	4.4.2	What Groups can do	75
	4.4.3	More Arrangements	76
	4.4.4	Realtime Groups	79
	4.5	A first brief summary	79

Chapter	**5**	**MIDI**	**81**
	5.1	A short history of MIDI	81
	5.2	The hardware	81
	5.3	Communication	82
	5.4	Bits and bytes	83
	5.5	Additional MIDI commands	84
	5.6	MIDI and sequencers	85

Contents

	5.7	Hard stuff: the data formats	86
	5.8	Still more numbers	87
	5.9	MIDI Program Change events	89
	5.10	Possible problems	90
	5.11	The General MIDI standard	91
	5.12	Chase Events	91
	5.13	Other non-note events	92
	5.13.1	Pitch Bend	92
	5.13.2	Tuning	93
	5.13.3	MIDI Channel Pressure & MIDI Poly Key Pressure ("Aftertouch")	94
	5.13.4	MIDI Control Change events	94
	5.13.5	The MIDI modes	97
	5.14	Tip	97
	5.15	Problems	97
	5.16	Tips on handling non-note MIDI events	99
	5.17	System Exclusive data	100
	5.18	Specialized MIDI knowledge	101
Chapter	**6**	**Data Management**	**103**
	6.1	Saving and loading	103
	6.2	Working with disks - tips and tricks	104
	6.3	The various Cubase file types	106
	6.3.1	DEF.ARR	106
	6.3.2	Song (extender .ALL)	107
	6.3.3	Arrangement (extender .ARR)	107
	6.3.4	Part (extender .PRT)	108
	6.3.5	Setup (extender .SET)	108
	6.3.6	Converting other formats	108
	6.3.7	Standard MIDI Files	108
	6.3.8	Loading Format 0 files with merge	109
	6.3.9	Loading Format 0 files without merge	109
	6.3.10	Loading Format 1 files with merge	109
	6.3.11	Loading Format 1 files without merge	109
Chapter	**7**	**Special Functions**	**111**
	7.1	Remix and Mixdown	111
	7.2	Useful: the Preferences	113
	7.2.1	Auto Save	113
	7.2.2	Mouse Speeder	114
	7.2.3	Additional options	114
	7.3	Multirecord	114
	7.3.1	Tip: using ready-made accompaniments	116
	7.4	Input Split	117
	7.5	Layer	118
	7.6	Remote control	118
	7.7	The Notepad	119
	7.8	Modules	119
	7.8.1	Operation	120
	7.8.2	Loading additional modules	122
	7.9	The Input Transformer	122
	7.9.1	The Filter function	123
	7.9.2	A summary of the Filter function	126
	7.9.3	The Transform functions	126
	7.9.4	A summary of the Transformer function	128
	7.9.5	A concrete example	128
	7.9.6	A few tips	130

Contents

	7.10	Transpose/Velocity	131
	7.11	The Track Classes	132
Chapter	**8**	**The Key Editor**	**135**
	8.1	The "normal" Editors	135
	8.2	The Key Editor	135
	8.3	The layout of the Key Edit window	136
	8.3.1	An important example	140
	8.3.2	The first edit	140
	8.3.3	Changes	140
	8.3.4	The graphic solution	142
	8.3.5	The Edit Loop	143
	8.3.6	The Toolbox	144
	8.3.7	Realtime correction	146
	8.3.8	Creating notes	146
	8.3.9	Step input	148
	8.3.10	Functions	150
	8.3.11	The Clipboard	151
	8.3.12	The Controller Display	151
	8.3.13	Modifying velocity data	152
	8.3.14	Handling data in the Controller Display	153
	8.3.15	Editing existing data	156
	8.3.16	A few facts about individual event types	158
	8.3.17	Some thoughts on the Controller Display	160
Chapter	**9**	**The List Editor**	**161**
	9.1	The event list	163
	9.2	The events' statuses	164
	9.2.1	Control Change	164
	9.2.2	Poly Key Pressure (aftertouch)	165
	9.2.3	Channel Pressure (aftertouch)	165
	9.2.4	Program Change	165
	9.2.5	Pitch Bend	165
	9.2.6	System Exclusive	165
	9.2.7	Special Events	166
	9.2.8	Text events	166
	9.2.9	Mute events	167
	9.2.10	The Stop event	167
	9.2.11	MIDI Mixer events	167
	9.2.12	The Display Filter	167
	9.2.13	The Grid	168
	9.2.14	What the Editors have in common	169
	9.2.15	Creating events	170
	9.2.16	A review of the List Editor's special functions	170
Chapter	**10**	**The Score Editor**	**175**
	10.1	The relationship between Parts/Tracks and the notation	175
	10.1.1	In general	177
	10.2	Practical applications	178
	10.2.1	The screen layout	179
	10.2.2	Display options	180
	10.2.3	Editing notes	184
	10.2.4	Moving notes	184
	10.2.5	Useful features	186
	10.2.6	Creating notes	188

	10.2.7	Additional Toolbox functions	190
	10.2.8	Note input via MIDI	191
	10.2.9	Another option	192
	10.2.10	Synopsis	192

Chapter 11 The Drum Editor   193

11.1	The initial steps	193
11.1.1	Adjusting the Drum Editor	194
11.1.2	Assigning notes	195
11.1.3	Input	198
11.1.4	The Info Line	200
11.1.5	Additional methods of input	200
11.1.6	Synopsis: the rules of the game	202
11.2	Additional functions	202
11.3	Identical functions in all Editors	204
11.4	A few tips	205
11.5	The Drum Map	205
11.5.1	Additional advantages	207
11.5.2	Converting Drum Maps	207
11.5.3	Drum Tracks and MIDI files	208
11.5.4	A tip or two	209
11.5.5	Drums and notation	210

Chapter 12 The MIDI Mixer   211

12.1	Introduction	211
12.2	Getting started	212
12.3	MIDI Thru while Mix Track is active	213
12.4	Initial steps	214
12.5	Recording MIDI Mixer events	216
12.6	Repairs	216
12.7	Problems and solutions	217
12.8	Snapshots and static mixes	218
12.9	Snapshot options	219
12.10	Replace	219
12.11	Basic rules	220
12.12	The Mixer Maps	220
12.13	The first edits	222
12.14	New objects	228
12.14.1	Sustain button	228
12.14.2	Panpot	228
12.14.3	Bank Select (e.g. for the Korg Wavestation)	229
12.14.4	Additional controls	229
12.15	Back to the beginning	229
12.15.1	The Master Fader	229
12.15.2	Text objects	231
12.15.3	The Remote Controller	231
12.16	Saving your maps	232
12.17	SysEx data	232
12.17.1	Sounds	232
12.17.2	Recording data	233
12.17.3	SysEx in various devices	233
12.17.4	More on SysEx	235
12.17.5	The checksum and some special cases	235
12.17.6	Some good advice	236

Contents

Chapter	13	**The Logical Editor**	**237**
	13.1	Starting is the easy bit	237
	13.2	The Presets	240
	13.3	The first operation	241
	13.4	Undo	242
	13.5	Exercises	242
	13.5.1	Additional criteria	247
	13.6	A first look at the Expert functions	248
	13.7	Brief review with examples	248
	13.8	Tips	250
	13.9	The edit options	250
	13.10	What you can do	251
	13.11	Examples of simple mathematical operations	252
	13.11.1	The Insert function	256
	13.12	Special data manipulations	258
	13.12.1	Dynamic operations	258
	13.12.2	Invert	260
	13.12.3	Flip	261
	13.12.4	Value 1 and Value 2	261
	13.12.5	Scale	261
	13.12.6	Reference to the Input Transformer	262
	13.12.7	Random	262
	13.12.8	Using Presets	263
	13.13	Final observation	264

Chapter	14	**Timing**	**265**
	14.1	Hardware limitations	265
	14.2	MIDI communication	266
	14.3	Cubase solutions	267
	14.4	Hardware solutions	267
	14.5	Synopsis	269
	14.6	The whole truth	269
	14.7	More on voice assignment	270
	14.7.1	Voice priority	270
	14.7.2	The actual number of voices	270
	14.7.3	Legato	270
	14.7.4	Doubled notes	271

Chapter	15	**Quantizing**	**273**
	15.1	The Cubase time grid	273
	15.2	Note lengths	275
	15.3	Challenge Cubase	275
	15.4	Back to note lengths	277
	15.5	How does quantizing work?	277
	15.6	Selecting the quantizing factor	278
	15.7	Quantize ... now!	281
	15.8	Two essential rules	281
	15.9	Critical observations on quantizing	281
	15.10	Quantizing with Cubase	282
	15.11	Manual quantizing	284
	15.12	The different types of quantizing	284
	15.12.1	Note On Quantize	284
	15.12.2	Iterative Quantize	284
	15.12.3	Analytic Quantize	288
	15.12.4	Match Quantize	288
	15.13	The influence of the quantizing factor	290

	15.13.1	First example	291
	15.13.2	Second example	291
	15.13.3	Third example	291
	15.13.4	Examples 4 and 5	291
	15.13.5	Creative Groove Quantizing	292
	15.13.6	Freeze Quantize	292
	15.13.7	Groove Quantize	292
	15.14	Your own grooves	293
	15.14.1	Changing reference points	294
	15.14.2	Lengths	294
Chapter	**16**	**Notation and Page Layout**	**295**
	16.1	Notation display difficulties	295
	16.2	The basic conditions	295
	16.3	The first important rules	296
	16.4	The essential corrections	297
	16.4.1	The correct key and clef	297
	16.4.2	Staff settings	298
	16.4.3	Flags	299
	16.4.4	The display quantization	300
	16.4.5	Additional guidance	301
	16.4.6	Polyphony	301
	16.4.7	The theory behind polyphony	302
	16.4.8	More on assigning notes to voices	304
	16.4.9	Drum notation	305
	16.4.10	Drum notes and MIDI Tracks	309
	16.4.11	Facts on drum notes	309
	16.4.12	The Drum Map as an Editor	310
	16.4.13	Rhythm notation: the single line drum staff	310
	16.4.14	Rhythm notation for guitarists	311
	16.5	The layout phase	312
	16.5.1	Choosing the printer	314
	16.5.2	The eternal printer problem	314
	16.5.3	The hardware	314
	16.5.4	Page size	315
	16.5.5	Special functions	316
	16.5.6	Special symbols	317
	16.5.7	MIDI Meaning	320
	16.5.8	Hiding displayed events	320
	16.5.9	The song title	321
	16.5.10	Layout	321
	16.5.11	Creating upbeats	322
	16.5.12	Numbering the staves	323
	16.5.13	The final polish	323
	16.5.14	Printing	323
	16.5.15	Troubleshooting	323
Chapter	**17**	**Synchronization**	**325**
	17.1	The Master Track	325
	17.1.1	Additional information	327
	17.1.2	The graphic Master Track	328
	17.2	Synchronization	328
	17.3	Cubase and simple MIDI synchronization	329
	17.4	Song Position Pointers	330
	17.5	Older sync formats	331
	17.6	SMPTE	331

Contents

	17.7	MIDEX+ and practical synchronization	333
	17.7.1	Generating a sync track	333
	17.7.2	Starting Cubase	333
	17.7.3	Post production synchronization	334
	17.8	SMPTE synchronization without MIDEX+	335
	17.9	The resolution	336
	17.10	MIDI Time Code	336
	17.11	Pros and cons	337
	17.12	Special SMPTE features	337
	17.12.1	Track Lock	337
	17.12.2	Creating polyrhythms	338
	17.12.3	Human Sync	338
	17.12.4	Additional functions	339
Chapter	**18**	**MIDI Processor and IPS**	**341**
	18.1	The MIDI Processor	341
	18.1.1	Other applications	343
	18.1.2	Quantizing	343
	18.1.3	Processing previously recorded Tracks	344
	18.2	The IPS module	344
	18.2.1	The first IPS phrase	344
	18.2.2	MIDI input parameters	346
	18.2.3	A brief review	347
	18.2.4	Interpreter settings	348
	18.2.5	The IPS modules	350
	18.2.6	The modulators	351
	18.2.7	IPS B	352
	18.2.8	Combis	352
	18.2.9	The Functions menu	352
	18.2.10	Recording IPS data in Cubase Tracks	353
Chapter	**19**	**M*ROS and Switcher**	**355**
	19.1	The M*ROS operating system	355
	19.1.1	The driver concept	355
	19.1.2	M*ROS and more	357
Chapter	**20**	**Cubase on the Macintosh**	**361**
	20.1	Hardware	361
	20.2	Available memory and the System	361
	20.3	For Macintosh IIfx Users only	362
	20.4	Installation	362
	20.4.1	Booting from floppy disk	362
	20.4.2	Booting from hard disk	363
	20.4.3	The Cubase Key	363
	20.4.4	Remove	364
	20.5	Cubase and the Finder (System 6.0.x)	364
	20.6	Cubase in the Multitasking mode	364
	20.7	Memory requirements	364
	20.8	Choosing an interface	365
	20.9	Differences from the Atari ST	365
	20.10	The Toolbox and value changes	365
Appendix			**367**
	Appendix 1:	Computer tips	367
		Hardware for the Atari ST	367
		Hardware for the Mac	367

12

Increasing the memory	368
Storage media for the Atari ST	368
Storage media for the Macintosh	369
Computers on stage	369
The mouse	370
Fan noise	370
Large-screen monitors	370
Useful software	371
Danger! Virus on the rampage!	371
Appendix 2: Conversion tables	372
Program Change table	372
Program Change table	373
Numbering formats	374
Appendix 3: The MIDI Data format	375
Additional Channel Messages	375
System Messages	375
System Common Messages	376
MIDI Realtime Messages	377
Appendix 4: Keyboard commands	378
The numeric keypad	378
Transport functions	378
The alphanumeric keypad	378
In all windows	378
In the Arrangement window	379
In all Editors	379
In the Key Editor	380
In the List Editor	380
In the Drum Editor	380
In the Score Editor	380
In the MIDI Mixer	380
In the Interactive Phrase Synthesizer	380
Appendix 5: Index	381

Contents

Foreword

When we launched Cubase Version 1.0 at the 1989 Frankfurt music fair, we at Steinberg were convinced that we had found the right concept, but none of us really knew whether the user would agree. We had, it's true, gained a large amount of experience programming MIDI recording software. We could look back on the success we had had with the Pro-16 on the C 64 computer, and we were responsible for developing the first MIDI sequencer for the Atari ST, the Pro-24. The Pro-24 saw in a new era in music software. It enabled musicians all over the world to relate to the new technology and all that it could do. Most of these musicians had had little experience with computers and were, essentially, navigating uncharted waters. All this happened in '86 through '88 in a way that exceeded our wildest dreams.

Something that we failed to predict was the variety of uses that musicians would find for the Pro-24. We had, and continue to maintain, a close relationship with our users, one which we feel is very important. The result is an on-going exchange of ideas, with suggestions, criticisms and ideas for improvement. Many of these were incorporated in the Pro-24 but, as happens in the studio, when you've filled up all the tracks, when you've used up all the effects and the desk's faders are all the way up, you either say: "that's as good as it gets", or you start over.

So we started over. The aim was to come up with a new concept; an open one, with plenty of potential for future expansion. A program that allowed the musician to concentrate on what he or she was good at: the making of music. The musician should have control over the musical arrangement at all times, with plenty of opportunity to try out ideas and to radically alter the arrangement and other things using simple tools. All this planning led to Cubase.

"Don't stop the music!" was one of our ground rules: no matter what the user wants to do, whether it be opening an editor, rewinding, adding a few notes or even saving the song on disk, the music should carry on playing. Very few musicians find having to wait for a whirring disk drive very creative, and waiting for the screen to refresh before you can carry on working can become very irritating.

This was one of the reasons we at Steinberg developed M*ROS = MIDI Realtime Operating System, a further milestone in MIDI software development, and at the heart of the Cubase concept.

But back to the beginning of my foreword. Cubase became a huge success. Its simple, straightforward concept speaks for itself, and every user has since spread the word as no advertising campaign can. Its success spurred us on to strive for further improvements in the concept, helped by the contact with Cubase users.

Music can be anything from a single note to interlocking, complex musical structures, from folk to jazz, pop to classical or movie soundtracks to avant-garde. Inevitably, this means that there are all kinds of ways of approaching the program. Although Cubase is easy to operate, and the

Foreword

user manual goes a long way to describing the individual functions, additional help in the form of practical examples makes it that much easier to get to grips with the software: that's what this book is intended to do. There are still secrets to be discovered in Cubase, in the score printing, the editors, synchronization, the Interactive Phrase Synthesizer, and much more. Following an example is often a better way of understanding a function than simply reading a description about what it does. MIDI recording is a world in its own right, and this book will help you to enter it.

But whatever you do, keep in mind that musicians love to play so above all, have fun!

I hope you enjoy this book, this world, and this program. Maybe you have a few ideas you would like to share with us and other Cubase users. We would certainly appreciate it.

Manfred Rürup
Steinberg Soft- and Hardware   *Hamburg, March 1992*

Introduction

During the early stages of electronic music, no-one could have foreseen the rapid development that has taken place in this field. Not only has the equipment become increasingly powerful, it has also gone down in price: a development more than welcomed by everybody. Instruments that used to reach the dizzy heights of $6000 a few years ago are now available at a fraction of that today - with the added bonus of increased power.

Although the concept of using computers with music was around a long time before the MIDI era, it was the introduction of the MIDI interface in 1982 that really got things going. Early experimentation with the Commodore C 64 computer hinted at the possibilities offered by the hardware, but it took higher performance computers such as the Apple Macintosh and Atari ST to raise the standard to a level acceptable for professional applications.

On the downside, the progress in technological development is making big demands on the user. Modern synthesizers and software programs often contain hundreds of functions which have to be understood before a program can be used to the best of its abilities.

This book is designed to familiarize you with one of the professional programs in this field: Steinberg's MIDI recording system, Cubase. Unlike Cubase's operating manual, this book is based on practical applications. Its numerous examples will help you to quickly grasp the program's functions. Strong emphasis is placed on the more complex parts of Cubase using practical examples to bring you and Cubase closer. It therefore makes sense to have your computer to hand as you work your way through this book: not only will you become completely familiar with Cubase but, as an added bonus, you will learn a lot about MIDI and computers.

The original version of Cubase ran on the Atari ST only. Since then, the Cubase family has grown, giving us streamlined Atari versions, and versions for the Apple Macintosh and MS-DOS computers.

You don't have to be a computer expert to be able to use Cubase or understand this book. All the steps you have to take are explained in detail. You will soon see that there are often several different ways of achieving the same result. Try them all out, and choose the method that suits you best. There's also additional information on computers and peripheral equipment, in so far as it affects Cubase, in the appendix.

There were a number of people directly or indirectly involved in the creation of this book, and I would like to take this opportunity to thank them for their input: Gunther Carstensen, Peter Gorges, everyone at Steinberg, especially Manfred Rürup, Karl Steinberg, Ralf Schlünzen and the programmers, Apple Germany, Sabine and Caro, the sub-editors for the English language edition and everyone else who in whatever way contributed to the final result.

Udo Weyers *July 1992*

Introduction

1 Installing the System

1.1 Versions

This book is based on Cubase version 3.0 for the Atari ST/TT. If you have not yet acquired this update, you should definitely consider doing so as it contains a number of useful new features and functions. The cut-down versions, Cubeat and Cubase Lite, are similar enough in operational terms to the larger Cubase program for most of the information in this book to apply to them as well. The same is true of the Macintosh and MS-DOS Cubase versions, although their user interfaces differ slightly from the Atari version. A separate chapter at the end of this book covering installation and operation is addressed to Cubase Mac users.

1.2 Installation

Let's first look at what you need to operate Cubase. All the examples in this book are based on an ST configuration consisting of an Atari 1040 ST/STE, Mega ST/STE or a TT computer with a high resolution monochrome monitor such as the Atari SM124 or SM144. If you own additional hardware, such as a hard disk, large-screen monitor or printer, you will find the relevant information in the appropriate chapters.

From version 3.0 on, Cubase users whose computers have a single megabyte of RAM may find themselves running out of memory, depending on the program configuration selected. We'll return to this topic later.

1.3 Setting up the computer

Connect all the computer components, i.e. the mouse, keyboard (for the Mega ST/STE and TT models), monitor and AC mains cable following the steps in your Atari manual. Use of a mouse mat is also recommended to keep your mouse clean.

You probably can't wait to switch your computer on, but please wait just a little longer!

1.3.1 The dongle

The Cubase package includes two manuals, two Additionals disks, and a "dongle", or key. This small red or black (depending on the version) electronic module ensures that Cubase cannot be copied or distributed illegally. Please note that version 3.0 has a new dongle: version 2.01 will not run using the 3.0 dongle and vice versa.

Installing the System

Using a dongle has both advantages and disadvantages. The main advantage is that you can (and should) make as many backup copies as you need of the program disks which themselves are not copy-protected. *Never* work with the original program disks in case you inadvertently alter or delete important files.

You cannot run Cubase without the dongle. It must be inserted in the computer before you start the program. If you lose the dongle, you effectively lose your program, so keep it in a safe place.

Insert the dongle into the ROM port located on the left side of your Atari, which is also where the MIDI ports are on the 1040 ST. The Mega ST has its keyboard port there, too. Please keep two important factors in mind: first, make absolutely sure your Atari is switched off before you insert the dongle; second, ensure the dongle is inserted with the "Steinberg - This side up" inscription facing up. Failure to observe these two caveats may lead to damage to the dongle or the computer. Or both.

Don't use brute force to insert the dongle - it's easy to plug in, and it's all too easy to damage the ROM port's terminals. If you run into problems after switching the power on (no picture, disk drive will not activate), more often than not the source is an incorrectly seated dongle. Turn your computer off and insert the dongle correctly.

1.3.2 Disks

Consult your Atari manual on how to make backup copies of disks, though you will find a better method described in the appendix of this book. You need 3.5" blank disks to make a backup copy of the program and save the results of the work we'll be doing - these are available from computer shops, mail order companies and large department stores' computer sections.

The Atari works with "double-sided, double density" (often labelled "2DD") disks. Do not buy High Density (HD) disks as your Atari cannot correctly process this format; however, some Mega STE and TT computers come with a high-density drive which is intended for HD disks. Besides the relatively expensive brand-name disks, many shops offer "no-name", unbranded disks. These disks are usually manufactured by brand-name companies, and appear to suit our purpose perfectly well.

Before you can use a new disk, you have to format it. An unformatted disk is a bit like a record without grooves - your computer will reject it. Formatting divides the disk into tracks and sectors which enables the computer to store data at specific locations on the disk and to retrieve the data later. Computer companies use different methods to apply tracks and sectors to disks, which means, for instance, that a disk formatted by an Atari computer cannot be read at all, or only under certain conditions, by an Apple Macintosh, and vice versa.

Along with your backup copy, format several more disks following the instructions in your Atari manual. We will later be saving the results of our work on these blank formatted disks. If at some point you discover you have created a musical masterpiece but do not have a formatted disk available, don't panic! You can format disks without leaving Cubase. But more on that later.

As your Atari manual will have explained, every 3.5" disk can be mechanically write-protected using the little tab in one corner of the disk. Your program disks (original and backup) should always be write-protected, though obviously you shouldn't write-protect disks you want to save songs and Arrangements on. Write-protecting does not stop the computer from reading a disk, only writing data to it or deleting data on it.

1.3.3 Hard disks

In the past, hard disks were generally peripheral to a normal Atari setup. The new TT and Mega STE models have changed all that: both versions come factory-fitted with hard disks, or at least offer them as options. The 1040 ST/STE cannot be fitted with an internal hard drive; the old Mega ST can be, though any Atari model will support an external hard drive.

Hard disk drive owners should copy all Cubase files on to the hard disk. For further details, see the appendix of this book.

1.4 Cable connections

Connect your MIDI master synthesizer and any other MIDI sound modules to your sound system.

(Please note: we will use the term "master synthesizer" or just "master" in this book to mean the MIDI synthesizer that you are using to transmit data to the computer. This catch-all term includes any MIDI device that produces a sound and that has a way of transmitting MIDI data - it could be a synthesizer, sampler with keyboard, MIDI "workstation", MIDI guitar with expander and so on. If you have a "mother" keyboard which produces no sound, this is essentially the same as having a master synthesizer for our purposes; example 4 below is for you.)

Next, connect the Atari to the other MIDI components in your system using good quality MIDI cables available from any music shop. Because there are lots of setup variations that depend on what instruments and peripheral equipment you use, this section contains a few examples of connections.

Whichever example you follow, set your master synthesizer's "MIDI Local Control" function to "Off", provided it supports this function. Disabling "Local Control" means that the circuit connecting the master's keyboard to its sound-generating section is internally severed. Some older models do not offer this feature: if this applies to you, use the method described in "The classic stumbling block: MIDI Thru".

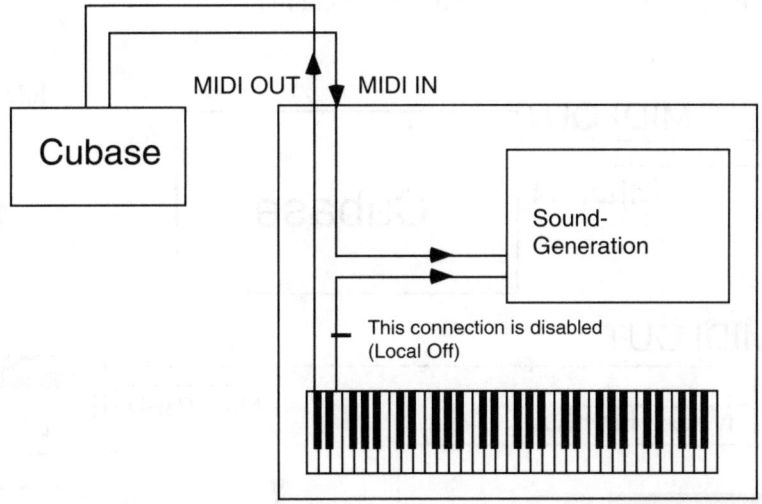

The MIDI Local Control function

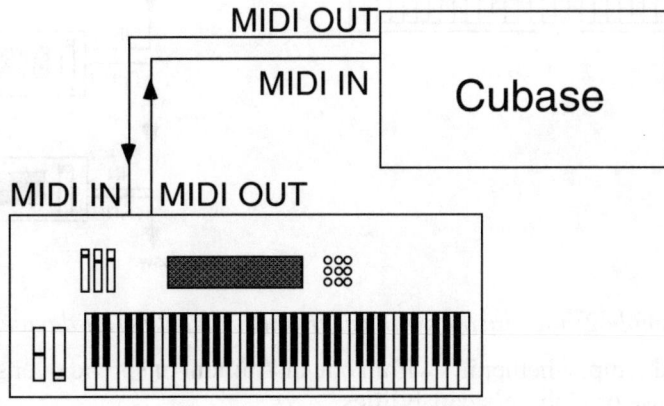

Example 1: connecting the master synthesizer to the computer/Cubase

Installing the System

Cubase as MIDI recorder: the information generated when you play your master's keyboard is transmitted from the master's MIDI Out port to the Atari's MIDI In - where it can be recorded by Cubase.

Cubase as realtime MIDI processor: furthermore, this data being generated by your master's keyboard can be instantly processed (in "realtime") by Cubase and immediately sent back from the Atari via its MIDI Out port to your master, even if you don't record it in the sequencer.

Cubase combining both of the above functions: the data being generated by your master's keyboard can be merged in realtime inside Cubase with the data already recorded and being played back, and both sets of data sent back from the Atari via its MIDI Out port to your master.

The last paragraph describes the standard configuration on which most of the exercises and examples in this book are based. However, these examples can easily be adapted to other configurations.

Whenever we discuss Cubase functions that require additional hardware or software (Midex, SMP 24 etc.), your attention will be drawn to it. If at all possible, create a multitimbral setup for the more advanced exercises in this book, either within your master synthesizer (if it is multitimbral) or using several additional synthesizers. Assign a piano sound to MIDI channel 1, bass to MIDI channel 2 and strings to MIDI channel 3. Add drums on MIDI channel 10, if available.

In case you're wondering, "multitimbral" means "able to respond to more than one MIDI channel simultaneously, allocating a different sound to each channel".

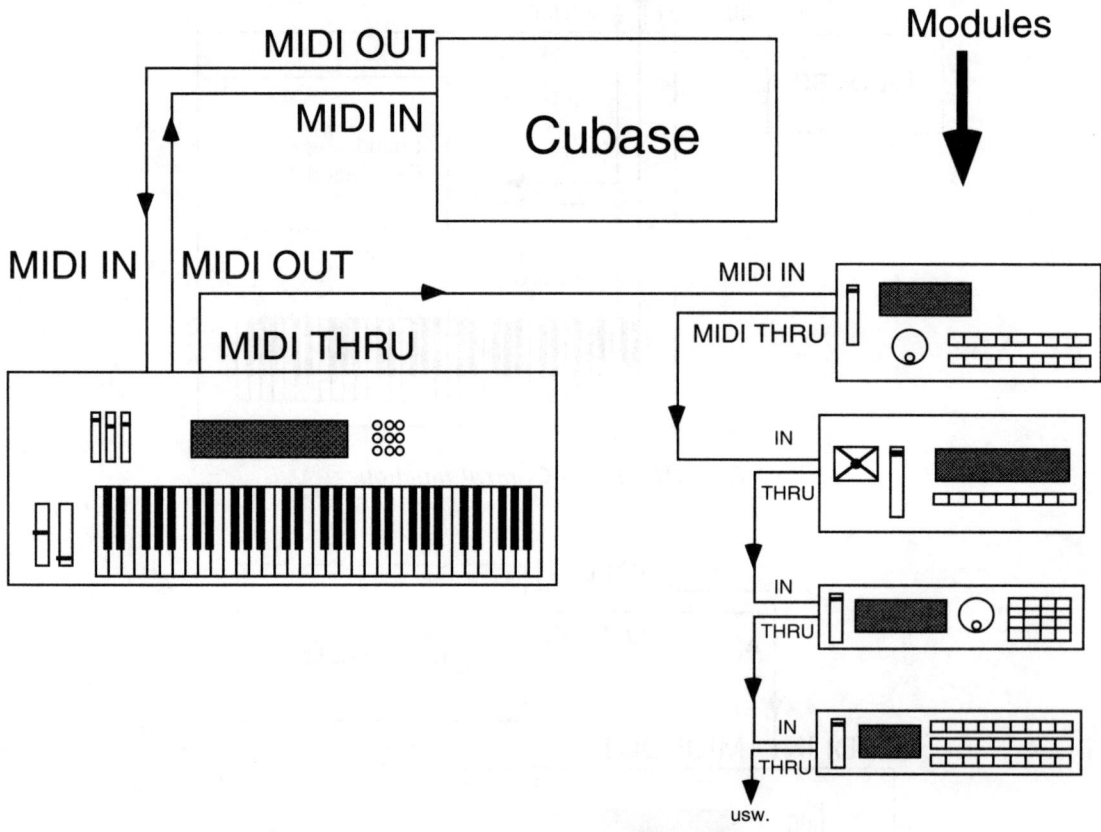

Example 2: the master synthesizer plus several MIDI devices

Use of a multitimbral setup, whether it's within one instrument or spread over several, is the best way of making full use of Cubase's capabilities.

Essentially, example 2 shows you the same setup as example 1, the only difference being that messages entering the master's MIDI In are instantly sent on to various additional modules via its MIDI Thru port.

This setup should not create any timing problems if you are using modern MIDI equipment. However, if you add too many (older) devices to this system you may run into response delays, which are perceived as timing fluctuations.

If you are fortunate enough to own several MIDI devices, do try and use a MIDI Thru box. This results in a "star" system, as follows:

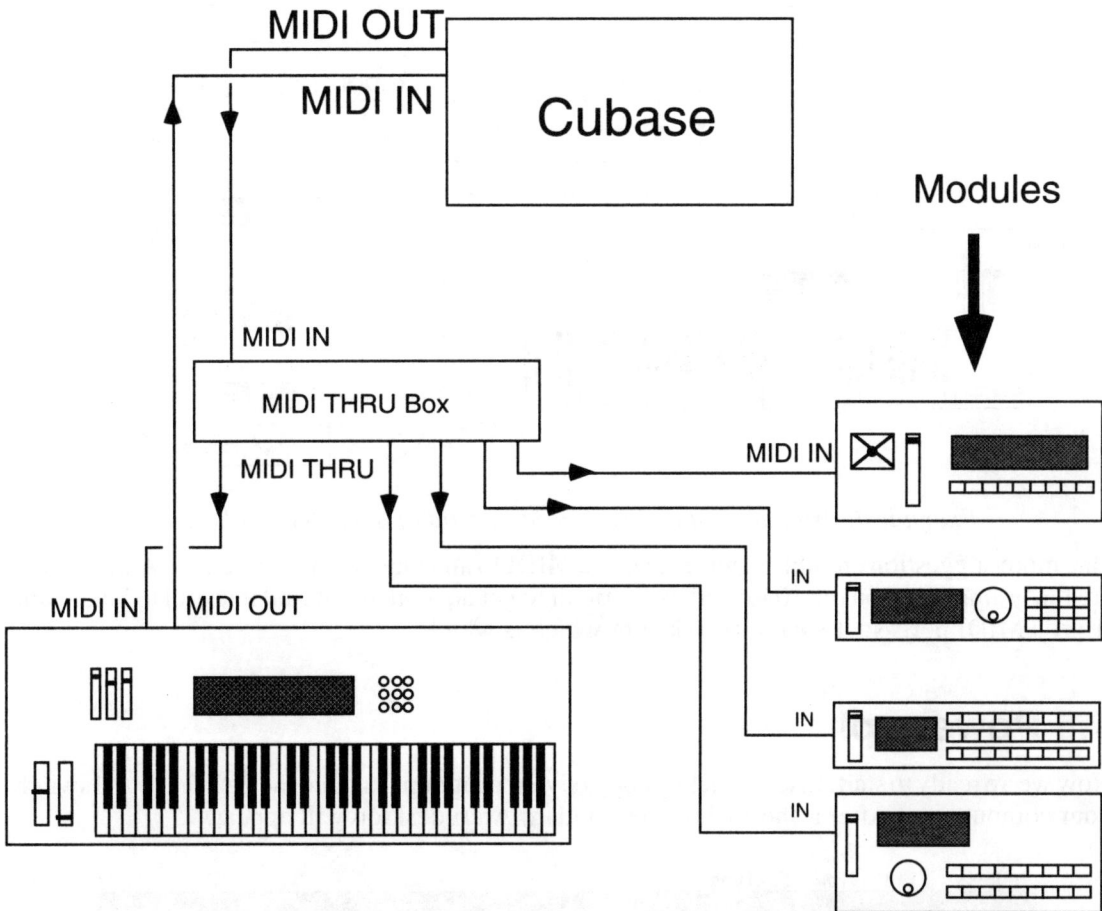

Example 3: the master synthesizer plus several MIDI devices and a Thru box

The Thru box instantly sends all the data it receives to the devices at the same time. This means that if you are using a MIDI device that has problems re-transmitting the Thru data on time, you are bypassing the problem altogether!

Plus, thanks to this "star" system, it's much easier to keep track of what cable is going where - and each device has only one cable going to it.

(Note, however, that it is rare for a MIDI device's MIDI Thru circuitry to give problems - MIDI timing problems are much more likely to be due to too much data being sent at the same time via the same MIDI port, or due to a device reacting too slowly to data being sent to it. Where MIDI Thru circuitry may well give problems is in devices that have a "soft" Thru, where you can switch a port between MIDI Thru and MIDI Out - but that's another story.)

You can, of course, replace the master synthesizer in our examples with a "mother" keyboard. Mother keyboards are sophisticated "mute" keyboards that don't generate sound, only MIDI commands. You don't need the MIDI connection back to the keyboard, and mother keyboards have no MIDI Local Control function as they don't need them:

Installing the System

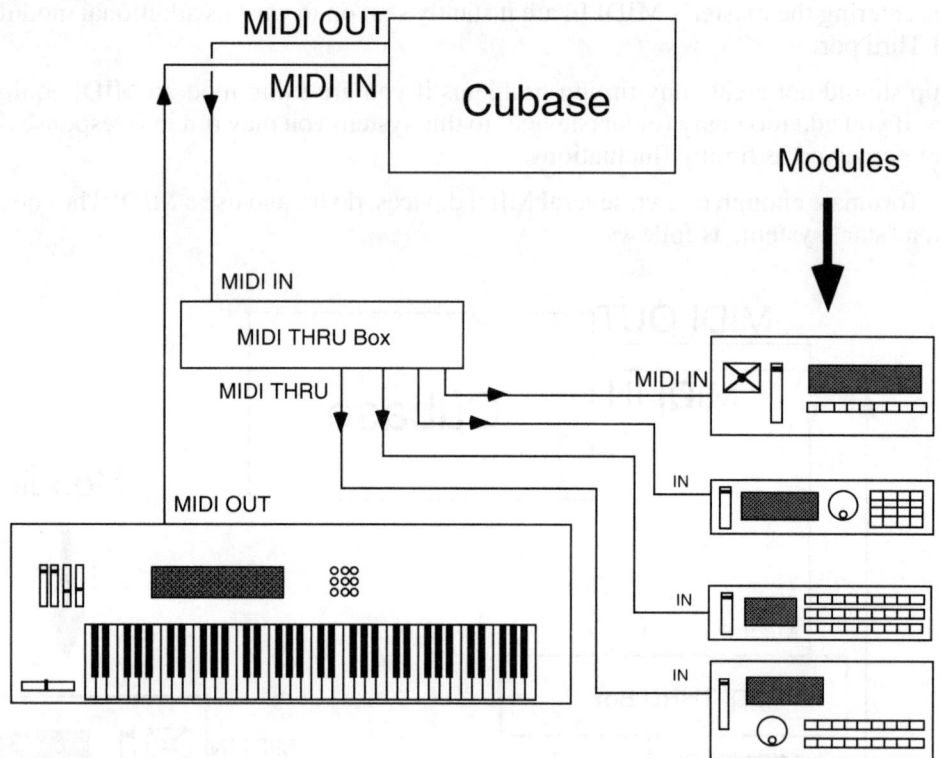

Example 4: using a "mother" keyboard instead of a master synthesizer

One more suggestion on cable connections: the MIDI In and Out inscriptions on the Atari's ports are fairly small, and on the 1040 models, difficult to get at. You might find it useful to label your Atari's MIDI ports so it's easy to make out which is which.

1.5 Power up!

Now we're ready to start. Insert a backup copy of your program disk into the disk drive and switch your computer on. After a short while the standard Atari desktop will appear.

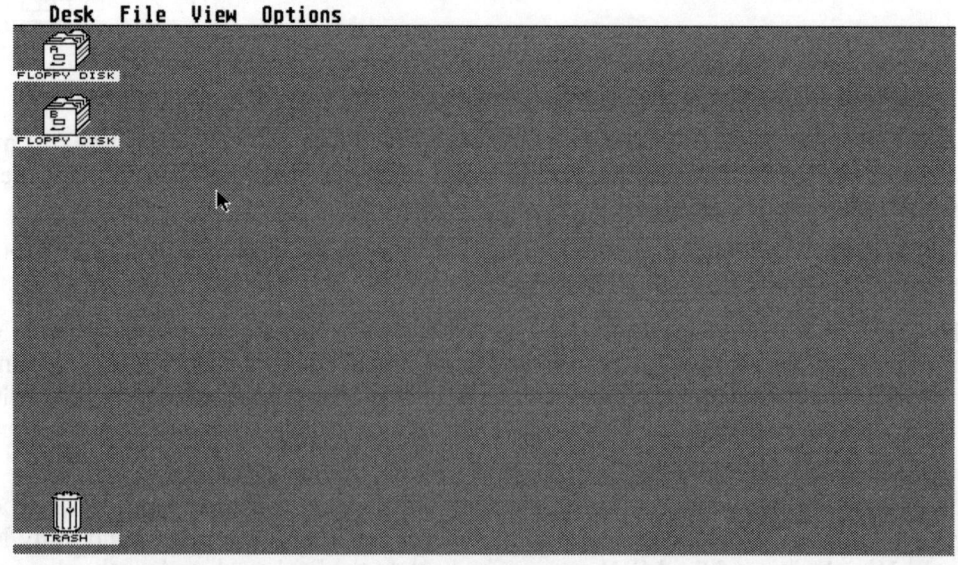

The Atari desktop

Your screen may differ slightly from the diagram above, depending on which computer model you use, whether hard drives are installed, and so on. However, in principle and for our purposes, operations are identical in all Atari ST, Mega and TT models.

Note that the contents of the disk may appear in a window that opens automatically. This is fine - all it means is that the disk was programmed to display its contents automatically on start-up. This doesn't stop you from carrying on with your reading!

There is not a great deal to see or change on the desktop. If you are already familiar with the Atari's basic operations, you will already know about the range of functions available here. However, if you are a computer novice you may want to investigate the desktop area. The best way of getting to know the Atari computer is by becoming familiar with its manual's contents. It covers basic operations such as handling the mouse, plus all the other useful things you need to know. This book on Cubase has to assume that you have read at least the basic topics in the Atari manual.

Let's look at the contents of the Cubase program disk, which you should already have inserted in drive A. To do this, activate disk icon A by placing the mouse pointer on it and clicking the left mouse button twice in rapid succession (called "double-clicking"). A window will now open displaying the contents of the disk.

A disk icon

Beginners may find double-clicking awkward, but you will soon get used to it. If, however, you are having real problems here, there is a simpler but more time-consuming alternative to double-clicking. Click disk icon A once (the icon is now "highlighted", i.e. it reverses shade). Place the mouse pointer on the File menu heading in the Menu Bar across the top of the screen: a "drop-down" menu appears. Move the pointer down to menu item "Open" (as you move the pointer to an item, it becomes highlighted) and click the left mouse button once. The disk's contents will now appear in a window.

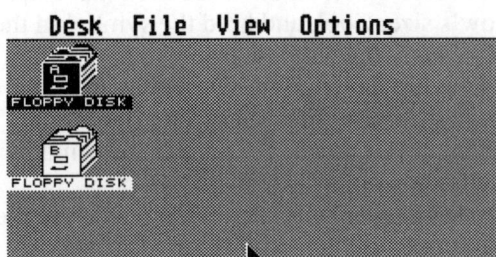

Selecting disk icon A

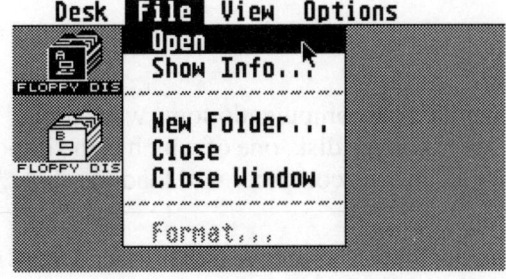

Selecting "Open"

Installing the System

The disk's contents will look something like this:

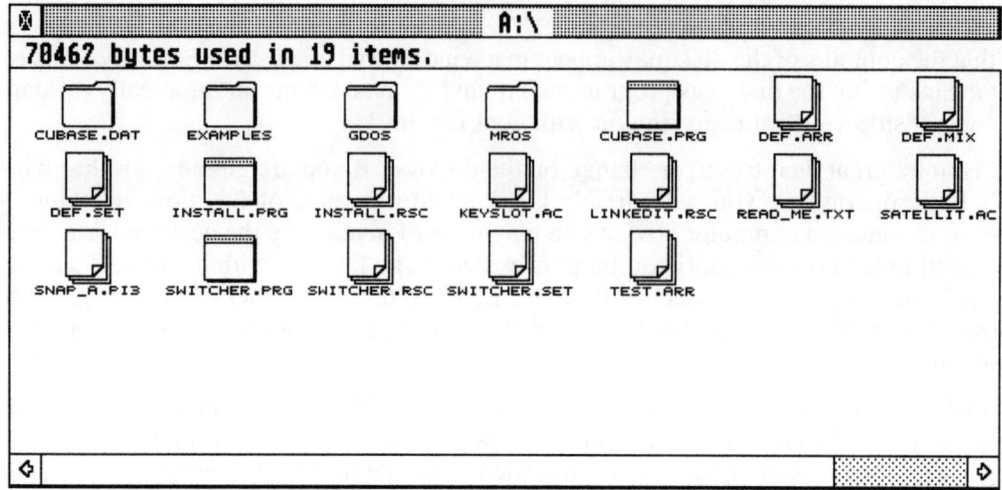

An Atari ST window displaying the contents of the Cubase program disk

If you are already familiar with the Atari's windows, so much the better: skip the following paragraphs and go to "Initial settings". If not, try the following exercises: they will help you make full use of Cubase in due course.

- Move the mouse pointer onto the shaded bar along the top of the window (the "Title Bar"). Press and hold down the left mouse button. You can now "drag" the window to another position on the screen by carefully moving the mouse pointer. Releasing the mouse button completes the operation.
- There are two "scroll bars" in the window: one along the bottom of the window and one down the right edge. The arrows at each end move ("scroll") the window's contents in the direction the arrow is pointing to. You may need to scroll a window's contents if you want to view information which is not currently in the window. A quick glance at the scroll bars will tell you whether there is more information to be seen. If the window's contents continue beyond its borders, the scroll bars become speckled in the corresponding direction, and a "scroll box" appears which you can drag along the scroll bar. For more on scroll bars, see the Atari manual.
- You can change the window's size. Click and hold the symbol in the bottom right corner (the window's "size box"), which causes the window frame to appear as a dotted line. Drag the size box until the dotted line is showing the window size you want, and release the mouse button.
- Click the diamond symbol in the top right corner (the "zoom box") to enlarge the window to its maximum size. Clicking the zoom box again returns the window to its previous size. This allows you to toggle between two window sizes.
- Click the symbol in the top left corner (the "close box") to close the window. Follow this by double-clicking disk icon A to open the window again.

For more on window techniques, see the Atari manual. As you get to know Cubase, you will come across these basic techniques again and again.

1.6 Initial settings

Being creatures of comfort we'll let the computer do some work for us. The window we have just opened contains all the file names on the disk, one of which is the important program file called CUBASE.PRG: double-click it, and the computer will load (or "boot") the sequencer program into its memory.

If you do not see this file on your screen, you have either loaded the wrong disk, or the window section on your screen is not displaying it: scroll the window's contents by clicking and holding the appropriate scroll bar arrow as described above. If you are having problems double-clicking

Initial Settings

the program file, use the alternative method ("Open" in the File menu) which we described earlier, but try not to make a habit of it.

Loading takes approximately one minute. This can be reduced to about 15 seconds if you use a hard disk. After loading is completed, Cubase's main screen, called the Arrange window, will appear.

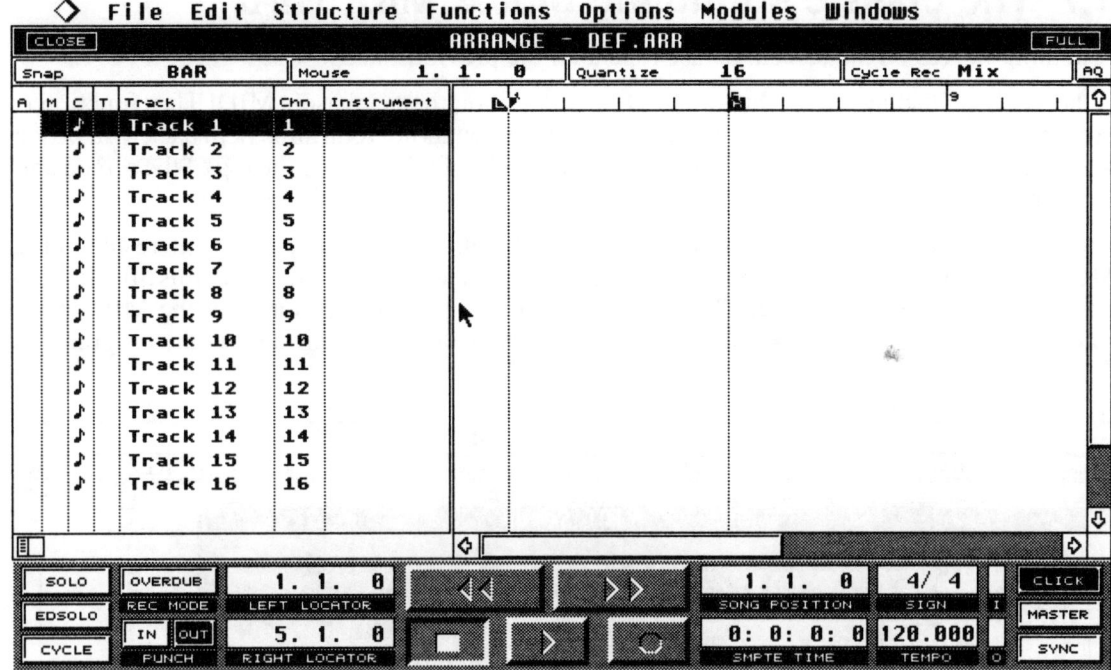

The Cubase 3.0 Arrange window

At first, the amount and variety of information in this window may confuse you. Don't worry, it's the job of this book to help you find your way around Cubase! You'll find that most operations take place in the Arrange window, including such basic and essential functions as recording, arranging, copying, and many more.

For your first Cubase steps, set your master synthesizer to receive on MIDI channel 1. Do not select a multitimbral program. Play a few notes on its keyboard. Two small displays, labelled I (MIDI In) and O (MIDI Out), should be moving in the lower right portion of the screen. This means that information is being received from your synthesizer (I) and is being sent out again from the computer (O). The master synthesizer, silenced by having its MIDI Local Control function disabled, is sounding again because its sound-producing section is now receiving MIDI messages.

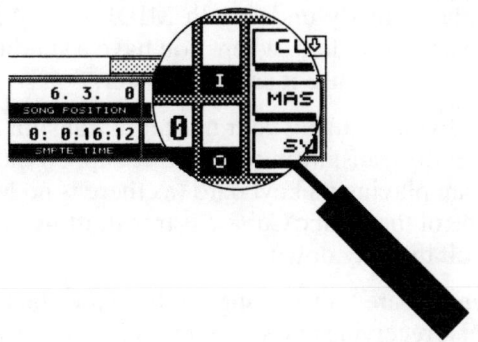

The MIDI In/Out displays

27

Installing the System

Please note: to ensure everything works the way that has been described, the first Cubase Track must be selected (Track 1 is highlighted), and its MIDI channel must be set to 1: these are the program's default settings. If for some reason this is not the case, do carry on for the time being. We will come back to this topic in a little while.

1.7 The classic stumbling block: MIDI Thru

If nothing moves on the screen, please repeat all the previous steps.

If the MIDI In display moves, but the MIDI Out does not, then Cubase's MIDI Thru function is not active. The Atari is receiving your master's signals, but is not returning them back to it. Move the mouse pointer to the Options menu heading in the Menu Bar across the top of the screen and select menu item MIDI Setup....

A new dialog box will appear on your screen. For the time being, we are only interested in the MIDI Thru Active function. There should be a checkmark in the box to the left of this title. If there isn't, click the empty box once. The checkmark will appear and denote that the MIDI Thru function is now active. Checkmarks are used to activate functions throughout the program.

Defining the Thru function

The Thru Off channel display directly underneath MIDI Thru Active can be significant. It provides the solution to a specific problem, where you have a synthesizer that does not support MIDI Local Control, but you want to use it as your master.

This is not really a problem if you are using your master to transmit data to the sequencer using a MIDI channel that Cubase is not transmitting on; all that happens here is that you will hear your master's sounds while you are playing its keyboard (as there is no MIDI Local function to turn it off) together with the sound of the device Cubase is transmitting to. If this bothers you, simply turn your master's volume all the way down.

A problem only arises when you are transmitting on the same channel that Cubase is set to re-transmit on. Here, the master is receiving two sets of messages as a result of the cable connections suggested in the examples above: one directly from its internal circuit, and the other from the Atari, via Cubase's MIDI Thru circuit. The result is an unwanted doubling of everything you play on that channel. By dialling in the offending channel in the Thru Off Channel function, you are blocking that channel from being passed through Cubase and back to the master.

Once you have entered the correct settings, exit the dialog box by clicking OK or tapping the Return key on your computer keyboard.

1.8 Control: mouse v keyboard

Let's end this chapter with a brief word on basic operations. There are two ways to execute many functions: via the mouse or your computer keyboard. For the time being, you will find yourself relying on mouse control, i.e. moving the pointer and clicking a mouse button, because mouse control is very intuitive. In the following examples you will be asked to execute functions with the mouse button: please ensure you *always* use the left button unless specifically told to use the right one.

Many functions, however, can be executed much more quickly using the computer keyboard. Once you become more familiar with the program, you will probably combine the two control methods, so this book describes both of them. Each operation is accompanied by its corresponding key command in brackets. Simply press the appropriate key or key combination on the alphanumeric keypad or the numeric keypad (the latter is the calculator-type cluster at the far right of the Atari keyboard).

Installing the System

2 The Basic Functions

Now that we have booted Cubase, we will spend some time looking at the Arrange window in detail.

It consists of three basic elements:

- The Menu Bar along the top of the screen is used to select additional commands or call up other areas of Cubase. Move the mouse pointer onto the Menu Bar: as it touches each menu heading, a drop-down menu appears, containing a number of items. As you move the pointer down a list of items, they highlight in turn: clicking a highlighted item selects its function.

To get rid of the menu without selecting any item, simply click anywhere outside the menu.

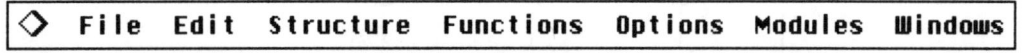

The Menu Bar

- The Transport Bar located along the bottom of the screen contains functions that correspond roughly to those of a tape recorder. It is used to start, stop, and execute other control commands.

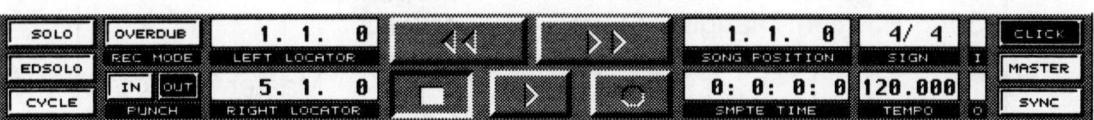

The Transport Bar

- Between the Menu and Transport Bars, which are identical throughout Cubase's various screen pages, you will find a window, which in this case is the Arrange window. This Arrange window can itself be divided into three elements:

- The lefthand area contains the sequencer Tracks with their MIDI channels and other assignment functions. Cubase defaults to displaying 16 Tracks, which can be increased to up to 64 if required.

- The major area of the Arrange window consists of a white surface which we'll call the Part Display: this is where graphic information is presented, showing you if and when the Tracks are playing. The line directly above it containing numbers (1, 5, 9, 13...) is the Position Bar which tells you where you are within the song at any given moment.

The Basic Functions

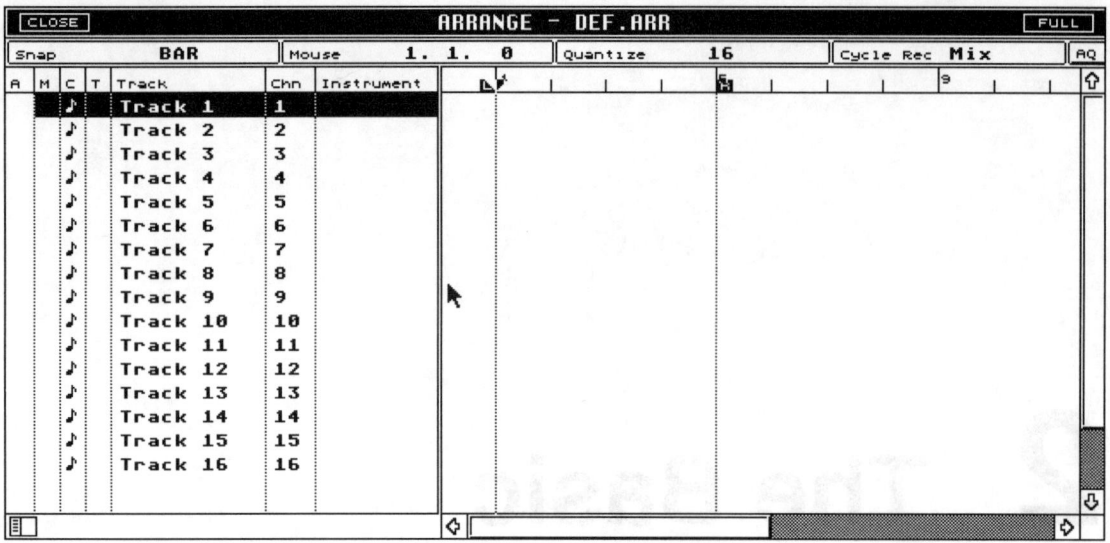

Now for an overview of the Transport Bar.

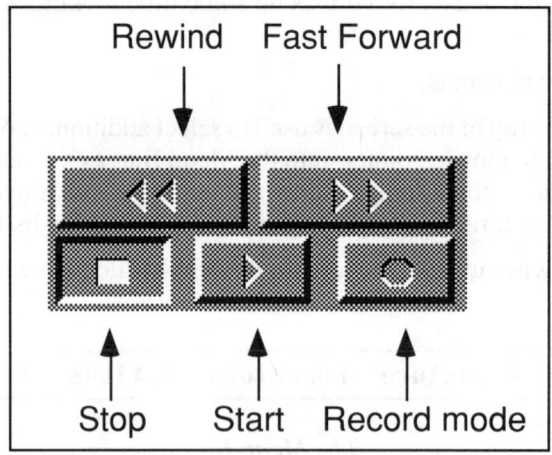

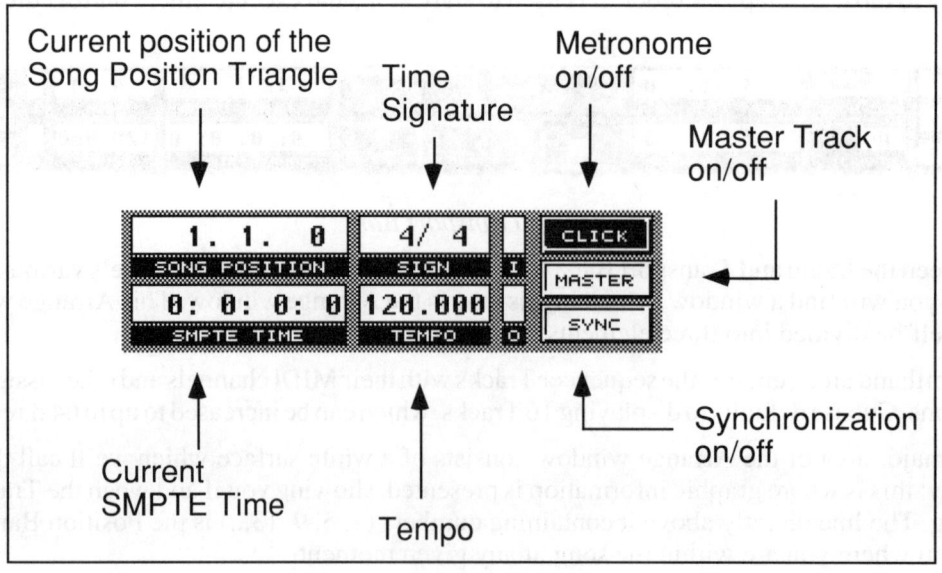

32

The Basic Functions

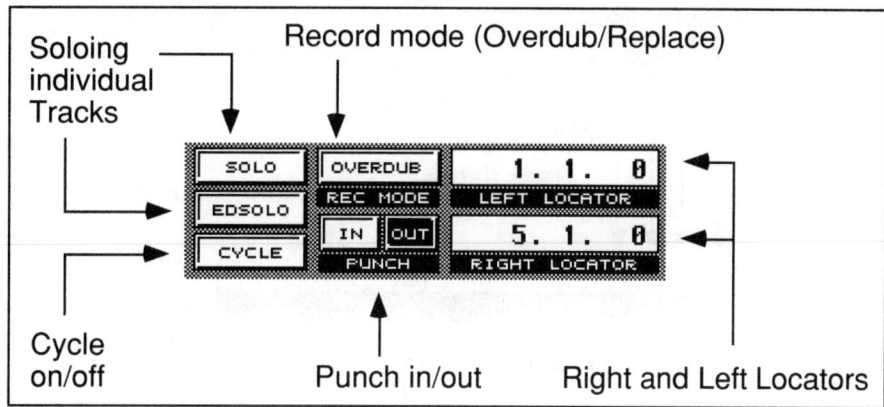

There's also the Functions Bar, containing terms such as "Snap", "Bar", "Mouse", etc., located between the elements of the Position Bar and the Menu Bar. We will learn more about this later; meanwhile, here's a quick overview:

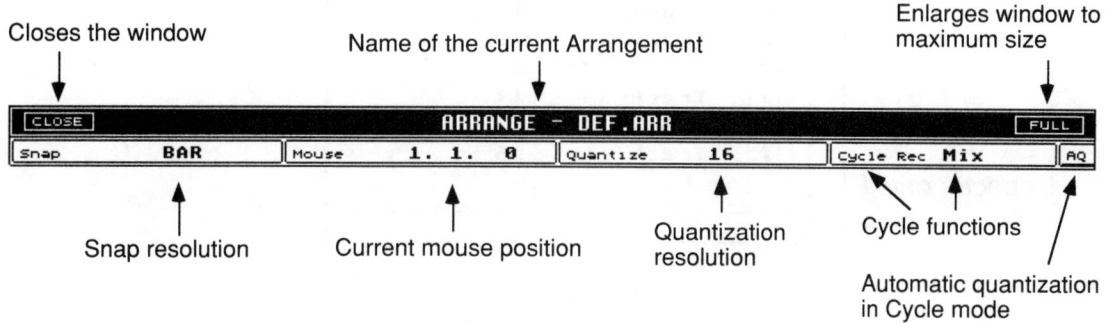

The Functions Bar

The following diagrams show you the individual elements of the Arrange window in detail.

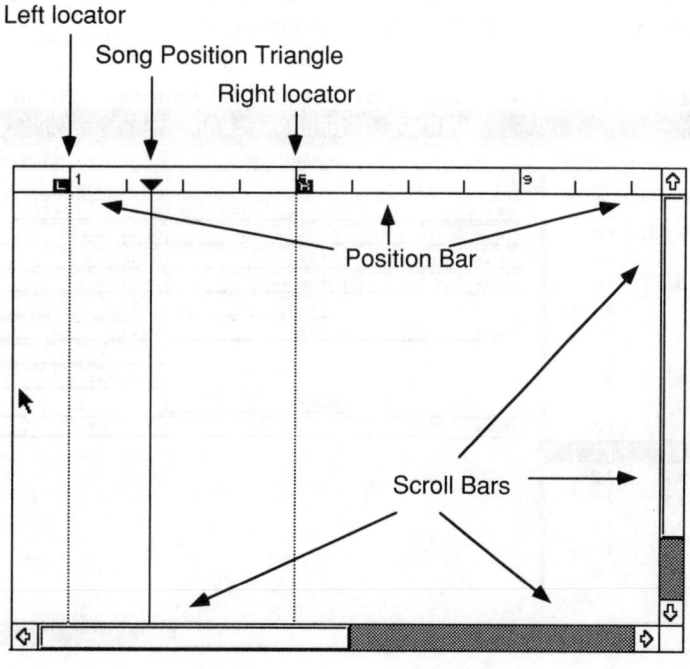

The Part Display

33

The Basic Functions

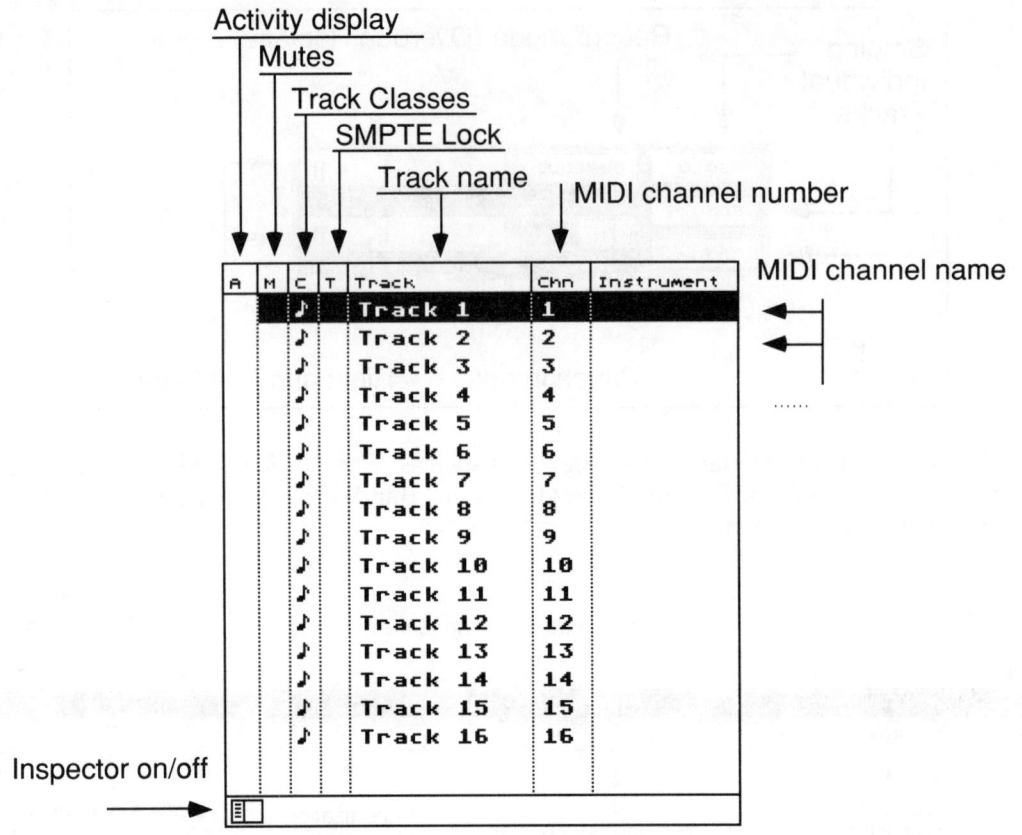

The Track List

If you record something in a Track, horizontal beams appear in the Part Display. Each beam represents the length and location of a recording. This beam is called a "Part", as it forms part of an overall Track. This is rather like multitrack recording on a tape recorder; in fact, the way Cubase works and is displayed leans heavily toward multitrack recording with tape. If you have ever seen a multitrack tape recorder's track sheet, you will find the following illustration familiar. Your Arrangements will look something like this later on.

The Arrange window containing recorded Parts

2.1 Your first recording

The best way to become familiar with the many functions and displays of the Arrange window is to try them out and experiment, so let's record something. Loosen up your fingers, we're ready to roll.

We will record a Part on the first Track. To do this, you must first select a Track. A selected Track is denoted by a black beam that highlights it.

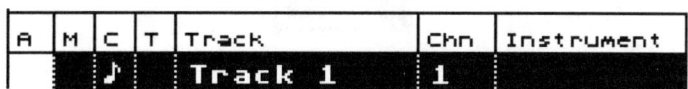

A selected Track

A Track that's not selected

After you have booted Cubase, the first Track normally defaults to MIDI channel 1. If this is not the case, click on the word "Track 1".

Move the mouse pointer to the first Track's MIDI channel display (Chn) and set the value to 1 as described in the following paragraphs.

2.2 Important! Entering values

There are two ways to enter values in Cubase. Try them both out.
- Click the MIDI channel's value with the left or right mouse button. The value will change with each click, moving up with the right button and down with the left. Keeping a mouse button depressed makes the values scroll further. To accelerate the scrolling in either direction, press the computer's [Shift] key in addition to the mouse button, or press the other mouse button in addition to the first one.
- You can also type in values. Double-click the value you want to change: an empty input field will appear. Enter the desired value via the top line of the alphanumeric keypad or the numeric keypad. Then press the [Return] key.

Go for the method you feel most at home with.

These two inputting methods, i.e. using the left and right mouse buttons or double-clicking and typing numbers + [Return], are used to enter all the values in the program. Use one of these two methods when you are asked to enter a value.

2.3 Back to the song

After this short but essential detour, we return to our recording. Ensure your computer monitor's volume is turned all the way up. Start the recording by clicking the Record button (computer keyboard: [*] on the numeric keypad).

The Record button

35

Cubase will provide you with a two bar count-in, after which the recording starts. Record something as long or as short as you like (a song can be up to 9999 bars long!) though around eight bars would seem like a good length to start with.

Stop the recording by clicking the Stop button (computer keyboard: [Spacebar], or [0] on the numeric keypad).

The Stop button

Cubase ends the recording process and stops at the current position in the song. We now want to listen to the results, so the sequencer must be "rewound". At this stage, there are two methods: click one of the spooling buttons to move freely throughout the song (computer keyboard: [(] for rewind and [)] for fast forward on the numeric keypad).

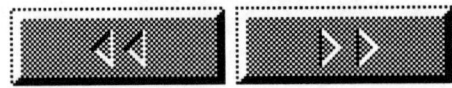

The spooling buttons

Pressing the [Shift] key in addition to the mouse button, or additionally pressing the other mouse button, accelerates the "spooling". However, we will use a much simpler method:

If you press the Stop button a second time, Cubase automatically returns to the beginning of the song. Do this, then start the playback by clicking the Start button (computer keyboard: [Enter] on the numeric keypad).

The Start button

You can interrupt playback at any given time, whereupon Cubase will stop at the current song position. When you start playback again, your song will continue from this position.

The Start button operates in a "Continue" mode, i.e. Cubase will always continue playing from the current song position when Start is pressed. If you have had the opportunity to work with other sequencers, you will notice a difference here as most other sequencers automatically return to the beginning of the song when Start is pressed.

2.4 Changes

During recording and playback, you may have noticed a few things that call for an explanation. After the two bar count-in, a little triangle called the Song Position Triangle begins to move in the Position Bar, accompanied by a vertical dotted line in the Part Display. It tells you where you are within the song. When it reaches the border on the right side, the Position Bar scrolls on, and the next bars are displayed.

At the same time, a counter bearing the inscription "Song Position", located in the Transport Bar at the bottom right of the screen, displays the exact bar position as a numeric value. Beneath this counter is another one entitled "SMPTE Time".

We will come back to that one later. The previously blank Arrange window now contains a black beam, representing our first recording, i.e. our first "Part".

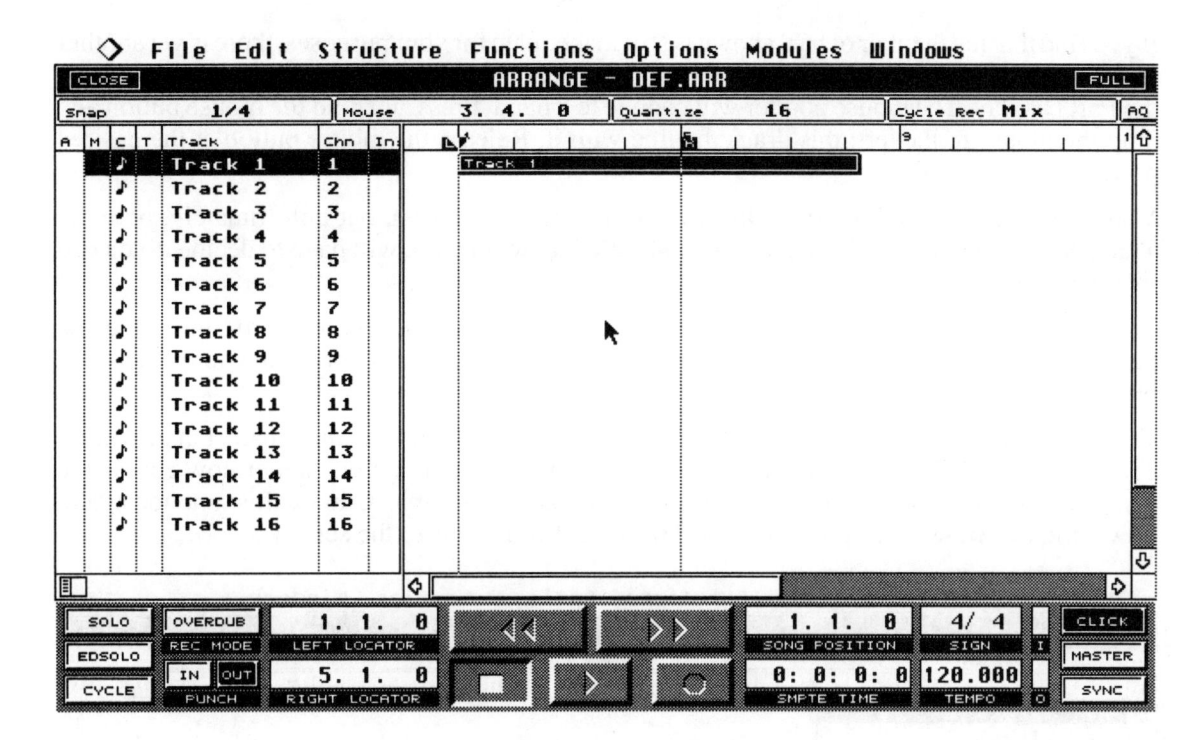

This is what your screen should look like now

When you are in playback mode, the activity display in column A (at the front of Track 1) shows when MIDI data is being sent.

If you are not satisfied with the results of your efforts, or if you have made a mistake, simply delete the Part with the help of the [Backspace] or [Delete] keys and record a new one. Later on, you will be introduced to far better methods for deleting errors.

If the problem is due to timing and not incorrect notes, the quantization function may help. Quantizing can correct timing errors within a certain framework. Move the mouse pointer to the Menu Bar and choose "Over Quantize" from the Functions menu (keyboard: [Q]). Cubase will now attempt to adjust your recording to the correct time. This function normally does the trick, but it might not. Listen to your recording again.

We will examine quantization and how it works later on in greater detail.

Did you record more than eight bars? If so, you have probably noticed that the Position Bar has moved. The Arrange window defaults to displaying approximately 16 bars. When you go beyond this limit, the Position Bar moves on. This is called "scrolling" as well, something which we will encounter again at later stages.

If you want, you can switch the scroll function off. Go to the Options menu and choose "Follow Song": its checkmark disappears, and the Position Bar no longer moves when the Song Position Triangle reaches the screen's right border. Click "Follow Song" again to reactivate it.

Despite this assistance, being able to see only a few bars on the screen can become bothersome. But don't panic, help is at hand. You can change the Position Bar's display resolution by "zooming" it.

Two scroll bars containing arrows at either end are located at the bottom and the right edges of the screen. Place the mouse pointer on the left arrow of the horizontal scroll bar and press the *right* mouse button.

The scale of the display has changed! More than 16 bars are now being shown. If you keep the mouse button depressed, the zooming will continue - upwards of 100 bars can be displayed at a time in the Arrange window. To reverse the scrolling and return to the original scale, click and hold the right mouse button on the righthand scroll arrow of the scroll bar.

The Basic Functions

If you find that the number of bars shown is still inadequate for your purposes, there is yet another method to enlarge the display area. Point at the vertical double lines between the Track List and the Part Display. The mouse pointer will change to a hand. Press and hold the mouse button and drag the mouse to the left: this drags the line with it. Release the mouse button at the desired position.

You have now enlarged the Part Display. More bars can be seen, but unfortunately, both the Track names and the MIDI channels are concealed. Later on, you will have to decide if you can live with this situation.

We will leave the Part Display at its standard size for our purposes. In other words, move the line back to its original location (mouse pointer on the line (hand appears), press and hold the mouse button, drag it back to the right).

The Transport Bar can be removed from the screen to not only display more bars, but also more Tracks. Go to the Windows menu and choose "Hide Transport". You cannot now access the Transport Bar with the mouse, but keyboard control is still possible. Choose this function again, now entitled "Show Transport", and the Transport Bar returns to the screen.

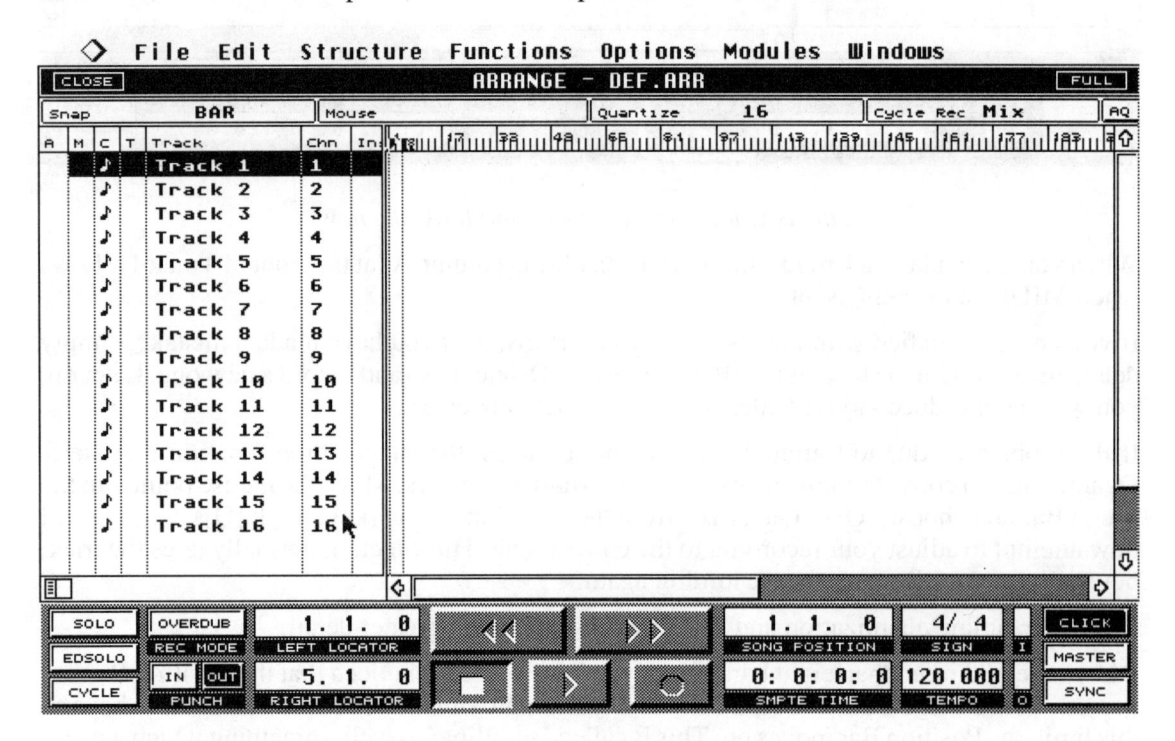

Zoomed Part Display

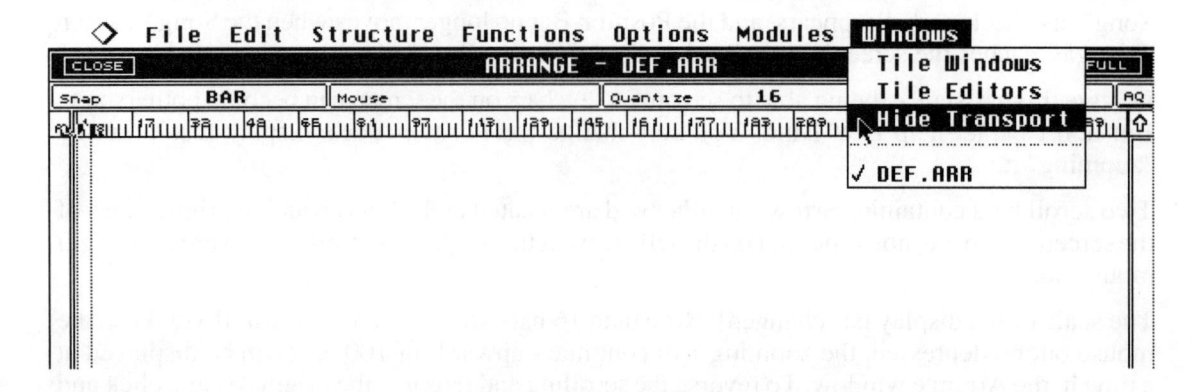

This menu command hides the Transport Bar

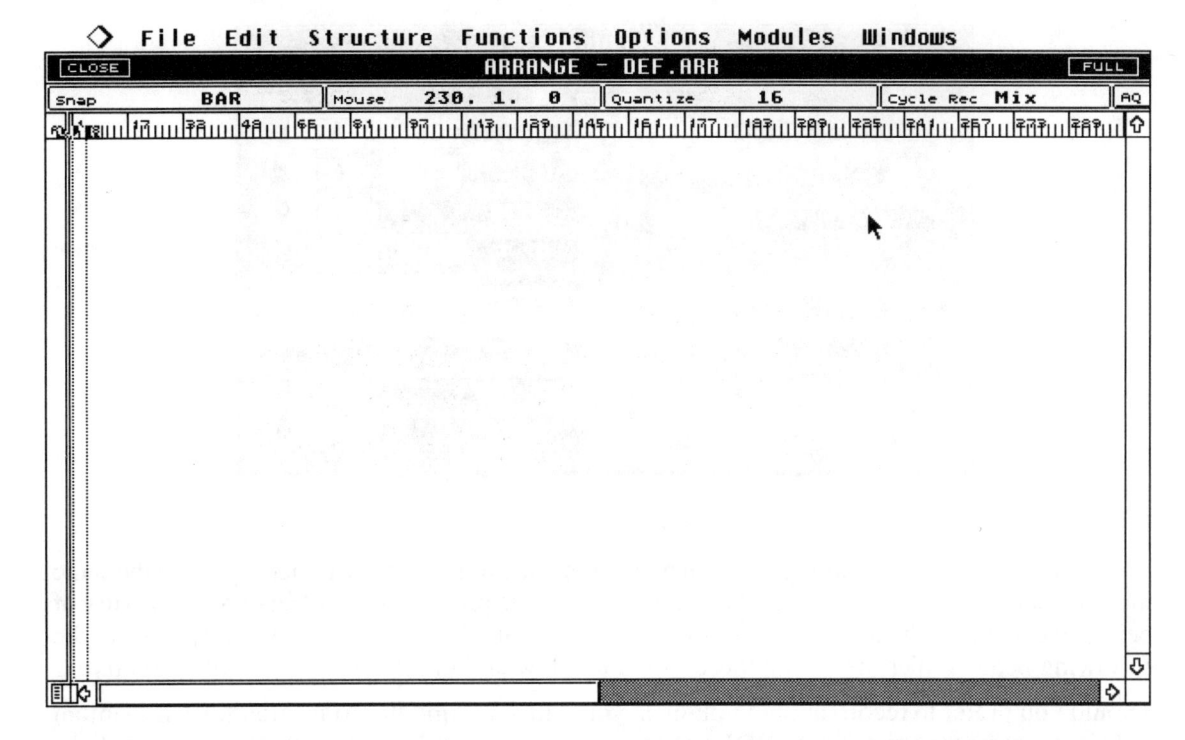

The Part Display at maximum size (on a standard monitor) with the border moved left

This principle of horizontal zooming applies to the vertical direction as well. Click the vertical scroll bar's upper (zoom out) or lower (zoom in) arrows to determine the number of displayed Tracks. Do you recall the information about how to handle the Atari's windows at the beginning of this book? The Arrange window behaves in the same way as a normal Atari window.

Go ahead and try a few things out. Go to the white square in the bottom right corner of the Part Display: this is the "size box". Press and hold the left mouse button and drag the size box to alter the size of the window. Click the Full button at the top right of the screen to return the window to its original size.

2.5 The tempo

If you liked neither the tempo nor the count-in, you can easily change them. The current tempo is displayed in the box next to the SMPTE time. It defaults to 120 when the program is first started. Place the mouse pointer in the box and change the value using one of the methods described above.

There is a third inputting method used for nothing other than changing the tempo: tapping the plus/minus keys on the numeric keypad.

2.6 The count-in

Was the count-in too long, too short, or maybe you didn't like the sound? No problem. Go to Options in the Menu Bar and choose "Metronome". A box containing a number of parameters appears, in which all sorts of changes can be wrought to the count-in.

First, we will turn our attention to the "Precount Active" function ("Precount" is what Cubase calls a count-in). The checkmark denotes that the count-in is active. Clicking the checkmark makes it disappear and disables the count-in. You can adjust the length of the count-in in the field to the right of the "Bars" inscription (you know how: right/left mouse button or double-click, enter number, press [Return]).

The Basic Functions

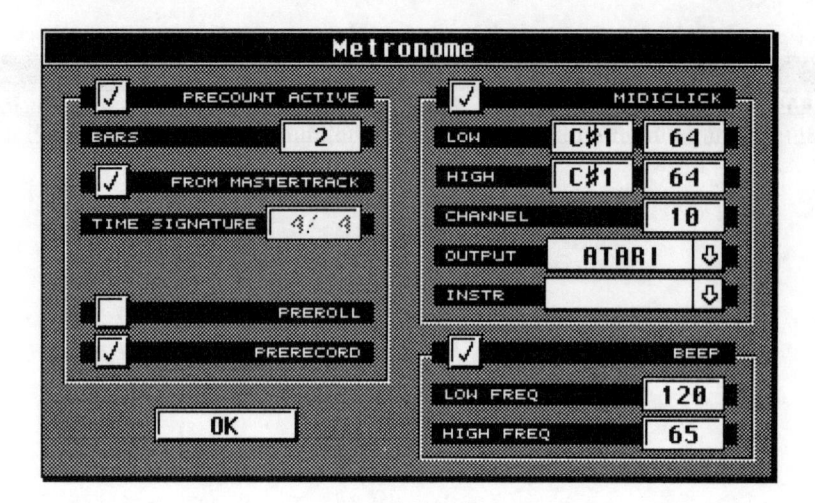

The Metronome box

The "Beep" inscription refers to the actual metronome itself. It can be switched off using the same method that we came across with "Precount Active". The program even offers you the luxury of being able to adjust the monitor metronome's pitch for the first beat of a bar separately from the following beats. Experiment with these functions (low and high) and find a setting you like.

Should you prefer to record at high volumes, you will soon find the Atari monitor's maximum volume level far too quiet. The "MIDIclick" function is the solution, where the metronome clicks are sent via MIDI to an instrument of your choice, allowing you to determine both volume and sound.

Set the MIDI channel to that of the sound module you've chosen, in this case MIDI channel 1. The pitch of the metronome signal can be adjusted in the same manner as that of the monitor metronome, i.e. separately for the first and the following beats. You can edit the volume and velocity of the MIDI clicks as well. Find the settings you prefer. To avoid dissonance and clashing notes, you might like to select pitches that are compatible with the key your composition is in.

Do you have a drum machine, sampler, or does your keyboard feature built-in drum sounds? Great! In this case, don't use just any old MIDI note, but choose instead a cowbell, sidestick, or hihat sample. Set the metronome's MIDI channel to the MIDI receive channel of your drum machine or sound module (this can also be a MIDI channel of your master synthesizer, of course). Many manufacturers use MIDI channel 10 for drum sounds, which explains why Cubase defaults to it. The MIDI note settings must match those of your MIDI device's samples: consult its manual to find out which sounds are assigned to which MIDI notes, or use the mouse to scroll through the low/high values until you hear the sounds you want. You can create an accent on the first beat by setting a higher velocity value.

When you have finished with the Metronome box, press [Return] to go back to the Arrange window. In some situations, you may not need the metronome, in which case click "Click" at the bottom right of the Arrange window to turn it off (keyboard: [C]). The MIDI metronome and the monitor's metronome are now disabled, and only the count-in for the recording will still be heard.

2.7 New Tracks - the MIDI channels

Let's now continue working on our song, recording another Track in addition to the first. Click Track 2 (keyboard: [down arrow]) to highlight it. Ensure that MIDI channel 2 is selected. Play a few notes on your keyboard. If you are using our initial multitimbral setup, you should be hearing a bass sound. If your instrument is not capable of playing several sounds simultaneously, and you have just the one instrument available, then set the MIDI channel of the second Track back to 1 and continue to work with the piano sound.

This example shows that Cubase's MIDI Thru function re-routes incoming MIDI signals (the keys that you are playing) to the MIDI channel you've selected in an empty Track. Your keyboard's transmit channel is ignored. There's one exception to this rather practical rule: if you set a Track's MIDI channel to "Any", then the incoming MIDI notes are not re-routed to a new channel, but go to the MIDI device dictated by your master's transmit channel.

Continue with the rest of the Tracks as you see fit. You are now in a position where you can play on virtually as many Tracks as you like on the same or on different MIDI channels. If the standard 16 Track setup is insufficient, you can call up additional Tracks by double-clicking a free (white) section of the Track List (keyboard: [Control][T]).

2.8 Mute and Solo

If you want to listen to only certain of the Tracks of your composition, you can silence those Tracks you don't want to hear with the help of the Mute function. Click the "M" column to the left of the Track's name. This Track is now marked with a dot, which denotes that the Track is muted. To reactivate the Track, click the mute dot. Ensure that you do not mute while recording, because the action of muting can be recorded and played back, too.

The first two Tracks are muted

It is advisable to listen to Tracks one by one when attempting to find mistakes. You can do this quite quickly by selecting the desired Track with a mouse click and clicking the "Solo" function in the Transport Bar (keyboard: [S]): every Track other than the one you have selected is now muted. Repeating this disables the soloing. By the way, the computer's up/down cursor keys can also be used to move between Tracks.

The Cueing function can also be useful here. Go to the beginning of the song and keep the *right* mouse button pressed on the Fast Forward button. Your Arrangement will now play back until you release the mouse button. Drag the mouse to the left to increase playback speed, to the right to decrease it. Simultaneously pressing [Shift] or the left mouse button achieves more rapid tempo changes. Note that the tempo change is only temporary: your song's actual tempo does not change.

Using Mute and Solo together is helpful for some applications. To listen to three Tracks out of a total of 24, you could manually mute the other 21, impractical as it might seem. A far better method is to select a Track, solo it, and switch the other two Tracks back on.

Additionally, Cubase offers a way of pre-programming up to ten Mute configurations:

First mute the desired Tracks as described above. Press and hold the [Shift] and [Alternate] keys, then press the [F1] function key at the top of your computer keyboard. The mute configuration is now saved. Let's try it out. Reactivate the muted Tracks by clicking each mute dot individually. Press [Alternate] and [F1] simultaneously. The mute configuration you just set up should reappear. As your Atari ST has ten function keys, so you can set up ten mute configurations.

To delete a stored mute configuration, set up and save a new one using the same function key, whereupon the previous configuration is replaced.

The Basic Functions

It's a good idea to have one configuration in which none of the Tracks is muted, so you can quickly switch back to normal. This is because it's not possible to switch off the pre-programmed mutes by simply pressing the same function key again. In order to make best use of the programmable mutes, it makes sense to get used to working in quite a structured way. When recording, make it a habit to always assign specific instruments to the same Tracks, such as using the first three Tracks for drums and percussion, the fourth for the bass, etc. This will ensure that you make best use of the mutes (e.g. muting just "drums" or "drums and bass").

2.9 Recording mutes

We mentioned earlier that Cubase records mutes if they are activated during the recording of a Track. You can stop this happening by going to the Options menu and looking at the menu item called Record Tempo/Mutes. A checkmark by the item denotes all mutes are recorded. Click the item once to remove the checkmark.

The recording of mutes can and should also be used creatively, such as for simple arranging within a lengthy song. Not only are manual mutes recorded, but you can also record the mute configurations described earlier by recalling them using the function keys during your recording.

2.10 Naming Tracks and MIDI channels

At the moment, the Tracks are entitled "Track 1", "Track 2," etc, which doesn't tell you very much. You can enter more descriptive names by double-clicking the name "Track 1": a frame will surround it. Delete it by pressing the [Esc] key on your computer keyboard, or by using the [Backspace] key. Enter a new name, such as "Piano" and confirm the entry by pressing the [Return] key. Name all the other Tracks recorded so far using the same method.

A blank space called "Instrument" is located next to the MIDI channel column, which is where you can assign names to MIDI *channels*. Select an empty Track and set it to MIDI channel 1. Double-click the blank space between the Track and MIDI channel: the naming frame will appear. Enter a name for MIDI channel 1. If you are using several instruments, the ability to name a channel according to its instrument is a boon. You may find that entering the name of a particular sound is not particularly helpful, as one Track could contain a number of different sounds. Nevertheless, the choice is up to you and how you organize your work.

Confirm the entry by pressing [Return]. Now set this Track's MIDI channel to 2. Name the second MIDI channel as described above. Of the remaining 14 channels, name those you are using for the composition. The Track List containing a recording, complete with a set of names, could look something like this:

A	M	C	T	Track	Chn	Instrument	Output
	●	♪		Basic	1	JV-80	ATARI
	●	♪		Drum Guide	10	R-8M	ATARI
		♪		Drum	10	R-8M	ATARI
		♪		Drum Add	10	R-8M	ATARI
		♪		Piano	16	SY-99	ATARI
		♪		Bass	3	Oberheim	ATARI
		♪		Groove	5	SY-77	ATARI
		♪		Strings	3	Oberheim	ATARI
		♪		Special	9	Microwav	ATARI
		♪		Adds	10	R-8M	ATARI
		♪		Zap	12	S-1100	ATARI
		♪		Zap Zap	12	S-1100	ATARI
		♪		Add Perc	13	D4	ATARI

The Track List

Track Handling

Naming Tracks and MIDI channels is not absolutely essential, but it does help you find your way around. Being able to name MIDI channels has another advantage: have you named several MIDI channels? Then click and hold on an empty Track's Instrument field. A "pop-up" menu appears, containing the MIDI channel names you've already entered. Drag the mouse through the list while holding the mouse button down - to select a name once it is highlighted, release the mouse button; this selects that name's MIDI channel as well. You can see why this is a good way to work: it means you can go by the instruments' names when you're assigning Tracks to instruments or sounds instead of having to memorize the individual MIDI channel numbers. This also allows you to quickly set the MIDI Thru function, and it's easy to alter the channel of already-recorded Tracks.

Now change the first Track's MIDI channel back to 1 if it's not already there.

A	M	C	T	Track	Chn	Instrument	Output
	●	♪		Basic	1	JV-80	ATARI
	●	♪		Drum Guide	10	R-8M	ATARI
		♪		Drum	10	R-8M	ATARI
		♪		Drum Add	10	R-8M	ATARI
		♪		Piano	16		ATARI
		♪		Bass	3	D4	TARI
		♪		Groove	5	JD-800	TARI
		♪		Strings	3	JV-80	TARI
		♪		Special	9	Microwav	TARI
		♪		Adds	10	Oberheim	TARI
		♪		Zap	12	R-8M	TARI
		♪		Zap Zap	12	S-1100	TARI
		♪		Add Perc	13	SY-77	TARI
		♪		More Perc	13	SY-99	TARI
		♪		Guitar	15	Wavestat	TARI
		♪		Strange	4		

The MIDI channel "pop-up" menu

2.11 Personalizing your Cubase

Many of the exercises we have completed so far have served to tailor Cubase to your personal needs. It would be rather tedious to have to re-install all these parameters every time you start Cubase. The good news is you don't have to - Cubase can save all the important settings so that they are automatically loaded every time you start the program. The chapter called "System Functions" describes in detail how you go about this.

By the way, the Track List's columns can be repositioned. This little luxury, available from version 3.0 onward, allows you to personalize the Track List's setup. Click and hold one of the column headings (A, M, C, T, Track, CHN, Instrument, or Output) using the left mouse button. The heading and its fields below are now framed by a dotted line. Keeping the mouse button pressed down, you can drag the entire column to the left or right until you reach the desired position. All columns can be repositioned by dragging them to where you want them.

2.12 Track handling

Now that you are familiar with the basic recording steps, let's find out more about what a MIDI recording system can do, and get to know many more of Cubase's functions.

The Basic Functions

2.12.1 Deleting Tracks

A Track's complete contents can be deleted, provided no Part is active (black) in the Part Display. Click any blank space in the Arrange window. Select the Track you want to delete as usual, i.e. click it or use the cursor keys [up] and [down].

The Track can then be deleted by pressing [Backspace], [Delete], or clicking "Delete Track" in the Edit menu, at which point the selected Track and its contents will disappear from the Arrange window. Try this out on Track 1.

Note: if you have accidentally activated a Part, then only the Part will be deleted, and not the entire Track. The menu item changes depending on what is selected, e.g. if you selected one or more Parts, then the menu entry will read "Delete Parts". Conversely, if a Track is active, the entry reads "Delete Track".

2.12.2 The Undo function

Almost every action can be reversed using the Undo function. Press the Atari's [Undo] key or select Undo in the Edit menu, and the deleted Track is back. Be aware that only the last step can be undone. For example, if you deleted two Tracks in succession, then the Undo function will only pull the last Track out of the hat. The other Track is lost forever.

Once you have executed the Undo function, you can rescind it by pressing the [Undo] key again. Delete a Track as described above. Press the [Undo] key. The Track re-emerges. Press [Undo] again, and the Track disappears again.

Be warned that Undo cannot recall all actions. Your attention will be drawn to the situations where it won't work as and when we encounter them in this book. By the way, the last action you have undone is entered in the Undo item of the Edit menu.

2.12.3 Moving Tracks

Click and hold Track 1 with the mouse button. It does not matter if there's a Part selected in the Part Display. The selected Track is now surrounded by a dotted line. Dragging the mouse up and down now inserts the Track at another position in the Track List.

Drag the first Track to Track 3's position and release the mouse button: this alters the order of the Tracks. The essential fact here is that this moves the (erstwhile) first Track's entire contents, complete with its MIDI channel and instrument name. You will soon see that this can encompass a great deal more than the one Part we have recorded on it so far.

2.12.4 Copying Tracks

You can not only move Tracks, but, using a similar method, copy them as well. Follow the steps described above for moving Tracks, but instead of using the mouse button on its own, press and hold the [Alternate] key throughout the operation as well.

Copying a Track, i.e. transferring its contents to another Track or another location in the Track List, copies its contents only (the MIDI data); the name and MIDI channel are those of the destination Track, i.e. the one to which you copy the contents of the original Track.

2.12.5 Overdub/Replace

What happens if you accidentally record on a previously-recorded Track? Try it out and see. Select Track 1, start the recording and play something. After a while, stop Cubase and listen to the result. You will hear both the original and the new recording. Cubase defaults to merging the old information with the new.

You can prevent this by using the Record Mode switch in the Transport Bar. When you start Cubase, this switch is set to "Overdub" which means that the recordings are merged. Click this box once and the mode changes to "Replace".

Track Handling

Switching between Overdub...

...and Replace

At this setting, any new information is not added to the original, but overwrites it: the old recording is deleted. If you stop the recording before the Part ends, then the original notes located between the current song position and the end of the Part are not deleted. Let's try this out. Set the Record Mode to Replace and start to record on Track 1. Play a few notes, say a bar, then stop Cubase. Go back to the beginning of the Track and listen to the result (to avoid confusion, activate the Solo function to silence the other Tracks). You should hear the new material only on the first bar of the Track, after which you should be able to hear your original recording.

Use the Undo function to recall your original material. Note the following:
- In Replace mode, Cubase deletes old Parts only if you actually play in something new.
- On the other hand, even if you only play a brief note in Replace mode, Cubase will continue to delete from that point on until you stop the recording.

2.12.6 Manual Punch In/Out

The two techniques discussed above are suitable for adding to a Track, as well as correcting minor mistakes. What if the position where you want to add or improve material appears much later in the song? Enter Punch In and Punch Out, terms used to describe the following:

Select the desired REC MODE (Overdub/Replace) and the correct Track. Start the *playback* (not the recording) of your song. You will hear the material you have previously recorded. Once you get to the point in the song where you want to record, "Punch In" by activating the Record mode (click Record, or better still, press the [*] key in the numeric keypad). Now you can replace material, or add to the original. "Punch Out" by pressing the Record key again to end the recording. The playback will continue. You can repeat this set of operations at any time during playback of a song.

2.12.7 The locators/automatic punching

You may think having to time the right moment for your Punch In, and having to play the new notes at the same time is a bit awkward, and you'd be right. A professional program should be able to provide better tools for situations like this.

Cubase has locators to help you here. They can help you define a specific point in your song for recording and have lots of other uses as well. In our Punch In / Punch Out situation, the left locator defines the starting point and the right locator the end of the recording. Replace any two bars in Track 1 of your song, such as bars 5 - 7. Switch to Replace mode to do this.

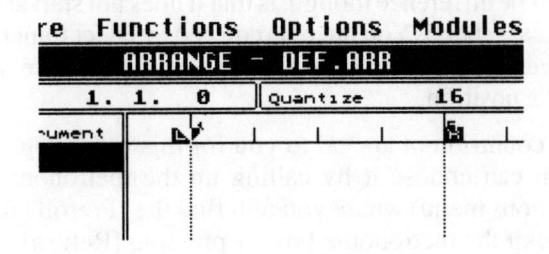

The locators' default positions

The Basic Functions

The locators default to bars 1 and 5 when Cubase is started. We will now change their positions. The program offers several different ways to go about this, so let's start by selecting the simplest. Use the *left* mouse button to click bar 5 in the Position Bar. The small field above the Position Bar labelled "Mouse" helps you to locate the position more precisely. When moving the mouse sideways across the Part Display, the Mouse display tells you what bar you are currently in. *Right*-click bar 7 in the Position Bar to position the right locator (R).

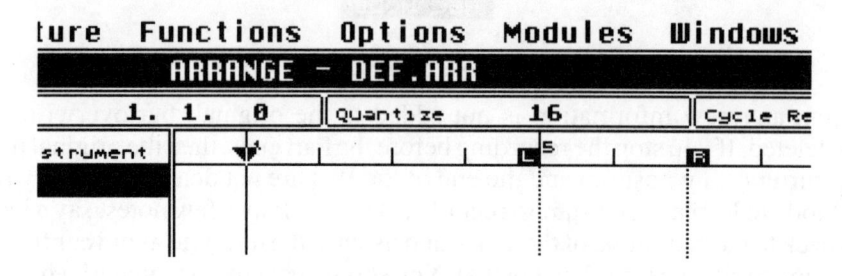

The locators in position

Now that we have defined the area in which we want to record, we have to tell Cubase what to do with it. For our purpose we will use the Transport Bar's Punch buttons. Click both In and Out so that they are highlighted. Cubase now knows that it is intended to switch on Record mode when the left locator is reached, and exit that mode at the right locator.

Go back to the beginning of the song. You may have to click the Stop button not once, but twice - you will soon see why. Remember that the position of the REC MODE defines the nature of the recording (Overdub/Replace).

When you are ready to record, start the *playback*. The sequencer starts and you hear the previous recording. Cubase starts to record upon reaching bar 5. For this exercise, play two bars of material, after which Cubase returns to Playback mode and continues in it until you press Stop. Go ahead and listen to the recording.

You are still owed an explanation regarding the stop button. To be precise, the stop button has three functions, two of which you are already familiar with: if you press it once during recording or playback, Cubase stops at the current song position. Press it a second time and the Song Position Triangle moves back to the left locator (provided the current song position is beyond the locator's position). Click the button a third time and Cubase returns to the song's start.

Reminder: until now, you have clicked the stop button twice to return to the start position. This was fine because the left locator's position was identical to the starting position of the song.

So far so good: start the playback and listen to the results of your work. In principle the procedure is the same as the one used for manual Punch In, only substantially easier.

2.12.8 Options

If the position you want to record at is well into the song, always having to listen to the bars before it may become somewhat tedious. Here's how you can steer clear of this problem: position the locators and instead of starting the playback, press Record. You now hear the count-in, then the recording starts as usual. The difference though, is that it does not start at bar 1, but at the position of the left locator: in this case, bar 5. You are not required to select Punch In as the program does it automatically. However, do select Punch Out, otherwise Cubase will continue to record beyond the right locator's position.

Should the metronomic count-in not appeal to you for this recording, you have another more musical alternative. You can choose it by calling up the metronome box discussed earlier ("Metronome" in the Options menu) where you will find the "Preroll" function. Click its box to select the function, and exit the metronome box by pressing [Return].

Now, start the recording again, refrain from playing, and listen: Cubase does not start at the left

Track Handling

locator, but one or more bars prior to its position, and plays the Tracks back in the normal manner. Once it reaches the left locator, the program switches to Record mode. If the click still bothers you, turn it off (key [C]). You can tell Cubase how many bars you want to hear before the Punch In commences in the Metronome box's "Bars" field. The length of the metronomic count-in and of the Preroll is identical.

2.12.9 Target practice

Cubase offers you variations to the locator positioning method in addition to the two methods described above. This will also give us the opportunity to look at a few more functions of the Transport Bar.

You will find the left and right locator displays to the left of the Transport buttons (stop, start, etc.). When you position the locators via mouse click in the Position Bar, these two boxes show the position as a numeric value. This value consists of:
- the first number (before the first decimal point), which corresponds to the bar,
- the second number (between the two points), which corresponds to the quarter note,
- finally, the third number is substantially more precise (up to 384 possible positions, from 0 to 383).

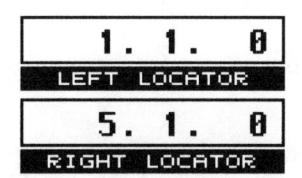

```
    1 . 1 .   0
   LEFT LOCATOR

    5 . 1 .   0
   RIGHT LOCATOR
```

The left and right locators

This of course requires an explanation. Cubase version 3.0 operates on an internal resolution that breaks down into 1536th notes, i.e. each bar is subdivided into 1536 positions. The shortest possible note is, therefore, a 1536th note. This smallest possible unit is referred to as a "tick". 1536 ticks equal a whole note, 768 a half note, 384 a quarter note, etc. Below, a list of note values and their relationships to ticks:

Value	Ticks
1/1	1536
1/2	768
1/4	384
1/8	192
1/12	128
1/16	96
1/24	64
1/32	48
1/48	32

To simplify the picture, Cubase not only divides musical time into bars and ticks, but also into quarter notes. An example should clarify the matter: the fourth eighth note in the first bar would be at position 1576. This is not exactly the clearest way of putting things, so the programmers used a clearer, more musical, measuring method, where every bar is subdivided into quarters. Cubase counts

Bar 1, first quarter: 1.1.0

Bar 1, second quarter: 1.2.0

....

Bar 2, third quarter: 2.3.0, etc.

Each quarter is then divided into 384 ticks as discussed above. If you want to position a locator

47

The Basic Functions

on the first eighth note in bar 1, then 1.1.192 is the corresponding value. The third eighth note is located at 1.2.0, and the fourth at 1.2.192.

The chapters 14 "Timing" and 15 "Quantizing" take a closer look at this somewhat unusual method of counting beats. Right now it is more important for you to understand how Cubase defines and controls positions and lengths.

Note: Cubase version 3.0 features an improved internal resolution. The value scale of 1536 ticks per bar is twice as precise as in version 2.01. This of course has ramifications for the display of positions and lengths in the program. The values quoted above apply to 3.0 users only; those of you using version 2.01 must divide the values by two, as you have only half the resolution!

2.12.10 Back to the locators

Let's get on with our target practice. As well as using the mouse to click locators into position in the Position Bar, they can also be positioned by directly manipulating the LEFT and RIGHT LOCATOR numeric displays. Change the locator values using the familiar methods: clicking with right/left mouse buttons, or via a double-click followed by typing the desired value (keyboard [L] or [R] plus value entry). The second method requires that you enter a period, a space, or a plus sign between values. If you just want to locate to a bar, and not a specific position within it, the bar number suffices (e.g. 5 for bar five). You will see that the locators move to the position you have just entered.

Clicking the LEFT LOCATOR or RIGHT LOCATOR displays moves the current song position to the respective locator position.

You may prefer to mark the position by listening to the playback and stopping at the desired position. In that case the following entry method may be of help to you. Press the [Shift] key and [1] in the numeric keypad simultaneously. The left locator adopts the current song position. Press the [Shift] key and [2] in the numeric keypad simultaneously to situate the right locator at the current song position. This method also works during recording.

2.12.11 Cue points

The recording method you have been introduced to thus far, i.e. recording entire Tracks, best meets the requirements of those of you who view songs as one complex entity, and use sequencers as virtual tape decks. Long songs can make the search for specific passages difficult and time-consuming. A solution is the use of what are commonly called "cue points" in tape recorders. Cubase also features cue points: these mark specific positions within your song.

You can program up to six cue points using a simple method. Go to the desired song position via the fast forward/rewind keys, or by typing the values directly in the Song Position box, or by listening to the song and stopping at the desired location during playback.

Press and hold the [Shift] key and one of numbers [3] - [8] on the numeric keypad. The current song position is saved as the number you have selected. Move Cubase on in the song. Recall the stored cue point position by pressing its number (this time without [Shift]). Cubase jumps back to that position. This feature is especially handy for marking changes of section within a song, such as intro to verse or verse to chorus.

Apart from those we have seen so far, there are a number of other ways of locating song positions. Go ahead and try these out:
- As with the locators, you can enter the song position directly using the right/left mouse buttons, or via a double-click (keyboard [P]), typing in the desired value and pressing [Return]. But there is yet another way. When entering a new value, you don't have to type in the desired numbers: you can also subtract from or add to the current value. Double-click the Song Position box, enter [+] then [10] and confirm with [Return]. The Song Position Triangle moves ten bars forward. This works for the locators as well.
- Another very simple pointer-positioning method: double-click the desired position in the Position Bar.

Track Handling

- Click the highlighted Left Locator or Right Locator box once, and the pointer moves to the respective locator position (keyboard [1] or [2]).
- The [Clr/Home] key moves the pointer to the left border of the Arrange window (this position need not be bar 1, as the Position Bar may have been scrolled forward).
- If you stop Cubase, re-start it, but now, for whatever reason, want to move back to the original Stop position, press [9] in the numeric keypad while the sequencer is running. Cubase jumps back to the last Stop position, and continues playback. You can jump back as often as you like, creating a sort of manual cycling.

All of these positioning functions can be used while the sequencer is running. Numeric entries are not executed until you confirm by pressing [Return]. Don't fret if you find the range of possibilities overwhelming: everyone feels that way at first. There is no iron-clad rule that says you have to use all the methods. Select those you feel best fit your way of working and you feel most comfortable with.

2.12.12 You've got the power - Snap!

After you have tried out all the different positioning methods, you will note that the locator is always placed at the beginning of a bar no matter where you click in the Position Bar, but positioning via the Song Position or by typing in values gives you the in-between values as well. This is because the Position Bar has a coarser resolution: Cubase defaults to a resolution of one bar. However, you can change the Position Bar's resolution using the "Snap" function: click and hold in the Functions Bar's Snap box with the mouse pointer, and a pop-up menu appears.

Snap settings

Now you can determine the resolution of the positioning by mouse click: Off (unrestricted), or to the nearest bar, half, quarter, eighth or sixteenth note. Select the Off position and try to place the locator at the beginning of a bar in the Position Bar. You will probably find positioning is a lot more difficult than it was before. Now select the 1/8 Snap setting and slowly move the mouse across the Part Display. The Mouse display changes in units of 1/8th notes, beginning with 1.1.0, then 1.1.192, 1.2.0, 1.2.192, 1.3.0, etc. The value of 192 is arrived at due to Cubase's resolution, as 192 ticks equal one eighth note.

Try the other settings and watch the Mouse display change. In a moment and later on, you will see that the Snap function is of great importance for other operations as well (e.g. copy and move functions).

2.12.13 Saving the work so far

Before we get to know new techniques, we should save the results of the work we have done so far. Insert a new formatted disk in the drive and choose "Save" from the File menu (keyboard: [Control][S]). *Never* save song or other such data on the program disk!

49

The Basic Functions

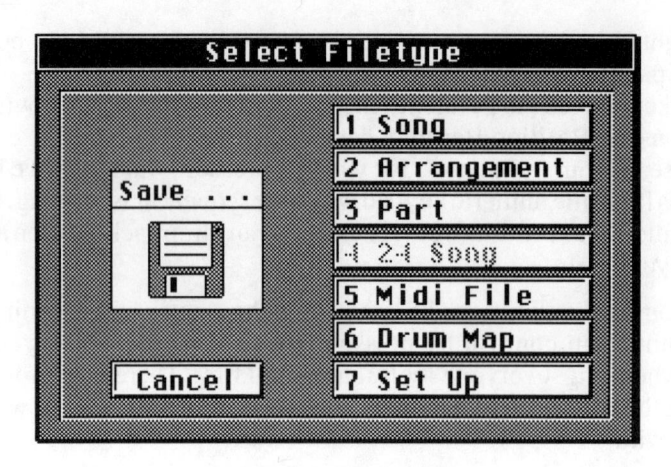

The "Save" dialog box

Select "2 Arrangement" in the dialog box (key [2] in the alphanumeric keypad). After a few moments, the Atari's Item Selector will appear. It is used for managing files on disk (loading and saving). The look of the Item Selector may differ from the one shown here, depending on your Atari's TOS version and whether you have a hard drive attached.

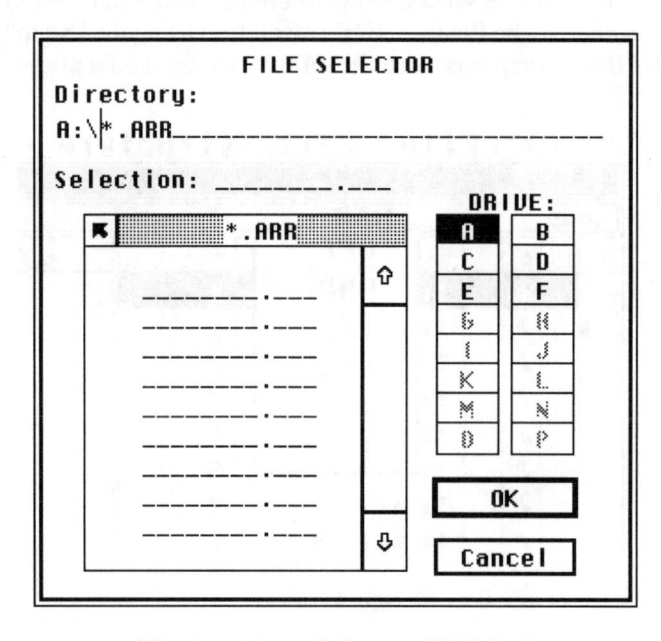

The Atari Item Selector (TOS 1.4)

Whatever the look of the Item Selector, the "Selection" line is always used to name files. A file could be a Cubase song, or the text of a word processing program. When you save an "Arrangement", the Selection line defaults to showing the name DEF.ARR. Delete this name by pressing the [Backspace] key several times, or by pressing [Esc] once. Enter a new name with a maximum of eight letters. Please use numbers or letters only. Do not enter anything in the three spaces after the dot as Cubase will enter the extension automatically. Once you have entered the name, confirm by clicking OK (keyboard: [Return]). You have now stored your first recording. Further essential information on saving, loading, disks, etc. is covered in chapter 6 entitled "Data Management".

Let's Go!

3 The Parts

Up to this point, we have recorded several Tracks and each Track contains only a single Part. This is, of course, not all Cubase has to offer. A Part is merely *one single* recording of a passage of a specific length, but you can determine the length and position of additional recordings thanks to the locators.

We need different examples for our next exercise, so delete the Parts you have created until now (but not the Tracks). To do this, simply select the first Part (it highlights) and press the [Delete] or [Backspace] keys. Select the second Part, delete it, and carry on until all the old Parts of our Arrangement have been deleted. If you find this method somewhat long-winded, don't worry as there are simpler ones coming up later in the book.

Our next goal will be to create a clearly structured song. We want to come up with identical results, so please follow the listed structure, otherwise your song's bar positions will not be the same as the ones in this example:

4 bars Intro

8 bars Verse

8 bars Verse

8 bars Chorus

4 bars Verse

You could, of course, achieve this with the information you have learned so far, but would have to record this structure as individual Tracks from beginning to end. The following method makes the assembly of the song easier and offers a number of other advantages.

3.1 Let's go

Place the left locator at the beginning of bar 1 if it isn't there already. Place the right locator at the start of bar 5. Assign the MIDI channels to the Tracks according to the devices in your MIDI system. If at all possible, stick to the format "piano", "bass", "strings", "drums". If you do not have several instruments at your disposal, don't worry. Simply record fewer Tracks with the different sounds you do have.

Activate Punch Out, and select the first Track. Start the recording and play an introduction. Cubase records the first Track, then switches from Record to Play mode at bar 5 and continues running until you stop it. If you haven't done so already, stop it now. The Part you have just recorded is exactly four bars long.

You can individually name all the Parts you record. Double-click the Part while holding the

The Parts

[Alternate] key down. Press the [Esc] key once to delete the previous name and replace it with one of up to ten letters.

Naming Parts is not absolutely essential, but you will see as we go on that naming things gives you a clearer overall picture. Confirm the name entry by pressing the [Return] key. If you press the [Alternate] key at the same time, all the Parts in the current Track will receive this name. We will see this feature again later.

In principle, you could select a second Track and name all its Parts, and so on with the other Tracks; however, there is a more user-friendly method which we'll discuss later.

3.2 The Cycle

Cycling in Cubase is what is known as "shuttling" in a tape recorder, where a section of tape is automatically repeated over and over, except that a computer can do instant Cycles whereas a tape has to spool back between them. In Cubase's Cycle mode, a specified number of bars is repeated as often as you want. The length of the Cycle is determined by the left and right locators which are already in position. Now all you have to do is switch to the Cycle mode by clicking the Cycle button in the Transport Bar (keyboard: [/] in the top row of the alphanumeric keypad).

Cycle mode on/off

Ensure that the song is at bar 1 and start the playback. Cubase will run to the end of bar 4, but then the Song Position Triangle will jump back to the first beat of bar 1, then start again. This will carry on until you stop the sequencer, and means that the material you recorded earlier on Track 1 is being repeated over and over.

You can play along during the playback. If you want a different sound on another MIDI channel, select the next empty Track, and assign its MIDI channel to the desired instrument. You're not required to stop Cubase. By the way, most functions can be executed while Cubase is running.

Back to our recording, where we'll now use the Cycle mode. Ensure that REC MODE is set to Overdub and not Replace, then click the Record button or activate Record mode at any time during playback. All the notes you record now will be played back in the next Cycle. You can continue to add to these notes since everything will be recorded. You can just as easily record the first Part in its entirety during the first Cycle and hear it repeated in the next one, as add bits of the Part in each Cycle until you have assembled the complete picture. Take your time, there's no need to add notes in every Cycle. There are different Cycle modes for different applications.

3.3 The Cycle modes

The Cycle modes are accessed by clicking the "Cycle Rec" field at the lefthand end of the Functions Bar. Of the three choices in this special menu, click "Mix".

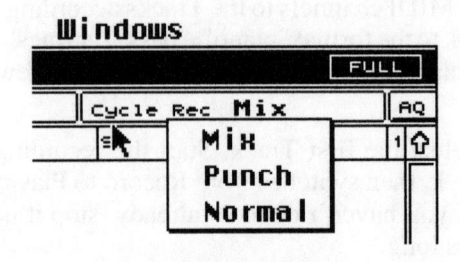

The Cycle modes

The Mix Cycle mode is the one we have just used in which you can add notes at any time. All data is recorded, and then played back during the following Cycle. Although it may seem as if it doesn't matter whether you are in Overdub or Replace mode, they apply to situations where you are recording on a Part that already contains notes:

If REC MODE is set to Overdub, all newly added notes are merged with what was already in the Part in each Cycle. In Replace mode, the Part's original notes are deleted, and only the new notes are recorded and mixed. The REC MODE has no significance if you are recording from scratch.

The Punch Cycle mode does something different. To see how it actually works, let's create a new working Part. First select an empty Track, assign it a MIDI channel and Solo it to silence the other Tracks. Activate the Punch Cycle mode and start recording.

Record a simple line of notes, such as eighth notes at the same pitch (C3), using a piano-type sound. Do not continue to play after the first four bars, but listen to the results in the second Cycle.

In the third Cycle, let the first two bars run unchanged. In bars 3 and 4, play eighth notes that are two octaves higher (C5). You will discover, based on this simple exercise, that this mode replaces the original notes. Listen to the result in the next Cycle without playing anything. Cubase has replaced the original notes in bars 3 and 4 (pitch C3) with those of your second take (pitch C5).

What exactly happens? The sequencer switches to Punch In mode as soon as you play something, and switches back at the start of a new Cycle. All the original notes are deleted from the point you start to play until the right locator, no matter how little you play. If you play nothing, the original is not affected.

Try it out: stop the sequencer and delete your last take using [Backspace] or [Delete]. Now create a new Part using the same method as before. First take: eighths at pitch C3, then listen to the second Cycle. For the third Cycle, play a single note at C5. The following Cycle will show that everything following the C5 is gone.

As before, the REC MODE (Overdub/Replace) setting applies to previous recordings only: original notes are immediately deleted in Replace mode, but are kept safe in Overdub mode.

What does the final Cycle mode, Normal, have to offer? Here too, a practical demonstration provides us with the answer. Delete your first working Part. Select the Normal Cycle mode, start the recording and play something. In the second Cycle you will find that the Track contains no notes! The entered notes are only saved if you stop Cubase before the end of the Cycle. The previous Cycle is deleted with each new Cycle! Once again, Replace and Overdub apply to previously recorded material only: Overdub keeps the original notes, whereas all notes are immediately deleted in Replace mode.

The following point should be clearly understood: the choice of Cycle mode (Mix, Punch, Normal) is only relevant for notes that are being recorded. Other previously recorded material will be handled according to the REC MODE switch. Overdub merges old and new notes. What then happens to the new notes depends, as you now know, on the Cycle mode. Either way, Replace mode deletes old material.

3.4 More on cycling

You may have made a mistake in one of your takes. You already know how to correct minor timing fluctuations with the Quantize function. While the recording is running, go to the Functions menu and select Over Quantize ([Q]). A simpler way is to activate the automatic quantization by clicking the grey letter combination "AQ" right at the end of the Functions Bar. After each Cycle, your previous take's timing is corrected by "Over Quantize". Bear in mind that this automatic function works in Cycle mode only.

If you are in Overdub mode, some puzzling things can happen while you are cycling. Your enthusiasm may take over, and you play through one Cycle and on into the next. If this happens and you get duplicated notes, choose the Delete Doubles command from the Functions menu,

The Parts

whereupon doubled notes of the same pitch and on the same beat are deleted. You can also do this while the sequencer is running. This function is important in other respects, too: see chapter 14 on "Timing".

Another critical point is the use and recording of performance controls such as a sustain pedal, pitch bender, modulation wheel or joystick. These can interfere with each other from one Cycle to the next. For instance: say you used a piano sound for recording the first Verse (bar 5 to 12). You pressed the sustain pedal in bar 11 and released it in bar 6 in the following Cycle. If you are listening to the Cycle only, everything seems alright. However, keep in mind that this Part is just a small portion of the overall Track. If you then play the Part back with Cycle mode disabled, you'll find the sustain off message comes *before* the sustain on message: the messages are the wrong way round!

Moral: always use performance controls carefully.

3.5 Useful items

Cubase offers several other helpful items in the Cycle mode. Delete your working Part and switch Cubase to Cycle Mix mode. Start the recording and play the repeated eighth notes again. During recording, click and hold the mouse button on the Cycle Rec field (not on the word "Mix"!). A new menu will appear, which can only be activated during recording.

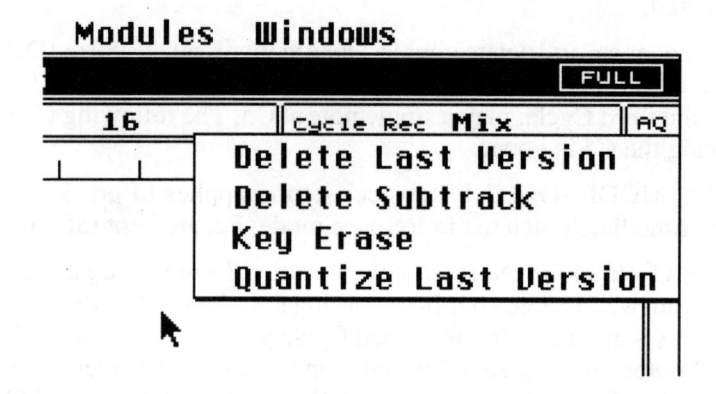

Cycle aids

Now temporarily leave the menu and play an additional note (C5) in the Cycle. Go back to the small menu and select Delete Last Version, or press [V]. This last note is deleted. The function deletes the most recent Cycle in which you actually recorded something, even if you followed it by listening to several Cycles without playing in anything new.

"Delete SubTrack" or [B] deletes all Cycles. The advantage here is you don't have to stop Cubase. Whatever you do, do not press [Backspace] or [Delete] while recording in the Cycle mode or you will delete the entire Track. However, should such a mishap occur, you can use the Undo function.

The last two Cycle aids are easy to explain. "Quantize Last Version" or [N] quantizes the most recent Cycle take using the Quantize value in the Functions Bar: this defaults to sixteenths.

"Key Erase" allows you to delete specific notes, ironing out minor errors. Start recording and play a wrong note at some point. Press and hold that wrong key on your instrument during one of the following Cycles and select Key Erase or [K]. The wrong note disappears.

But be careful: this function deletes *all* notes of the same pitch within the Cycle. If you want to remove a specific note from the Cycle, but this note also appears at other positions in the Cycle which you want to keep, you end up deleting those too. This function is good for correcting basic mistakes, such as accidentally hitting the wrong key when you really wanted to play the one next to it, and so on.

3.6 Let's get started

So far, we have been learning about the Cycle mode. Now let's see how this knowledge can be applied. You will find out the quickest way to transfer your ideas to the computer's memory.

Use the take on the first Track as a foundation or record something new. Ensure the basic settings are correct:
- Left locator: 1.1.0
- Right locator: 5.1.0
- Cycle active
- REC MODE: Overdub
- Cycle mode: Mix
- No Tracks muted
- Automatic quantization: On
- The MIDI channels of Tracks 1 to 4 should be set so they address drums, bass, strings and piano, and select these sounds on your instrument(s). The instrument/sound you begin this exercise with is up to you.

Select Track 1. Keep in mind that you want to create some kind of introduction. Start recording and play for four bars, e.g. drums. You don't have to do this within one Cycle. Take your time: you can first enter the bass drum, then the snare, hihat, etc.

Do not stop Cubase. Remember, you can delete the last Cycle or the results thus far via the Cycle Rec menu's Delete Last Version or Delete SubTrack. Keep the other Cycle aids in mind, too.

Once you are satisfied with the first Track, select the next one. Here again, do not stop Cubase.

You can now enter the bass line. As you have already preset the MIDI channel, Cubase automatically activates the MIDI Thru function. The same options discussed above apply to this Track as well. Once the bass line is in, record the other Tracks in the same manner.

Following these simple steps, you can create a section four or more bars long, depending on the locators' positions, using almost any number of Tracks; all this without stopping Cubase, even for a second. This section of music is called a *Pattern*.

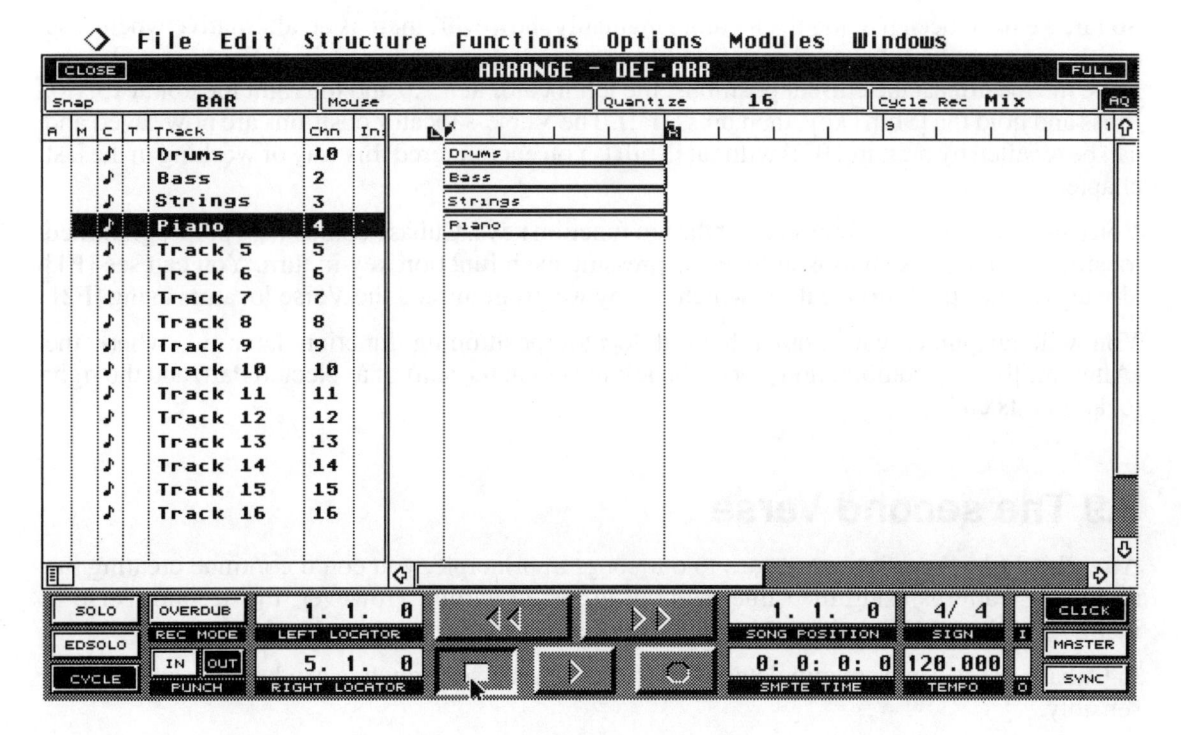

The finished Intro

The Parts

3.7 The first Verse

Next on the agenda is the first Verse. You will obviously want it to start after the Intro, so you must re-position the locators. Our first four bars are already in the can, so place the left locator on bar 5 and the right on bar 13 so that our Verse is eight bars long. You *cannot* position locators during recording, only in Stop or Playback modes.

Start your Verse Pattern on Track 1. As a rule, you should work within the Cycle, but the Preroll or Punch In methods, which we encountered earlier, can also be used. Switch Punch In on and place the Song Position Triangle at the start of the song. Start the playback. Cubase plays the Intro. Once it reaches the left locator, it goes into Record mode. You can record now. From bar 5 on, the Cycle takes over. The same holds true for the Preroll function: Cubase starts before the beginning of the Cycle, then the Cycle takes over, and repeats the Verse indefinitely.

Note that the cycling is between the two locators only - it does not include any Preroll.

The reason for listening to what comes before the Verse Cycle is so that you can hear upbeats and so on in their correct musical context: you can hear, for instance, a run-up to the Verse, allowing you to record the final note of the run-up on the downbeat of the Verse.

If you want to hear something of the Intro each time you record a new Part in the Verse, you must stop Cubase each time you have finished recording a Part and start the sequencer in the new Track from the desired position prior to the Cycle.

Of course, you don't have to line up a song's patterns exactly on the bar as in this example. This would make the recording of upbeats unnecessarily difficult.

Say you want to start the Verse's upbeat on the Intro's "four and...". Place the left locator at position 4.4.192 instead of 5.1.0. The Intro and Verse will slightly overlap, but Cubase doesn't mind, and it makes the recording of upbeats so much simpler. Ensure the Snap function is at the appropriate resolution or you will not be able to locate the proper position on the Position Bar.

3.8 Programming the locators

So far, we have been placing the locators manually; however, there is an alternative where you can program up to ten locator configurations and recall them when required. For the first Verse, leave the locators at the current positions: the left locator at 5.1.0 and the right locator at 13.1.0. Press and hold the [Shift] key, then press [F2]. The Verse's locator positions are now saved and can be recalled by pressing [F2] without [Shift]. You encountered this way of working in the last chapter.

You can save a locator pair on each of the ten function keys. Cubase comes with preprogrammed locator positions: take a look at them by pressing each function key in turn. You can see [F1] already defines the Intro locators, which is why we programmed the Verse locators using [F2].

You will encounter yet another helpful locator positioning function later on, where the [Alternate][P] key combination places the left locator at the start of a selected Part, and the right locator at its end.

3.9 The second Verse

After this little excursion, we return to our song. In principle, you could continue creating the remaining Patterns using the same method discussed earlier. However, the second Verse is identical to the first! So why go through the hassle of recording the same thing again?

In Cubase, Parts can be manipulated very flexibly. Let's see how this can be done quickly and sensibly.

Select the first Track's Verse Part by clicking it so that it is highlighted. Keep the mouse button pressed down: the Part is framed by a dotted line. Drag the Part to the desired position by moving the mouse: forward, back, or even to other Tracks (in which case, the Part adopts the destination Track's MIDI channel assignment). Drag the Part to position 13.1.0 on Track 1 by watching the position display in the Mouse field. The Snap function will help you position the Part properly.

Once you have found the correct position, release the mouse button. You have just *moved* a portion of the Verse and left a gap between bars 5 and 13 of Track 1. If you haven't already done so, zoom the display to get a good view of this portion of the song.

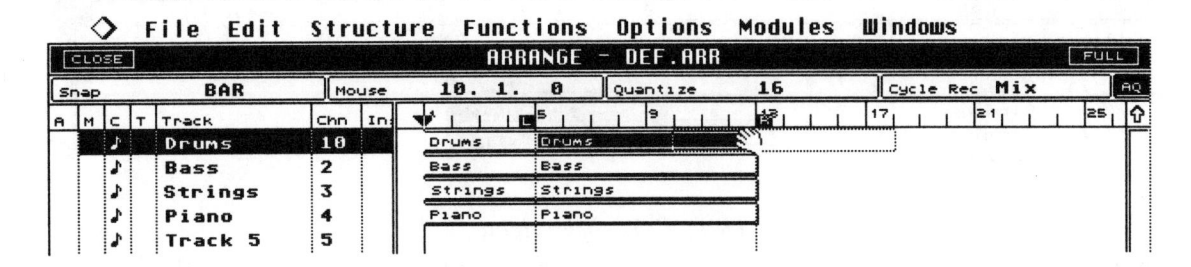

Moving a Part on Track 1

The result we have achieved is not the one we intended, as the idea was to *copy* the Part. So drag the Part back to its original position, but this time, press and hold [Alternate], or press and hold the right mouse button as well as the left one once you have selected the Part.

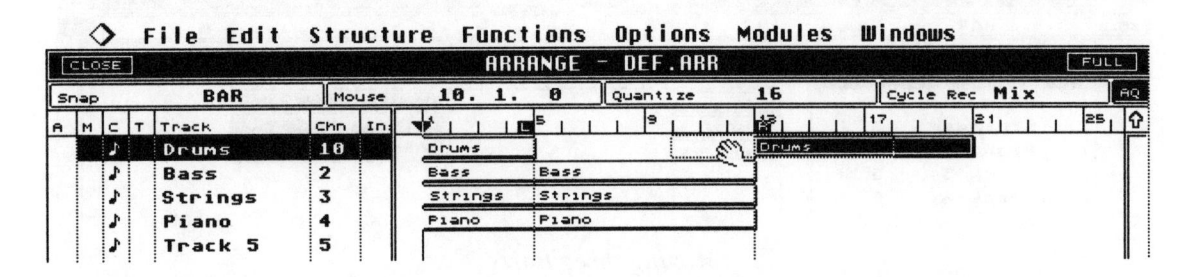

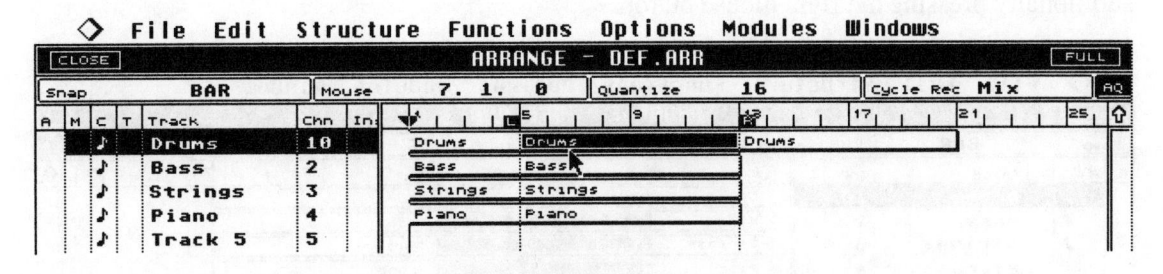

Copying a Part on Track 1 by pressing and holding [Alternate] or the right mouse button

After you have done this, you will discover you have copied the Part. It occupies bars 5 to 13, and bars 13 to 21.

The Parts

All you need to do now is copy the remaining Verse Parts to the desired positions. Fear not, there is an easier method. Select the remaining three Parts simultaneously by clicking them one after the other while holding [Shift] down. The Parts are highlighted. If you selected the wrong Part by mistake, you can deselect it by clicking it again, provided you keep [Shift] depressed. If you want to deselect all the Parts, click any free area of the Part Display without pressing [Shift].

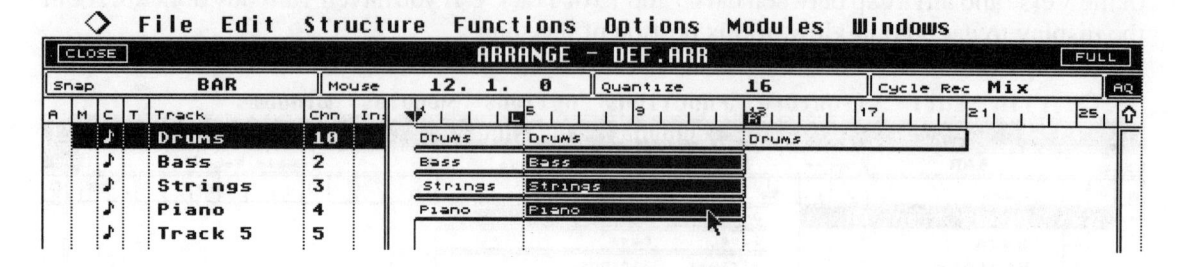

Three Parts are selected

Release [Shift], then click and hold one of the three Parts. All three Parts are surrounded by the dotted line, denoting that they can now be dragged. Keep the mouse button depressed and drag this trio to bar position 13.1.0. Watch the Mouse field as it tells you where the mouse pointer currently is.

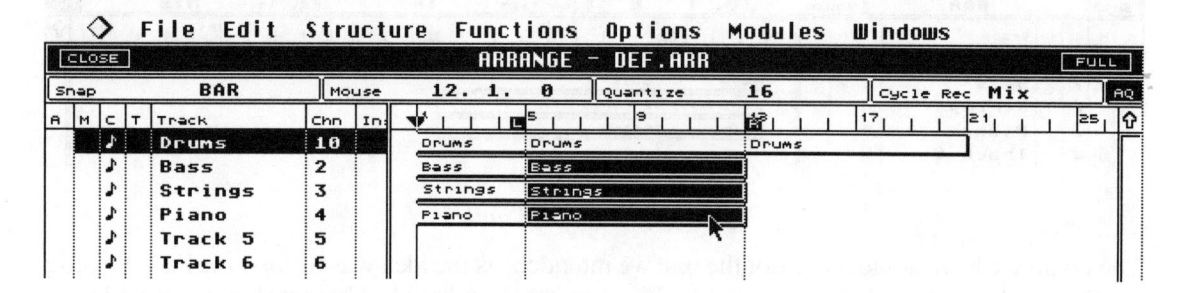

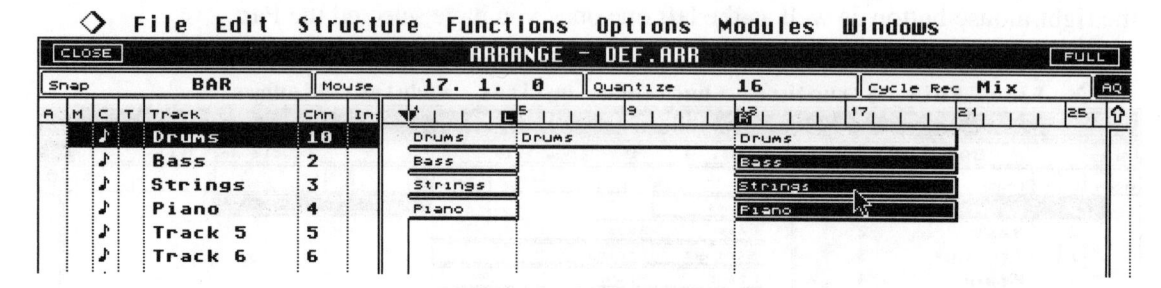

Moving three Parts

Copy the three Parts back to their original positions by pressing and holding [Alternate] or additionally pressing the right mouse button.

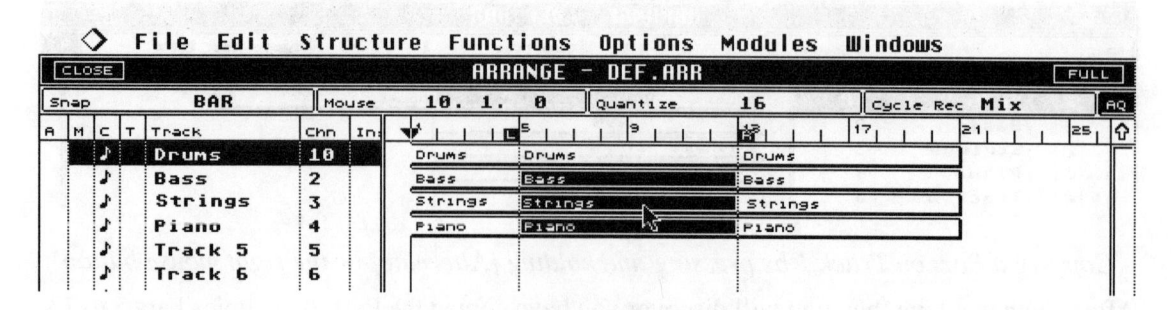

The result

3.9.1 Selecting Parts

The techniques discussed above are some of Cubase's best features. Here are more exercises and hints on selection techniques.

Select the Parts of *one Track*. There are several ways of doing this:
- Clicking the Parts one after the other while pressing [Shift].
- Pressing [Shift] and double-clicking any free portion of the Track.
- Selecting the Track, holding [Shift] and pressing the right or left keyboard cursor keys.

To select Parts of *several Tracks*, click them one after the other while pressing [Shift]. You can select as many Parts as you like. They do not have to be consecutive or touching.

There are two other possibilities. The Select All command (keyboard: [Control][A]) in the Edit menu does exactly what it says, by selecting all the Parts of an Arrangement.

The final option is provided by a feature referred to as "rubber banding". This is described in the Atari owner's manual, but here's a quick run-down. First, copy several Parts to Tracks 13 - 16. This will look something like this:

Parts copied to other Tracks

Now click a blank space just before/after and above/under the Parts and, keeping the mouse button pressed, move the mouse diagonally across the Parts. You will see that you are drawing a dotted "rubber band" around the Parts.

The rubber band

The Parts

All the Parts touched or surrounded by this rubber band are selected when the mouse button is released.

This method is recommended for selecting large groups of adjacent Parts. If you want to select Parts that abut each other and which are surrounded by other Parts, you probably won't find a free space in the Part Display to start the rubber band. Here too, there is a solution you will not find documented in the manual.

Press [Shift] before and while you are drawing the rubber band. This enables you to separately select Parts that are close together. Keep in mind that a Part does not need to be completely surrounded by the rubber band, but only needs to be touched by it.

Parts, once selected and regardless of how you selected them, can be moved and copied as you please. The gaps between the Parts are maintained. Parts may overlap partially or completely, in which case they are played back simultaneously. You will discover a few things during your experimentation:
- If you copy or move a selected Part and wander beyond the screen's right border, the Position Bar is automatically scrolled on.
- If you release a Part below the final available Track, Cubase automatically creates a new Track.

3.10 Repeating Parts

There is yet another useful function available should you want to copy Parts one after the other. Select the desired Parts, go to the Structure menu and select Repeat, or press [Control][K]. Designate the desired number of copies and confirm by pressing [Return].

The selected Parts are copied from the end of the original Part for as many times as you chose. Try it, then delete the Parts using the technique you have learned: [Backspace] or [Delete]. The "Ghost Copy" parameter will be discussed later.

3.11 Deleting Parts

You already know one method by which a selected Part may be deleted: using [Backspace] or [Delete] on a selected Part. You can also use the Delete Part(s) command in the Edit menu. Both of these variations delete all the selected Parts.

Delete all the Parts that you have created in these exercises with the exception of those designated for the original Arrangement.

3.12 Merging Parts

Say you move one Part so it partially or completely overlaps another. No problem. Both Parts are played back, and their contents remain complete.

Pressing [Control] and [Alternate] together gives you another option if you actually want to *merge* two Parts. Here, the selected Part, the source Part, is merged with another Part, the destination Part. The source Part's MIDI data, as well as that of the destination Part, remains unchanged.

This applies when REC MODE is set to Overdub. The same operation in Replace mode deletes the destination Part's notes and replaces them with those of the source Part.

Now we know that it is unlikely that both Parts will have precisely the same length. So what happens if two Parts of different lengths are merged, or if the source Part is not placed at the start of the destination Part, but somewhere in its middle? In this case, the additional notes are attached to the end of the destination Part. Let's do an experiment that will help us distinguish copying and merging.

The Toolbox

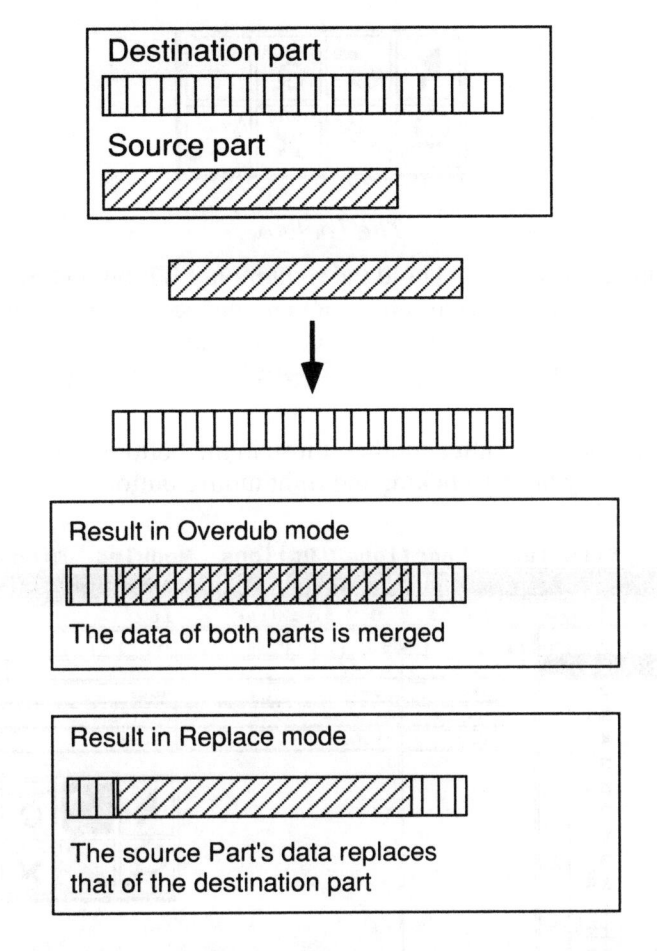

Merging Parts while pressing [Control] and [Alternate]

Select a blank Track and silence all other Tracks via their mutes so that they don't interfere. Use the locators to enter a Part with a length of four bars, and ensure its MIDI channel is correctly assigned. Go to the next blank Track and enter a Part eight bars long. Record low notes in the first Part and high ones in the second so you can distinguish between them in the experiments below.

Ensure Overdub mode is active for the following experiment. Press [Control] and [Alternate] and move the longer Part onto the shorter one so it starts at 1.0.0. It would appear that nothing has happened. Let's take a look. Mute the Track containing the longer Part and start the playback. The shorter Part now actually comprises the contents of *both* Tracks. Even after the Part has reached its end on the screen, you can still hear data being played: a phenomenon which we're about to look into.

Reverse the merge via [Undo] and again copy the longer Part onto the shorter one, this time starting at 3.0.0 and not at 1.0.0. Listen to the result. The notes of the copied Part are merged starting from 3.0.0. Try the same thing when Replace mode is active.

Before we can return to our song, we must first delete both new Parts. Instead of doing it the way we learned earlier, this time we'll use the Toolbox.

3.13 The Toolbox

Cubase has another surprise in store concerning the handling of Parts. If at some time you have accidentally clicked the Part Display with the right mouse button, you will already know what the surprise is. If not, click and hold the Part Display with the right mouse button. A new box appears containing a set of symbols: the Toolbox.

The Parts

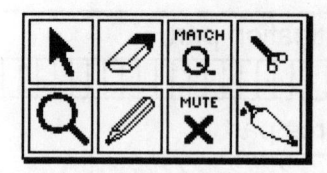

The Toolbox

Tool selection is quite easy. Press and hold the right mouse button on top of the Toolbox, then move the mouse slowly to the right. One after another, the tools are highlighted. To select a tool, release the mouse button when it is highlighted. Select the Scissors tool: the mouse pointer disappears from your screen, replaced by the Scissors. You can move it the same way you move the mouse pointer.

Select all the different tools, one after another, those in the bottom row too. You can recall the normal tool, the Arrow, by briefly clicking the right mouse button.

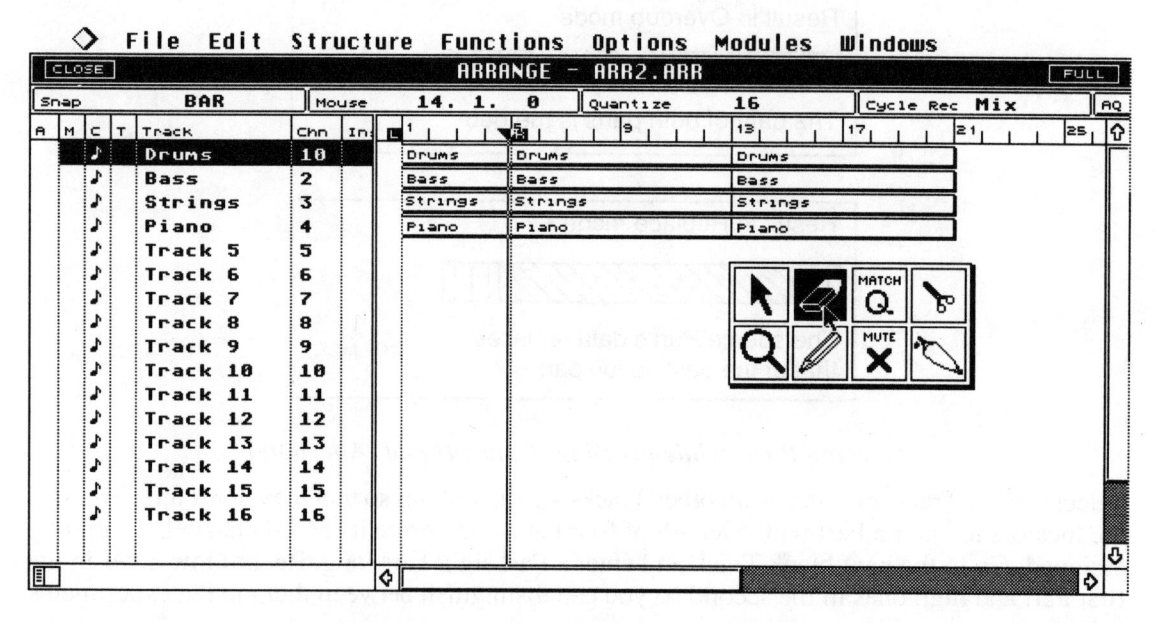

Selecting the tools, in this case the Eraser

Now that you know how to access these tools, you're probably asking yourself what they are used for. The first and most important tool, the mouse Arrow, has been covered to a certain extent in the previous sections, so let's move on to the next one, the Eraser. Press and hold the right mouse button and select the second tool from the left in the upper row: the Eraser. We will save the neighboring "Match Quantize" tool for the "Quantizing" chapter.

The "Match Quantize" tool

3.13.1 The Eraser

The Eraser tool

This tool's function is easy to explain. You can use it to delete ("rub out") Parts quickly and easily. In contrast with the methods we have learned so far, it is not necessary to select the Part first. Place the Eraser on one of the two Parts created for the last exercise, that are now no longer needed. Click the left mouse button: the Part disappears. You can press [Undo] to recall the deleted Part. Please note: under normal conditions, you only delete the Part that the Eraser is on. Delete the second superfluous Part, too.

To delete all the Parts in a Track, press and hold [Alternate] and click on the first Part of the Track. All the following Parts are deleted right along with it. The important thing to note is all the Parts *after* the selected Part are deleted.

3.13.2 The Magnifying Glass

The Magnifying Glass tool

The Magnifying Glass is not just amusing, but is also a useful tool. A short example will clarify this. Select the Magnifying Glass from the Toolbox. Click the first Part of the first Track with the mouse button. Keep the mouse button depressed.

The Magnifying Glass alters the Part's appearance

The appearance of all the Parts in the first Track has changed. Instead of the name, you see a number of vertical black lines. These lines represent the individual notes and their respective time values. Move the Magnifying Glass slowly over the first Part while holding the mouse button down. As soon as you reach a black line and move across it, its corresponding notes are played. You can move the Magnifying Glass at any speed you like. You can even move it backwards to hear the Part played back to front.

This function enables you to quickly spot mistakes without having to mute the other Parts, engage Solo or use the transport commands. Bear in mind that the Magnifying Glass can only be moved across the selected Part. If you want to listen to all the Parts in a Track, you must first click the initial Part, move the tool across it, briefly release the mouse button, click on the second Part, move across it, etc.

The Magnifying Glass can also be helpful during playback. If you click a Part while pressing [Alternate], this Part is played along with the Arrangement, even if the song position is nowhere near where the Part is. The Part is played once, beginning from the next bar.

You can make the display of all the Parts in an Arrangement stay the way they are described in this section by choosing Part Appearance from the Options menu. Click Show Events in the Part Appearance dialog box and confirm by pressing [Return]. All Parts now display the events they contain. This feature is especially helpful when you are dealing with sparse musical passages where there are long gaps between notes: you can see when and where notes will play.

The Parts

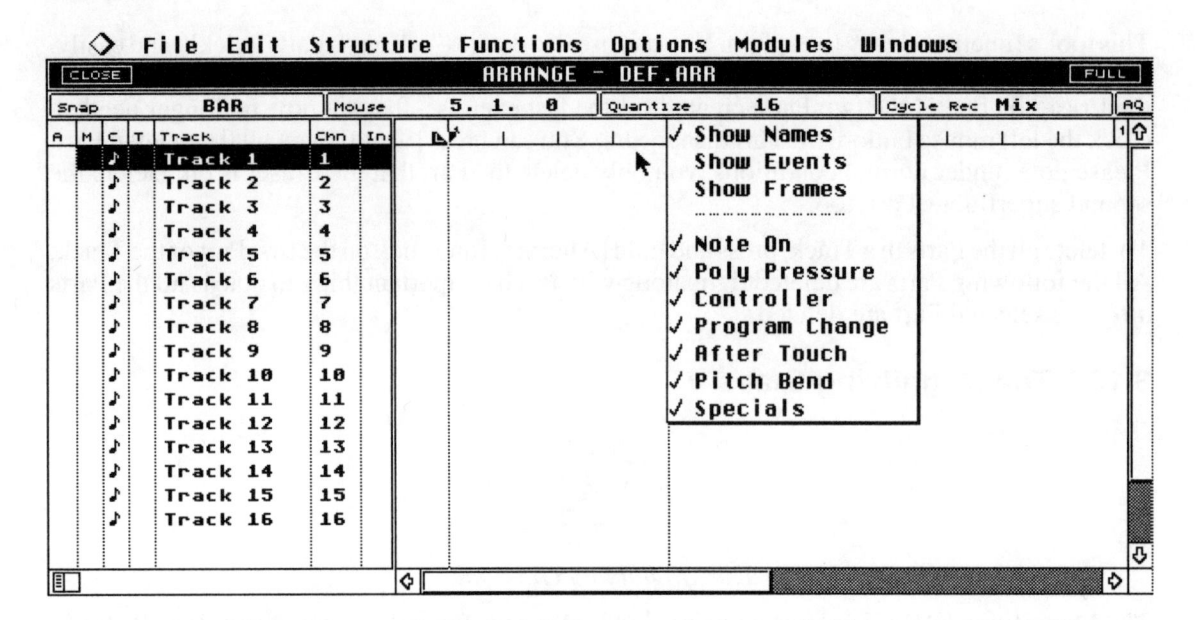

The Part Appearance dialog box

The Part Appearance dialog box contains a number of other display options. "Show Names", the default option, displays the Part names. "Show Frames" displays only the empty Part beams. Below, a number of display filters are listed allowing different types of MIDI data to be excluded from the display

Cubase defaults to showing every type of data when "Show Events" is selected. If all you want to see is notes, switch off the other types of event such as Poly Pressure, etc. These settings affect the *display* only, and do not affect the data in the Parts nor its playback.

3.13.3 The Part Mute

The Mute tool

The Part Mute tool is also easy to explain. Once you select it, the mouse pointer changes to an X. Parts clicked with this X are muted and become speckled grey. Click again to unmute. You can mute as many Parts as you like.

Muted Part and non-muted Part

3.13.4 Pencil, Scissors, Glue and a little relaxation

Before we approach the remaining three tools, you should kick back and relax for a while. Now it is time to create the Chorus for your song. Record four Parts on the four Tracks from bar 21.1.0 to bar 29.1.0. Note that the normal display size does not include the last portion of the Chorus in the Arrange window. The right locator must be placed slightly outside the screen.

There are two ways to go about this. Either enter the position as a numerical value, i.e. 29.1.0 in the right locator display, or if you prefer to work with a graphic display, scroll the Position Bar forward. Here again, you have two options. You can zoom the display scale, or click in the Position Bar's outermost left corner. Each click moves the left locator later by two bars.

The method you ultimately use is entirely up to you. For now, zooming the display scale is preferable as it gives a better overall picture of the song.

Now that you have recorded the Chorus, your first song is virtually complete. Your next goal should be to record the third and final Verse. It should be identical to the first two, with the one difference that it is only half as long. Copy the Parts of the first Verse to bar 29.1.0, i.e. directly after the Chorus. Put your new-found knowledge to work!

To refresh your memory:
- Press and hold [Shift] and click the four Parts (bar 5.1.0 to bar 13.1.0) on Tracks 1 through 4.
- Press and hold [Alternate].
- Drag the Parts to position 29.1.0, and release them there. By the way, if you are not using another display magnification, the Position Bar is automatically scrolled forward/back when you reach the right/left borders of the Arrange window.

You have now copied the Verse to the position right after the Chorus. Here is where the remaining tools come into play. Select the Scissors from the Toolbox and click the following position: the middle of the third Verse, i.e. position 33.1.0 in the first Track. You have just cut the Part in half!

The Scissors tool

You will not hear a change as all notes are still intact. Click anywhere free in the Part Display to deselect the Parts. Now you can see the cut you have just made more clearly. Drag the latter portion of the Part further back. You can now see that the Part is indeed cut. Return the latter portion of the Part to where it was. Select the Glue tool and click the first half of the severed Part. The two portions are again restored to a single Part, and can be moved and copied as such.

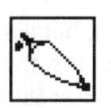

The Glue tool

We wanted the final Verse of the song to be half the length of the others. To achieve this, you could use the Scissors to cut the Parts at Position 33.1.0 and use the Eraser to delete the severed portions. However, there's an even easier method: select the Pencil from the Toolbox and click bar 33.1.0 of all four Parts. The superfluous portions are removed (bars 33.1.0 to 36.1.0).

The Pencil tool

3.14 Summary and useful tips

The final three tools are powerful performers, so a brief synopsis with some additional information is in order:
- The Scissors divides Parts at the selected position. The remaining portions can be handled in the same manner as normal Parts. Bear in mind that the Scissors can cut large structures, allowing you to record a long Track, then use the tools to keep the best bits.
- Pressing [Alternate] at the same time as using the Scissors divides the Part into equal lengths. Let's assume you recorded a Part 20 bars long. If you cut at the end of bar 2, Cubase dissects the Part into ten two-bar Parts. Cut at the end of bar 4, and the result is five four-bar Parts.

The Parts

- The Glue connects a Part with the next one situated *after* it. Any gap between two Parts will be closed. Clicking the newly connected Part again adds the following Part to this original Part. Continued clicking in this manner merges all the Parts in the Track.
- Pressing [Alternate] automatically glues all the Parts located after the selected Part together.
- The Pencil shortens a Part. This always functions from *back to front*. You can only delete the latter portion of a Part via this method. To remove the front portion, Scissors the Part at the desired spot, and delete this front Part.
- The Mouse field and the Snap function really come into their own when using the Scissors and Pencil tools.
- Cubase handles all Parts in such a manner as to avoid cutting notes that are still sustaining, so preventing the dreaded MIDI drone. Its method of recording notes is the decisive factor. Normally, a sequencer records the start of a note and its end (see the following chapter on MIDI). If you shorten a Part, you could theoretically lose the Note Off command and be saddled with a drone. Cubase follows the same routine at first by recording the beginning of the note, but then it computes the note's length after it receives the Note-Off command. This length remains intact, with the following example being the sole exception.
- What this all means is easily demonstrated by a practical application. Select a sound that can be played sustained or staccato. Record an eight-bar passage containing quarter note chords, plus a sustained note beginning with the downbeat of the first bar, lasting throughout the Part. Use the Pencil to shorten the Part to half its length. You will notice that the last four bars of chords have gone, but the sustained note carries on playing for the full eight bars.
- This tells us that all MIDI data after the cut disappears. Data initiated prior to the cut is executed for its designated length. This can confuse, as the display is showing four bars, yet you are hearing eight, and might be undesirable where you wish to append other Parts after the first four bars.
- To avoid this problem, utilize the Cut Notes command from the Structure menu. This function ensures all notes are cut at the designated point. The selected Parts now actually end at precisely the position displayed on your screen. If the notes in the Part started prior to the cut, but their endings extended beyond the cut, Cubase simply moves the note endings earlier to the cut position.
- The Pencil allows you to not only cut Parts, but also extend them. Click and hold anywhere in the Part. Move the mouse to the right keeping the mouse button depressed. Once you have reached the length you want, release the mouse button. The Part is extended. If you shortened a Part earlier, the notes you cut away are retrieved, provided you did not use the Cut Notes menu command. Lengthening a Part does not change or move its notes in any way.
- The Pencil can also be used to make copies. Press and hold [Alternate], click a Part and drag the mouse to the right. Release the mouse button when you have reached the desired position to create a copy of the selected Part.
- You can easily create a blank Part. Select a Track and place the locators at the start and end positions of the Part you want to create. Double-click somewhere in the Part Display or press [Control][P]. The purpose of this function will be explained later on.

4 Additional Arrange Functions

4.1 The Inspector

So far, we have been moving, copying, deleting and merging Parts and Tracks as a whole. It is also important to be able to alter a Track or Part in its own right. Cubase has numerous options available to achieve this. We are about to see how this works in practice.

Select a Part and click the "Inspector" symbol in the bottom left corner of the Track List.

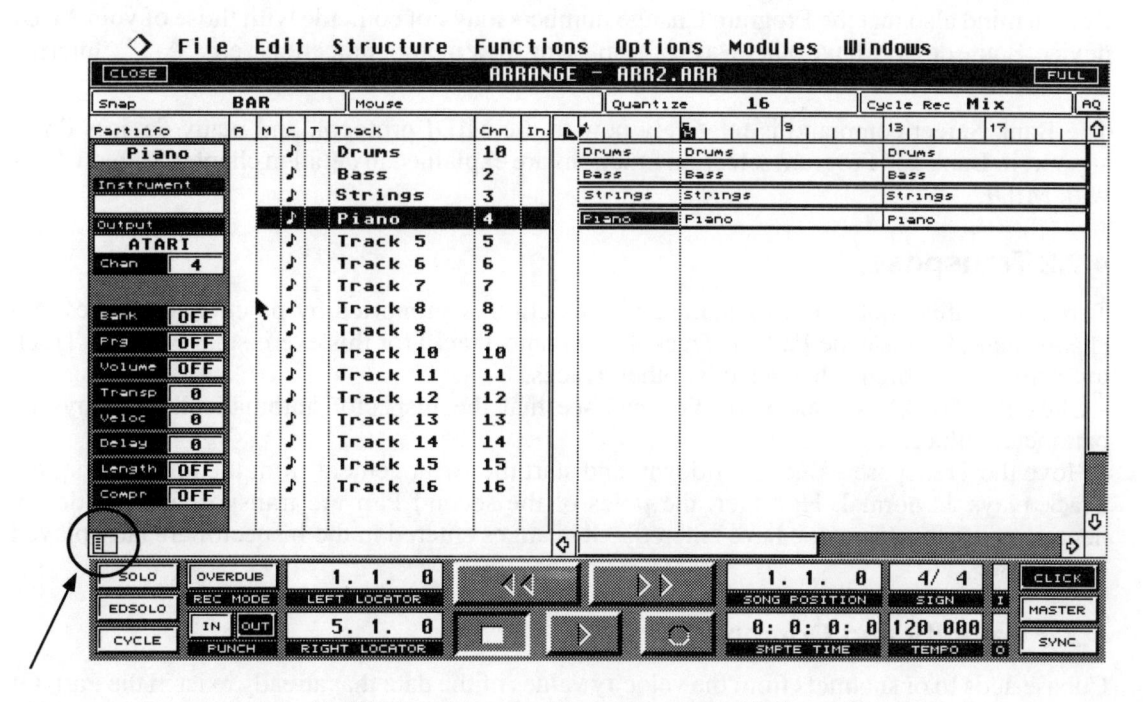

This is where the Inspector is enabled

The Inspector is a new display that appears next to the Track List and contains essential data about the selected Part. If you have not selected a Part, the Inspector displays the data for the selected Track. This means you have the choice of editing the entire Track, or individual Parts. After you

67

Additional Arrange Functions

have done your edits, you can move on to other Tracks and Parts by simply clicking the desired Track/Part, or choosing the right/left cursor key to select Parts of the same Track, or using the up/down cursor key to select other Tracks.

The Inspector will then switch to the corresponding Track or Part without your having to leave it. It will always display the current Track's or Part's name. This is just one example of why it is important to name Parts and Tracks, to help you distinguish one from another.

All the parameters accessed here are "play" parameters, i.e. they solely affect the way data is played back, not the way it is recorded. For this reason, you can always reverse alterations or enter new ones.

4.2 The Inspector's functions

The functions available for manipulating Tracks and Parts are identical. The first few items in the Inspector will be familiar to you from the Track List.
- The Part/Track name is displayed at the top. A single click on the box allows you to enter a new name.
- The Instrument field is the name of the MIDI channel.
- The Output field is covered in one of the following chapters (M*ROS Timing).
- The MIDI channel.

Changes to these fields are made in the usual way.

4.2.1 PRG Change and Volume

You can insert Bank Select, Program Change, or Volume Control Change messages at the beginning of each Part. Simply enter the desired values. Bear in mind that these Program and Volume commands are transmitted *while* you are entering the values: this allows you to audition the alterations as you make them.

Bear in mind also that the Program Change numbers may not coincide with those of your MIDI device. Some devices have other ways of displaying their memory locations, e.g. "A-1", "Internal 6-6", etc. Refer to the conversion table in the appendix for the most common formats.

The Bank Select command is relatively new to the MIDI protocol, and many devices don't support it. Bank and Program selection functions are explained in detail in chapter 5 which deals with MIDI.

4.2.2 Transpose

Throughout this book, the explanation of a function is supported by practical examples. No change here: let's use the Parts in Track 4 (the piano Track) for this exercise. Switch the Track to "Solo" so you aren't distracted by other Tracks.
- Click the Track's second Part. You can see that the Inspector automatically displays its parameter values.
- Move the Transpose value up or down, and start the Arrangement from the top. At first, the Track plays as normal. However, the notes of the second Part are transposed up or down, depending on the value you have entered. All changes entered in the Inspector are later played by Cubase.

4.2.3 Velocity and Compression

Cubase adds to or subtracts from the velocity values of the data that already exist in the Part. Of course, this can only work if your instrument supports velocity. This function is used to do things like reduce the aggressiveness of a sound, etc.

Compression works in a similar way. However, the velocity values are dictated by percentage and not absolute values. A 50% setting halves all velocity values, 200% doubles them, subject to the maximum MIDI value of 127. This function is suitable for, amongst other things, balancing different instruments' velocities.

4.2.4 Length

The Length parameter, too, uses a percentage scale. A Length value of 50% halves the duration of all notes in a selected Part. Values exceeding 100% add to the original notes' lengths. Remember that this function, like all the others in the Inspector, applies to the playback only. You can recall the original values simply by resetting the parameter to "0" or "Off".

4.2.5 Delay

Delay enables you to move the positions of the notes of a Part earlier (a "negative delay" or "push") or later, relative to the other notes in the Arrangement. The value is expressed in ticks. We will take a detailed look at what this means in a later chapter. Experiment with values of 48 and 96, which equal a thirty second and sixteenth note. Notes can be moved only within the boundaries of a Part. If you use a "negative delay" to push a Part's notes, those whose start times come before the Part's start will no longer be played. The same principle holds true for the end of the Part if you delay notes. The Delay function is useful in all sorts of ways, quite apart from the fun aspect:
- Some synthesizers, especially some vintage models, react rather slowly to MIDI commands: you can compensate for their timing delays by moving the Track earlier in time.
- Enter various drum instruments on several different Tracks and, especially for the snare, try some minor delay value changes to create a different feel for each instrument.
- Play a Part featuring eighth notes. Copy this Part to two other Tracks. Set the first copy's Transpose parameter to 12 and Delay to 96, the second copy's Delay value to 48. Listen to the result.

You can see that experimentation and the careful use of various parameters can lead to interesting effects.

4.2.6 Exercise

To get to know the Inspector's functions better, let's Cycle the working Part so that it is continuously repeated. As a reminder: position the left and right locators at the start and end of the Part. The easiest way to do this is to select the Part and press [Alternate][P]. Switch Cycle mode on and move the Song Position Triangle to the left locator, or press [1]. Start the playback, and Cubase continuously repeats the Cycle. Experiment with the Transpose, Velocity, Delay, Length, Compression and Volume values while the sequencer is running.

As mentioned earlier in the chapter, values in the Inspector apply to the MIDI data in playback only, and do not affect the data itself. In some situations, however, it is necessary that the data itself adopt the play parameters, e.g. when exchanging songs between different sequencer programs. For this purpose choose Freeze Play Parameter from the Functions menu. You can find detailed information on this function in the "System Functions" chapter.

4.2.7 Ghost Parts

In the previous example for the Delay parameter where identical Parts were copied one after the other, it was not actually necessary to make a complete copy, because only the play parameters of the Parts were altered. So next time, press [Control] instead of [Alternate] during the copy operation. The copy you make using this method is distinguished by the dotted line that surrounds it. You can move these "Ghost Parts", copy them, assign other MIDI channels to them, and change their play parameters.

But there is one fundamental point to bear in mind: any changes you make to the source Part (the Part they're ghosting), e.g. via the Editors (we will get to these in due course), apply to the Ghost Parts as well. On the other hand, as soon as you cut, merge or add a Ghost Part to a regular Part, it is automatically converted into a normal Part.

Additional Arrange Functions

4.2.8 Part Info

Each Part has its own Part Info box, where certain data can be excluded from the playback. To do this, just click the type of data you want to filter out. This function is of use when you want to suppress data-intensive MIDI information such as Aftertouch. The chapters on "MIDI" and "Timing" take a closer look at this function. The Part Info also allows you to move a Part or alter its length.

Activate a Part of your choice, then choose Info from the Edit menu or press [Control][I]. You can use the skills acquired thus far to change the settings in the dialog box. Bear in mind that the changes affect the *selected* Part only. You cannot select another Part while the dialog box is on your screen. You must first press [Return] to go back to the Arrange window, select another Part, and then open its dialog box again.

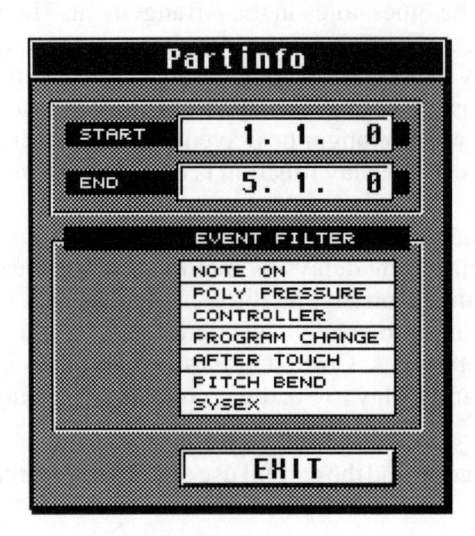

The Part Info box

By the way, from version 3.0 upward, all of these types of dialog boxes can be treated like conventional windows and moved around the screen. If at some time you are uncertain about which Part is currently selected, click and hold the top bar of the dialog box and drag it aside so you can see the Part Display.

4.2.9 The realtime aspect

So far as Program Change and Volume Control Change messages are concerned, we have seen that they are sent via MIDI directly to the instruments while they are edited. The same principle applies to Transpose, Velocity, and Compression: you can hear the effect of the edits as you execute them. Change a Part's Transpose value when the sequencer is in Stop mode; at the same time, play something on your instrument. Your computer executes the changes in realtime, which allows you to set the parameters prior to recording.

Program Changes and Volume Control Change commands are also very handy options for live applications. Create two successive blank Parts on one Track. Enter a Volume setting and a Program number in the first Part's Inspector. Assign different values to the second Part. Start the playback from the beginning of the first Part and play anything you like. When the first Part is over, Cubase changes programs in your synthesizer and changes its volume setting, provided your instrument supports this kind of information. This exercise shows that you can execute functions similar to those of a mother keyboard via Cubase, using a blank Track containing merely the play parameters.

Although this experiment is not complex, it shows that you can get maximum results with a minimum of effort. Experiment away! You will encounter tricks and shortcuts as you continue working with Cubase that will dwarf the one above.

4.2.10 The Clipboard

Apart from selecting a Part and copying it with the aid of the mouse, there is a another copy function which can be used in other areas of the program too: the Clipboard. The Clipboard is unassigned computer memory which you can access to temporarily save various items. The following example illustrates how the Clipboard can be used for Arrangements.

Select all four Parts of the first Verse. Choose Copy from the Edit menu ([Control][C]). The four Parts are now copied to the Clipboard. Place the Song Position Triangle at bar 35 or later. Choose Paste from the Edit menu or press [Control][V]. The four Parts are inserted at the current song position. Select the four Parts again, if they are not already active, and this time, choose Cut, not Paste, from the Edit menu ([Control][X]). It seems that the Parts have been deleted, but actually they are in the Clipboard. You can insert them at any given song position.

The way the Clipboard works is easy to explain. Copy enters a copy of the selected Part(s) in the Clipboard, leaving the original(s) in the Arrangement; Cut removes the Part(s) from the Arrangement and lodges it/them in the Clipboard. Paste copies whatever is in the Clipboard to the Arrangement's current song position. You will see later that Clipboard Parts can be inserted in other Arrangements as well. Once something is in the Clipboard, it can be pasted as often as you like.

Try the following exercise. Select the Verse Parts again and copy them to the Clipboard. Set the song position to bar 40.1.0. Activate the Paste function, and the Verse is inserted in the Arrangement at bar 40. Set the song position to bar 48.1.0. and activate the Paste function again. As you can see, the Verse is inserted again, which shows that it does not matter where you insert the Clipboard contents. You can even overlap Parts.

There are two important rules to keep in mind concerning Clipboard operations. The information you copy to the Clipboard is saved *temporarily*. As soon as you Cut or Copy new material to it, the previous contents are lost. You can use this to your advantage. Once a Part is no longer needed, remove it with the Cut command, and just leave it in the Clipboard. That way, the Clipboard assumes another function, that of the trash.

The second important rule: Parts copied to the Clipboard can be inserted anywhere within an Arrangement, but only on the same Tracks. The four Parts you just copied from Tracks 1 to 4 can be moved forward and back, but must remain on their respective Tracks.

You will encounter these Clipboard functions again and again. Work with them for a while so you are familiar with them when they crop up again.

4.3 More Arrange functions

Several additional features round off the Clipboard's attributes. Are the Verse Parts still in the Clipboard? Then copy them to the end of your song, three times in succession from position 40.1.0. Position the locators at bars 42.1.0 (left locator) and 45.1.0 (right locator). Choose Global Cut from the Structure menu and watch what happens. Cubase cuts the information between the locators and moves the remaining portions after the right locator to the left locator. This allows you to quickly remove sections from the Arrangement and join the remainder seamlessly to the first portion. All the material between the locators is removed. The exceptions are muted Tracks which are excluded from the cut and remain unaffected.

The counterpart to Global Cut is Global Insert, which is also in the Structure menu. Check out this feature. This time the section between the locators is not removed, but a blank space is inserted. This is useful when you want to create a break in the Arrangement. Here too, muted Tracks remain unaffected. You can fill the blank space using the skills acquired so far.

Two other similar commands are listed in the same menu. Global Split is comparable to the Scissors in the Toolbox, but here all the Parts in the Arrangement are divided at the left and right locators. If you want to execute a single Scissors cut only, either place both locators at the same position, or put one in a blank space somewhere in the Arrangement.

Additional Arrange Functions

Copy Range executes a function you are already quite familiar with, but more simply: the section between the locators is copied and inserted at the current song position. For these two functions the following also applies: muted Tracks are excluded from any alterations.

4.4 Group Tracks

You are by now familiar with all the basic techniques used for creating songs. You know the Arrange window's layout and how to utilize its features to record a song and edit the results. If you prefer to record one complete Track after another you probably knew it all after the first few pages anyway. If you work in a more pattern-oriented fashion, you have already mastered the basics.

However, Cubase has another jewel in its crown for those who prefer to work along pattern-oriented lines: the Group Tracks. Before we get down to business, ensure the original song structure is intact. Delete all Parts created during the last few exercises, provided they are not an integral Part of our basic song structure.

Now save the results so far. Click "Save" in the File menu or press [Control][S]. Select "Arrangement" in the dialog box that appears or press [2]. You will be confronted with the Item Selector. If a name is already in the Selection line, use [Esc] to delete it. Enter a name for your new Arrangement, e.g. "Basic" (bear in mind that the name may not exceed eight letters) and press [Return].

4.4.1 Creating and editing Groups

Your song is divided into five separate sections: the Intro, three Verses, and the Chorus. Up to this point, when you wanted to manipulate a section within the structure, you were forced to select all its relevant Parts, and then move them. The Clipboard makes things a bit easier, but Cubase has an even easier method in store for you.

Activate all four Intro Parts. Go to the Structure menu and choose Build Group ([Control][U]). A dialog box appears. Delete the default name "Group 1" by pressing [Esc] and enter a new name, e.g. "Intro". Confirm the entry by pressing [Return] or clicking the New button.

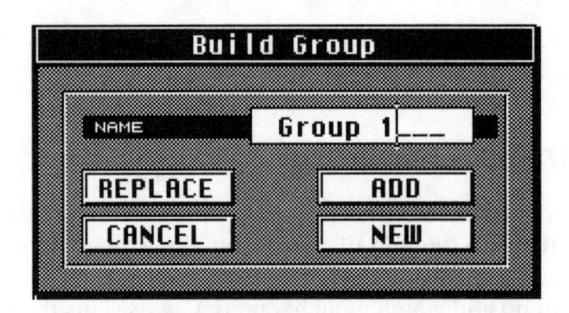

The Intro's four Parts are grouped...

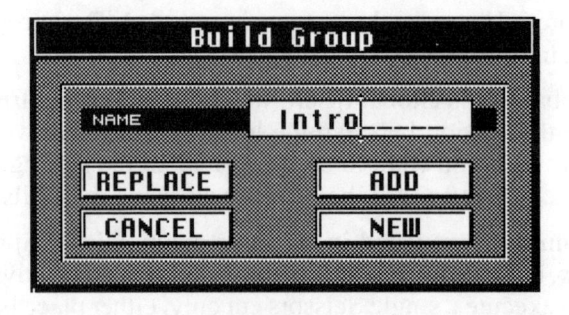

...named...

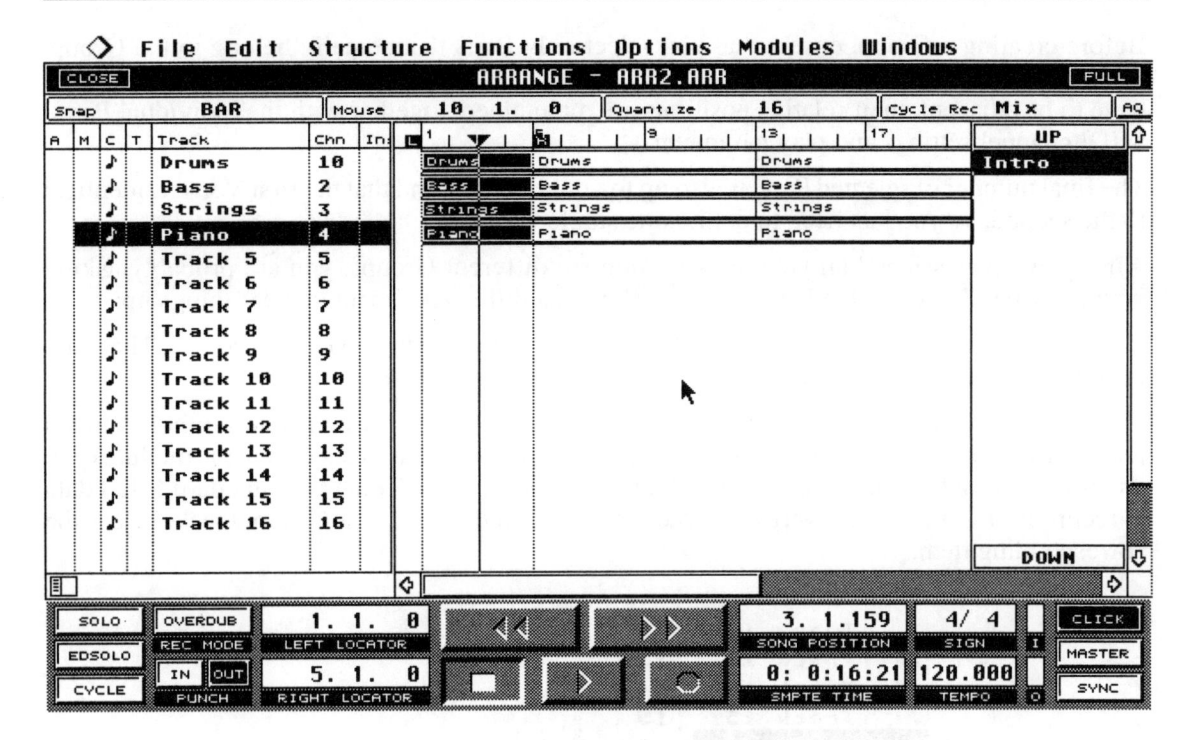

...and added to the Group List

Cubase returns to the Part Display. A new column appears to the right, in which the Groups you create are listed. You can hide the display by choosing Hide Groups from the Structure menu ([Control][J]). To recall the display, activate this command again.

Now let's define the next Group. Select the Parts of the first Verse. Call up the Build Group function again ([Control][U]), assign a new name, e.g. "Verse", and enter the new Group in the Group List by pressing [Return]. Use the same method with the remaining sections of the Arrangement. The Group List should then look like this:

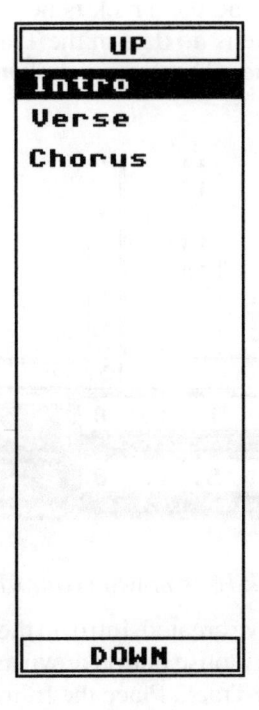

The Group List

Additional Arrange Functions

Before creating a Group, ensure that you select only Parts that actually belong to the Group. Cubase doesn't really care what you define as a Group. The Parts you select for a Group do not have to be adjacent; their relative positions are maintained, together with the individual Parts' MIDI channel settings and play parameters.

The final number of selected Parts is also up to you. Bear in mind that the first Verse is identical to the second, so you just need to define one single Group.

After you have assigned all your song sections to different Groups, you are probably asking yourself what the reasoning behind this is. Here is a little experiment to clear things up:

We first need to define a Group Track. The Track Classes are what you use to do this. These are called up for every Track using the "C" column of the Track List.

Click and hold column C of, say, Track 16, which is currently showing a note symbol. A menu featuring five or more choices will appear, depending on the Cubase version and the modules you are using. The default position is "MIDI Track", denoting a Track on which standard MIDI data is recorded. In order to convert this Track from a MIDI Track to a Group Track, select the corresponding item.

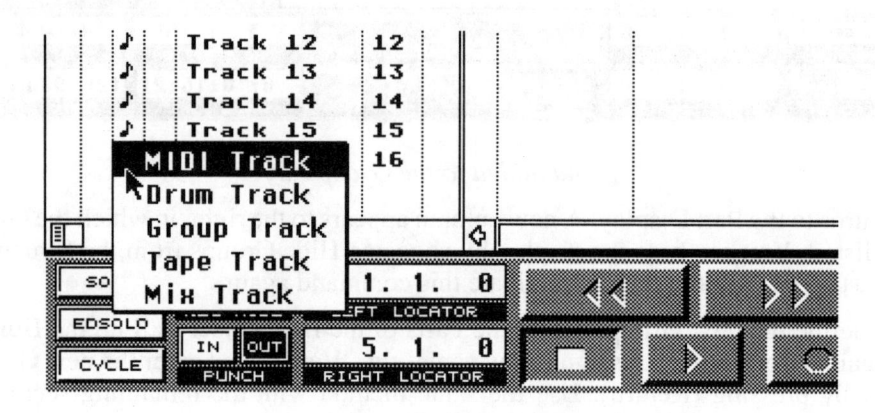

Selecting the Track Classes

The symbol in the column changes and the Track is now a Group Track. You can cancel this definition at any time, provided there is no data in the Track. Essentially, any blank Track can be made into a Group Track. The other Classes such as "Drum Track", etc. are discussed in later chapters.

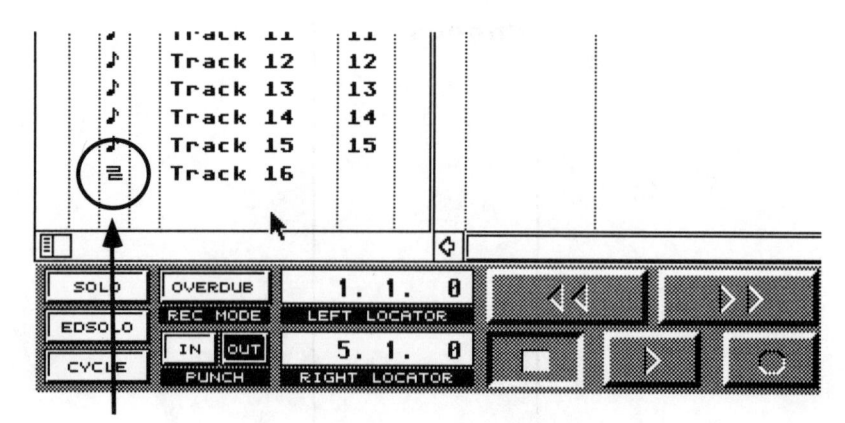

Track 16 is now a Group Track

Click and hold the first Group you have created, Intro, in the Group List. You can drag this Group as you would any Part by holding the mouse button down as you move the mouse. Drag the Intro Group to position 1.1.0 of the Group Track. Place the following Groups behind it, in any order. The result should look like this:

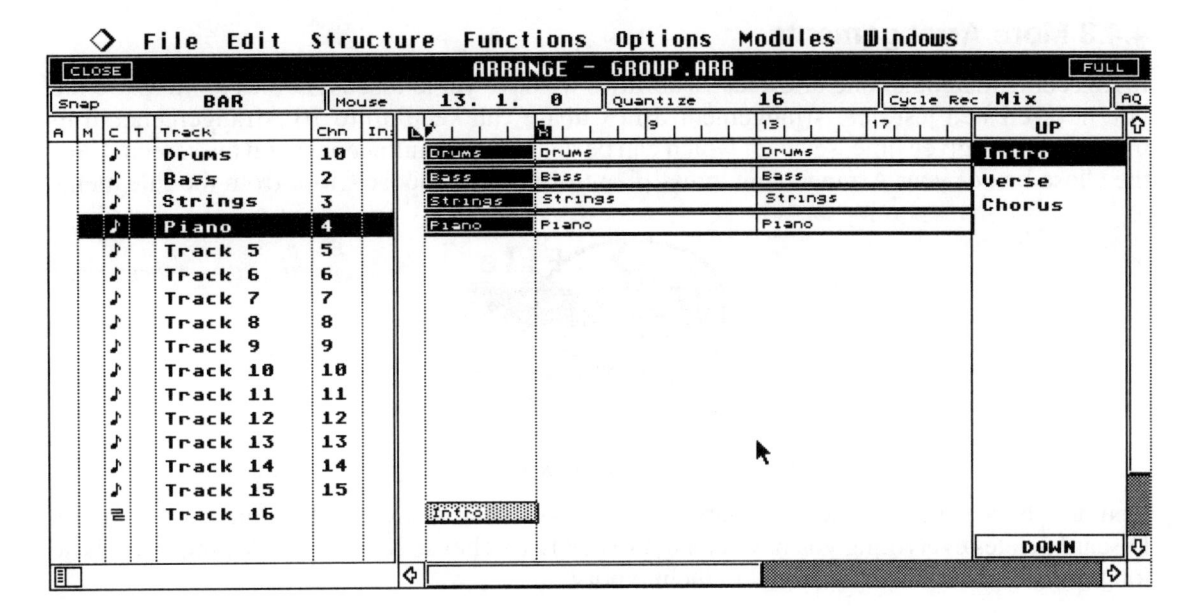

The Intro Group is in place

Mute all Tracks other than this Group Track. Play the results back. Even though you muted all the other Tracks, you can still hear their original notes: this is because the Groups contain all the necessary information.

To recap: a Group can contain as many Parts as you want. The Groups can then be arranged in any order on a separate Group Track. Of course, you can name or completely delete a Group Track just as you would any other Track. A Group Track cannot have a MIDI channel assigned to it, for the MIDI channel is determined by the Tracks of the individual Parts that make up a Group.

The Group Track's components can be regarded as normal Parts. You can move, delete and mute them, edit them via the Pencil and copy them using [Alternate]. However, you cannot merge, Scissors nor Glue them, nor can you record on a Group.

If you copy a Group to a position occupied by another Group, then the rest of the Groups are moved later. In other words, the Group is inserted into the Arrangement. You can superimpose a Group on another one. Double-clicking a Group allows you to rename the entire Group.

Change the structure of your Arrangement again and watch how the defined Groups always correspond to the original Parts. If you delete a Part that was assigned to a Group, then that Part is removed from the Group as well. If you delete all the Parts assigned to a Group, then the Group disappears too. You can add new Parts to a Group whenever you want: press and hold [Shift] and select the desired Part and the destination Group. Open the Build Group menu and click Add instead of New. The selected Part is added to the Group.

"Replace" in the Build Group menu replaces all the Parts in a Group you had defined previously with those currently selected in your Arrangement.

Double-clicking a Group in the Group List allows a new name to be assigned to it. Dragging a Group and moving it up or down out of the Group List deletes it.

4.4.2 What Groups can do

Now that you know how to create and edit Groups, let's take a look at their many versatile applications. One of these we have already applied during a practical exercise, namely how to quickly change the order of sections in an Arrangement.

You don't always have to assign Groups as Choruses or Verses. You could just as easily group together percussion or wind Parts and insert them at the desired position within the Arrangement.

Additional Arrange Functions

4.4.3 More Arrangements

In this context, another one of Cubase's abilities we have yet to discuss comes to mind. So far, you have created just *one* Arrangement. But Cubase can keep up to 16 Arrangements in its memory at any given time, seven of which can be displayed simultaneously on the screen. Click the Close box of your Arrangement, press [Control][W], or choose Close from the File menu.

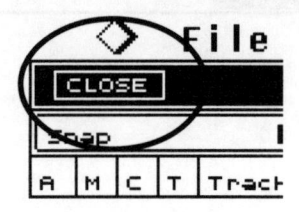

The Close box

You now have several choices available. Cancel does what it says, it abandons the operation. Discard deletes everything you have created so far! Let's choose Keep. Your Arrangement is no longer visible, but it is still lodged in the memory.

Go to the Windows menu. You will find the name of your Arrangement listed here. Click it to display it on your screen again. After this little exercise, we return to the Groups.

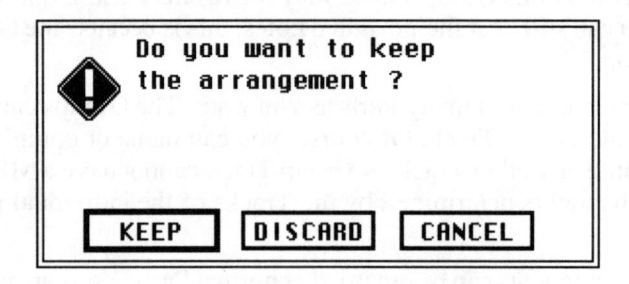

Discard deletes the Arrangement, Keep saves it

Choose New from the File menu or press [Control][N]. A blank Arrangement appears in which you can still see the Group list. Create a new Group Track and arrange the Groups in any order you like. At some point in time, you will have to zoom the Position Bar display. Now listen to the results of your efforts.

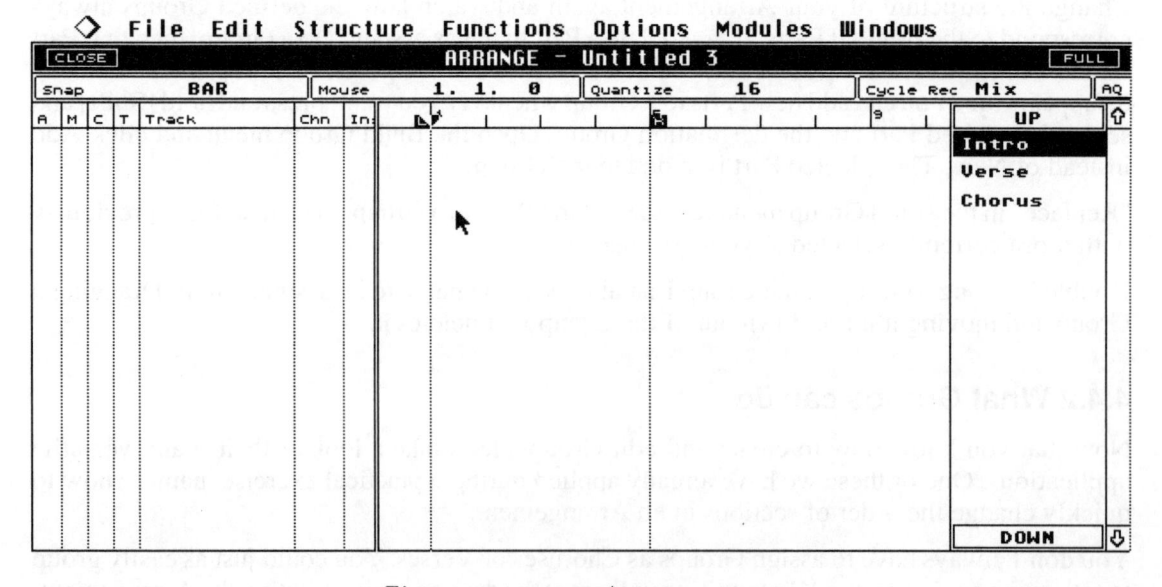

First create a new Arrangement...

Group Tracks

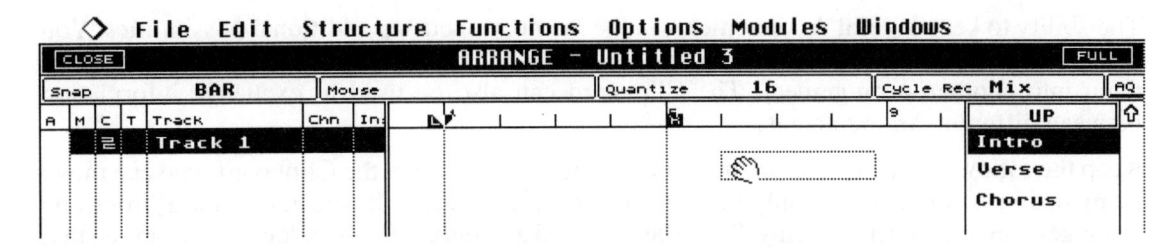

...then drag the Groups to the Group Track

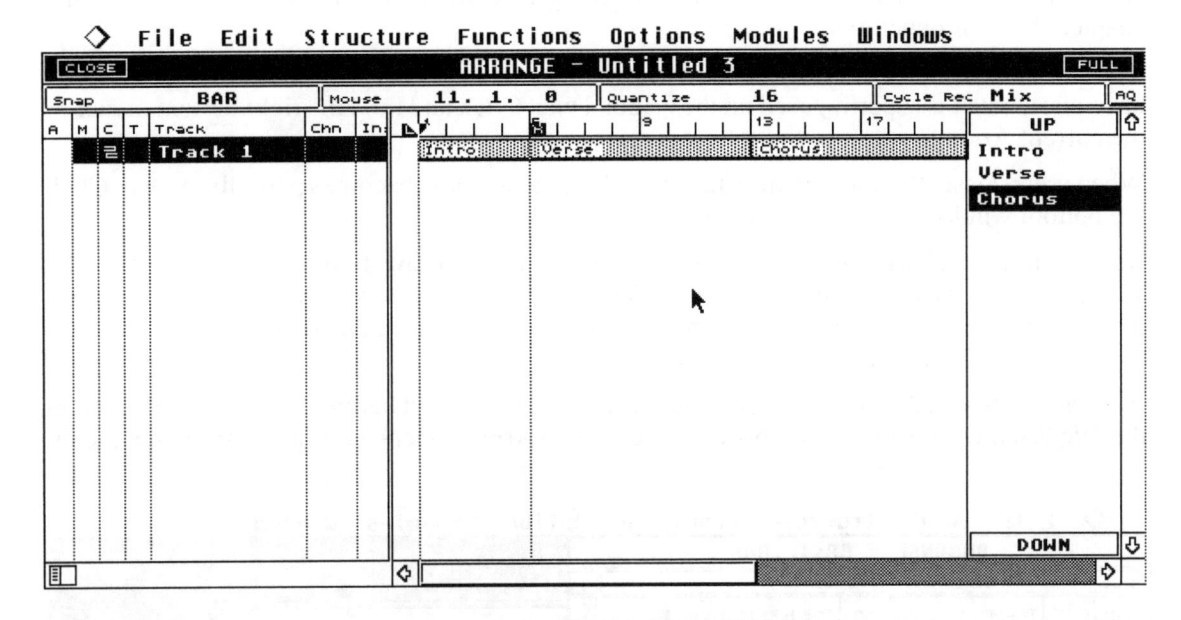

The basic Arrangement is completed

Create a normal Track with [Control][T], or double-click the Track List. Assign it to the MIDI channel of your piano sound and record a Track to accompany the Arrangement as it plays. Do not position the locators nor activate Cycle mode, and switch the metronome off. Record more Tracks if you want.

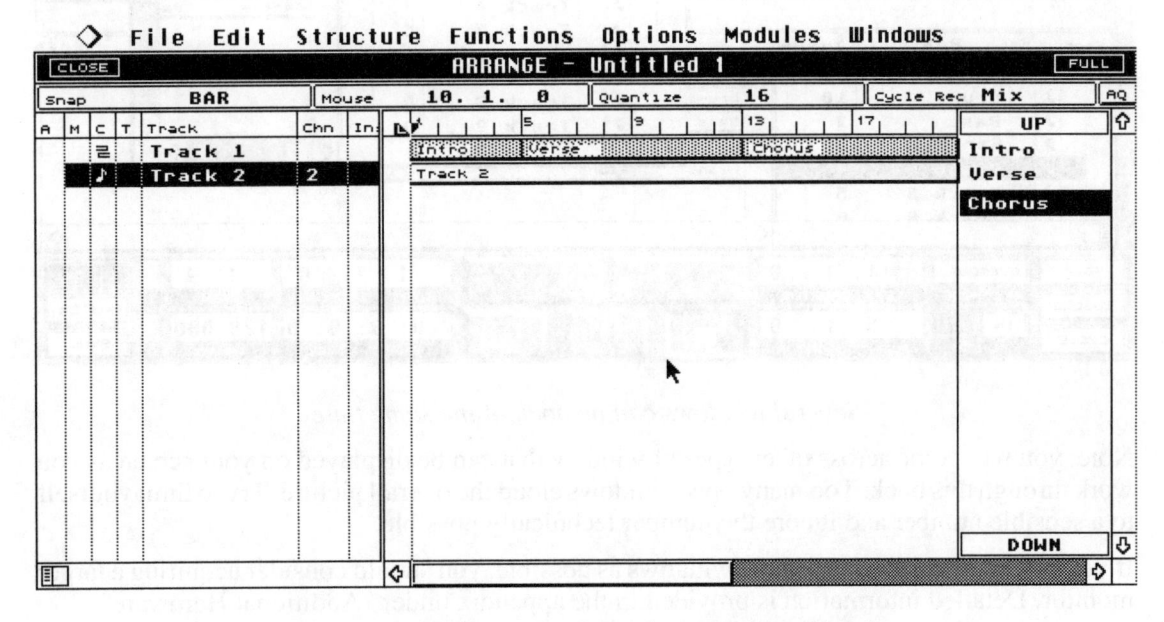

You can record new Parts on the remaining Tracks

Additional Arrange Functions

The ability to keep several Arrangements in the memory opens up additional possibilities. You could for instance create drum Parts in one Arrangement, define them as Groups and then insert them into another Arrangement. The Clipboard can also be used to exchange information between different Arrangements.

Keep the following differences in mind: once Parts are entered in the Clipboard, you can move them within a single Track only, and not on to other Tracks. If you move Parts from one Arrangement to another, as many Tracks as required are automatically added. You can see that the Clipboard functions somewhat differently in this sort of situation.

All Arrangements can be saved together as a "Song". Detailed information can be found in the chapter "System Functions".

You can simultaneously display up to seven windows on the screen. The new Arrangement you have just created is superimposed on the original one. Click and hold the right bottom corner of the current Arrange window and reduce its size.

When you release the mouse button, the other Arrange window becomes partially visible. Click the bottom window to move it to the top.

Keep in mind that windows can be reduced, enlarged, or moved about as you see fit. Tile Windows in the Windows menu is a handy function: it lays out the available Arrange windows in such a way that they are all fully visible - in so doing, it adjusts their sizes: the more windows there are, the smaller each window has to be.

Arrangements saved with the Keep command need to be opened before they can be included in the Tile Windows operation. Simply click the desired Arrangement name in the Windows menu.

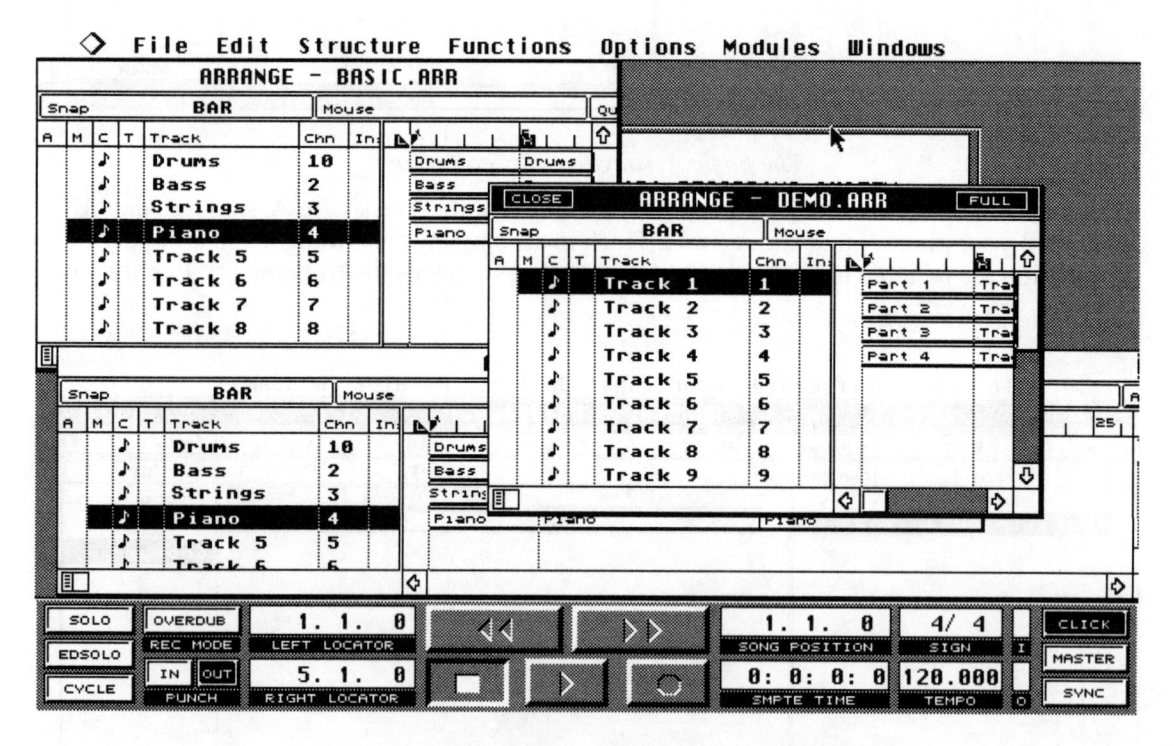

Several windows can be open at the same time

Note: you will come across other types of window that can be displayed on your screen as you work through this book. Too many open windows cloud the overall picture. Try to limit yourself to a sensible number and ignore the number technically possible.

If you prefer to work with as many windows as possible, you should consider acquiring a larger monitor. Detailed information is provided in the appendix under "Additional Hardware".

A First Brief Summary

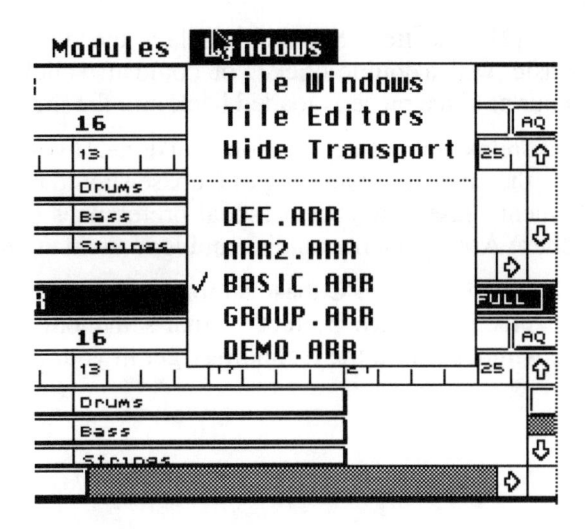

Tile Windows adjusts the window sizes

Due to the Atari's operating system, only one window at a time can be active, and you can make changes in the active window only: you'll recognize it by its highlighted black Title Bar.

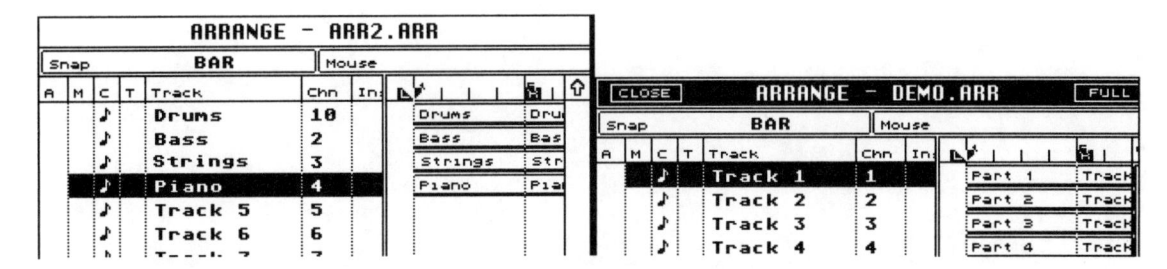

The left window is inactive, the right active

An inactive window can be activated by clicking anywhere on it. Note that only one Arrangement at a time may be played.

4.4.4 Realtime Groups

As a crowning glory, we will insert Groups in the Group Track in realtime. Choose New from the File menu to call up a new Arrange window. Create a new Group Track and place the Intro at Position 1.1.0. Place the Song Position Triangle at the beginning of the Arrangement and start playback. Cubase plays the Intro. While the Intro's final bar is playing, press [Control] while you click a Group in the list. This Group is inserted right after the Intro and is played back.

Cubase places Groups selected using this method on the downbeat of the following bar. For instance, if you click a Group while bar 4 is playing, then the selected Group is inserted at position 5.1.0. This function allows you to create an Arrangement structure and listen to it at the same time. This way you could, for example, insert additional horns or strings into an existing Arrangement.

4.5 A first brief summary

Now we have gone through all the Arrange functions. Close the windows one after another, and this time, confirm with Discard instead of Keep. All the Arrangements are being deleted. Do not forget to activate and delete the Arrangements saved in the Windows menu.

You can load your basic Arrangement at any time from the disk you saved it on: choose Open from the File menu and "Arrangement" from the dialog box that then appears, or press

Additional Arrange Functions

[Control][O] followed by [2]. The Item Selector displays the disk's contents. Select your Arrangement entitled "Basic" with a double-click. You could also click the file name and select OK or press [Return]. Your practice piece is loaded back into the memory.

Now it is time to kick back, relax, and reflect on a job well done. If you have run through all the exercises conscientiously, then the basic handling of Cubase should no longer pose a problem. You can create Arrangements based on your personal preferences using long Tracks and/or Patterns. You can save these Arrangements on disk and load them at any time.

The next chapters delve more deeply into Cubase's more advanced features. Here too, please keep experimenting, as "practise makes perfect" - that's the only way you'll be able to concentrate on the music without letting the technology get in your way.

5 MIDI

If you have worked with Cubase this far, you have been introduced to the basics of MIDI. Yet the power of the MIDI standard goes far further than these basic applications. A thorough understanding of MIDI is necessary before you can really know the ins and outs of Cubase. This chapter will give you the necessary technical background, and establish the connection between technology and practical application.

5.1 A short history of MIDI

Sequencers were in existence well before the era of digital technology. At first, these were limited to analog devices, which were usually monophonic and operated on control voltages. The first sequencers featuring digital communication were roughly comparable in operation to the principle of MIDI, but they had one major disadvantage: they only supported certain synthesizers from the same manufacturer as the sequencer. For example, the Oberheim DSX sequencer did not support the Sequential Circuits Prophet V, an extremely popular device at the time: you had to use the Sequential sequencer, which in turn could not communicate with the Oberheim OB-Xa, OB-8, or the Roland Jupiter 8. Everyone was confronted with a problem to which there seemed to be no real solution.

To get to grips with this problem, electronic musical equipment manufacturers set about developing a universal interface. The goal was to establish a communications medium for all the diverse models of different manufacturers. After a lengthy developmental phase, the MIDI standard was first introduced in 1982. The first MIDI devices, a Roland Jupiter 6 and a Sequential Circuits Prophet 600 were connected at a trade fair, and the long-awaited communication standard was established. The Prophet could by driven by the Roland's keyboard, and vice versa. This new development was given the title, "Musical Instrument Digital Interface", in short, MIDI. Its enormous success can be measured by the fact that today virtually no device reaches the market without the obligatory MIDI ports.

5.2 The hardware

Cost considerations dictated a relatively modest hardware configuration. Most devices incorporate three standard ports:
- MIDI In receives information sent by another instrument or computer.
- MIDI Out transmits the information a device produces.
- MIDI Thru passes on the information it receives at its MIDI In to other devices without modifying the data, which means several devices can be connected in series. Some economy

MIDI

models do not feature this port and in some cases, it may be integrated in the Out port. However, the function remains the same.

MIDI data is transferred via a standard five-pin cable, comprising two wires and the shielding.

5.3 Communication

In addition to the hardware question, the manufacturers had to agree on a common communications protocol in order to make sure that musical devices could communicate with one another. This MIDI standard, with a few additions along the line, remains the standard today.

To gain an understanding of data transmission in general, and MIDI and sequencer applications in particular, let's now take a look at the basics.

In order to transfer the information that is created when you hit a key on your keyboard in the form of a digital MIDI command, the information needs to be broken down into individual steps. The source instrument tells the destination instrument which note was played, and the velocity with which the key was struck since most instruments now respond to velocity dynamics.

A computer processes only numbers, which is where its strength lies. For this reason, it is necessary to translate musical information into numeric values.

The MIDI protocol performs this task as follows: to switch a note on, the source instrument sends three consecutive numeric values to the destination instrument. The first value is referred to as the "status byte". It tells the destination device what type of MIDI message will follow, in this case, the command to play a note. The next value defines the note in question. Finally, the velocity tells the device how hard or softly the key was struck. These second and third messages are called "data bytes".

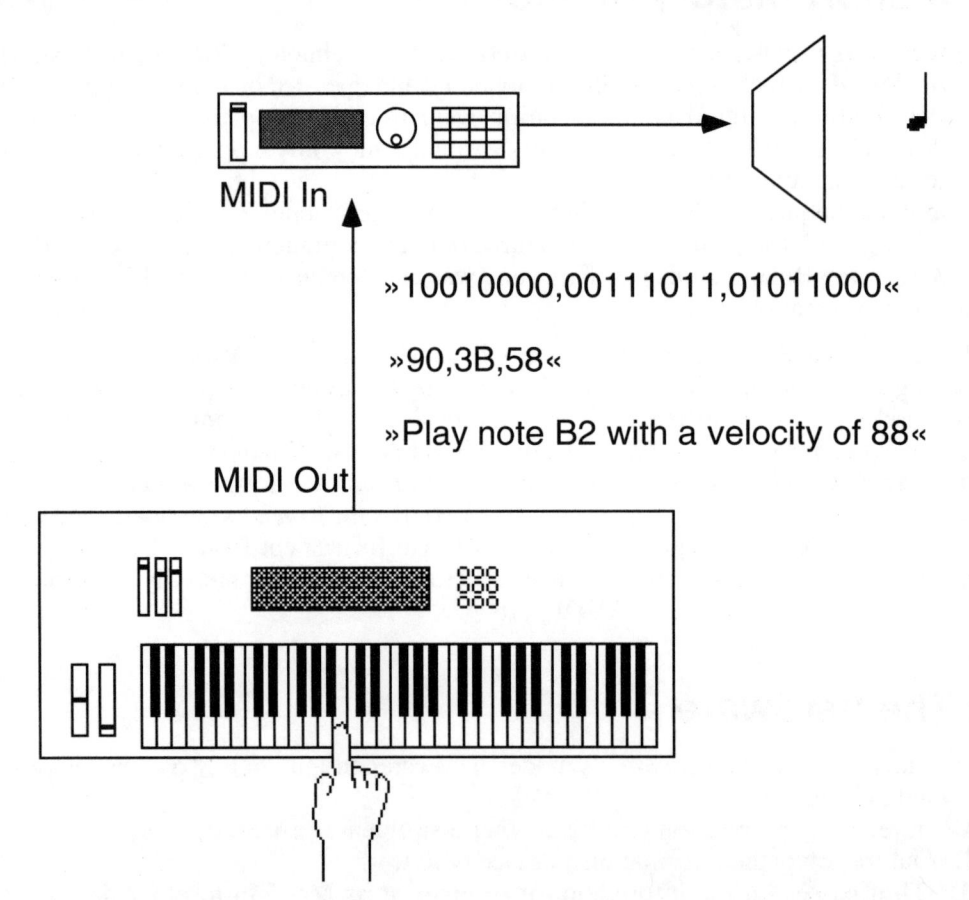

A MIDI message prompts the sound module to generate a note

5.4 Bits and bytes

The term "byte" is derived from the computer world and is transmitted in a specific numerical format, i.e. binary. Let's take a brief look at the mathematics involved. A detailed analysis is reserved for the section entitled "Hard stuff".

Computers process data and numbers using a switching process, and MIDI messages are treated the same way. Computers distinguish between just two states, on and off, and they translate this by switching a current between two numbers, 1 and 0. The digital representation of these values is called a "bit". In order for a computer to be able to deal with larger numbers, it combines eight bits together to form a byte. A byte can represent up to 256 different numbers.

The MIDI protocol is based on this eight-bit concept. The computer uses the first bit to distinguish between a status and a data byte. If the first bit is set to one, the byte in question is a status byte. Conversely, a zero in the first position denotes a data byte.

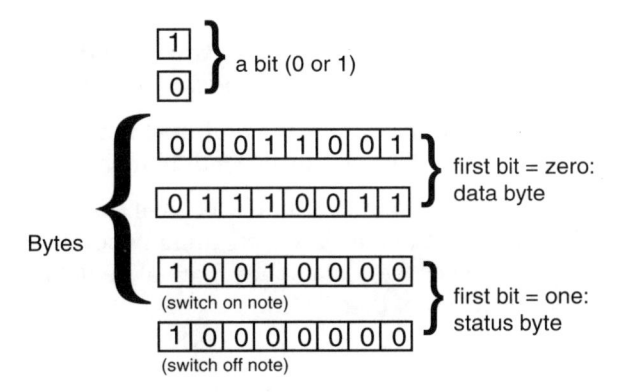

Bits, status bytes and data bytes

By distinguishing between 1 and 0, the computer or synthesizer is able to transmit the necessary information. Your instrument and the computer are exchanging virtually endless sequences of numbers telling each other what to do in response to what you or Cubase are playing. The important fact here is also the source of some irritation among many MIDI users: MIDI is a *serial* protocol.

Within the MIDI cable, only one of the wires is used for MIDI data transfer, which means that the MIDI messages have to be sent one after another, not simultaneously. In the example above, the status byte is sent first, followed by the two data bytes. Even though this occurs at a very fast rate, you should always keep in mind that an incredible amount of information has to be transmitted while you play. A situation involving a complex Arrangement of instruments and a large number of MIDI Tracks full of notes can, under some extreme circumstances, cause the data transfer to lag behind the song's tempo.

The correct timing of notes and other data is essential in music, so you can see where you might run into problems. That some MIDI messages are much more data-intensive than those that simply convey information on notes means that the problem is compounded.

However, before you decide to chuck away all your MIDI gear, let me reassure you on a few points: despite certain disadvantages, MIDI allows for a great deal of headroom in musical applications before you even come close to encountering these problems. Plus, there are a number of ways of coping with or even preventing them altogether. We will take a closer look at both of these points later on.

Now back to our MIDI note. A MIDI Note On message comprises three sections which are sent as three separate bytes, and interpreted by the receiver. Note commands and their velocity can contain up to 128 different values, so for velocity, this means that a note can be played at one of 128 steps of velocity. The following diagram gives you an idea of the musical range that can be achieved via MIDI:

MIDI

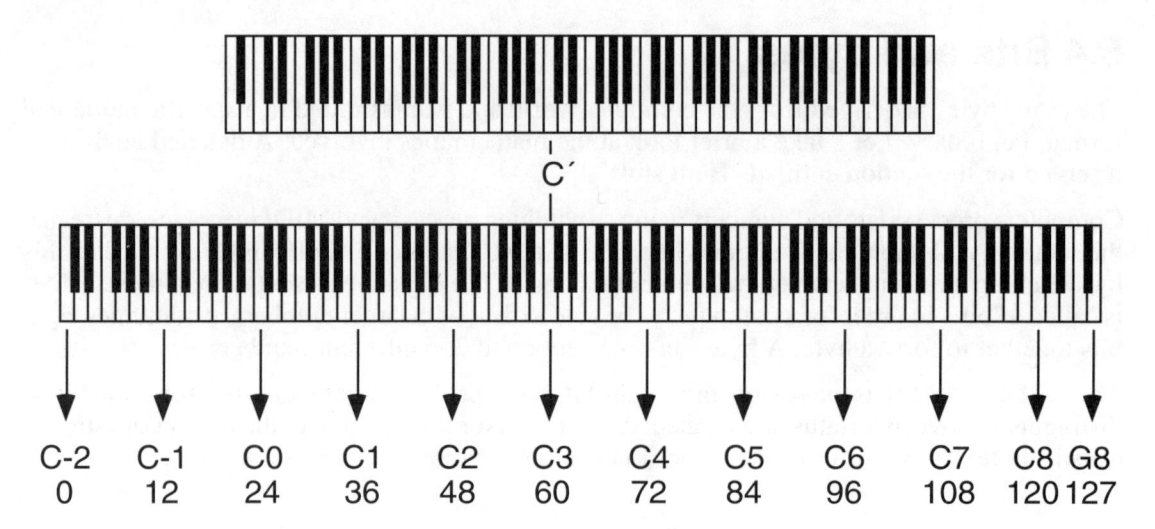

The tonal range of MIDI (with a standard piano keyboard above for comparison) showing note pitches and their corresponding MIDI note numbers

C-2	C-1	C0	C1	C2	C3	C4	C5	C6	C7	C8	G8
0	12	24	36	48	60	72	84	96	108	120	127

The range exceeds that of a standard piano. Each MIDI note number is sent with a preceding status byte which tell the receiver to play the corresponding note.

There are lots of other types of MIDI commands, not just note messages, and we'll be discussing them all in due course. All MIDI commands have one thing in common: they all have a status byte. It is usually followed by one or two data bytes. Special applications such as sound data transmission can have huge numbers of data bytes.

5.5 Additional MIDI commands

The MIDI message telling the receiving sound module to play a note is called a "Note On event". Obviously, you will release the key sooner or later. This entails a similar process: a status byte is sent containing the Note Off event. The two following data bytes specify the note number and the speed at which the key was released. The latter is called "release velocity". This means that on some (very rare) devices, you could program the decay time of the sound to correspond to the speed with which you release the key. However, very few synthesizers can send or interpret release velocity.

If no Note Off followed the Note On, the note would simply sustain until you switched the device off. You can try this out: select something like a string sound, press any key and hold it. Now unplug the MIDI cable from the receiving module. Even if you release the key the note will drone on. Some devices have a way of stopping such drones: if yours doesn't, simply switch the receiver off.

Apart from the Note Off message, the MIDI standard includes another way to switch notes off, where a Note On command is sent with a velocity value of zero. This is a default setting in Cubase. This may lead to problems in very few devices which don't recognize this command.

Almost no-one has ever run into this problem with a sound module. It is less rare when using a mixer automation system that uses Note On/Note Off commands to mute audio channels. If you are using a device which recognizes Note Off commands only, choose MIDI Setup from the Options menu. The Note Off entry in this dialog box is not usually activated. Click the blank box to activate the Note Off mode. Only do this when you are left with no other choice. You will later see that this function adds even more data to the MIDI load.

In some especially difficult situations you may have to resort to the Length Correction function in the MIDI Setup dialog box. Length Correction puts a little gap after Note Off commands if they are followed by more Note On commands of the same pitch and on the same MIDI channel This is because some synthesizers with slow reaction times sometimes have problems. So, if your device has problems reacting to rapid staccato notes, try experimenting with the Length Correction values.

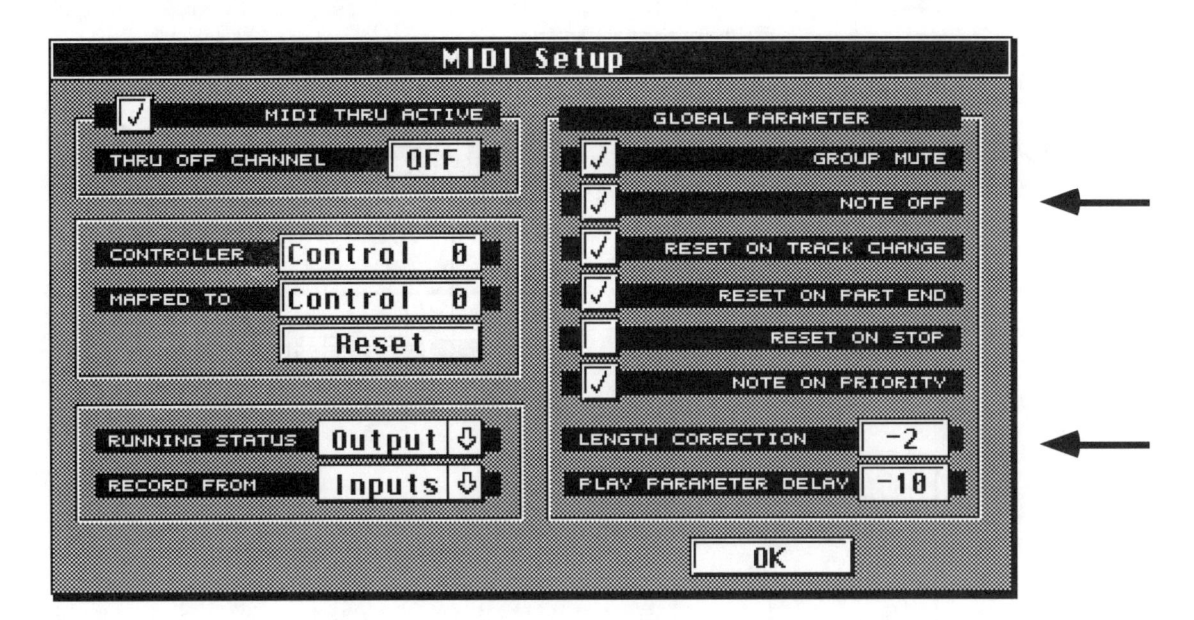

The Note Off and Length Correction functions

5.6 MIDI and sequencers

We have seen how one or more notes of a sound module can be played and stopped in any order via MIDI messages. Switching notes on and off in any order is usually referred to as playing music (think about it!). This takes us away from technical matters and back to the music.

If we carry this logic a step further it will shed some light on the way sequencers and hence Cubase operate. A sequencer is no more than a recorder that sends messages to an instrument, telling it when and with what velocity to switch notes on and off. The sounds themselves are not recorded, but simply the note parameters. What kind of sound this note information triggers depends entirely on the receiving synthesizer or sampler.

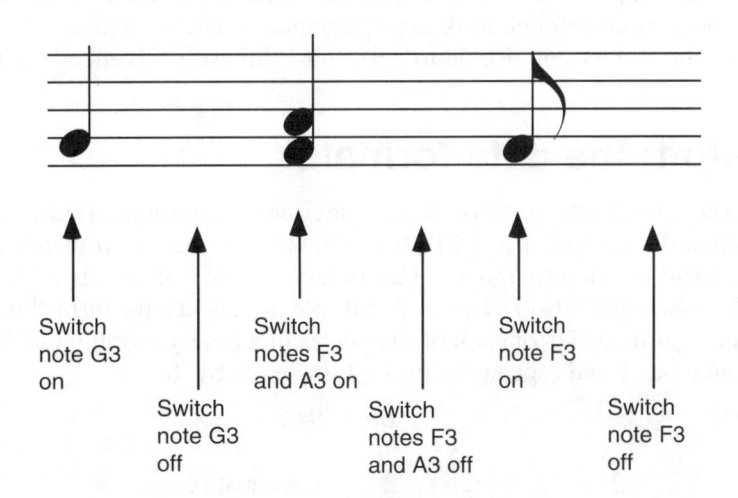

How a Note On and Note Off sequence relates to notes

However, complex music consists of more than just a number of notes playing the same sound: it normally comprises many different sounds produced by one or more different instruments. The MIDI standard must do more than just generate notes in an instrument via remote control; it must

MIDI

also be capable of controlling *several* devices at the same time via one simple cable. This is accomplished with the help of MIDI channels, of which there are 16.

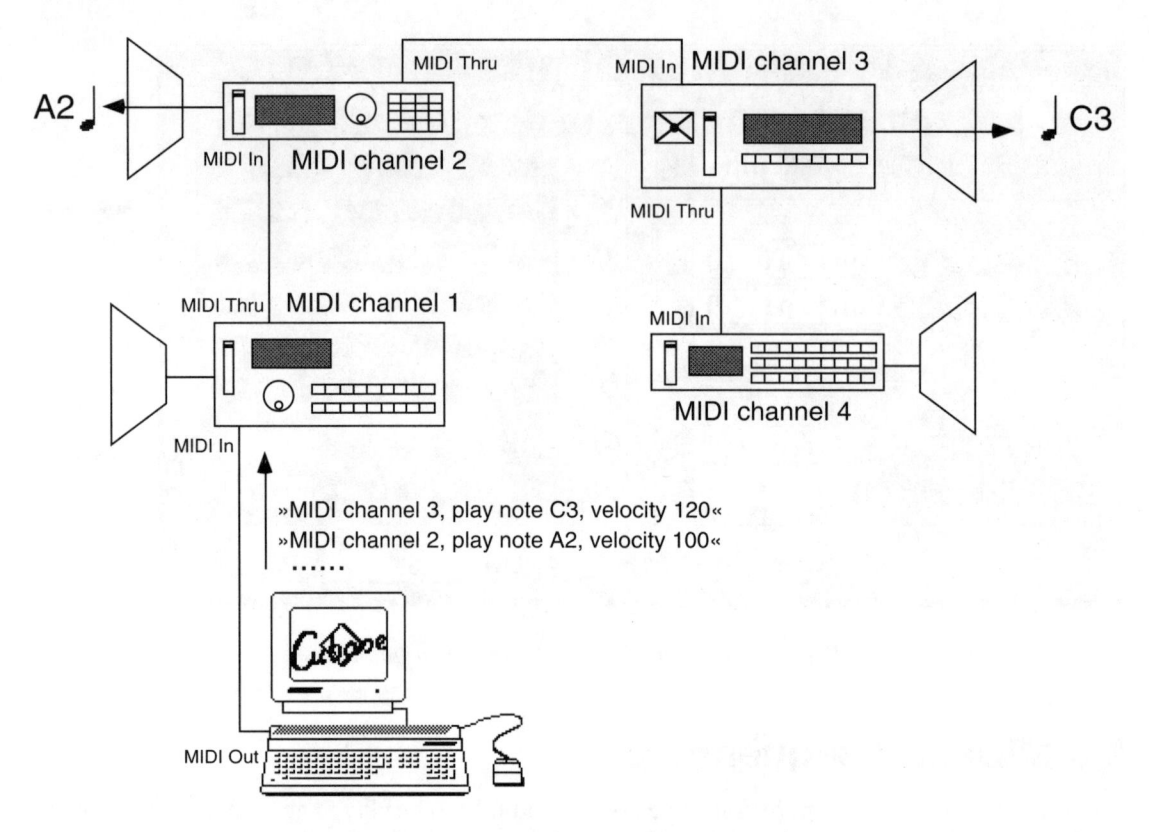

Sending commands via MIDI channels

Sound modules that are programmed to listen to a certain channel will only react to MIDI messages sent on that channel. In the diagram above, the modules can "hear" if a MIDI message is sent intended for them: the devices set to channels 2 and 3 recognize their respective MIDI messages and each of them executes the command to play a specific note. The other two modules are not addressed, so they remain silent.

Why does MIDI feature only 16 channels? The answer is based on the structure of the MIDI data format, and requires a more detailed look at the technical aspects. In practise, you won't have to deal with the maths, unless you decide to delve into Cubase's advanced applications.

5.7 Hard stuff: the data formats

Every decimal number (that's the way normal people count) can be converted to a binary number. We've just seen that the computer and MIDI use binary numbers to transmit commands and subsequently translate them into music. The binary system of numbers is fairly easy to understand. Each of the eight bits in a byte is a multiple of 2, hence the term "binary". As a mini rule-of-thumb, the significancies of each of the places in a binary number can be computed by starting with the number 1 and repeatedly multiplying each by 2.

Bit 8   *Bit 1 Byte*

2^8	2^7	2^6	2^5	2^4	2^3	2^2	2^1	power of two
128	64	32	16	8	4	2	1	product in decimal numbers

The following byte

0	0	0	0	0	0	0	1

corresponds to number 1. The byte

1 0 0 0 0 0 0 0

corresponds to number 128. The following method simplifies the conversion of decimal into binary numbers. Just split up the decimal number by 2. So, 120 is

(0 x 128) + (1 x 64) + (1 x 32) + (1 x 16) + (1 x 8) + (0 x 4) + (0 x 2) + (0 x 1)

The number 120 is therefore represented in the binary system as:

120 = 0111 1000.

The number 129 is factored as

(1 x 128) + (0 x 64) + (0 x 32) + (0 x 16) + (0 x 8) + (0 x 4) + (0 x 2) + (1 x 1) = 1000 0001.

The highest value which can be represented by a byte is 255. In computer terminology the two halves of each byte, each containing four bits, are called "nibbles".

(1 x 128) + (1 x 64) + (1 x 32) + (1 x 16) + (1 x 8) + (1 x 4) + (1 x 2) + (1 x 1) = 255 = 1111 1111.

In this example all bits in the byte are set. If you include the value 0 (0000 0000), there are a maximum of 256 different values. MIDI distinguishes between status and data bytes when transmitting messages. The computer does this by taking the left bit as a reference. If it is set to 1, you are dealing with a status byte. If not, the byte concerned is a data byte. In equation form, it looks like this:

Byte ≥ 1000 0000 (decimal 128 and higher) = status byte

byte ≤ 0111 1111 (decimal 127 and lower) = data byte

So we can conclude that data byte values cannot exceed 127 as all values above 127 are treated as status bytes. This applies to a large number of MIDI messages such as note range and velocity values. If a higher data resolution than 127 is required, MIDI uses a little trick, but more on this later.

We still haven't explained why there are only 16 MIDI channels. The information you have been given so far gives you a clue. The channel coding is always lodged in the second Part of the status byte, its second "nibble". Let's look at a Note On event in more detail:

First nibble   Second nibble

1001   0000

There are sixteen possible values for the second nibble:

8 4 2 1

0 0 0 0 = 0

0 0 0 1 = 1

0 0 1 0 = 2

0 0 1 1 = 3

....

1 1 1 1 = 15

0 through 15 gives sixteen different values.

5.8 Still more numbers

If you wade your way through one of your devices' operating manuals, you are bound to run into character combinations such as F0, 11, 12, B0 or F7. Sometimes these codes are preceded by a $ symbol or followed by an "H", e.g. $F0, $11-F0H, B5H. These codes are derived from a format

MIDI

used in MIDI based on the hexadecimal system. The dollar sign or the H serve to distinguish hexadecimal numbers from decimal numbers.

We looked at binary numbers in order to gain a better understanding of how a computer operates. Hexadecimals in turn are *essential* for programming some of Cubase's more advanced features, such as creating your own MIDI Mixer applications.

The hexadecimal system is a more compact way of representing numbers. One hexadecimal place can represent 16 different values, as opposed to two in the binary system and ten in decimal. The values are represented by the following symbols:

Hexadecimal : Decimal

0 = 0

1 = 1

2 = 2

......

9 = 9

A = 10

B = 11

C = 12

D = 13

E = 14

F = 15

Because MIDI uses 256 values, we need two places in the hexadecimal system. The first place is computed following the method depicted in the table above. The decimal value of the second place is the result of a multiplication by 16. The hexadecimal value of $FF is therefore:

F (= decimal 15) x 16 = 240 + F (= decimal 15) = 255. We know that this must be a status byte.

The hexadecimal value $61 is: 6 (= decimal 6) x 16 = 96 + 1 (= decimal 1) = 97. This number is a data byte.

More examples:

$AO = 160 (10 x 16) + 0

$34 = 52 (3 x 16) + 4

We don't need to get into too much detail regarding this data format. However, there's an easy way to convert hexadecimal into binary numbers and vice versa. The binary number is divided into its two nibbles. Each nibble can represent 16 different values. This is exactly the range of values which one place of the hexadecimal value can represent. And here's how the conversion works:

	1st Nibble 1000	2nd Nibble 0000	from 1000 0000
equals decimal	8	0	
equals hexadecimal	8	0	you get ($)80(H)

	1st Nibble 1111	2nd Nibble 1111	from 1111 1111
equals decimal	15	15	
equals hexadecimal	F	F	you get ($)FF(H)

You can now breath a sigh of relief. The following dissection of a MIDI Note On event will represent the end of our mathematical excursion:

	binary	hexadecimal	message
Status byte	1001 0000	144	Note On MIDI channel 1
Data byte	1000 0000	40	MIDI Note 64 = E3
Data byte	0000 1101	0D	Velocity = 13

This knowledge won't directly benefit you in your musical endeavours, but it will help when you want to program, say, a MIDI Manager application that Steinberg hasn't included in the Cubase package.

The appendix includes a complete conversion table for binary, decimal and hexadecimal numbers.

5.9 MIDI Program Change events

Back to the MIDI interface. It has many more applications than just controlling notes. For instance, you may want to switch to a different sound on your synthesizer at some place during a song. You can call up any sound with a simple MIDI command. The message consists of a status byte and one data byte, so up to 128 programs can be accessed.

Program Change events are bound by the 16 channel limit, allowing a maximum of 16 different sound modules to be addressed. This, of course, includes the virtual "devices" within a multitimbral synthesizer.

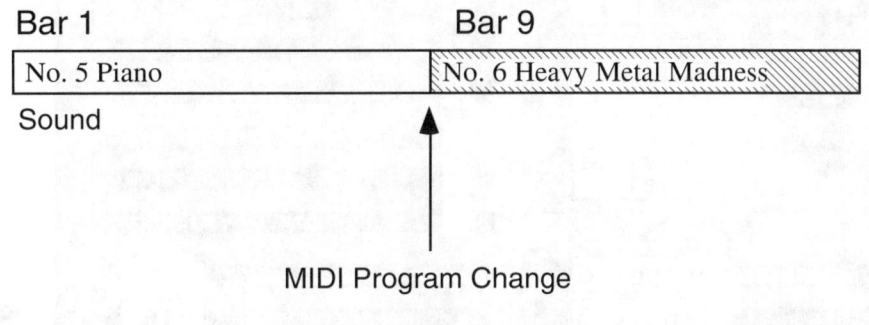

A Program Change

The example above illustrates how Cubase switches to another sound upon reaching bar 9 of a particular Part. The section on the Inspector in the previous chapter showed how you can do this. The Program Change event simply calls up a memory location in the receiving device on a specific MIDI channel: the sound in this memory location depends on the receiving device.

Record a Part of your choice and at the same time switch programs at the device itself. Cubase records the Program Changes (providing the device is transmitting to Cubase) and plays them back.

MIDI can address a total of 128 programs. The majority of modern devices offer substantially more sounds, so the manufacturers of MIDI equipment decided some time ago to expand the MIDI standard, which led to the introduction of the Bank Select command. In theory this command can access 16,384 banks, and within each bank you get the 128 standard Program Changes. This means you could address a total of 2,097,152 programs. Satisfied? The Bank Select command can also be found in the Inspector.

There is a ground rule that governs all MIDI options, including the Bank Select command: regardless of all the great things Cubase and MIDI have to offer, the receiving device must be capable of processing the information it receives, which is far from the case. As of yet, few devices can deal with Bank Select commands. The actual MIDI command consists of a combination of two "Control Changes" which we'll take a closer look at in one of the following sections.

MIDI

5.10 Possible problems

Basically, a Program Change is a simple process. However, you can still run into problems. The good news is there is a solution for each of these problems.

If you send Program Changes in rapid succession, your device may react to them rather slowly. The root of the problem is fairly obvious: some Program Changes require the device to reset literally hundreds of parameters. Depending on the device's performance specifications, this can take a brief moment and may even cause extraneous noise. Such noise can occur when a Program Change is received while notes are still sounding, or where a program has a fairly long envelope release phase, even if you can no longer hear the sound. Most devices abruptly cut the sound off when the next Program Change command is received, though some instruments are quite capable of dealing with this problem.

To avoid this kind of problem, you should avoid sending Program Changes on the downbeat of the bar, but slightly before it. For this reason, Program Changes executed by the Inspector are sent prior to the downbeat. If you are still having difficulties with Program Changes, i.e. delays and noise, change the Play Parameter Delay in the MIDI Setup dialog box. Negative delay values move the Program Changes to a position before the downbeat, which is usually prior to the new notes. Try different settings until you have resolved the problem.

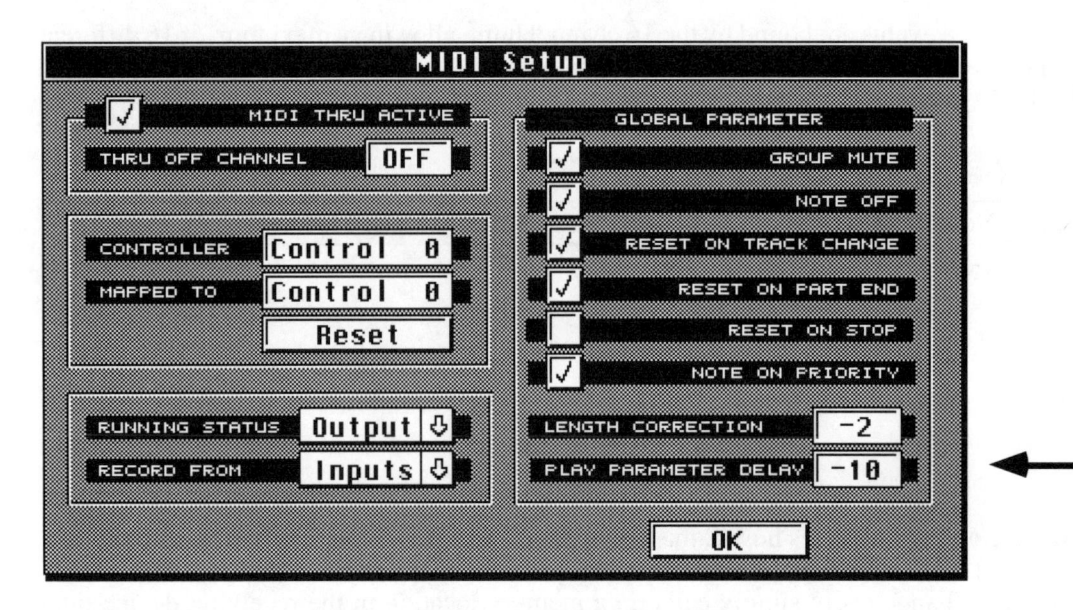

The Play Parameter Delay

As a rule, you should keep Program Changes to a minimum in your songs. Program Changes can be annoying in other respects. If you load new sounds into your instrument via MIDI or from a cartridge, the Program Change commands are still valid but the sounds called up by the numbers will be completely different. This is particularly irritating if you prefer to work with sounds you have programmed yourself.

Let's assume you have modified a sound without saving it afterwards. You naturally want to hear the edited version in a musical context. You play the song back. If a Program Change comes along, it may destroy the results of all your efforts. Why? Many synthesizers temporarily store edited sounds in a buffer. If you accidentally switch to a new program in Cubase, the corresponding sound is loaded into the buffer, deleting your edited sound.

Cubase displays Program Changes as decimal numbers, from 1 to 128, such as in the Inspector. However, some synthesizers use other counting systems: the Roland D-50 operates on an octal system (11-18, 21-28,...), the Kawai K1 on a bank system (A-1, A-2,...). Others don't offer the whole range of programs allowed by MIDI (the first Yamaha DX7 had just 32 programs). Others such as the Oberheim Matrix 1000 have way more than 128 program locations.

These devices interpret MIDI Program Change events differently; for instance, Program Change 3 could call up Program 203, and so on. Please make up a conversion table when using devices that count differently to MIDI.

5.11 The General MIDI standard

The General MIDI Standard (abbreviated as GM) further helps to co-ordinate Program Changes. In the GM standard, sounds are assigned to categories such as piano, strings, etc. Similar sounds are allotted to the same program numbers in a GM device. This means that you can configure your channel assignment, knowing that the sounds will be correct, no matter which GM device you play back on, as in the following situations:
- you have bought a new instrument and you want to play your old sequences on it.
- You want (or have to) play a finished Arrangement on another instrument.
- You are exchanging Arrangements with another musician.
- You have bought MIDI disks containing ready-made songs.

If you stick to the GM standard, your Program Change commands will call up similar sounds, whatever the device, though of course no two devices from different manufacturers will sound identical. The Yamaha TG 100 and the Roland Sound Canvas each offer different sounds. You can recognize a similarity in the sound material though, and then select the ideal sound or take such a sound as the starting point for further editing. Without the GM standard, a piano Track might trigger drum sounds, your bass line could be played by Ukrainian cowbells, etc. In short, your masterpiece might not sound like one! Note that Roland use something called the "GS standard" which is a version of GM.

5.12 Chase Events

Cubase automatically deals with a problem which all sequencers face: you may have Tracks containing Program Changes and start the sequencer, not at the beginning, but halfway through the Arrangement: this means the MIDI devices don't get the Program Changes that are located earlier on in the song, so that it starts off with the wrong sounds. The solution is the "Chase Events" function: go to the Options menu and enter a checkmark by that function. Cubase will now comb the Tracks for MIDI commands prior to the position where you started the playback. In a way, the program simulates what would have happened if you had started from the beginning, and executes the previous commands. You can decide what type of MIDI commands Cubase should search for.

Choose Chase Events from the Options menu. In the menu which now appears you can switch Chase events on and off and designate which type of MIDI message Cubase should search for. You might not recognize all of these commands yet, but we'll discuss them later on. Unfortunately, you can only select one command at a time. You have to access the menu again for each new item.

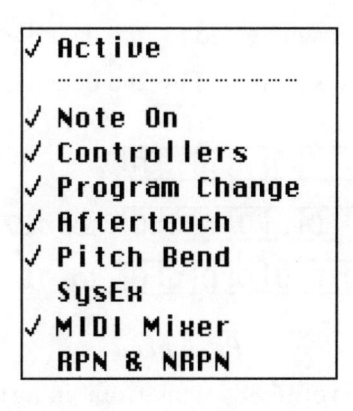

```
√ Active
..........................
√ Note On
√ Controllers
√ Program Change
√ Aftertouch
√ Pitch Bend
  SysEx
√ MIDI Mixer
  RPN & NRPN
```

The Chase Events menu

5.13 Other non-note events

The term "controllers" has become rather over-used in the MIDI world, and this is not helped by Steinberg being equally vague within the software itself: in this book we attempt to rectify the situation as follows:
- "MIDI Control Change events" are the MIDI events that come under the MIDI Control Change status byte: they do specific jobs such as modulation, sustain, volume and so on;
- "performance controllers" are the physical devices which produce these MIDI Control Change events, such as a pitch bending *wheel*, sustain *foot switch*, volume *pedal*, etc;
- Cubase lumps all non-note events under the generic, unofficial title "controllers": its Controller Display (see later in the manual) displays everything from velocity to Pitch Bend events. We are forced to follow the same nomenclature in the book, but where possible we'll make a distinction.

MIDI non-note events represent an interesting area of MIDI. They are the software equivalent to faders on a mixing desk, or knobs on an analog synthesizer in that they carry out specific functions of your MIDI device. Your synthesizer probably features several performance controllers, such as a pitch bending wheel or joystick, a sustain or a volume pedal, etc.

On the face of it, performance controllers simply affect the synthesizer's internal sound generator and have, in principle, nothing to do with MIDI. But at the same time their use can generate different kinds of MIDI non-note events which can be transmitted to other devices.

Ideally, the receiving device should be able to support all kinds of MIDI information; this is not always the case as many devices don't have the necessary functions. Many drum computers, for example, do not understand the MIDI Control Change event for Volume, so that if you send volume commands from Cubase or your master keyboard to your drum computer, nothing happens. Let's take a closer look at the different types of non-note MIDI events.

5.13.1 Pitch Bend

MIDI Pitch Bend data is used to smoothly alter pitch values in the destination sound module. As with note commands, Pitch Bend commands are MIDI channel-specific, so that a maximum of 16 instruments can be addressed. The same holds true for all MIDI non-note events. After all, not too many players would appreciate it if their pitch bending efforts during a solo affected the pitch of the entire Arrangement! A MIDI Pitch Bend event is similar in structure to a Note On/Off event: a status byte is followed by two data bytes. The data format for all MIDI events is listed in the appendix.

The human ear is very sensitive to pitch changes, so when laying down the MIDI standard the manufacturers decided to use a higher-resolution pitch bending scale than the 128 steps used in most MIDI applications. The purpose was to ensure that MIDI pitch bending sounds smooth, not jerky. This is achieved by having the two data bytes interact, where each value in the first data byte is divided into a further 128 values in the second data byte. This is how it works:

Value of 1st data byte = 1, is then subdivided by 2nd data byte (0 - 127);

Value of 1st data byte = 2, is then subdivided by 2nd data byte (0 - 127), etc.

Status byte	▶ $En	1 1 1 0 n n n n
1st data byte	00, $00,	0 0 0 0 0 0 0 0 to 127, $7F, 0 1 1 1 1 1 1 1
2nd data byte	00, $00,	0 0 0 0 0 0 0 0 to 127, $7F, 0 1 1 1 1 1 1 1

Pitch Bend

This scale provides for a resolution of 16,384 steps. Combining two data bytes to achieve a higher resolution is called an "LSB/MSB combination". The 1st data byte is the "Least Significant

Byte", the 2nd data byte the "Most Significant Byte". The diagram above is shown in decimal, hexadecimal and binary.

The status byte is the exception to the rule: its exact value is determined by the second nibble, which includes the MIDI channel address. Its value can therefore vary between 1 and 16. The variable "n" is used to illustrate this in the diagram.

In reality, very few devices support the "LSB/MSB combination", either when receiving or sending, probably because there is a fear amongst manufacturers of too much data being generated at one time, for little perceivable benefit. Most devices use the information in the second data byte only, which gives a resolution of only 128. In practise, this seems to be fine.

5.13.2 Tuning

A few things should be borne in mind regarding MIDI Pitch Bend operations:
- The maximum range of the bend is determined by the receiving device. The MIDI Pitch Bend events regulate *how far* the pitch bends within the maximum range. If you have set the maximum Pitch Bend to a value of 12 semitone steps in the receiving device, then the pitch increases by an octave when you push the pitch wheel all the way up. Conversely, if you set the maximum to a single (semitone) step, pushing the pitch wheel all the way up moves the pitch up by a semitone. Later on, we'll be looking at a more advanced method that enables greater pitch change intervals.
- If your instrument is limited to a resolution of 128, and you set the pitch bend to intervals greater than an octave, you will start to hear the individual steps in the pitch bend.
- Pitch bending can go down as well as up, so the 2nd data byte value when it's at rest is 64, not 0. You will need to remember this when working with Cubase's Editors.
- In some situations, the receiving device might not return to the resting value of 64 after it has received Pitch Bend events, such as when you fast forward Cubase in the middle of pitch bending. It is then out of tune with the other instruments. If this happens, move the pitch wheel up and down once and release it in the center position to reset the value, ensuring that the Cubase Track containing the Pitch Bend data is active, so that you have selected the right MIDI channel.

Cubase offers a number of options in the MIDI Setup dialog box designed to avoid these types of problems. They also apply to the other types of MIDI events we are going to discuss below.

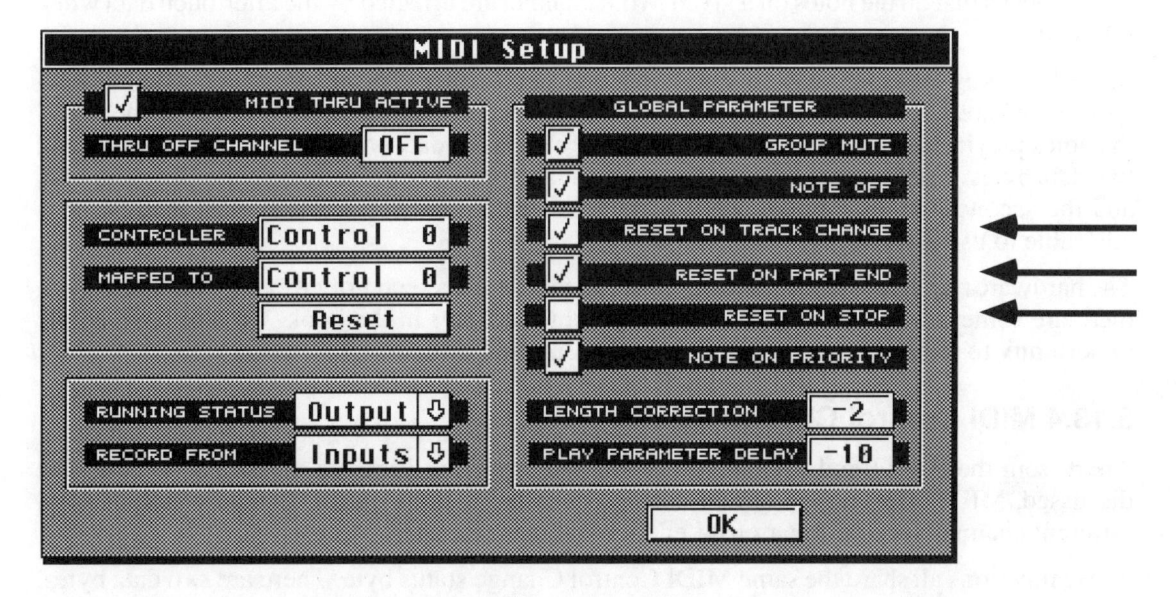

Reset parameters

The relevant MIDI Setup functions are:
- "Reset on Track Change" returns Pitch Bend, Control Change 1 (modulation) and Channel Pressure (aftertouch) back to their resting values when you switch to another Track. What

happens, for instance, if you go to another Track assigned to a different MIDI channel while you are executing a Pitch Bend? The Pitch Bend gets stuck at the current pitch, and is not reset because you are now on another MIDI channel. The reset function takes care of this for you, so avoiding tuning problems.
- "Reset on Part End" does the same thing at the end of each Part, and applies to the Pitch Bend, Control Change 1 (modulation), Channel Pressure (aftertouch) and Control Change 64 (sustain pedal) functions. If you are recording a four-bar Part, you don't have to worry about placing the performance controllers back to their resting positions at the end of the Part. If it wasn't for this function, the next Part might start out with all sorts of extra MIDI data you didn't want, or at least you would have to manually ensure that the above non-note data was all at rest before the end of the Part, a time-consuming operation.
- "Reset on Stop" automatically resets Pitch Bend and all other non-note events and sends an All Notes Off command over all channels as soon as you stop Cubase.

Although these parameters help to avoid a number of problems, you should use them with caution. For example, let's suppose you have activated modulation at the beginning of a long Track and you want it to be active all the way through: if you change Tracks while Reset on Track Change is enabled, the modulation would disappear.

5.13.3 MIDI Channel Pressure & MIDI Poly Key Pressure ("Aftertouch")

Here are two more types of MIDI message that Steinberg lump together under the generic term "MIDI Controllers" even though they each have their own, distinct status bytes. Furthermore, Steinberg mis-name MIDI Channel Pressure by calling it "Aftertouch" in the program - in fact, the term "Aftertouch" is the layman's term applied to both MIDI Channel Pressure and MIDI Poly Key Pressure.

So, both these types of "aftertouch" event are transmitted when you apply more pressure to a key *after* the initial strike (the initial strike provides velocity, additional pressure provides aftertouch) and is detected by sensors under the keys. What effect aftertouch data triggers is determined by the receiving device: you can choose volume changes, vibrato, or other similar effects.

A number of synthesizers and samplers offer at least the most common form of aftertouch, MIDI Channel Pressure. It consists of a status byte and one data byte and is MIDI channel-specific, which means that all the notes on a given MIDI channel are affected by the aftertouch data when it is sent.

MIDI Poly Key Pressure takes this principle one step further. This is aftertouch which is *key-specific*, whereby pressure on individual keys applies aftertouch to those notes only, not to all the notes playing on that MIDI channel. Poly Key Pressure data consists of one status byte and two data bytes. The first data byte designates the note number, similar to the Note On command, and the second one the amount. Poly Key Pressure can transmit a heavy data load, so it is advisable to use it sparingly.

The hardware required is not without its costs, so few devices send Poly Key Pressure; however, there are some devices that will at least respond to it. Later in the book, we will have ample opportunity to experiment with this data in the Cubase Editors.

5.13.4 MIDI Control Change events

Apart from the Pitch Bend, Channel Pressure and Poly Key Pressure messages we have just discussed, MIDI offers a type of non-note event called MIDI Control Change which has 128 different channel-specific functions. Let's look at them in detail.

These functions all share the same MIDI Control Change status byte. There are two data bytes. The first data byte determines which one of the 128 functions is active, the second one gives its amount.

Each function has an amount range of 128 (0 - 127). Control Change functions weren't properly defined during the early years of MIDI, which caused a great deal of confusion. MIDI Control

Changes are basically nothing more than neutral transmitters of data; in theory, each of the 128 functions should have a defined job, but these jobs have never really been standardized, and the effect they produce depends on the device being addressed. Over time, though, manufacturers have agreed that certain MIDI Control Changes should have specific functions.

The following list contains the 128 Control Changes and their functions, where agreed:

0	Bank Select MSB
1	Modulation
2	Breath controller
3	not defined
4	Foot pedal
5	Portamento Time
6	Data Entry MSB
7	Volume
8	Balance
9	not defined
10	Pan
11	Expression
12, 13	Effects Control Changes 1 + 2
14, 15	not defined
16 - 19	Multi-function Control Changes 1 - 4
20 - 31	not defined

Control Changes 32 - 63 are LSB for Control Changes 0 - 31 and so provide a higher resolution.

64	Sustain pedal
65	Portamento
66	Sostenuto
67	Soft pedal
68	not defined
69	Hold 2
70 - 79	not defined
80 - 83	Multi-function Control Changes 5 - 8
84 - 90	not defined
91 - 95	Effect Intensity 1 - 5
96, 97	Value Changing plus/minus
98, 99	non-registered parameters LSB/MSB
100, 101	registered parameters LSB/MSB
102 - 121	not defined
122 - 127	Channel Mode commands

In the early stages of MIDI development, MIDI Control Changes were divided into two categories: "continuous" and "switch". These categories were based on the functions as interpreted by the receiving device and not on the actual data format.

In general, though, it makes more sense to distinguish between Control Changes which can almost double in resolution (mainly Control Changes 0 - 31 as MSBs and those which are necessary to achieve this higher resolution, 32 - 63 as LSBs), and those with the standard 128 step resolution (Control Changes 64 - 127). According to the MIDI standard, these higher-resolution Control Changes can be combined as MSB/LSB combinations to increase the parameter range, rather like Pitch Bend, except that here two status bytes and two data bytes are used.

In reality, however, with the sole exception of the Bank Select command we discussed earlier in the book, hardly any manufacturer supports this option: those Control Changes which can support the higher resolution use either the LSB *or* the MSB, so producing the standard 128-step resolution. The Bank Select command consists of Control Changes 0 and 32 plus a Program Change event.

MIDI

Considering that the Bank Select command makes it possible to select thousands of sounds and that modern synthesizers are increasing in memory size, use of the Bank Select command's MSB/LSB combination would appear to be justified. Generally, though, contemporary devices feature two to a maximum of ten banks of sounds, for which the LSB value remains at "0". This means that only the MSB value, i.e. MIDI Control Change 0, is relevant, accompanied by a normal Program Change message.

It would appear that the manufacturers cannot agree on how to interpret the standard here: some Roland devices operate a kind of "reversed priority", using only the LSB values. The result is that Bank 1 of these devices relates to Cubase's Bank 128, Bank 2 to 256, etc. Keep this in mind when you are setting values in the Inspector and watch how individual devices actually process the data.

The decision not to support the theoretical high resolution available for the other Control Changes is probably a good thing: if we assume that you use the a MIDI performance controller to its fullest extent, this would produce 128 x 128 = 16,384 possible values: moving the modulation wheel all the way to its end stop would almost certainly produce a data logjam in the MIDI system (remember it's serial) and maybe lead to timing delays.

Control Changes 64 - 95, which used to be called "switch" Control Changes, are used merely as on/off switches despite their possible 128 step resolution. Since different interpretations led to a great deal of confusion, the following 2nd data byte values have become standard: values from 0 to 63 are "off", 64 to 127 are "on". Older instruments may interpret these commands differently, for instance 0 = off and 1 - 127 = on, or 0 = off, 127 = on, and 1 - 126 are ignored. If you encounter this type of problem, you can modify the data with the help of the Cubase Editors, the Logical Editor in particular.

The registered/non-registered parameters represent a relatively new development. Here too MSBs and LSBs are used for higher resolutions. These two types of Control Change were developed as a response to the uncoordinated way manufacturers were using Control Changes. Only a few Control Changes are defined by a specific function, e.g. Control Change 7 for volume, Control Change 1 for modulation, etc. Manufacturers have been using the undefined controllers for their own purposes, which would ultimately lead to a communications breakdown between devices.

We have seen that a MIDI Control Change is merely a source of values with a specific address. What happens at that address in the receiving device is determined by the receiving device. Supposing a manufacturer decided that his device's filter frequency should respond to and transmit the undefined Control Change 25: this data would then be sent to another manufacturer's device, where it might affect a completely different function.

As a solution, the manufacturers agreed on the use of registered and non-registered Control Changes. Non-registered Control Changes allow the manufacturer to assign functions as they see fit, and possible incompatibilities are accepted. Registered Control Changes, on the other hand, are only assigned after extensive consultation. The first registered Control Change is number 0, which regulates Pitch Bend sensitivity. It allows you to remote control the Pitch Bend range.

Control Changes can produce a massive amount of data, so extensive use of them in realtime situations is not advisable. Apart from the MSB/LSB Control Change values which merely define the parameter, Control Changes 6 or 96/97 still have to be used to define the specific values. This involves a huge amount of data - stage lighting may open up a new field of application.

Control Changes 122 - 127 have a special application. You can use Control Change 122 to switch your keyboard/synth to Local Control Off via MIDI. Control Change 123 gets rid of MIDI drones by switching all notes off. This generally useful Control Change can cause problems: some Roland synths send this command as soon as you release all the keys. Other devices may switch their notes off in response to this command, even though this is totally uncalled for in your Cubase Arrangement. You should filter this controller out in Cubase's MIDI Definition box. Follow the method described below.

5.13.5 The MIDI modes

The remaining Control Changes are used to select the various MIDI operating modes. Some of you may feel that these modes are anachronisms in an age of multi-functional, multitimbral, polyphonic work stations. However, we'll take a quick look at them for the sake of completeness. The receiver can be set to any of four modes which determine how it will recognize voice messages. The modes are set with two mode messages: Omni On/Off and Poly/Mono:

Mode 1	Omni On,	Poly
Mode 2	Omni On,	Mono
Mode 3	Omni Off,	Poly
Mode 4	Omni Off,	Mono

In Poly mode, the receiver assigns voice messages to multiple voices (more than one note) which are played polyphonically.

In Mono mode, the receiver assigns voice messages in a single channel just a single, monophonic voice. For instance, if an instrument has six voices, it can simultaneously be addressed on six different channels. It translates different information into different notes, i.e. one note per channel. Mono mode does not mean that you can assign different sounds to each of these notes - this used to be a popular misconception. Mono mode is now used primarily for guitar synthesizers, where each string is assigned a different MIDI channel to enable pitch bending, because MIDI Pitch Bend events are channel-specific. If all the strings were on the same channel, and you bent a note, the Pitch Bend would bend all the notes that were being played at the same time.

In Omni On, the receiver reacts to all data received, regardless of its MIDI channel. Obviously, this mode is not very useful when working with sequencers. However, there are several older instruments that operate exclusively in this mode, and some of them can offer some very good sounds. If you want your device to react to one channel only, you either need a little add-on MIDI filter device to filter out those channels you dont want it to react to, or you can employ additional hardware such as Steinberg's MIDEX which enables you to assign Cubase Tracks to specific MIDI outputs. More on this subject later.

In Omni Off, the receiver reacts only to data that is sent on the channel to which it is set.

The four modes are therefore combinations of the above. To cut a long story short, Mode 3 (Omni Off, Poly) is the mode to use whenever you are in a sequencing situation, and this book assumes this is the mode you are in the whole time. The others are very rare.

5.14 Tip

Make sure you finish up by returning all non-note values back to zero via MIDI when you are experimenting with the Cubase Editors. Otherwise, they may remain "active" and produce undesirable effects.

The exception is MIDI Control Change 7 (Volume), whose resting value is 127 (maximum volume). Remember that the resting values of Pitch Bend's two data bytes are 0 and 64 respectively.

5.15 Problems

All performance controllers' MIDI non-note messages have one thing in common: they produce a deluge of data. We've already given this subject a good airing, but let's finish by taking a quick look at what a single movement of a pitch wheel produces when viewed in one of the Cubase Editors - and that's not even using the higher resolution:

MIDI

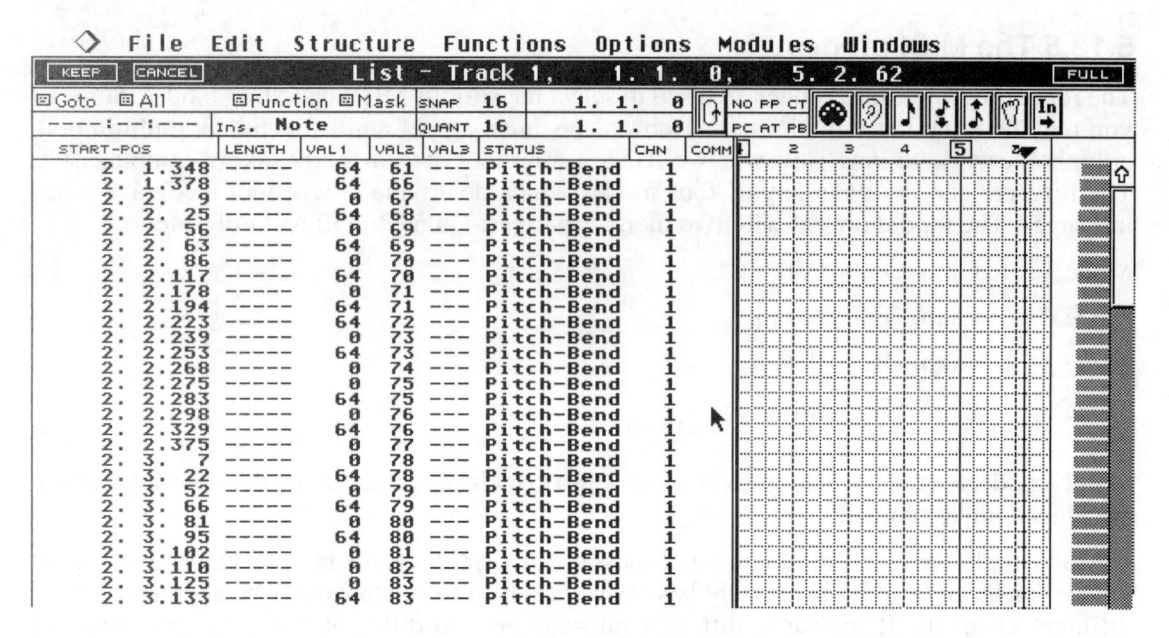

A single upward movement of the pitch wheel in Cubase's List Editor

MIDI tries to limit this flood of data with the aid of the "Running Status". It suppresses the status bytes of consecutive MIDI events if they all share the same status. So, if you use, say, the modulation wheel, its first event will have the status Control Change 1 followed by the channel and amount data bytes, but all the subsequent stream of events will contain the data bytes only without the status.

Running Status for a particular stream of events is cancelled as soon as a different status byte interrupts, such as when a note is played in the middle of the modulation events described above; but is renewed again whenever two events are transmitted that have the same status. This is the reason why Cubase usually sends a Note On command with a velocity value of "0" instead of an "official" Note Off command to switch notes off: it means notes all share the same status whether they are being switched on or off, allowing optimum exploitation of Running Status.

However, this useful function also has a few drawbacks. Some devices require the use of Note Off commands, and older ones have serious problems with Running Status communication. A sure sign of this is when your instrument plays the first note only, and not the following ones. It needs the status bytes ahead of the data bytes which the Running Status has filtered out. In this case, switch Running Status off in the MIDI Setup dialog box.

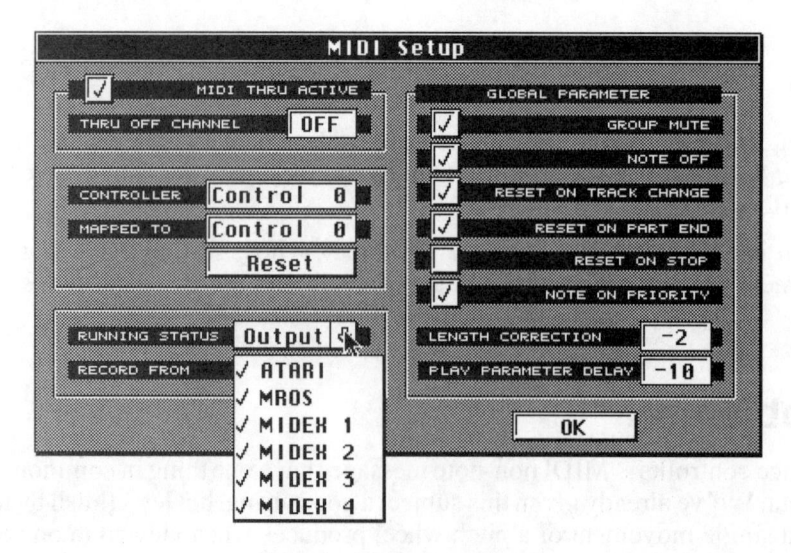

Running Status settings

98

Click and hold the arrow to the right of the term "Output"; in the pop-up menu that appears, switch Running Status off for the output your device is on by dragging the mouse pointer down the menu and releasing the mouse pointer when the correct output is highlighted. You can see that Cubase apparently has more outputs then the Atari can offer. Additional hardware is required, and we'll discuss this later.

5.16 Tips on handling non-note MIDI events

Because the use of hardware performance controllers (e.g. the pitch bend wheel) or other means of generating non-note MIDI events (e.g. the MIDI Mixer) can produce massive amounts of data which needlessly clog the MIDI circuit, the only real solution is to use them as little as possible. Aftertouch data (either type) is a continuing source of problems, and is often generated accidentally. Cubase offers an elegant solution.

Again go to the Options menu and choose MIDI Filter. Two extensive data filters are listed with which you can prevent specific MIDI data from being recorded and transmitted via MIDI Thru. Click the desired filter, which highlights, meaning that it's activated. Aftertouch data is usually created inadvertently, and should not even be recorded in the sequencer. You should always filter it out unless you really want to record this type of data.

You can filter out Note On, Poly Key Pressure and similar data over all MIDI channels, though you can also do it on a per-channel basis, or even per-status basis, e.g. the "All Notes Off" command. Simply click the desired MIDI channel or event type. A total of four freely definable Control Changes can be filtered out using the right or left mouse button to select the desired ones in the four boxes.

The MIDI Filter box applies to the MIDI input only so that this kind of data is not recorded. What happens if undesirable data has already been recorded in a Part? Here, too, Cubase offers several solutions.

The MIDI Filter

If you want to permanently remove the values delete them with "Logical Edit" or another Editor. We'll look at this in one of the following chapters. Another possibility is provided by the "Delete Controller Data" command in the Functions menu ([Control][F]), which deletes *all* the selected Part's non-note MIDI data.

MIDI

The third option solves the problem without deleting data. The Part Info box (you came across it in the previous chapter) contains a data filter that stops specific MIDI data from being played back from Tracks or Parts.

The fourth method involves the "Reduce Controller Data" command, and it is a very useful one. It does not delete MIDI controller data, it only thins it out. Usually, there is no audible difference, but the MIDI data load is lightened.

Although early MIDI devices were limited in the type of non-note data they could produce, modern devices, especially mother keyboards without internal sound generation, incorporate user-programmable performance controllers, where you can designate which type of MIDI data is created by a wheel, joystick, pedal etc.

Cubase provides an option for those instruments that are not able to do this. Let's look at a possible application: your master synthesizer features a wheel which can produce modulation (MIDI Control Change 1) only. However, you would like to address the breath controller function in a Yamaha FM sound module (Breath Controller is MIDI Control Change 2).

Go to the MIDI Setup dialog in the Options menu where you will find the "Controller Map". Set the source to "Modulation", and the destination ("Mapped To") to "Breath Control" using the mouse. The modulation wheel now generates breath controller data.

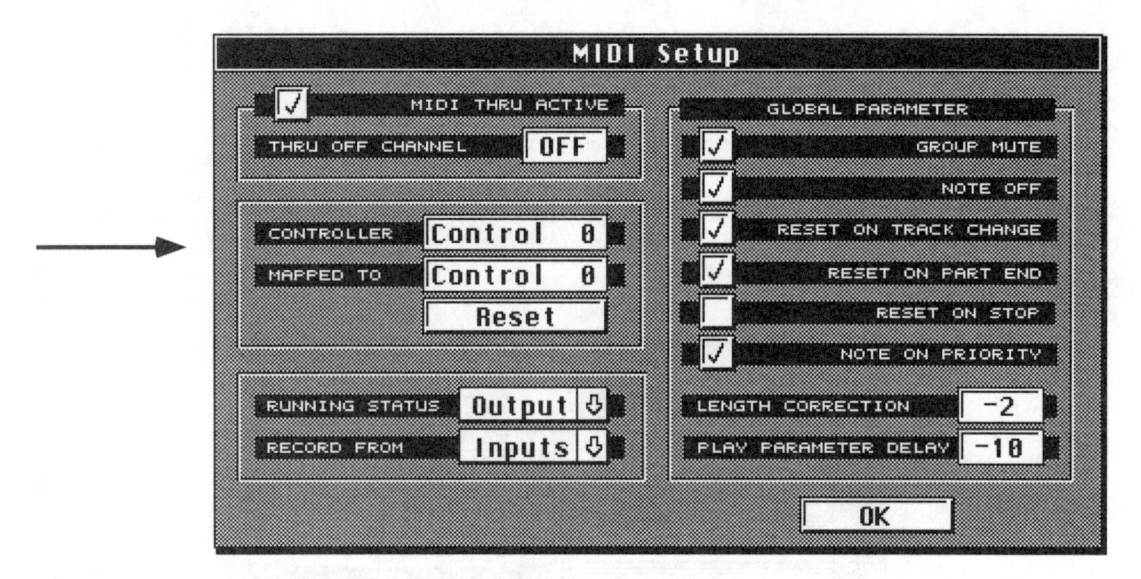

The Control Change Map

Generally, you can redefine Control Change data as you wish, such as controlling MIDI volume from the modulation wheel. This will not work if the receiving device is unable to interpret those MIDI commands; in that case, even Cubase can't help, not even with the use of foot pedals or a mother keyboard's clever programming.

Your devices' manuals list the type of MIDI information they support, usually in their MIDI Implementation chart. You don't have to look for this chart in the Cubase manual - there isn't one - as it can record, playback and create every possible type of MIDI event.

5.17 System Exclusive data

So far we've had a look at normal MIDI data, which is the communications medium for all brands and models of MIDI devices. However, there is another type of data tailored to specific manufacturers and instruments: System Exclusive (SysEx).

This type of data is used to transmit sounds and other device-specific data via MIDI. This enables you to edit sounds in your instruments with the aid of a software Editor, or load sound data into the computer and store it on disks. Cubase can record and play SysEx data. We'll run through an exercise in the MIDI Mixer section.

Every device has a different internal architecture, so SysEx data has to have an open, flexible structure. Only the beginning and end of a SysEx message is defined by the MIDI standard: what comes in between is up to the manufacturer. A status byte marks the beginning of a SysEx message ("F0" hexadecimal ("240" decimal or "11110000" binary)). Another status byte ends the message ("F7" ("247", "11110111")). Any number of data bytes, though no status bytes, can be contained between those two status bytes.

The only other common characteristic is the manufacturer's ID, which immediately follows the first SysEx status byte. Any manufacturer can request an exclusive ID number from the MIDI Manufacturers' Association, which is then listed in the second byte of a SysEx message.

Sound data can only be exchanged between MIDI instruments with identical sound structures. You cannot exchange sound data between different instruments, such as between a Roland JD-800 and a Yamaha SY99. One reason is that the Yamaha device needs data to define its various FM algorithms, a concept which doesn't exist in the Roland synthesizer's sound generation system. You can send data between the Yamaha device and the JD-800 via MIDI, but neither will respond to the messages.

The reason for this is as follows: the SY99 sends a status byte ("F0"). The Roland synth registers the message and stands by for SysEx data. The next data byte contains the Yamaha ID code. The JD-800 recognizes the code as alien and ignores all subsequent information. You could try to send SY99 data to another Yamaha model such as a DX7. It recognizes the Yamaha ID code, but the ID number of the synth model is listed next in the SysEx message, so the DX7 also ignores the message. Manufacturers always use a model ID number, even though it is not strictly required by the MIDI standard.

So what happens when SysEx messages are exchanged between identical or compatible models? The SysEx status byte with its ID bytes is called the "Header" in SysEx jargon, and is followed by the data bytes. Once the destination instrument accepts the Header, it then assigns the information to its sound parameters as defined by the data bytes; in other words, the sound settings are transmitted.

In contrast to most other types of MIDI data, SysEx messages are not MIDI channel-specific. However, some manufacturers assign internal channels, so you might run into communication problems even between identical devices. As a precaution, use the "Any" Track channel setting when playing back SysEx messages from Cubase. You shouldn't mix sound data SysEx and notes on the same Track. Some devices can transmit "Parameter Change" SysEx messages while you make changes directly at the instrument (e.g. the movement of a cutoff slider on the Roland JD-800); these can be recorded by Cubase and played back. For this to work you must ensure you have not activated a Cubase filter to block SysEx messages.

In general, SysEx is a complex subject matter; we'll be dealing with it again when we work with the MIDI Mixer. Until then, please avoid working with SysEx or you may accidentally delete or change sound data, and then where will you be...!

5.18 Specialized MIDI knowledge

This chapter covered the basic MIDI subject areas. Specialized functions such as sound data exchange, synchronization, and how to deal in detail with SysEx data will all be discussed in later chapters. You will find a detailed technical listing of the MIDI data format in the appendix.

6 Data Management

Cubase features a number of ways you can administer your songs, Arrangements, etc. on floppy disk or hard disk. This chapter covers all the relevant information you'll need.

6.1 Saving and loading

In a previous chapter we looked at the method to save and load Arrangements to and from disk. Let's quickly review this information and then take an in-depth look at the subject. Everything you record in Cubase is lodged in your computer's memory. However, this memory is volatile, and once the power is switched off or interrupted in any way, the data is lost. So before you switch the power off, you have to store the data permanently. The medium for this is either a floppy disk or a hard disk.

The first chapter gave you a basic understanding of disk operations. Data is stored on disks in file form. A file is a self-contained unit of data which can be recognised by Cubase.

You will know by now that loading and saving data basically always starts with the same routine: choose Open in the File menu ([Control][O]) to load a file, or Save ([Control][S]) to save a Cubase file to a disk. A dialog box then appears asking you what you want to save. We will look at the difference between the listed entries in a moment. Click the desired entry or press a number between 1 and 8 on the alphanumeric keyboard (not the numeric keypad).

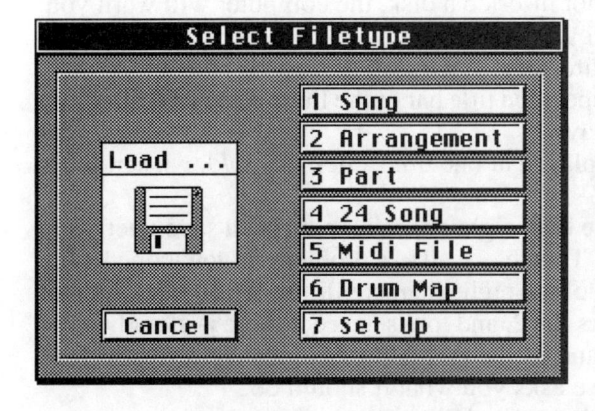

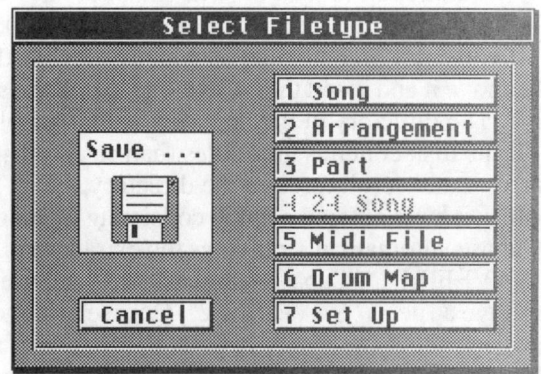

The Open dialog box on the left, Save dialog box on the right

At this point the Atari Item Selector appears, showing you the disk's contents. Enter a name of up to eight letters and press [Return] or click OK.

Data Management

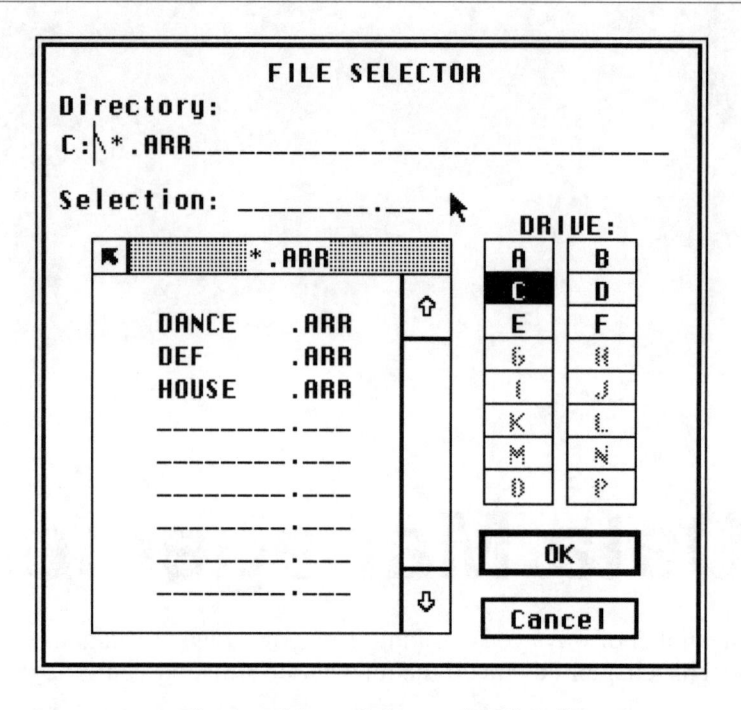

The Atari Item Selector (TOS 1.4)

There are a number of ways to select a file:
- Double-click the desired file in the Item Selector's directory list. If the disk contains many files, use the scroll bar to scroll through the list until you find the one you want; or
- click the file in the list once (it is highlighted), and press [Return] or click OK; or
- if you know the name of the file, type it in the selection line and press [Return] or click OK.

If you are loading a file, any of the above operations will load the file into the computer's RAM.

6.2 Working with disks - tips and tricks

We have already talked about disks on a number of occasions in this book. You will not find disk operations difficult; nevertheless, some musicians may be computer novices and may run into small problems, which we will discuss now. Feel free to skip this section if you are at home with disks, and consult it later if you do encounter problems.

- *Never* remove a disk from the disk drive when the drive indicator lamp is illuminated - you may destroy data.
- If you attempt to load or save data, but have not inserted a disk, the computer will warn you. Insert the disk and confirm with the [Return] key.
- If you can't find the file you want in the disk directory, you may have inserted the wrong disk. Remove it and insert the correct one. Click the speckled title bar of the Item Selector's directory list. The directory of the new disk is then displayed.
- If the disk contains more files than can be displayed at one time, click the up/down scroll bar arrows and scroll through the directory.
- If you have entered a name consisting of more than eight characters during a save operation, Cubase automatically removes the extra letters. This may lead to a problem. If you named a file "SAVEFILE1", Cubase removes the 1 because of the eight character limit. If you later attempt to save a file as "SAVEFILE2", Cubase removes the 2, and looks to see if there is already a file bearing the same name. It finds the first one, and as the computer cannot save different files bearing the same name to the same disk, Cubase asks you what it should do.
- You are given three choices. "Replace" deletes the original file and saves your new Arrangement as SAVEFILE. "Backup" renames the original file under the same name, but with a new "extender" (see below). The option "Cancel" allows you to exit the Item Selector without saving the file.

Working with Disks - Tips and Tricks

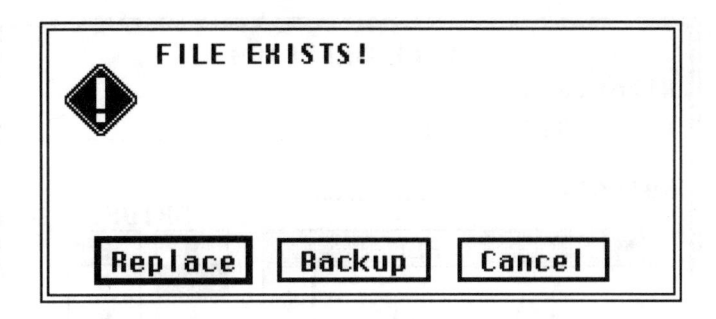

A file bearing the same name already exists on disk

Cubase adds an "extender" to each file name. It consist of three letters, and Cubase *always automatically* adds a period and an extender to the end of a file name. The type of file dictates which letters are in the extender. More on this in a moment.

Cubase automatically changes the original file's extender when you use the backup function described above.

The extender tells Cubase what type of file it is dealing with during disk operations, and tells the Item Selector to display only those files of the same type as the one being saved/loaded etc. During load operations, for instance, not all files on the disk are displayed, only those you can actually load: for instance, if you want to load an Arrangement, Cubase displays the Arrangements on the disk with their respective extenders, and not songs, setups, etc, nor even backup files, even though they may be on the disk.

The extender is displayed in the Item Selector's pathname line (under the word "Directory") and in its directory lists's speckled title bar.

To display all the files on a disk, irrespective of their extenders, click in the pathname line: delete the three extender letters using [Backspace], and type in a [*]; follow this by clicking in the directory list's speckled title bar. However, bear in mind that if you have told Cubase you want to load, say, a song, you cannot then select and load an Arrangement, etc.

Although you cannot save files of the same name and extender on a disk, you can save two files with the same name whose *types* are different: these are distinguished by the extender.

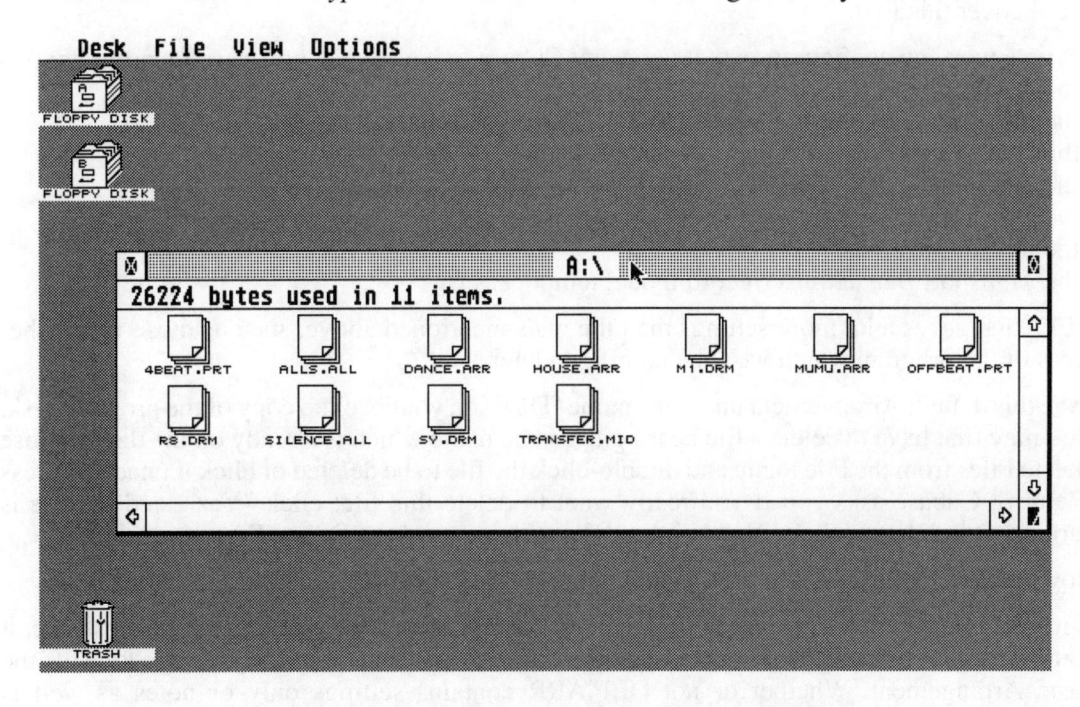

A comparison between those files actually on a disk...

Data Management

```
            FILE SELECTOR
 Directory:
 C:\CUBASE\*.ALL_____

 Selection: |_____.___
                                       DRIVE:
      |K|░░░░░░*.ALL░░░░░░|        | A | B |
                                   | C | D |
                              ⇧    | E | F |
        ALLS    .ALL                | G | H |
        RTRAK01 .ALL               | I | J |
        SILENCE .ALL               | K | L |
        _____.___               | M | N |
        _____.___               | O | P |
        _____.___
        _____.___                 |  OK   |
        _____.___
        _____.___        ⇩        | Cancel|
```

...and those displayed under "Song" in the Item Selector

6.3 The various Cubase file types

Cubase allows you to save and load various configurations and files. Let's take a closer look at these. A basic understanding of the different file types is essential to load and save operations.

6.3.1 DEF.ARR

At the beginning of the Arrange chapter, we discussed the ability to tailor Cubase to your needs. We'll cover this first.

Set up a working configuration that you want Cubase to have when you start the program; this can include:
- the metronome (monitor click and MIDI), Part Appearance,
- the count-in ("Precount"),
- the Tracks' respective MIDI channels in your order of preference,
- the MIDI channel names,
- the locator positions,
- the Transport Bar settings (record mode, tempo, etc.).

DEF.ARR saves a lot more settings than the ones mentioned above, such as those from other areas of the program which we'll be coming to later.

Save this default Arrangement under the name "DEF" on your backup copy of the program disk. You may first have to delete a file bearing the same name which is already on the disk: choose Delete Files from the File menu and double-click the file to be deleted or click it once and press [Return]. Cubase asks you if you really want to delete this file: click "Yes", and the file is permanently deleted (click "No" or press [Return] to cancel the Delete Files operation).

Now, whenever Cubase is booted, it looks for the file DEF.ARR and loads it automatically.

If it suits your way of working, DEF.ARR can contain recorded Parts as well. For instance, it could be useful to have the computer load the drum groove that you always use to kick off the basic Arrangement. Whether or not DEF.ARR contains settings only or notes as well is irrelevant: the important thing is that the file be correctly named "DEF".

Using the same principle, the name "DEF" can be used with all the following extenders to provide default start-up configurations, which the program will look for and automatically load when booting.

Tip: To create a DEF.ARR file from an existing Arrangement without saving any of its musical Parts, use the following trick: select all the Parts of our basic Arrangement ([Control][A]) and press [Backspace] or [Delete]. The Parts are gone. Ensure you have inserted the right disk. Press [Control][S] and then [2] on the alphanumeric keypad (i.e. you are saving an Arrangement). In the Item Selector, enter "DEF" and confirm with [Return]. If another file bearing the same name already exists on the disk, Cubase will make you aware of this. You can overwrite the file, or tell Cubase to change its name. After the file is saved, you are back in the Arrange window. Press [Undo] and your Parts reappear, but have not been saved on disk.

Note: ensure you follow the above steps in the same sequence, otherwise you may not be able to recall the Parts with [Undo].

Delete your basic Arrangement after this little diversion as we'll load it from disk when we need it again.

6.3.2 Song (extender .ALL)

A Song saves or loads the *complete* memory content of the computer. This can include up to 16 Arrangements with all their respective settings (e.g. Groups). Loading a song deletes everything else in your computer's memory such as Arrangements, Groups, etc., even if you abort the operation and do not load the song. Cubase will ask you if you really want to do this.

6.3.3 Arrangement (extender .ARR)

An Arrangement saves the currently active Arrange window, or loads one of your choice. The name you enter when saving is assigned to the window, and it remains on your screen after it has been saved. The window size and its position on the screen are saved as well.

When you load an Arrangement, you are presented with several options after which the Arrangement appears on the screen. The Arrangements that were on your screen before are not gone, but covered up. Activate Tile Windows, or modify the window sizes to meet your needs. The Arrangement you have just loaded is immediately active.

Basically, all save and load operations can be executed while Cubase is running. A newly loaded Arrangement replaces the current one. You have the option to stop this from happening, as it could be annoying in live gig situations: press and hold [Alternate] while the sequencer continues to run. Load in the usual manner. After a while, a dialog box will appear with two options: "Replace" does what it says and replaces the current Arrangement that's playing with the new one; "Background" loads the Arrangement but holds it in reserve - you can call it up when you need it from the Windows menu. The current Arrangement continues to run.

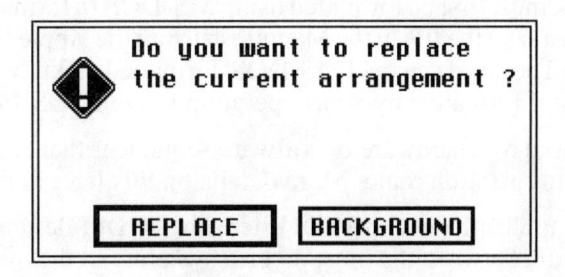

Replace or Background

Arrangements can be loaded while the sequencer is running, which avoids embarrassing delays on stage, provided your computer has enough memory available. If you try to load an Arrangement and you've run out of memory, Cubase will alert you to this fact. You must then abort the loading operation, but your current Arrangement continues to play.

Data Management

6.3.4 Part (extender .PRT)

Parts can be saved individually and in an Arrangement. All selected Parts are saved. If no Parts are selected, Cubase saves all the Parts of the current Track.

The following rules apply to loading Parts from a disk: Parts are inserted into the Arrangement at the left locator's position. Their relative positions are maintained, as are their original Track assignments. If the current Arrangement contains fewer Tracks than the one from which the Parts originated, the missing Tracks are automatically created.

6.3.5 Setup (extender .SET)

In principle, a Setup is the same thing as a DEF.ARR file, with the difference that no Parts are saved in it, so no Arrange window is generated during the loading operation. You can even load a Setup into an existing Arrangement.

The "Drum Map" and "MIDI Mixer Map" options in the Save/Open dialog boxes are covered in the chapters on Editors.

6.3.6 Converting other formats

Apart from the normal loading and saving operations of Cubase-specific data, it is possible to load and save other formats as well.

Have you ever worked with Cubase's predecessor, Pro-24? If you have, you can load its songs directly into Cubase using the "24 Song" option in the Open File dialog box. Due to the difference in program structures, some of Pro-24's song parameters are not converted to the Cubase format.

If the Pro-24 song was synchronized to tape in any way, you will have to use a special conversion routine on it: the chapter on synchronization has all the details.

6.3.7 Standard MIDI Files

The MIDI standard includes a special format which allows disk-based data to be exchanged between different sequencers: the Standard MIDI File Format. It is supported by Cubase.

Arrangements saved as MIDI Files can be transferred via disk to another program (not another Cubase), provided the other sequencer can read this format. First you have to save the Cubase Arrangement you want to transfer as a MIDI File. Then you can load it into another program as described below. The process of course works in the opposite direction as well, i.e. from another program to Cubase.

The program does not necessarily have to be an Atari ST program. Other computers support a number of programs that can read and write MIDI Files. Bear in mind, though, that other operating systems use different disk formats; for instance, the ST cannot directly read an Apple Macintosh disk. The disk must first be formatted using MS-DOS (a format that both the Mac and the ST can read); you then save the file in the Macintosh using the Apple File Exchange program onto that MS-DOS disk. The Atari can read MS-DOS-formatted disks. MS-DOS computers can read Atari ST disks only if formatted by Atari operating system TOS 1.4 or later.

If you want to add material to a hardware or software sequencer that cannot write MIDI Files, you have to go the synchronization route. More details on this later in this chapter.

Let's try some practical applications with MIDI Files. The MIDI File standard is designed to be a communications medium between the most diverse systems, so the manufacturers agreed on the lowest common denominators, which means there are limitations of which you should be aware. A Cubase MIDI File saves:
- the active Arrangement *only*, not complete songs with several Arrangements,
- the contents of all the recorded Tracks. All the Parts of a Track *must* be connected, and this can be done with the Glue tool,
- the tempo, Track name and time signature.

Save the Cubase file not as a song or an Arrangement but as a MIDI File. Cubase automatically assigns the extender ".MID". Transfer this file to another program, bearing in mind you may have to convert the disk format as mentioned above with the Mac.

Cubase always saves MIDI Files using Format 1 (see below), if you only recorded data on a single Track.

You can also load other programs' MIDI Files into Cubase. Choose Open from the File menu, and then the MIDI File entry. Cubase asks you what it should do with the MIDI File you want to load. If you want to create a completely new Arrangement, select "No" ([Return]). If you want to merge the MIDI File with the current Arrangement, click "Yes": the data in the MIDI File is inserted in the current Arrangement, starting at the position of the left locator.

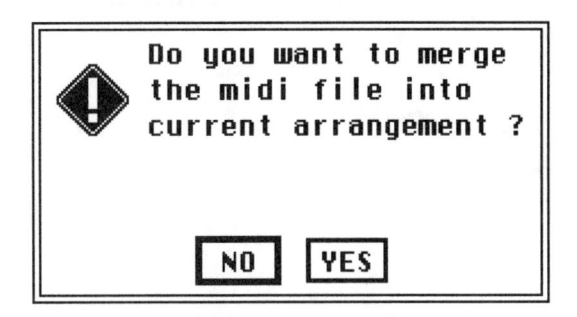

Loading MIDI Files

It is important to know that the MIDI standard includes two types of MIDI Files: Format 0 saves all data on *one single* Track. Format 1 generates as many Tracks as there are MIDI channels in the Arrangement.

Here's a brief look at what steps Cubase takes when loading MIDI Files:

6.3.8 Loading Format 0 files with merge:

Beginning at the left locator, Cubase inserts a Track containing all new information on Track 1. It adopts the current Arrangement's Track name, tempo, time signature and MIDI channel. If other Parts already exist at this position, they are covered up, but not removed.

6.3.9 Loading Format 0 files without merge:

Cubase creates a new Arrangement containing one Track which contains all the new data. Its MIDI channel is set to "Any", which means that the events' original MIDI channels are honoured. Tempo and time signature are also adopted from the MIDI File. To regain the original separate Tracks that existed in the donor sequencer, you'll need to "remix" the Track. We'll take a look at this process in a moment.

6.3.10 Loading Format 1 files with merge:

Cubase inserts as many Tracks as are contained in the MIDI File with all their new data, starting at the left locator. The current Arrangement's Track name, tempo, time signature and MIDI channel are maintained.

6.3.11 Loading Format 1 files without merge:

Cubase creates a new Arrangement containing as many Tracks as the MIDI File contains. Their MIDI channels are set to "Any", which means that the events' original MIDI channels are honoured. Track names, tempo and time signature are also adopted from the MIDI File.

Data Management

7 Special Functions

7.1 Remix and Mixdown

If you have created a new Arrangement on a MIDI File in Format 0 (one Track contains all the data), you are confronted with a problem. You can play the song as usual and you can hear all notes on their respective MIDI channels, so long as the Track's MIDI channel is set to "Any" but you cannot manipulate individual instruments. The Remix function, which also has wider applications in Cubase, is the answer. You may not have a MIDI File in Format 0 handy, so we will use a different route and create a similar Arrangement for this exercise.

Delete any remaining Parts from your Arrangement and record new ones in two to four Tracks, about twelve bars in length will do. Your recording should look something like this:

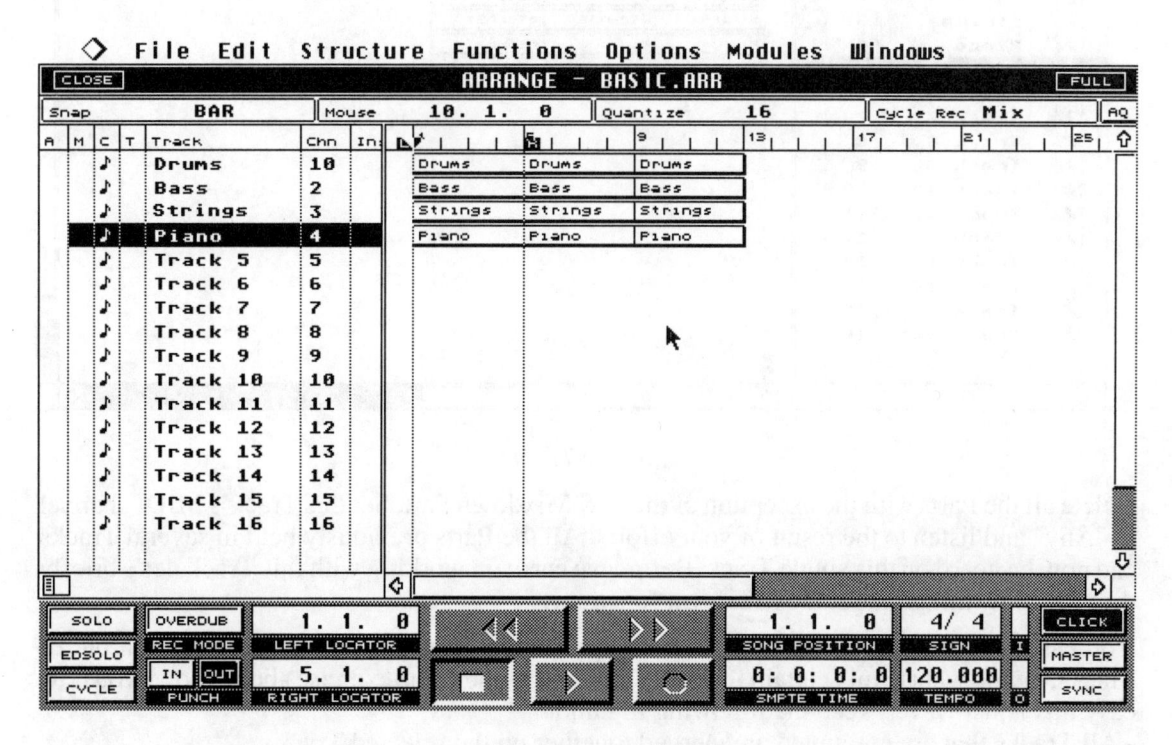

A demo recording

Now we'll mix the Tracks together to form a single Track. Select an empty Track located above

Special Functions

or below your Tracks. Set the locators to the start and end of the Parts. Execute the Mix Down command in the Structure menu. After a moment, a Part entitled "Mixdown" will appear in the Track you have selected.

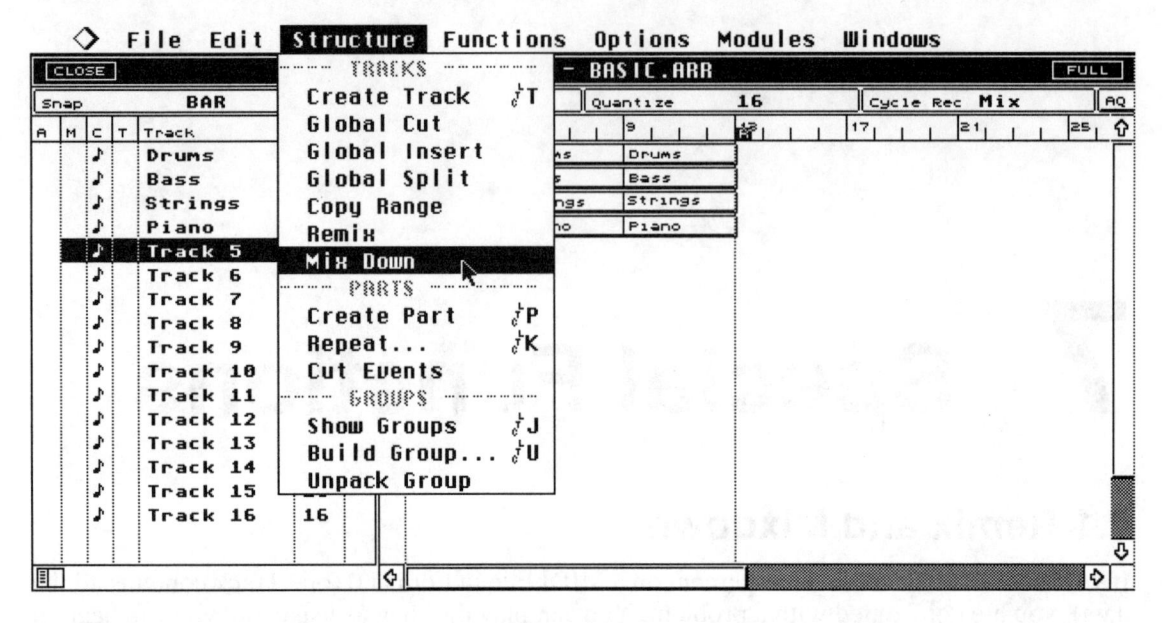

Mixdown creates...

...a new Track

Delete all the Parts with the exception of the new Mixdown Part. Set this Track's MIDI channel to "Any" and listen to the result of your efforts. All the Parts previously held in several Tracks can now be heard on this single Track. Before we carry on working with this Track, let's briefly discuss a few things about the Mixdown function.

You can use this function for other Cubase applications, such as where you have run out of Tracks, or you want to mix certain Parts and Tracks together. The exercise above shows you how easy this is. However, keep the following in mind:
- All Tracks that are not muted are merged together on the selected Track.
- Cubase only merges the bit of your Arrangement that is framed by the locators, allowing you to merge portions of Tracks. Try it! Create two new Tracks 16 bars long. Set the locators

somewhere in the middle of these Parts, say bars 5 to 9 and execute the Mixdown command. You have now created a new Part that contains bars 5 to 9 of the source Tracks.
- The data's original MIDI channels still apply. You must set the Mixdown Track's channel to "Any" to be able to hear these.
- You can happily delete the original Tracks because they are easily recreated.
- The play parameters of the individual Tracks and Parts are now permanent components of the new Track. You can no longer reverse them in the Play Parameter box; for this, you must use Cubase's various Editors. Consult the appropriate chapter in this book for what needs to be done in this sort of case.

Move the Mixdown Part you have created to Track 1. You have just simulated the loading of a Format 0 MIDI File (a single Track containing several merged MIDI channels-worth of data). Recording from a sequencer without the MIDI File capability gives you the same result, as would playing a mother keyboard which is able to transmit on several channels at once.

To separate the data according to the individual MIDI channels, follow these steps: select the Track you want to split up, mark the section with the locators and execute the Remix command in the Structure menu. Cubase generates a new Track and new Parts for each MIDI channel in the source Part. The Tracks are automatically assigned to the correct MIDI channels.

You should follow this by deleting the original Mixdown Part, otherwise its notes are doubled. If the Track or Part you want to split contains only one MIDI channel, then it's plain that you cannot Remix it.

7.2 Useful: the Preferences

The File menu contains some very handy functions. Format Disk is used to format brand new disks. The formatting is executed in the standard Atari way, and is largely self-explanatory. You can also use it to format disks that have already been written on, though this deletes all the data on the disk.

The Preferences dialog box is accessed from the File menu, and contains even more useful items.

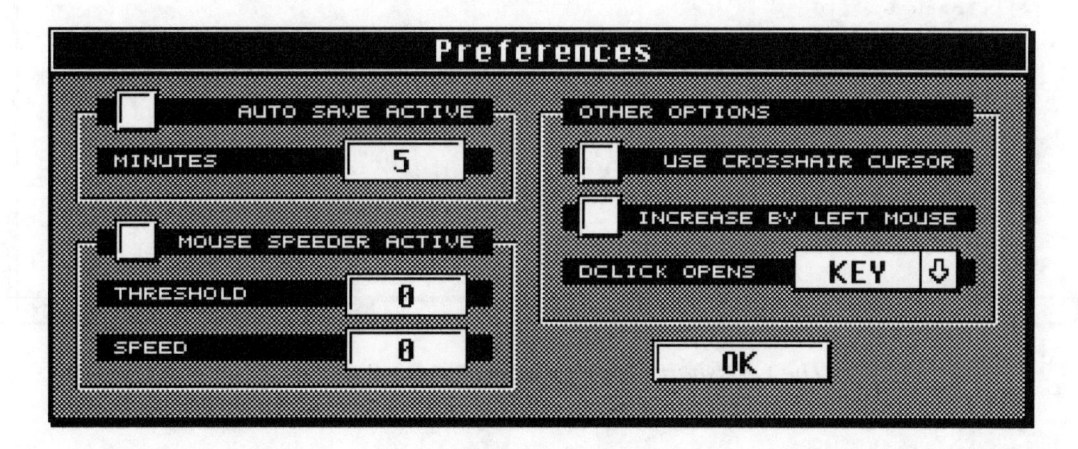

The Preferences dialog box

7.2.1 Auto Save

It is advisable to save your work at regular intervals. Although Cubase is a safe and reliable program, one can conceive of a number of situations where you can lose the results of your efforts.

Cubase features a neat way of saving your data regularly. Activate Auto Save in the Preferences box and enter an interval of between two and 30 minutes. Cubase then automatically saves the current song as BACKUP.ALL at the intervals you have specified.

Special Functions

7.2.2 Mouse Speeder

The Mouse Speeder does what it says: it controls the speed of the mouse. Different values make the mouse pointer move slower or faster than usual across your screen. Switch it on and change the values. The mouse pointer moves faster at "2" than at "1", even though you are moving the mouse at the same rate. This can be helpful when you want to move from one screen corner to the other, especially if you have a large-screen monitor.

You may run into problems when you have to move only short distances on the screen, such as when you are moving or copying Parts. The mouse pointer may move too fast to position them accurately. The Threshold Factor provides a neat solution. It determines the point at which the mouse is accelerated: move the mouse slowly and the pointer will also move slowly, move the mouse more rapidly and the pointer will pick up speed. Set the Threshold Factor to a value you feel comfortable with.

7.2.3 Additional options

In Cubase, you usually use the left mouse button to reduce values, the right one to increase them. You can reverse the assignments if you are accustomed to another program's clicking. Simply click "Increase By Left Mouse".

"Use Crosshair Cursor" changes the mouse pointer's appearance. This is useful for more precise positioning operations such as when you are copying or moving items. We'll leave the "DClick Options" to the chapters on Editors.

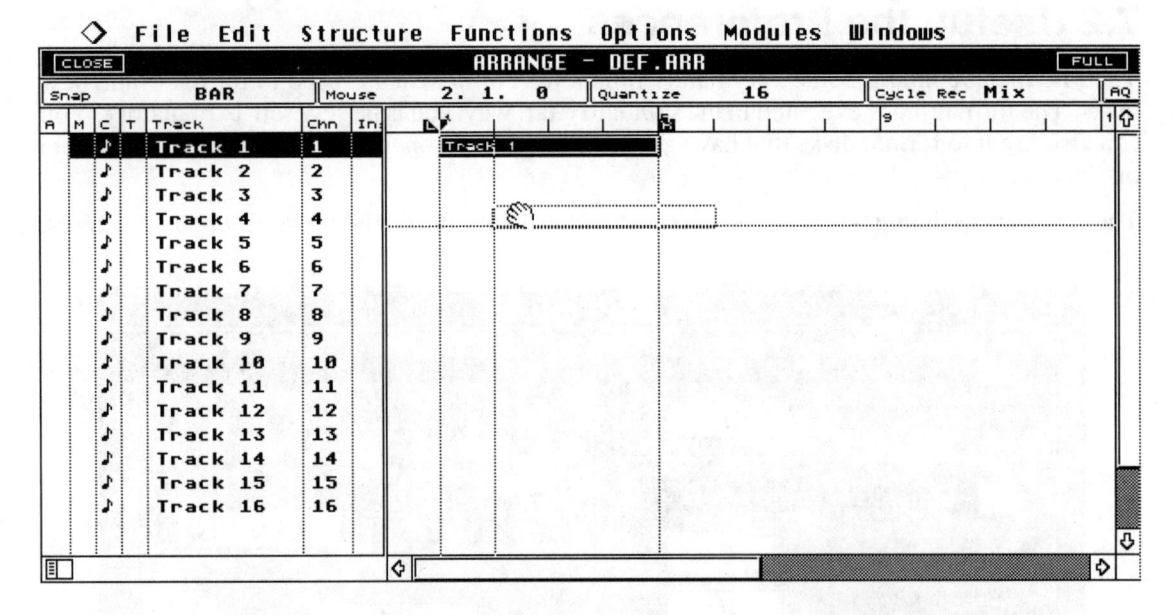

The Crosshair Cursor used for moving an event

7.3 Multirecord

Until now, you have played on one Track at time and pieced your Arrangement together Track by Track. However, you can also record several MIDI channels simultaneously or successively on a single Track (set the Track's MIDI channel to "Any"). This usually entails some additional processing afterwards, in that the Track has to be split up according to its MIDI channels with the help of the Remix function. We encountered this when we were discussing the transfer of MIDI Files.

Again, if you record from a sequencer lacking the MIDI File option, the same method applies (see the "Synchronization" chapter). If you have several synthesizers at your disposal, or one that

Multirecord

can transmit on several MIDI channels at the same time (e.g. a MIDI mother keyboard), you can address them all simultaneously "live".

The Multirecord mode is available for this and similar applications. Before going into details, choose Multirecord from the Options menu. In the dialog box that appears, enable "Active". The Multi-Player mode is now active, and a new column with the heading "R" appears on the Arrange window.

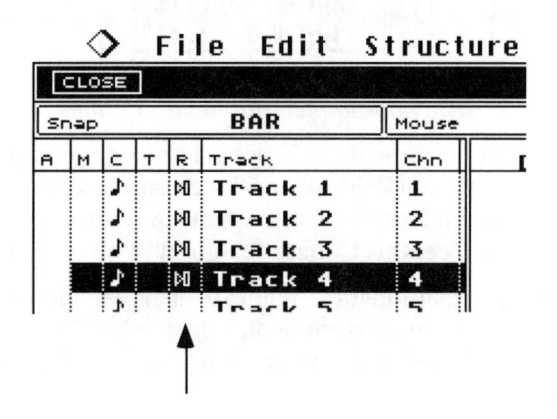

The new "R" column

The Multirecord menu features four different operating modes. These four options can also be selected in the Options menu. The function with the checkmark is the active one. If you want to change a function, click the desired one: "Merge" is the normal recording mode. A maximum of four Tracks can be addressed by the Multirecord mode. To allow this, click any four Tracks in their respective "R" column slots; they do not have to be neighbouring Tracks. Depending on the operating mode, symbols or numbers will appear in the column; these denote that the Track is in Multirecord mode, and in some cases, enable additional options. Track assignment is absolutely essential. If you don't assign at least one Track to the Multirecord mode, you can't record.

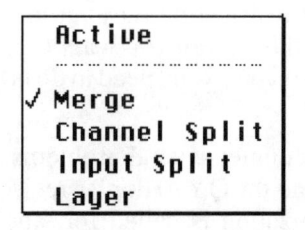

The Multirecord menu

Now you are probably wondering what exactly the Multirecord mode does. Its advantages and applications are best demonstrated with a number of practical exercises:

Delete all previous recordings, enclose four bars with the locators, and activate Cycle mode. Select the Multirecord mode "Channel Split". Multirecord mode must, of course, be active.

For the following exercise, your master synthesizer must be capable of sending information on at least two different MIDI channels. Set your synth so that it transmits one sound on Channel 1, and another on Channel 2, such as bass on the lower half of the keyboard, piano in the higher registers. Ensure that the sounds are not just addressed internally, but also sent to Cubase via MIDI as two separate channels. Otherwise, you will not be able to see what exactly happens.

Click the "R" column of Track 1. A pop-up menu appears: select the following setting: 1, 5, 9, 13. Do the same for Track 2, but select 2, 6, 10, 14. You have just determined which of the incoming channels are assigned to which Cubase Track. Start recording and play a Part. Obviously, both sounds should be recorded at the same time.

Special Functions

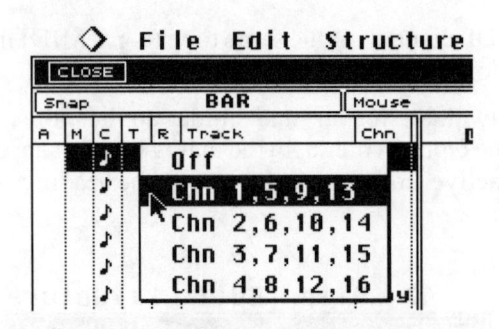

The pop-up menu in the R column

Stop the recording: Cubase has generated two Tracks. The first contains the data of MIDI channel 1, Track 2 the data of MIDI channel 2. Mute one Track and then the other for audible proof. If you are keen on playing Parts and Tracks in a single take with an instrument that can transmit on several MIDI channels at once, this Cubase feature will be of immense help to you.

The Track's channel setting doesn't matter. You can change it and reassign the MIDI channel. If you want to return to your original assignment, select MIDI Channel "Any" or the channels you actual used, in this case 1 and 2. All other functions, e.g. Cycle, Overdub, etc. are also available in the Multirecord mode.

7.3.1 Tip: using ready-made accompaniments

The Channel Split option is designed for those who like to work with accompaniments, such as those used in domestic "contemporary keyboards" or similar devices. Let's look at one of the popular devices, the Yamaha QY10, although the Yamaha only serves as an example: this function works with all of these sorts of devices.

Connect the QY10 (or any other similar device) MIDI Out to your Atari's MIDI In. Select Multirecord and the Channel Split operating mode. In the "R" column, assign different channels to Tracks 1 through 4 (Track 1: 1, 5, 9, 13; Track 2: 2, 6, 10, 14, etc.). Set their MIDI channels to "Any". Cubase now adopts the QY10's MIDI assignments. If you already know how long you want the Pattern to be, place the locators at the desired positions, which means you immediately have the correct length and don't have to resort to any cutting operations. You don't require Cycle mode or similar functions. Select the pattern you want to transfer in the QY10. It would seem that you are now ready to record. All you would need to do is to just start Record mode in Cubase, and the playback of the QY10.

However, you would probably encounter several problems. Play and record operations are not "in sync": the tempos of Cubase and the QY10 don't precisely match, even if they both display the same tempo value. Synchronization is called for, and MIDI makes it possible. Choose Synchronization from the Options menu: a wide-ranging dialog box appears.

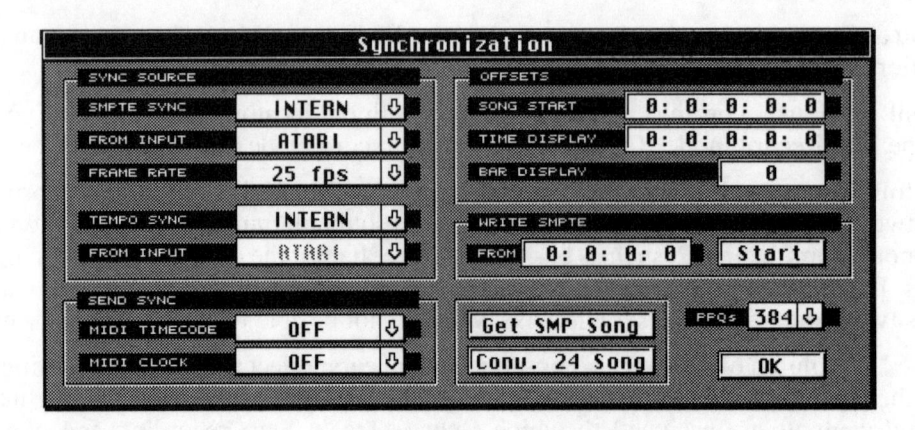

The Synchronization dialog box

116

For the moment, we are only interested in "Tempo Sync". Click and hold the arrow pointing down, located to the right of this term. Select MIDI CLK and exit the dialog box by pressing [Return].

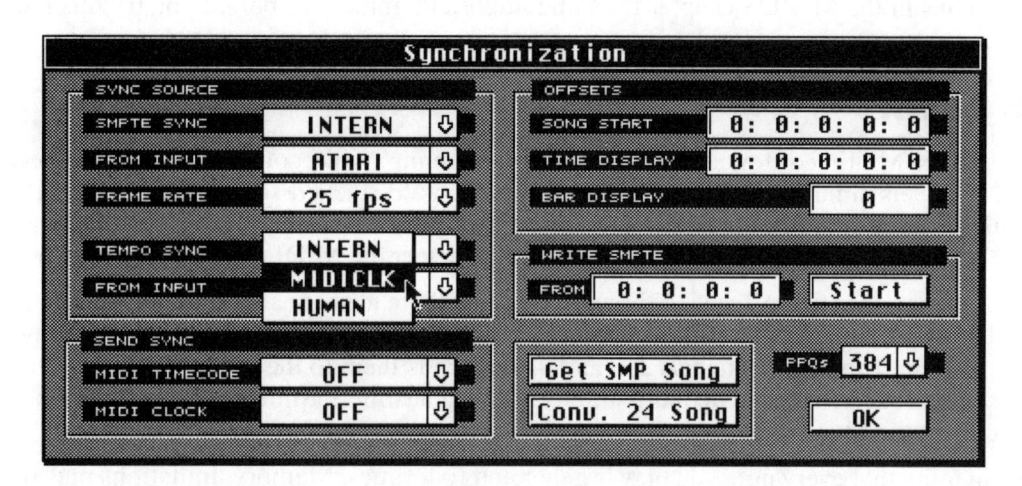

Activating the MIDI Clock

Now click SYNC (keyboard: [X]), located at the righthand end of the Transport Bar. We have now carried out all the preconditions for recording. Click Cubase's Record button. Cubase switches to record status, but does not actually start. It won't begin until you start the QY10's pattern. Do so, and the QY10 pattern is recorded in Cubase. Stop the QY10 after the pattern has run through once. Go back to Cubase, switch SYNC off and listen to the recording. Cubase has recorded the QY10 pattern on four individual Tracks, divided into bass, drums, and two other instruments. You can edit the Parts as usual. Here are a few guidelines:

- If you leave the MIDI channel settings at "Any", then Cubase adopts the QY10's MIDI channel assignments. You can, of course, reassign channels as you please, and recall the original settings at any later stage via "Any".

- The above method is not limited to the QY10. It can be extended to other devices, provided they are capable of sending their accompaniment patterns via MIDI and support the MIDI clock required for synchronization. You may have to switch on the MIDI clock of your donor synth before proceeding - see its manual for instructions.

- Do not use Cycle mode as you could end up with doubled notes.

- Even if you synchronize the two, you may still get little movements in timing due to things like the tempo of the donor device being too high for the amount of data being transmitted. This data recorded by Cubase tends to be around 1 - 3 ticks late, which is normally not a problem. If this bothers you, carefully apply some quantization. You should acquire a solid background on quantizing before you try things like this as it is all too easy to delete the finer details of the recorded pattern. In any case, consult the chapter covering quantizing for more information.

- You can reduce problems by reducing the tempo before recording. You can then speed the pattern up to its original tempo for playback purposes. Further tips on synchronization and recording can be found in chapter 17.

- The above method is limited to recording on four channels. If your accompaniment device sends data on more than four channels at the same time, record the pattern on a single Track, with the same synchronization procedures. Ensure that this Track is set to "Any", and that the Multirecord mode is not active, then "Remix" the Track.

7.4 Input Split

This allows several keyboards, drum machines, MIDI, etc. to be recorded simultaneously in a live situation.

You need additional hardware if you want to use this Multirecord operating mode. Steinberg's

Special Functions

SMP 24 or MIDEX give you two additional MIDI inputs; add the Atari MIDI input, and you have three input ports through which you can record simultaneously. Once you activate MIDI Input Split, incoming signals are assigned to three Tracks via use of the "R" column. However, you should consult the M*ROS chapter for some important guidelines before you try this mode.

7.5 Layer

In the Layer Multirecord mode, Cubase routes incoming MIDI commands to four selectable MIDI channels simultaneously. It means you can create stacked sounds from several sound modules even if your master synthesizer doesn't transmit on more than one channel at a time. Activate the desired Tracks in the "R" column and select the MIDI channel you want to use.

Let's assume you activate Tracks 1 through 4 - assign them to channels 1 through 4 respectively, and play on MIDI channel 1. While you play, Cubase duplicates the information it receives on MIDI channel 1 to MIDI channels 2, 3 and 4, and sends them to the output. That way you can control up to four different devices in realtime. At the same time, the information is simultaneously recorded on the four Tracks you've selected.

Keep in mind that every note you play is generated four times. Memory limitations may dictate that you use a different method to create layered sounds, such as the method described in the Arrange chapter for creating Ghost copies.

7.6 Remote control

The list of useful little details that make Cubase so easy to work with is not yet complete. There are quite a number of sequencer functions you can carry out from your MIDI keyboard which mean you don't have to touch your computer to execute recording and playback functions.

Go to the Options menu and select Remote Control. Click the Remote Active box to enter a checkmark.

The remote control function is now active. Exit the dialog box by clicking OK ([Return]). You can also simply press [Y] to activate or deactivate the remote control function, provided you are not in its dialog box at the time.

The remote control is designed to be very user-friendly. Press and hold the C6 key. If no transposition function is active, then this key is the highest note on a five-octave keyboard. Press the A#5 key while holding C6 down. Cubase starts playback. Stop the sequencer by pressing C6 and B5 together.

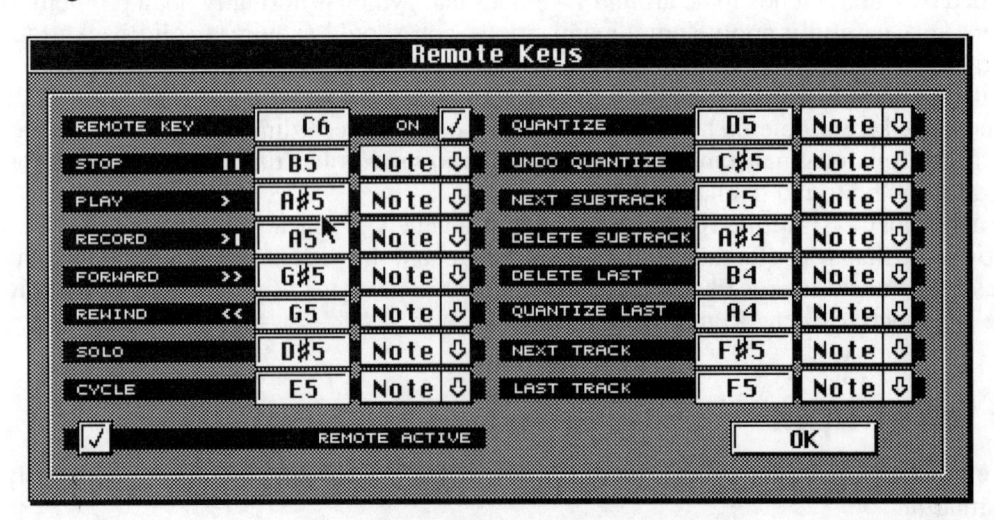

Remote Control settings

By pressing and holding the C6 key (the "Remote Key"), you are letting Cubase know that a remote control command is on its way, as defined by the next key press. The available commands are listed in the dialog box shown above. Remember to press and hold the C6 key first, as without this command the keys below the C6 play normally. Avoid using this key when you are in Remote Control mode since you may accidentally stop the recording or alter something.

You can tailor the key assignments to your preferences: the Cubase defaults are just an example. Use the mouse to change key assignments in the dialog box, making sure that you don't assign the same key to two functions.

MIDI data other than note events can also be used, such as Control Changes. Click and hold the arrow pointing down adjacent to the Note field. You can now use Control Change or Program Change commands for remote control. The number on the left defines the command.

Although use of the Remote Key is intended to avoid confusion between remote commands and normal note playing, there can be problems when you play chords in the upper register. If your keyboard has more than five octaves, it is easier to define a region of your keyboard that your playing doesn't interfere with. It makes sense to use Control Change messages that are never otherwise used, but take care not to run out of functions. Consult your master synthesiser's MIDI Implementation Chart to find out which Control Change messages are generated and used.

7.7 The Notepad

The Notepad provides a simple but very useful additional function as it allows you to type in comments and such like. Call up the Notepad from the Edit menu ([Control][B]). There is no "word wrap" function so you have to press [Return] at the end of each line. [Backspace] deletes characters before the cursor.

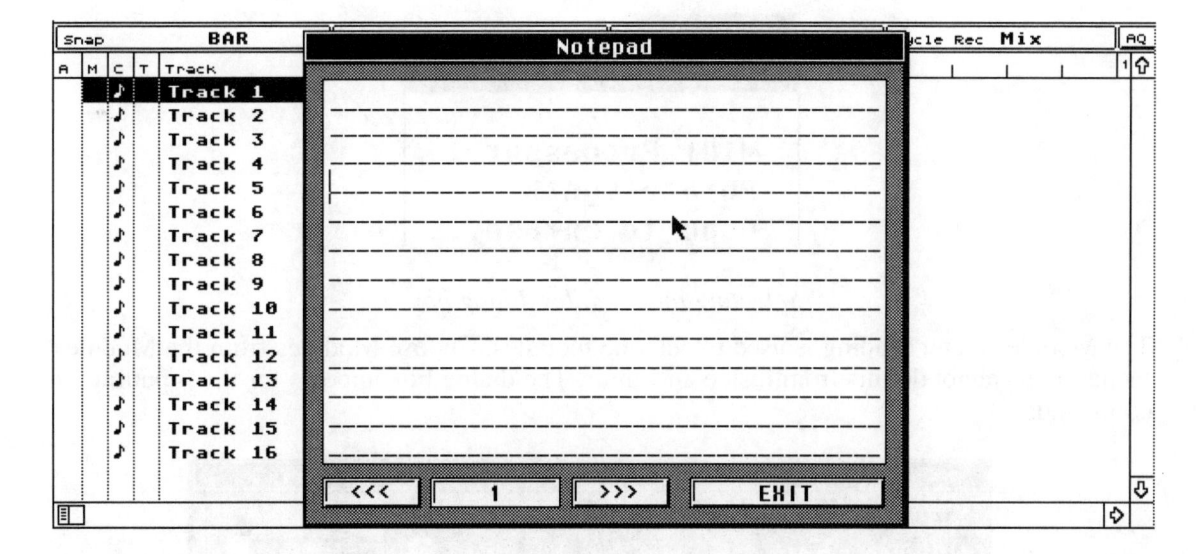

The Notepad

The cursor keys on your computer keyboard are used to move from line to line or between characters. The Notepad has a number of pages which are accessed by clicking the ">>>" and "<<<" buttons. Once you have finished your typing, click Exit. Each Arrangement has its own Notepad.

7.8 Modules

When you start Cubase, all the necessary data is loaded into the computer's memory or "RAM" (Random Access Memory). All activities take place in the RAM, including your recording. As

Special Functions

the RAM is not buffered by a battery, its contents are lost when the power is switched off or otherwise interrupted. This is why you have to save your work at regular intervals, and load Cubase every time you start.

Every computer's RAM is limited; for instance, the Atari ST usually comes with one megabyte (MB). Much of this MB is taken up by the program; what's left is available for your data, i.e. notes and other MIDI events. Cubase's increased performance specifications take its toll on the available memory. The program uses more memory, at least when you use all of its functions.

To allow Cubase to be workable in a single MB environment, Version 2.01 had the option of removing components of the program. Cubase 3.0 has become even more flexible in this respect. As well as providing the basic functions, it has an "interface" which allows you to "plug" in additional modules. This means you can load and remove certain program components to and from the memory as required. Not only do you make best use of the available memory, you can also upgrade the program with more modules.

The basic Cubase package comes with four modules: the Score Editor, IPS, the MIDI Mixer and the MIDI Processor. Additional modules such as Styletrax and Cuetrax are available as optional extras. You can load any of these modules at any time. You, of course, require more memory with each additional module: you cannot, for instance, load all four into a single MB computer at once. If you want to use several modules at the same time, you have to increase the RAM. The Atari's RAM can be easily and inexpensively upgraded - please consult the appendix for additional information.

7.8.1 Operation

All modules are inactive when you install Cubase. This makes sense, as users have varying requirements and varying RAM.

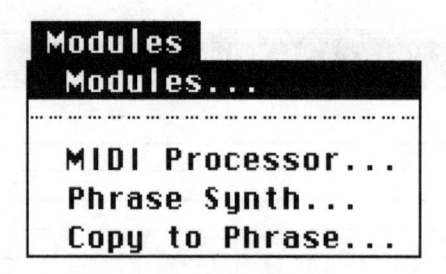

Selecting the Modules dialog box

The Modules menu heading is used to activate modules. Choose Modules from the Modules menu. You cannot do this from inside an Editor. The dialog box appears for the inputting of commands.

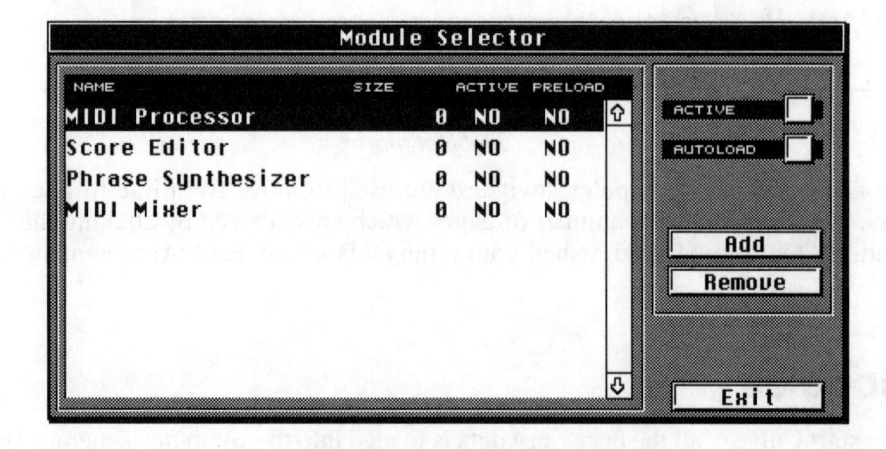

The Module Selector dialog box

The large area in this box displays the available modules. They are shown as active when there is a memory size displayed beside them. Please note that the available modules are limited to those in the CUBASE.DAT folder on your hard disk or floppy disk.

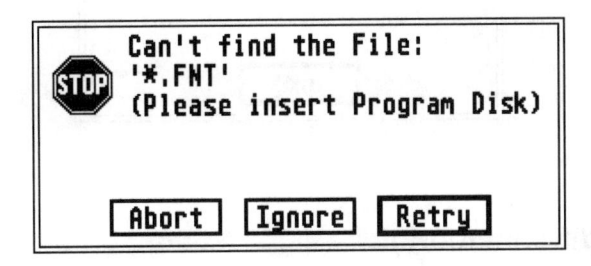

```
          Can't find the File:
   STOP   '*.FNT'
          (Please insert Program Disk)

          [Abort]  [Ignore]  [Retry]
```

The CUBASE.DAT folder is missing

If you want to load a module, your program floppy must be inserted in the disk drive. If you're using a hard disk, the folder containing the file must share the same path as the CUBASE.PRG file.

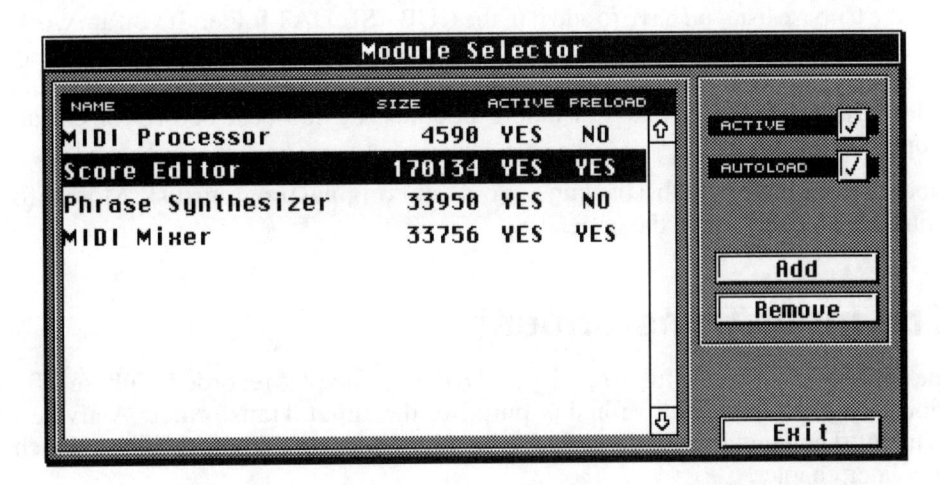

```
                      Module Selector
   NAME                SIZE    ACTIVE  PRELOAD       ACTIVE    [√]
   MIDI Processor      4590    YES     NO
   Score Editor        170134  YES     YES           AUTOLOAD  [√]
   Phrase Synthesizer  33950   YES     NO
   MIDI Mixer          33756   YES     YES
                                                     [  Add   ]
                                                     [ Remove ]

                                                     [  Exit  ]
```

Four modules are loaded, two of which are loaded automatically

Apart from the modules, this folder contains other important information, e.g. character fonts and printer drivers.

You can start Cubase without the data in this file, but then you have to make do without important functions. Cubase alerts you to the missing file several times if you do decide to give it a try.

To install a module, click the desired one (e.g. MIDI Processor or Score Editor) to highlight it, then put a checkmark in the box next to "Active". The selected module then loads.

The memory being used is displayed, and the Active status changes from No to Yes. Follow the same method to load any additional modules. Having to load modules every time you start the program can become rather tedious, so Cubase offers automatic loading.

Select a module and click the Autoload box. The Preload status changes from No to Yes, and the selected modules are automatically loaded next time you start the program. Cubase makes a note about which modules it needs to load by writing to disk, so make sure that, if you are using a floppy, it is not write-protected.

Module activation and the Autoload status can be reversed by clicking the appropriate checkmarks of the selected module once more. This way you have more memory available, and you won't encounter the following warning:

Special Functions

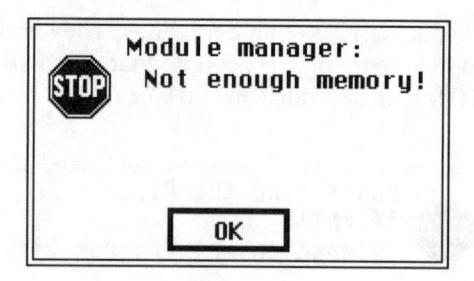

Too little memory

7.8.2 Loading additional modules

You can also load modules not contained in the CUBASE.DAT folder. Click the Add field and select the desired module in the Item Selection box which now appears. Cubase adds it to the list. The module is not actually loaded, just added to the list. Follow the steps described above to load it. Use Remove to delete a module from the list.

These Add settings are lost when you exit the program. If you want a module to permanently appear on the Cubase list, you have to add it to the CUBASE.DAT folder. If you are working with a floppy, not a hard, disk, you may run out of memory. A "DD" floppy disk has a capacity of around 720 kBytes, which is simply not enough for the Cubase program, its fonts, and dozens of modules. Therefore, you have to first delete modules you don't use before you can add others to the floppy.

Remember to always work with a backup *copy* of your original program disk. More information on computers can be found in the appendix.

7.9 The Input Transformer

For some applications, it is useful to modify MIDI data *before* it is recorded. Cubase 3.0 provides a function designed specifically for this purpose, the Input Transformer. Activate it in the Options menu. The Input Transformer dialog box is related to the Logical Editor, which we will cover in a later chapter.

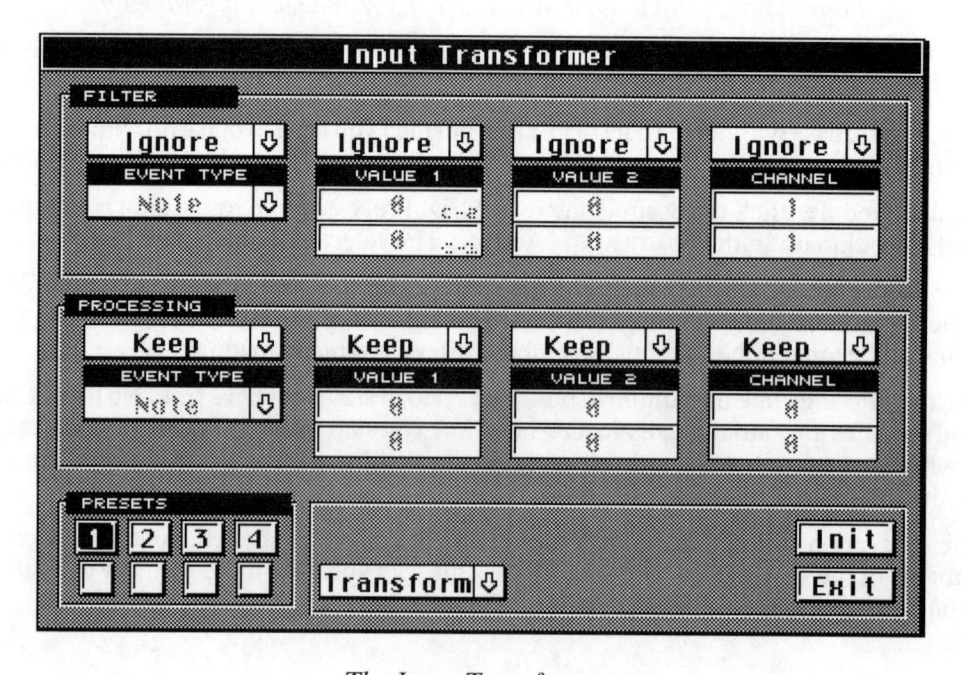

The Input Transformer

The Input Transformer

The Input Transformer has two functions. Firstly, data can be filtered out of the MIDI data stream. Although this is also possible with the filters you have encountered so far, the Input Transformer offers far more specific options.

Secondly, the structure of incoming data can be altered, making it possible to convert, say, Pitch Bend data into modulation or volume commands.

All processing is executed in realtime: incoming MIDI data is immediately altered, recorded (if you wish), and then sent via the MIDI Thru to your MIDI devices.

Up to four presets are available which can be activated individually or together. Click the "1" and the white box below it. Both are located in the Presets box. You have just selected and activated the first Input Transformer preset. All the settings that you can see apply to the currently selected preset only.

Preset management: Preset 1 is being edited, Presets 1 and 2 are active

To define more presets, you have to first click the desired number, and then edit the settings. A preset is not activated *automatically* by doing this: you must enter the usual checkmark to do so.

7.9.1 The Filter function

You need to know about the MIDI data structure to make best use of the filter functions. The previous chapter has already supplied much of the relevant information. You need to define the Transformer's operating mode before you can use it to filter specific data. Click and hold the down arrow to the left of the Init and Exit fields.

Basic setting: Filter or Transform

Select "Filter" because we want to filter specific MIDI messages in this exercise. We only need the upper third of the Transformer box for this purpose. The four boxes that are arrayed side by side are where you enter the relevant settings. "Ignore" means no messages are filtered. Click and hold the down arrow above the Event Type entry, and select the condition "Equal".

Selecting the condition that defines the type of event

Cubase uses different "conditions" which have to be met before something is processed, one of

123

Special Functions

which is the entry you have just selected, "Equal". The entry in the Event Type box was grey: it is now highlighted, i.e. active.

Play a few notes on your master synthesizer. You shouldn't hear anything. Why? Because Cubase is filtering all notes from the incoming MIDI data. This is what you have just determined: everything "Equal" to the Event Type "Note" is removed, i.e. all the notes you play are filtered out. Now click and hold the down arrow in the Event Type box.

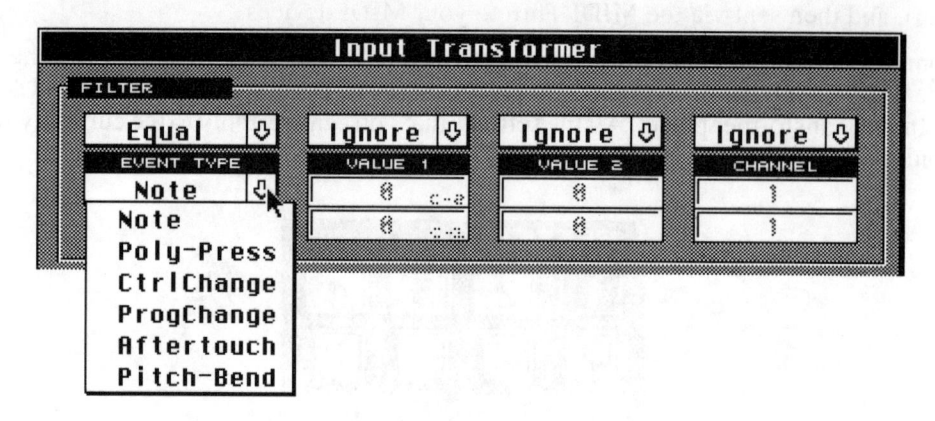

The types of event (as defined by their MIDI status)

You can select any available event type from this list. If you select Aftertouch (MIDI Channel Pressure), it filters out all that data. If you have studied the chapter on MIDI, you will know how Cubase does this: it simply analyses the incoming status bytes and recognizes which ones are Channel Pressure messages. It then simply ignores them.

In addition to this method for selecting and filtering out specific types or status of MIDI data, there is its "reverse" variant, as it were: the condition "Unequal" is the one to use here.

Let's stick with the example above: activate "Unequal" and keep the Event Type as "Note". Cubase now filters out all messages that are *not* note commands, e.g. Control Changes, Program Changes, Channel Pressure, etc.

Next to Event Type, you can define three further conditions with their criteria which exactly define which events are to be filtered. Exactly what these boxes contain depends on the event type.

Let's look at an example using note commands. Leave "Note" as the event type, and set its condition to "Equal". Set the "Value 1" condition to "Equal" as well, and enter a value of 60 in the upper field (this is MIDI Note 60 (C3)). The lower field remains dimmed, so you can't enter anything in it for the moment.

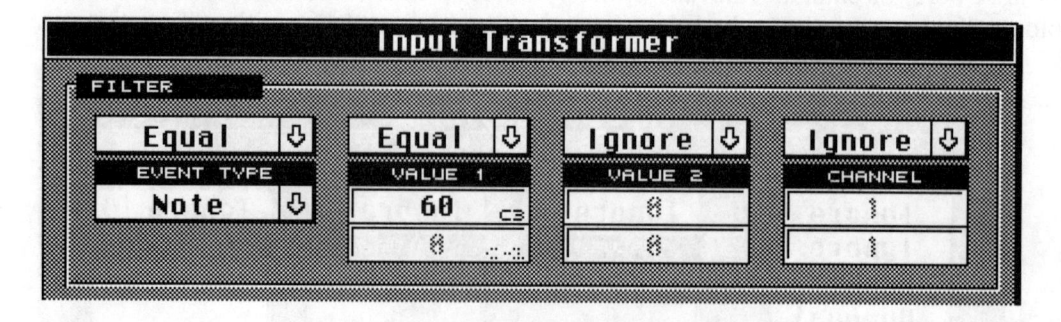

Filtering out the note C3

Play chromatically up or down the keyboard. You will notice that C3 cannot be heard: its key is now muted. You can mute any key by entering its value in the Value 1 box. This process can also be reversed by replacing the condition "Equal" with "Unequal": all keys *except* C3 are muted.

The Input Transformer

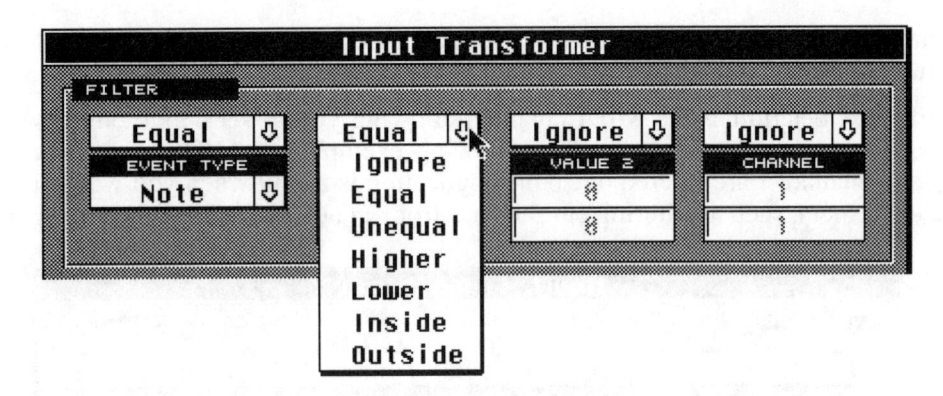

The conditions: these determine the range for further processing

You can see there are other conditions for defining the Value 1 range. Try Higher (than) and Lower (than). These are used to divide the keyboard into sections.

Inside and Outside also define ranges. With these conditions, you must enter an upper and a lower limit. Try the following settings:

Event type "Note" with condition "Equal":

"Value 1"   "Value 1"

Condition	Value	Result
Higher	C3	All notes higher than C3 can be played, the rest are muted.
Lower	D4	All notes lower than D4 can be played, the rest are muted.
Inside	C3 - C4	All notes between C3 and C4 can be played, the rest are muted.
Outside	C3 - C4	All notes outside C3 and C4 can be played, the notes between these two keys are muted.

In each of these exercises, you have divided the keyboard into playable and non-playable sections. So far, two conditions have been interconnected: notes and range. There are other criteria available. Value 2 (which represents the 2nd data byte of a MIDI event) is used to define velocity values for notes. Enter the following settings in the Input Transformer:

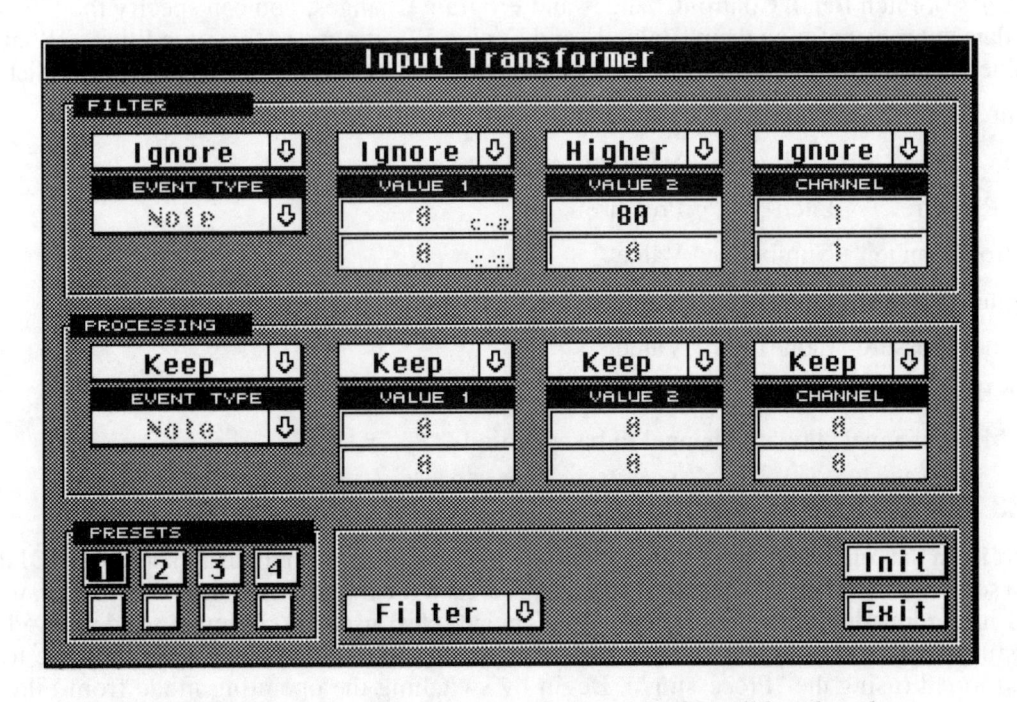

Only notes with a velocity value lower than 80 will be played

Special Functions

Play something with varying velocities on your keyboard. All notes exceeding the 80 velocity value limit are filtered out. Experiment with different values and criteria.

The fourth box determines the MIDI channel, allowing you to set conditions based on the channels of incoming messages. In the following example, all MIDI channels except for ("Unequal") channel 2 are filtered out. This application is useful when you want to specify a specific instrument, such as filtering out the bass from an auto-accompaniment program.

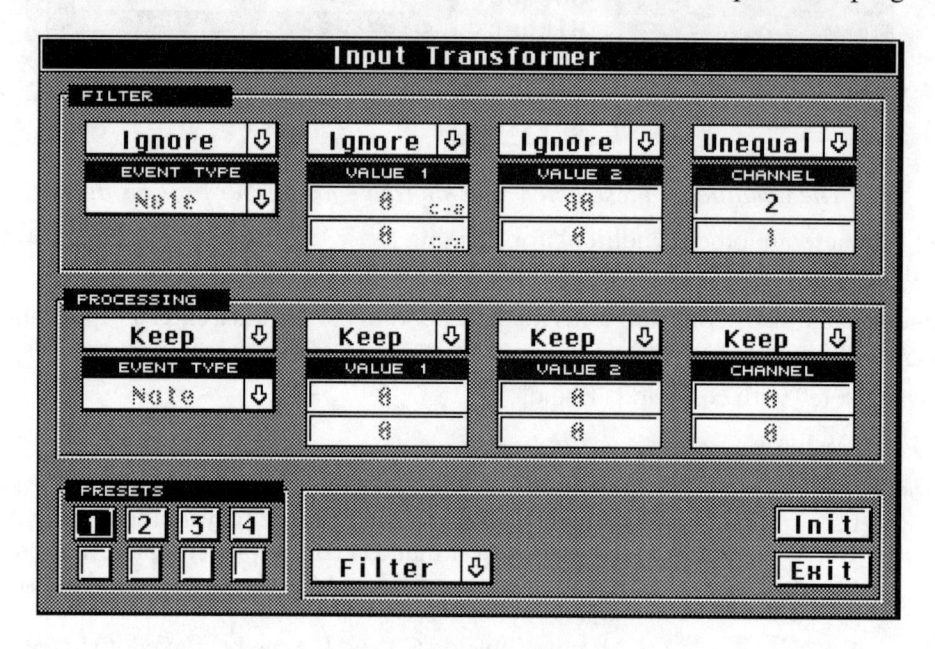

Specifying a MIDI channel

7.9.2 A summary of the Filter function

The filter settings define the MIDI events you want to filter. As well as being able to define the "event type" (MIDI status), i.e. notes, Poly Key Pressure, Channel Pressure (called "Aftertouch" in Cubase), Pitch Bend, Control Changes and Program Changes, you can specify their 1st and 2nd data bytes by defining their "Value 1" and "Value 2" settings and their conditions. What the "Value 1" and "Value 2" boxes refer to depends on the "event type". Here's a detailed list:

Event Type	Value 1	Value 2
Note	Pitch	Velocity
Poly Pressure	Pitch	Pressure
Control Change	Number	Value
Program Change	(none)	Number
Channel Pressure	(none)	Value
Pitch Bend	(none)	Value

The MIDI channel allows a channel to be specified.

7.9.3 The Transform functions

Apart from the relatively simple Filter function, you can also manipulate all sorts of MIDI data in all sorts of ways. This is what the "Processing" area of the Input Transformer is used for, when used in conjunction with the "Filter" area. Their boxes, used in conjunction, define which incoming events are eligible to be transformed (using the "Filter") and how they are to be transformed (using the "Processing"). Begin by switching the operating mode from Filter to Transform:

The Input Transformer

Switching to "Transform"

The event types can be accepted as they are, or modified as per the example at the end of this section. "Value 1" and "Value 2" tell Cubase what to do with the individual events. You can transform incoming values by adding to or subtracting them from a value (plus/minus), defining a fixed value for them (Fix), inverting them (Invert), processing them with the Value 1 or Value 2 value, or scaling them with Value 1. Most of these operations will become clear as you apply them. Enter the following settings:

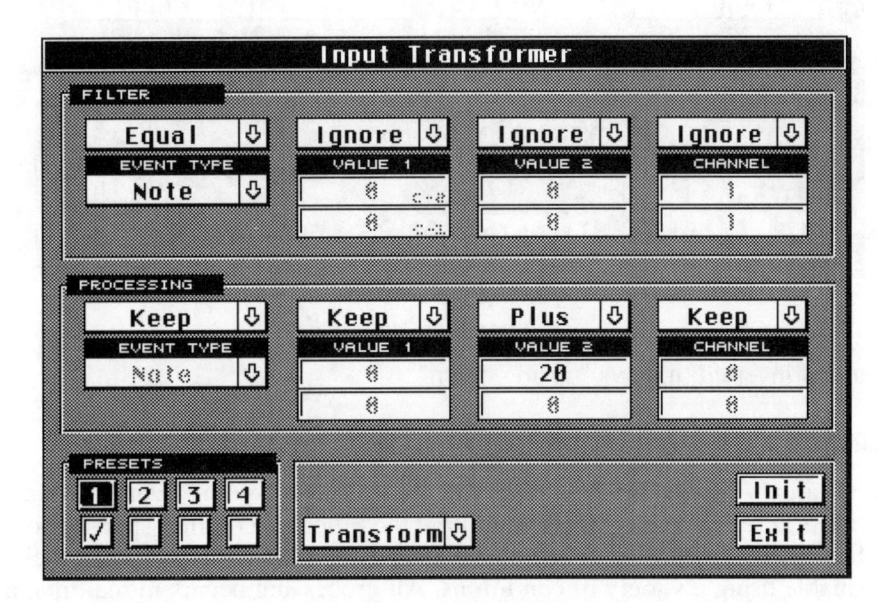

Increasing velocity values

All the incoming notes' velocity values are raised by a factor of 20. A value of "20" becomes "40", "60" becomes "80", etc. "Note" must remain as the event type (this is why you enter "Keep" for the "Processing Event Type"), otherwise additional notes would be generated by incoming notes.

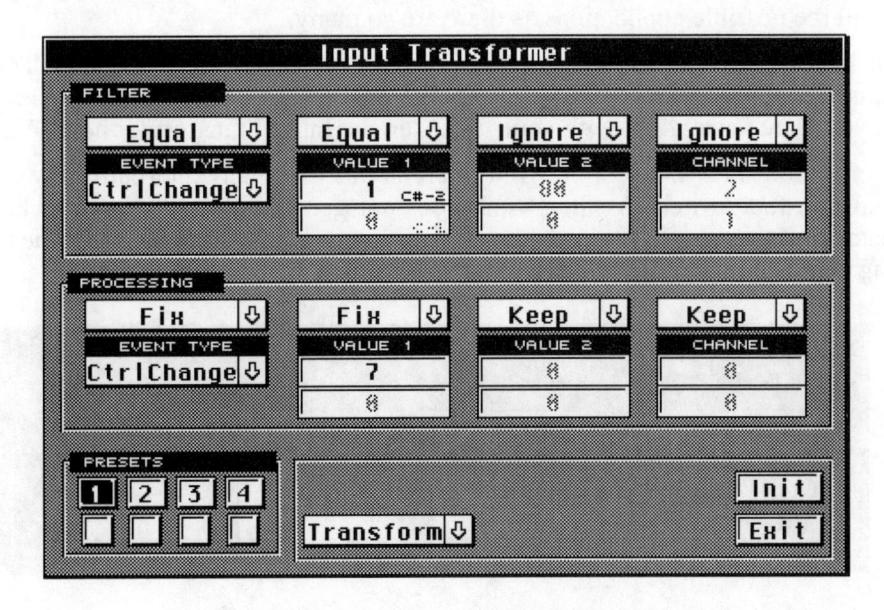

Using the mod wheel to control volume

127

Special Functions

The above example shows how Control Change 1 (modulation) is transformed into Control Change 7 (volume).

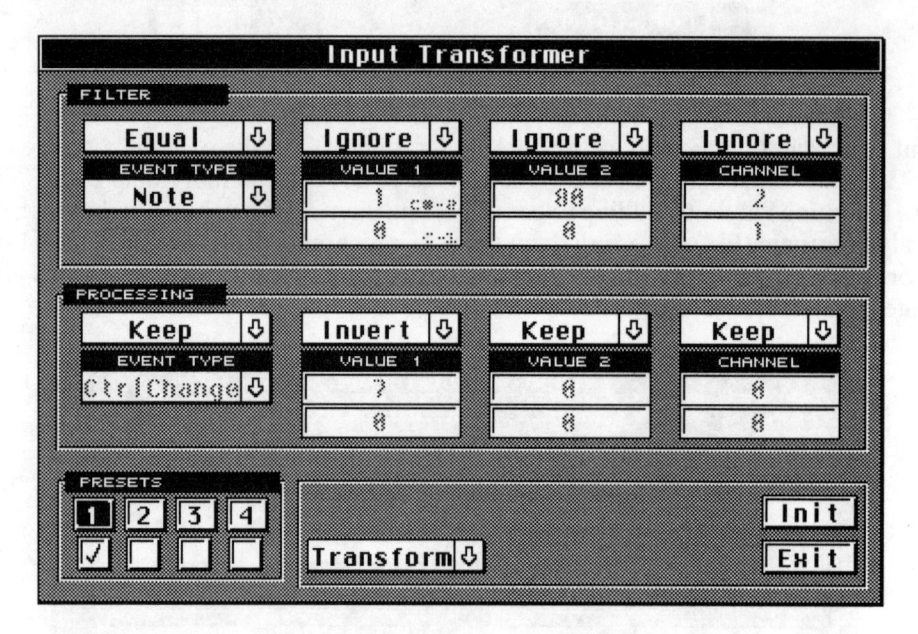

To invert the keyboard

The keyboard is inverted: it plays "upside down".

7.9.4 A summary of the Transformer function

If the "Filter" area's various boxes are set to "ignore" all incoming events, it means that all incoming events are eligible for transformation; if the Filter area defines specific conditions for specific values, then only those will be transformed. The MIDI status bytes and their data bytes are transformable using a variety of conditions. All processing occurs in realtime, and can be heard as it happens.

7.9.5 A concrete example

The preceding examples cover only a fraction of what is possible. It would be impossible to document all the possible applications as there are so many.

What you have learned so far should allow you to create all sorts of Input Transformer applications. Let's use a concrete example to apply that knowledge: say you want to record a kick drum, but you want to trigger it with your foot. Can the Input Transformer help? Yes, it can!

When it comes to using your feet in MIDI, there aren't that many alternatives: we'll use the master's sustain foot switch. As the switch does not generate note commands, but Control Change data, you have to specify that that is the data you want to work with, using the Filter area. The setting depicted in the following diagram shows this:

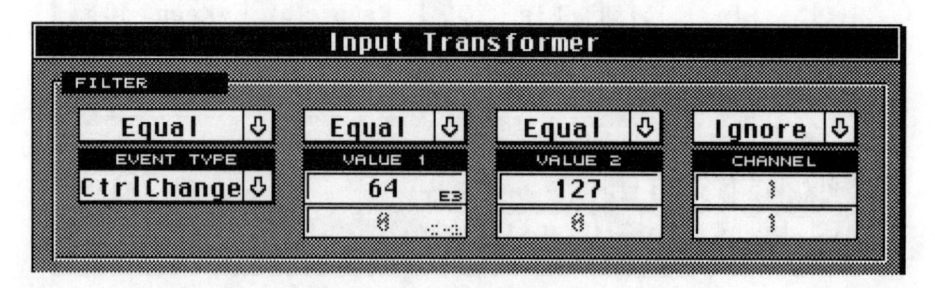

Our example's Filter setting

MIDI Control Change 64, which is generated by the sustain foot switch is the one you want to process. This switch produces two values: "0" is transmitted when the switch is released (off!), and "127" denotes that the switch is pressed (on).

For this example, we need the "127" value only, so enter it in the Value 2 box. If you don't, the switch will generate two notes, one when you press it, the other when you release it.

Now that you have set the Filter conditions, hold on a minute and think of how to proceed. You want the Control Change event to generate a (drum) note of a certain pitch. The sustain switch does not produce velocity values, so you have to create one. The result is the following Transform setting:

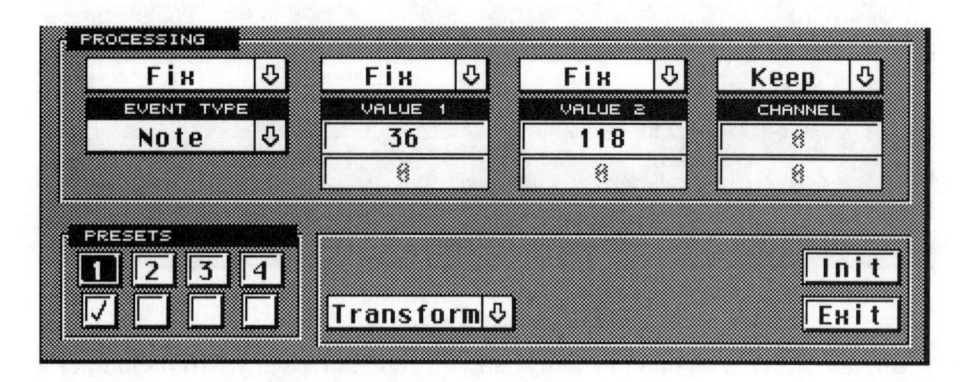

The Transform setting

The above diagram shows that we are creating a "Note" event type. Value 1 must be set to the kick drum's MIDI Note Number, which of course does not necessarily have to be "36". Value 2 defines the velocity, so set it at the value you want.

The currently selected Track on the Arrange window determines the MIDI output channel, so make sure it is set to the drums' channel.

You can also combine more than one Preset. Our final example shows how to create a keyboard split, and also demonstrates the Input Transformer's versatility.

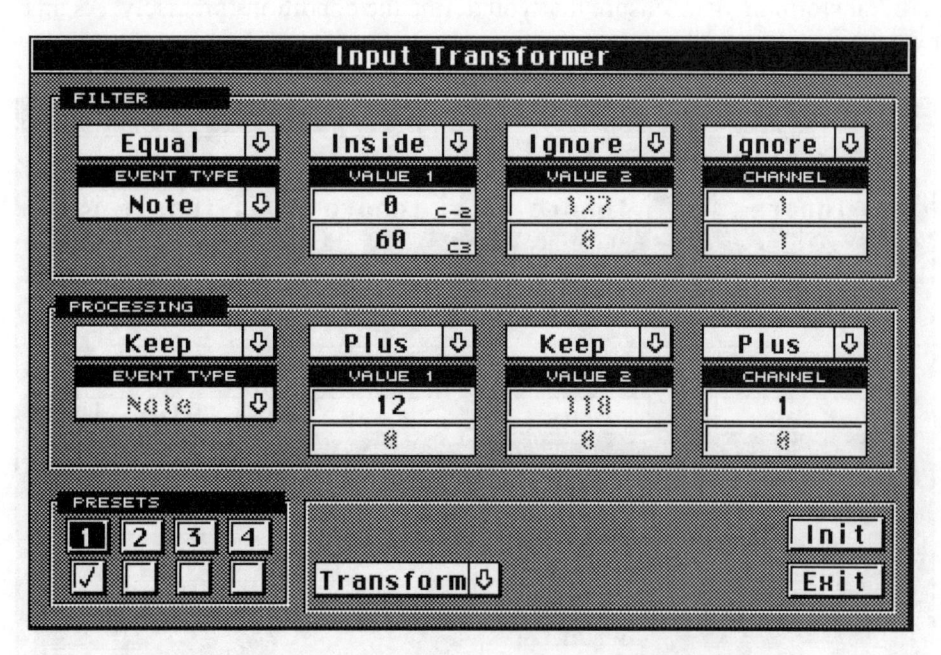

The Preset 1 setting. Combine it with the following Preset 2

Special Functions

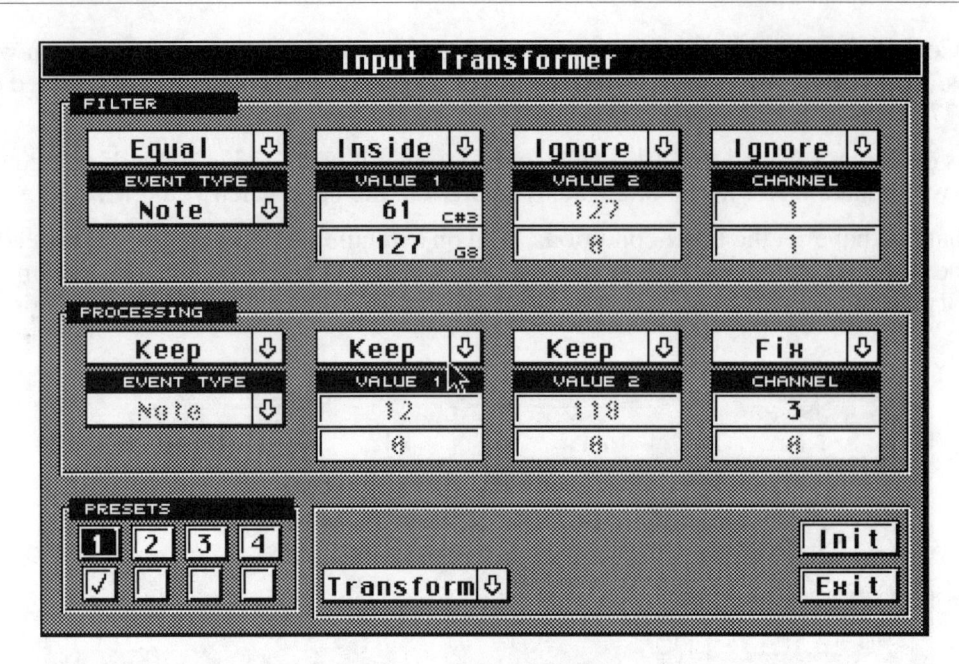

The Preset 2 setting

Start by setting the Track's channel to "Any" so you can address any MIDI channel when you play. Thanks to Preset 1, Cubase plays everything up to C3 on MIDI Channel 1, and everything above C3 on MIDI Channel 3 thanks to Preset 2. So you have a keyboard split that addresses two different channels. Moreover, Preset 1 is adding 12 semitones (an octave) to the lower register.

7.9.6 A few tips

Here are two tips that should help you to avoid unnecessary difficulties:
- If you are using the Input Transformer to alter MIDI channels, make sure the selected Track's channel is set to "Any" on the Arrange window, or you won't be able to hear the results of the alteration.
- If you are transforming data, ensure that you define the conditions precisely. As an example, say you want to transpose all incoming notes up an octave:

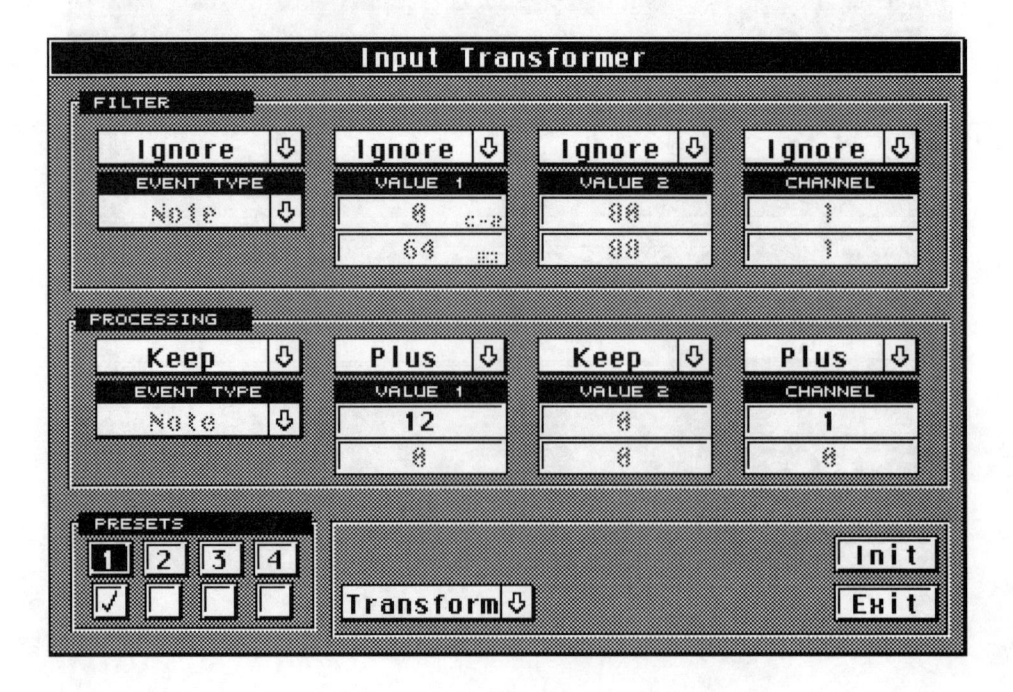

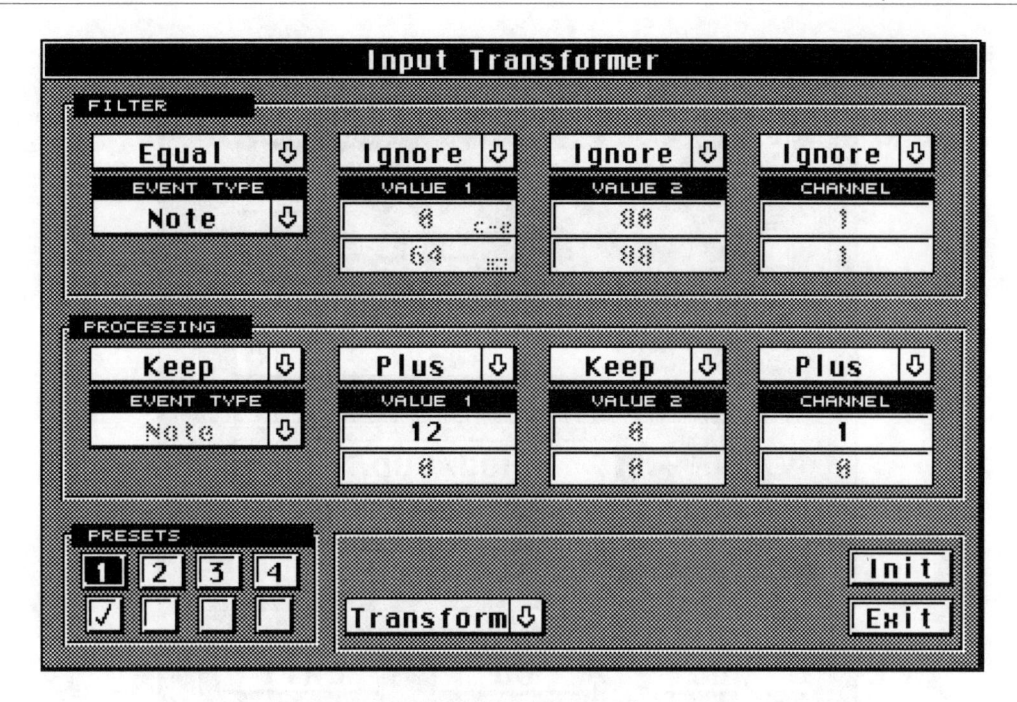

Two ways of transposing

Of the predecing two diagrams, only the second one will work, because the Filter is specifying that all *notes* should be transposed.

In the first diagram, incoming notes are also transposed, but because the Filter is not specifying "Note", *all* incoming events, whatever their type, will have their first data bytes altered by a factor of +12. The result is that, say, incoming MIDI Control Change 64 events become 76, 1 becomes 13 and so on.

Your synthesizer now receives invalid sustain foot switch commands and other weird data that might make it behave oddly.

From time to time in the Input Transformer, you may encounter the dreaded MIDI drone: the notes are correctly switched on, but not switched off. This can happen, especially when you transform Control Change or other MIDI commands into notes.

Cubase is not the problem. The culprits are the little quirks of MIDI communication. If you get a drone, press the Cubase Stop button to cut them off. If the "Reset on Stop" function is active in the MIDI Setup dialog box, all notes that are still sustaining will be switched off.

7.10 Transpose/Velocity

The Transpose/Velocity item in the Functions menu allows you to do things to all the Parts selected in the Arrange window, or all events selected in one of the Editors.

The method is very simple: it's a matter of entering the required values and activating "Do". To use the Transpose function, activate it by entering a checkmark by it. The events are transposed up or down according to the entered value, between +/-127.

Do not transpose drum Tracks as you will change their MIDI note assignments! If you make a mistake, you can undo what you've done via the Undo button.

Special Functions

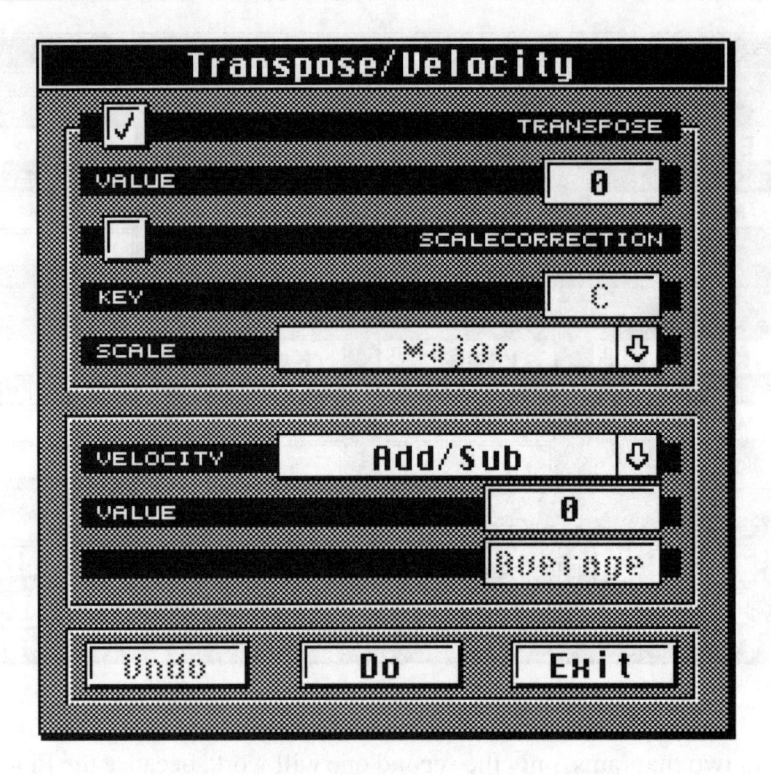

The Transpose/Velocity dialog box

You can also transpose material using a scale correction, where notes are modified to match the selected scale. You must determine the key and the scale.

Click and hold the Scale box. Select a scale, then enter the key in the box above it. Chapter 13 on the Logical Editor describes how scale-corrected transposition works.

The Velocity section allows specific changes according to specific criteria. Select its basic mode under "Velocity". "No change" is self-explanatory. "Compress/Expand" processes the velocity values of the selected Parts or events.

Enter the percentage value in the "Ratio" box. Additionally, in the Centre box, enter a value around which the processing occurs: this is what is sometimes called the "centre key" in compansion, and is the one that is not affected by any processing: if you enter 100, say, then all values above and below 100 are increasingly compressed or expanded as the values move away from 100.

Alternatively, you can let Cubase compute the mean centre value from all the available velocity values by selecting "Average".

"Limits" enables you to define areas in which velocity value changes should occur. Notes within the defined area are left unchanged, all others are modified to the maximum or minimum settings. "Add/Sub" changes all values by the amount entered here.

7.11 The Track Classes

Cubase 3.0 has introduced a new term, "Track Classes". These are used to define what kind of data is recorded on a given Track.

Each Track can be assigned any Class. The basic setting is "MIDI" and applies to recording and playing every kind of MIDI event. The second option is one that we've met before: "Group" defines a Track as a Group Track.

The other Classes are discussed in detail in the appropriate chapters. The number of Track Classes will increase with the development of additional Cubase modules.

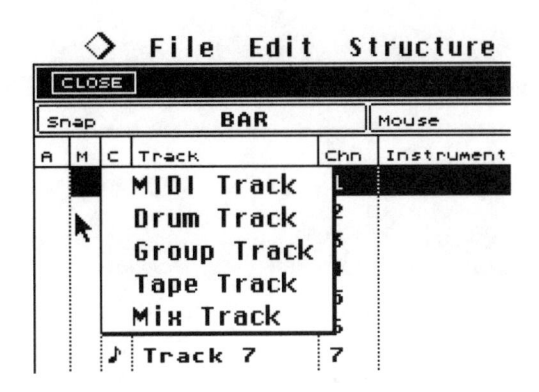

The Track Classes

Some Track Classes feature a relationship with the Part Display, allowing you to call up an Editor by double-clicking a Part. This applies to Drum, MIDI and Mix Track Classes. This is how it works:

By double-clicking a Part in a
- MIDI Track, you enter the Key, List or Score Editor
- Drum Track, you enter the Drum Editor
- Mix Track, you enter the MIDI Mixer.

To assign a Class to a Track, click and hold, using the mouse pointer, the desired Track's C column. Select the desired Class from the pop-up menu. It is always best to assign the Class before you record on a Track.

As mentioned above, three different double-click options are possible for the MIDI Track Class. You must decide which Editor you want to enter via the double-click. The File menu's Preferences dialog box is where you enter your choice. Select the desired Editor under "DClick Opens". This setting applies to all MIDI Tracks.

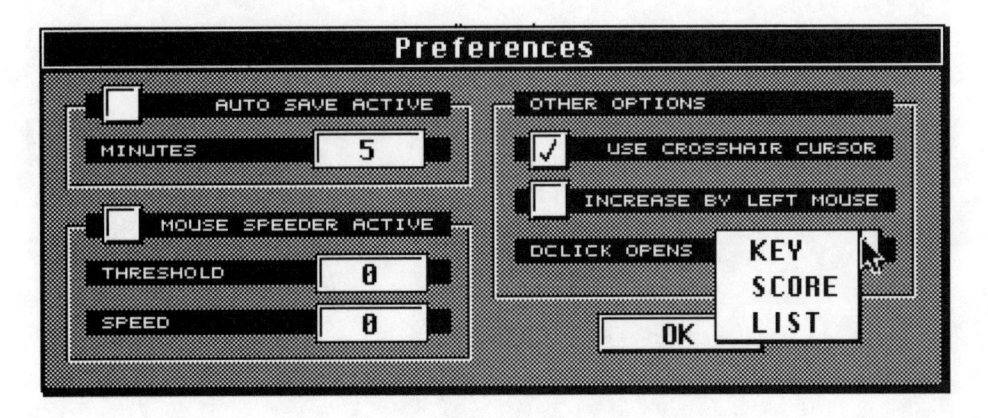

The double-click options of the MIDI Track Class

8 The Key Editor

In this chapter, we'll change the focus of our discussion and take a look not at Parts or Tracks but at the MIDI events contained in them. Cubase features a number of Editors that enable you to have direct access to Notes, Control Changes and all the other types of MIDI data. Knowledge about how MIDI basically works, as laid out in Chapter 2, is extremely useful here.

The Editors are designed to edit specific note and other MIDI data. You can also use the Cubase Editors to generate notes step by step, allowing difficult passages to be created in non-realtime.

The following chapters are divided into two sections. The first section covers the Key, List, Score and Drum Editors, i.e. the "normal" Editors; the second section features the remarkable capabilities of Logical Edit, the MIDI Mixer, IPS and the MIDI processor. Although these components of the program differ substantially from the other Editors, they are also used to create and change events and can therefore also be called "Editors" of a sort.

8.1 The "normal" Editors

The normal Editors, i.e. the Key, List, Score and Drum Editors all have certain handling characteristics in common, which we'll be discussing in this chapter. In the remaining Editors, your attention will be drawn to any difference in handling from the Key Editor, so by getting to know how the Key Editor works, you'll be learning about the other Editors, too.

To enter an Editor and be able to access single notes and other MIDI data, you must first select one or more Parts or a complete Track. The number of Parts you can select is defined by the type of Editor. You can also create an empty Part: by selecting it you enter the Editor, too.

8.2 The Key Editor

Create an Arrangement featuring several Parts on different Tracks. We want to come up with similar results, so please create an Arrangement similar to the one in the illustration below. You could also use the basic Arrangement we created in Chapter 1. Select the first Part in Track 1 and select the Key Editor in the Edit menu ([Control][E]) to enter the Key Editor.

A completely new window opens which you can size to your specifications: remind yourself about how to move, size, etc. windows - things you learned with the Arrange window. In the process you will notice that the Arrange window has not disappeared off your screen, but is merely covered up by the Key Editor window.

You could use the familiar Tile Windows function to display equal-sized Arrange and Editor windows on your screen, but for now, leave the Editor window at its maximum size.

The Key Editor

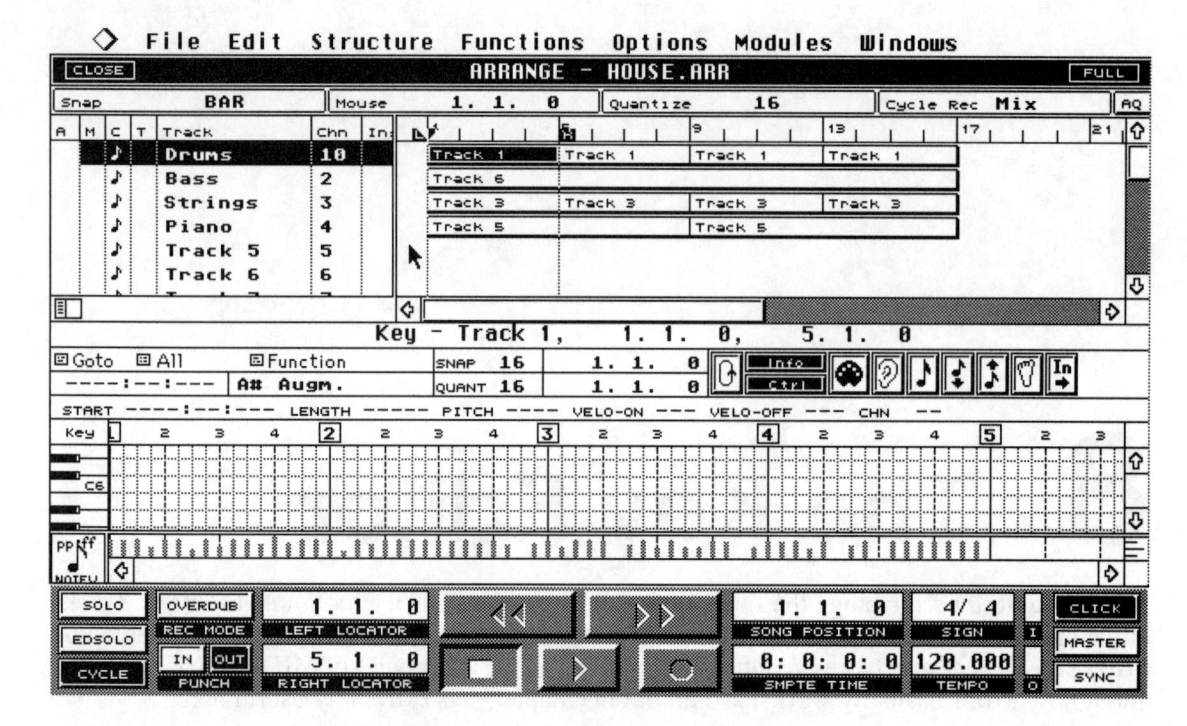

The Key Editor and the Arrange window (Tile Windows)

The Transport and Menu Bars below and above the Editor window are the same in all the "normal" Editors. Their functions operate as usual. You can access an Editor while the sequencer is running in playback or record modes.

If you are not yet used to operating a sequencer while it's running, do all the exercises below when the sequencer is stopped.

8.3 The layout of the Key Edit window

Let's take a closer look at the Editor window. This is a good opportunity to discuss the differences between the various Editors.

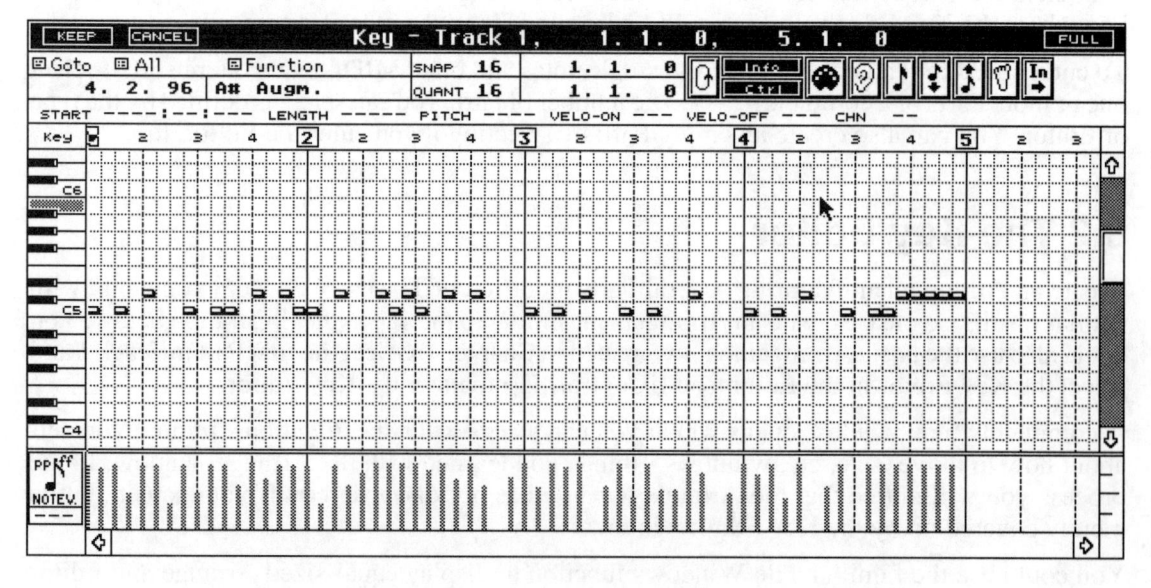

The Key Edit window (without the Menu Bar or Transport Bar)

The Layout of the Key Edit Window

The Key Edit window is divided into four distinct sections:

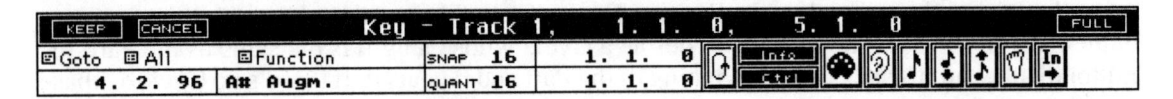

```
[KEEP] [CANCEL]        Key - Track 1,    1. 1. 0,    5. 1. 0        [FULL]
⊞Goto  ⊞All   ⊞Function    SNAP  16   1. 1. 0 | Info |            | In |
       4. 2. 96  A# Augm.  QUANT 16   1. 1. 0 | Ctrl |             |  → |
```

The Functions Bar

- The Functions Bar also contains a number of icons (symbols that act as switches). It exists, with minor differences, in all four Editors.

```
START ----:--:---  LENGTH -----  PITCH ----  VELO-ON ---  VELO-OFF ---  CHN --
```

The Info Line (without information as yet)

- The Info Line displays information concerning a single, selected note. The List Editor doesn't have it.

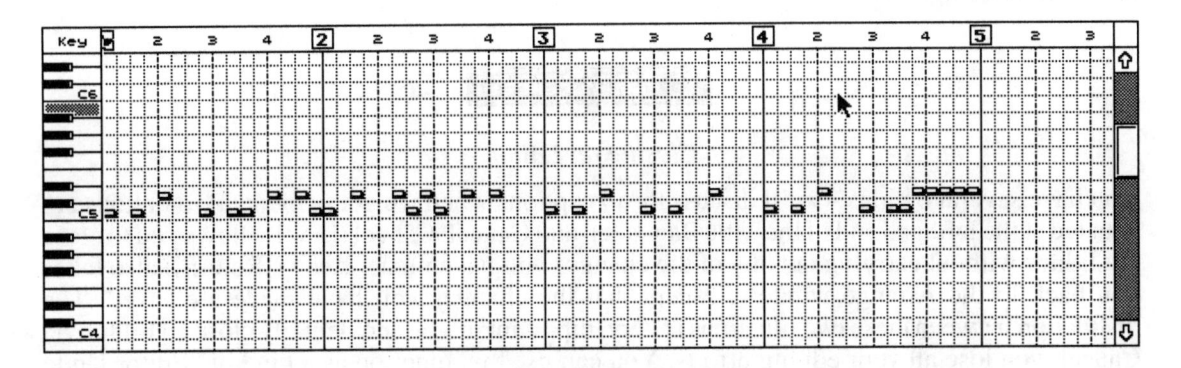

The Key Editor display

- The Key Editor display has a graphic keyboard on the left, and most of it is covered by a grid pattern. This is the area where there are substantial differences between the Editors.

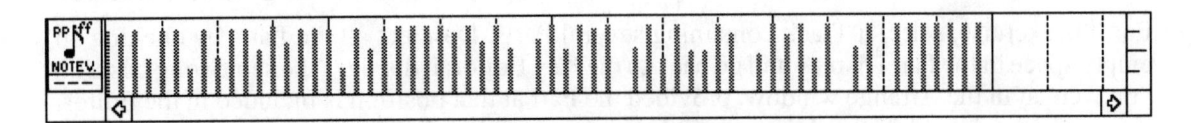

The Controller Display

- The Controller Display features either small vertical beams or grey areas, depending on the setting. The Drum Editor also has this display.

You can remove the Info Line and Controller Display from the window, or if you cannot see them, you have to activate them so they can be seen. The "Info" and "Ctrl" buttons in the Functions Bar are used for this purpose ([Control][I] and [Control][C]). Click both of them and see what happens. By removing these two features, the dimensions of the grid display increase correspondingly. Activate both features for our purposes.

MIDI notes are displayed in the Key Editor in a manner resembling a player piano's perforated roll. Each of the little rectangular beams represents a note.

The pitches of the beam notes are shown on the keyboard at the left edge of the screen. The length and position of the notes can be taken from the Position Bar, which you probably recognize from the Arrange window. Generally, the Arrange window and the Editors covered in this section share several common features.

The Key Editor

Start Cubase. The Song Position Triangle in the Position Bar begins to move in the same manner as in the Arrange window. When it reaches a beam note, it plays it. Once the Song Position Triangle reaches the right edge, the Position Bar is scrolled forward to show you the next notes in the Part. If you used the locators to define a Cycle whose length is the same as the Part, the Editor display jumps back to the beginning of the Part and repeats it. If there's no Cycle, Cubase runs through the Arrangement as usual, i.e. the Editor window is scrolled to the end of the Part and stays there. The Song Position Triangle disappears and starts its journey through the following Parts in the Track, though you cannot see this.

As with the Arrange window, you can tell Cubase to scroll the Position Bar according to the song position: choose Follow Song from the Options menu ([F]). As usual, you can use the scroll bar along the bottom edge of the window to access elsewhere in the Part.

Even if you have only a single Part in the Editor, the Parts of other Tracks which run parallel to this one are played unless you previously muted these Tracks. Once in the Editor, you can prevent other Parts from playing by clicking the Ed Solo button in the Transport Bar so that only those Parts in the Editor are played.

It's also possible to have several Parts in the Editor. For this purpose let's close the Editor window for the time being.

Closing an Editor

You have several options - we'll discuss the exceptions when we get to them. Two buttons are situated at the lefthand end of the Title Bar, Keep and Cancel. Cancel ([Esc]) allows you to close the Editor without carrying out any of the changes you have made. Keep ([Return]) also takes you back to the Arrange window, except that the changes you have made are saved. The distinction between these two functions is very important: if you accidentally close an Editor via Cancel, you lose all your editing efforts. You can use this function as a kind of "Editor Undo function". As we haven't made any changes, you can exit anyway you want.

For our next exercise, we'll enter several Parts in the Editor. There are differences between the Editors regarding this operation, and we'll discuss them when we get to them. The following applies to the Key Editor: all selected Parts, regardless of which Track they happen to be in, are entered. If no Parts are selected, then all the Parts of the currently selected Track are entered.

For this exercise, select a Track containing several Parts. Deselect all the Parts by clicking an empty space in the Part Display and go back to the Key Editor: it displays the same song position you were at in the Arrange window, provided the Part at that position is included in the Editor: if you were at bar 14 in the Arrange window, you are still at bar 14 in the Key Editor; if you selected a single Part ending at bar 5, you will find yourself at the end of that Part in the Editor.

You can use the rewind and fast forward functions or use the horizontal scroll bar to scroll through the song. You can also type in the position in the Song Position box, or click the desired position in the Position Bar to move through your song.

Even if you have entered several Parts in the Editor, only one of them is active at a time. Special operations such as recording, step input and changes via MIDI are *always* executed in the active Part.

In our example, the first Part is active. According to the Arrangement we created in the first chapter, this first Part covers positions 1.1.0 to 5.1.0. This active Part range is displayed in the Key Edit window's Title Bar, along with the Editor and Track names.

The active Part's range

The Layout of the Key Edit Window

This display, too, is identical in every Editor. Go from the first Part to the next, i.e. to position 5.1.0: the contents of the Title Bar change, and the note beams before position 5.1.0 change from having solid outlines to dotted ones.

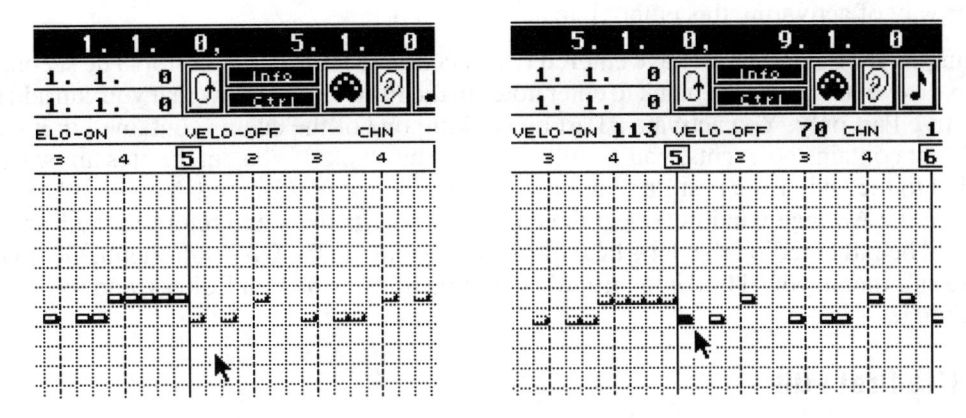

Activating Parts

Click one of the dotted beams: the display changes. Now the events prior to position 5.1.0 are dotted, and those *following* position 5.1.0 are solid. You have just activated the second Part of your Track. The Part's start and end positions are entered in the Title Bar. If you selected parallel Parts that play at the same time in the Arrange window, these Parts are displayed in the Editor window at the same time, although just one Part can be active at a time: this means you will see solid and dotted beams in the same Part of the display at the same time. Clicking a beam selects its Part, but you run into problems where the parallel Parts contain notes of the same pitch at the same positions, as they will lie one on top of the other; here, it's impossible to select some notes.

The Goto sub-menu in the Functions Bar is designed to solve this problem. Click and hold Goto with the mouse pointer. A menu appears featuring a number of selections, some of which we will now get to know.

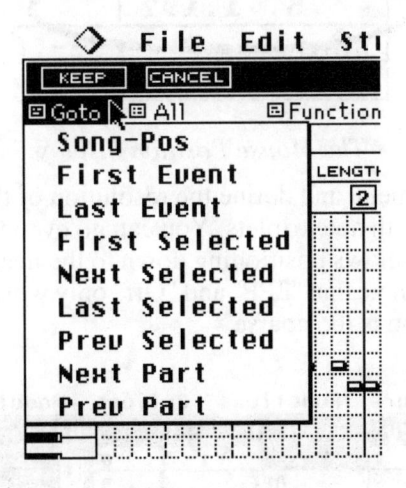

The Goto sub-menu

Choosing Song Position in the sub-menu moves the window display to the Song Position Triangle's position. First Event and Last Event move the window to the first or final events in the active Part. Next Part and Previous Part move the window to the following or preceding Part; these two functions only make sense if you have transferred several Parts into the Editor. All the commands in the Goto sub-menu are used to move the window display: no data is edited, nor are any Parts selected.

The only exception is that if one of the Parts which has been selected with the command is empty, it is automatically activated.

The Key Editor

8.3.1 An important example

This Next Part or Previous Part operation is important if you later want to enter notes with the mouse, or step by step. If you entered an empty Part along with Parts containing notes, you have no other way of activating this empty Part.

For example, let's assume you have entered two successive Parts in the Editor. The second Part contains no events - you left it blank to enter notes in the Editor. You know that you can add notes to an active Part only. You activate a Part by clicking one of the events contained in it. As the second Part contains no events, you would appear to be stuck. If you enter notes anyway, they are added to the end of the first Part, and not in the new one you wanted. You could of course go back to the Arrange window, select the empty Part on its own, and return to the Editor, but this would be rather tedious, so let's take the easy way out via the Goto sub-menu. Get to know the Goto sub-menu; you'll find it in virtually the same form in the four Editors, and its operation never changes.

8.3.2 The first edit

You now know how to move about in the Key Editor, which we'll use as the basis for the following exercises. We will run through two operations in the following sections:
- changing existing notes in various ways,
- creating completely new events.

8.3.3 Changes

If you move the mouse pointer across the grid of the Key Editor, Cubase keeps you updated with two displays. Below the Goto sub-menu in the Functions Bar, you can see the Mouse Position display. You will recognize it from the Arrange window.

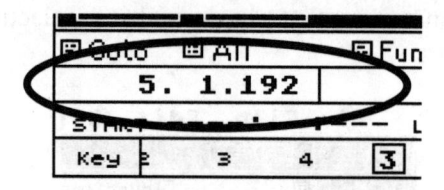

The Mouse Position display

Click and hold the Snap sub-menu and define the resolution of the mouse pointer movements, from a dotted whole note to 64th note triplets. You can go even finer than this: "2PP" to "7PP" equals 2 to 7 ticks, and "Off" allows positioning down to the nearest tick, the smallest possible unit of time in Cubase. Please note that "2PP" and "Off" only work when you zoom the window, otherwise the screen resolution is too coarse.

Snap resolution values

140

The Layout of the Key Edit Window

You can change note values in all windows including the Arrange and Editor windows, using your computer keyboard, via the alphanumeric, not the numeric, keypad:

1 - whole note
2 - half note
3 - quarter note
4 - eighth note
5 - sixteenth note
6 - thirty-second note
7 - sixty-fourth note

The "T" stands for triplets, the dot for dotted notes.

Apart from the time components (note length and position), each note has its own pitch. These are displayed in the keyboard at the left edge of the window.

The pitch display (in this case, B4)

Move the mouse pointer up and down. The keyboard displays the pitch corresponding to the pointer's position. Click one of the keys, and the note is sent via MIDI to your instrument (ensure the Track's MIDI channel is set correctly).

The keyboard display does not show the entire range possible. Don't worry if an event is not visible on the keyboard: the note is probably out of the display range. Move the keyboard display by scrolling the righthand vertical scroll bar or arrows.

You can zoom the display resolution in the same way as the time axis: click as usual the vertical scroll bar or arrows with the right mouse button to reduce or increase the display size. You have to decide what size is best for you in terms of clarity and range of information.

Now, click the first event in the Key Edit window. It is highlighted, i.e. selected. You can tell Cubase to play all the notes you click via MIDI by activating the "Ear" icon with a mouse click.

Auditioning notes by activating the Ear symbol

The Info Line displays additional information about the selected note: its starting point, length in ticks, pitch, velocity, release value and the MIDI channel on which the note was first recorded, i.e. the channel your synthesizer transmitted on. Cubase records this information, though the

141

The Key Editor

channel is normally ignored since it is overridden by the Track's channel setting. The original MIDI channel is only used if you set the Track's MIDI channel to "Any".

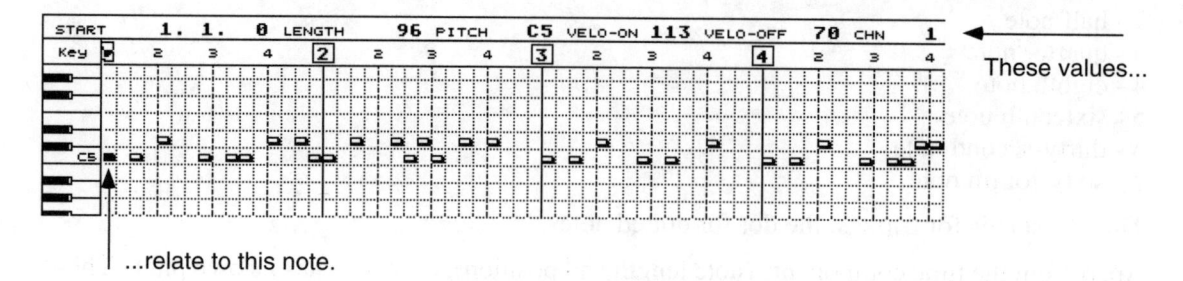

These values...

...relate to this note.

The Info Line

You can change all the values in the Info Line using, as usual, the right and left mouse buttons, or a double-click followed by direct, typed entry.

Change the selected note's pitch. You can see that the graphic display reacts immediately. The note display moves upwards in the grid. Now change the starting point and the length, and watch the graphic display adjust to the changes.

8.3.4 The graphic solution

In addition to this method of numerically accessing a note, you can also treat notes as you would Parts. You can move, copy, etc. them with the mouse. Some of the options described below are available in other Editors as well, and you'll be asked to refer to the following explanations when you go through the other chapters.

Select a Snap value of "8" and move the mouse pointer to the first event in your Part. Click and hold it with the mouse button. The note is selected, and the mouse pointer becomes a hand symbol. You can now drag the note around while holding the mouse button down.

Pitch changes are registered on the keyboard to the left and in the box in the Functions Bar beside the mouse position display which shows by how many notes up or down you are transposing.

The mouse position display registers how far you are moving in time. In our example, you can only move the note in eighths. If you require a different time value, set the Snap resolution accordingly. Once you reach the desired position, release the mouse button to fix the note.

This allows you to "manually" quantize a note. Let's assume you played a note at position 1.4.377, which means that it's situated 7 ticks before the second bar's downbeat. Select a Snap value of "8" or "16" and drag the note to the next Snap position, i.e. the "1" of the next bar.

On the whole, handling events in this Editor is very similar to handling Parts in the Arrange window. There you learned how to copy and delete Parts: before you drag the note, press and hold [Alternate], then drag it. Delete the note with [Backspace] or [Delete].

You can execute all the above operations with as many notes as you want simultaneously so long as you select the notes first. Selecting is the same as for Parts in the Arrange window:
- If you hold [Shift] down, notes are selected one after another as you click them;
- The rubber band selects all the notes it touches or surrounds. Activate the rubber band by clicking an empty space in the grid and dragging the mouse while holding the mouse button down;
- The Select All function in the Edit menu selects all the notes in the active Part;
- Click an empty space in the grid to de-select all selected notes;
- Use the right/left Atari cursor keys to jump from one note to another. If you hold [Shift] down at the same time, the notes are selected or de-selected. If you select more than one note, the Info Line displays no information as it can handle only one note at a time.

The remaining functions in the Goto sub-menu are used to access specific events:

- First Selected moves the display window to the first event that is selected;
- Next Selected to the next selected event;
- Last Selected to the last-selected event;
- Previous Selected to the previously selected event.

These functions do not modify the data, but simply scroll the display to another position. They are often the source of misunderstandings. If all the events in the current window view are selected, Cubase does not respond to any of the above commands as it cannot scroll to a position it is already at.

These functions are only really suitable for events that are further apart. The following two examples illustrate the best use for Goto functions:
- If you're working on a piano Track, some notes are probably pitched too far apart for them to be displayed at the same time. Select a relatively high note (transpose one if you cannot find one in the current Part). Using the vertical scroll bar, move the display down to the lower register and select a low note, pressing and holding [Shift] at the same time, otherwise the first note will be deselected. Choose First Selected from the Goto sub-menu, and the high note is returned to the display. Choose Next Selected, and the low note is returned to the display. In other words, these functions replace the scroll bar.
- The second example is an even more practical application. An Editor is designed for locating and correcting mistakes, amongst other things. As it's impossible to say where you might have made a mistake, let's fabricate an error or two. Go to different positions and move some notes to the wrong pitches and positions. Go back to the beginning, activate Ed Solo and start playback. Watch the events in the Edit window. When incorrect notes appear and are played, click them, holding [Shift] down as you do so. It may be an advantage to slow the playback down so you have time to react to what you hear. Stop Cubase after the Parts have been played to the end. You've now marked the mistakes: the Goto functions allow you to move from one wrong note to the next and correct them.

Did you have trouble recognizing the incorrect notes in the Edit window even though you could hear them clearly? No problem - simply mark any event close to the position of the incorrect note. You then use the Goto functions to localize the general area in which a mistake occurred, restart Cubase, and have a closer look.

All the methods used to select one or more events are applicable in the other Editors as well. If you can read music, searching for mistakes might be easier for you in the Score Editor which we'll come to later.

8.3.5 The Edit Loop

An Arrange Cycle created with the locators will also be played when you're in the Editors. There is a further "edit loop" which acts as a "loop within a Cycle". It is useful if you want to hear a certain passage several times to discover mistakes. Cubase again offers several ways of defining the loop's length:
- Use the left and right mouse buttons to directly set the values in the loop boundary boxes on the Functions Bar. You can also call these up by double-clicking ([Alternate][L] and [R]) and typing in the values.
- Drag directly on the Position Bar in any direction. The speckled beam defines the loop's length and position.

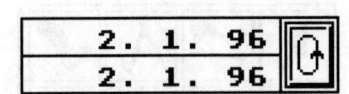

The Edit Loop button with the boundary boxes

The Key Editor

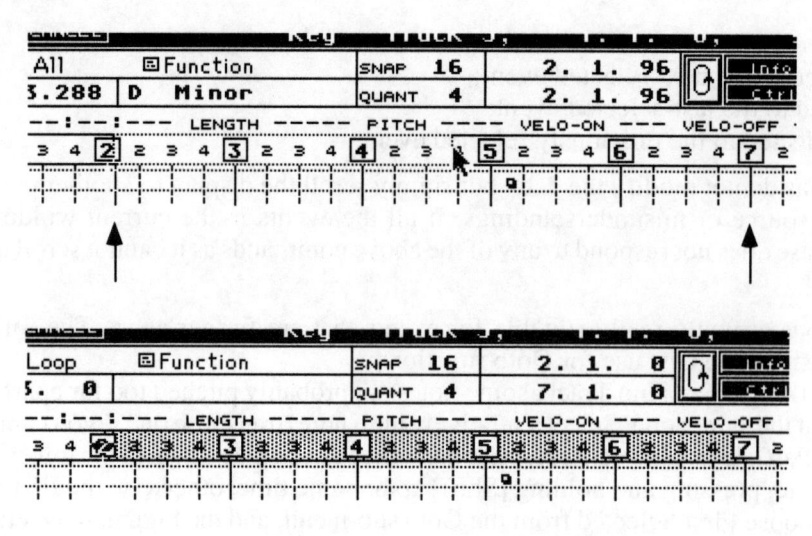

Dragging to define the edit loop

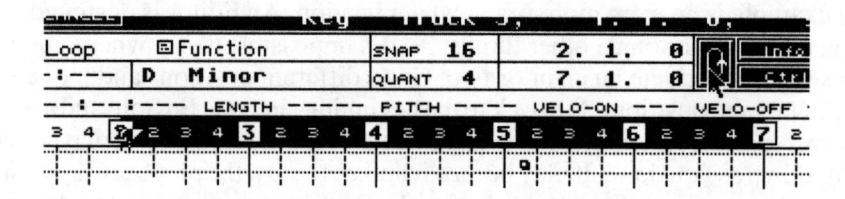

The edit loop is active

Click the Loop button to activate the edit loop ([Alternate][O]). An active edit loop is shown in black on the Position Bar, and speckled when it is inactive. Define an edit loop in the Key Editor and start playback.

An edit loop can be re-defined as much as you please by simply dragging the mouse across the Position Bar again. The new edit loop replaces the old one. To delete an edit loop, simply click any position outside the loop within the Position Bar.

If you haven't activated a Cycle with the locators in the Arrange window, everything should work as described.

If a Cycle is active, then this edit loop cannot exceed the Arrange Cycle's length. The Arrange Cycle jumps back to its start once it reaches the right locator, regardless of where the edit loop happens to be.

A number of editing options are available for editing events within edit loops. We'll have a look at these in a moment.

8.3.6 The Toolbox

Another similarity between the Arrange window and the Key Editor is the familiar Toolbox. Click the grid with the right mouse button, and it will appear.

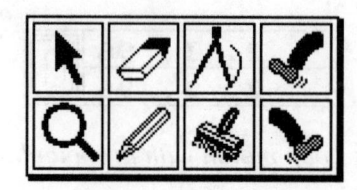

The Editor Toolbox

You know how to select a tool. You probably recognize some of them.

The Layout of the Key Edit Window

The Eraser deletes notes with a mouse click

The Magnifying Glass is used to audition notes by clicking and holding them

Kicking notes earlier

Kicking notes later

The two Kicker tools are used to move notes. Select the upper one and click a note. It is "kicked" earlier by the number of ticks or the note value in the Snap box. If you set it to eighths, the note is kicked earlier in eighths steps with each click. The same happens with the other values. The lower Kicker tool performs the same function in the opposite direction, by kicking the notes later by an amount equal to the Snap value.

The Pencil tool

The Pencil tool allows you to create notes (we'll get to this in a moment) and change their lengths. Click and hold any ending of a note with the Pencil. The note is surrounded by a dotted box. Use the Pencil to change its length: the Snap function helps by quantizing the length. Release the mouse button when you have reached the desired position.

At times, you may find it difficult to locate the correct position of a note. You may accidentally create a new event instead of modifying an existing one. Use the zoom function to enlarge the note beams, or press and hold [Alternate] before the first click to prevent new events from being created.

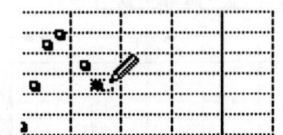

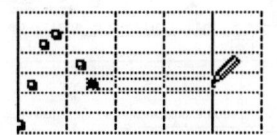

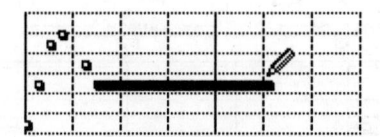

Modifying the note length by dragging the Pencil tool to the right of the selected beam

To shorten a note's length, simply click the intended end position with the Pencil, which avoids having to drag the beam to the left to shorten it.

We'll save the remaining two tools, the compass and Paint Brush, for later. Keep in mind that it's always only the latest operation that can be recalled with the Undo function.

The Key Editor

8.3.7 Realtime correction

You can also edit existing notes via MIDI in realtime. Activate the MIDI In icon in the Functions Bar with a mouse click and choose which of the event's parameters you want to adjust: pitch, normal note-on velocity or release velocity. Each parameter is represented by an icon. You can select all of them or any combination thereof. Active functions are highlighted.

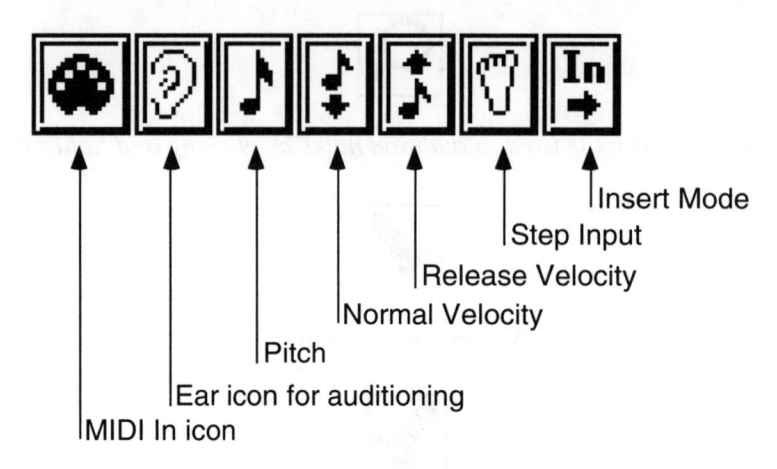

The Functions Bar icons

Let's assume we want to change the normal velocity values of the notes. Activate the velocity icon and select the first note in your Part. Play a note on your keyboard. The Key Editor registers only this note's velocity and assigns it to the note you have selected. It then moves to the next note. Change the velocity values of every note as you go in this way. If you want to change the values for a specific note, click it first or select it with the Atari keyboard's cursor keys. The same applies to pitch changes: just select the pitch icon.

8.3.8 Creating notes

Until now we have merely modified existing notes. However, Cubase enables you to generate new notes and other MIDI events. We'll use some exercises to work our way through the process. Press [Esc] to exit the Key Editor. All the edits we've done till now are deleted, and we're left with the original Part. Create an empty Part on any empty Track. Set the Track's MIDI channel to your piano sound and return to the Key Editor. The grid is empty, and you are going to fill it with new notes.

Select a Snap value of "4" and enter the same value in the Quantize box. Select the Pencil from the Toolbox and click position 1.1.0 at the C3 pitch. If the Ear icon is on, you can hear the corresponding note via MIDI.

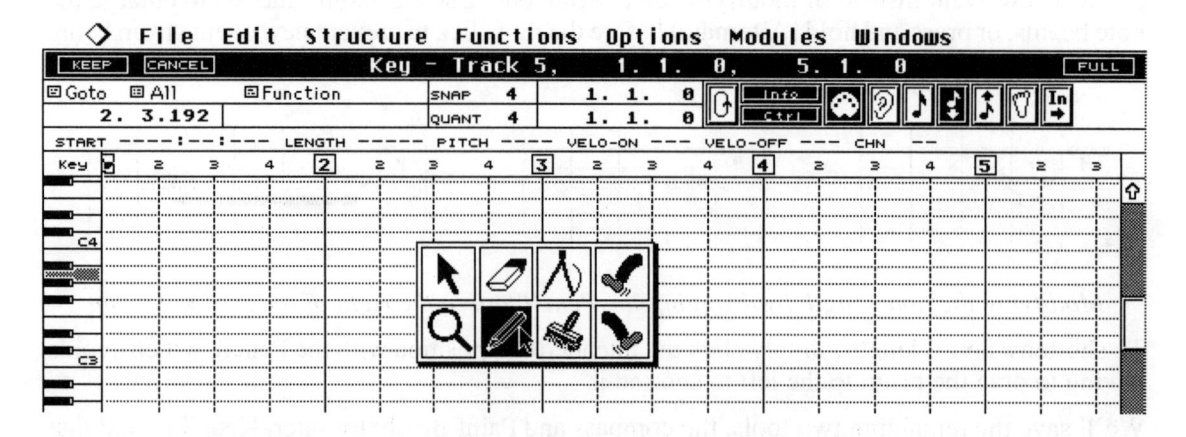

Select the Pencil from the Toolbox (Quantize and Snap at "4")...

The Layout of the Key Edit Window

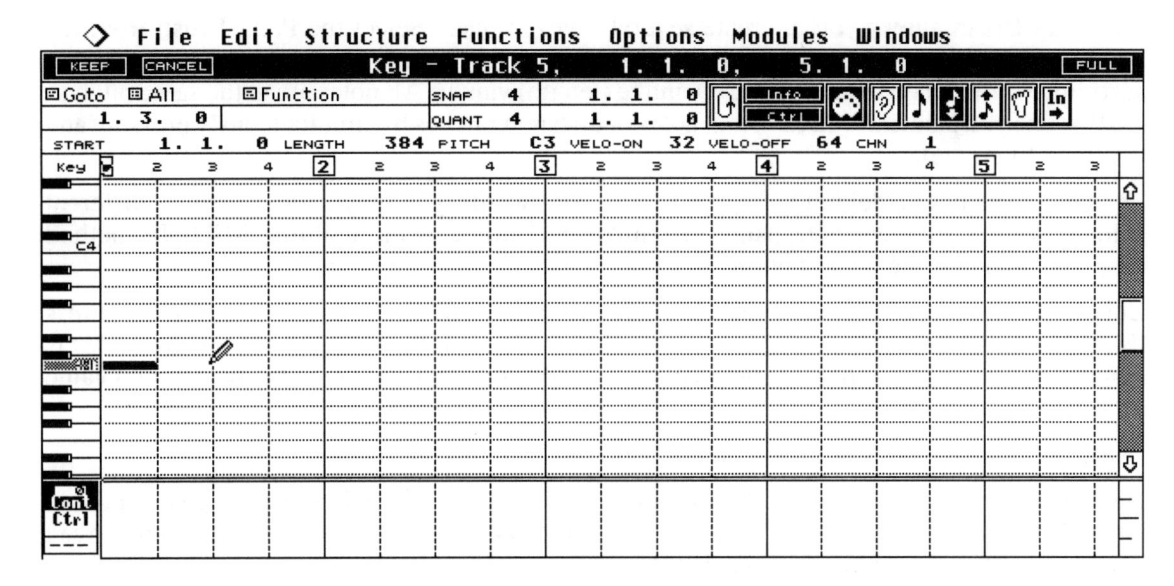

...insert a note at 1.1.0...

...and follow it with three more

If you've been following the diagrams, you have just entered four quarter notes at 1.1.0, 1.2.0, 1.3.0 and 1.4.0. You can't miss, as the Snap resolution ensures that you only hit quarter note intervals, and the Quantize resolution dictates that you can create quarter notes only. The new notes can be edited in the same way as you would any other notes. You can even add notes to Parts already containing notes.

By changing the Snap and Quantize resolutions you can enter notes of any length and at any position in the Key Editor's grid. The Quantize setting defines the length of the note. If, however, you hold the mouse button down while positioning a note, you can modify the note's length by dragging the mouse to the left or right. In other words, the mouse movement overrides the Quantize factor. Of course, you can also draw notes parallel to one another to create chords.

The Paint Brush tool

The Key Editor

The Paint Brush allows you to create several notes at once. Select the Paint Brush from the Toolbox, press the mouse button, and drag this tool through the grid. Notes are entered in the grid according to the Snap (distance) and Quantize (length) values. All notes are at the same pitch as the first one you painted. You can paint notes of different pitches by simultaneously pressing and holding [Alternate].

The new notes have a default velocity of "32". Afterwards, you may choose to enter different velocity values for each note using the Info Line, although the realtime MIDI In method described above is the better option.

Cubase offers a way of entering three other velocity values while you are painting the notes. Press [Shift][Control] to assign a velocity value of "110", [Control] for "96", [Shift] for "64"; "32" is assigned automatically when no computer keys are pressed. Release velocity always has a value of "64".

There are other methods of manipulation which we will discuss later.

New notes are usually entered at the current mouse pointer position in the grid. If you activate the In(sert) icon in the Functions Bar, the new note is inserted and the following events are moved later by an amount equal to the Snap value.

8.3.9 Step input

Step input is possible via MIDI. Delete all the events you've entered so far and activate the Foot icon. This makes the Step Position box appear in the horizontal scroll bar, which shows you where note input will occur. Normally, this position is identical to the current song position in the Transport Bar. However, during step input, it moves independently: New notes are always entered at its current position.

You can change the Step Position via mouse click, or a double-click followed by typing with the keyboard. As soon as you change the position in the Transport Bar's Song Position box, these two displays are again identical.

Set the song position to the beginning of your Part so that we can get started. We want to enter a simple four-bar passage.

Enter Snap and Quantize values of "8". Play the chords Am, G, F and G eight times each. Don't play too quickly so that Cubase can assimilate the data. Every time you release the last key, Cubase advances to the next Snap position.

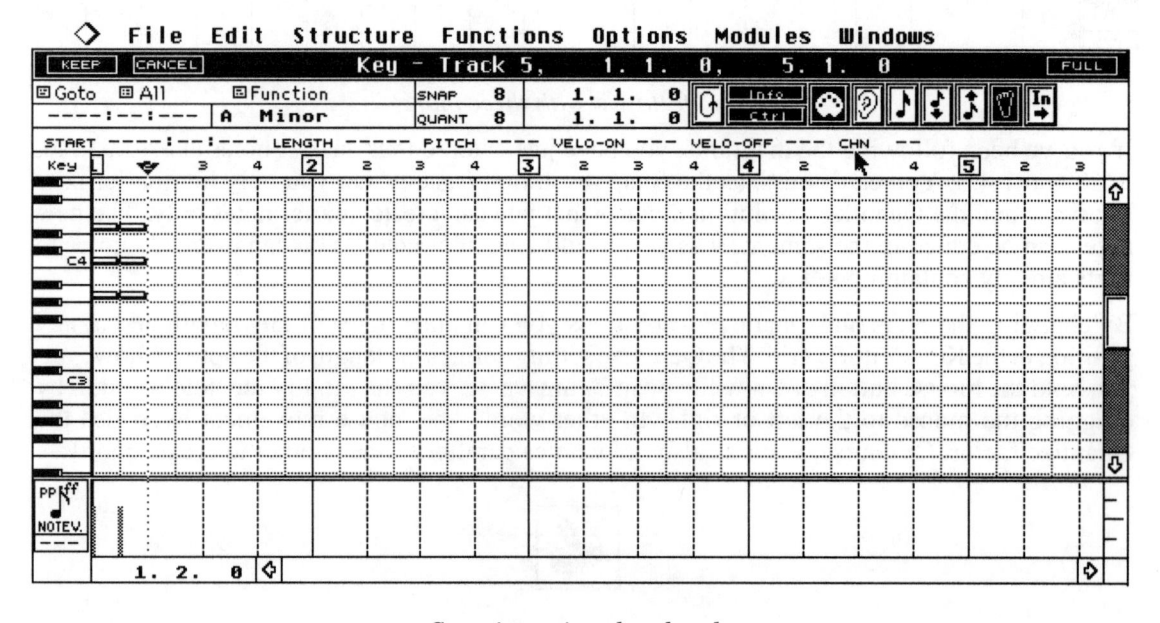

Start inputting the chords

The Layout of the Key Edit Window

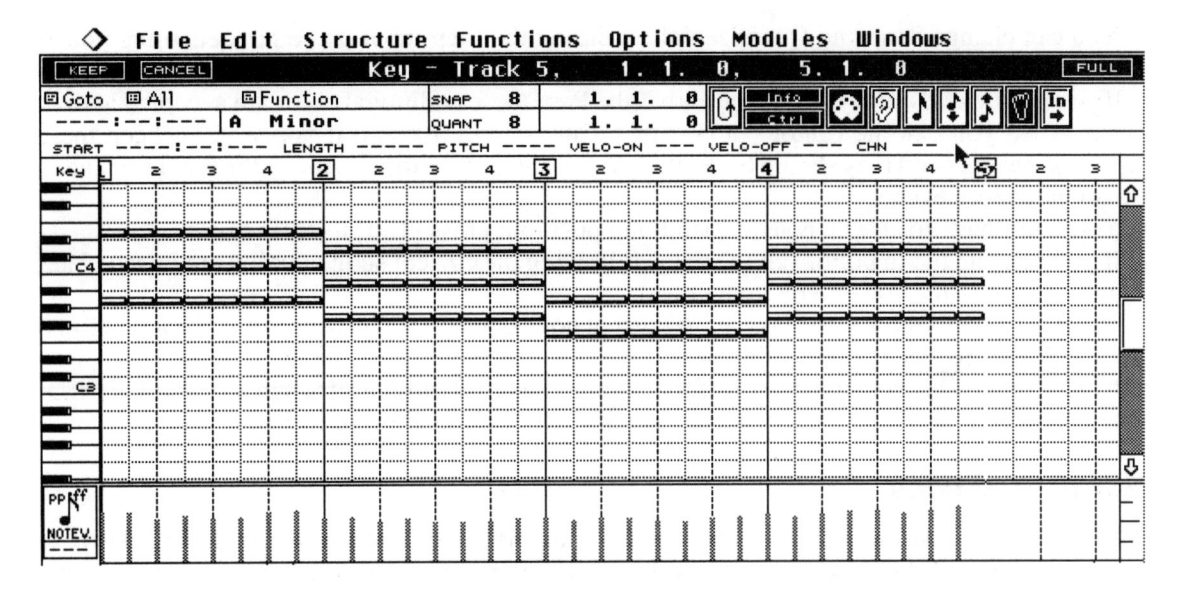

The result of your work

You entered the chords during the first run through. Listen to the result. Deactivate the Foot icon so the Song Position Triangle can be followed. Cubase has inputted the chords over four bars. Each chord is an eighth note long, and there's a chord at every eighth note interval. The velocity values will be read and inputted with the notes. Go back to the first bar's downbeat: the quickest way is to press the Stop button. Make absolutely sure the Step Position box returns to position 1.1.0. If it doesn't, press [Clr/Home]. Let's now add a bass line: set Snap and Quantize to "4" and play four bass notes for each chord. Cubase inserts the notes in the grid, but this time as quarter notes at intervals of a beat.

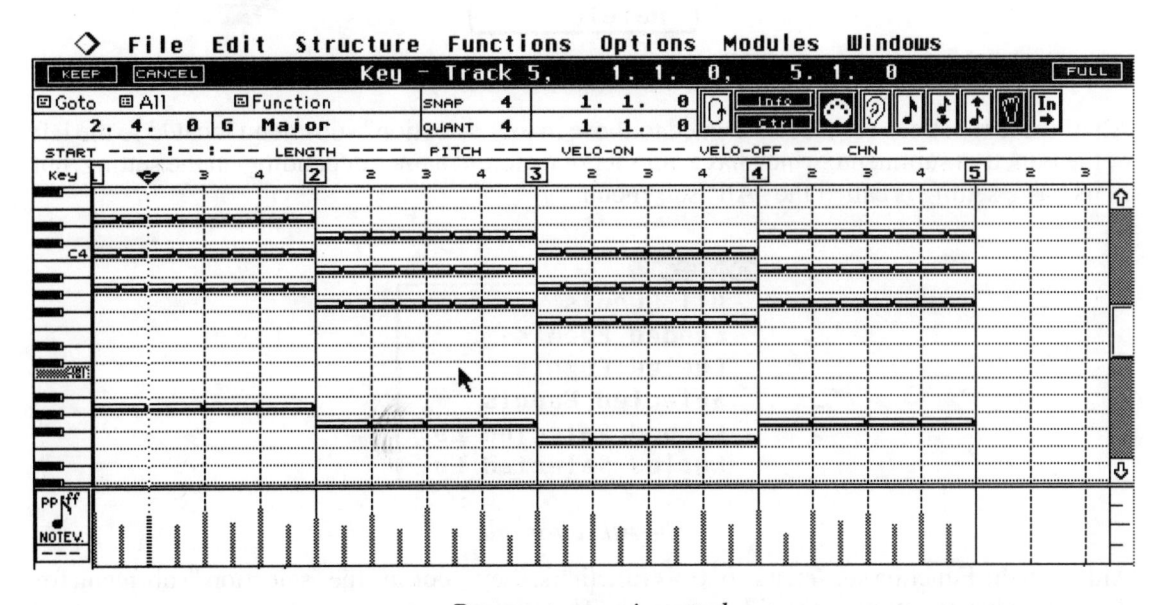

Bass notes are inputted

Step programming is capable of a great deal more than this simple example can show. Here are a few tips and suggestions:
- Cubase always places new notes at the current song position.
- You can combine step input with normal realtime recording. Exit the Editor via [Return] and record the notes in realtime, using the overdub technique described in the Arrange chapter.
- Snap and Quantize values can be combined any way you like. If you want to play staccato, use small Quantize values combined with wide Snap values (Quantize: thirty-seconds, Snap: eighths, so thirty-second notes are placed every eighth interval).

The Key Editor

- You can change Snap and Quantize values during the Step Input procedure, enabling you to devise complex rhythmic structures.
- If you accidentally play beyond the end of the Part, these additional notes are accepted at first. Then when you exit the Editor via [Return], Cubase will ask you if you want to keep these appended events or if they should be deleted. If you tell Cubase to keep them, the Part is extended to include these events.
- You don't have to enter a note at each Snap position: press [Tab] to enter a rest.
- If you activate the In button, all the notes following the current song position are pushed later by a step each time you enter a note or rest.
- The [Insert] key enters a new note at the current note's position. The new note's pitch is defined by the Fill entry (see paragraph below).
- Cubase places all new notes on MIDI channel 1. This is only used when the Track's MIDI channel setting is "Any". Otherwise the Track's MIDI channel has priority.

8.3.10 Functions

Cubase features two other Editor sub-menus in addition to the Goto sub-menu, designed to ease editing. Click and hold Function in the Functions Bar. The Function pop-up menu appears containing a number of choices. Don't confuse this menu with the large Functions menu in the Menu Bar across the top of your screen.

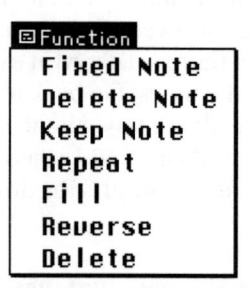

```
Function
  Fixed Note
  Delete Note
  Keep Note
  Repeat
  Fill
  Reverse
  Delete
```

The Function sub-menu

All of these functions are closely related to those in the "selection" sub-menu located to the left of the Function sub-menu, which has a number of different names depending on the setting, but in its basic setting is called the "All" sub-menu.

```
All
  All Events
  Looped Events
  Cycled Events
  Selected Events
  Looped Selected Ev.
  Cycled Selected Ev.
```

The All sub-menu

Although the Function sub-menu controls functions, they "look at" the "selection" sub-menu for deciding what events they should operate on. The choices are:
- All Events: all the events of the Part(s) in the Editor.
- Looped Events: all the events inside an edit loop.
- Cycled Events: all the events inside an Arrange Cycle, even if the Cycle is not currently on.
- Selected Events: all the selected events.
- Looped Selected Events: all the selected events inside an edit loop.
- Cycled Selected Events: all the selected events inside a Cycle.

Once you've activated an item, its name is adopted as the sub-menu heading. This sub-menu's settings can affect the Quantize function: we'll get back to this in the appropriate chapter.

The Layout of the Key Edit Window

Now that you know what you can edit, you need to find out how this is done. Go back to the Function sub-menu. The first three selection options work for a *single* selected note only. By now, you should know enough to be able to try these out without a practical example from the book!

- Fixed Note forces notes to adopt the pitch of the selected one: the affected notes are defined in the "selection" sub-menu (All, Looped, Cycled, etc.).
- Delete Note deletes notes of the same pitch as the selected note.
- Keep Note keeps notes of the same pitch as the selected note and deletes all the rest.
- Repeat repeats a section of the Part until the end of the Part. Cubase generates the new events that are required. You define the "repeat Cycle" by setting the loop or the Cycle. If you choose Repeat, the events in the loop or Cycle are copied over and over up to the end of the Part. The "selection" sub-menu determines what happens here:
- Looped Events and Cycled Events replace the original events located there;
- Looped Selected Events and Cycled Selected Events merge new and existing events.
- Fill fills the defined area with notes whose pitch is determined by the center pitch of the graphic keyboard as it is currently displayed at the window's left border. Their positions and lengths are determined by the Snap and Quantize settings. This function can only be executed when the "selection" sub-menu heading is set to All, Looped Events or Cycled Events.
- Reverse reverses the event order. They are played back to front.
- Delete deletes all events in the defined area.

8.3.11 The Clipboard

The Clipboard is available in the Editors as well. Its use is identical to the Arrange window. Select the events, cut them or copy them, and paste them at the current song position. Remember you have just one Clipboard available. As soon as you Copy or Cut events to the Clipboard, the previous data in it is lost.

8.3.12 The Controller Display

Until now we have been editing notes. Now we'll get to work with the other non-note MIDI events which we discussed in the chapter on MIDI. The Controller Display enables you to quickly and easily manipulate non-note MIDI events. You know how to switch it on and off: [Alternate][C]. You can enlarge it by clicking and holding the dividing line between the Controller Display and the Key Edit grid: the mouse pointer turns into a hand. Keep the mouse button depressed and drag the dividing line down. All this operation does is give you a clearer view of the display; the whole range of values is available, regardless of the display size.

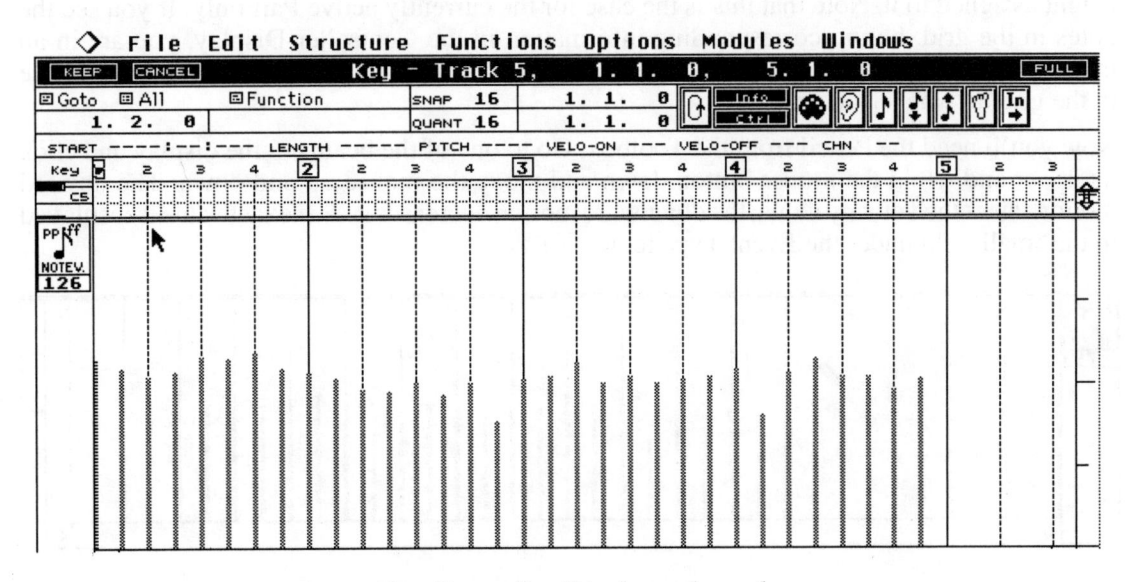

The Controller Display enlarged

The Key Editor

There's a little icon box in the upper left corner of the window. This box serves two purposes. It displays the currently selected event type, and the vertical mouse position, which denotes this event's amount value. Move the mouse up and down in the Controller Display and watch it change the value. The actual value range depends on the event type you select.

Note: Steinberg have called this function the "Controller Display". The Controller Display displays all kinds of non-note MIDI data (Pitch Bend, Poly Key Pressure aftertouch, Channel Pressure aftertouch, Program Changes, Control Changes and so on, plus data that has no status of its own, such as velocity). You might have expected that something called a "Controller Display" would display MIDI Control Change events only - this is not the case; we have had to use the same term as the one in the official Cubase manual and the program.

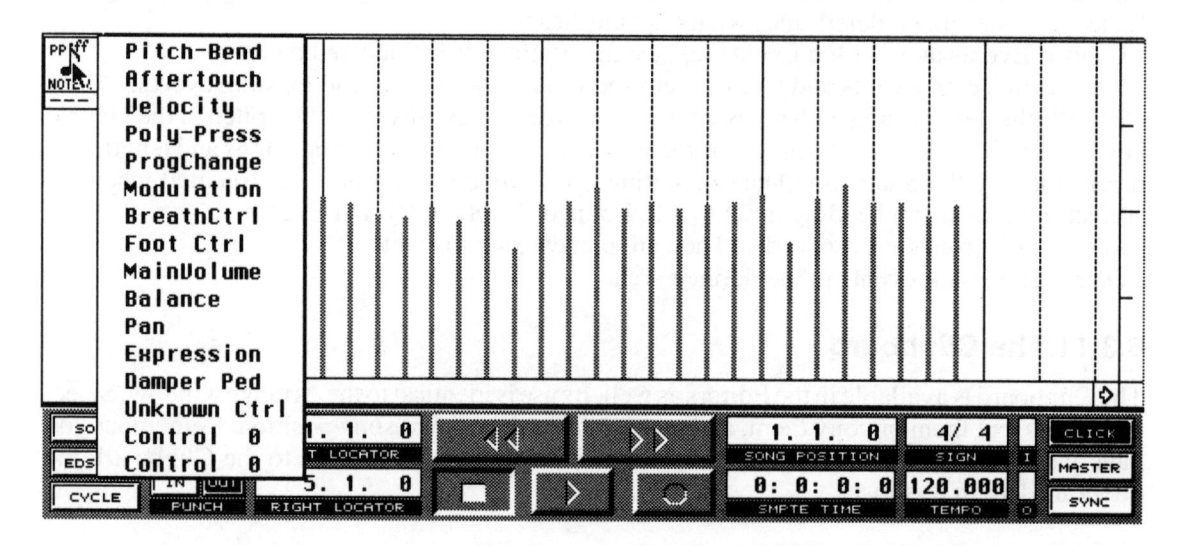

The Event Type box's pop-up menu

In the following section, we'll run through a few standard operations to demonstrate Controller Display functions.

8.3.13 Modifying velocity data

Click and hold the small event type icon. A selection of the most common options appears in a pop-up menu. Choose Velocity from this list. Each note in the grid now has a beam of varying height assigned to it. Note that this is the case for the currently active Part only. If you see the notes in the grid, but no corresponding information in the Controller Display, you are in an inactive Part. Controller Display data can be manipulated in an active Part *only*. Clicking a note in the grid activates its Part.

Now you'll need the Pencil from the Toolbox. Go to one of the beams in the display and click its upper end. Hold the mouse button down and move the mouse up and down. The upward motion raises the velocity value, the downward motion decreases it. The exact value is displayed in the small field under the Event Type icon.

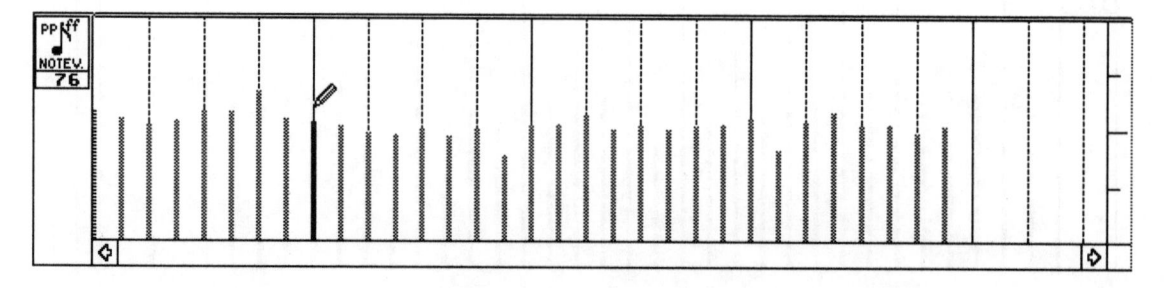

Editing a note's velocity

The Layout of the Key Edit Window

You can also click any point in the beam with the Pencil to change the value immediately.

If several notes are at the same position, you will only be able to see one beam. When you modify the beam, *all* the notes at the same time position are affected. To edit individual beams in this situation, use the Info Line as we've done in the past.

You do not have to click each and every note you want to modify. Press and hold the mouse button, then drag the Pencil across the beams. All the beams will move according to the mouse movement. The Toolbox contains a compass tool for special applications. Select it and the mouse cursor appears as a crosshair.

The Compass tool

Find a group of about five to ten neighbouring velocity beams. Click a value somewhere between 0 and 20 in front of the first beam and drag the mouse to the right. As long as you keep the mouse button depressed you can draw a line. Ensure the line extends from the first to the last beam. Select a value between 120 and 127 for the last beam and release the mouse button. All the velocity values of the group are scaled linearly according to the line you have drawn. The following diagrams depict how this should look:

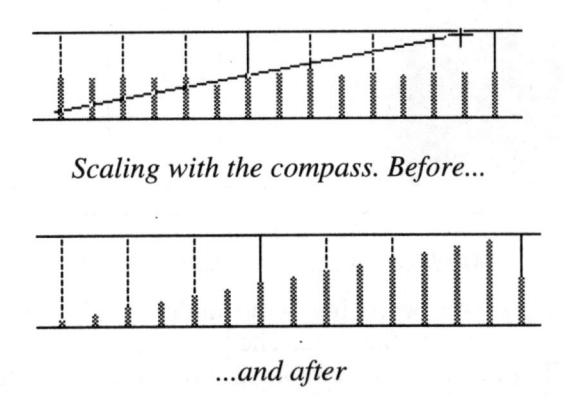

Scaling with the compass. Before...

...and after

The compass can be used to create fade outs and other similar effects. You can include as many events as you please. Draw the line as long as you like: the Controller Display is scrolled further when you reach the left or right boundaries of the window with the dragged mouse pointer. The line's angle is up to you: you can scale upwards, downwards or horizontally.

8.3.14 Handling data in the Controller Display

Cubase allows you to record non-note data and edit it, as well as manually create new data. Let's start with the former. You need a master synth capable of generating the necessary non-note data. Most synthesizers incorporate performance controllers, i.e. one, two or three wheels or levers; maybe a joystick; various foot pedals and foot switches. For this exercise, we'll choose the wheel/lever/joystick used to generate vibrato or tremolo effects. You have read the MIDI chapter and know that vibrato is MIDI Control Change #1. Do not use the pitch bender for this exercise, even if your synthesizer allows you to route it so it transmits Control Change 1 events.

Create a new Part along these lines: record a four bar chord and at the same time move the modulation performance controller (wheel, etc.) to its maximum position, hold it there for a bar, then return it to the zero position before the end of the four bars. Later, of course, you can use the synthesizer's performance controllers to produce all kinds of data which can then be edited to your heart's content, but for now, please stick to the above example so you can follow the exercise in the book.

Select Modulation from the Event Type pop-up menu. Cubase displays the most common non-

The Key Editor

note events by name, not by their MIDI numbers. Don't worry if you can't find all the MIDI event types listed in the MIDI chapter: we'll discuss those in due course. Cubase offers a separate display for every conceivable event type, but only one can be displayed at a time.

The velocity beams are no longer to be seen, but nevertheless they still exist. Instead, a grey area resembling the one in the diagram below appears. If you don't see it, scroll back (using the horizontal scroll bar) to the beginning of the new Part. Enlarge the Controller Display as described at the start of this chapter to get a better view. Put the mouse pointer on the line between the display and the grid and hold the mouse button down; the pointer appears as a hand. You can now drag this double line up and enlarge the Controller Display.

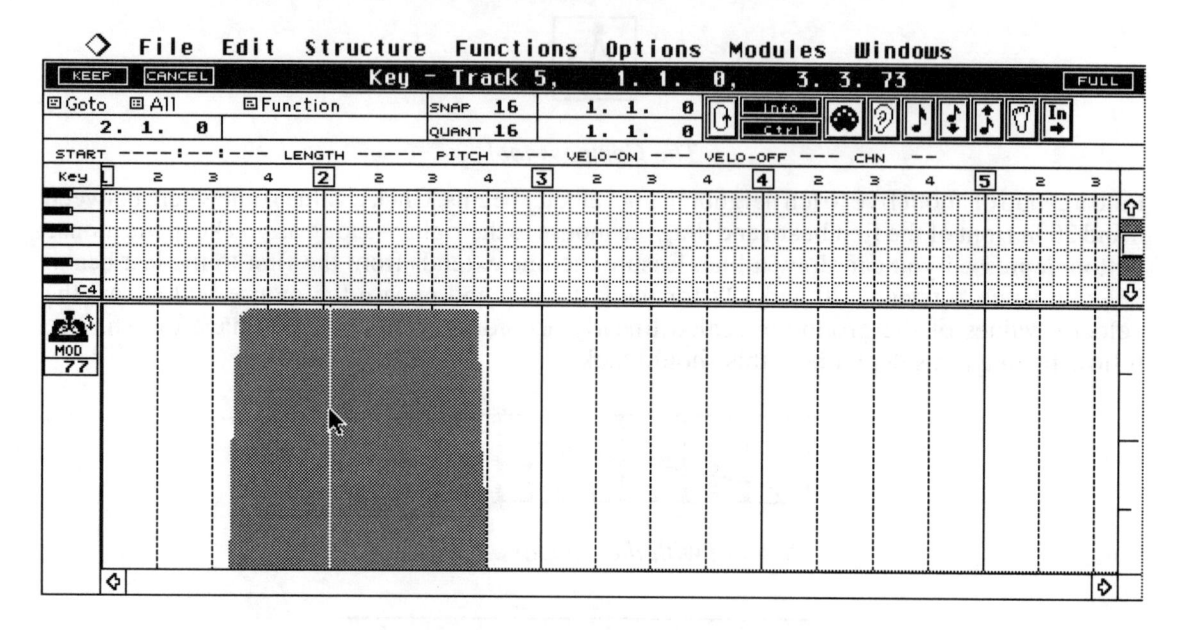

Modulation events in graphic form

Use the mouse pointer to go to the beginning of the modulation "mountain". Press and hold the mouse button and drag the mouse to the right. The line you are drawing should entirely frame the whole heap of data. Release the mouse button: the grey area is now highlighted in black. You can delete the selected data via [Backspace] or [Delete]. The Clipboard can be used here too. Before you start experimenting, here are a few important guidelines.

The data is selected

As you know from the MIDI chapter, movements of performance controllers can generate a great deal of data. In this example, MIDI data is generated in two places. One is at the beginning of the mod wheel, etc. movement (on the incline, up to a maximum value of 127), and the other at its end (on the decline, down to a minimum value of 0). The Controller Display contains no values in the area between these two places. The control change value remains at 127, as illustrated by the central area in the following diagram:

The Layout of the Key Edit Window

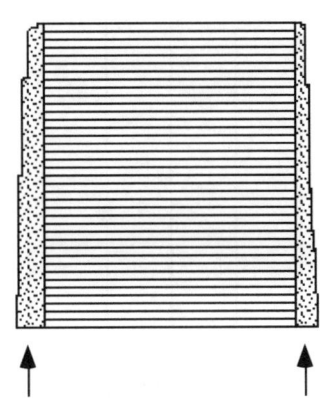

Data was generated in these two places only

We have just learned how to select data in the Controller Display. Try to select a small area between the incline and decline positions. When you do, Cubase selects the two highest neighbouring values (before and after the clicked point). In our example, these are the highest point of the incline and the start of the decline.

Partially selected data

Select just the incline and delete it with [Backspace]. Not only is the incline gone, but also the entire area until the next controller movement, i.e. the decline. This interrelationship will be very important for our later work, as it is a prime source of confusion. You can only edit data that *actually exists*, which was generated when the performance controller was *moved*: When it is not moved, it *ceases to produce data*, and Cubase "fills in" the period of non-movement with a graphic area that looks like the "real" data, but is in fact a visual trick.

Cubase does this for even the shortest periods of non-movement, so that the result of moving, say, the mod wheel is a series of "steps" as the wheel is moved up and down: there is always one event at the beginning of a "step", but *none* between that first event and the next one, i.e. none wherever the display is horizontal.

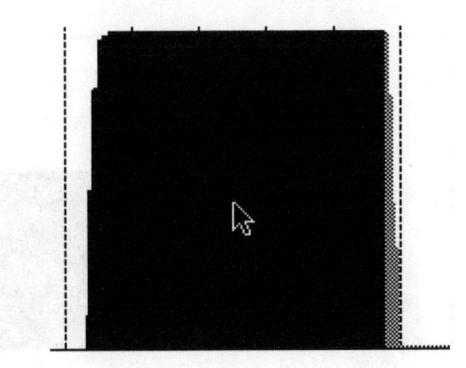

The beginning of the modulation is selected...

155

The Key Editor

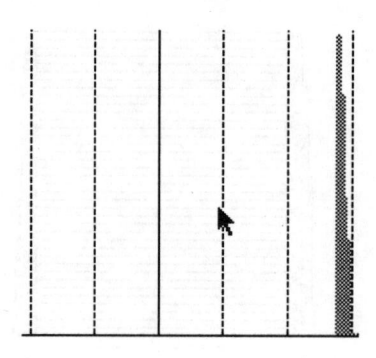

...and deleted

Recall the deleted data with [Undo]. Let's get started with some detailed operations. Sharpen your crayons and let the art class commence.

8.3.15 Editing existing data

First we'll reduce the maximum modulation value slightly to make the modulation less intense. As we have seen that there's always an event at the start of a step, the maximum value event must be situated at the beginning of the long horizontal plane. Cubase helps you to locate its position, so you don't have to place the Pencil at the exact spot. Press and hold the mouse button and drag the value down. The display in the Event Type value box shows the current value. Set it to 70. The display should now look something like this:

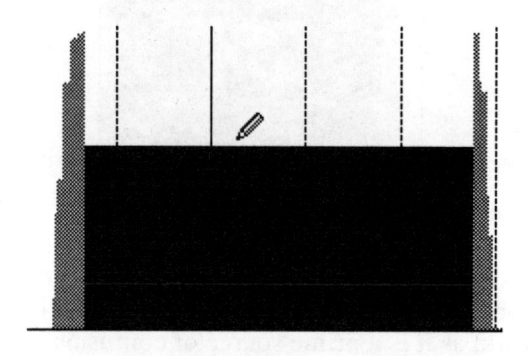

The maximum value is reduced...

As you can see, we have decreased the maximum value, but the task is not finished yet. The modulation overshoots at the start and end, so we must now modify the incline and decline to suit the new maximum level. There are two ways to correct this. Place the Pencil at the beginning of the modulation and slowly draw it up the incline until you reach the maximum value. The values are scaled according to the Pencil's movement. Smooth the curve out so that you have a gradual rise.

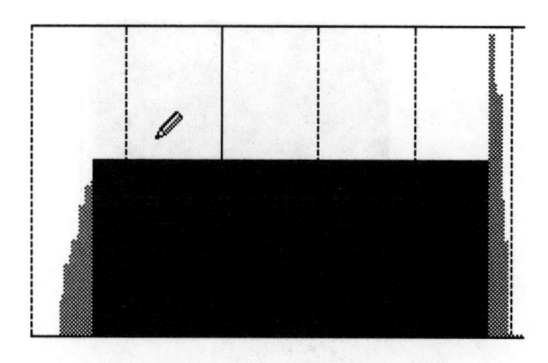

...then the start phase is redrawn

The Layout of the Key Edit Window

We'll use a different method for the end phase. Select the compass from the Toolbox. Set the compass at the projected beginning of the decline and draw a line down to zero, keeping the mouse button pressed. Watch the value display of the Event Type box to ensure the end value is actually 0.

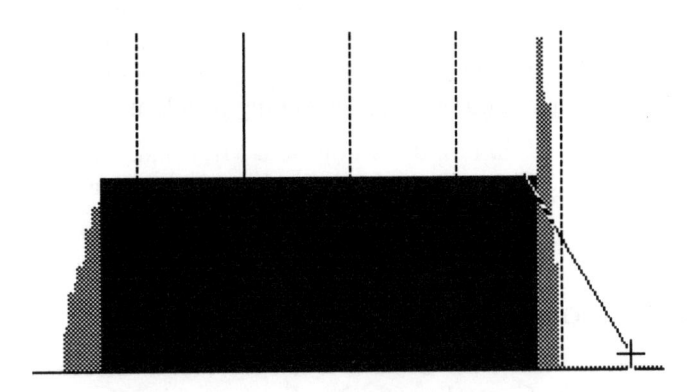

The end of the modulation is redrawn with the compass

The next exercise involves adding the time dimension to our work. This time, we are not modifying the maximum value, but the amount of time it takes to reach the maximum value. If the curve starts earlier, the rise (and therefore the onset of modulation) is more gradual. The only way to achieve this effect is to create new modulation values. Until now, we've only modified *existing* data with the Pencil. To produce *new* data, hold [Alternate] down while drawing with the Pencil.

Before we start, here's another important piece of information. Values are generated at the positions defined by the Snap function only. We'll soon see what this means in practical terms. For our first exercise set the Snap value to "Off".

Hold [Alternate] down and draw a curve with a gradual rise. The angle determines the length of the rise. Your curve should resemble the one in the following diagram.

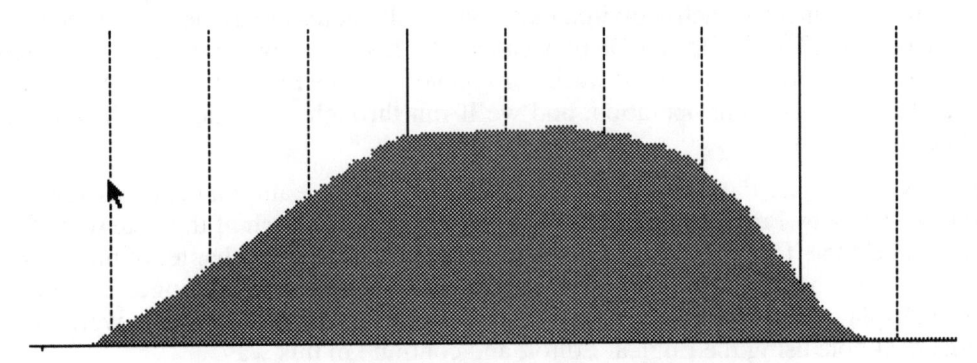

This is what our new modulation could look like

You could also use the compass to achieve the same effect. Here too, hold [Alternate] down. New events are generated along the line the compass is drawing.

Now delete all the data by selecting the area and pressing [Backspace] or [Delete]. You can also use the Eraser from the Toolbox, but keep in mind that it only deletes single event values, never an entire group of events. If that is the aim of your work then choose "Delete Cont. Data" from the Functions menu. It deletes all the non-note events of the Parts in the Editor.

You are probably still waiting for an explanation of how the Snap function relates to the Controller Display, so here it is. We'll draw a new curve, first setting the Snap resolution to "4", which denotes quarter notes. You will find that only coarse increments are possible because Cubase is inserting the new events at quarter note positions. However, this is not subtle enough for modulation.

The Key Editor

You must use the Snap function to determine what resolution you want for the events. The ideal compromise is to find a resolution where the events are close enough together so that they do not produce audible steps between the events (this largely depends on the type of MIDI data you're generating: the human ear is more sensitive to pitch changes than to minor modulation intensity differences) but not so close that you are using an unnecessarily large number of events for the job in hand. In other words, use the coarsest Snap setting you can get away with. Controller Display drawings at the "Off" Snap setting create a great deal of data: too much data places a heavy load on the MIDI system, and may lead to timing problems.

The following is a good rule of thumb: draw non-note MIDI data at Snap settings of "Off" or "2PP". Then choose "Reduce Cont. Data" from the Functions menu. Cubase deletes what it considers to be the superfluous events from the data you have drawn: you won't hear a difference, but the MIDI system's load has definitely been lightened.

8.3.16 A few facts about individual event types

Now that you know how to handle the Controller Display, let us discuss the characteristics of some of the event types in the Controller Display. Some of this information is dictated by the MIDI standard. Let's go through the event type pop-up menu list.

Pitch Bend data can go up or down; this is why Cubase divides the Controller Display into two horizontal halves. Downward pitch changes are drawn in the lower section, those going up in the upper section. The center position has a numeric value of 4096 and is displayed in the field under the Event Type box. Keep in mind that the maximum pitch bend range is defined by the internal setting of the receiving instrument, and by not the MIDI values it receives: these determine the amount.

What Cubase calls "Aftertouch" events (MIDI Channel Pressure) can be handled the same way as Control Change data, as illustrated by the modulation exercise above. We covered velocity in the first exercise.

Poly Key Pressure represents a special case. As you know, Poly Key Pressure is aftertouch information for each individual key. Poly Key Pressure requires a graphic display to be able to show pressure amounts for each individual key even if the notes are at the same time position (such as in a chord). The Controller Display cannot do this on its own: you have to combine it with the Logical Editor, which we're covering in chapter 13 "The Logical Editor". For now, read and remember the following operation, and we'll run through a practical application in the Logical Editor chapter.

Draw Poly Key Pressure data at the first note's position. Cubase automatically assigns the C3 pitch to new Poly Key Pressure data. Alter this C3 to match the pitch of the note with the help of the Logical Editor. This is explained in detail in the Logical Editor chapter of this book. The amount values can be left as they are. The pressure values can now no longer be seen in the Controller Display. Now draw Poly Key Pressure events for the next note. Convert the C3 to match this next note using the Logical Editor, and continue in this way.

You can draw Program Change data, but it's much better to use the List Editor (see below).

Modulation, Breath Control, Foot Control, Main Volume, Balance, Pan, and Expression are all functions of the MIDI Control Change status and can be drawn in the usual manner. Balance and Pan are similar to Pitch Bend in that they can go up and down (actually, left and right) and feature a center position.

Damper Pedal (also called sustain foot switch) is another special case. We have seen in the section on Control Change events in the MIDI chapter that this type of event is assigned different resolutions in the MIDI standard. Control Change #64 is responsible for the damper pedal. In theory, it has a resolution of 128 steps, but as it's a switch, only the values 0 (pedal not depressed) and 127 (pedal depressed) are recognized.

This is why some event types that act as switches allow you to enter only two values (0 and 127) in the Display. Try to enter damper pedal data and you'll soon see how this works.

The Layout of the Key Edit Window

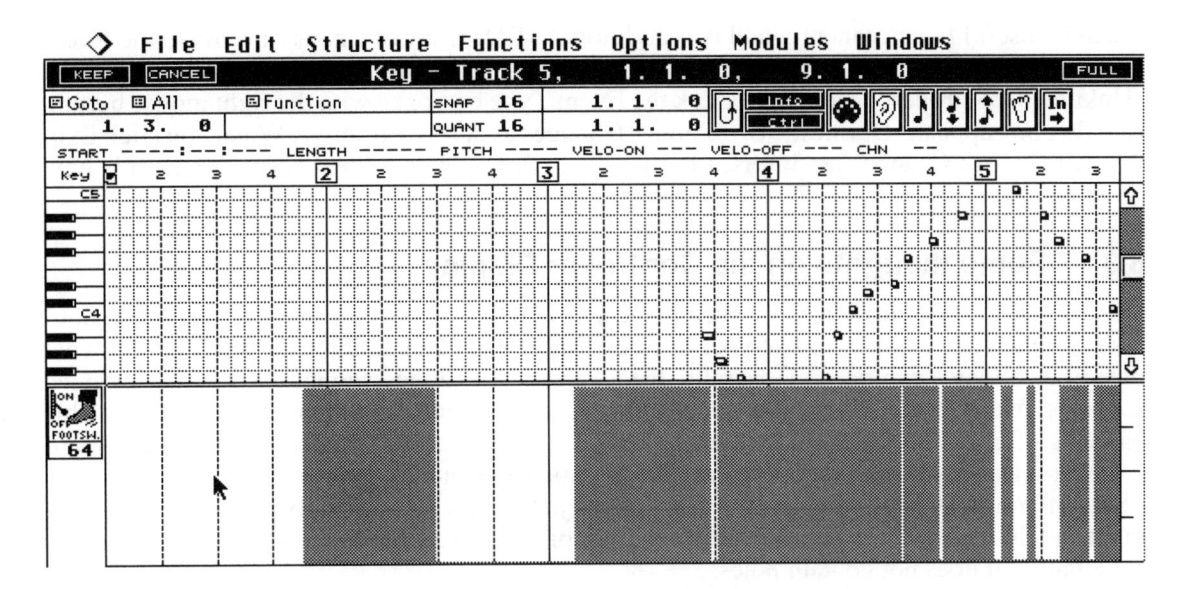

Switch-type events are limited to two values: 0 and 127

You have several options if you want to use an event type not included in the event type pop-up menu. To temporarily insert a new event type, choose Unknown Controller from the Event Type menu, and a dialog box appears where you can select any MIDI Control Change event.

Click and hold the arrow next to the "Control 0" field. Yet another list appears. You can scroll through the list keeping the mouse button pressed, and as you do this, the selected event name highlights. As soon as you reach the arrows at the end of the list, the list is scrolled on and you can read the event names that lie "beyond the horizon". Release the mouse button once you have found and highlighted the desired name. This Control Change name is then adopted by the event type menu list. If your Part already contains these events, you will suddenly find them displayed since the Controller Display can now recognize them (it only recognizes data that is listed in the pop-up menu). You can now also draw the new event values in the Controller Display. Keep in mind that each MIDI event type has its own display.

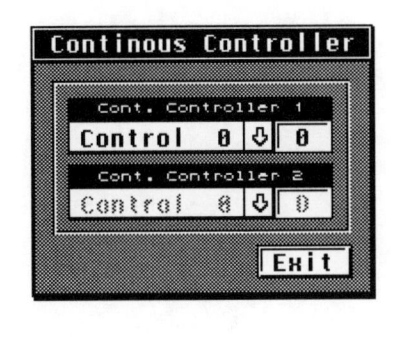

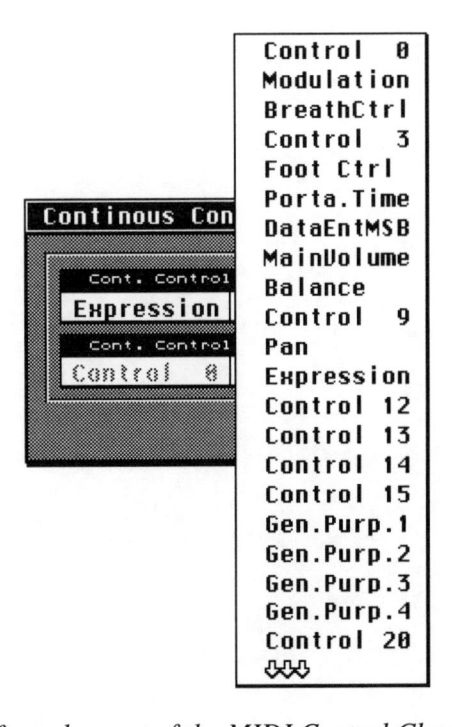

The "Unknown Controller" setting on the left, and a part of the MIDI Control Change list

The Key Editor

It can be useful to permanently add two additional MIDI Control Change events to the Event Type menu if you're going to be using them regularly - this would avoid having to redefine the "Unknown Controllers" each time. Click the Event Type box once with the right mouse button. A dialog box appears. Define the two Control Changes as described above. When you click Exit, the two Control Changes are inserted in the Event Type list and direct access to them is now possible.

8.3.17 Some thoughts on the Controller Display

- Instruments vary quite radically in their respective MIDI capabilities, especially regarding non-note events. Take a quick look at your devices' MIDI Implementation Charts to find out what type of data they can process. Generally, the Chart shows all the available events that a device supports. Many devices can receive and process more event types than they can send. This happens often with Poly Key Pressure as it is easier to receive than to send. The keyboard hardware needed to send Poly Key Pressure is expensive and complicated.
- Lots of non-note data is designed to work in conjunction with notes only. After all, it doesn't make much sense to draw data such as either sort of aftertouch, modulation, damper pedal, etc. for a Part that does not contain notes.
- To stop the effect of modulation, pitch bend and so on, it must be returned to its zero value. This can lead to problems, especially if several Parts are situated one after another on a Track. Say you draw a damper pedal On command prior to the end of a Part without the necessary command to end it. The command tells all notes in the following Parts to sustain the notes. Although Cubase will automatically correct some problem areas - especially those involving pitch bending - you should still keep potential problems in mind when drawing and editing non-note data.
- Ensure the Reset on Part End function in the MIDI Setup dialog box is active. This ensures that certain event types (Pitch Bend, Control Change 1 (modulation), Control Change 64 (sustain), Channel Pressure (what Cubase calls "Aftertouch")) are reset at the end of a Part. This can avoid some of the problems discussed above.
- Reset on Stop is a valuable tool as well: it sends All Notes Off and Reset All Controllers commands every time you stop Cubase. Notes that don't receive a Note Off command because you stopped Cubase before they arrived are switched off anyway, and all non-note data is reset.

9 The List Editor

Commands are almost identical in all of Cubase's Editors. Once you are familiar with the handling in one Editor, you will quickly get used to the others. Lots of operations discussed in the Key Editor chapter apply to the List Editor as well, though you will find some differences because the List Editor is different in concept.

Either a selected Part or all of the Parts of a Track can be presented in the List Editor. To display the whole Track, ensure none of its Parts are selected. It is not necessary to return to the Arrange window prior to entering the List Editor - you can directly move back and forth between Editors. For example, if you leave the Key Editor to go to the List Editor, Cubase automatically closes the Key Editor.

You can also call up several Editors at the same time by pressing and holding [Alternate] while calling up the Editors.

This allows all sorts of configurations:
- different Editors with different Parts,
- different Editors with the same Parts,
- identical Editors with different Parts.

The one general limitation is that a maximum of seven windows can be opened at one time. If you have opened several windows, you'll have to watch their sizes, depending on how big your monitor is. The Windows menu's Tile Editors command is a handy function for this purpose as it allows all the selected Editors to be displayed on the screen, each of which has the largest possible dimensions for the configuration you have selected.

Seven windows still take up a lot of space and will appear rather small, so a large-screen monitor is definitely an advantage. Those of you with 12" screens can still work with several Editors at a time if you use the Tile Editors command to help you optimally position all the selected Editors on the screen. The Full button at the upper right corner of the active Editor enlarges it to its maximum size. Another click returns it to the smaller format.

Remember that only *one* window can be active at a time. The Song Position Triangle runs in the active window only. To activate a window, click it anywhere within its borders. Although only one window is active, all the Editor windows are affected by changes in the active one: changes made in one Editor are immediately adopted by the other Editors.

If a Part is contained in an Editor, it cannot be copied, deleted, moved or shortened in the Arrange window.

Select any Part in the Arrange window and go to the List Editor via the Edit menu ([Control][G]). Double-clicking the Part serves the same purpose, provided the Preferences setting for the Track Classes is correctly entered. The new window looks something like this

The List Editor

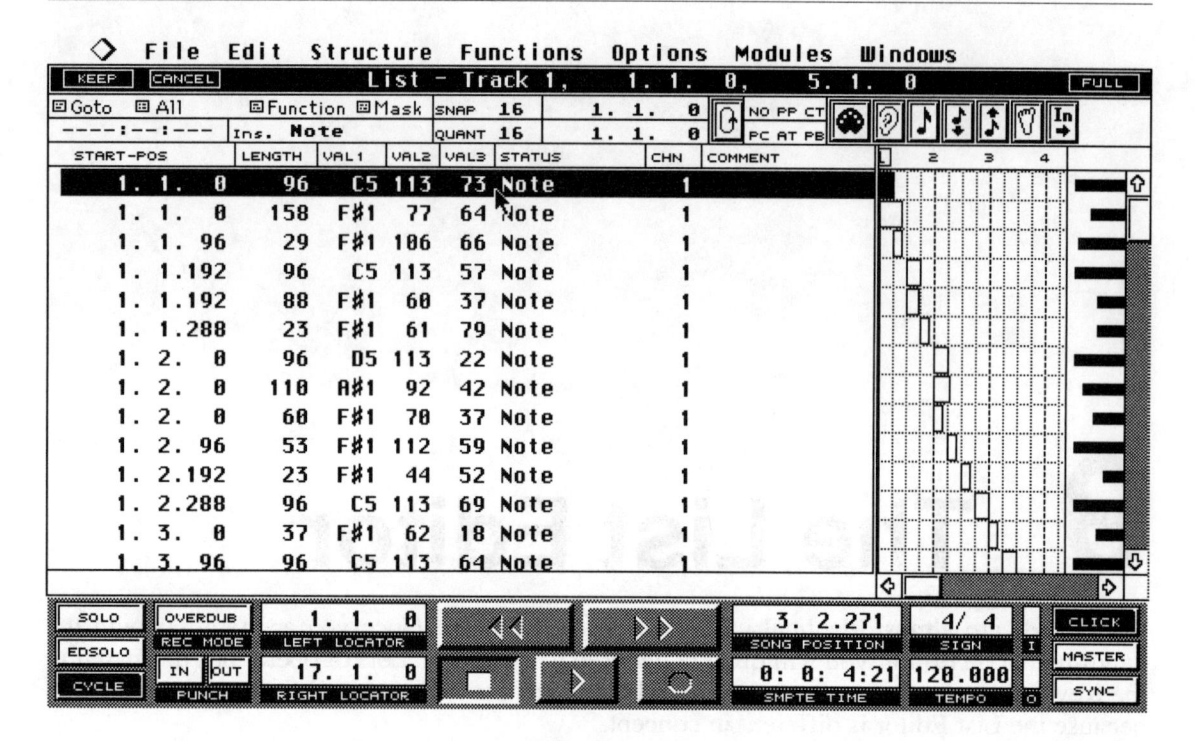

The List Editor

The Functions Bar is identical to the one in the Key Editor, with a few minor differences. You won't find an Info Line, nor is one required, as you will see.

Two large areas occupy most of the Editor. The right side should remind you of the Key Editor's grid; the left side lists numerical values whose meanings depend on what's in the active Part(s).

You can change the size of one half in relation to the other by dragging the vertical dividing line that lies between them to the left or right.

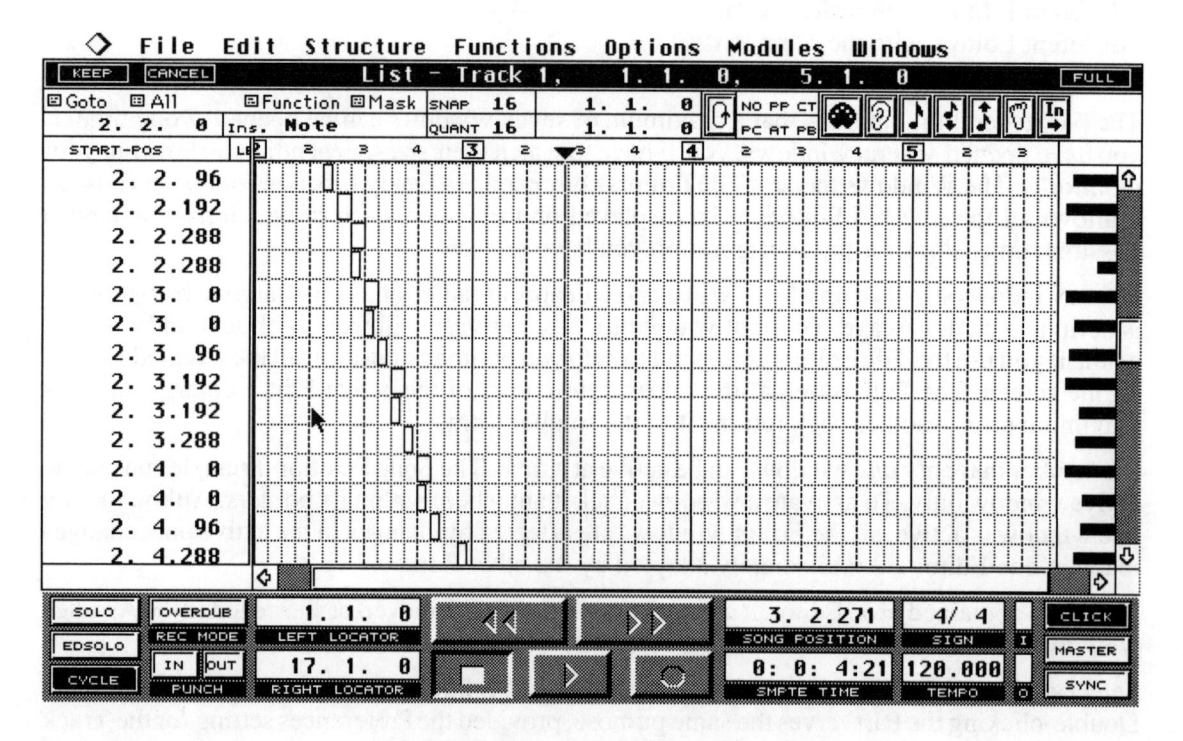

The grid display has been enlarged

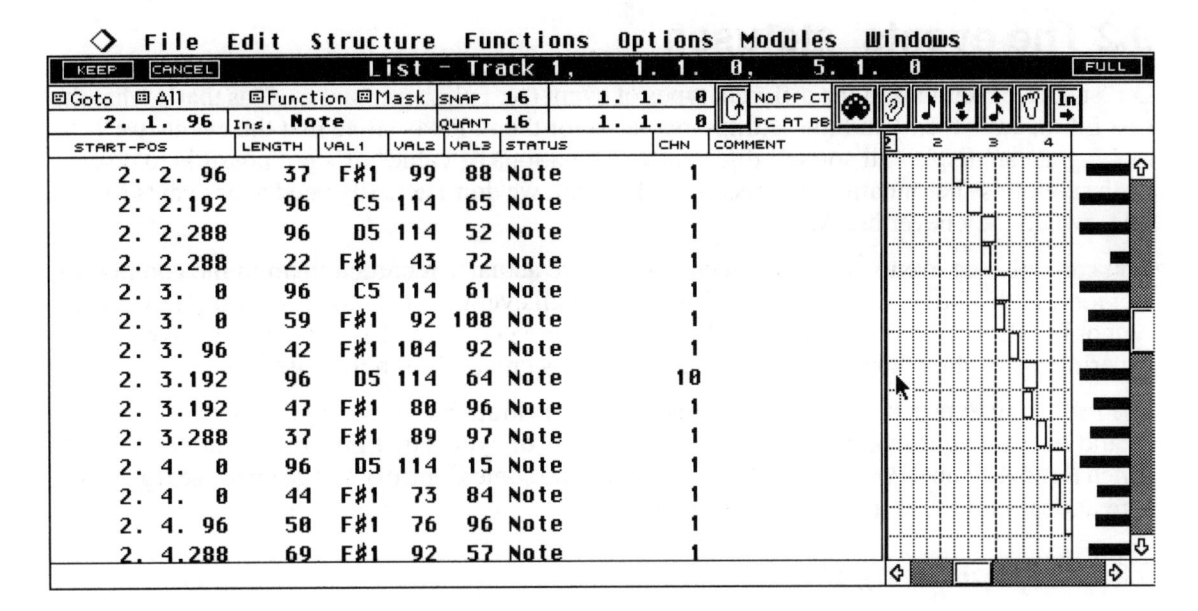

The Event List

START-POS	LENGTH	VAL1	VAL2	VAL3	STATUS	CHN	COMMENT
2. 2. 96	37	F#1	99	88	Note	1	
2. 2.192	96	C5	114	65	Note	1	
2. 2.288	96	D5	114	52	Note	1	
2. 2.288	22	F#1	43	72	Note	1	
2. 3. 0	96	C5	114	61	Note	1	
2. 3. 0	59	F#1	92	108	Note	1	
2. 3. 96	42	F#1	104	92	Note	1	
2. 3.192	96	D5	114	64	Note	10	
2. 3.192	47	F#1	80	96	Note	1	
2. 3.288	37	F#1	89	97	Note	1	
2. 4. 0	96	D5	114	15	Note	1	
2. 4. 0	44	F#1	73	84	Note	1	
2. 4. 96	50	F#1	76	96	Note	1	
2. 4.288	69	F#1	92	57	Note	1	

And now the event list has been enlarged

The List Editor does not have a Controller Display. The window's right edge contains two items you'll recognise from the Key Editor: the scroll bar and the beam display.

You can zoom the window's display scale in the same manner as for most of the other windows: horizontally (for the grid only) and vertically (for the grid and the list). To do this, click the appropriate arrows in the scroll bars with the right mouse button. For now, leave the List Editor window at its original size.

9.1 The event list

The screen's left half contains the event list. All the events of a selected Part or Track are displayed as lines of text, one below the other, in the order in which they occur. The following diagram depicts a note (Status column) at position 1.1.0 (Start Position), whose pitch is C3 (Value 1) and 96 ticks long (Length), which is a 1/16th. The note was played with a velocity of 32 (Value 2), and the release value is 64 (Value 3). The MIDI channel the Track was originally received on is displayed to the right (but this is not necessarily the MIDI channel that Cubase is transmitting this Track on, as that's determined by the Arrange window settings).

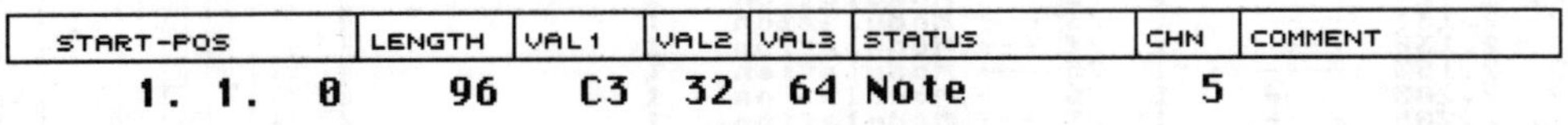

START-POS	LENGTH	VAL1	VAL2	VAL3	STATUS	CHN	COMMENT
1. 1. 0	96	C3	32	64	Note	5	

The parameters of one Note

You can edit almost any of these note parameters immediately by simple clicking. This selects the event. Editing is the same as always: left or right mouse button click; or double-clicking followed by typing in the input box that appears. If you move the Start Position value beyond the preceding or following event's position, the event is moved to a new position in the list.

You cannot change the status of most events in this Editor. The list displays all the events' statuses you recorded in the Part, i.e. Notes, Control Changes, Program Changes, etc. plus a few special Cubase events. Not every event has a value for each of the list's columns. For instance, notes are the only events featuring a Length value, Control Changes do not have a pitch value, etc. The exact structure of individual events is dictated by the MIDI data format.

However, all events have a time value in the Start Position column. You can delete a selected event from the list via [Backspace] or [Delete].

9.2 The events' statuses

Let's take a closer look at the different types of event (we call them "statuses" as that's what the List Editor calls them) and the settings available for them. Please note that the events we'll be looking at can display all sorts of different combinations of values; it's not possible to discuss all the countless permutations of possible values, but we don't actually need to as events follow rules which they never break.

You can only see events on your screen if you have actually recorded them in the computer's memory. In this book, we haven't yet done that for all events. There are also types of event that cannot be recorded nor sent out via MIDI, but are created in the List Editor only. We will do experiments to show how you can modify as well as create data in the List Editor.

The following explanations are each supported by illustrations showing you how the operation should look on your screen. Keep in mind that types of events that give out "continuous" data (Pitch Bend, Channel Pressure, Poly Key Pressure and some Control Change messages) generate a great deal more than just one single event.

9.2.1 Control Change

The list displays two numeric values next to the start position. Value 1 defines the Control Change number, i.e. modulation (#1), volume (#7), etc. Value 2 is the Control Change's amount. The Status column confirms that the event is a Control Change and lists its number again.

START-POS	LENGTH	VAL1	VAL2	VAL3	STATUS	CHN	COMMENT
1. 1. 3	-----	60	32	---	Control 60	1	

MIDI Control Change 60, amount 32, at position 1.1.3, recorded on channel 1

Record some Control Change events (no notes) in an empty Part and return to the List Editor. There are four ways to move through the list: using the computer keyboard's up/down cursor keys, fast forward and rewind, the vertical scroll bar, and by starting playback.

A single movement of the modulation wheel produces all these events, as displayed in the List Editor

An arrow appears down the lefthand side of the Event List, pointing to the event that is currently being played. Choose one of the four positioning options and move through the Event List. Depending on the type of MIDI status you have just recorded, you can see how some generate a large amount of data.

9.2.2 Poly Key Pressure (aftertouch)

Poly Key Pressure can generate even more data, especially if you are not aware that it is active: each key can generate up to 128 amount values. In addition to its position and status, each Poly Key Pressure event has two values: the key pressed (Value 1) and the amount of pressure applied to the key (Value 2).

START-POS	LENGTH	VAL1	VAL2	VAL3	STATUS	CHN	COMMENT
1. 1. 2	-----	C3	32	---	Poly-Press	1	

Poly Key Pressure on C3, amount 32, at position 1.1.2, recorded on Channel 1

9.2.3 Channel Pressure (aftertouch)

Steinberg call MIDI Channel Pressure events by the generic term "Aftertouch" which is misleading since the description "Aftertouch" applies just as much to Poly Key Pressure events. Bear this in mind when you see the status "Aftertouch" in the List Editor - they are referring to Channel Pressure. Either way, the list shows the position and the Value 1 value which defines the amount of pressure applied to the keys (remember that Channel Pressure is monophonic - apply aftertouch to one key and it affects all the notes on the same MIDI channel).

START-POS	LENGTH	VAL1	VAL2	VAL3	STATUS	CHN	COMMENT
1. 1. 5	-----	60		---	Aftertouch	1	

Channel Pressure amount 60, position 1.1.5, recorded on Channel 1

9.2.4 Program Change

This event also has just one variable value (in the Value 1 column). It determines which program is selected in your synthesizer. As with all the events in the list, this event is immediately sent to your synth if you click or edit it when the Ear icon in the Functions Bar is active.

START-POS	LENGTH	VAL1	VAL2	VAL3	STATUS	CHN	COMMENT
1. 1. 4	-----	61		---	ProgChange	1	

Program Change to program number 61 at Position 1.1.4

9.2.5 Pitch Bend

The Pitch Bend status has two variable values, scaled from 0 - 127. Pitch bending can go up and down, so the Value 2 column's resting value is 64 (not 0!), and Value's 1's is 0. Very few MIDI devices actually use the high resolution made possible by the combination of these two values.

START-POS	LENGTH	VAL1	VAL2	VAL3	STATUS	CHN	COMMENT
1. 1. 6	-----	60	32	---	Pitch-Bend	1	

Pitch Bend amount 60 + 32, position 1.1.6, recorded on channel 1

9.2.6 System Exclusive

As you know, this data is device-specific. Cubase displays the manufacturer ID in the Status column, provided it is known. Value 1 displays the MIDI channel or device number sometimes contained in SysEx messages. Change this entry only if you want to send this message on a different MIDI channel or to a different device. If you have no experience of working with SysEx data, please *don't* change anything as you may corrupt sound data.

The List Editor

START-POS	LENGTH	VAL1	VAL2	VAL3	STATUS	CHN	COMMENT
1. 1. 7	-----	60		---	SysEx	1	F7

A SysEx event header

If you move the dividing line between the list and the grid all the way to the right, you will see more columns. The Comment column lists the beginning of a SysEx message.

SysEx messages can be very long, depending on the device and type of message, so Cubase displays the initial bytes only. The remaining data is stored, but not displayed.

You can also edit SysEx messages. Click the Comment field, and the following editing line appears:

```
F0,F7
```

The SysEx editing line

This editing line contains the SysEx message in the hexadecimal format. The Atari's cursor keys are used to access individual values to change them. This editing method is suitable for short SysEx messages only. If you try to work on a message that is too long, Cubase will warn you with an alert box:

⚠ That's too much!

[OK]

You can edit brief SysEx messages only

If you are unsure about what you are doing, don't change anything. SysEx data cannot be auditioned while you are in the Editor, so you must do it from the Arrange window. You'll be introduced to better ways of generating and editing SysEx data later in the book.

9.2.7 Special Events

These are Cubase's internal control commands which you can use to tell Cubase what should be done. The Status column displays the type of Special Event. You can click the Status field in order to move between the different types. Special events, like SysEx messages, are transmitted during playback only when you are in the Arrange window, so close the Editor before you start the playback.

9.2.8 Text events

Text events are simply comments that you can enter in the Editor, such as naming SysEx messages. No MIDI data is generated or modified. Click in the Comment column and type in the desired text in the entry line that appears. Confirm it with [Return], and the text is entered in the Comment column.

The other values shown are of no relevance. Text events can be created in the List Editor only, and then only manually.

The Events' Statuses

```
| START-POS | LENGTH | VAL1 | VAL2 | VAL3 | STATUS | CHN | COMMENT |
   1. 1.  8   -----   60     32    ---   Text
```

Text is entered in the Comment column

9.2.9 Mute events

These events are created when you mute/unmute a Track during recording (refer to the Arrange chapter). Value 1 denotes the Track, Value 2 denotes whether a Track was muted (value = 1) or unmuted (value = 0).

```
| START-POS | LENGTH | VAL1 | VAL2 | VAL3 | STATUS     | CHN | COMMENT |
   1. 1.  9   -----   1      0     ---   Track-Mute   --   Drums
```

Track 1 entitled "Drums" is unmuted at position 1.1.9

9.2.10 The Stop event

This function allows you to set a Stop point where Cubase ends the playback. You can see how this might be helpful in a live situation. You can line up several songs in an Arrangement and separate them with the Stop command. Cubase plays the first piece, stops at the designated point, and starts the next piece when you activate playback again. You could insert an empty bar between the two pieces, and add a count-in to it. Stop events are created exclusively in the List Editor.

```
| START-POS | LENGTH | VAL1 | VAL2 | VAL3 | STATUS | CHN | COMMENT |
   1. 1. 10   -----   ----         ---   Stop    --
```

Cubase stops at position 1.1.10

9.2.11 MIDI Mixer events

MIDI Mixer events are those which have been generated in the MIDI Mixer. For now, it suffices to know that Value 1 denotes the object number, and Value 2 its amount. Both values can be edited. The Comment column contains the name of the object and the instrument to which it is assigned. Right now, you are probably wondering what the purpose of this information is: we'll get to these events in due course.

```
| START-POS | LENGTH | VAL1 | VAL2 | VAL3 | STATUS | CHN | COMMENT |
   1. 1.  8   -----   7      1     ---   Mixer   --   VOL10 -
```

A MIDI Mixer event

9.2.12 The Display Filter

If you want to work on specific types of events only, it may be distracting to see all the other types in the list. Cubase has something called a Display Filter, which you'll find situated between the Loop and MIDI In icons.

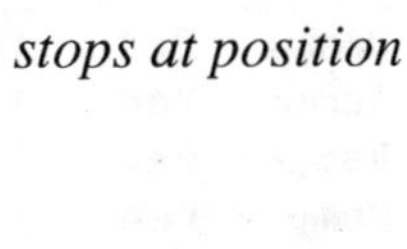

```
| NO PP CT |
| PC AT PB |
```

The Display Filter

Six different event types can be filtered out of the display. Click NO, and all the notes in the event list disappear. Poly Key Pressure (PP), Channel Pressure ("Aftertouch") (AT), Program Change

The List Editor

(PC), Pitch Bend (PB) and Control Change (CC) events can be filtered out of the display by simply clicking the desired type. The events themselves are not deleted, but continue to be heard: it's just that they are excluded from the graphic display.

```
 ◇   File   Edit   Structure   Functions   Options   Modules   Windows
[KEEP] [CANCEL]         List - Track 5,    1. 1.  0,    9. 1.  0              [FULL]
▣Goto  ▣All    ▣Function ▣Mask  SNAP  16    1. 1.  0   [↻] no PP CT  [🎨][?][♪][↕][♩][👣][In→]
----:--:---   Ins. Note          QUANT 16    1. 1.  0       PC AT PB
 START-POS    LENGTH   VAL1  VAL2  VAL3  STATUS       CHN  COMMENT    2       3       4     [2]    2
    1. 4.221  -----    64   127   ---  Damper Ped    1
    1. 4.372    60     A#2   93    41  Note          1
    2. 1. 80    63     G#2   83    53  Note          1
    2. 1.178    48     F#2   90    67  Note          1
    2. 1.278    34     G2   112    93  Note          1
    2. 2. 85    58     F2    73    29  Note          1
    2. 2.186    38     D3    66    39  Note          1
    2. 2.368  -----    64     0   ---  Damper Ped    1
    3. 1.180  -----    64   127   ---  Damper Ped    1
    3. 3.307   100     A#3   96    10  Note          1
    3. 3.352  -----    64     0   ---  Damper Ped    1
    3. 4. 21    83     G3    74    64  Note          1
    3. 4. 34  -----    64   127   ---  Damper Ped    1
    3. 4.171    53     F3    63    37  Note          1
```

```
 ◇   File   Edit   Structure   Functions   Options   Modules   Windows
[KEEP] [CANCEL]         List - Track 5,    1. 1.  0,    9. 1.  0              [FULL]
▣Goto  ▣All    ▣Function ▣Mask  SNAP  16    1. 1.  0   [↻] no PP CT  [🎨][?][♪][↕][♩][👣][In→]
   1. 2.192   Ins. Note         QUANT 16    1. 1.  0       PC AT PB
 START-POS    LENGTH   VAL1  VAL2  VAL3  STATUS       CHN  COMMENT    2       3       4     [2]    2
    1. 4.221  -----    64   127   ---  Damper Ped    1
    2. 2.368  -----    64     0   ---  Damper Ped    1
    3. 1.180  -----    64   127   ---  Damper Ped    1
    3. 3.352  -----    64     0   ---  Damper Ped    1
    3. 4. 34  -----    64   127   ---  Damper Ped    1
    4. 3.160  -----    64     0   ---  Damper Ped    1
    4. 3.186  -----    64   127   ---  Damper Ped    1
    4. 4. 52  -----    64     0   ---  Damper Ped    1
    4. 4. 87  -----    64   127   ---  Damper Ped    1
    5. 1. 55  -----    64     0   ---  Damper Ped    1
    5. 1.116  -----    64   127   ---  Damper Ped    1
    5. 1.188  -----    64     0   ---  Damper Ped    1
    5. 1.292  -----    64   127   ---  Damper Ped    1
    5. 1.345  -----    64     0   ---  Damper Ped    1
```

A piano Track with and without notes in the display. Only the sustain pedal events remain

The Display Filter shows if data is being filtered from the display: capital letters mean that the status is not being filtered; lower case letters mean that it is. Special Events are always displayed.

9.2.13 The Grid

Let's take a look at the other half of the Editor. Every event has a corresponding beam in the grid located in the right half of your screen, whose length varies according to the event. Select any note in the list. It becomes highlighted, and at the same time its graphic beam in the grid is selected. List entries and their grid beams always share the same horizontal line.

The rest of the grid display is similar to that of the Key Editor. An event's position and length can be read off in the Position Bar. Its velocity value can be changed via the beams at the right edge of the window. When you move the mouse pointer over the velocity beams, the pointer becomes a Pencil: click a beam and change its length by dragging it to the left or right. Its current value is displayed in the event list. The pitch of note events and the status of an event are displayed in the Event List only.

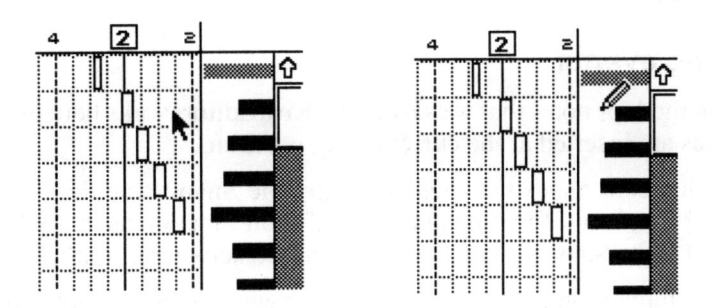

Modifying a velocity using the Pencil

9.2.14 What the Editors have in common

Only within the grid does the List Editor offer lots of functions that you will recognize from the Key Editor. Since we discussed these functions when we covered the Key Editor, all you need is a memory refresher:
- Key Editor functions such as dragging events, copying with [Alternate], deleting, selecting several events with [Shift] or with the rubber band, etc. can all be used in the List Editor's grid as well. Try out all these variations. Note that if you move an event in time, the list to the left takes a moment to restructure itself according to the event's new position. This may lead to a little confusion, but the event you selected remains selected.
- The Toolbox is also at your disposal. Press the right mouse button and select a tool. All tools have the usual functions, except the compass which has no function in this Editor.

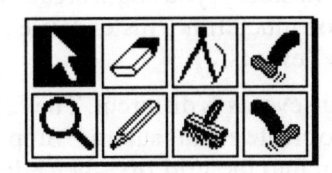

The familiar Toolbox

If you have entered a complete Track in this Editor with all its Parts, the events of the currently active Part are framed in black. The events in the inactive Part(s) are framed with a dotted line, the same way they were in the Key Editor. Activate a Part simply by clicking one of the dotted events.
- The familiar edit-loop function and Goto, "selection" and Function sub-menus are also available in the List Editor. Use them at your discretion. If you have trouble remembering exactly how they work, look in the Key Editor chapter.

Goto	All	Function
Song-Pos	All Events	Fixed Note
First Event	Looped Events	Delete Note
Last Event	Cycled Events	Keep Note
First Selected	Selected Events	Repeat
Next Selected	Looped Selected Ev.	Fill
Last Selected	Cycled Selected Ev.	Reverse
Prev Selected		Delete
Next Part		
Prev Part		

All the Key Editor options are available in the List Editor

The List Editor

- Note On velocity, pitch, and release velocity values can be changed via MIDI: use the icon functions. Their uses are identical to those in the Key Editor.
- The Clipboard can be used as usual.

9.2.15 Creating events

The step input method for notes that we saw in the Key Editor works here too. Activate the Foot icon and the notes are inserted at the current song position.

The Quantize value determines the event's length, the Snap value the time interval between events. The [Tab] key, Insert function and the "In" icon function as in the Key Editor. Keep in mind that with all Editors, events can be entered in the active Part only.

The List Editor features another new way to create events. Enter an empty Part in a blank Track and return to the List Editor. Activate the Pencil from the Toolbox. Click and hold the Insert box. Select the event type you wish to create. All the events discussed above are available. Let's choose a note event. Click the desired position in the grid. This creates a C3 note whose length is specified by the Quantize setting and whose position is determined by the Snap value.

As in the Key Editor, velocity values are affected by [Shift], [Control], or a combination of both. If you don't release the mouse button when you insert a note, you can simultaneously determine its length - we saw this in the Key Editor as well. New notes are always assigned a pitch of C3. Set the desired pitch in the Event List. In contrast to the Key Editor, not only can you create notes, but all other event types, too.

9.2.16 A review of the List Editor's special functions

Although the List Editor can do so much, it's a fact that each Editor is better at some things than at others. Let's look at a few examples. Moving a pitch bender, volume pedal, etc. can produce vast numbers of individual events. In theory, you could create these events step by step in the List Editor, but it would simply take too much time. Instead, use the Controller Display of the Key Editor which allows you to "draw" events.

The situation with Program Change events is different. They are difficult to generate in the Key Editor, so do it in the List Editor. To create events such as "Stop" and "Text", which can be created in the List Editor only, insert them into the grid first then edit them in the list.

The following paragraphs list operations that are easier to execute in the List Editor than in the other Editors:
- Select the Program Change command from the Insert menu. Click the event at the desired position in the grid using the Pencil-pointer that automatically appears. The event will also appear in the list. Enter the required program number in the Value 1 column. If the Ear icon is active, the changes are sent via MIDI to the synthesizer whose receive channel matches the Track's MIDI channel, allowing you to immediately audition the Program Change.
- Delete the event(s) you have just created using "Delete" in the Function menu. Select the Stop command from the Insert menu and click it at the desired position in the grid. Ensure that the event is at a position beyond 1.1.0. Position 3.1.0 is fine for our purposes. Press [Return] to close the Editor and start playback from the beginning. Cubase stops at the position where you inserted the Stop event.
- Go back to the List Editor and delete the Stop event. Select Control Change from the Insert menu and enter a Control Change event in the grid. It defaults to number 0, with an amount of "0". This Control Change event, combined with Control Change 32 as an "MSB/LSB combination", denotes the relatively new Bank Select command. Let's assume that you want to access the various internal sound banks of a Korg Wavestation (as it happens, the Wavestation uses the LSB value (control change 32) only and ignores any MSB (control change 0)): enter a Control Change 0 event at the desired position in the grid and change it to Control Change 32 in the list. Its Value 2 determines the bank number: a value of "0" selects the RAM 1/2 bank, "1" the ROM/Card bank. You then *must* follow this by specifying the program within the bank using a Program Change event.

The Events' Statuses

- Keep in mind the following: according to the MIDI standard, the Bank Select command should consist of an MSB/LSB combination. However, the Wavestation ignores the MSB value, so you don't have to use it. Other devices may process Bank Select commands differently, so be sure to always take a look at the MIDI Implementation Chart of the device in question.
- Unfortunately, the number of devices capable of understanding Bank Select commands is rather limited at this time. Those that cannot, simply ignore them.
- The Key Editor is usually the preferable option for inserting and editing notes individually as the display is clearer and can show more notes at a time. If you still prefer the List Editor, use its display filter to simplify matters.
- The Mask, found only in the List Editor, is a valuable function. The Display Filter suppresses one or more complete statuses from the display; Mask, on the other hand, allows you to exclude certain events from any editing you are doing, e.g. using the commands in the Function sub-menu next door.
- Proceed as follows: supposing you accidentally entered a C4 note in a Part several times, select the note in the event list and click and hold the Mask sub-menu: select "Mask It" from the menu that appears. Now select Delete from the Function sub-menu, and all C4 notes are deleted from that Part. Select "No Mask" from the Mask menu, and all other events reappear.
- You can see that Mask It selects all the identical events in the Part and allows you to process them. "Identical" means that the status and the Value 1 column value have to be the same. "Mask Event Type" is used to mask all the events of a certain status. For our example, this would mean that *all* notes, not just C4's, are masked. One conceivable Mask application is deleting undesirable aftertouch data. The following diagrams illustrate how this is done.

Select the first Channel Pressure (aftertouch) event in the event list.

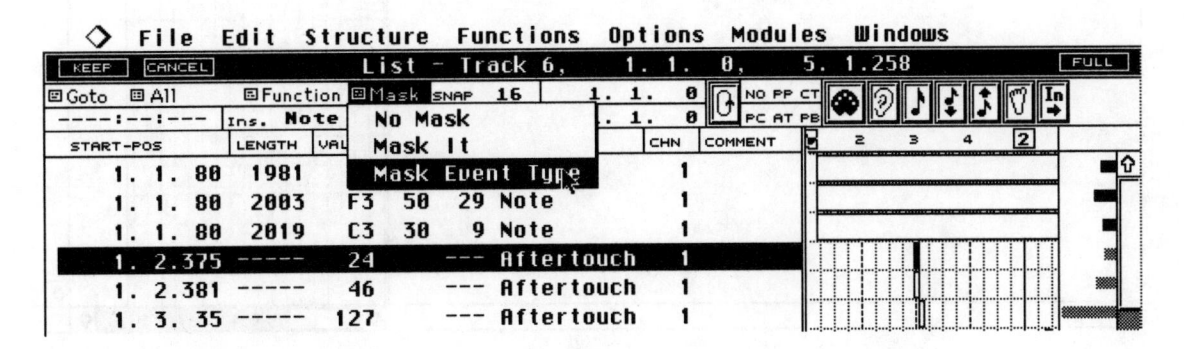

Activate Mask Event Type.

The List Editor

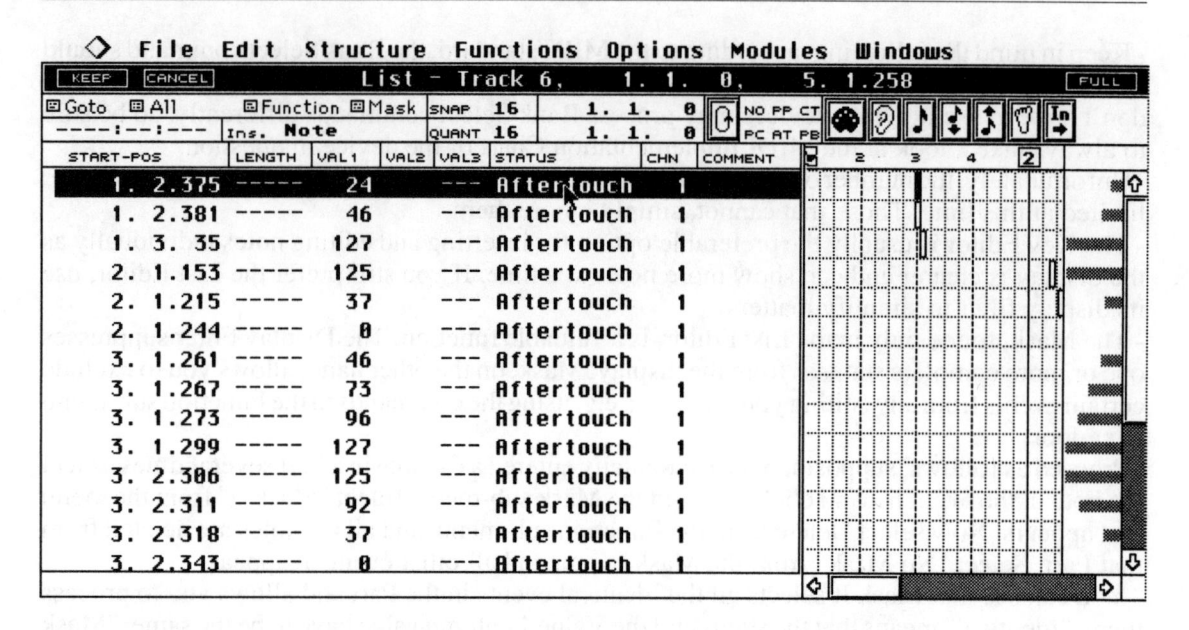

The list now displays Channel Pressure events only.

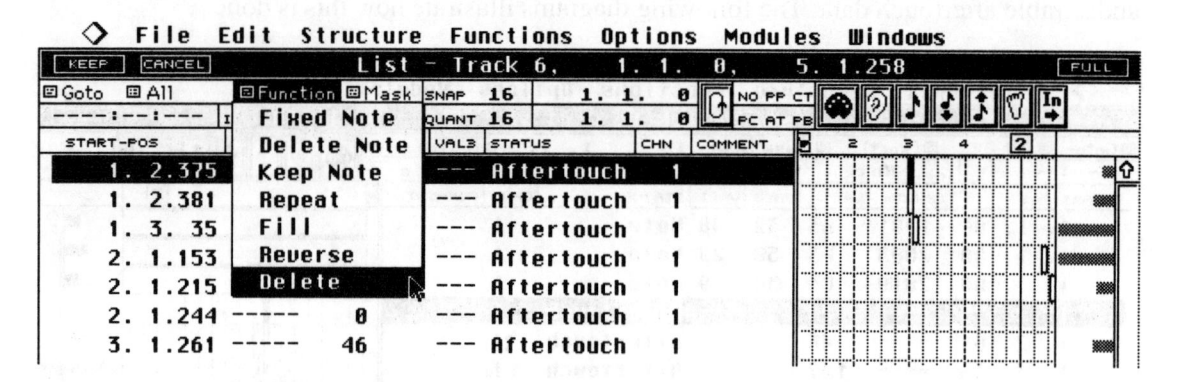

Ensure you activate All Events, then choose Delete in the Function sub-menu.

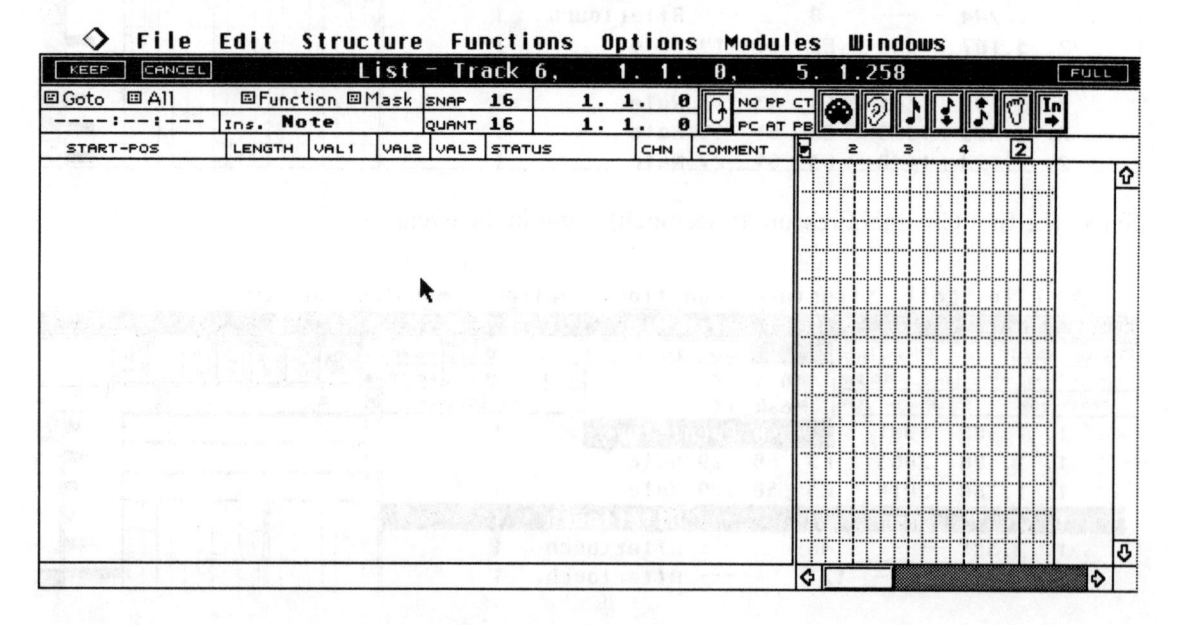

All Channel Pressure events are deleted.

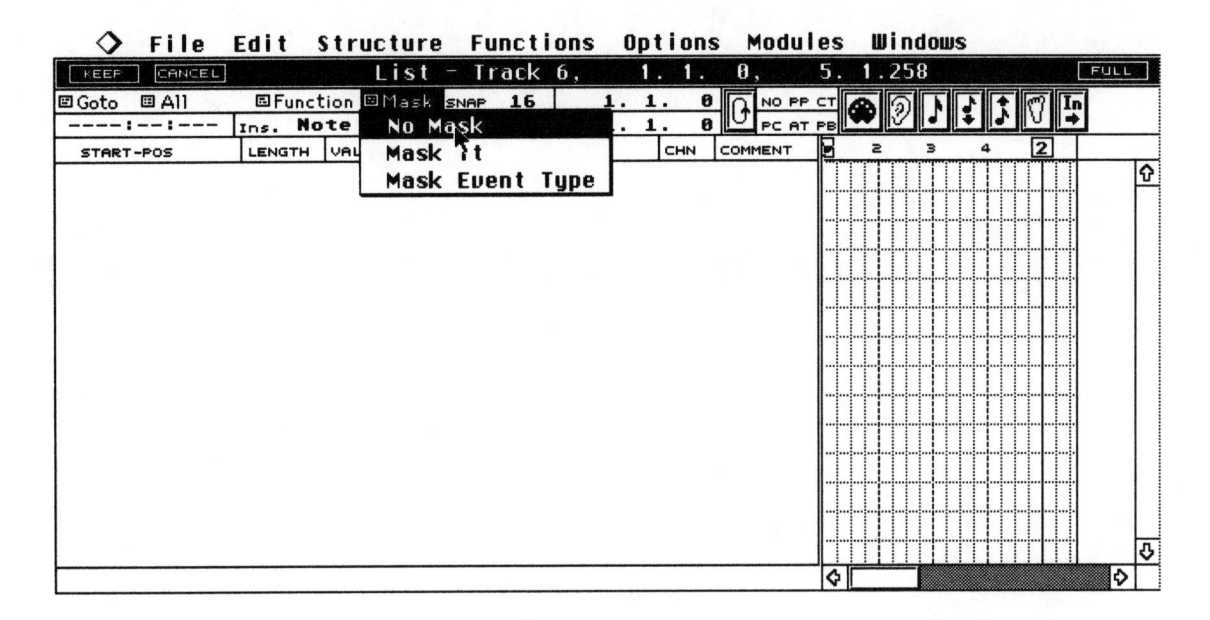

Now choose No Mask....

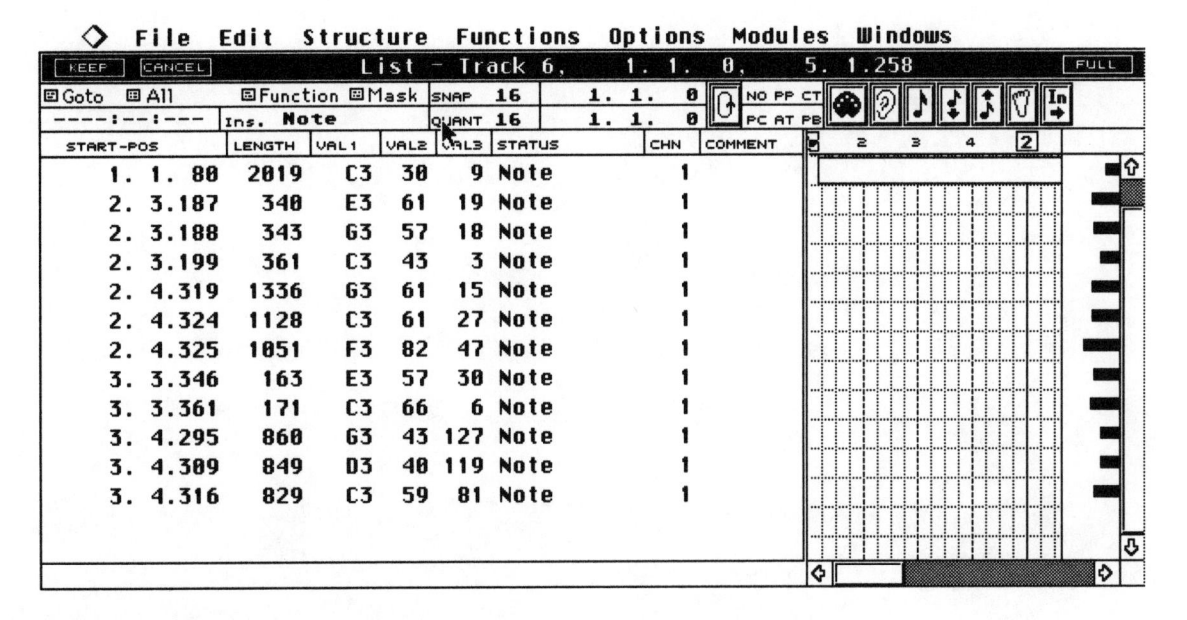

...and the notes return to the display.

Although you will encounter even more powerful editing tools, the Mask function is still a quick and easy way to process specific data of your choosing.

The List Editor

10 The Score Editor

The Editors we've looked at so far mainly rely on numerical graphics for editing operations; the Score Editor, however, is designed for those who prefer to work a bit more musically as it displays notes as regular notation.

The Score Editor is similar to the other Editors in many respects, so you should be able to find your way about it fairly quickly. It has two basic functions: editing notes in the context of a sequencer application, and management of staves and score. This chapter is concerned with the editing function; we'll cover its other faculties in a separate chapter.

We have mentioned before that the Score Editor is a Cubase module, which means that you must load it separately after Cubase is first started as described in chapter 7 on "Special Functions". If you habitually work with this Editor, you can have it load automatically whenever you start Cubase.

We need to define what is meant by a:

- Staff: a line of bars belonging to the Parts of one Track, e.g. "drum staff";

- Staves: the plural form of "staff", i.e. one staff, two staves;

- System: two or more staves that "belong together", e.g. a string quartet's staves constitute a system if they are included in a "score" (see below);

- Split System: sometimes called a double-staff or piano staff, this is where a Part is divided into a treble staff and a bass staff, e.g. "piano system";

- Score: what the conductor would look at, i.e. the entire collection of the music's staves arranged one below the other, e.g. if the string quartet (see above) were on its own, its four staves would constitute a score.

10.1 The relationship between Parts/Tracks and the notation

Cubase presents all selected Parts in the Score Editor. If no Parts are selected, it presents all the Parts of the active Track. Because Cubase is Part-oriented, the Score Editor display is dependent on the type and number of Parts presented in it. The following examples should help to explain this.

The Score Editor

A Part in the Editor

If you enter a Part of one single Track, Cubase displays as many bars as possible in staves, one above the other. Use the vertical scroll bar down the window's right edge to get to the remaining bars of a lengthy Part.

Two or more Parts of a single Track in the Score Editor

The same applies to several Parts of a single Track. Here as well, Cubase displays as many Parts as possible. The line at the bottom of the diagram above represents the screen's lower edge.

The remaining notes cannot be seen as they go beyond this line: use the right scroll bar to access them.

If you select one or more Parts on *different* Tracks, or *all* the Parts of an Arrangement, Cubase creates a separate staff for each Track, and will attempt to display as many notes as possible across the screen.

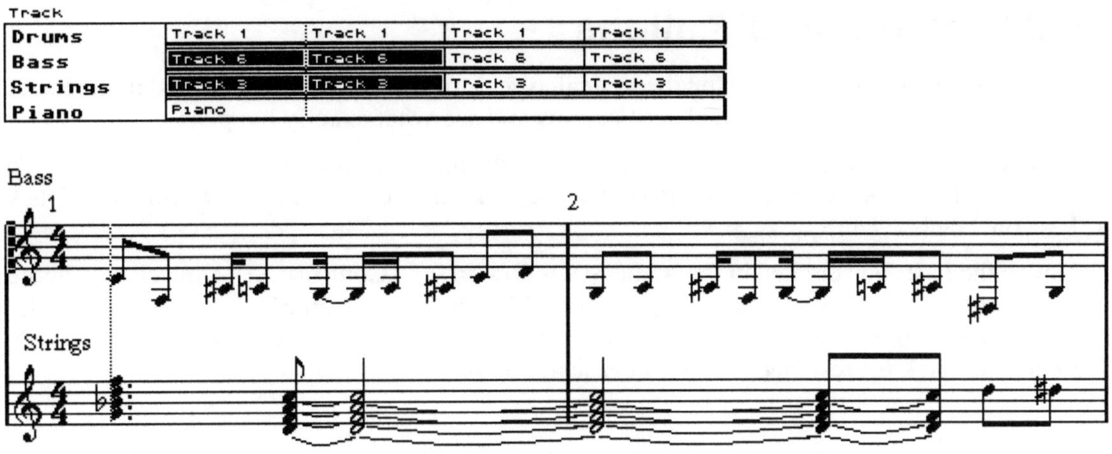

The Relationship between Parts/Tracks and the Notation

Several Parts on different Tracks in the Score Editor

This time, the bars disappear beyond the right screen edge. Use the horizontal scroll bar along the lower edge to access them.

The vertical scroll bar has another function when several Tracks are displayed in the Editor. Staves are laid out one below the other, so it accesses the staves that lie below the lower screen edge when there are too many to be seen at once. A maximum of 16 Tracks can be presented in the Editor, though these can each contain as many Parts as you like.

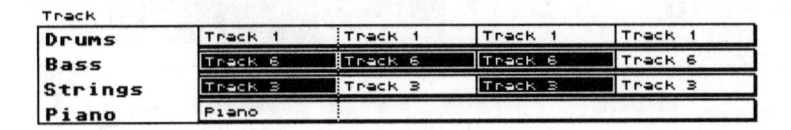

Several non-sequential Parts in the Score Editor

The selected Parts do not have to be in sequence. Cubase creates rests for the missing Parts: these rests are seen in the Score Editor only; the notes in the Parts are still there and are played as normal, except you won't see them in the Score Editor.

The above illustration shows position 5.1.0, between the first two Parts. Both bass Parts are selected and appear in the display, but whereas the strings' first Part is selected and displayed, the second Part is not selected, so Cubase displays rests even though the Part actually still contains notes. The lower scroll bar moves the display horizontally to access the notes before or after what's currently on the screen, the right scroll bar moves it vertically to access other Tracks' staves.

10.1.1 In general

Make sure you thoroughly understand the relationship between Parts/Tracks and the way they are displayed in the Score Editor. As you read through the chapter, experiment with one or more Parts.

The Score Editor

10.2 Practical applications

So far we have merely discussed the theoretical aspects of how Parts are presented in the Score Editor. Now let's try some practical applications and see what exactly happens.

For our first exercise create a new Arrangement featuring several Parts on several Tracks. To benefit from the book's examples, try to stick to the structure we used before, i.e. drums on Track 1, bass on Track 2, etc.

Select all the Parts you created in the Arrange window so far ([Control][A]). Now choose Score Editor from the Edit menu ([Control][R]). You could, of course, enter the Score Editor by double-clicking a Part provided the setting in the Preferences dialog box is correct, but in this case only the Part you click is presented, not all the selected Parts.

All the Parts in an Arrangement are selected...

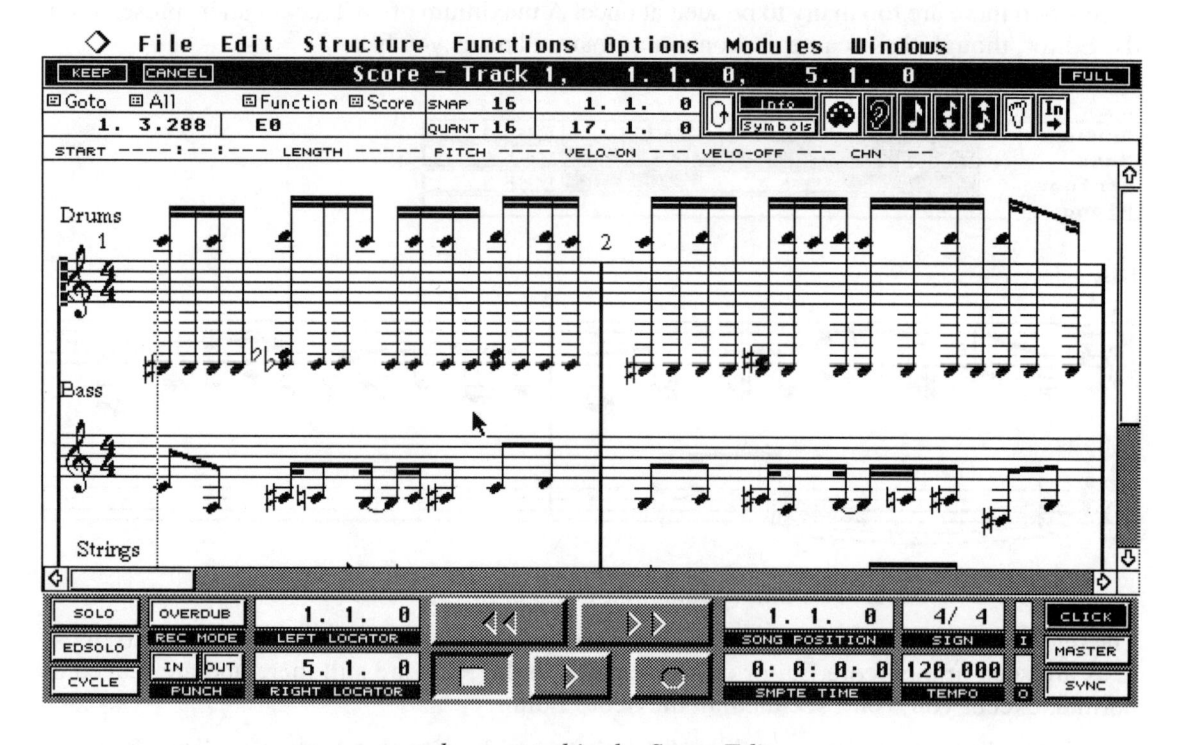

...and presented in the Score Editor

Cubase now displays all the Parts as notation. Each Track has its own staff, with the Parts arranged one after the other in their respective staves. The staves are arranged one below the other according to the order of the Tracks in the Arrange window.

If you change the order of the Tracks in the Arrange window, the Score Editor displays the changes accordingly.

The bars which lie beyond the screen are accessed by the scroll bars, as we have discussed. A click on the horizontal arrows scrolls the notation forward/back a bar. A click in the speckled bar "turns the page". You cannot zoom the Score Editor display in the usual fashion. More on this topic later.

Practical Applications

Start the playback. The Song Position Triangle starts to move and shows the current song position. Once it reaches the right edge, the score display automatically flips to the next bars. This may take a moment, depending on the number of notes involved and your computer's performance specifications. Here, too, you can switch the automatic scrolling off using Follow Song in the Options menu or [F].

The options used in the previous Editors to access particular song positions apply here as well:
- The fast forward and rewind buttons.
- Enter the desired position in the Song Position box via a double-click and typed input or use of the left/right mouse buttons.
- Press [Clr/Home] to move the song position to the first bar displayed in the Editor window.
- Press and hold [Alternate] and then click a position in the notation with the right mouse button to move the song position to this spot.

You can work in this Editor during recording and playback, as with the other Editors.

Now stop Cubase and set the song position back to the beginning.

10.2.1 The screen layout

You now know how Parts are presented in the Editor and how to move about in the notation. So let's take a closer look at this Editor.

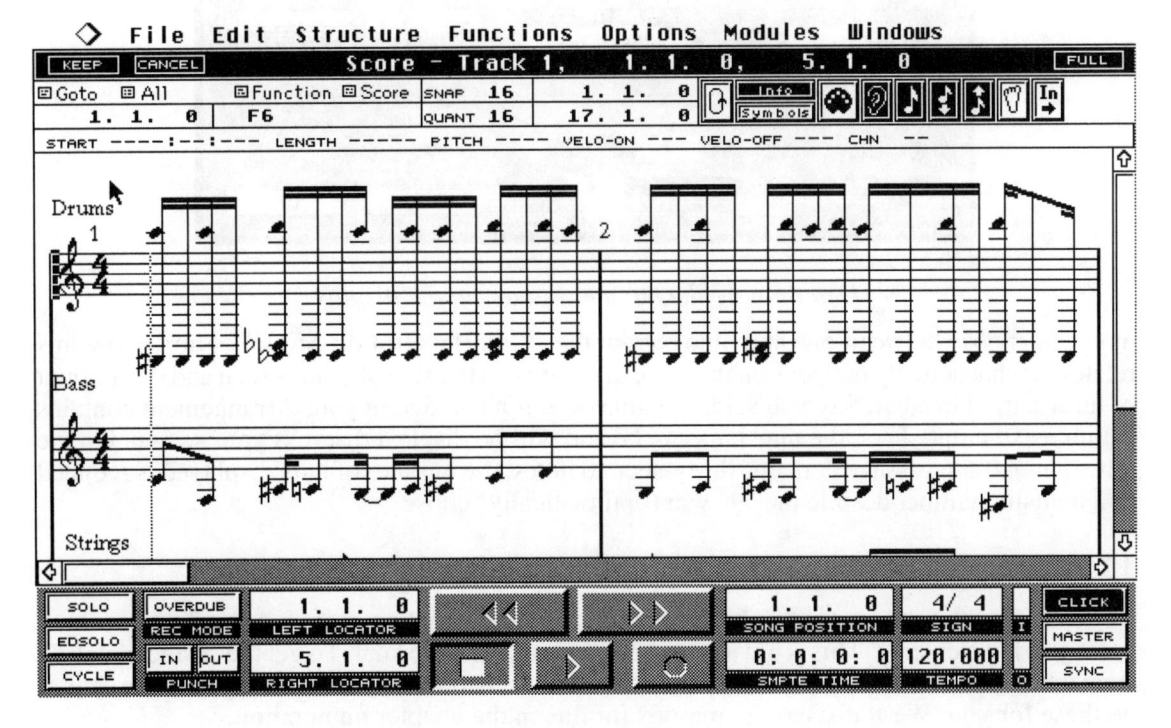

The Score Editor

The Title Bar across the top of the screen displays the currently active Part and Track.

Below it comes the Functions Bar with the usual functions (Goto, Selection and Function menus, etc.); a number of icons which you will be familiar with; the Snap, Quantize, Mouse Position displays; and the edit loop boundaries. You will recognize these from the previous Editors, but you will find out as we proceed that some functions are different.

The Info Line, which we came across in the Key Editor, is situated between the notation display and the Functions Bar, and gives detailed information on selected notes. It can be removed from your screen by clicking the Info button or pressing [Alternate][I]. You can determine how many bars Cubase displays at a time by clicking and holding "Global Settings" in the Score sub-menu.

179

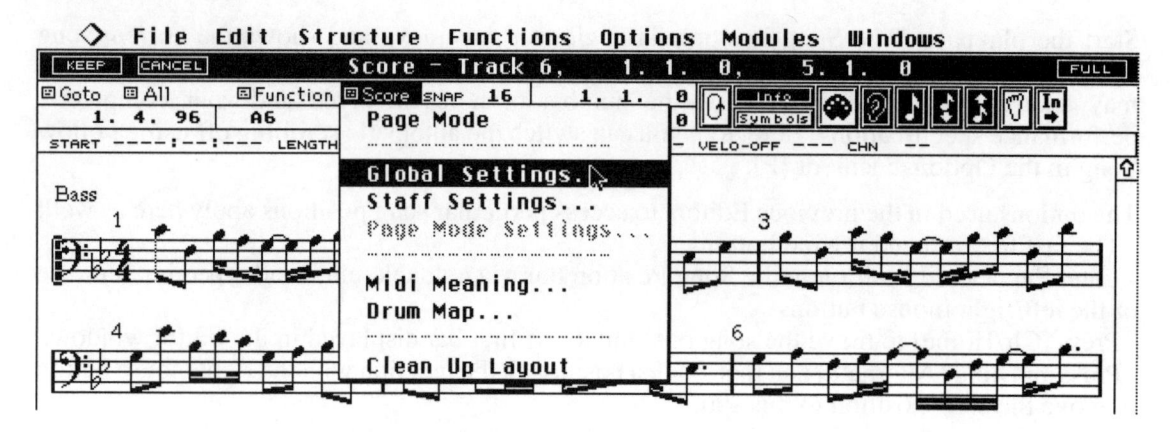

The Score Editor

Global Settings in the Score sub-menu

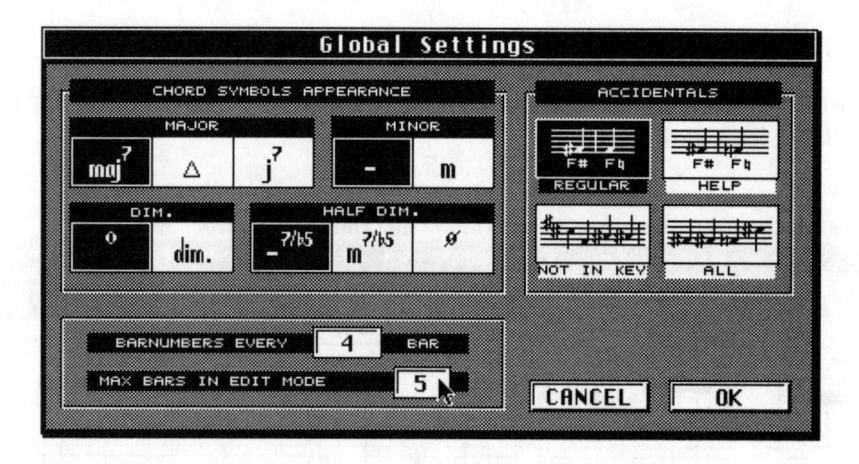

Determining the number of bars in the display

You can choose between one and nine bars in the "Max Bars in Edit Mode" option. How this relates to what actually happens on the screen depends on the size of your screen and the amount of information in a bar. Say you select a value of 9. If a passage in your Arrangement contains a number of empty bars, the nine bars can be and will be displayed across your screen. On the other hand, if the passage contains thirty-second notes, the number of bars displayed is reduced to a realistic number despite the "9" you (optimistically) chose.

10.2.2 Display options

You may find some aspects of Cubase's notation slightly irritating at first, depending on which notes you have entered. This is not a program error; it's quite normal. To get the correct notation from what you have played, there are parameters you need to set manually - sadly, Cubase cannot do these for you. We'll discuss the reasons for this in the chapter on notation.

What we want to do at this stage is to eliminate the major inconsistencies so that the editing of notes is made easier. This is done using a large number of things called "display options" that help make the display clearer and more realistic.

The basic display of staves
Click anywhere in the first staff to select it - a little black rectangle appears before the clef. Double-clicking a staff's clef enables you to select its clef and key: there are lots of display options available, only a few of which relate to the editing of notes.

The correct clef and key
If you have recorded a bass line or other passage in the lower/upper registers, Cubase makes use of ledger lines which can hinder readability, depending on which clef is in use. To change the

Practical Applications

clef to one that suits, double-click that staff's clef (let's assume it's the bass staff we are discussing - leave any drum Tracks as they are for now).

You can now enter the correct clef and key signature in the dialog box that appears. Click the clef with the left or right mouse button to select all the available kinds of clef, one after the other, i.e. bass, treble clef, etc.

The second option concerns the key signature. Click the staff next to the clef with the left or right mouse button. Each click moves the key up or down by a fifth. If you start at the default key of C, the right button calls up G, D, A, etc. and the left button F, B, Eb, etc.

Close the dialog box after you have entered all settings by clicking OK or pressing [Return] and Cubase will enter the settings in the display. Cancel or [Esc] takes you back to the Score Editor without executing any of the settings in the dialog box.

The following diagram illustrates how a bass Track was assigned the correct clef and the key of Bb major. Keep in mind that any alterations you make apply to the selected staff only, and that alterations are displayed only after you have pressed OK or [Return]. Use of Cancel or [Esc] aborts any settings you may have made.

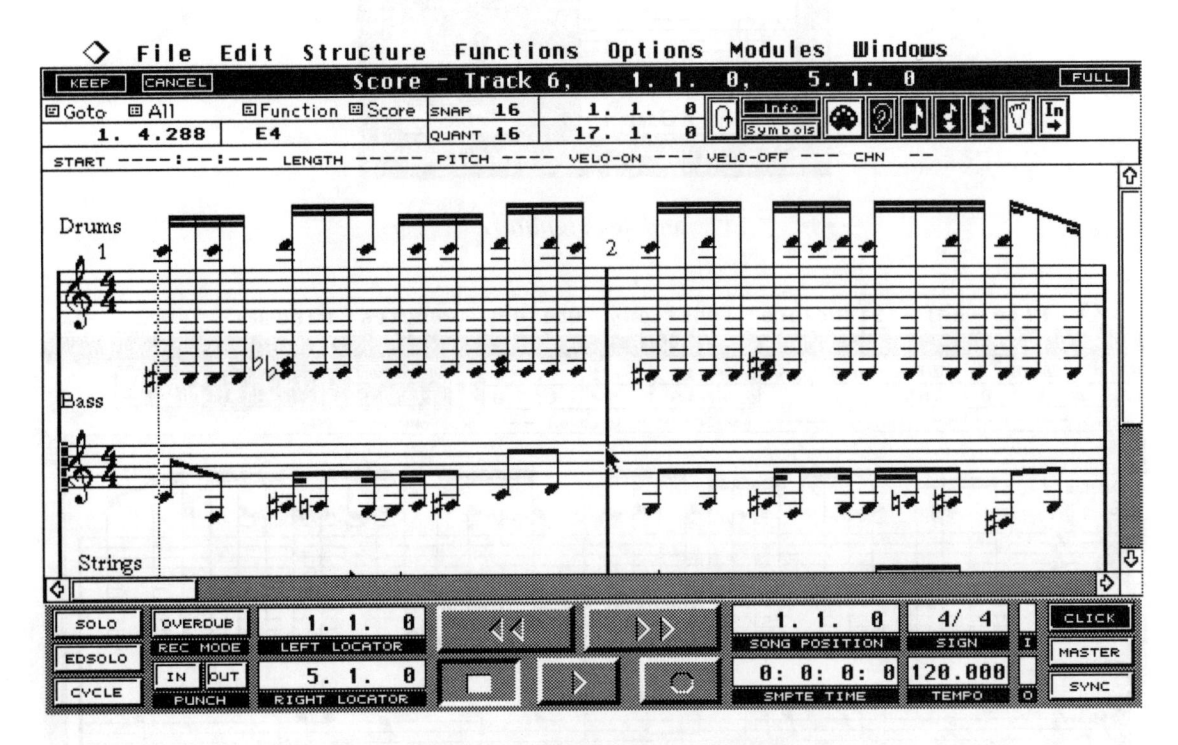

The bass Track has been selected for editing

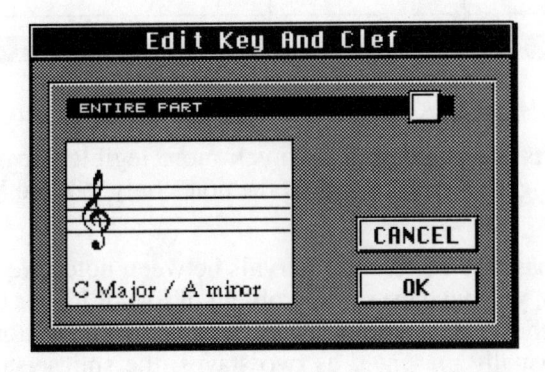

Double-clicking the staff's clef symbol opens the dialog box

181

The Score Editor

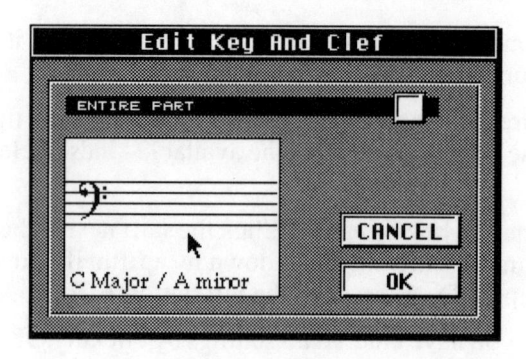

Clicking with the left or right mouse button selects the desired clef...

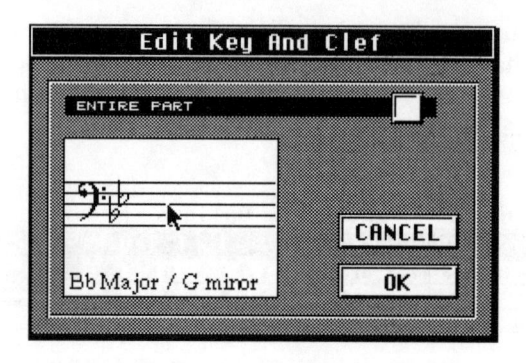

...and key signature

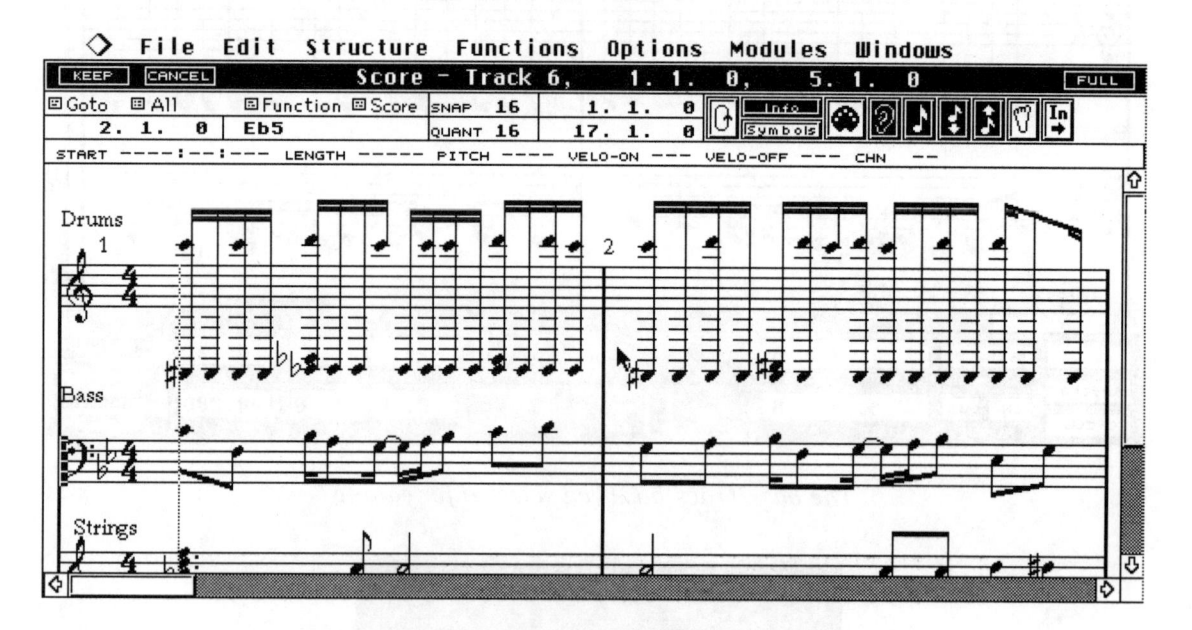

Use of "OK" applies the settings to the display

The result of your efforts is notation that is much more legible. Bear in mind that all these alterations you are making affect the *display* of the notes only, not the MIDI notes themselves.

Split systems
If you have recorded a passage where the intervals between notes are substantial, as happens when you play the piano, you have the same problem of lots of ledger lines getting in the way. The following example shows a piano Part in the Editor. This illustration shows a fairly chaotic scene. Piano Parts are usually presented as two staves, the split system. Click and hold the "Score" sub-menu and select "Staff Settings" in the pop-up menu that appears.

Practical Applications

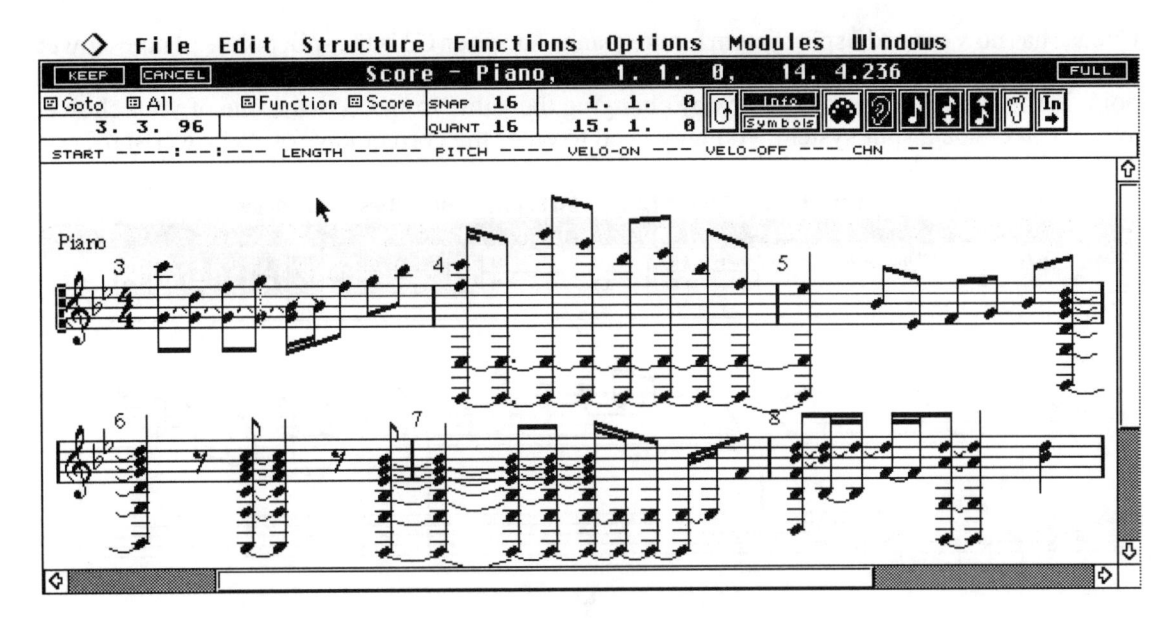

The original piano Part already features the correct key

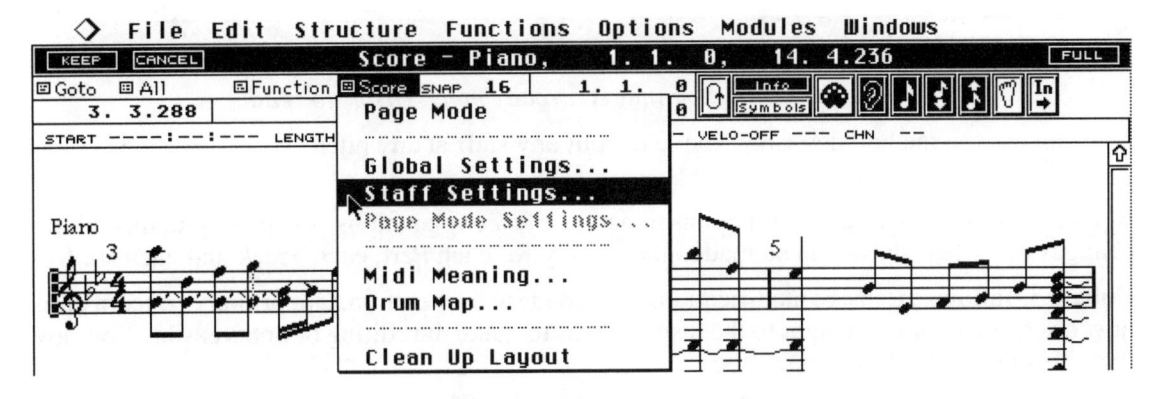

Selecting "Staff Settings"...

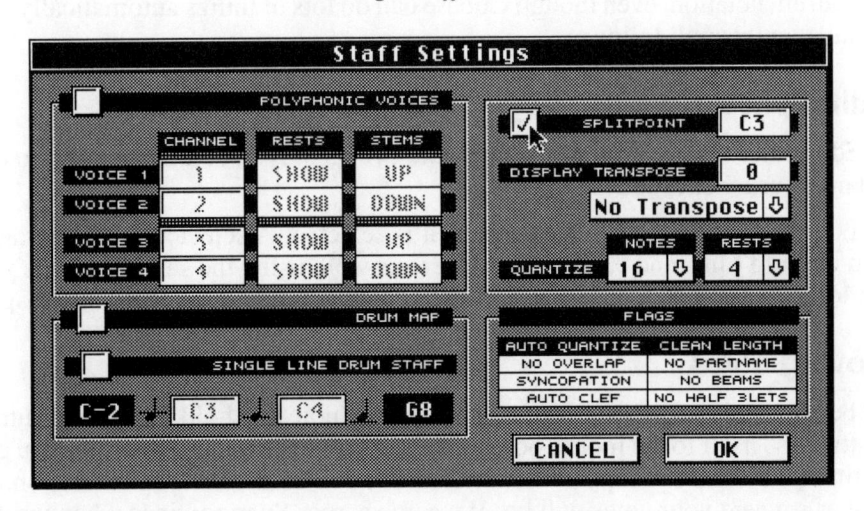

....and choosing the split point

The dialog box contains a number of options: for the moment, we are interested in the split point only. Activate it by clicking the empty box to its left so a checkmark appears and close the box via OK or [Return].

The Score Editor

Cubase has now created a split system for the piano. The pitch C3 is the split point: all notes lower than C3 are displayed in the bottom staff, those above it in the upper one. You can alter the split point in the Staff Settings dialog box by changing the value from C3 to the one of your choice. When you create a split system, you may need to enter the correct key for the lower staff.

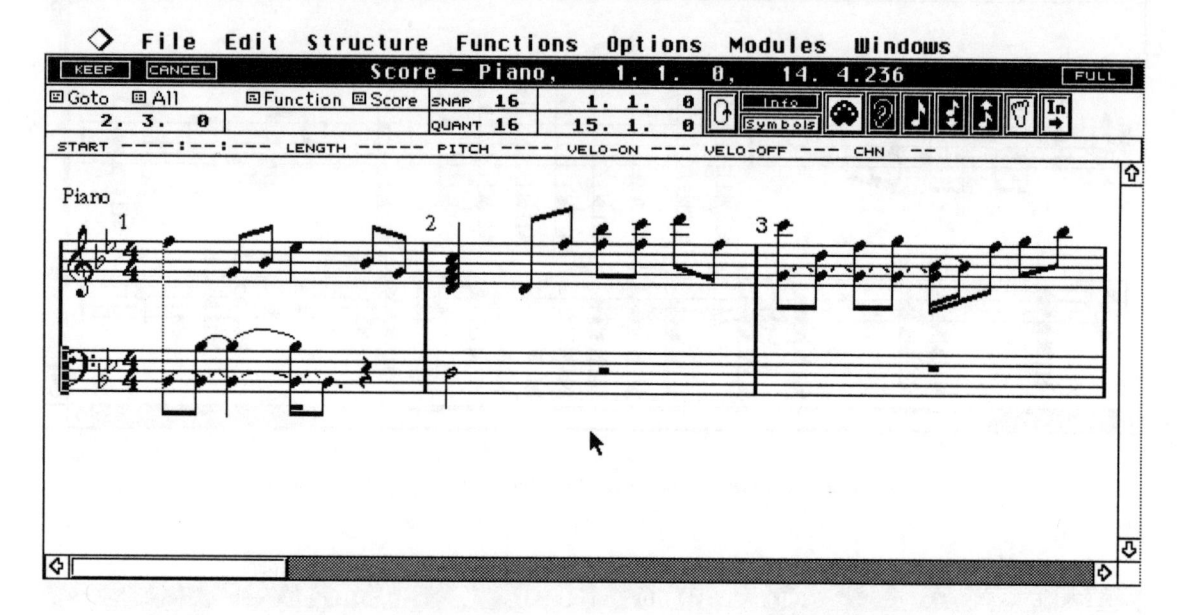

The result is notation that is already much easier to read

You can use the method described above to split any staff at any pitch.

Summary
Before we go on to the editing functions in detail, a few explanations. Keep in mind that all the changes described above can be made individually for each Part, each Track and each staff.

Cubase 3.0 allows extensive modifications to be made to the notation. Our primary concern until now has been to make changes to the display so as to make the editing of notes easier. You saw that this only took a few simple steps.

These few steps are not sufficient for detailed, absolutely correct notation, especially for special cases such as drum notation, even though Cubase can do lots of things automatically. However, fear not, details on this will follow.

10.2.3 Editing notes

The Score Editor allows you to view and edit note events only. You cannot use it to edit MIDI Control Changes or other events.

Click the first note. It highlights, which means it is selected. A selected note's parameters are displayed in the Info Line, and can be edited there as well, using the same methods you met in the Key Editor. Changes made via mouse click are immediately reflected in the display.

10.2.4 Moving notes

Events can be edited directly in the notation. Select any note and hold the mouse button down. The note "attaches" itself to the mouse pointer. If you move the note right or left you change its position in time. It can only occupy positions that are allowed by the Snap resolution. If it is set to eighths, that's where your notes will go. We came across Snap routines when we dealt with the other Editors.

Moving the note up or down changes the selected note's pitch accordingly. The amount of transposition is displayed as semitone intervals in the "Transpose" field which appears next to the Mouse Position field.

Practical Applications

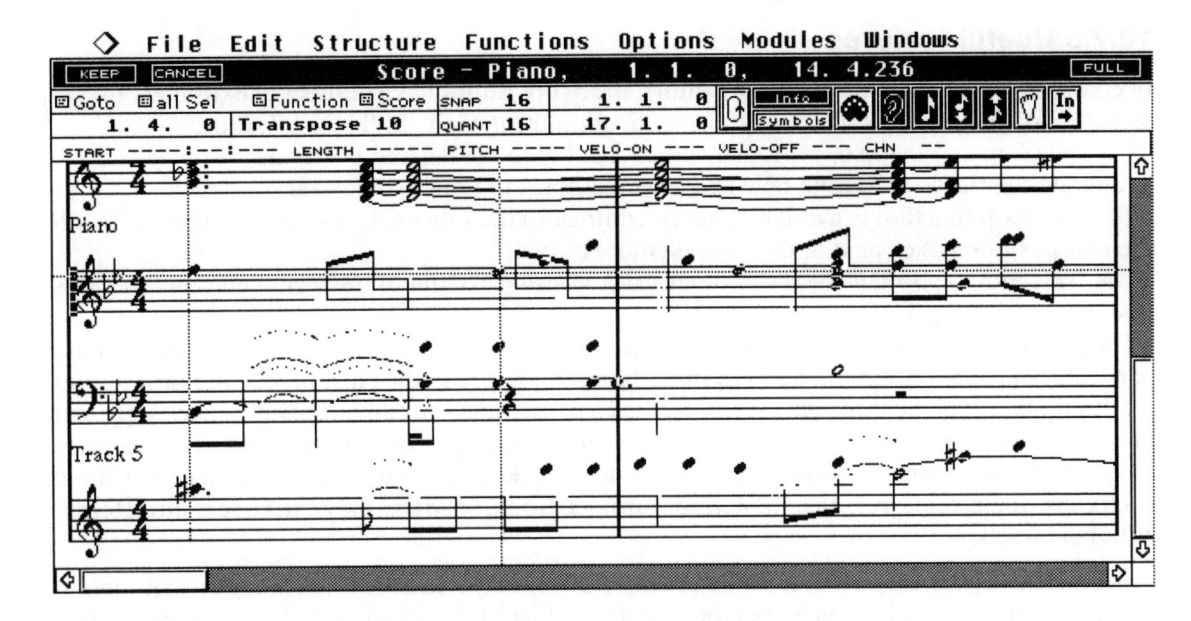

Notes can be moved in a number of ways

Several basic rules apply when working with notes, which are ones you will recognize from the other Editors. Here's a brief review:
- Several notes can be selected simultaneously in different staves and then edited together: press and hold [Shift] and click the desired notes one after another.
- The familiar rubber band can also be used here: activate it by clicking an empty space and dragging the mouse while holding the mouse button down. It selects all notes it touches or encloses, even if they are in different staves.
- Use the right and left cursor keys to jump from one note to another within a staff. If you hold [Shift] down at the same time, the notes are selected.
- The up and down cursor keys are used to go from one staff to another. If you hold [Shift] down at the same time, additional notes are selected.
- If you select and move several notes at the same time, the relative intervals between them are maintained.
- Pitch changes are normally "diatonic", i.e. the pitch intervals are dictated by the selected key: say you are in the key of C major, and you want to transpose a "C" note. The intervals you are able to change to will be those of the C major scale: D, E, F up, and B, A, G down. If you need the "in-between" (chromatic) values, hold [Control] down while transposing the note, and you will be able to access the semitones (C#, D#, Bb, etc.).
- You can change a note's pitch and position at the same time. Just release the mouse button when the note is where you want it to be.
- Don't rely on the notation display when you reposition a note, but watch the Mouse position display for its precise position.
- If you want to change just the pitch, or just the position, first select the note by clicking it, and keep the mouse button pressed down. Press and hold [Shift]. Your next mouse movement tells Cubase what your intentions are: if you move the note vertically, Cubase assumes that you want to transpose it and will prevent you from moving it in time. On the other hand, if you start by moving the note horizontally, you can only change its time position, and transposition becomes impossible. These two options are very useful as they ensure you make the right move.
- Pressing [Alternate] at the same time as selecting a note creates a copy of it. Copies, too, can only be transposed diatonically unless you press [Control][Alternate] to access the chromatic semitones. Use [Shift] to limit the range of this operation.
- Notes can be moved from one staff to another with the help of the key combinations described above.
- [Delete] or [Backspace] deletes the notes that are selected.

The Score Editor

10.2.5 Useful features

In common with all the other Cubase Editors, the Score Editor has a number of extremely useful features. We ran through these, from a practical point-of-view, in the Key Editor:
- Use the Goto sub-menu to move the screen display to the desired position.
- Activate the Ear icon to send new and selected notes to your synthesizer.
- The edit loop function is available, but in contrast to the other Editors you can define it with the two position boxes next to the Loop symbol only.
- The "selection" sub-menu next to Goto is used, as usual, to limit the effect of certain functions (Quantize, Clipboard, etc.) on specific notes.
- The Function *sub-menu* contains the same features you have already met, plus others that are particular to the Score Editor. Most of these functions apply to the page layout and printing, so we'll skip these for the moment. However, the Explode function can be useful for Arrangement purposes as it divides a multi-voiced staff into single-note lines in separate staves (i.e. separate Tracks): if you recorded a string ensemble on one Track, you can use this function to distribute each constituent voice to a separate staff for further editing, or so that they can be sent on different MIDI channels.

To "explode" a staff, select it first. You can only work on *one* Track at a time, though it can contain as many Parts as you like (remember that a staff = a Track). Unselected Parts remain untouched by any exploding.

Try it out. Record a Track containing chords in the Arrange window and select it. Go to the Score Editor.

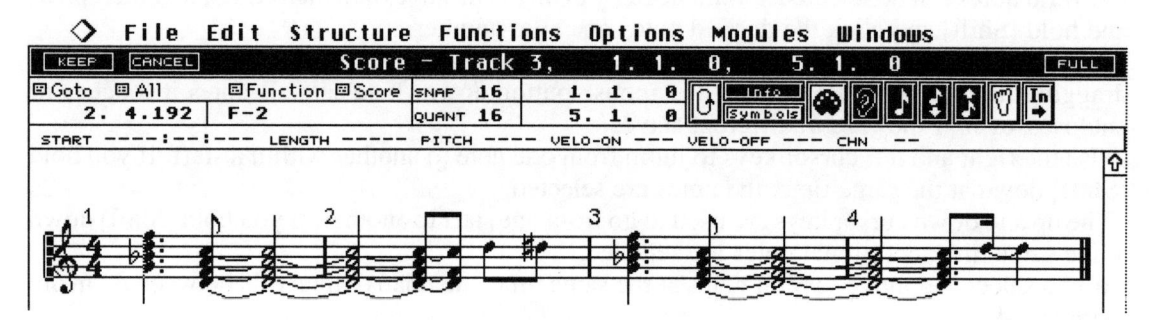

This is the Part to be "exploded"

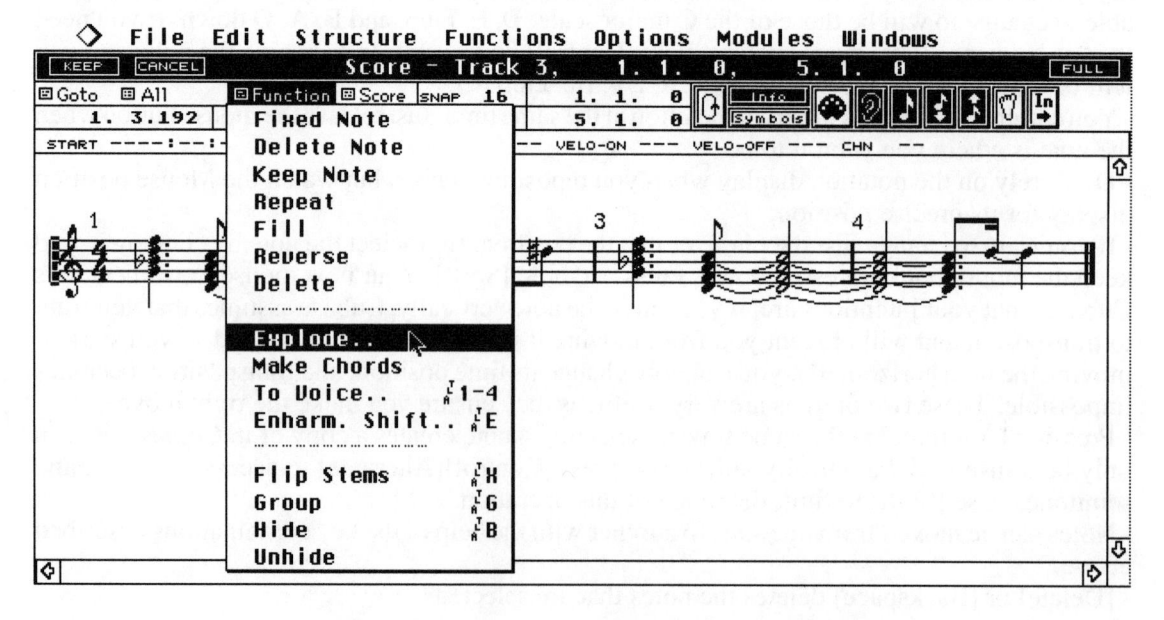

Select Explode from the Function sub-menu

Practical Applications

Selecting Explode makes the following dialog box appear:

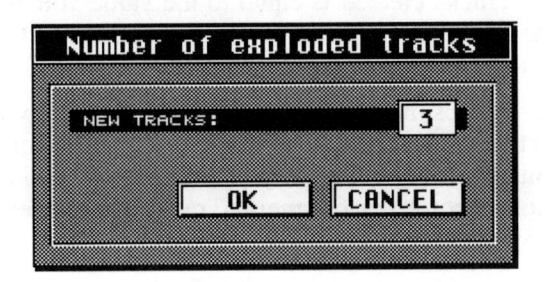

How many new Tracks do you want?

Tell Cubase how many separate staves you want to extract. Enter a value of 3. Once you confirm via OK or [Return], the Track "explodes". Cubase creates new Tracks containing the new Parts and appends them below the existing Arrangement. The original Track now contains the highest note of each position where there was a note or chord; the remaining notes are assigned, in descending order of pitch, to the new Tracks which have been appended below the Arrangement's existing Tracks.

The result is new Tracks...

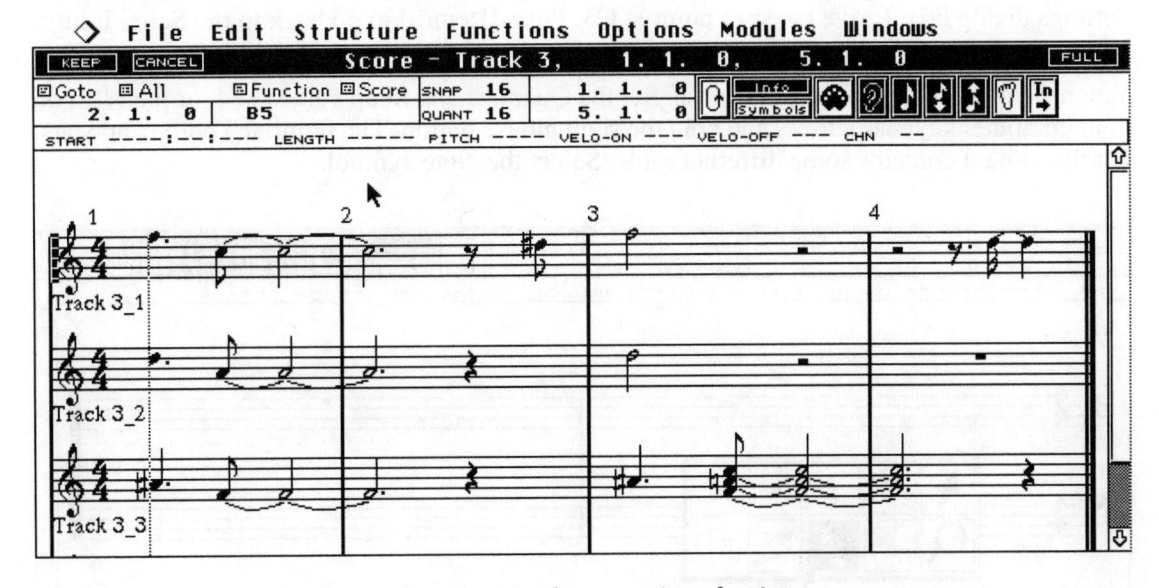

...that contain the re-assigned voices

Out of a chord consisting of Bb, G, Eb, and C, the original Track retains only the Bb, which is

187

The Score Editor

the highest one of the notes at that particular time position. G is moved to a new Track of its own, and so on. The number of Tracks created is equal to the value you entered. A value of 1, for instance, would extract the upper melody line only. Keep in mind that Cubase sorts notes strictly by pitch only, not by musical, quasi-polyphonic criteria.

To quickly achieve the desired result, you have to know what the maximum number of notes is at any position: remember to include the original Track in your calculations. To create a "one line per Track" situation, the number of new Tracks you define must be one less than the number of notes in your most polyphonic chord. You can merge Tracks you have exploded at any time using Mixdown in the Arrange window.

10.2.6 Creating notes

Step inputting and the direct entry of notes is, in the main, identical to the methods used in the other Editors. To practise a little, we'll step-input a short musical phrase. Create a blank Part in an empty Track in the Arrange window and make it two bars long (1.1.0 to 3.1.0). Assign the Track's MIDI channel to a synthesizer capable of producing piano sounds and go to the Score Editor. Ensure you have only entered this one Part in the Editor.

We'll use a simple phrase to demonstrate all the more complex step input functions. The following diagram illustrates how this phrase will look when we've finished.

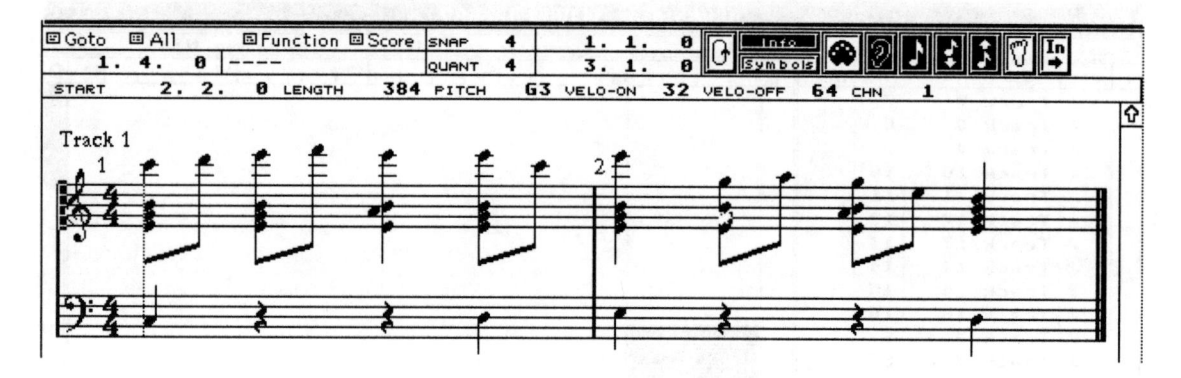

Step-inputting a simple example

First we want to use a split system: go to the Score sub-menu and activate Split Point in the Staff Settings dialog box. Leave the split point at C3. Press [Return] to go back to the Score Editor. Now enter the bass line in the lower staff.

You need quarter notes for this purpose. Set the Quantize and Snap values to 4, or press [3] on your computer keyboard. Press and hold the right mouse button. The familiar Toolbox appears, but this time it contains some different tools. Select the Note symbol.

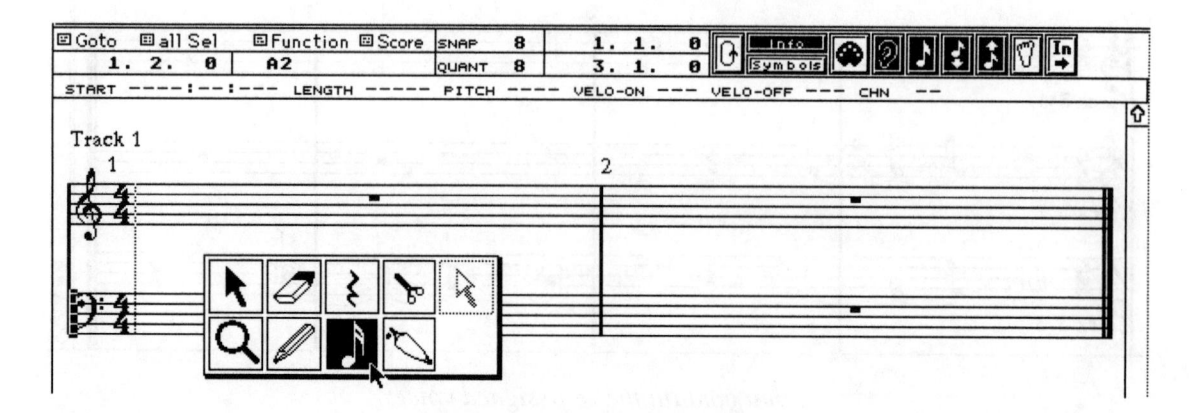

Select the Note from the Toolbox

Practical Applications

The mouse cursor changes from the Arrow to the Note. The Note tool's value always reflects the selected Quantize value - in our case, a quarter note. Do you remember the relevance Snap and Quantize values have when you're entering notes directly? The Quantize value dictates the length of the note about to be inserted, the Snap value its position in so far as it determines where you can move the mouse pointer.

Move the Note tool to position 1.1.0 of the lower staff. You may have to rewind Cubase back to the start. The Mouse position display helps you with this.

Move the mouse horizontally. You can see that the mouse pointer moves in quarter note intervals as dictated by the Snap value. The current pitch is displayed in the field beside it. Move the mouse vertically and you will see that the mouse moves in C major diatonic intervals only. If you need semitones, press and hold [Control] while entering notes.

Luckily, we don't need semitones for this exercise. Go to the lower staff's 1.1.0 position, at a pitch of C2. Click that position once. A C2 note is created. If the Ear icon is active, the note is sent directly to your synthesizer.

Keep the golden rule in mind: a staff must be active before you can enter a note, as designated by the little black rectangle in front of the clef. In our example, it is possible that the upper staff was the active one; if this was the case, our first click in the lower staff did not insert the note, but merely selected it: you need to click again to insert the note. This only applies to the first operation in an inactive staff.

Now insert an E2 at position 1.4.0, keeping an eye on the position displays. If you need to correct a note's positioning, call up the Toolbox, activate the Arrow and use it to drag the note to the correct position.

Insert the four bass notes.

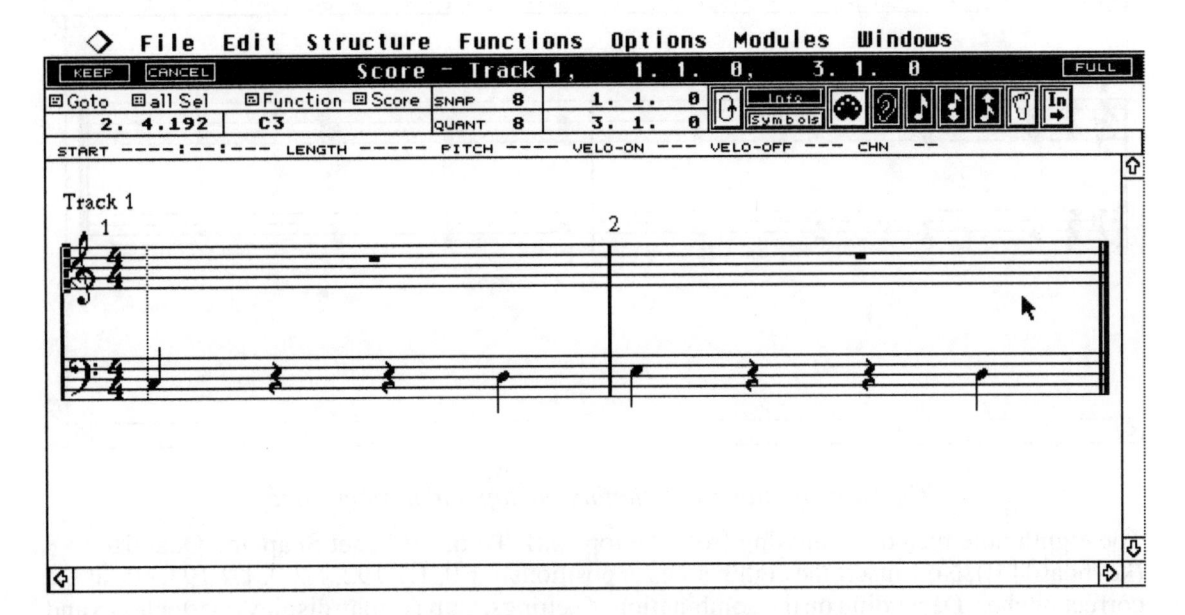

The bass notes are in place

Let's go to the upper staff. Click it to activate it. If it was already active when you clicked it, you may have accidentally entered a note! There are two ways you can remove this note. Select the Eraser from the Toolbox, place it on the incorrect note and click once. The other method is a little more versatile: select the mouse Arrow from the Toolbox, select the incorrect note by clicking it and press [Delete] or [Backspace] to remove it. This method has the advantage that pressing and holding [Shift] allows you to select as many notes as you please and delete them. Moreover, you can select the rubber band for this operation.

If you have activated the "In" symbol in the Functions Bar, you are in a position to delete notes

The Score Editor

from a staff and the notes that follow it will automatically move earlier by a corresponding amount.

Back to our example. Use the Note tool to go to position 1.1.0 and E3 in the upper staff. Insert the note. We also need G3 and B3 at the same position, with their respective pitches above the E3. Make quite sure the "In" symbol in the Functions Bar is not active, since if it is, the notes cannot be inserted as a chord; instead, each time you enter a note, Cubase moves the existing notes later by one Snap position.

The second chord is identical to the first, so you can copy the first one: use the mouse arrow and the rubber band function to select the whole chord. Press and hold [Alternate] and click the chord with the mouse pointer, press and hold [Shift] and copy the chord to position 1.2.0.

Now release [Alternate] and [Shift]. You have just copied the chord. [Shift] ensures you alter the position, not the pitch.

Now enter the third chord. Place the fourth chord at position 1.4.0 using the same copying operation. The same holds true for the second bar: select all the chords in the first bar with the rubber band and copy the whole lot to position 2.1.0.

The upper staff is halfway finished. Let's listen to the result: activate Ed Solo in the Transport Bar and create an edit loop two bars in length. Here's a quick memory refresher: activate the loop symbol, set the bar positions next to it to 1.1.0 (top) and 3.1.0 (bottom). Click Ed Solo and start playback. Cubase repeatedly plays the two bars.

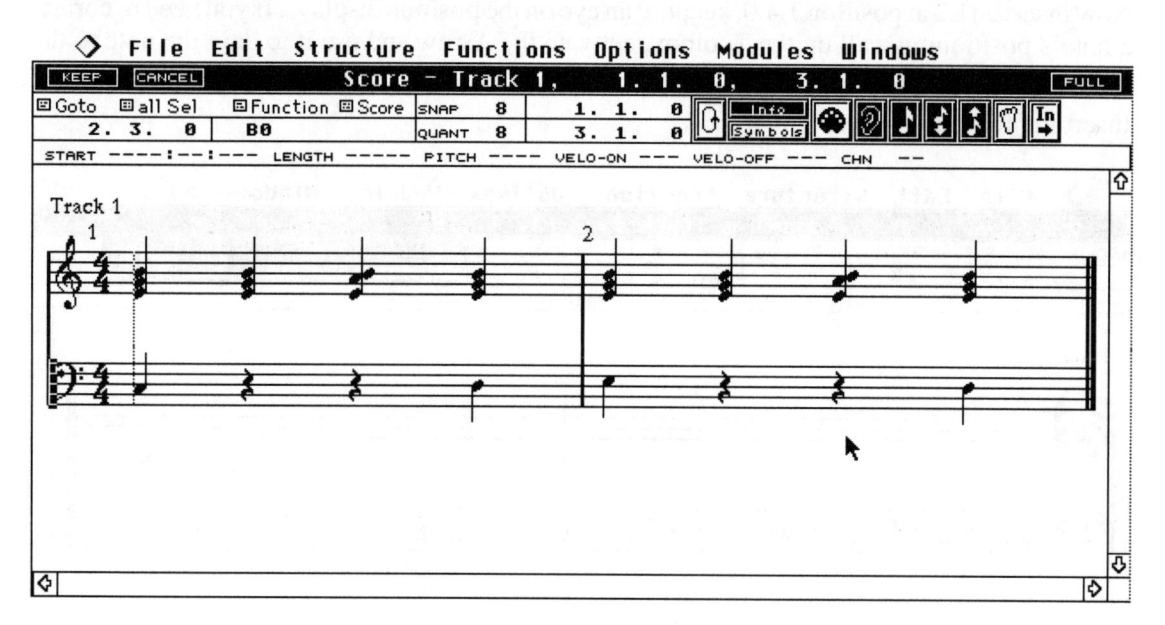

The halfway stage: auditioning the top and bottom staves

The eighth note melody is missing from the top staff. To insert it, set Snap and Quantize to 8 (keyboard [4]). Now insert the eighth notes at positions 1.1.0, 1.1.192, 1.2.0, 1.2.192, etc. at the correct pitches. Depending on the combination of settings, Cubase may display quarter notes and not eighths: don't let it worry you, since the entries are correct. It's just that Cubase hasn't recognized these notes as being of the melody voice yet, and so begins by assigning them to the chords values.

While you are inserting notes, bear in mind that you can manipulate the velocity values using [Shift] and/or [Control] as in the other Editors.

10.2.7 Additional Toolbox functions

The Toolbox features two additional functions. We'll save the Pencil tool for the chapter on score printout. The Glue tool merges two notes of the *same* pitch: where, say, two eighths of the same

190

pitch are next each other, clicking the first one with the Glue tool converts the two eighths into a quarter note. You can use this function to create notes not featured in the Quantize menu, such as a sixteenth tied to an eighth note.

We have already covered the Magnifying Glass extensively. The Rest tool is obviously used to insert rests. Rest lengths are dictated by the Quantize value. The effect of inserting a rest is to move all the following events later, regardless of whether the "In" icon is active or not.

10.2.8 Note input via MIDI

We covered this function in the Key Editor. The following section may serve as a quick review.

Let's create a new Part in the Arrange window, open the Score Editor and create a split system. Activate its upper staff to enter new notes. Activate the Foot icon in the Functions Bar for step entry. Notes entered via MIDI are always entered at the current Step Position: the insert position is displayed to the left of the bottom scroll bar.

We covered the basic function of this display and its relationship to the Song Position box in the Transport Bar when we discussed the Key Editor. In contrast to the other Editors, the Step Position in the Score Editor window does not follow the display in the Transport Bar. This means that you can only change the position manually, and not via fast forward/rewind or similar operations.

Go to position 1.1.0 and click it. For the above reason, refer to the Step Position display in the Editor window, not the one in the Transport Bar. Snap and Quantize should be set to eighths. Play the first chord of the upper staff on your master MIDI keyboard. The velocity values you are generating are recorded as well.

Cubase jumps to the next Snap position once you release the keys, i.e. to 1.1.192. Enter the chord sequence till the top staff's three bars are full. Cubase places the chords automatically at the correct positions thanks to the Snap function: all you have to think about are the pitch and velocity values.

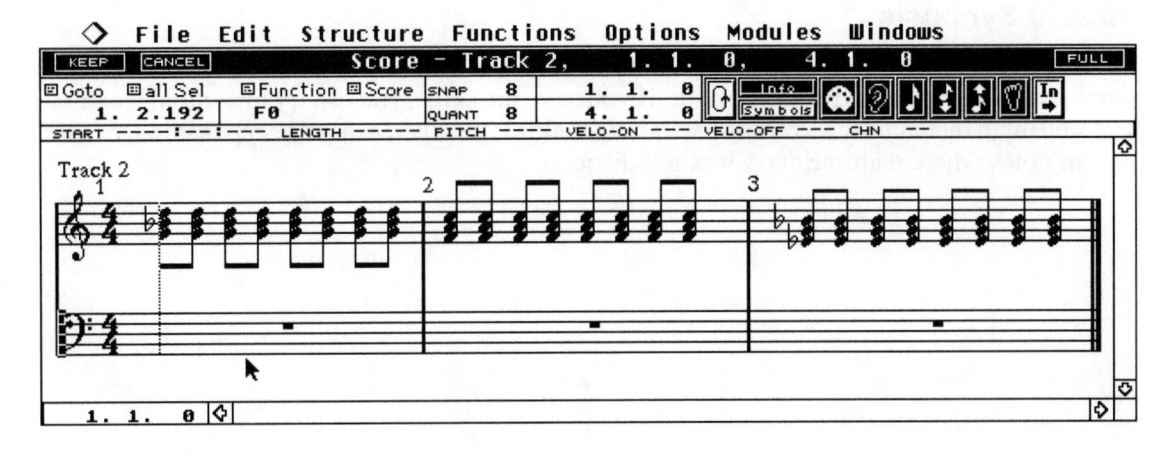

The top staff is done

The entering of notes for the lower staff is just as easy. Select the bottom staff and set Snap to half notes and Quantize to quarter notes, the Step Position to 1.1.0, and play the required notes one after the other up to the beginning of the third bar: quarter notes are being inserted at half note intervals. Quantize dictates the note lengths of the notes entered, and Snap their positions. You control the pitch and velocity.

The third bar requires different Snap and Quantize values. The Eb is a half note, this means that Quantize is "2". The following notes should be entered at position 3.3.0, i.e. the midpoint of the bar. The Snap value is also 2, i.e. a half note. Now play the note. If you make a mistake, call up the eraser from the Toolbox. Ensure the Step Position display at the lower left screen corner has not been altered.

The Score Editor

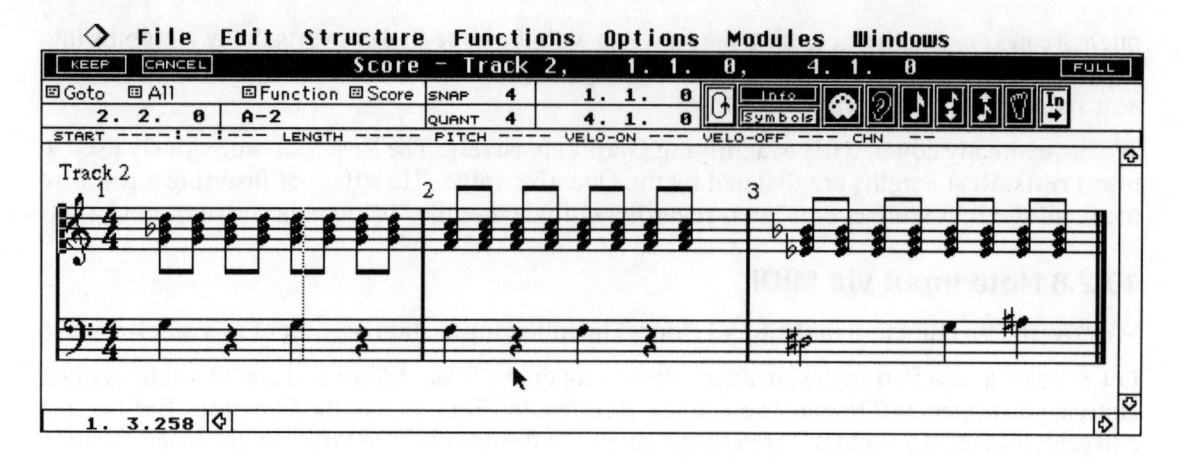

Adding the bass line

When you reach position 3.3.0, the Snap and Quantize values have to be changed to quarter note values. Play the final two notes, and listen to the result. Remember to turn off the MIDI In function, otherwise you'll insert a note every time you inadvertently touch a key of your MIDI master.

You may need to enter rests, depending on the type of music you want to create: press the computer's [Tab] key and Cubase jumps to the next Snap position leaving a gap.

10.2.9 Another option

You already know that you can edit existing notes by using the MIDI In function in conjunction with the note, velocity and release velocity icons. If you can't recall how this works, review the section that covers these functions in the Key Editor chapter. The only difference here is that Cubase does not move from one symbolical note stem to the next, but from actual note to note.

10.2.10 Synopsis

As usual it is entirely up to you which of these methods of entering notes you use. You can also combine the input methods as you see fit. If you have the skills, you can try to combine realtime and step input methods by recording the Parts in realtime and then using the step method to insert or edit notes where realtime entry was too difficult.

11 The Drum Editor

The Drum Editor has been specifically designed with the creation of drum and percussion Parts in mind. "Pro-24" users will already be familiar with the way this Editor displays its data. Before we get down to its practical use, we should clarify a few technical points which are vital to understanding how the Drum Editor works. Each MIDI note you play is assigned to a specific sound in the destination sound module. Hit the note C3 on your keyboard and depending on the way your sound module has been set up, you will hear, say, a bass drum; D3 might trigger a snare sound, and so on. It is always the destination module which determines which sound will be triggered.

Although an assignment of sounds to specific MIDI notes has been not been laid down, a standard assignment has been established between most manufacturers for the most common sounds. Nevertheless you may experience unexpected difficulties: say you entered a drum Part on a Cubase Track, but you want to use a different sound module for the final recording. This sound module may well use a different MIDI note assignment. The most likely result is that you will hear the basic pattern you played, but without the original sounds that you used. What was originally a fat kick drum is now wimpy toms, your amazing hihat is replaced by an orchestral hit, and the snare has disappeared altogether; in short, complete chaos reigns.

Of course on most sound modules, you can change the MIDI note assignment to match your Part, but Cubase offers a much simpler and substantially more efficient facility: the Drum Map. There are two ways to use the Cubase Drum Editor, one with the Drum Map, the other without it. It is the selected Track Class which governs whether the Drum Map is active or not. We'll keep it simple for the initial introduction to this Editor and record drum notes on a normal MIDI Track. Ultimately though, it is far better to activate Drum Track in the Arrange window's Track Class column. You'll save yourself a lot of unnecessary work.

11.1 The initial steps

You will probably have to configure the Drum Editor to match your setup before you can start using it. Although in principle the Drum Editor is not limited to controlling drum or percussion sounds, it is tailored to this specific purpose. You should therefore use drum sounds in some shape or form for the following exercises. It doesn't matter whether they come from a drum computer, drum sound module, or a sampler. Nowadays, many synths and workstations feature a respectable collection of drum sounds.

Delete any Parts left over from previous editing of your Arrangement. Select Track 1, create an empty two-bar Part, and then select it. Make sure that the Track is set to a MIDI channel which is triggering drum sounds on your instrument. Before you open the Editor, have a listen to the

The Drum Editor

sounds. Make sure that each note triggers a specific drum or percussion sound. If this isn't the case, check the MIDI channel assignment and the internal setup of your sound generator.

Enter the Drum Editor via the Edit menu, or the [Control][D] key combination. This is the only way to do this if you want to enter several Parts on different Tracks in the Drum Editor. Later, we will see that by setting the Track Class to Drum, you can enter the Drum Editor directly by double-clicking a Part. The edit window that is called up has certain things in common with the other Editors. The main section of the window is reminiscent of the Key Editor.

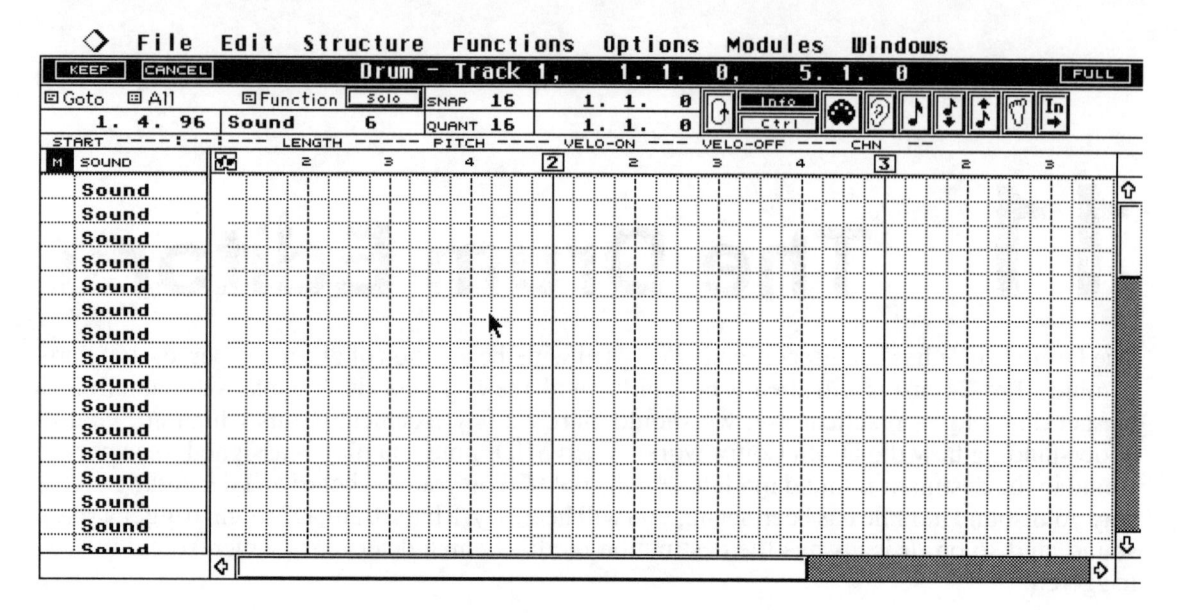

The Drum Editor

Before you can start to use the Drum Editor, you will need to adjust the note assignment to that of your sound module. These settings can be saved on disk and reloaded as required. This enables you to set up and archive configurations for various different instruments and applications. Note assignment is a necessary, but very lengthy process, so Steinberg supplies note assignments for most popular synthesizers with Cubase.

Remove the program or song disk from the disk drive and make a backup copy of the Cubase Additionals 1 disk. Choose Open from the File menu ([Control][0]) and then the Drum Map entry in the dialog box ([6]). Drum sound assignments are in the Drumsets folder. Click Drumsets twice. The Drum Maps contained on the disk will appear. If you find a drum set with your instrument's name, double-click the name in order to load it.

If this is the case, skip the following sections and go directly to the section on note input. You may want to ensure that this drum set is loaded automatically from now on every time you boot Cubase: copy the file onto the backup copy of the program disk, or to the Cubase file on your hard disk. Rename this file "DEF.DRM".

If you own a device that Steinberg has not developed a preset Drum Map for, then you will have to configure the drum set to your instrument yourself.

11.1.1 Adjusting the Drum Editor

The following operations are somewhat tedious, but you only have to do them once which will save you a lot of work later on. The left half of the screen displays the available parameters for each sound. We'll look at these in greater detail in a moment. The grid in the right half of your screen is used to create the required rhythmic structures via mouse click. First you have to assign the MIDI notes to the drum sounds in such a way that your receiver will respond appropriately. Once you have done this, Cubase automatically places the MIDI notes in the correct place on the grid.

Each line in the left half of the screen contains the parameters for a MIDI note, i.e. the corresponding parameters to trigger a sound in your sound generator. Now let's set up a completely new note assignment. This system allows you to deal with up to 64 sounds and assign MIDI notes to each of them. The initial display lists 16 sounds and their respective parameters. The vertical scroll bar allows you to access the remaining sounds. You can zoom the display if necessary.

The dividing line between the grid and the parameter columns can be moved in the same way as in the other Editors. Click the line as accurately as possible. The pointer turns into a hand. Keeping the mouse button held down, drag the line as far to the right as possible.

Now you have access to all the parameters. The number of visible columns depends on whether you are dealing with Drum Tracks or regular MIDI Tracks. At the moment, we're working with MIDI Tracks, so your window should look like this:

MIDI note assignment parameters

11.1.2 Assigning notes

Each line, and consequently each sound, should be assigned a MIDI note, which in turn is assigned to a sound in your instrument. If you try to assign two identical notes on the same MIDI channel, Cubase will advise you of your mistake. If you decide not to use all 64 assignment options, you can switch the note assignment to "Off" independently for each line.

Before you start assigning notes, we want to set all notes to the same starting point: "Off". This will prevent you being hindered by the constant re-appearance of the "Double defined INote in your drum-set!" warning.

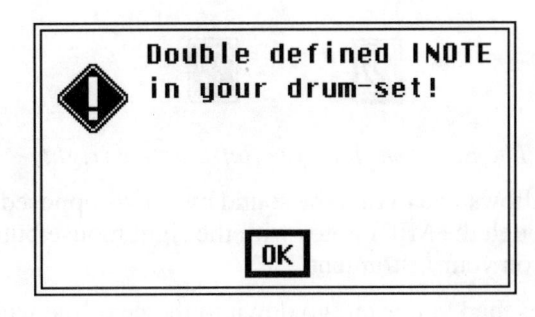

Warning: two identical notes on the same MIDI channel

The Drum Editor

Scroll to Sound No. 1 at the top of the list using the vertical scroll bar. Hold down the [Control] and [Shift] keys. Using the right mouse button, click and hold the little box in the first line under the "INote" heading. You will see the value changing. Wait until "Off" appears then release all keys. All the "INote" values will now be set to "Off". Whenever you hold the [Control] key down whilst assigning a value to the current parameter, that value will be entered in the appropriate column for the remaining 63 sounds. As you know, holding down the [Shift] key speeds the value change by a factor of 10.

Now we can make the first assignment. Set the first sound's INote to your instrument's bass drum sound.

The first note assignment: C1 triggers the bass drum

How do you know which note this is? Simple! It is the same note you have to play on your keyboard to trigger this sound. If you have to hit C2 to play the bass drum sound, set this field to C2. Change values in the normal way using the two mouse buttons, or double-click and direct input. Input from the Atari keyboard is probably the best method for this particular case.

Always name the sound assigned to each line so that you can see all your note assignments at a glance. Double-click "Sound 1" (or hit [Alternate][N] on the keyboard). Delete the old name by pressing [Esc], and enter a new name. Every time you click this name or its line from now on, Cubase will send out the corresponding MIDI note and the connected sound module will play that note. This acts as an auditioning mechanism so that you can hear which sound you are dealing with.

By activating the Ear icon, you can cause any changes you make in the INote column to be sent out via MIDI. This means you can hear the sound which will be triggered as you assign the note.

The Ear icon: inactive (left), active (right)

This auditioning facility allows you to find the sound by ear, as opposed to knowing the precise pitch required. Scroll through the MIDI notes with the right mouse button and audition which sound each click triggers on your instrument.

Once you have set up the sound you want, go down to the next line with a mouse click (or the up/down cursor arrows) and assign the next MIDI note.

You may accidentally assign the same note twice via the mouse/direct input methods. Cubase will alert you with a warning box. OK this and then make sure you find and remove the double assignment.

Although you cannot delete list entries, you can change their order. Click and hold any of the list entries and drag the field to the desired position. The entry will be inserted at this position, with the following entries moved down accordingly.

Normally, the entire input process would have to be done for each sound and its associated MIDI note. However, Cubase has a far simpler method that you can use. Click the INote box and activate the MIDI In symbol in the Functions Bar.

The MIDI In icon: inactive (left), active (right)

Now Cubase will check the MIDI input for the note played so you can find the correct note on your keyboard. Play across the keyboard until you find the right sound. Its assigned MIDI note will be automatically entered in the INote box. Bear in mind that this only works in the currently active line. Name the sound in the Sound column. Select the following lines in turn with a mouse click (or the down cursor arrow on the keyboard), and assign the other sounds. If you have enough sounds available, you can assign up to 64 of them.

The sounds are assigned one after the other until the basic configuration is complete

You should now save your setup to disk so you don't lose the results of your efforts. To do this, use the Drum Map option in the Save dialog box. Remember that the INote column should only be active (i.e. highlighted) whilst assigning MIDI notes. As soon as you are finished, select another column. Otherwise, you may run into difficulties in other operations, especially during MIDI step input.

For our purposes, create a simple setup with bass drum, snare, two toms, open and closed hihat in the top six lines. These sounds are standard, and should be available on any drum machine or sampler. You can, of course, assign them to different sound modules by using different MIDI channels. The MIDI channel for each individual MIDI note is entered in the Chn column. The MIDI channel of the Track must be set to "Any" for this application, otherwise Cubase will ignore the MIDI channel settings entered in the Editor.

The Drum Editor

11.1.3 Input

Now that we've finished the important preparation, let's start entering some notes and rhythms. Drag the dividing line between the grid and the parameter list as far as you can to the left, so that only the M, Sound, and Quantize columns are visible. The grid should now display several bars. The Drum Edit window can be enlarged, reduced, zoomed, and moved in the same way as all other edit windows.

For our first attempt, we need to see just two bars. Zoom the display scale by clicking the bottom scroll bar's left arrow until two complete bars are visible.

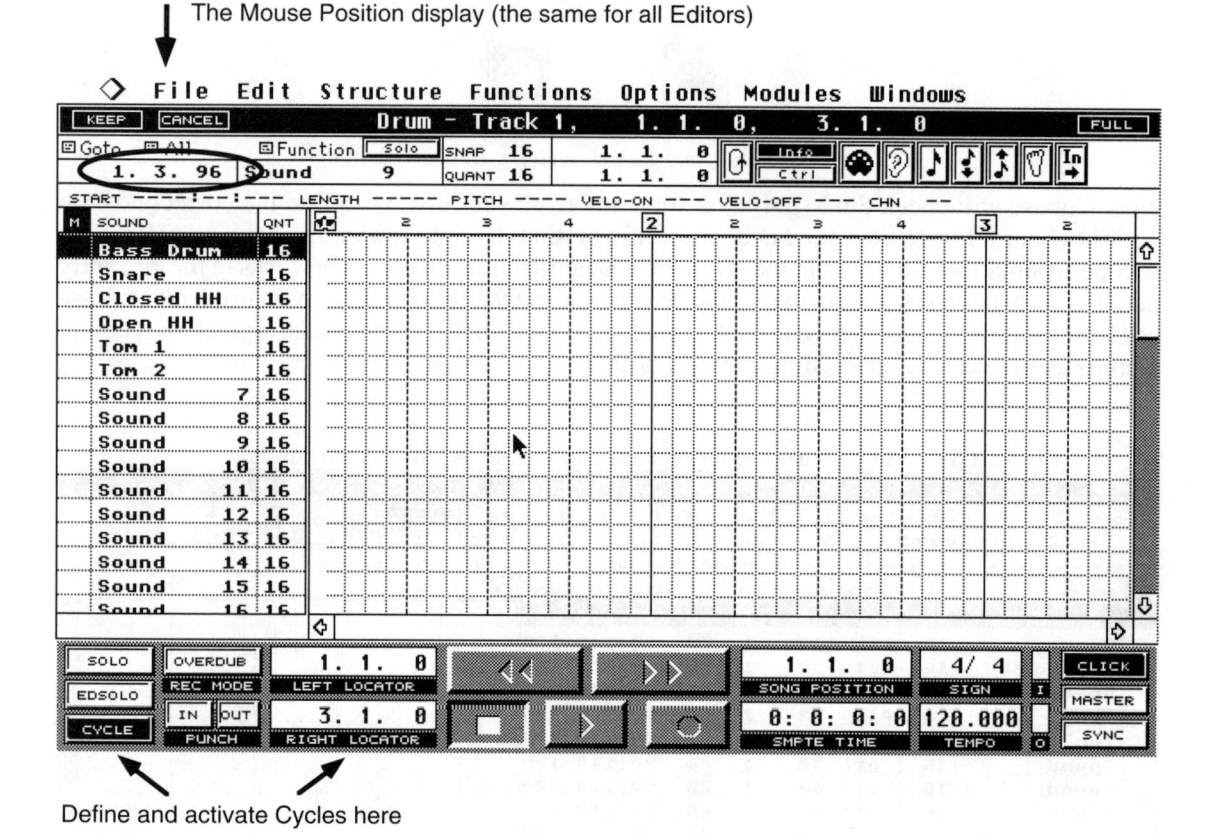

Ready for note input

Now we'll create a pattern in the same way as conventional drum machines to familiarize ourselves with the various functions of the Drum Editor. Our pattern should be two bars long. Set up a two bar Cycle. You can use either a Cycle defined by the locators, or an edit loop created via the Loop icon in the Functions Bar. You can "draw" the loop in the Position Bar the same way you did in the Key Editor. Start playback, not recording. Press the right mouse key somewhere within the grid to call up the Toolbox. Select the Drum Stick from it.

The Drum Stick in the Toolbox

198

The Initial Steps

Now you can use this tool to enter notes. Click position 1.1.0 in the bass drum line. Keep one eye on the Mouse Position display. The note will be placed here and played during the next Cycle. Enter more bass drum notes at positions 1.3.0, 1.4.192, 2.1.0, 2.3.0, and 2.4.192.

The notes are displayed as small diamonds. The Mouse Position display will help you to place them correctly.

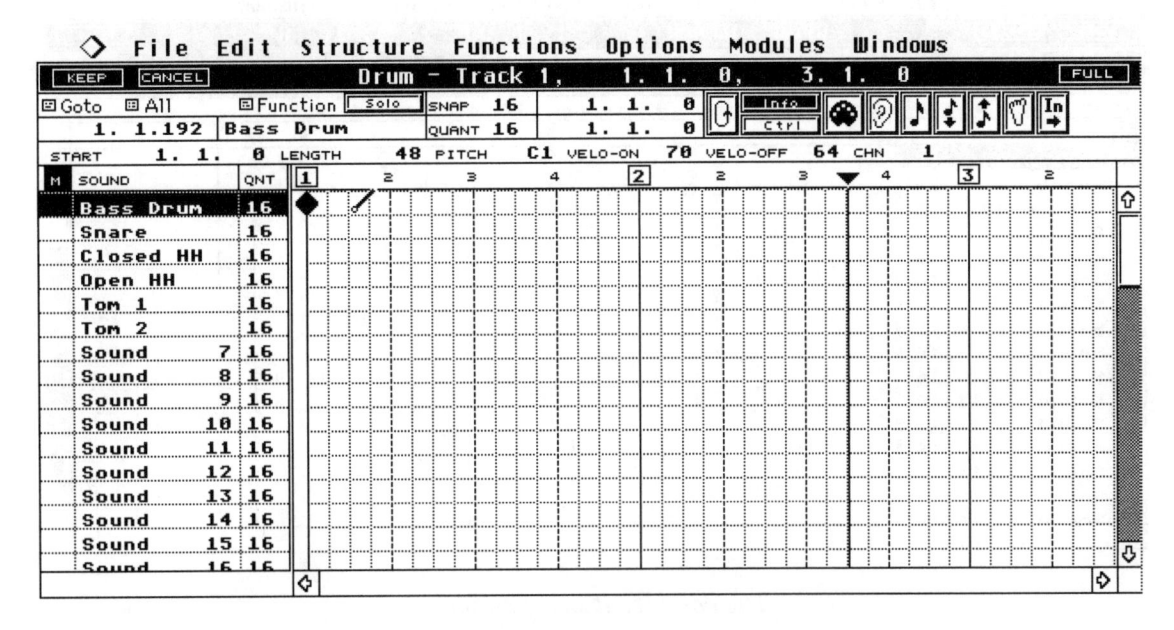

The first bass drum beat is in place

The Quantize value assigned to each note dictates on which bar position the notes can be placed. In the above example the QNT column is set to sixteenths for each sound. We'll utilize these in a moment. The Snap and Quantize settings in the Functions Bar (so important in the other Editors) have no effect whatsoever during Drum Editor note input.

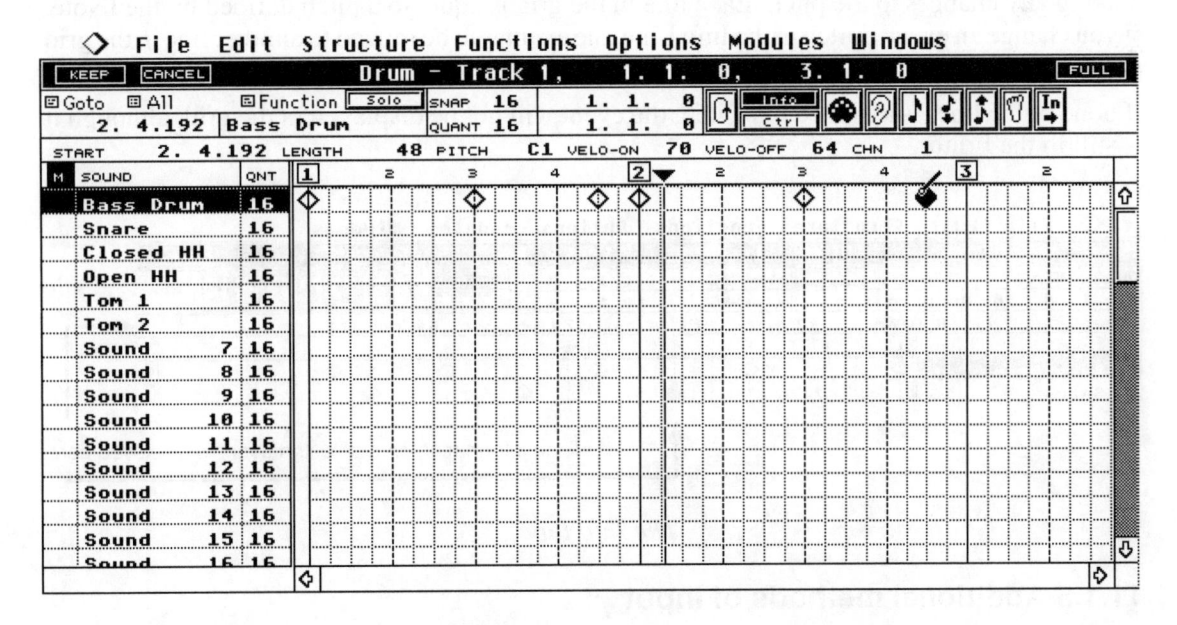

The above bass drum pattern entered

Now we'll enter the positions of the snare notes. Place a snare beat at positions 1.2.0, 1.4.0, 2.2.0, and 2.4.0 in the second line. You can delete a note in several ways: click the drum stick tool again to remove the note. You can also use the Eraser from the Toolbox. You are also already familiar

199

The Drum Editor

with the third method: select the mouse arrow from the Toolbox and highlight the events you want to delete with a mouse click. You can use the click/[Shift] method, or the rubber band to select several notes. Selected events are highlighted and can be deleted via [Backspace] or [Delete].

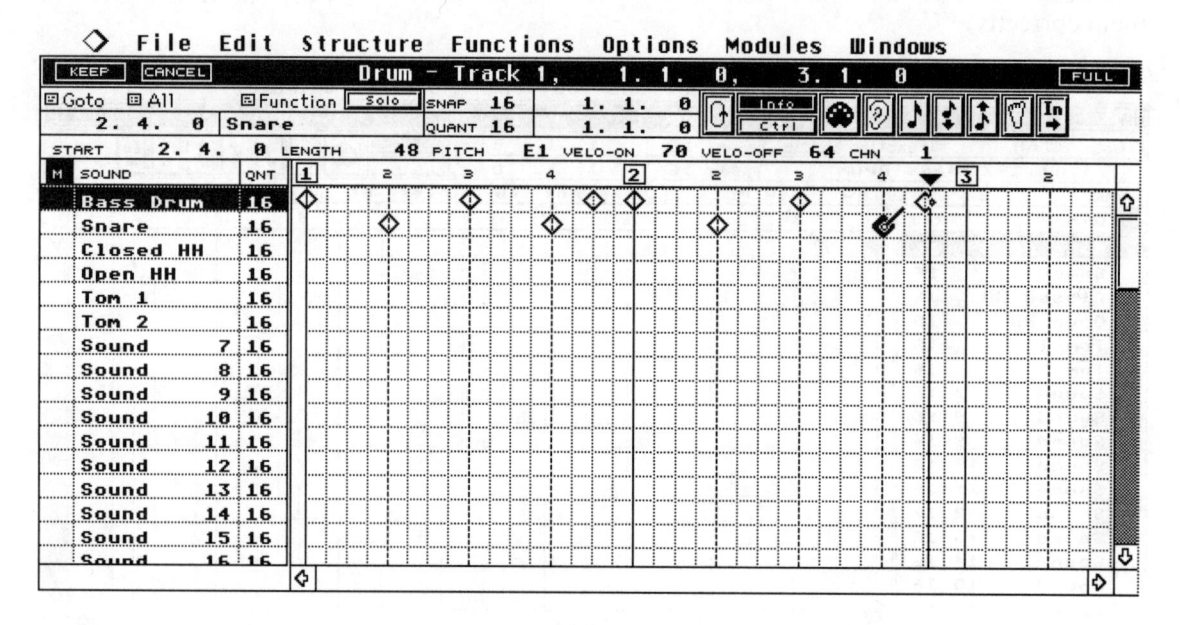

The completed snare pattern

11.1.4 The Info Line

If you select just individual notes, you can see their parameters in the Info Line. Any changes you make there with the mouse are also reflected in the grid.

For percussive sounds, the length value normally has little effect. Think carefully before you start making any changes to the pitch. Each line in the grid is equal to a pitch defined by the INote. If you change an event's pitch in the Info Line, the event will be moved to another line in the grid corresponding to the new pitch.

If none of the lines is assigned this pitch, the event will not be displayed in the grid, although it is still in the Editor.

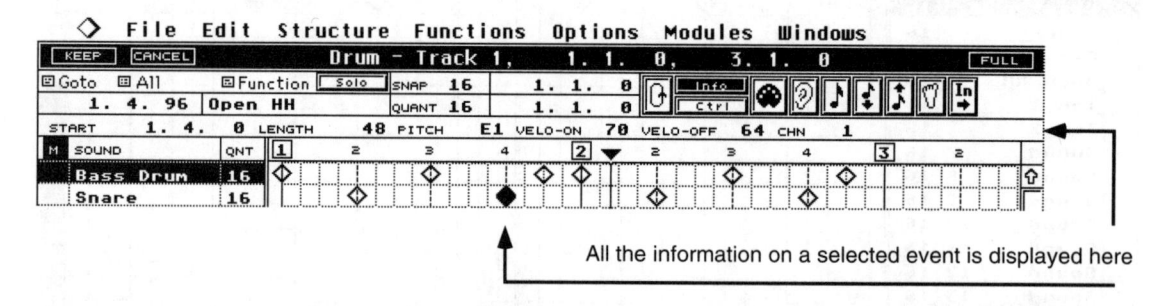

All the information on a selected event is displayed here

The Info Line

11.1.5 Additional methods of input

Until now, we have only been inserting single events. In the following exercise, an eighth hihat pattern, a number of notes will be entered with a single operation.

Enter a Quantize value of 8 for the closed hihat. Click and hold in the hihat line's Quantize column. A box will appear in which you can enter this value.

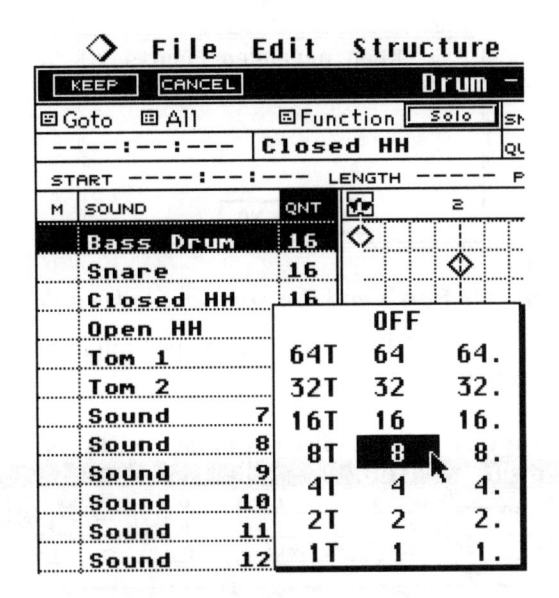

Select a Quantize value of "8"

Activate the drum stick from the Toolbox and place it at position 1.1.0 in the hihat line. Press and holding the mouse button, drag it to the right. A note is entered at each eighth position in the grid. It is the Quantize value which dictates the grid intervals. "16" equals sixteenth steps, "4" are quarter intervals, etc.

The grid gives you a graphic representation of where notes can be placed. The current display scale is insufficient for small values, i.e. 32nds and 64ths. You will need to zoom the display in order to see these.

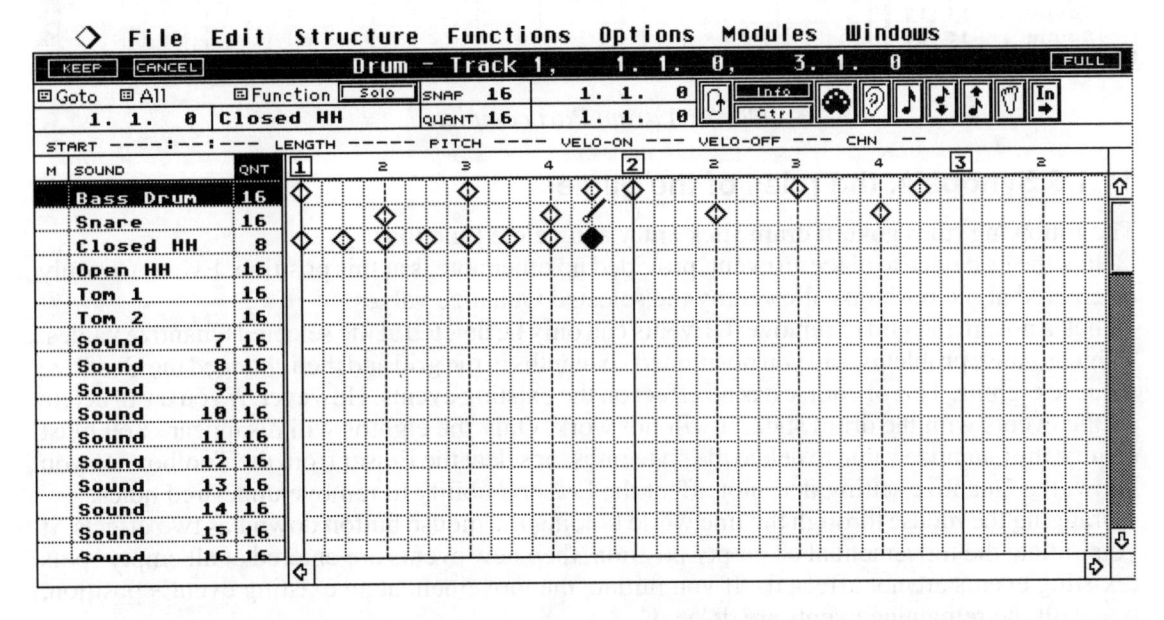

Drag the mouse to the right while holding the mouse button down:
the hihat pattern will be entered

In our example, we have entered eighths. You won't make any mistakes when entering as notes can only be entered in the current line. Even if you move the mouse up and down, the notes are still only entered here.

Bear in mind that you can continue to draw beyond the end of a Part. Cubase will ask you if you want keep the additional notes when you leave the Editor. If you answer Yes, Cubase will add the notes to your Part.

The Drum Editor

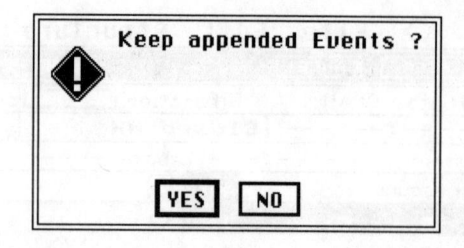

You've drawn beyond the Part's end. Do you want to keep the additional events?

Delete the hihat event at position 2.4.192 and enter an open hihat note in the line below it. You can also enter some toms if you like.

Our first drum Part completed

11.1.6 Synopsis: the rules of the game

The following rules govern drum stick entry and delete functions:
- Click the grid once to place an event, provided no other note is at this position. Events can only be entered at the positions allowed by the selected Quantize values.
- Click a note in the grid to remove it. Events can only be deleted at the selected Quantize values. This can cause problems: say you positioned sixteenths in the grid and then changed the Quantize value to eighths. This of course has no effect on the existing events. However, if you try to delete all the events with the drum stick, it will not work. Only the eighths will disappear. You must change the Quantize value to delete the sixteenths, or select the Eraser from the Toolbox. As you know, the Quantize setting does not affect the Eraser's ability to remove undesired notes.
- Dragging the mouse through the line while holding the mouse button down has two effects: if you initiate the movement at an empty position, then new events are entered at all empty spots (existing events are not affected). If you initiate the movement at an existing event's position, it and all the remaining events are deleted.
- If you press and hold [Alternate], new notes are entered in every line you touch, not merely in the line that is active.
- The Paint Brush tool works the same way as the drum stick.

11.2 Additional functions

The note length is set to a 1/32nd note. The length is of no consequence to most drum samples, because they are automatically played to the end once they have been triggered. You may,

Additional Functions

however, need a different note length, depending on the sound or channel. You can set a new note length individually for each pitch in the Len (length) column.

A hihat pattern with exactly the same velocity values throughout sounds very mechanical and boring in most types of music. You could of course edit each value individually for every note in the Info Line after you have entered it. However, you know how to control velocity values during the entry process from your experience with the other Editors. One of the available methods is to use certain key combinations. The Drum Editor also offers this option, with the added benefit of even more precision.

Move the dividing line between the parameters and grid all the way back to the right. The columns headed by "LV 1" through "LV 4" are the ones we are interested in. Velocity values will be assigned to the notes according to the key combinations you hold whilst entering notes. The different diamond patterns graphically represent the different velocities. During normal entry, the notes are assigned the Level 1 velocity value. Holding down [Shift] assigns Level 2, [Control] sets Level 3, and holding down both keys assigns Level 4 to the notes. You can specify which velocity values these actually represent for each instrument.

Velocity values are fairly abstract, i.e. difficult to picture because you just don't know how your instruments interpret these changes. As a result, you may prefer to input notes directly via MIDI. Activate the MIDI icon and select a sound. The entire line will be highlighted.

You can set individual velocity values in each of the columns "LV 1" through "LV 4"

Click the LV 1 column and play a note at the desired velocity. Your velocity value is entered. It doesn't matter which note you play, because the INote is already set. However, it is advisable to play the assigned note to hear the actual sound that you are entering these velocity values for.

Repeat these steps for the remaining levels. Click the desired column and play a note at the desired velocity. You can do this for every sound, but normally you would set these four values once and then copy them to the other sounds. Use the standard copy function via [Control]. Proceed as follows:

Deactivate the MIDI icon and the Level 1 value you want to copy to the remaining sounds while holding down [Control]. This setting will be carried across to all other sounds. The current value may move up or down an increment during this operation. If this happens, adjust the entry back to its original value with a mouse click whilst still holding down [Control].

The second method consists of entering values directly: hold [Control] down and double-click the value. Once the empty input box appears, release [Control] and enter the value. Hit [Return] to confirm. The new value will be copied to all other sounds.

The Drum Editor

Equipped with this new knowledge, let's have another go at the hihat pattern. Delete all the hihat notes. As you know, there are a number of methods available: the rubber band, drum stick, or the Function sub-menu, which you probably remember from the other Editors. Select a hihat note in the grid and choose Delete Note from the Function menu. Any notes of this pitch, in this case all the hihats, will be deleted.

Retrieve the drum stick from the Toolbox and slowly drag it through the hihat line. Vary the velocities by engaging different key combinations. Do not release the mouse button. The result should resemble the following diagram:

The hihat pattern entered with varying velocities

You can use the key combinations randomly or in a specific order to create accents. Your receiver must of course be able to respond to these varying velocity messages. Listen to the results of your efforts. The column at the far right of the parameter list is headed by an M. Its function is the same as in the Arrange window, although here you can't mute Tracks, but you can mute individual drum sounds. Simply click the sound's Mute column. The dot denotes the sound is muted. Click again to re-activate the sound.

This speedy process can, for example, be used to program rhythm patterns with two different bass drums. Mute one, then the other, to hear which one sounds better in context. In contrast to the Mute in the Arrange window, this mute can't be recorded. If you want to listen to one sound at a time, the Solo function is very handy as it mutes all the sounds in a pattern except the one you have selected. Click Solo or press [Alternate].

11.3 Identical functions in all Editors

We should review those functions that are virtually identical in all the Editors. In addition to the Goto, "selection" and Function sub-menus there are the icons used for the step input method, or to be more precise, editing via MIDI. However, it is most unlikely that you will ever need to use the MIDI step input option in the Drum Editor, as Cubase's graphic handling capabilities in this Editor are quite exceptional.

Controlling velocity data via MIDI In would seem to be a more sensible application. Let's go back to the hihat in our pattern for a second. Clear the hihat pattern again and select the hihat line. Activate Fill in the Function sub-menu. Cubase will enter a hihat pattern with identical velocity values at each grid position. The Quantize setting should still be "16" for the hihat line. We've now entered the required events. Now go back to the beginning of the pattern to start on the velocity values. Activate the MIDI In icon, the velocity icon, and the first note you want to edit.

Enter a new velocity value via MIDI for each note. As soon as you press and release a key on your keyboard, Cubase will enter the velocity value and move on to the next note. That way you can effortlessly enter all the velocity values, one after the other. If you want to leave an event's velocity unchanged, skip it using [Tab].

Make sure the dividing line between the parameters and the grid is moved at least as far left as the Quantize column, otherwise you may have problems with INote and ONote.

11.4 A few tips

The preceding examples were limited to the graphic and MIDI input options. You can also work on previously recorded Parts in the Editor, or go to the Drum Editor during recording (as with all the other Editors). Remember though that the events entered in this Editor are displayed only when the corresponding INote has been defined. If you play a C#4 note, then all graphic information is displayed in the C#4 line. If you haven't assigned C#4 in the Drum Editor, then the information is not displayed in graphic symbols.
- Events that are not exactly on the correct grid position, as is usually the case when you enter notes in realtime without Quantize, are deleted via the Eraser, and not a click with the drum stick tool.
- The Magnifying Glass and the two Kicker tools have the same functions as in the other Editors.
- You can move any number of selected events to other bar positions or pitches by clicking and dragging with the mouse pointer. Hold down [Alternate] to copy, delete, or move the selected notes.
- Most key commands and applications should be familiar from your experience with the other Editors. If you feel the need, refresh your memory by browsing through the Key Editor chapter.
- The Controller Display we met in the Key Editor is also available here. Click the Ctrl button in the Functions Bar or press [Alternate][C]. We've already looked extensively at the way Controller Display works. Here it is best used for editing the velocity values of individual notes. Click the desired sound in the Sound column and adjust the velocity column the way you did in the Key Editor. The majority of the remaining controllers and editing options are less useful in conjunction with drum sounds. Keep in mind that virtually all MIDI non-note commands are channel specific: you cannot control MIDI volume, modulation, or pitch bend data individually for each drum sound. The only event type applicable on a per-MIDI note basis is Poly Key Pressure - however, most drum samples are too short and percussive to achieve any worthwhile results through Poly Key Pressure.

If you do assign notes to several MIDI channels in your drum set, then Cubase operates in the following manner:
- The Controller Display displays only those events assigned to the same MIDI channel.
- New data entered in the display is assigned to the same MIDI channel as the selected sound.
- Poly Key Pressure data is assigned and displayed at the sound's INote pitch.

11.5 The Drum Map

Now that you've been introduced to the Drum Editor's most important features, let's go on to the "Drum Map" and "Drum Tracks" that were mentioned at the beginning of the chapter. In our exercises up to now, Cubase has accepted INote values input during recording. For instance, if you assigned the bass drum to the C2 note, then it was recorded and later played back whenever you played C2 on your keyboard.

If you're a creature of habit, and always use the same setup, then this setting is entirely sufficient. However, say you bought a new drum machine, or you want to use a different sampler in the studio. Your drum set may control completely different sounds, or even none at all. The snare you had assigned to C1 may correspond to the C#4 command in another device.

Most MIDI devices allow you to change MIDI note assignments to avoid this type of problem.

The Drum Editor

Be prepared for a long and extremely boring task. But don't despair! Cubase's Drum Map gets around this problem speedily and elegantly.

The Drum Map allows you to define both the INote and an additional ONote (output note) for the MIDI notes to be sent. To work like this, you must define each Track containing drum Parts as a Drum Track as discussed in the introduction to this chapter.

Create a new Part and move the dividing line between the sound parameters and the grid to the far right.

Drum Track parameters

Two new columns have now been added to the familiar ones: "Instrument" and "ONote". Instrument displays the name of the selected sound's MIDI channel, provided you assigned it a name in the Arrange channel. If you didn't, enter a name with a double-click.

The ONote column is of particular interest to us. You can assign the same values to a sound line's INote and ONote columns for your own recordings. However, these functions are especially useful in the following applications:

Let's assume you have created a drum Track with the conventional drum note assignments, in the same way as in our practical exercises. Now you are in a situation where you want or have to utilize a different setup. Cubase has recorded the events in the Parts according to the INote settings. You would have to change every single event on the Track to change the note assignments. For example, you assigned and recorded a bass drum and snare drum in the Editor. The MIDI trigger notes are set to C3 and D3, respectively. Not a problem if you continue to work with the same devices. However, another sound module may require C4 and E4 to trigger bass and snare drums.

Conventional editing techniques offer two options in such a case: either you change the note number assignments in the Editor, or you utilize the Logical Editor, which we haven't covered yet. In principle these methods are fine, they will work.

However, as a rule the Part also contains other MIDI notes that in turn trigger other sounds. Once you start transposing, you may accidentally assign them to pitches that are already assigned to other MIDI notes/devices. In this case, you won't be able to separate different events of the same pitch in the Editors. Your drum groove would be lost.

This is where the Drum Map comes in. When the Drum Map is in full use, Cubase reroutes the recorded notes according to your instructions. In our example, you would simply set the bass and snare drums' ONotes to C4 and D4, respectively. The recorded events are not affected in any way.

The Drum Map

You enter ONote values in the same way you entered those for the INote. This also makes it possible to enter changes via MIDI. Activate the MIDI In symbol, select the ONote heading by clicking it, select the required sound in the column and play the correct note on your keyboard. Select the next sound and repeat the procedure. That way, the notes of a finished drum Track can be assigned in a user-friendly manner without having to change the recording. In contrast to the INote, an ONote value can be set twice so that a single event can trigger two different instruments.

The INote can also be independently assigned when the Drum Map is active, so enabling you to reconfigure your keyboard sounds.

During recording, Cubase converts all incoming notes to an internal, fixed assignment for each of the 64 drum sounds in the Drum Editor list. The following example demonstrates how this works:

Without the Drum Map

note played	note recorded	note assigned
C3	C3	C3

The C3 note is required to trigger a bass drum sample in a module. This note must be played on your keyboard and recorded, so the sample can later be played.

With the Drum Map

note played	note recorded	note assigned
C2	C2	C3

The module's bass drum is still triggered by C3. If you want to trigger another drum sound, use the ONote to do it. Recorded events will then be remapped to the ONote. The INote value can be sent to any note number, so you can configure the sounds you need to trigger from your keyboard as required. If you prefer to play the bass drum at a higher position, simply change the INote. The event is recorded at the C2 pitch, but it is played back at the C3 pitch.

Cubase assigns fixed pitches for the first 64 drum sounds. The first of these is C2, the second C#2 the third D2, and so on. This scheme may cause some confusion when working in the other Editors. You will need to move the Key Editor's keyboard display on the left-hand edge of the screen all the way down to the bottom. The List Editor displays the drum sound's name in the Comment column for each event. If you use a sensible scheme to assign names to the 64 available sounds, you will find that this simplifies the entire editing operation.

11.5.1 Additional advantages

Setting up a complete map for a drum Track takes a considerable amount of time, but the advantages that a Drum Map has to offer are also considerable. Using Drum Maps is well worth the effort. Always record drum notes on Drum Tracks. For example, if you're in the production phase of a project where time becomes critical and you want to replace a cowbell at D5 with maracas at C4, whilst retaining the rhythmic structure. If you've recorded it on a Drum Track, all you have to do is change the ONote. If you haven't used the Drum Map, you're forced to move every D5 individually, or transpose them. The danger in this of course, is that you may end up transposing an instrument's note to the same pitch that another instrument is using, mixing them up.

Be sure to save your Drum Map separately via the Save dialog box, under Drum Map. The Drum Map is also saved along with a song, but not with an Arrangement. Only one Drum Map can be held in memory at any one time.

11.5.2 Converting Drum Maps

You may get so involved with a particular song that you end up recording drum patterns on a normal MIDI Track, forgetting all about using Drum Tracks and Drum Maps. No need to panic! You can convert the Parts or Tracks to a Drum Track.

The Drum Editor

Go to the Track Class column of the MIDI Track and set it to Drum Track. Cubase will ask if you want to convert the Parts to Drum Parts. The existing notes will be entered in the list according to the Drum Map's INote settings. Once this has been done, you can change the input and output notes without affecting the original data.

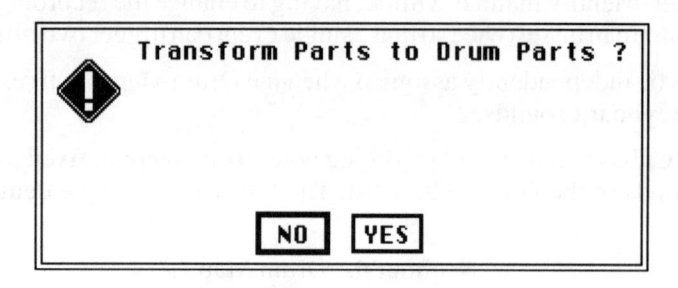

Transform MIDI Tracks into Drum Tracks?

Take this as an example: there are several companies that sell finished drum grooves. These can normally be loaded into Cubase. But if they're not available in the Cubase format, they may at least be available as MIDI files. In this case, you will need to load the file into the List Editor to find out the note assignments so that you can identify the notes and their roles in the Drum Editor.

When the MIDI file has finished loading, convert the song's drum grooves to Drum Tracks via the pop-up menu of the C column. Click on OK or press [Return] in response to the question shown in the above diagram. Go to the Drum Editor. Cubase will assign the notes according to its INote settings. If the MIDI file's bass drum was assigned to C1, then it will be entered in the line with a INote assignment of C1. If the snare drum was assigned to D1, then it will be entered in the line with a INote assignment of D1, and so on.

It is strongly recommended that you name the sounds in the relevant column of the Drum Editor as soon as you have loaded them. If the sounds are spaced a long way from each other in the list, you should move them closer together.

Cubase assigns each pitch an internal Cubase note during conversion. This means you can change the INote and ONote assignments, i.e. use the snare note for a tom sound, etc., as soon as the conversion procedure is completed.

11.5.3 Drum Tracks and MIDI files

You can see that Cubase uses an internal note assignment system that does not make use of the entire note range available via MIDI. The output notes are actually assigned via the Drum Map. If you export Cubase Arrangements as MIDI files, you may encounter some problems. The recorded low notes will be used, but not the assigned Drum Map notes. Most MIDI sound devices won't be able to process this data. This means you must convert Drum Tracks to normal MIDI Tracks first.

Go to the Track Class column of the Track and switch the setting from Drum Track to MIDI Track. Cubase will ask how notes should be converted. You must decide whether you want them converted to the assigned input or output notes.

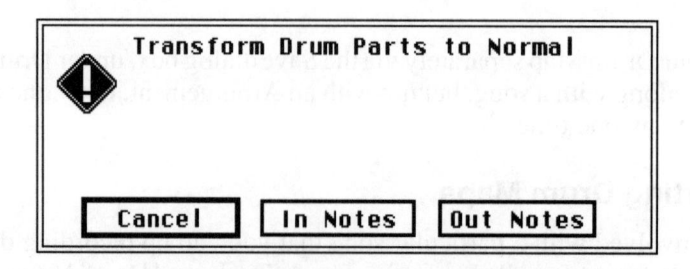

Converting Drum Tracks to MIDI Tracks

11.5.4 A tip or two

The Drum Editor's best feature is the quick and easy way it allows you to create rhythms. This is particularly true if you prefer working with patterns. In contrast, very few musicians attempt to enter the drum Arrangement for a 150 bar song in a single take.

Many musicians use a continuous groove as the song's skeleton, and then flesh it out as they go. Once the basic outline of a song is clear, they then concentrate on the detailed drum work. If this method of working appeals to you, create a Part several bars long, then use the Repeat function discussed in the Arrange chapter to copy it the desired number of times. Use Ghost Parts.

The reason many musicians use a drum machine even though they have a sophisticated software sequencer is obvious. Aside from the authentic sounds it has, a drum machine gives quick access to rhythms and grooves created/loaded earlier. But as a Cubase user, you don't need to miss out on this advantage. Create Parts and Tracks in keeping with the basic groove you have in mind. You can buy prefabricated grooves on disc if required. Load these new rhythms and edit the Tracks to suit your material by changing Parts, cutting them, etc. MIDI Files and external Drum Maps will need to be converted to Drum Maps which match your drum set. This should give you an Arrangement consisting of a number of such basic grooves.

There are two ways of managing your files efficiently:
- Save each Part using a name easily associated with its potential use. Later you can load this Part directly into your Arrangements and songs. Use a disk which you reserve exclusively for drum Parts. The Parts are always entered at the position of the left locator. Remember that saved Parts retain their original Track allocations. If a Part was on Track 1 when you saved it, it will be re-loaded in Track 1 of your Arrangement. If there are other Parts on this Track, then the Drum Track will be overlaid. You can then drag the drum Part to another Track. If you want to avoid this overlaying, always copy drum Parts to a particular Track reserved for drums.
- Save it as a complete Arrangement together with all the rhythmic structures you will need. As you already know, Cubase can hold up to 16 Arrangements in memory simultaneously. One of these can be demoted to act as your drum buffer. Whenever you want to use a drum groove, load the complete drum Arrangement, select the desired drum Part, and then use the Clipboard's Copy function. The drum Part will be copied to the Clipboard. Then call up the destination Arrangement.

Use Paste to insert the Part at the current song position in the destination Arrangement. You must set the song position to be the spot where you want to insert it. Each time you use Paste, the Part will be entered immediately after the previous Paste.

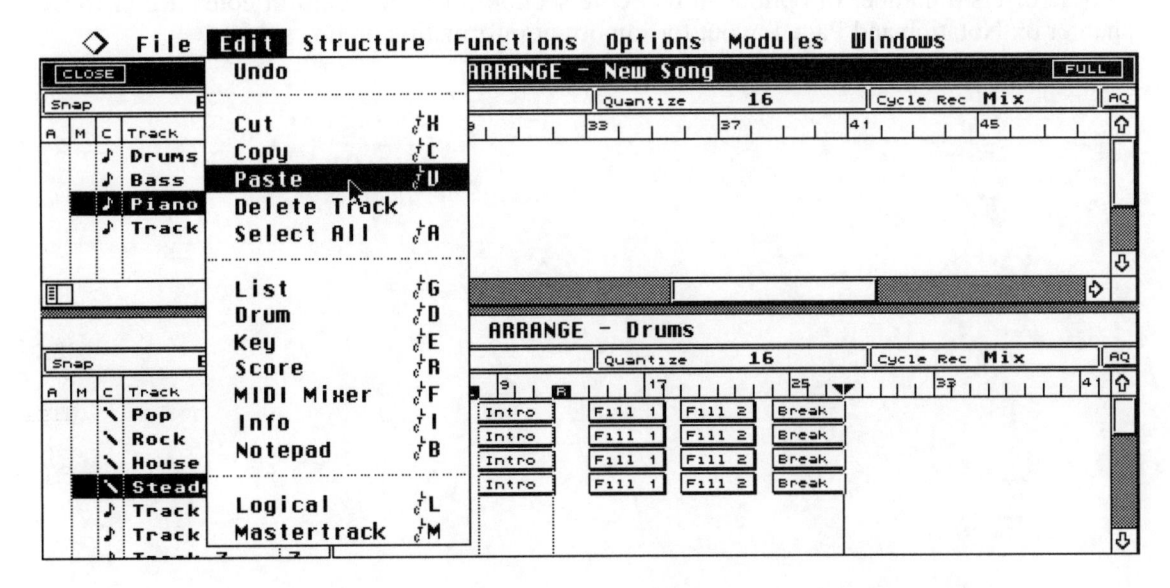

A special drum Arrangement containing several drum Parts. They can be...

The Drum Editor

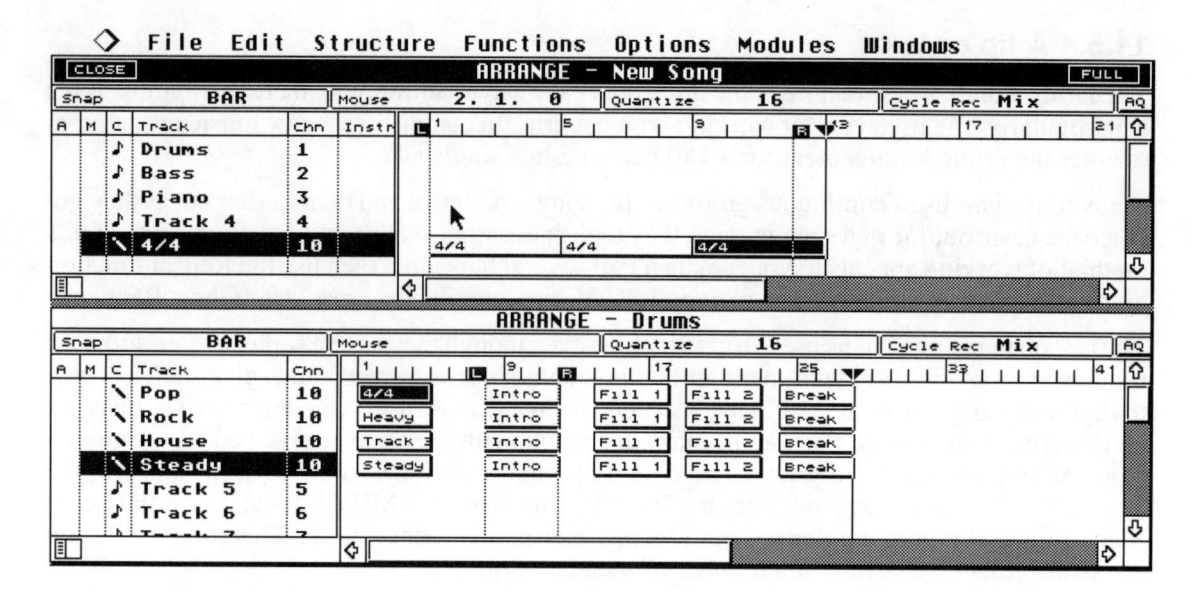

...entered in a new Arrangement

Once you have entered Parts in a new Arrange window as shown in the above illustration, new Tracks will be generated for these Parts to be placed on. You may just need to move them to the desired positions. Here too, pick names you can recognize easily for the groove Arrangement's individual Parts so you get a clear picture of your Arrangement.

Which of these methods you will prefer in the long run depends on two factors. If you store the Parts separately you may well use less memory. However, you will need to keep accessing the disk, which is rather time-consuming. The second solution, using the drum Arrangement, allows faster access. It allows you to copy around Parts quickly to try out different rhythms in the same context. This method uses substantially more memory because you are holding the drum grooves in it as well. If it's a big Arrangement, and your drum Arrangement contains a lot of grooves, you may run out of memory if you only have 1 MB available. In this case, remove all the modules of the program which you are not using, or don't load them in the first place. Refer to the Special Functions chapter for more details.

11.5.5 Drums and notation

Cubase offers a number of options in its Score section for notating drum notes. Refer to the chapter on Notation and Page Layout for important information on this subject.

Introduction

12 The MIDI Mixer

The MIDI Mixer is one of Cubase's most powerful features. It allows access to virtually all MIDI events in the form of a graphic display. You can use it to control volume, pan and other MIDI non-note data, as well as editing sound timbres and other device-specific parameters using SysEx data. You can even use it to create editors for MIDI devices. Steinberg supplies a number of current instrument adaptations on the Additionals disk which is included in the Cubase package. As a result, you don't need any specialized MIDI knowledge for basic Mixer operation.

This chapter is divided into two sections. The first section covers practical usage of the MIDI Mixer based on the preset applications supplied by Steinberg. In the second section we will look more closely at the theoretical background behind the Mixer. This will enable you to create your own Mixer applications.

12.1 Introduction

The MIDI Mixer is one of Cubase's modules, so you have to load it (as described in the "Special Functions" chapter) before you can start to work with it. Mixer data can be created on any track, but the track you choose must be assigned to the "Mix Track" Class before you start recording. The "Mix Track" assignment is the only way to enter the MIDI Mixer.

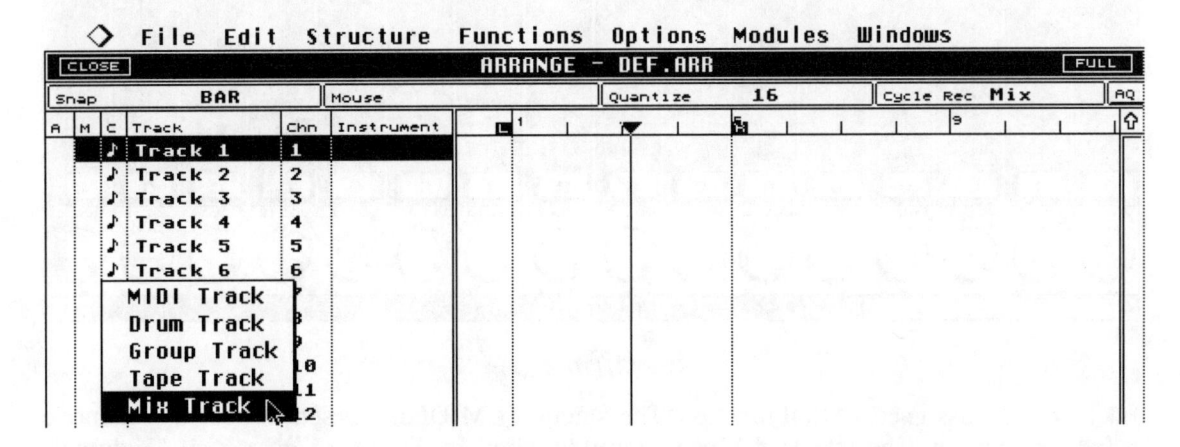

Setting the Mix Track Class

A Mix Track can only ever be a Mix Track. You cannot convert it to another Track Class as you can in the case of the Drum Editor. Like the Logical Editor, the MIDI Mixer has very little in common with the other editors because it only affects a single Part. Before you can work in this

211

The MIDI Mixer

editor, there must be a Part available and selected on the Mixer track. If no Part has been selected, then Cubase will enter the first Part of the current track. If the track does not contain any Parts, the MIDI Mixer cannot be activated. Cubase assigns a special data format to events created in the MIDI Mixer and uses this data to generate the required MIDI information in realtime or during playback. Keep this in mind when reading the following explanation as it is an essential condition to understanding how the MIDI Mixer operates.

We have already seen in the section on the List Editor that Cubase records MIDI Mixer data as "special events".

12.2 Getting started

- First of all enter several lengthy Parts on different tracks. Then create an empty Part on a new track for the Mixer by double-clicking or using[Control][P]. It should have the same length as the passage you have just recorded.
- Set its Track Class to Mix Track.
- Select this Part and choose Mixer from the Edit menu ([Control][M]), or double-click on the Part to go to the Mixer.

You can only enter the Mixer from the Arrange window, not from another editor. Similarly, exiting the MIDI Mixer always returns you to the Arrange window. The only similarities between the MIDI Mixer and the standard editors we have already seen is that you can move, enlarge, and reduce the MIDI Mixer as you would a normal window. However, you cannot zoom it.

Most of the Mixer is taken up by a number of control elements, the "objects". The MIDI Mixer can contain up to 128 objects. The vertical and horizontal scroll bars are used to access elements off-screen.

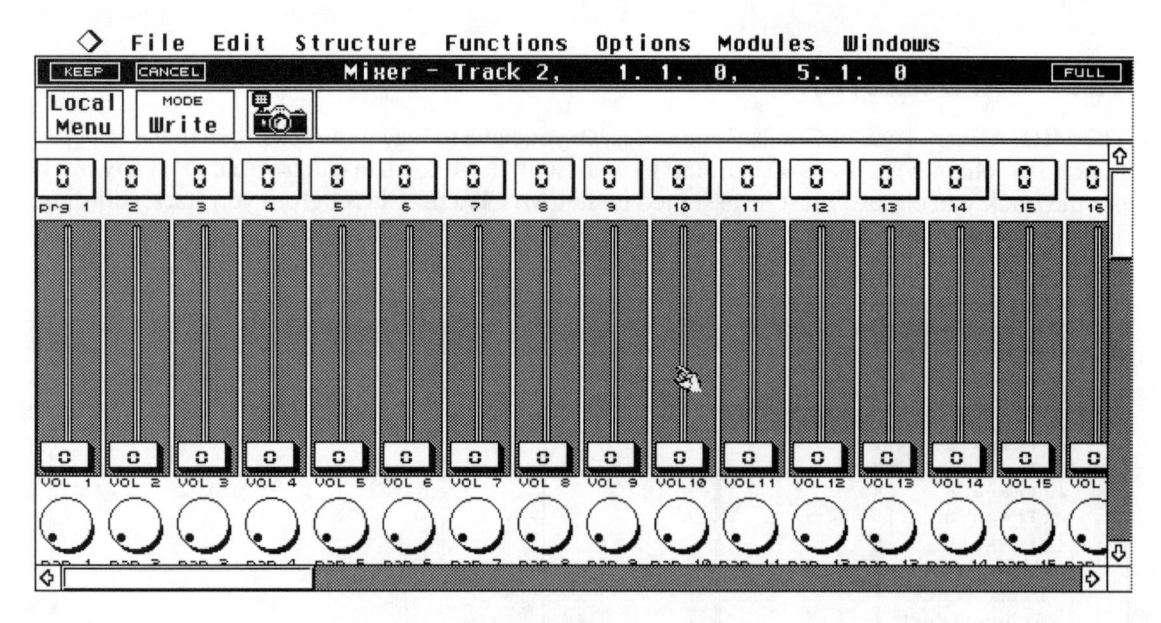

The MIDI Mixer

Each object is assigned a MIDI function. The function's MIDI data is sent as soon as you move a fader or button. The standard Mixer preset supplied by Steinberg gives you "Volume", "Program Change", and "Balance" objects for all 16 MIDI channels. Additional configurations can be loaded, created, and saved.

Each Mixer object sends on its own MIDI channel which can be freely defined. This is why setting the track channel in the Arrange window is neither possible, nor necessary.

However, the MIDI Thru assignment works slightly differently here, which at first encounter may be a little irritating to those of you familiar with earlier Cubase versions: if you have selected a MIDI track, the MIDI Thru connection corresponds to "Any". Your keyboard's MIDI signals will be passed unaltered through the computer.

If your keyboard happens to be sending on channel 1, then that is the channel on which data is sent through the computer. This cannot be changed as long as a Mixer track is selected.

For some situations this way of working is not recommended, such as if you want to try out something on different channels, and at the same time input a few notes on the corresponding MIDI channel. You could of course keep changing the MIDI send channel on your keyboard. However current instrument user interfaces mean that this is far too time-consuming a way of working. Use the following technique.

12.3 MIDI Thru while Mix Track is active

- Go to the MIDI Mixer as described above.
- Reduce the size of the window so that you can still see the elements you will need later. You need to be able to see at least part of the Arrange window.
- Activate the Arrange window with a mouse click to bring it to the front of the screen. Reduce its height until you see a narrow section with several tracks.

This diagram depicts how your screen should look. Owners of large-screen monitors will have a lot more space available for this:

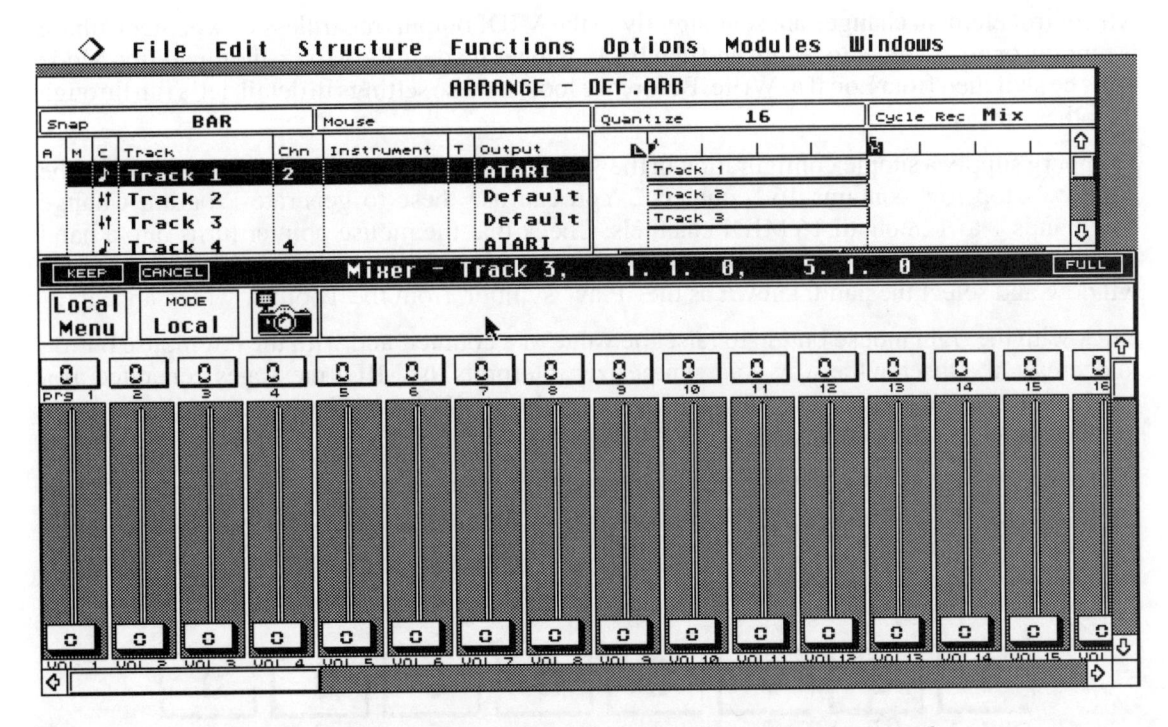

The Arrange window and MIDI Mixer in use simultaneously

Now you can activate any other track in the Arrange window, change its channel assignment, and so use the MIDI Thru function as usual. If you make any movements in the MIDI Mixer, they are recorded on the output track indicated in the MIDI Mixer's Title Bar, and not on the track currently selected.

During our first experiments you can play on your master keyboard throughout Mixer recording. Cubase will distinguish between the two types of data so that the Mixer uses only the data it created, and no other.

The MIDI Mixer

The MIDI Mixer has a special recording mode which is different from the usual one. MIDI Mixer events cannot be recorded via the usual recording method; on the other hand, this special mode can only be used to record MIDI Mixer events. All normal recording operations are invalid for as long as the MIDI Mixer is open. If you decide to try it anyway, the following message will appear:

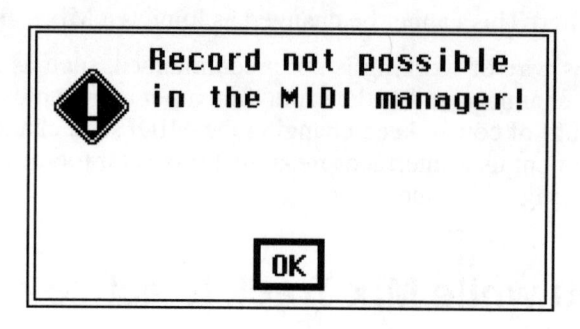

You cannot record in the normal way within the MIDI Mixer

12.4 Initial steps

The upper half of the window contains several options next to the camera symbol, one of which is the Mode sub-menu, used to determine the operating mode. This is critically important to your work in the MIDI Mixer.

All control element changes are sent directly to the MIDI output, regardless of whether Cubase is running or not. In order to record and playback changes made in the Mixer, the Operation Mode must be switched from Local to Write. Before we look at these settings in detail, let's run through the other options.

Steinberg supply a simple configuration in the "DEF" file which is loaded on program start. The window's top row contains 16 "counters". You can use these to generate Program Change commands 1 to 128 on all 16 MIDI channels. Check that the mouse pointer turns into a hand symbol when doing this. If this doesn't happen, press and hold the right mouse button in the Mix window and select the hand, known as the "Play" symbol, from the Toolbox which appears.

Click with the right mouse button to raise the value of a counter, and with the left mouse button to decrease it. Observe the way your synthesizer interprets the MIDI messages generated as a result. You must of course have selected a counter whose MIDI send channel corresponds to the input channel of your synthesizer.

Make sure that the synth is not on a patch which has been edited but not yet saved, otherwise all your editing work may be lost. If your machine is set to a combination program or Multi, on some devices (e.g. Yamaha SY77 or SY99, Roland JV-80) you can switch from program to program within the Multi.

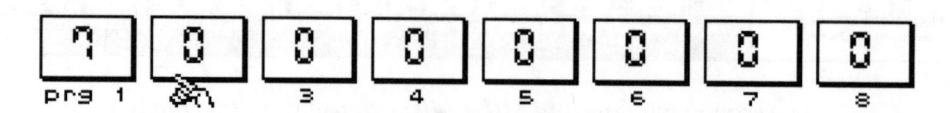

Program Changes using the counters

The fader objects below the counters control the MIDI channel volumes of your MIDI device(s) which must of course be capable of responding to MIDI Control Change 7, the volume message. Click and hold the first fader and move the mouse up and down. The fader will follow your movements and the changes in value will be displayed in the counter and sent out via MIDI. Play a few notes on your keyboard while doing this to hear the volume changing. You can also click directly on the desired fader position and the fader will jump straight to it.

214

Initial Steps

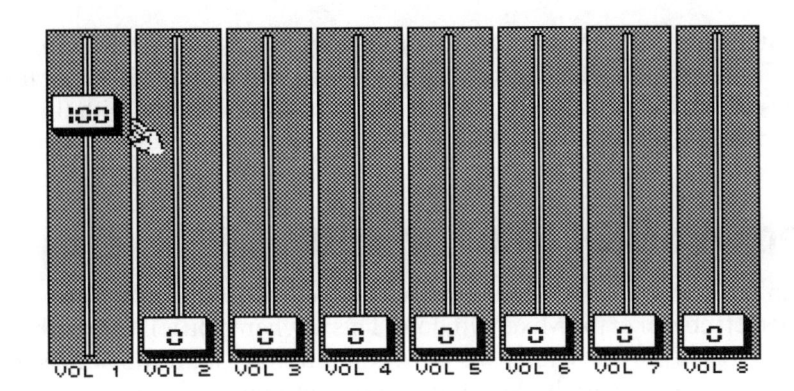

Volume changes with the fader

Keep in mind that in these exercises the recording channel (and therefore the MIDI Thru channel) must correspond to that of the volume fader, or the volume changes will be sent on another channel so that no volume changes will be heard. This applies to all the following exercises as well.

The final row of elements of the preset Mixer controls the pan settings of your MIDI device(s). The knobs only display the current position graphically. If the little black dot is below and to the left, i.e. the 7 o'clock position, the value is set to minimum. The maximum value is achieved by turning all the way to the right. Click and hold when the mouse pointer is in the centre of the pot. Keeping the mouse button down, move the mouse down or to the right to raise the value. Move the mouse up or to the left to decrease the value. Here too, your instrument must be able to recognize MIDI Control Change 10 (Pan), otherwise your movements will have no effect.

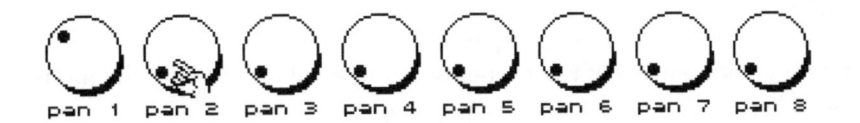

Pan change on MIDI channel 2

Apart from these elements, the Mixer contains a number of other types of object. We'll look at these later. Each control element can be moved using the computer keyboard. To do this, the desired control element must be selected. Click the desired control element (be it fader, counter display or knob) and press and hold [Shift]: this highlights the object. Make sure that only one object is selected as you cannot make changes with the keyboard if more are active. Now the up/down cursor keys can be used to change the value of the selected object. The values change in larger increments if you hold [Shift] down at the same time.

In addition to the 16 knobs, faders, and counter displays, to the far right there is a master fader. Try moving it up and down. You will notice that the volume faders follow the master fader's movement. The master fader regulates the sum of the other faders' volumes.

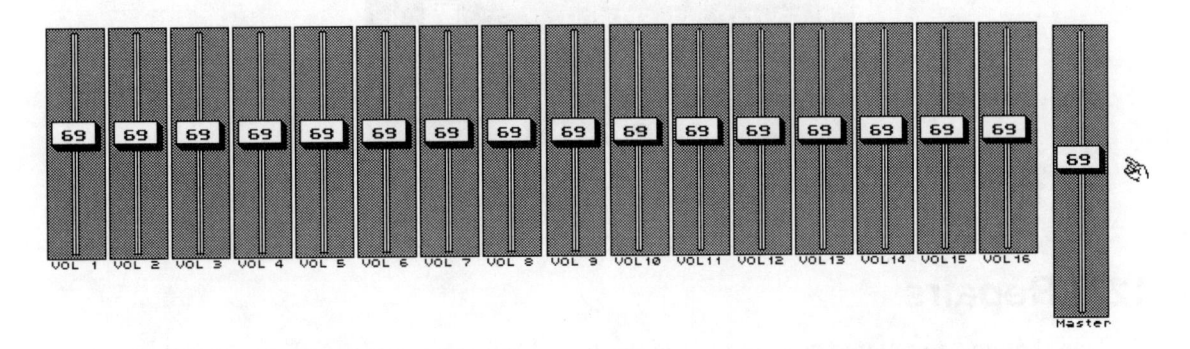

The master volume fader controls all the associated volume faders

215

The MIDI Mixer

You can use the Steinberg MIDI Mixer configuration to preset your entire setup. You can also call up the Mixer during playback and make changes in realtime, which will be immediately sent to the appropriate MIDI channels. Keep in mind that you cannot record with the conventional record mode when the Mixer is active.

12.5 Recording MIDI Mixer events

Of course you can record the changes you make with the control elements. The Mode switch is located at the upper left corner of the Mixer window. This is where you tell Cubase how to process the data you enter. "Local" is the setting we've used until now: it allows access to all control elements and sends the changes to the MIDI output in realtime.

Click Local and it will change to Write. This is the only operating mode where MIDI Mixer actions are recorded during *playback* to the Arrange window's selected Mix Track for later replay. For instance, you could change your instruments' volume levels dynamically, thereby create and record a MIDI mix.

Try the following experiment:
- Enter four tracks containing lengthy Parts.
- Use MIDI channels 1 - 4.
- Define a fifth track as a "Mix Track".
- Create an empty Part equal to the length of the Parts on the first track and select it.
- Enter the MIDI Mixer.
- Set the Mode switch to Write.
- Move all volume faders to the maximum setting, i.e. 127, with the master fader.
- Ensure you are not in Cycle mode.
- Start playback.
- Move the first four volume faders as required.
- Before you press stop, pull the master fader down to a value of 0 with the mouse.
- Stop Cubase.
- Return to the beginning of the Arrangement and start playback.
- This time, don't change anything, just listen and watch.

Not only are the fader movements you made played back via MIDI, but the objects on your screen also move accordingly, provided the Continuous Redraw function is active. To activate it, click and hold the Local menu at the upper left corner of the Mixer window. Choose Options from the menu which appears, and a dialog box appears: if not already active, switch on Continuous Redraw.

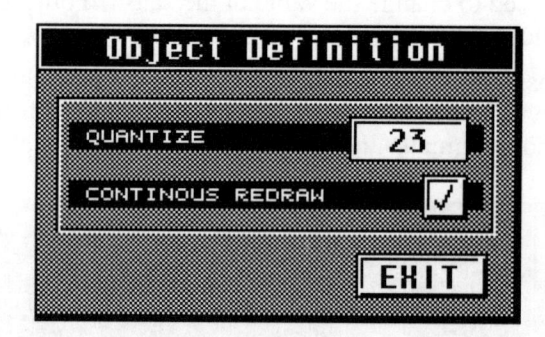

Activate Continuous Redraw

12.6 Repairs

You can change a completed dynamic mix at any time. To do so, simply click and hold the control element you want to edit. Move it during playback keeping the mouse button down. The previously recorded control movements during this section will be deleted, and the new movements recorded in their place. This works for as long as you hold the mouse button down on the control element. Once you release the object, the new recording is terminated and the following events are replayed unchanged. Essentially, this can be seen as a special manual Punch In/Out function for individual MIDI Mixer objects.

If you are unhappy with major portions of your Mixer recording, you can delete these completely. Click the right mouse button. The Toolbox contains three tools you can use for this purpose.

Deletes from the current song position to the end of the Part

Deletes from the beginning of the Part to the current song position

Deletes between the Locator positions

The first tool deletes all the data of one object from the current song position to the end of the Part. The second tool removes all the data of one object from the beginning of the Part to the song position. The final tool deletes all the data of one object between the Locator positions. This means you can define the range with the Locators. Try deleting all the events of one object from your mix. Select the desired tool and click the object for which you want to delete the events. The object is briefly highlighted so you know this selection has actually happened.

You can delete the events of all objects in a specified range if necessary. Use the Locators to define the range and then choose Delete Range from the Local menu. This will delete all Mixer events in the range you have defined.

All the events recorded in an entire Mixer session can be removed using an even simpler method. Exit the MIDI Mixer with Cancel or [Escape] instead of Keep ([Return]). All events entered since you last entered the MIDI Mixer will not be stored. However this does not apply to any changes made manually to the MIDI Mixer objects themselves.

12.7 Problems and solutions

When you move a Mixer object, Cubase records these movements as special events and converts them to MIDI data. In the preceding exercises and numerous other uses, Cubase uses these special events to generate normal MIDI Control Changes. Depending on the number of changes and the extent of the object's movements, a large amount of data may well be generated. As large data loads can cause timing delays and similar problems, Cubase offers a number of options which can be used to reduce data loads to a minimum.

You will find the Quantize function in the Options dialog box of the Local menu. It defines the time intervals at which the object element changes are produced in the Mixer. The display defines this in ticks. Higher quantize values produce larger intervals when an object's value moves slowly from 0 to 127 during playback. This may result in jumps or steps. You must decide if these jumps are acceptable. Keep in mind that even small jumps in volume and pitch are easily audible. In this case, select lower quantize values and let Cubase deal with the larger data load.

The MIDI Mixer

However, a fine resolution is not necessary when it comes to changes in Pan. Here you can select higher Quantize values to reduce the data load. The standard Reduce Controller option in the Function menu does not work in this context. Similarly, the MIDI Mixer movements cannot be displayed in the Key or Drum Editors' Controller Display because Cubase records object movements in the MIDI Mixer as special events (not detectable by the Controller Display) and converts them only afterwards.

12.8 Snapshots and static mixes

One of Cubase's special functions not only reduces the data loads generated, but comes in handy for other uses as well.

At the beginning of a Mixer recording, the objects are in a particular starting configuration. You must ensure that Cubase records this initial configuration. There are two ways of doing this. With the song position set to 1.1.0 and the Write mode active, set the objects to the required positions. This ensures Cubase records object changes at the current song position. You should not start playback for this exercise. You are recording a single definition at a single song position, so the Mixer does not save any dynamic changes, but just the final positions of the movements.

You can place this sort of static set-up at any song position. Go to the desired spot, activate Write, and set the objects to the desired positions. The last position for each object will be the one used.

This set-up recorded in this way can also be saved as a Snapshot. Set up any object configuration, making sure the Mixer is not in Write mode, otherwise, the set-up will be saved as a static mix. Now click the Camera icon.

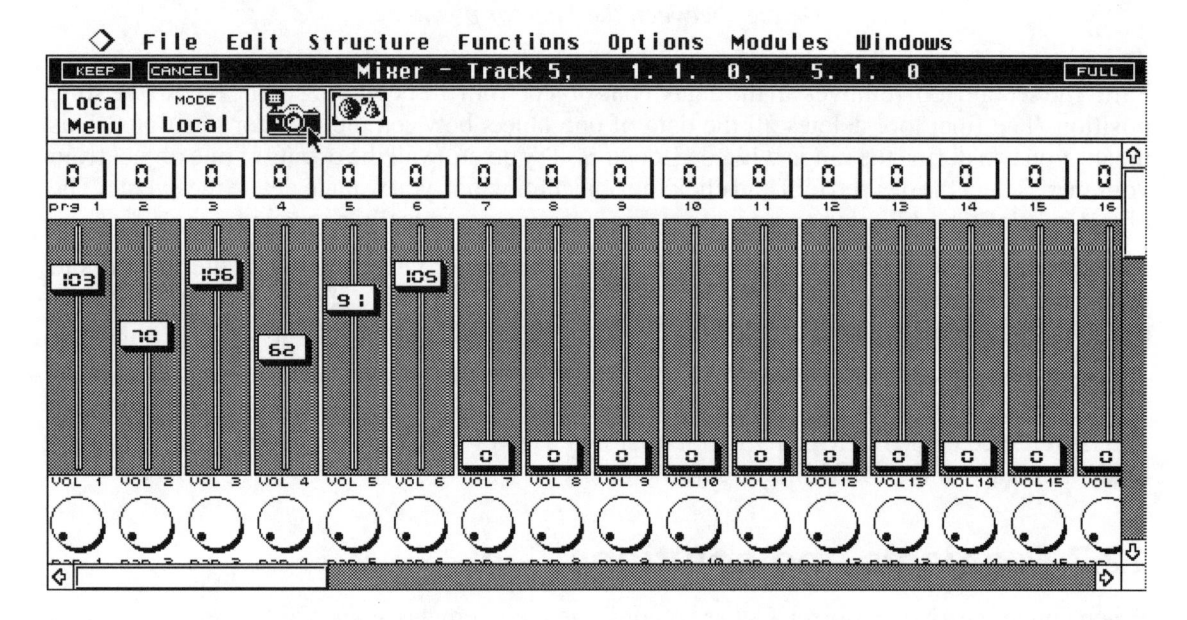

The fader positions are saved as a Snapshot

The empty line to the right now displays a small picture which represents your Snapshot. Move the faders and record a new Snapshot. Altogether you can make up to twelve Snapshots.

You can store up to twelve Snapshots using the Camera

Now click the first Snapshot. You will see your first fader settings displayed. Click any Snapshot to see its settings displayed. The advantage of this option is that only static settings are recalled, and not any movement operations. As with the static mix, the amount of data generated here is substantially lower.

A Snapshot is saved in a temporary buffer. However, this does not mean it is automatically assigned to your recording. You must activate Snapshots in the Write mode to add them to your recording - only then will they be played back. In this case, it doesn't matter whether they were recorded during playback or as a static mix when Cubase was stopped.

12.9 Snapshot options

You can of course name your Snapshots. Double-click the icon and enter a five letter name in the box.

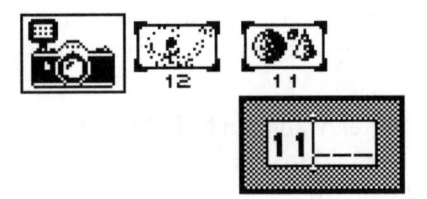

Naming Snapshots

Click a Snapshot icon with the right mouse button in order to delete it. Click on Delete in the dialog box which appears.

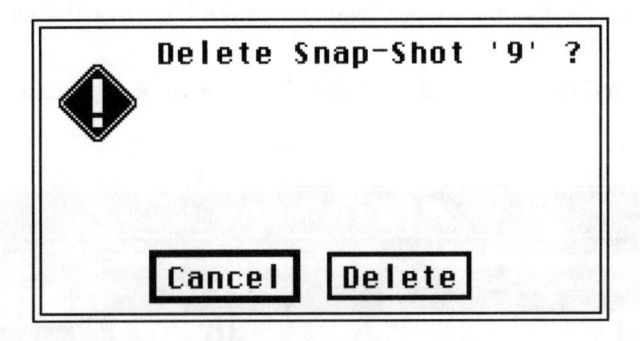

Deleting Snapshots

Snapshot settings can be reprogrammed. Activate the desired Snapshot, set the objects to their new positions, and then click the appropriate Snapshot symbol whilst holding [Shift]. Any changes made will now be recorded. Make sure you've selected the appropriate mode - Local - because in Write mode your new settings would be stored at the current song position as a static mix in the current Arrangement.

If you have already placed the original version of the Snapshot in an Arrangement then these new settings will not be used.

12.10 Replace

In order to alter already placed settings, particularly Snapshots, you must use the Replace function. This function allows Cubase to record new data to replace pre-recorded information. This can include the setting of a single object or a complete Snapshot.

Go to a song position situated just behind the event you want to change. Activate Replace in the Mode menu. Use the appropriate objects to enter the new events or activate a Snapshot and edit it. Cubase inserts the recording from the current song position and replaces the first corresponding object it comes across with the new object settings.

The MIDI Mixer

12.11 Basic rules

When trying to keep the amount of data down, you should follow these rules:
- Wherever you can, use Snapshots instead of dynamic mix operations.
- It is better to click the desired fader position than to move the fader there linearly.
- Use the Quantize function in the Local menu.
- Try to insert operations of this type between playback notes.

These basic rules will help you to avoid timing problems creeping in.

12.12 The Mixer Maps

The abilities of the MIDI Mixer are not limited to the features discussed above. The Additionals disc contains several preset Steinberg Mixer applications in the Mixer Maps file. Most of these Mixer Maps are small editors for popular devices such as the Korg M1, Kawai K1, Oberheim Matrix 1000, and others.

Within Cubase, eight different Mixer Maps can be held. A Mixer Map is a self-contained editor featuring a number of objects. These Maps are loaded into "Slots". You can define which Slots you want to use in the Arrange window.

Follow these steps:
- Return to the Arrange window.
- Move the dividing line between the Part Display and the Track List to the right until you can see the Output column.
- Activate Setup Mixer Maps in the Options menu or double-click the Output column of your Mixer Track in the Arrange window.

The dialog box depicted below is used to assign the eight slots. You can load or remove maps at will.

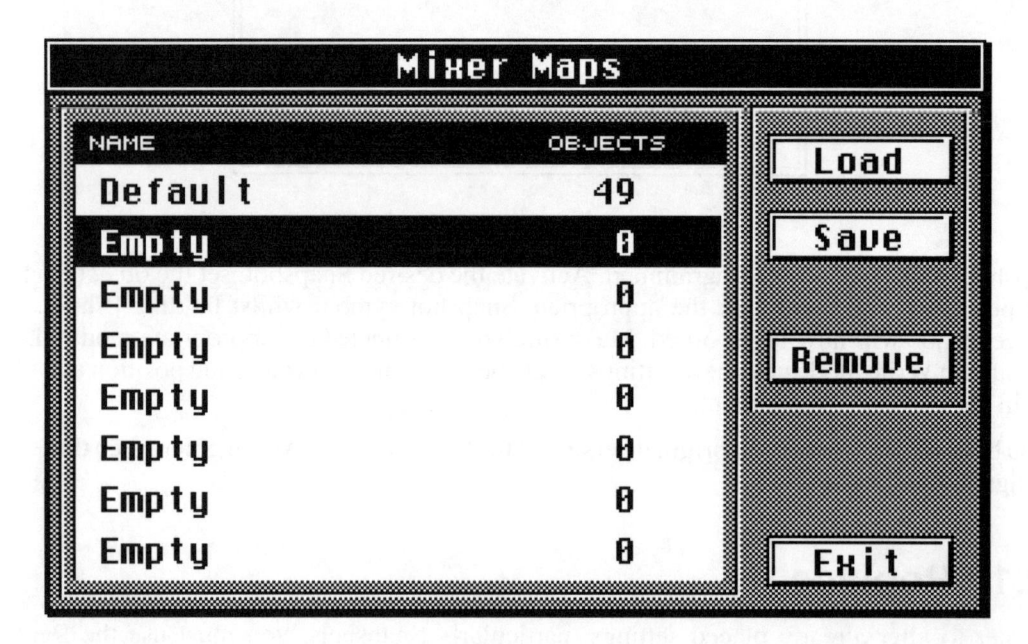

The Mixer Map dialog box

Now we'll load a few maps:
- Insert the Additionals disk containing the Mixer Maps.
- Click one of the eight Slots to select it.
- Click Load.
- Select the desired map from the Mixer Maps file in the Item Selector. Confirm via [Return].

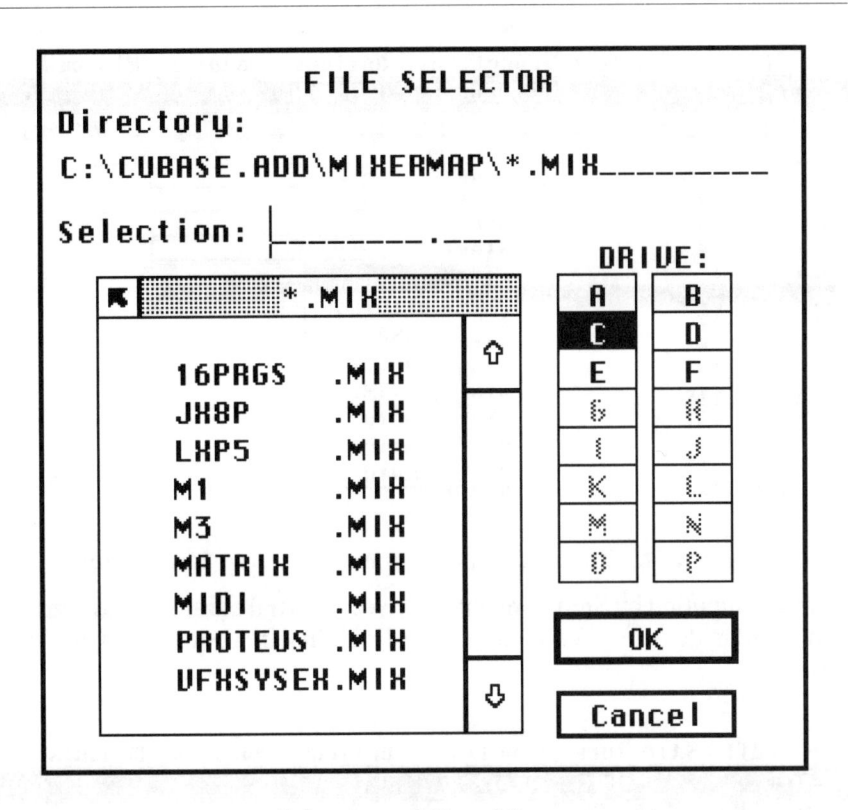

```
              FILE SELECTOR
  Directory:
  C:\CUBASE.ADD\MIXERMAP\*.MIX_____

  Selection: |_____.___
                                            DRIVE:
           *.MIX                         | A | B |
                                         | C | D |
           16PRGS  .MIX                  | E | F |
           JX8P    .MIX                  | G | H |
           LXP5    .MIX                  | I | J |
           M1      .MIX                  | K | L |
           M3      .MIX                  | M | N |
           MATRIX  .MIX                  | O | P |
           MIDI    .MIX
           PROTEUS .MIX                    OK
           VFXSYSEX.MIX
                                          Cancel
```

Selecting a Mixer Map

- Cubase will load the Map into the selected Slot.
- You can now select additional Slots and load Maps into them.

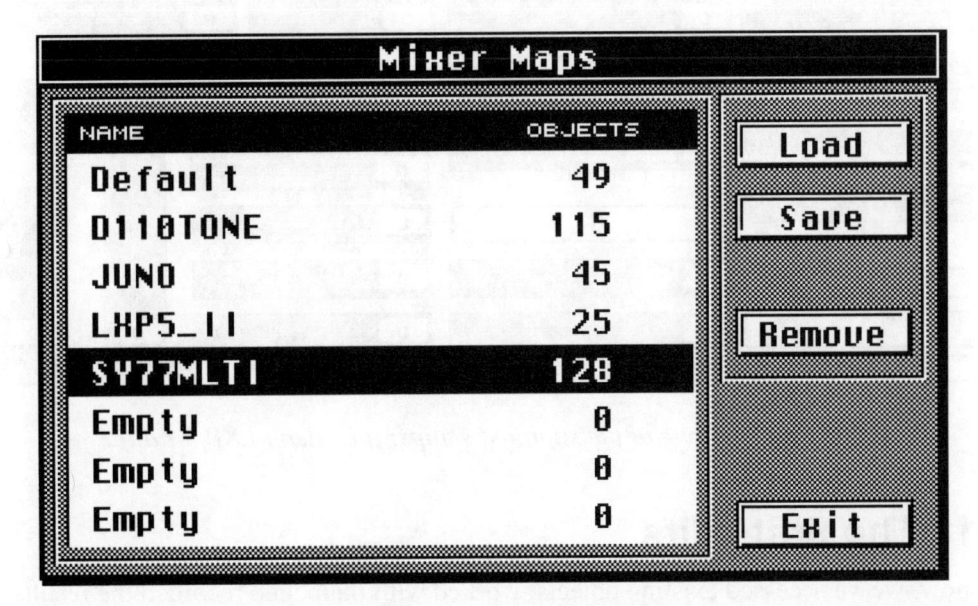

```
                  Mixer Maps
  NAME                    OBJECTS      | Load |
  Default                    49
  D110TONE                  115        | Save |
  JUNO                       45
  LXP5_II                    25        | Remove |
  SY77MLTI                  128
  Empty                       0
  Empty                       0
  Empty                       0        | Exit |
```

Loading several Mixer Maps

The Mixer Maps are now held in the memory of your computer. The number of objects in each is displayed in the dialog box. Each Map can contain up to 128 objects. A Mixer Map can be removed just as easily by selecting the Map you want to clear and clicking Remove.

Each Mix Track you create can have a different Map assigned to it. Click and hold with the mouse pointer on the Output column of the Mix Track: a selection list appears from which you can choose one of the eight Mixer Maps. Each Part you create in this Track accesses the Mixer Map entered in its Output column.

The MIDI Mixer

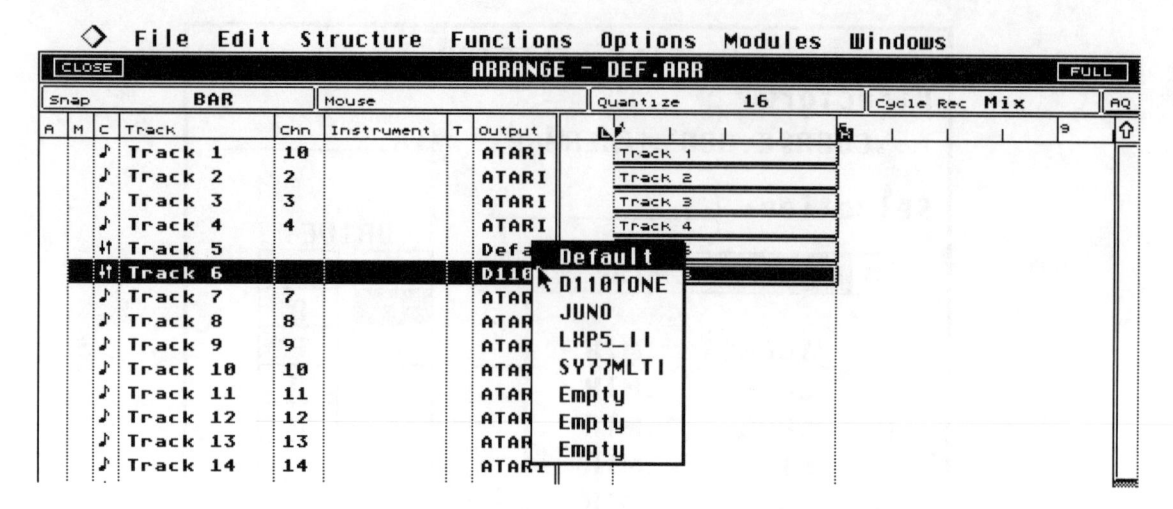

Each Mix Track can access one of the eight Mixer Maps

Most of the Maps supplied by Steinberg enable at least partial parameter editing of synthesizers, Mixers, and similar devices. We'll take a look at this in detail when we cover advanced applications.

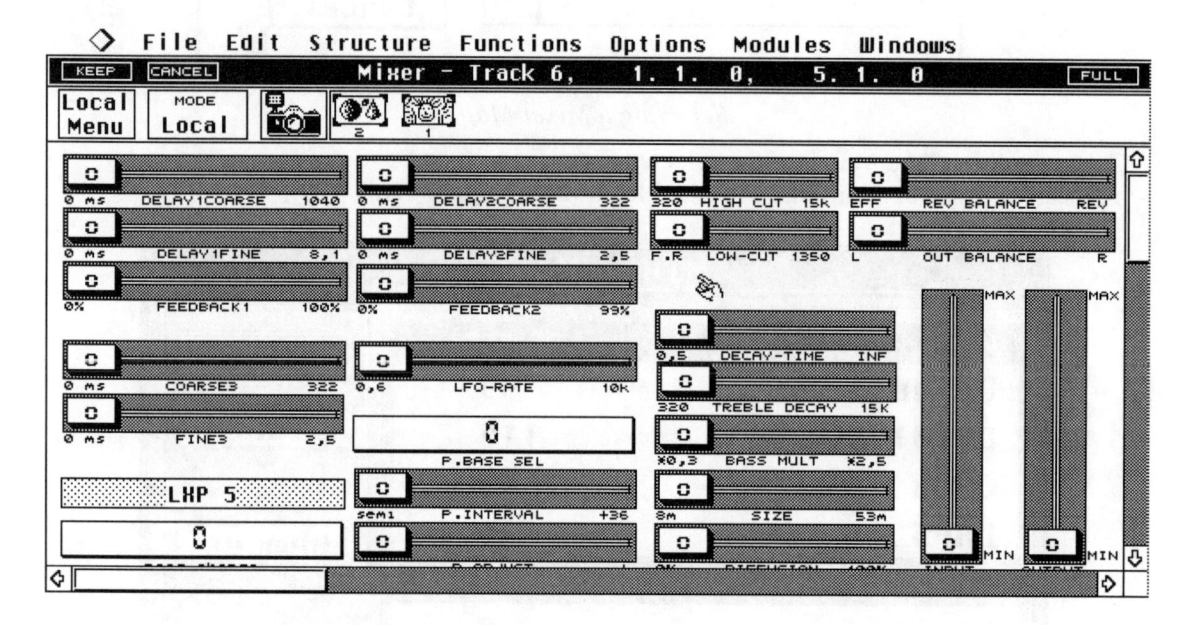

An example of one of the supplied setups: a Lexicon LXP 5 Editor

12.13 The first edits

Until now, we've accessed existing objects, worked with them, and recorded the results in the Arrangement. We haven't actually edited the objects themselves. This is what we will do now. So as to work with familiar events to start with, let's begin by creating the Map used at the beginning of this section for setting volumes, pan, and program changes. But first we must delete the existing elements.
- Return to the Mixer.
- Select the Arrow tool from the Toolbox.
- Select all Mixer objects using the Select All command from the Edit menu. ([Control][A]). All the objects will be framed by a dotted line.
- [Backspace] or [Delete] will now delete all objects.

222

The First Edits

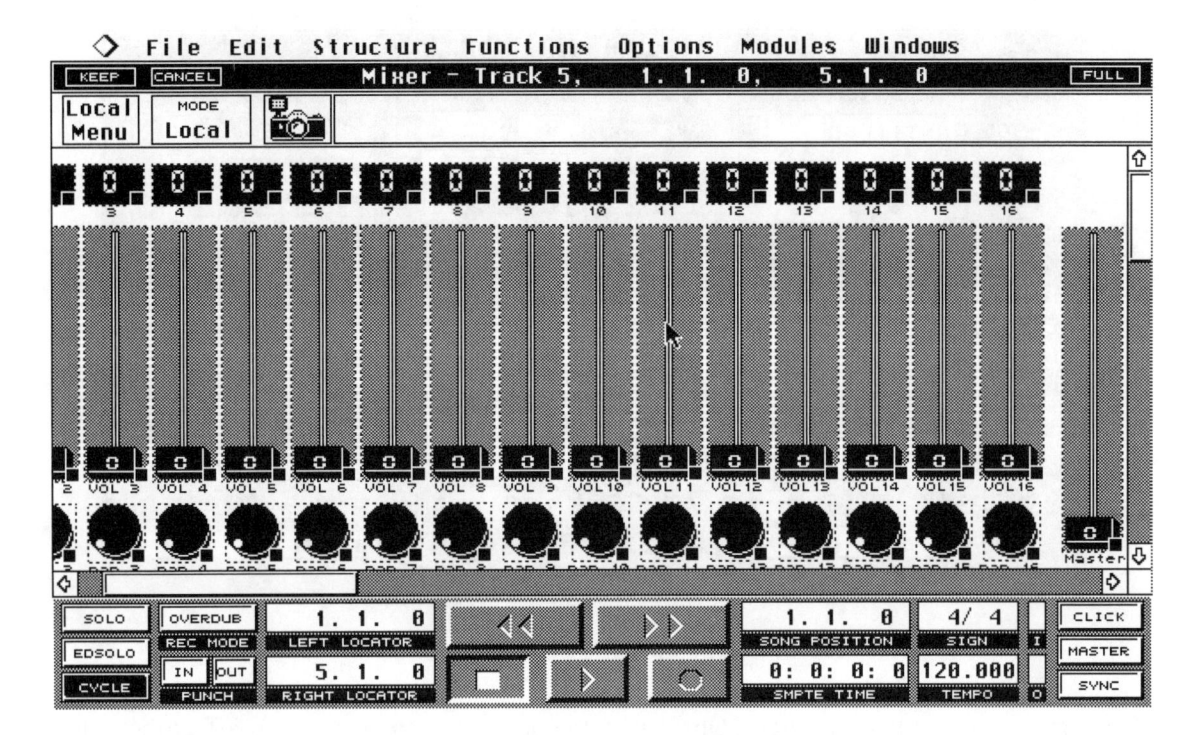

First all objects are selected...

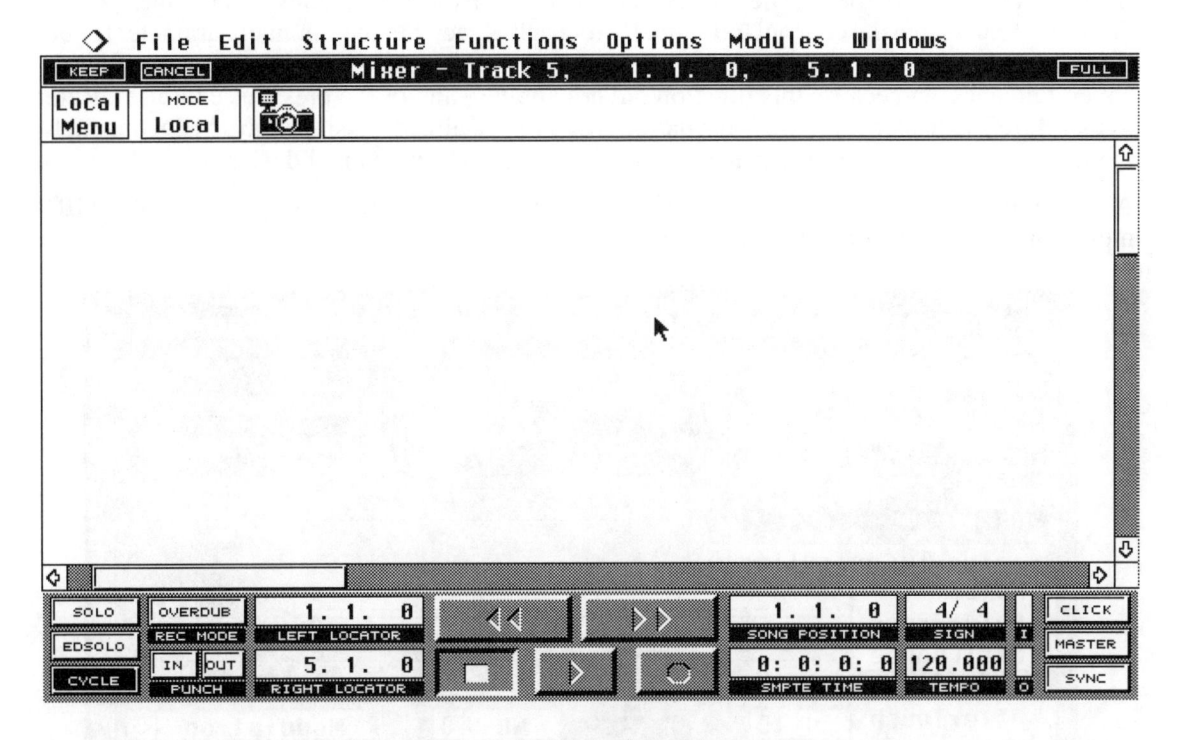

...and then deleted

You should have an empty Mixer window in which we will now place objects. Select the New tool from the Toolbox. The mouse pointer will become a cross.

First we want to install a counter display for a Program Change. Click with the cross in the required position, ideally in top left corner. An extensive dialog box will appear when you release the mouse button.

223

The MIDI Mixer

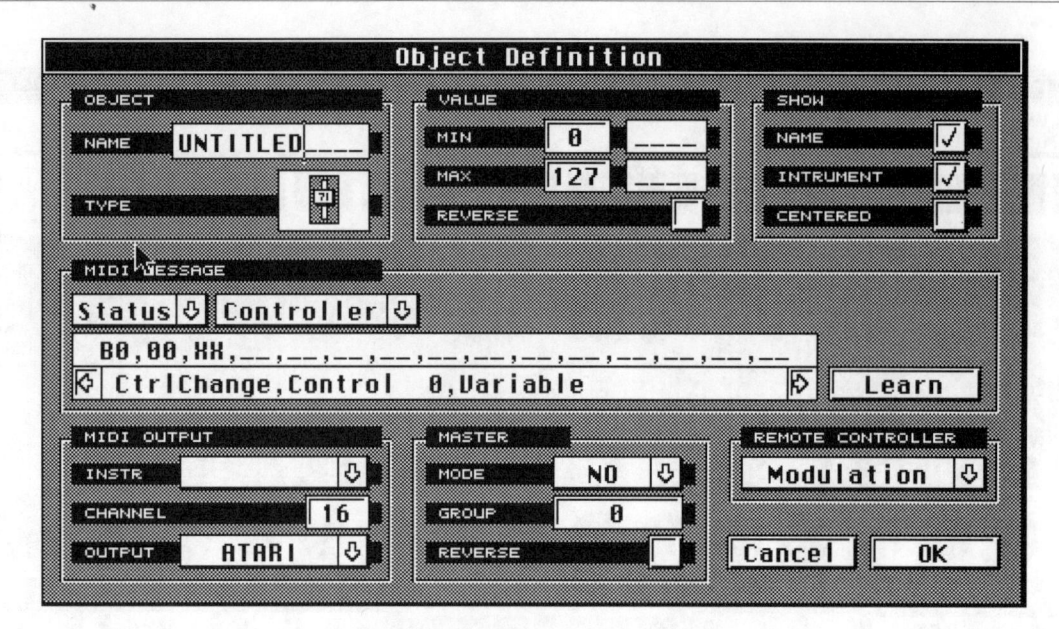

The dialog box used to create new objects

Enter a name for the new object in the Name box, e.g. "1". The only limitation for names is that they can not exceed twelve letters. Obviously, the name you enter does not affect the object function in any way.

In the next step, we will define the MIDI Channel on which the object sends its messages. As you know, you can assign the channel individually for each object. Set the Channel parameter for our first object to "1". You can also route each object to different MIDI outputs, something we haven't done as yet because this function did not apply to any of the previous exercises. Refer to the M*ROS chapter for more information. If you have already assigned the MIDI channels, the Instrument field's pop-up menu contains the correct MIDI channel designation.

A very important aspect of the MIDI Mixer object creation process is specifying the MIDI message you want the object to generate.

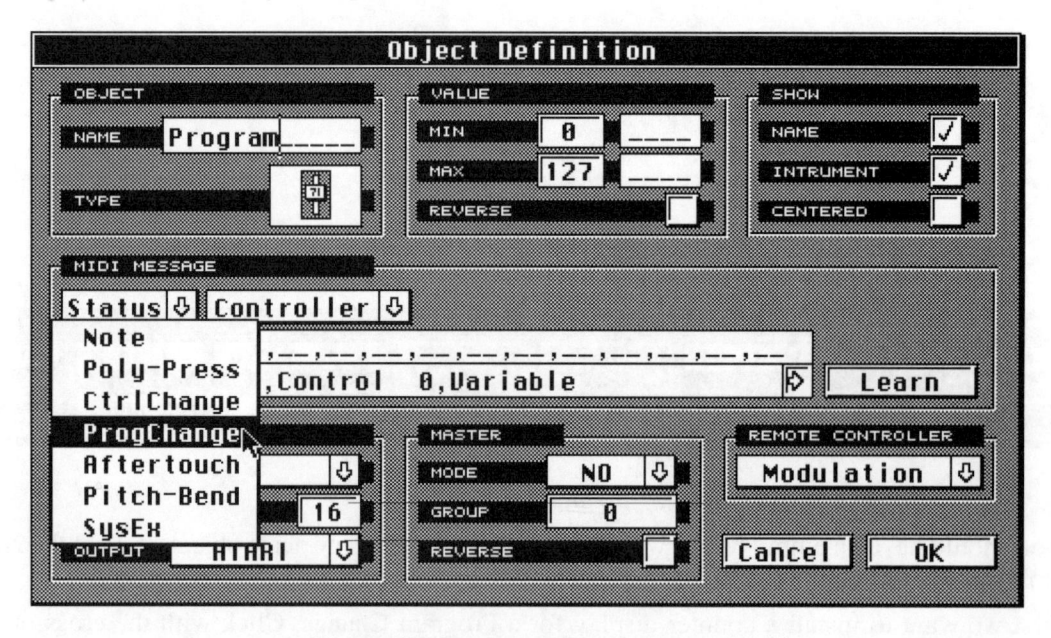

Selecting the Program Change status byte

The MIDI Message field in the dialog box is used to define this. For the first exercise, let's keep this setting fairly simple. Click and hold with the mouse pointer on the Status field, which is

224

where you select the status byte of the MIDI event you want to generate. Let's select ProgChange (which is short for Program Change). You will have learned from working through the MIDI chapter that a MIDI event's status byte defines which MIDI operation will be carried out.

The Input Line located under the Status field contains the following information:

```
C0,XX,__,__,__,__,__,__,__,__,__,__,__
ProgChange,Variable
```

The Input Line: the hexadecimal numbers above, their meaning below

The display consists of two components: the hexadecimal code above and the code's meaning below, provided the program recognizes it. You don't need to have a thorough understanding of the hexadecimal number system for the examples in this section. However, the sections which follow and more complex applications require this knowledge.

MIDI Program Change commands consist of two bytes, the status byte, in this case "C0", and a data byte that specifies the program you want to call up. The second byte is entered in the Input Line as "XX", which is a variable that represents the byte you will edit with the control elements in the MIDI Mixer. We'll take a closer look at this in a moment.

This already completes the MIDI message assignment for our Program Change object. The following operations apply to this object's graphic display and its specific function. The Object field is used to define its graphic display. You already know three of the options - the fader, the knob and the counter display. Three other objects are available:

The familiar objects

The function of the horizontal fader is identical to that of the vertical fader, only the graphic display is different:

The horizontal fader

The push button is different from all other objects in that it can only send two different values.

The push button

The "Text" event fulfils no MIDI function. It is simply used to label the Mixer or to describe its elements. You can use the Text function to add comments on the Mixer Map or to designate certain elements.

Entering text

The only other settings that are also important to our first object are the Value Min and Value

The MIDI Mixer

Max entries. Leave these at "0" for the minimum and "127" for the maximum values. These parameters are used to limit an object's value adjustment range. Most synthesizers and MIDI sound modules accept Program Change commands from 0/127, so no changes are necessary. However, if you have assigned MIDI Channel 1 to a sound module that has a more limited number of programs, then you should enter this device's highest program number.

N.B. Different instruments use radically different numbering systems. Some devices use a bank system (A-1, A-2...D-16), others start at "1" rather than "0". This does not affect the MIDI message because MIDI always counts from 0 to 127. However, you have to know which programs these numbers address. Refer to the appendix for a conversion table.

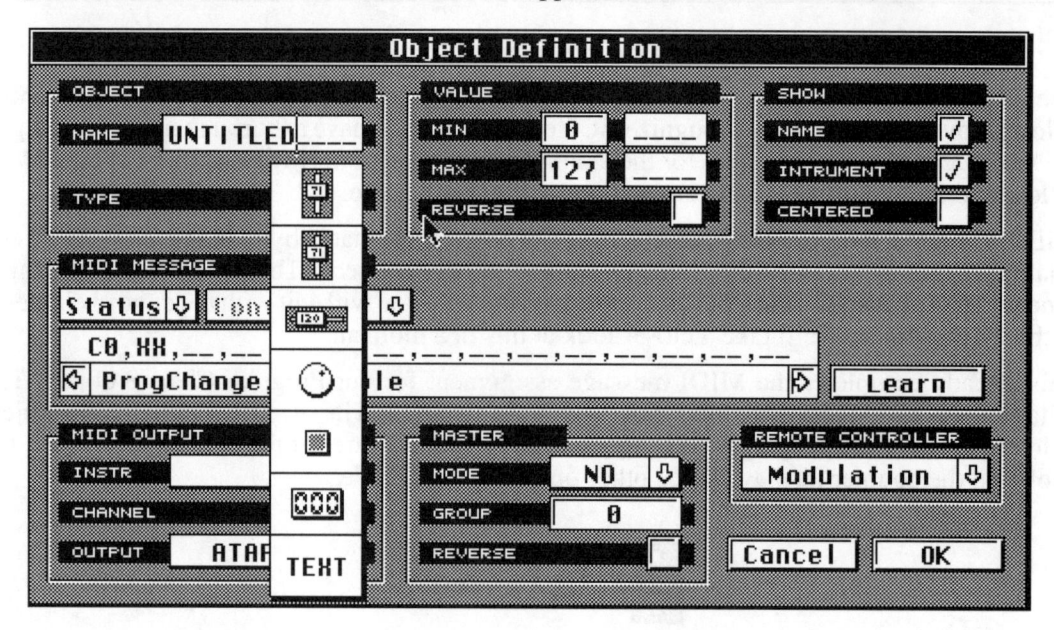

The different types of object

Select the counter object. This is all we need to do to define the first object, so now click OK ([Return]). The counter display is at the desired position in the Mixer. Before we try it out, here's a brief explanation of the tools in the Toolbox and their functions:
- The Hand is used exclusively to manipulate objects.
- The Arrow allows you to change existing objects.
- The New tool creates new objects and calls up the definition box exclusively for this purpose.

Select the Hand tool and move the values in the counter display up and down. Follow the results these movements produce on your sound module. If you defined a maximum value other than 127, that is as high as the counter will go. Press and hold [Shift] and the value changes will be larger increments. Ensure you are in the Local and not the Write mode, otherwise your experiments will be entered in the current Arrangement.

Now activate the New tool in the Toolbox and define fifteen more counter displays. Note that the cross position corresponds to the object's left upper corner. Don't feel you have to work through the following steps to enter the remaining counter displays. Steinberg has, after all, supplied you the completed Map. These practical exercises are designed to help you understand how objects are created, not to force unnecessary work upon you.

The procedure for the remaining objects is as follows: click the desired position with the cross. Now all you need to do in the Object Definition box is move the MIDI channel setting up by one for each object, select the desired object shape, in this case a counter display, and enter a name for it. You can copy existing objects: select the Arrow tool from the Toolbox and drag the counter display to the desired position while holding [Alternate] and the mouse button down.

As soon as you release the keys, the Definition box will appear. You can now enter the desired parameters. The object type is already set to the counter display.

The First Edits

You can prevent the object and instrument names (if indeed you have set any) from being displayed via the Show fields, if you wish.

If you run into any space problems, you can move any existing objects at any time. Select the Arrow tool from the Toolbox and select an object with a mouse click. Hold the mouse button down and drag it to another position. Cubase places the objects on an invisible grid, which makes precise positioning much easier. Press and hold [Control] to disable the invisible grid. This allows you to move objects very small distances. One or more selected objects can be deleted via [Backspace] or [Delete].

An existing object can be edited as much as you want later on. Double-click it or select it and press [Control][I]. This opens the Object Definition box in which you can enter any parameter changes.

Now we'll go on to the next item in the Map, the volume faders. We will create at least one of them to get some practice. Select the New tool from the Toolbox and click the desired position. Enter the name and the MIDI channel. Click and hold the Status field and select Control Change. A MIDI Control Change event consists of three bytes: the status byte "B0", which defines it as a Control Change message, and two data bytes. The first data byte specifies the Control Change function.

For our example, we need Control Change number 7 for volume. The input line contains Controller 0, so it must be changed. You have two options. If you click the inputting field, a cursor appears. Use the keyboard cursor keys to move this cursor to the second byte. Delete it with [Backspace] and enter "07". You can delete the entire line via [Escape] if this should become necessary. Keep in mind that the input field displays hexadecimal numbers. Volume's hex value happens to be the same as the decimal number, but this does not apply to all values. For instance, sustain Control Change 64 has the hexadecimal number 40. Refer to the appendix for a complete conversion table.

Direct typed input is only necessary for values which, for instance, refer to SysEx data. Cubase offers a simpler option for handling Control Changes: click and hold the down arrow next to the Controller field. A Control Change selection list appears. Select "MainVolume": the first data byte is automatically entered in the input line.

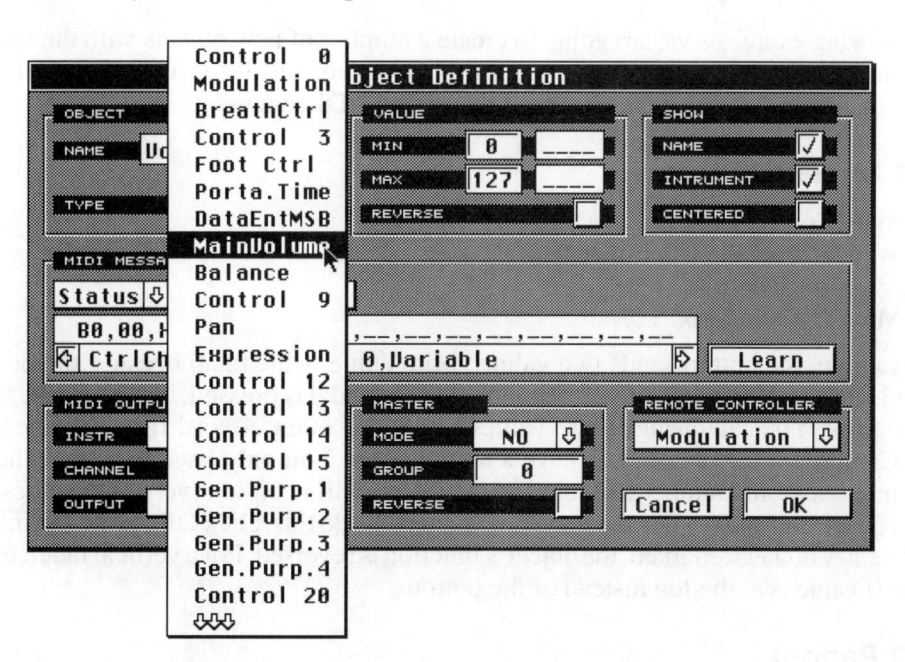

Quick access to the Control Change first data byte

This list may seem too long to scan comfortably, but as soon as you click and hold the bottom arrow, the list scrolls down automatically giving access to the remaining entries. The second data byte, i.e. the variable value, doesn't change of course as this value is generated using the object.

227

The MIDI Mixer

Select the correct object type, in this case the vertical fader, and exit the Object Definition box.

Now that we've created the desired object, we want to adjust its size. Select the Arrow tool from the Toolbox and click the fader. It will be framed by a dotted line. A black square is located at the bottom right corner. Click and hold here with the mouse button and then drag downwards with the mouse. In this way you can change the object to any size you like.

The size does not dictate the maximum value range, but keep in mind that you cannot access the finer resolution intervals if the object display is too small. Object enlargement is designed for fader, text and button objects only.

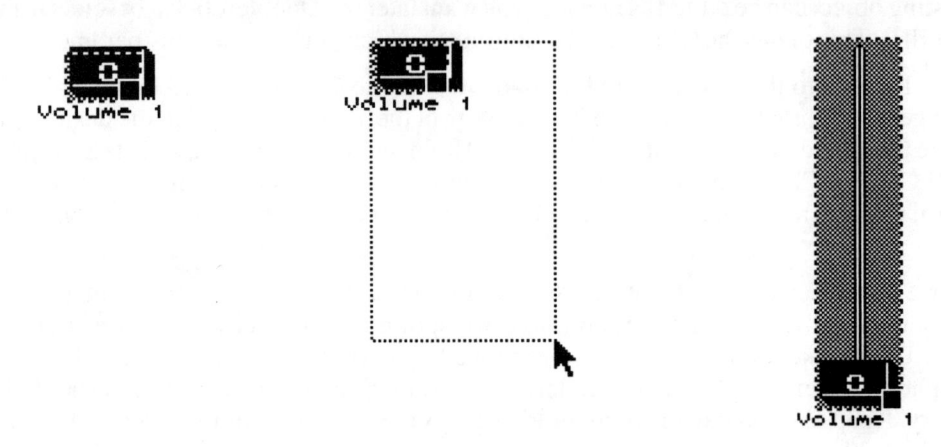

The defined object entered ... and ... enlarged to its final size

You can't start changing values in this mode. For that you have to activate the correct tool, i.e. the Hand tool.

12.14 New objects

In the following exercises we are going to create a number of new objects with the instructions in shorthand. Please follow these in the order they are listed. Set all new objects to MIDI channel 1. Check that the receiving device is set to the same MIDI channel.

12.14.1 Sustain button

- Status byte: Control Change.
- Damper Pedal from the Controller field.
- Object type: push button.
- Value Min: 0, Value Max: 127.

In our example, the button sends two values: Min Value, which is 0 because the pedal is not depressed, and the Max value of 127 denoting that the pedal is pressed, in which case the button is shaded grey. You can change these values to achieve other effects. If you define a volume Control Change for the button, you have a mute button. You only have to change the Control Change number from Damper to Main Volume. You will need to reverse the values, i.e. 127 when not depressed and 0 when the mute is activated. To do this, click DIR in the Definition box. If the Rev entry is check-marked, the object's function is reversed. For a vertical fader, this would mean the 0 value is at the top instead of the bottom.

12.14.2 Panpot

- Status byte: Control Change.
- Pan from the Controller field.
- Object type: rotary knob.
- Value: 0 - 127.

A pan control has a special characteristic which you can allow for in the Definition box. Pan is usually moved from the centre position to the left or right. The corresponding MIDI values are 64 at the centre position, 0 to the far left, and 127 to the far right. Activate the Centered parameter in the Definition box by clicking on the box at the right. The knob display has a centre mark so you can get to see its position better - it has no effect on the MIDI output. You can enter names for the values to help with identifying the function. Use "L" for the minimum value, "R" for the maximum value. Both will be displayed in the MIDI Mixer, but they have no effect on any operations.

12.14.3 Bank Select (e.g. for the Korg Wavestation)

- Status byte: Control Change.
- Control 32 from the Controller field.
- Object type: push button.
- Min Value: 0, Max Value: 1.

You can use this configuration to button between the banks of the Korg Wavestation. Press once for the RAM 1/2 bank, press twice to activate the ROM and Card bank. This only works when you specify a program in the bank after the Program Change command. Therefore, create another counter display with a Program Change status. Limit the value range from 0 to 99. Program changes from 0 to 49 select the programs in the first two banks, ROM or RAM 1, 50 through 99 address the programs in the other two banks, Card or RAM 2.

Limiting the value range in this way ensures that you do not send values to the sound module that it can not recognize. If you send Bank Select values greater than 1, the instrument will not respond.

12.14.4 Additional controls

The number of possible status bytes tells you that there are virtually no limits to what you can do. You can create Pitch Bend, Modulation or other non-note MIDI data. You can also create "note buttons" which allow you to remote-control mutes in some mixing desks via MIDI. The process is the same as the one discussed in the exercises above.

Many instruments allow you to control various parameters via MIDI. For this the manufacturers use the standard MIDI Control Changes. If one or more of your instruments allow realtime Control Changes to affect their internal reverbs or filter parameters, you can use this to your advantage: find out which MIDI Control Change is assigned to which parameter.

A number of devices even allow you to define these assignments. Create an appropriate object in the MIDI Mixer. Ensure the MIDI channel and Control Change number settings are correct and define the appropriate value range. For example, if you can access 50 different reverbs in an effects device, it is unnecessary to assign a value range of 0 to 127 to a Mixer control object.

The majority of MIDI devices allow internal parameter changes at least on a System Exclusive basis. You should leave trying to use this way of working until we have run through some practical exercises on SysEx data.

12.15 Back to the beginning

For the following exercises, we'll return to our starting point, so recall the Steinberg Mixer preset. We'll take a look at the remaining three topics: Master Fader, Text objects, and Remote Controllers.

12.15.1 The Master Fader

Switch to the mouse Arrow tool and open the Object Definition box via a double click on the master fader.

The MIDI Mixer

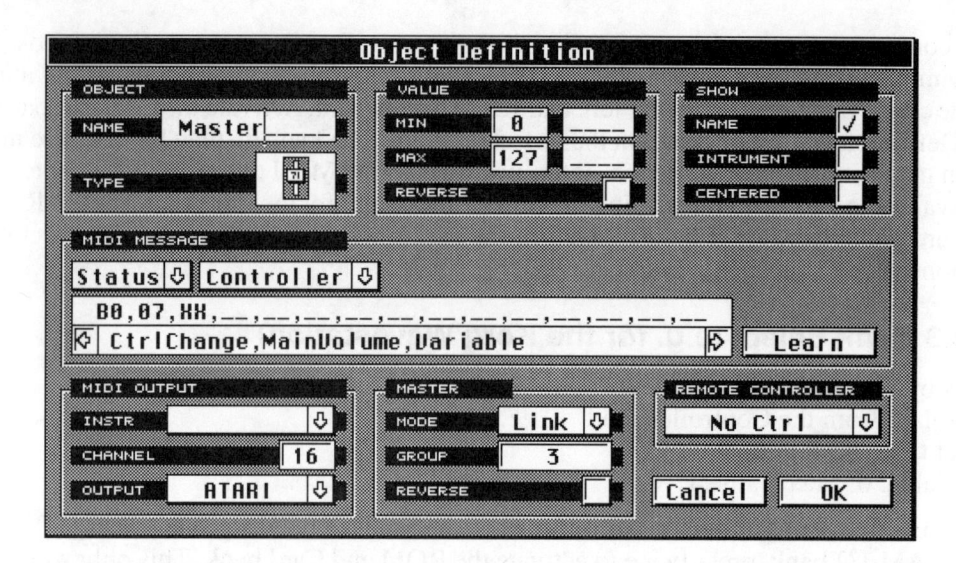

The Object Definition box for the master volume fader

In order to create a configuration where one fader becomes the master and several others its slaves (i.e. they follow its movements), several characteristics must first be programmed. So that Cubase can create several independent masters, all the objects in a group are assigned to Master Groups: all objects including the master fader must belong to the same master group. You can check this by looking at the master group settings of the master fader and other faders. They all belong to the same group, in this case 3.

Up to 128 different master groups are possible. Try changing a fader's master group setting and then return to the Mixer. Now move the master fader: the fader whose group assignment you just changed will not follow its movement anymore. The Reverse parameter next to the master group causes the opposite movement to that of the master fader. In other words, in the standard setting, the fader follows the master fader's movement. If you click the empty box beside Reverse, then it reverses to move in the opposite direction. If you move the master fader down, all the other faders in the same group move up.

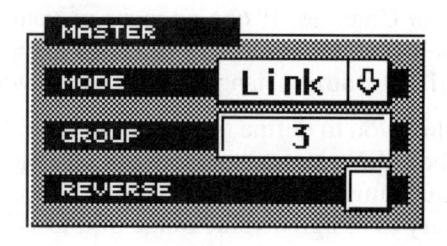

The master fader's parameters

Now that we know how to assign a fader to a master fader group, we have to find out how to redefine a fader as a master fader. The Mode field serves this purpose. You can only assign one master fader per master group.

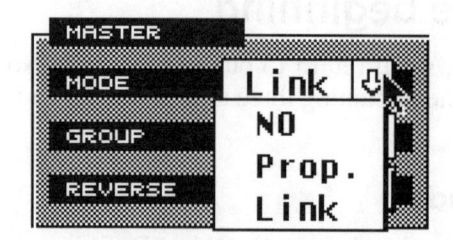

The Mode field's options

230

Click and hold the downward arrow. You can select one of three options form the list. "No" means that the object is not a master fader. Link and Prop assign the fader to a defined master group. The two settings have different connotations: Link ensures all faders in the group follow the master's movement exactly. Prop(ortional) ensures the proportions between the individual faders remain. Try this little experiment. Set the setting of the master volume fader to Prop in the Definition box and return to the Mixer.

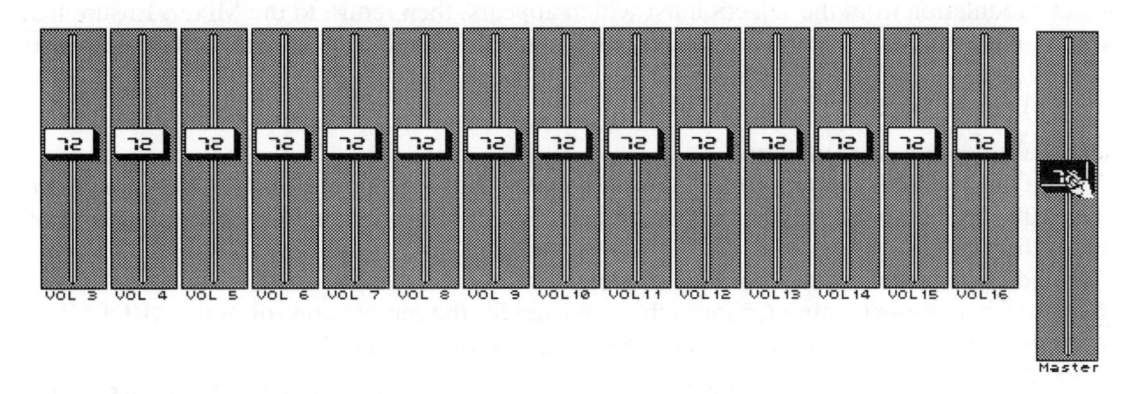

All assigned faders follow the master fader's movement exactly in Link mode

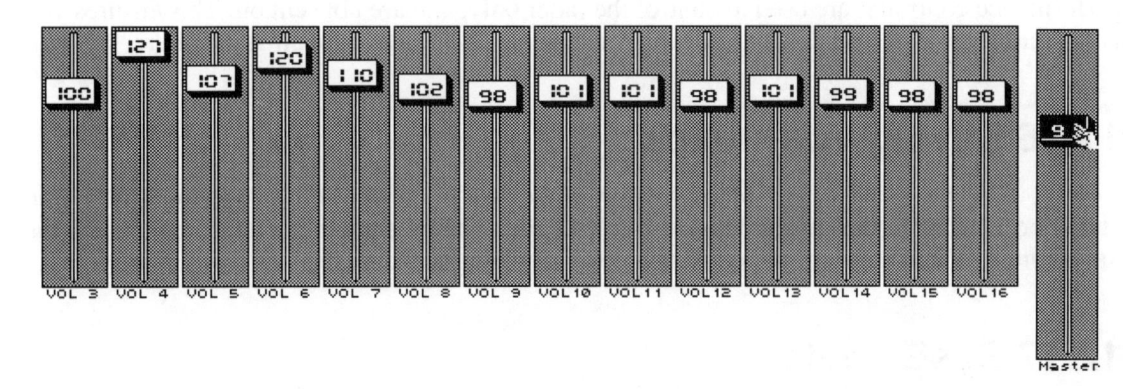

The relative positions between faders remain in Prop mode

Set the master to a value around 50, the 16 faders to different values, and then move the master. You can see the relative positions between faders remain. Drag the master fader to its upper limit. The faders all move to the upper limit, but as long as you hold the mouse button down, the relative positions are still valid. Drag the master fader back down. The faders return to their initial relationships. However, if you move the master fader and the others to the upper limit and release the mouse button, the original positions are deleted. This holds true for the bottom limit as well.

12.15.2 Text objects

The text object is specifically for labelling your MIDI Mixer. Select New from the Toolbox and click any open position with the cross. The only two parameters we'll concern ourselves with for the moment are the object type (select Text), and the Name box above it. You can enter up to twelve letters. They are then entered in the Mixer's Text box. If you need more letters, you have to create another text object. Keep in mind that you only have a total number of 128 objects available, so don't have too much text in the Mixer when you are using lots of objects.

12.15.3 The Remote Controller

Each individual object can be remote-controlled using a MIDI Control Change. The Remote Controller field is used for this function. Go to the Object Definition box of the master fader and click and hold the downward arrow of the Remote Controller.

The MIDI Mixer

Setting the Remote Controller

Select Modulation from the selection list which appears, then return to the Mixer. Ensure that you are in Play mode. If the mouse pointer has turned into a hand then you are. Select the master fader by pressing [Shift] and clicking it. You can now use your master synthesizer's modulation wheel to remote control the master fader.

Bear the following rules in mind:
- Ensure the messages coming from the master match the fader input Control Change number.
- The same applies to the MIDI channel numbers. Select MIDI Output in the Object Definition box of the master.
- The fader(s) must be selected in Play mode.
- Cubase filters those Control Changes that are used for the remote control of the MIDI Mixer out of the MIDI Thru circuit to avoid the possibility of data overspill.

This allows you to redefine Control Changes in real time. For instance, if you assign the modulation wheel as an external performance controller for a fader that is generating Pan values, you can then control the Pan from the modulation wheel in realtime. The values of the performance controller are used to control the fader only, and are not sent on. This ensures you only control the pan, and don't accidentally cause modulation to happen somewhere.

12.16 Saving your maps

You should always save Mixer Maps you have modified or created. First go to the Mixer Map dialog box in the Options menu. Double-click the current Slot and enter a new name. Click the Save button. The map is permanently saved to floppy or hard disk.

12.17 SysEx data

Until now, we've worked exclusively with MIDI Control Changes and in areas where the majority of devices react the same way to standard commands. The MIDI chapter covered the basic structure of SysEx messages. These MIDI messages can be used to access virtually all parameters in your device, edit them, or exchange complete sounds and sound banks.

A detailed introduction to all aspects of SysEx data would exceed the bounds of this book, so we will concentrate on the important aspects only. Not all of this information is necessarily related to the MIDI Mixer, but we will use this opportunity to get to know SysEx data in this context.

12.17.1 Sounds

Each sound in a sound device is the sum total of its parameter settings, i.e. filters, waveforms, envelopes, etc. This data can be sent via MIDI as SysEx messages. You can use Cubase to archive sound data and complete sound banks for each of your devices.

This method has a few disadvantages when compared with conventional editors and sound banks; for instance, the sounds' names are not displayed. However, it also has decisive advantages. Although you can use Program Change commands to select the correct memory locations for different songs, if you have changed the sounds in your synthesizer via MIDI or cartridge, the correct program number is activated but the sound currently stored with that number may be different.

This is why it is advisable to archive the sound data assigned to the program numbers. This method ensures that at the start of a song the right sounds are transferred to your sound modules.

12.17.2 Recording data

Sound data can be recorded in complete blocks in the normal way in the Arrange window. Whether the data block consists of a single sound or a complete sound bank is immaterial. Recording sound data is a lengthy process and generates large data loads. You should not mix this kind of data with normal data such as notes. Keeping these types of data at different points avoids the annoying side-effects that occur when normal data is mixed with SysEx MIDI messages.

Reserve several empty bars before the music begins for sound data. Of course, handling SysEx data is only required if you change the sounds in your synths from time to time, or if you have an enormous library of sounds to choose from. If you never exchange sounds in your devices, you can skip the following exercises.

A large number of synthesizers and MIDI devices allow you to transfer their memory contents at the push of a button. This is the simplest and best option to use to save sound data in Cubase. With some MIDI devices, you can even choose if you want to transfer all the sound data, just some specific sounds in a bank, or individual sounds.

If your instrument features this option, data transfer to Cubase should present no problems. We'll use the Roland JV-80 as our example. Save the internal sound data on another storage medium such as a sound card to avoid permanently losing data during our experimentation.

This is what you do:
- Ensure first of all that the MIDI Thru Filter in the Options menu's MIDI Filter function is active to avoid a MIDI loop.
- Make absolutely sure that the MIDI Record Filter is set to allow SysEx data to pass: the System Exclusive entry must not be highlighted.
- Select a free track and mute any tracks you may have already recorded on. Return to the beginning of the Arrangement.
- Press the Write/Compare button at the top right corner of the JV-80's control panel. You are now in the JV-80's communication menu.
- Select the Bulk entry from the Roland display with the arrow keys. The entry flashes.
- Press Enter on the JV-80. You can now choose what kind of data you wish to send to Cubase. Let's stay with the Internal presets for now.
- Press Enter, which puts the unit into stand-by mode.
- Start Cubase recording.
- Press the Roland's Enter button again as soon as the Cubase count-in is finished to initiate the transfer of data.

Do not use Cycle mode and ensure Punch Out is switched off. Never start the recording before the count-in is finished, otherwise the MIDI data may be recorded incompletely. The track channel must be set to "Any". The same holds true when you send data back to the instrument.

The JV-80 display shows Now Sending. A row of dots denotes the MIDI data transfer, and Cubase's MIDI Input display indicates a continuous activity. Stop the recording as soon as no more MIDI data is being transferred. Go to the List Editor and take a look at the massive data mountain you have generated.

You have effortlessly duplicated the JV-80's sound data from its internal memory to the sequencer. The transfer from Cubase to the Roland is just as simple. Return Cubase to the beginning. Ensure the JV-80's Memory Protect function in the Write/Compare menu is deactivated. Set Cubase to playback. All sounds will be sent back to your instrument. Do not stop Cubase until the load operation is completed.

12.17.3 SysEx in various devices

This example should familiarize you with how data is recorded and transferred. Many devices have quite a few options enabling you to transfer the entire memory content or portions thereof via MIDI. Data transfer for complete sound banks or single sounds is too complex a subject to

The MIDI Mixer

go into the details here. The following gives an overview of the various data transfer options, so you at least have some help in choosing the best method for your situation.

- Data transfer with the push button method as in the above example. This method should be fairly simple in most cases, as you can see by the JV-80 example.
- Loading sounds via the normal MIDI transmission. This is the simplest download method. There isn't much to worry about.
- Some devices do not allow you to initiate a dump by a button push. You will need a Dump Request to cause them to send their data. You can create a dump request in the List Editor, such as for the Yamaha DX7: create an empty Part, select it, and go to the List Editor. Use the Insert menu to enter a SysEx event in the first bar. If you can't remember how to do this, refer to the chapter on the List Editor. Move the dividing line between the grid and event list to the far right until the Comment column is visible. Double-click the Command column of the SysEx event you have generated. An input line will appear which already contains the two entries, "F0" and "F7". All entries in this line must be made using the hexadecimal number system.
- Now you need to enter the Yamaha DX7's dump request code. We want to transfer all 32 internal sounds to the Atari's memory. Go to the DX7's operating manual and find the correct command in the MIDI Implementation Chart. In case you don't have this available, here is the information: Yamaha lists the command structure in binary numbers, not in hexadecimal (the table in this book's appendix can be used for converting). The command's structure looks like this:

1. Byte "F0": Tells Cubase a SysEx message is on its way.
2. Byte "43": The Yamaha company ID.
3. Byte "20": A sub-status byte that defines the MIDI channel.
4. Byte "09": Tells the DX7 to send all 32 sounds via MIDI.
5. Byte "F7": Ends the SysEx message.

- Enter the number sequence, "F0", "43", "20", "09" and "F7", in that order in the Editor line. Each byte must be separated by a comma. If you forget a comma, Cubase will let you know immediately. Exit the input line via [Return] and go back to the Arrange window.
- The MIDI channel of the dump request track must be set to "Any" and the DX7 to MIDI channel 1. Select a new track and start recording. Cubase sends a dump request and the DX7 responds by sending the 32 internal sounds to its MIDI output. This data will be recorded by Cubase on the new track. Do not stop Cubase until the MIDI Input display ceases to move.
- To download the data back to the DX7, proceed as follows: delete the DX7's internal data or load several cartridge sounds to its memory so you can monitor if it has received the sounds correctly. Mute the track containing the dump request. Deactivate the Memory Protect function on the DX7, otherwise data loading will be impossible. Leave all other settings as they are and start playback. The sounds will be transferred back. Once the transfer is complete, you can listen to the results.

This method can be used for other devices. However, there are a few things which might prevent data transfer:
- Some synthesizers operate on specific MIDI channels when using SysEx data, even though this is not a binding MIDI standard. The DX7 is one of these devices. This means that several identical devices within one MIDI system can be addressed independently. Always leave the Cubase MIDI track channel containing the sound data at the "Any" setting. This ensures the MIDI channel setting of the send device is used. If you change the MIDI input channel of a device after sound transfer, you may run into problems when you attempt to download, as the sound module may ignore the SysEx data being sent on the original channel.
- Other devices use a "Device number" that can be set in the module. Leave the MIDI channel and device numbers at their standard settings. If you have two identical devices you will obviously need to assign a different device number to each.
- Edit the recorded MIDI data only when you know exactly what you're doing and how you're going to achieve your aim. Extremely long SysEx message chains such as sound banks cannot be edited in Cubase.
- Many devices use what is known as Handshaking for uploading and downloading. The sender and receiver communicate in both directions during the load procedure.

- This type of transfer technique requires extensive programming, so we will avoid handshaking routines for the time being.
- Keep in mind that most devices cannot produce any sounds when transferring large amounts of SysEx data. Data transfer from Cubase to MIDI devices should be carried out at a suitable point, i.e. where it does not interfere with timing.

12.17.4 More on SysEx

Let's go back to the MIDI Mixer. As well as SysEx messages allowing the transfer of complete sound banks, they can also be used to edit individual parameters, such as a synthesizer's filter frequency during recording. Some devices, e.g. the Roland JD-800, transmit Parameter Change SysEx messages in realtime, i.e. as you change the settings on the device. You can record these changes in the Arrange window using the normal Record mode.

The MIDI Mixer offers extensive applications for most devices that do not send Parameter Changes via MIDI, but can still interpret SysEx data. We've already discussed the Mixer Maps Steinberg has supplied that work on the basis of SysEx data. Now we will take a closer look at them.

Go back to the MIDI Mixer and load the Steinberg Editor Mixer Map for the Lexicon LXP 5. If for some reason this map is not included, select another one. You can include all object movements in your Arrangement during Cubase Mixer recording. For instance, you could record changes in the LXP 5's effect intensity. The same applies to synthesizers. In many cases, the Mixer Map can be used as an editor to create new effects when Cubase is stopped. You will need to bear three things in mind:
- The positions of the Mixer objects will not normally reflect the current settings in your MIDI receiver. This may cause undesirable effects: a synthesizer's filter may be completely open and you want to change this setting via the appropriate MIDI Mixer object and record it. The object you want to use to control this filter frequency is at the zero position. As soon as you click it with the play hand to move it, the filter setting will jump to the zero position and must then be moved back up to the desired value. You'll hear an unpleasant glitch when playing back your recording.
- If you edit a device using the MIDI Mixer, keep in mind that the changes are temporary: most devices store these changes in a temporary buffer. If you want to retain an edited sound or effect, you must save it in the respective device.
- Some editors are tied to a particular channel, i.e. they process SysEx data on a single specific MIDI channel. Your device must be set to that MIDI channel, otherwise it won't follow the MIDI Mixer edits.

Let's return to the LXP editor. Select the Arrow tool from the Toolbox and open the Object Definition box for the LFO Rate. This controls the modulation rate of, say, a chorus effect. You'll recognize most settings from the previous exercises. The input box in the MIDI Message box is of special interest here. It contains neither controllers nor events, but exclusively SysEx messages. You can find the appropriate bytes in the operating manuals of the respective devices. All you need to find out is what the structure of the parameter's SysEx code looks like so you can enter the correct code here. Cubase has a "Learn" mode for all MIDI messages, where incoming MIDI messages are automatically analyzed. Cubase finds out the required status bytes, message length, and the positions of the variables for you. Try it out: click Learn, move a performance controller on your master back and forth, and click Learn again. The input line will display all the necessary information. You can even design a new object. This extremely simple solution can be applied to SysEx data, which makes the creation of your own editor a simple affair. However, the device must be able to transmit these Parameter Changes via MIDI and send them to Cubase. Unfortunately, very few devices can do this, so you are usually forced to enter the SysEx code manually.

12.17.5 The checksum and some special cases

In the last few years, the MIDI implementation of all devices has grown more complex and more confusing. The different methods used to structure and transmit data require a great deal of specialized knowledge on the part of the user. In the past, creating a fairly simple editor for the first Yamaha DX7 was quite feasible. However, many new devices require a great deal more knowledge and time for such an endeavour.

However, even Cubase cannot generate all the messages needed for SysEx activities, since each manufacturer has developed his own way of dealing with SysEx.

Many devices use a "Checksum" during parameter changes. This checks if all bytes were correctly received at the end of a data transmission. If even a single byte is missing, an error message is sent. If the Checksum is not sent and recognized, SysEx message cannot be sent. Cubase automatically computes the Checksum for most Roland devices.

The Controller field has additional options available for special SysEx messages sent to devices by various manufacturers. Some of these applications, such as sound settings using sample selection in a ROM player, require you to enter higher values then the 128 maximum possible via MIDI.
- "LXP Uni" and "LXP Bi": both are specifically tailored to the Lexicon LXP 1.
- "MIDI-Byte>2 Nibbles": in this case a MIDI byte is divided into two 4-bit packages (nibbles) and sent in the MIDI format.
- "Full Byte>2Nibbles": The variable is extended to a full byte. The value from 0 to 255 is divided into two and sent in two bytes. The Ensoniq VFX uses this function, for example.
- "14 bit": The variable is converted to a bipolar 14-byte format used for example by the M and T series Korg synthesizers.
- „"7 bit +MSB": The variable is extended to a full byte format (0 - 125). This format is used by Oberheim Matrix synthesizers, among others.

If you want to use one of these formats, enter the variable in the input line of the SysEx message at the position you want to change. The following byte must be set to "00", to leave room for the extensions discussed above.

It would take too much time and space to discuss all the details here: please refer to the operating manuals of your devices.

12.17.6 Some good advice

Do not work with SysEx data until you are absolutely sure you know what you are doing. Only a few experts succeed at programming complex Mixer Maps for sound editing. If you want to try it anyway, use Steinberg's Mixer Maps or special editor programs. Find out if it is possible to change your instrument's sound parameters via MIDI Parameter Changes. This is a much simpler method than dealing with SysEx messages. The results are the same, just the effort and complications are so much less than with SysEx messages. Besides, Parameter Changes don't suffer from the typical SysEx communication problems that occur when other MIDI messages are sent at the same time.

13 The Logical Editor

The four Cubase editors we've already looked at enable you to edit and create various MIDI events simply and clearly. You have probably noticed that the major differences in the editors are basically due to the form of display. The basic functions and editing possibilities are not that different; it's just the graphic representation that varies. You can select your favourite editor for any particular situation, as each editor has a use to which it is especially suited.

The editors we will cover in this chapter, and the next one, are different to the editors we have covered so far, both in their function and operation. MIDI is an essential factor here, so prepare yourself by reviewing Chapter 5 if you still don't feel at home with this subject.

The Logical Editor enables you to extensively manipulate your recorded material. It does however require more abstract thought, but don't let the sheer magnitude of features bother you. Once you understand its basic functions, you'll see that the Logical Editor is a valuable creative tool. We'll approach this editor in the usual way, with the help of practical examples. At first, we'll stick to the basics so you quickly get an idea of what it's all about. Then we'll use other examples to show what logical editing is ultimately capable of.

13.1 Starting is the easy bit

Logical edit functions work on all the selected Parts. If no Part is selected, then all the Parts on the active Track are edited. This differs from the way the other editors work, where you select the Parts and work on them one after the other. Here, all Parts are edited at the same time.

Note: if you call up the Logical Editor from another editor, pay attention to the setting in the "selection" sub-menu. If the setting is "All", then all the events in the Part are edited by the Logical Editor. The "Selected" setting means that only the events that were previously selected in the other editor will be edited.

If you didn't select an event before you changed to the Logical Editor, then editing is impossible. If you are not quite clear about the significance of the "selection" sub-menu and its options, refer to the relevant section in the chapter on the Key Editor. The top field in the Logical Editor shows which selection is active (if you entered from another editor), or how many Parts you are currently editing (if you entered from the Arrange window). There are lots of other ways to limit operations to specific events or event types. We'll cover these as we move along.

The Logical Editor

Get ready for our first exercise:
- Delete all Parts, select track 1, and play in a piano Part of any length. Try to make it one where your left and right hands play independently. Avoid overlapping notes.
- Copy the Part to another track and mute it.
- Make sure that the original Part is selected and go to the Key Editor, so that you have a visible display of the results of the Logical Editor later. The "selection" menu should be set to "All Events". Go from the Key Editor to the Logical Editor via the Edit menu or by pressing [Control][L].

The Logical Editor appears. The display resembles the Input Transformer in many respects. There are no graphic aids, and the window cannot be altered in any way. The Title Bar at the top of the window shows how many Parts you have selected, or which editor selection is currently active. You can move the window if necessary. Click and hold the Title Bar with the mouse button, then drag the editor to the desired position. There is obviously more room to do this on a large screen monitor than on the small SM124 or SM144.

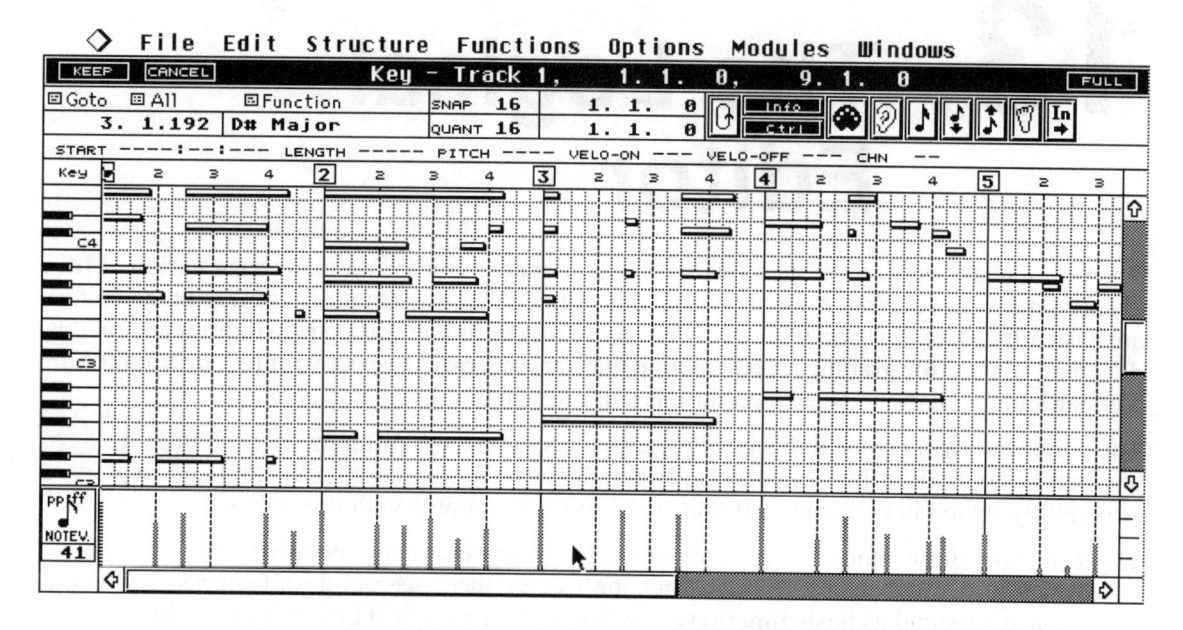

Create a Part and go to the Key Editor

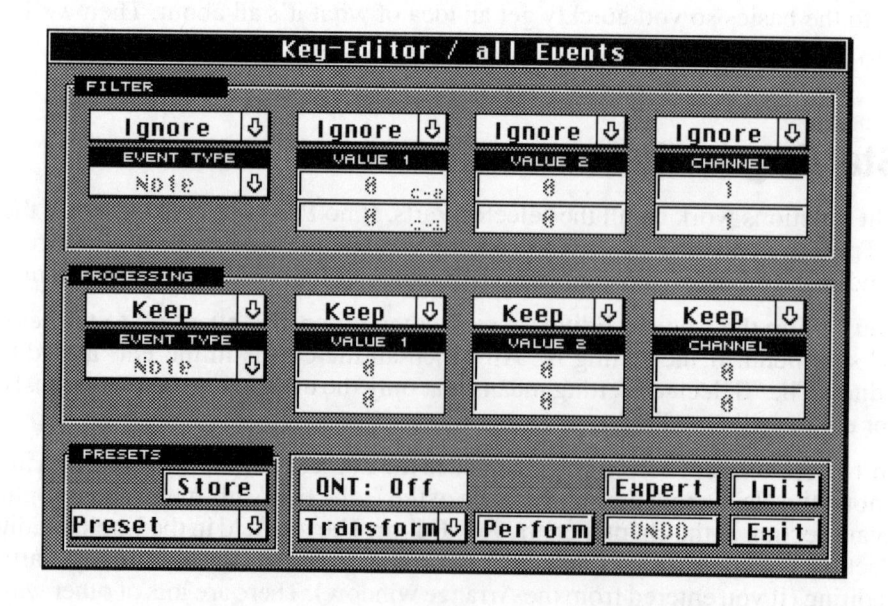

Go from the Key Editor to the Logical Editor

Starting is the Easy Bit

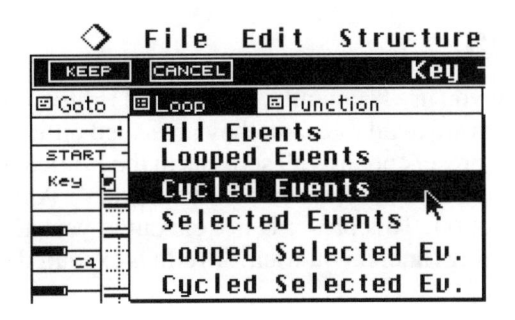

If you go from another editor to the Logical Editor, the heading displays...

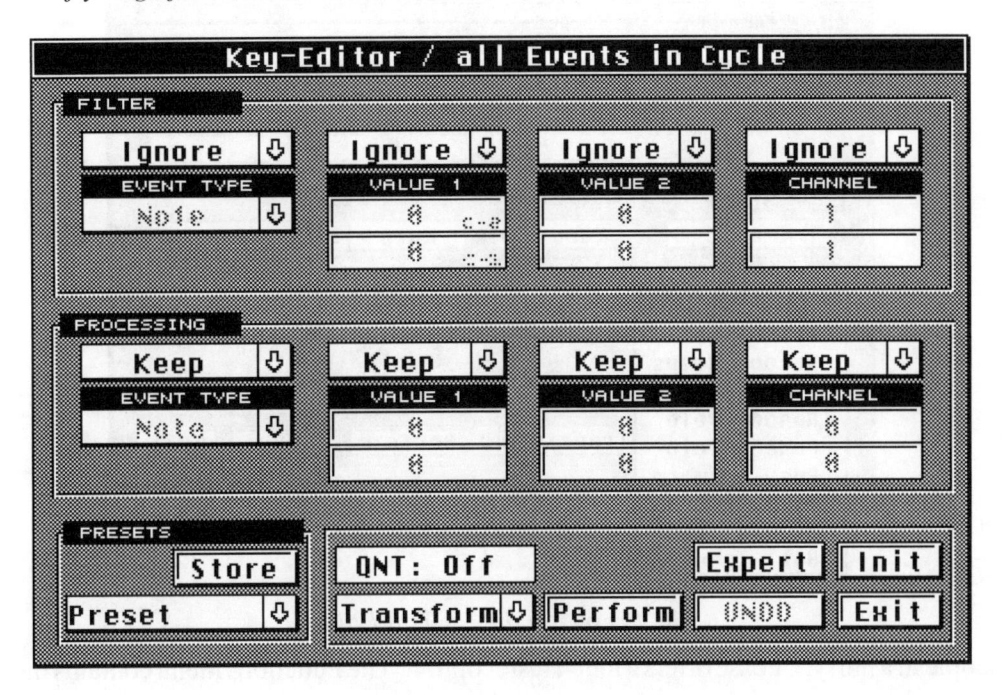

*...which setting was active in the first editor's "selection" sub-menu
(in this case, all events in the cycle)*

One Part : Track 1

One Track : Track 1

*If you enter the Logical Editor from the Arrange window, it displays how many Parts,
if any, are being processed, or which track is being processed*

The Logical Editor can be compared to a very specialised musical calculator that manipulates the events in the selected Parts according to the settings that you make. We won't waste time with lengthy explanations, but get down to the basics with some practical applications. In this editor, you must be sure about what you want to do, and how you are going to do it. Every conceivable kind of MIDI data manipulation is possible, including things that may be unusable like generating program changes from note commands.

To make it easier to become acquainted with the Logical Editor, there are two versions known as "Easy" and "Expert". You can swap between the two by clicking the field next to "Init", which tells you which version you will change to. If "Expert" is displayed, you are in the "Easy" version; by clicking the word "Expert", you enter that version, and vice versa. For now, we'll stick with the "Easy" version.

The Logical Editor

13.2 The Presets

To simplify operations that you use frequently, the Logical Editor allows you to save settings as a preset. Ten of these presets are available, and they are saved either with a set-up or a song, but not with an arrangement. A preset contains all settings in the Logical Editor. There are two ways to call up a preset. Click the downward arrow next to "Preset". A list appears from which you can select the desired operation. This preset is not executed yet, it's simply set in the Logical Editor. You can alter the settings later if you want. An edit is executed when you click the Perform button.

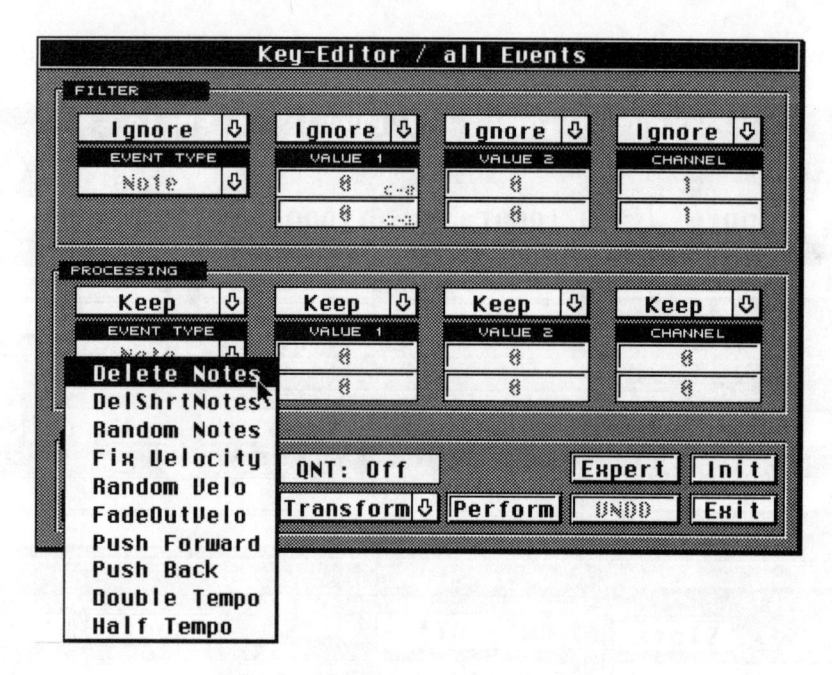

The Presets in the Logical Editor

For people in a hurry, Cubase offers a much faster option. The Functions menu contains the entry "Logical". When you click this a list of presets appears. You can select any preset you want from the list. This is executed as soon as you click it, and doesn't have to be confirmed.

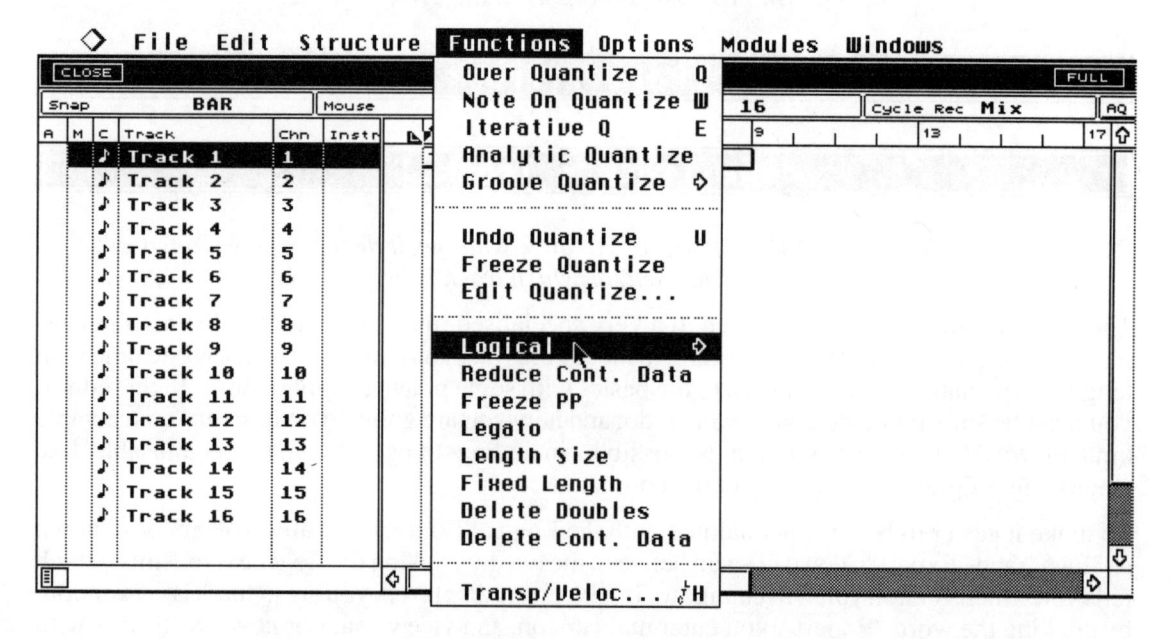

From the Arrange window, you can activate Logical in the Functions menu...

```
Delete Notes
DelShrtNotes
Random Notes
Fix Velocity
Random Velo
FadeOutVelo
Push Forward
Push Back
Double Tempo
Half Tempo
```

...which gives you access to the presets

We'll look at how presets are generated and used later. First, we'll try to understand exactly what the Logical Editor does.

13.3 The first operation

Click "Init" to put the Logical Editor in the neutral setting. It's always a good idea to do this when you want to enter a completely new setting. The bottom screen border of the Logical Editor contains a pull down menu to the left of the inscription "Perform". This has a number of functions which determine what Cubase will do with the events you have selected.

Click and hold the arrow with the mouse button. Now select the "Delete" option. To execute a selected action in the Logical Editor, you must click "Perform". If you do this now, you'll see that all events in the selected Parts are deleted.

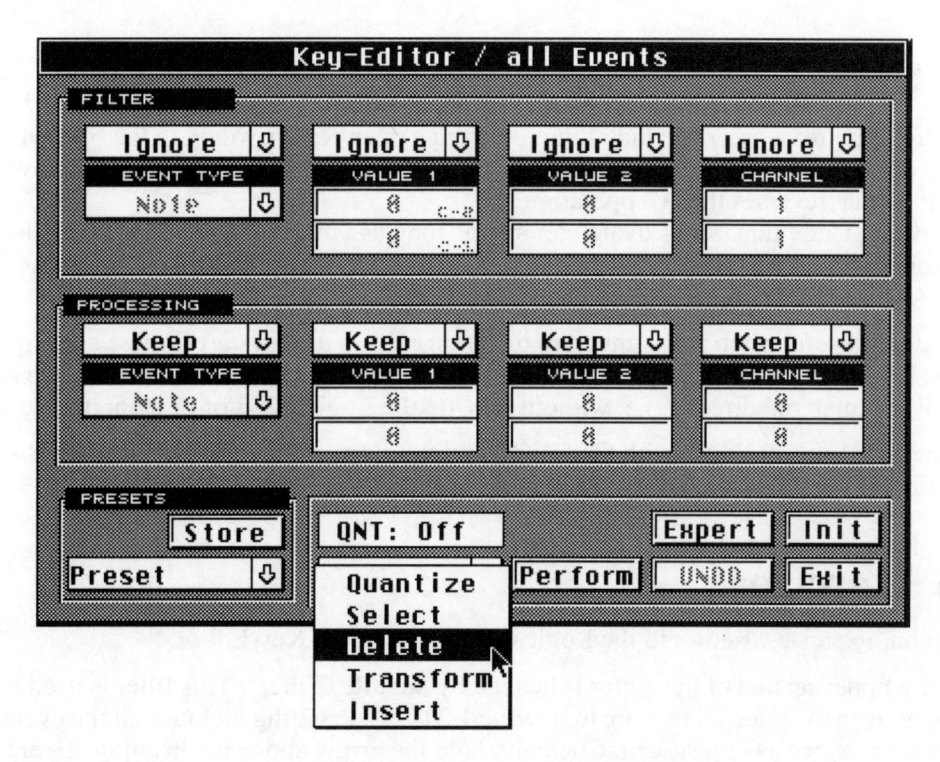

Select Delete and click Perform

The Logical Editor

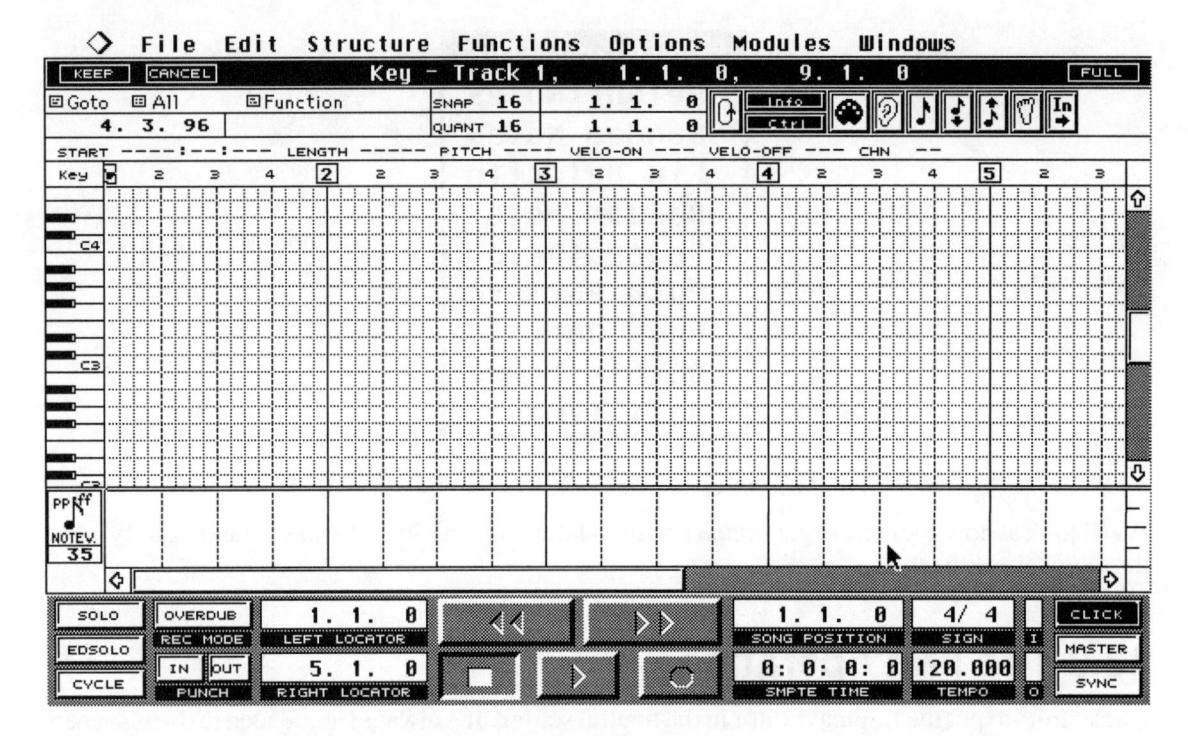

The events have disappeared

Exit the Logical Editor via "Exit" ([Return]). You are now back in the Key Editor, and the events have disappeared. Press "Undo" to bring them back. You can enter the Logical Editor from the Arrange window, as well as from the other editors. However, there are some differences, depending on where you start from. We'll take a closer look at these later, but for the time being make sure you enter the Logical Editor from the Key Editor, not from the Arrange window.

13.4 Undo

This editor features a separate Undo function, which operates according to the following rules:
- Every operation executed by using Perform within the Logical Editor has its own Undo function, which reverses the last operation.
- This special Undo function is available only as long as you stay in the Logical Editor.
- The normal Undo function (press [Undo]) is only available when you have left the Logical Editor. As usual, only your last command is reversed.

This option is useful when you want to try different edits. You can start Cubase and experiment with the Logical Editor during playback. If the results are less than thrilling, you can return to your original material directly, i.e. without leaving the Logical Editor or stopping Cubase.

You leave the Logical Editor with the "Exit" command (press [Return]). You always return to the portion of the program that you called up the Logical Editor from.

13.5 Exercises

Back to our exercises. Return to the Logical Editor from the Key Editor.

The entire upper section of the editor is headed by the title "Filter". This filter is used to define which events in the selected Part are to be edited. The basic setting includes all the events in the selected Part, as we have just seen. Click and hold the arrow above the heading "Event Type". A list featuring three options appears. These options define the logic used to define the type of events that you want to edit. Select "Equal".

Exercises

Initial logical settings

The "Note" entry, which was previously shaded grey (meaning it was not selectable) now turns black. Now you can also make changes in this field. Click the arrow next to "Note" and hold the mouse button down.

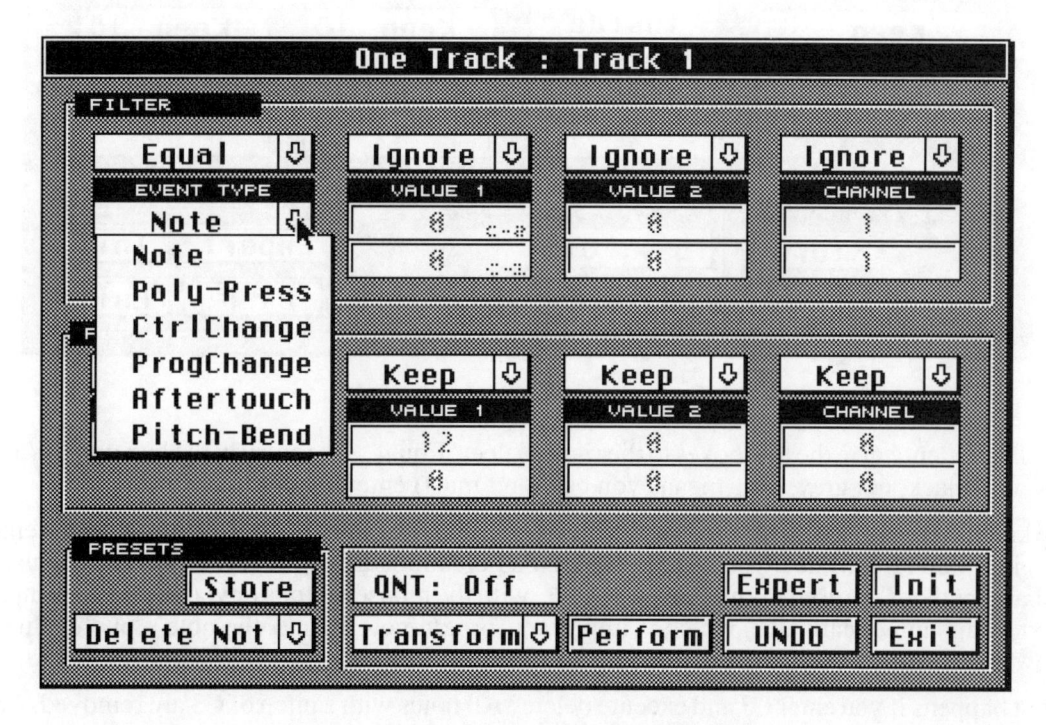

Selection of the event type to be edited

A new selection list appears offering a selection of many MIDI events. You're familiar with these from the other Cubase operations that we've encountered so far. Leave the setting "Note" as it is. The filter settings define the conditions which must be met by the events to be edited. All events that do not meet these requirements remain unchanged. This is the same principle you came across in the Input Transformer.

243

The Logical Editor

In our example, we have already defined one criterion for an operation: if you were to execute the "Delete" function again, Cubase would now delete all events from the selected Part that are identical ("Equal") to note commands. All other events, such as program changes, Control Changes, and so on, remain intact. If you select "Unequal" instead of "Equal", all other events are deleted, and the selected event type remains intact. In our example, the notes would remain, and all other types of event would be deleted.

This method of defining criteria defines the basic way that the Logical Editor operates.

The boxes next to the Event box are used for further definitions. As long as "Ignore" is displayed above the black dividing line, all events specified in the Event Type box are edited in the way you have selected; in this case they are deleted. Value 1, 2 and Channel further define the precise events that are to be processed. Here are few examples:

Leave the Event Type settings as they are (Note = Equal). In other words, we want to edit all note events. Click and hold with the mouse pointer the box above Value 1. The Selection list that you have just seen appears again, with a few additional entries (see the following diagram).

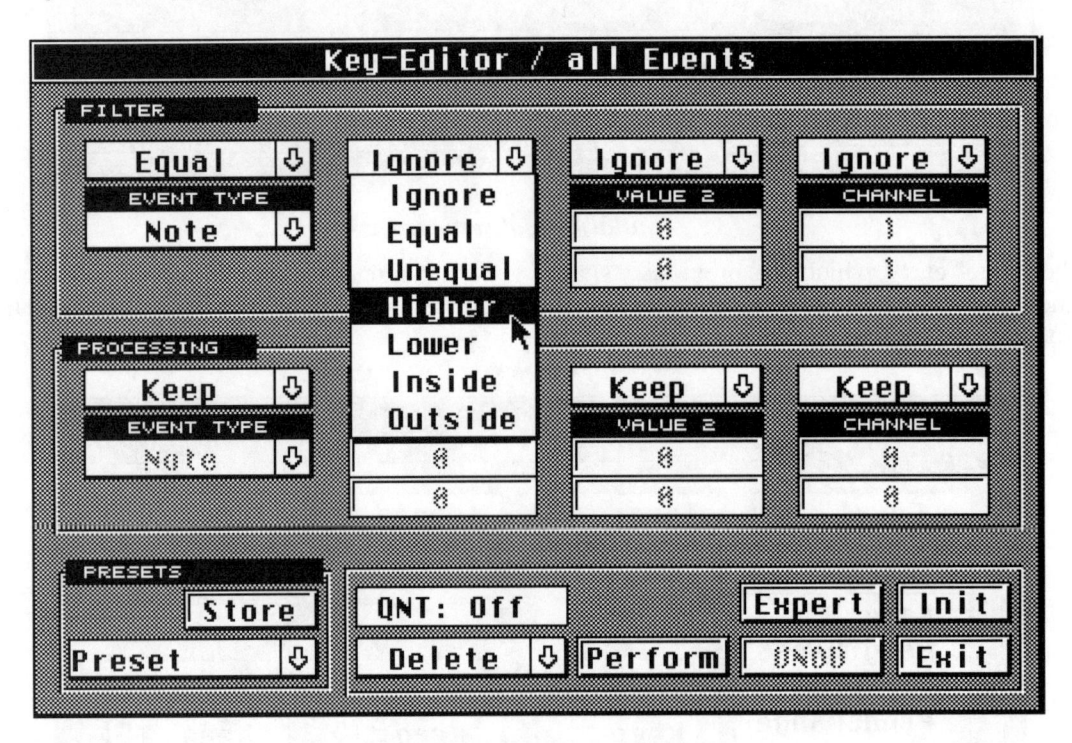

Defining events for editing

The list is identical in the two boxes to the right. Select "Equal". The entry in the box under Value 1 is now black, not grey. This means you can (and must) enter a value.

We know from previous exercises that "Value 1" defines the pitch for note events. You can enter the pitch value for the note you want to edit in the field immediately under "Value 1". The usual Cubase methods are used to enter this value, i.e. with the mouse buttons or via direct typed input. Next to the numerical value, which is important for non-note events, the note's pitch value is shown.

What happens if you enter C3 and execute delete? All notes with a pitch of C3 are removed. Any other data in the selected Part remains untouched. You can see that minor problems can be solved with a minimum of effort. If the "Unequal" setting was active, Cubase would retain all note events with the pitch C3, and delete all other notes.

The Selection list also features the entries "Higher", "Lower", "Inside", and "Outside". You'll probably already be able to guess what these mean. Select "Higher" from the box above Value 1, and enter "Value 1 = C3". The Event Type selection (Note = Equal) remains unchanged. Select

Exercises

Delete, click Perform, and start playback. All notes above the note C3 have been deleted from your Part.

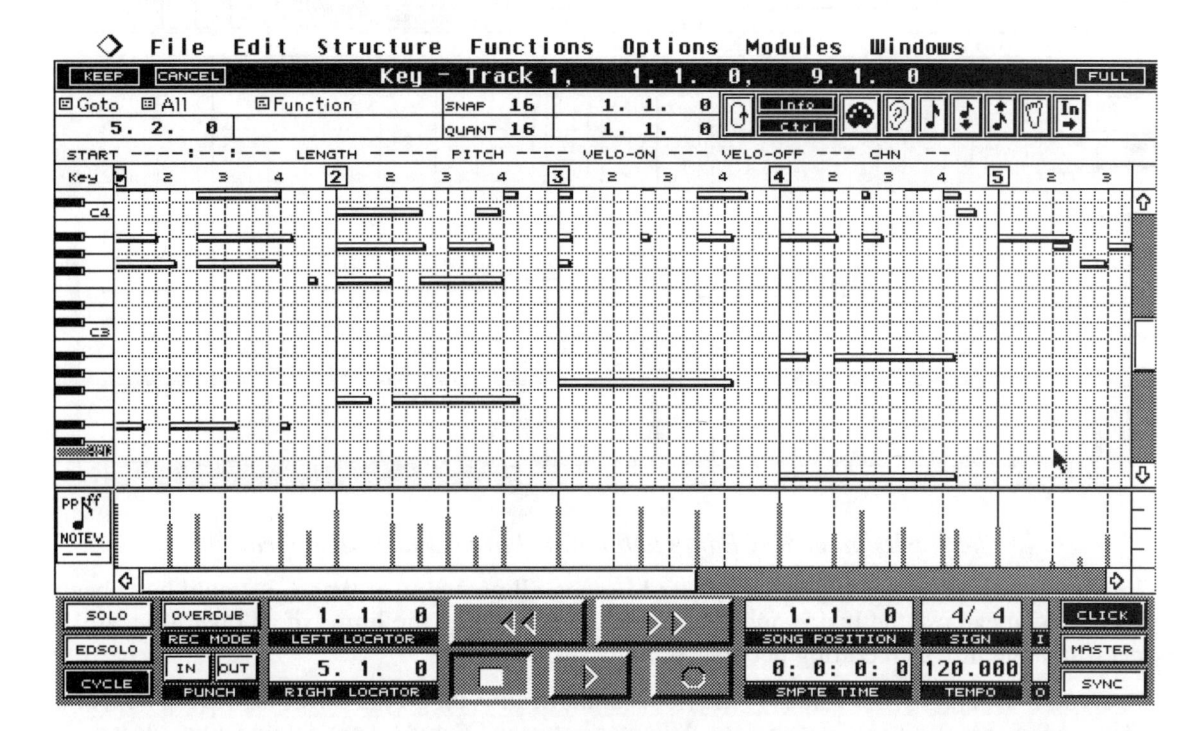

You want to remove the notes above C3

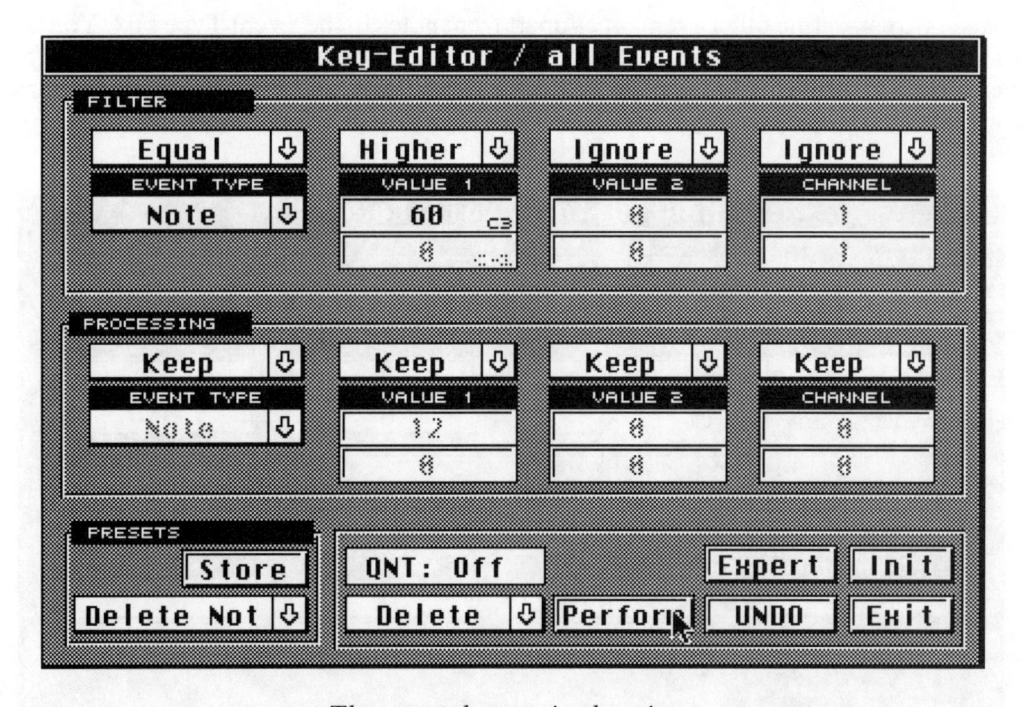

These are the required settings

245

The Logical Editor

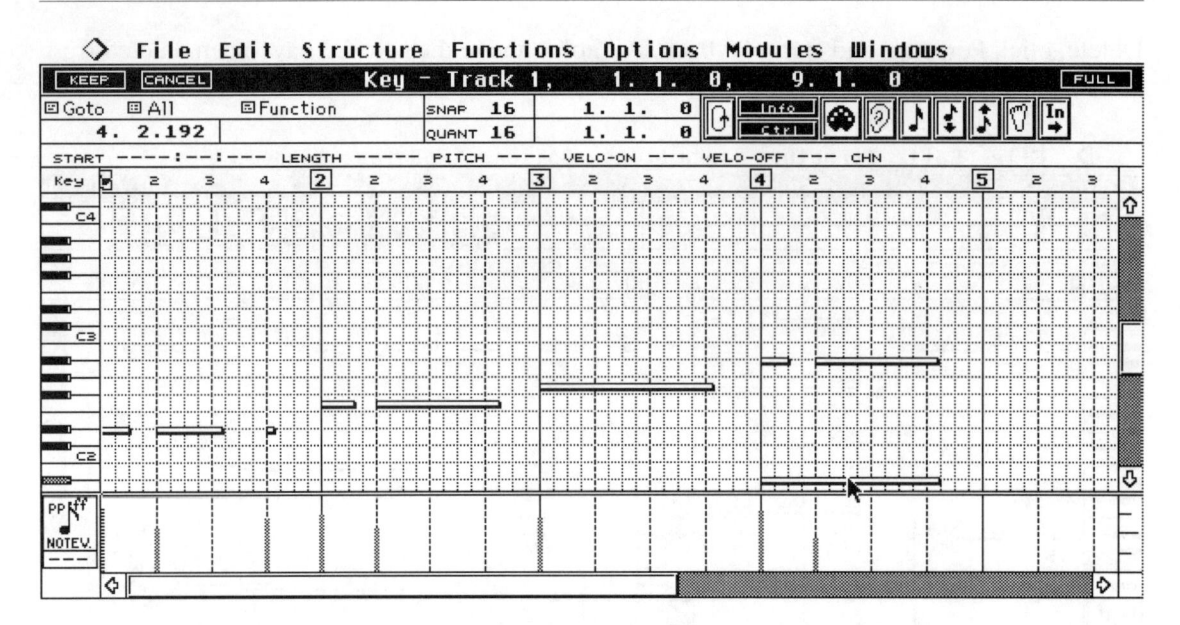

The results in the Key Editor: all notes above C3 have disappeared

Now undo the operation. If you've selected Lower, all notes lower than C3 would have been deleted. You can use the Inside and Outside options to define the limits of an operation, and a specific range in which editing occurs. Activate Inside.

Now you must enter some values in the fields underneath Value 1. Enter C3 in the top box, and F3 in the lower box, and activate delete. All notes between C3 and F3 are deleted. Outside would have left all notes inside this range where they were, and deleted the notes outside the range.

Of course, we can define other event types apart from notes in the Event Type box. You have to know what meaning Value 1 has in the individual cases, in order to understand exactly what happens in each case. Here's an example. Let's assume you enter the following settings and activate delete.

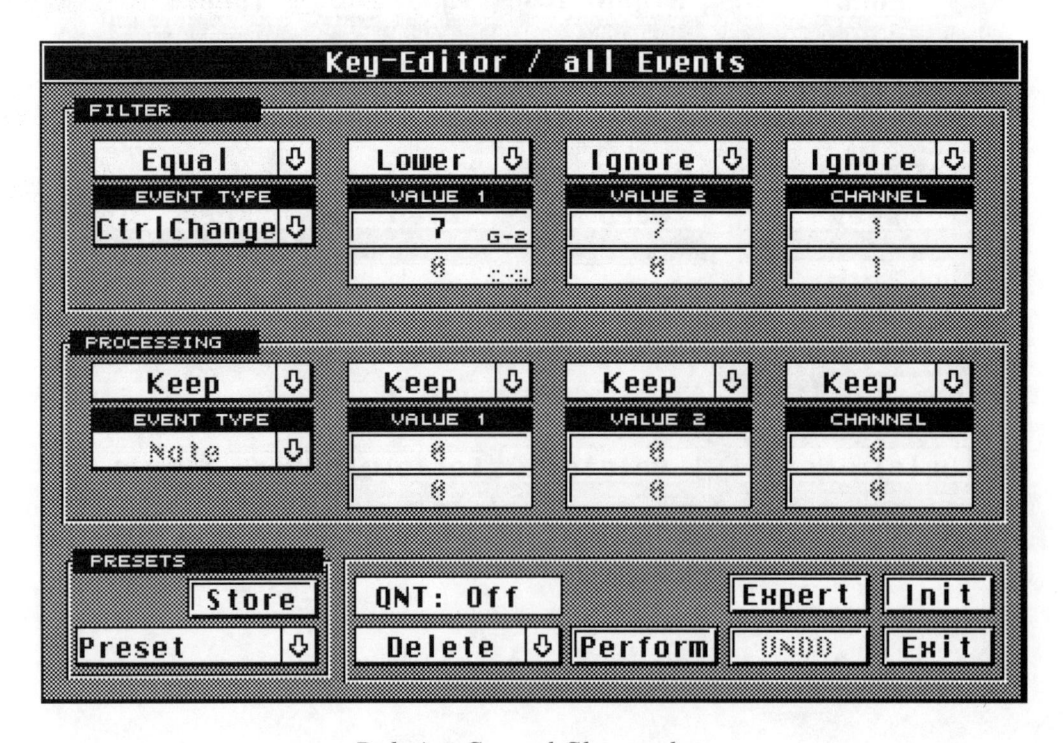

Deleting Control Change data

Exercises

In this case, all MIDI Control Changes lower than number 7 are deleted. Here Value 1 defines the Control Change function. This setting allows you, for example, to delete specific Control Changes from a Part. If you select the event type Control Change, and enter "Equal 1" in Value 1, you can delete all modulation data (Control Change 1 is responsible for modulation).

Bear in mind that Value 1 has different meanings for different event types. For notes, it defines the pitch, for Control Changes the Control Change address, for program change commands the program number, and so on. The section on the Input Transformer contains the complete list.

If you're not sure how Value 1 is related to a specific event, refer to Chapter 5, MIDI, or better still, the relevant section in the List Editor chapter.

13.5.1 Additional criteria

Let's look at the other definitions. Value 2 is used in the same way as Value 1. Remember that Value 2 has different meanings for different event types. Some event types, such as program changes, have no Value 2.

The "MIDI Channel" option is relevant only to the Part's events' actual MIDI channels: these are the channels that your master was sending on when Cubase was recording. Don't confuse these with the Track's channel setting that you assigned in the Arrange window.

Say you have played in a layered sound with your synthesizer. You used your keyboard to control modules on MIDI channels 1 and 2, and the track setting was, of course, set to "Any". Now you want to remove the notes played by the first sound.

The sound is layered, so all note values (pitch, length, velocity) are the same. The only distinguishing features are the different MIDI channels. Set the "Ignore" event type only, because you want to edit all MIDI events on a channel. Then, as the only distinguishing feature, set the Channel to 1 or 2 (depending on which channel you want to delete). All other values have no significance, so set the box above the Channel heading to "Equal". As soon as you activate delete, all the events on the MIDI channel you have selected are removed.

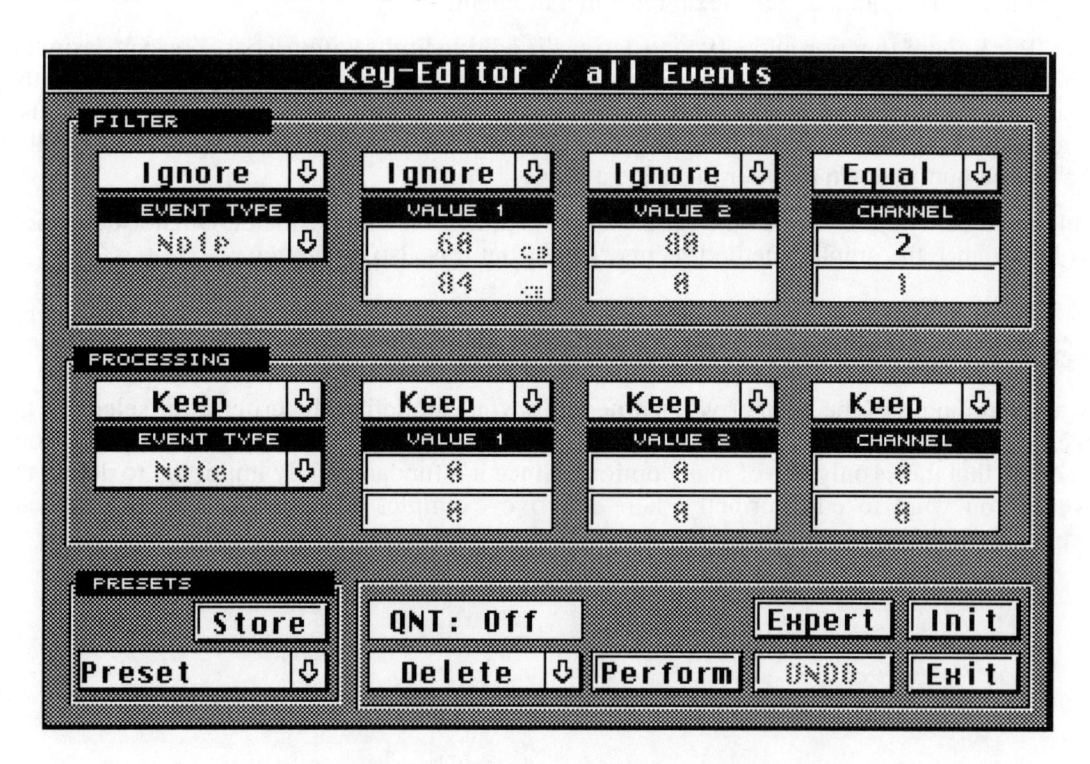

Deleting all MIDI channel 2 data

The Logical Editor

13.6 A first look at the Expert functions

The Expert mode features additional definition options. Click "Expert"; the larger box that now appears has two further options in the filter section.

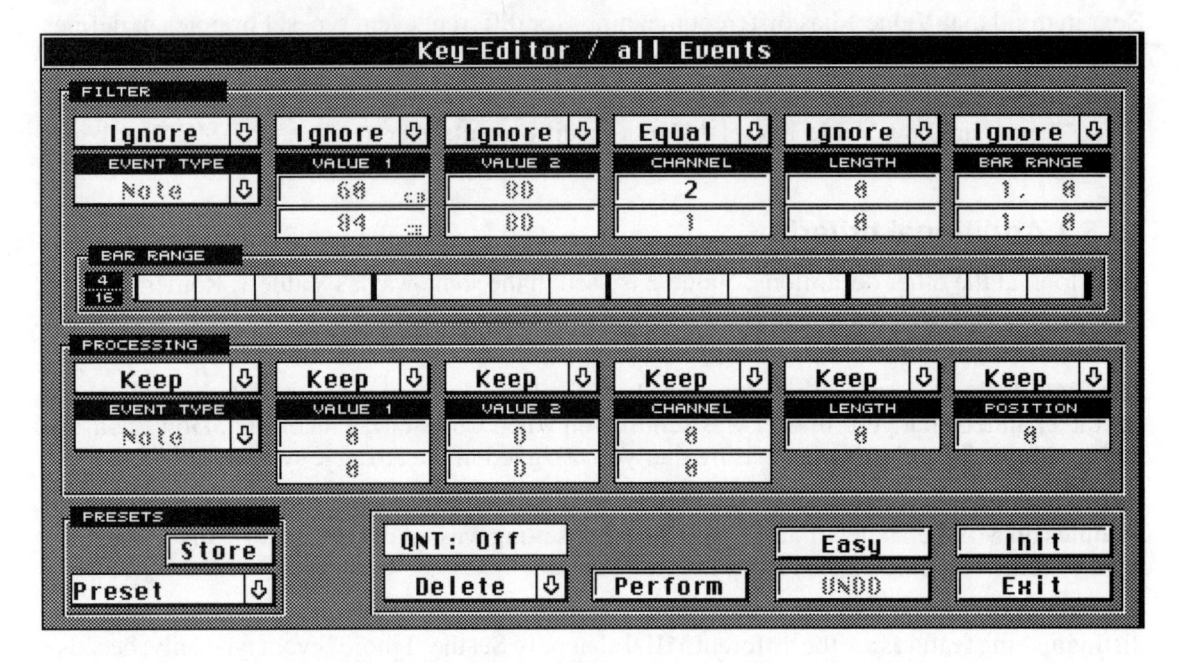

The Logical Editor's Expert mode

The "Length" filter option only applies to note events, because other event types do not have a length value. If you want to designate notes of a certain length for deleting, enter the desired length here. We'll look at a few examples in a moment.

The "Bar Range" function allows you to define the editing limits within a bar. You can designate which portion of the bar is to be selected and processed; the settings are in quarters and sixteenths. You can also enter the value in the Bar Range line at the bottom of the editor with the mouse. Click within the line to define a bar position. Drag the mouse to the left or right while holding the mouse button down in order to define a range.

This setting only makes sense when you use it in conjunction with the Inside/Outside definition. At first glance the graphic method seems clearer, but it is also less precise.

13.7 Brief review with examples

At the beginning of the chapter you learned how you can define the criteria for selecting the events you want to edit. In these examples you just deleted the selected events, but you'll soon discover that this is only one of many options. Since it's fundamentally important to define the events you want to edit correctly, here are five examples of settings, with the relevant explanations.

A Brief Review With Examples

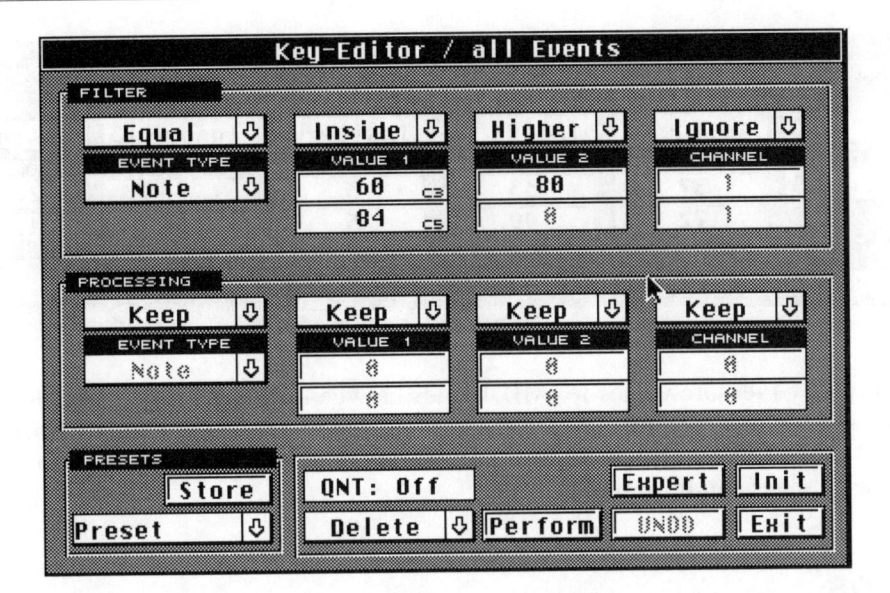

All notes between C3 and C5 with a velocity value greater than 80 are selected.

All notes on the downbeat of every bar are selected.

All MIDI Control Change number 7 (volume) events with a value greater than 90.

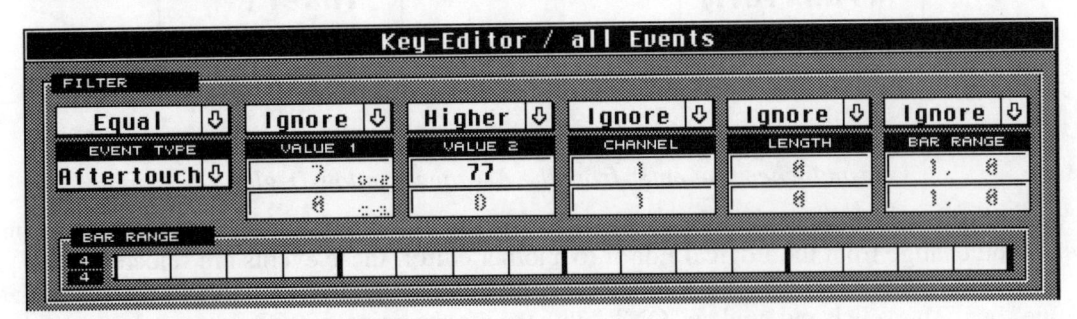

All Channel Pressure values greater than 77.

The Logical Editor

```
                    Key-Editor / all Events
 FILTER
    Equal  ⇩   Inside ⇩   Inside ⇩   Inside ⇩   Ignore ⇩   Inside ⇩
    EVENT TYPE  VALUE 1    VALUE 2    CHANNEL    LENGTH    BAR RANGE
  Poly-Press⇩    57   A2     33          3          ⦸         2. 34
                 72   C4     99          5          ⦸         4. 55
 BAR RANGE
   4
   4
```

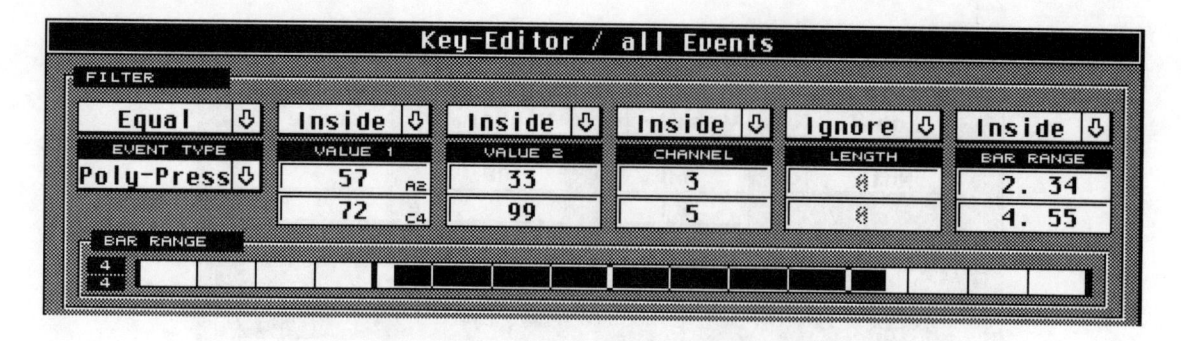

Here, all Poly Key Pressure values for MIDI notes between A2 and C4, with a velocity value between 33 and 99, recorded on a MIDI channel between 3 and 5, and situated between bar positions 2.34 and 4.55, are selected. This example uses very specific settings to show how precisely these ranges can be defined.

13.8 Tips

- It's essential that you know exactly which MIDI events you want to select. It's definitely an advantage if you know about the different types of MIDI events, and the meanings of Value 1 and 2. Cubase won't stop you from entering values that don't make sense.
- When you are entering two different values for a single setting, i.e. Inside/Outside limits, always enter the higher value in the bottom box first. The value in the top box cannot exceed the value in the bottom one.
- Remember that the Bar Range values apply to every bar. Say you entered a Part in the Logical Editor that is four bars long (1.1.0 to 5.1.0). You then set "Event Type: Equal Note" and "Bar Range: Equal 1.0", thereby deleting all notes at the first bar position. In this case, all notes at the positions 1.1.0, 2.1.0, 3.1.0 and 4.1.0 are removed.

13.9 The edit options

Deleting events is the simplest exercise in the Logical Editor. Click the arrow in the box to the left of the Perform heading with the pointer and hold the mouse button down. We'll take a look at the many editing options available here. The "Copy" and "Extract" functions are only available if you have entered the Logical Editor from the Arrange window. If you entered this editor from another editor, these functions are not present, but you can use the Select function.

```
   Quantize              Quantize
   Select                Delete
   Delete                Transform
   Transform             Insert
   Insert                Copy
                         Extract
```

Logical Editor functions when you enter from another editor (left) and when you enter from the Arrange window (right)

- "Select" does not process the defined events, it just selects them in the editor. This means that when you change from the Logical Editor to another editor, these events are selected there.
- "Quantize" quantizes the events you have defined. Enter the desired value in the "Quantize Value" box. Then click and hold on "QNT" with the mouse pointer, and select the desired value from the list.

What You Can Do

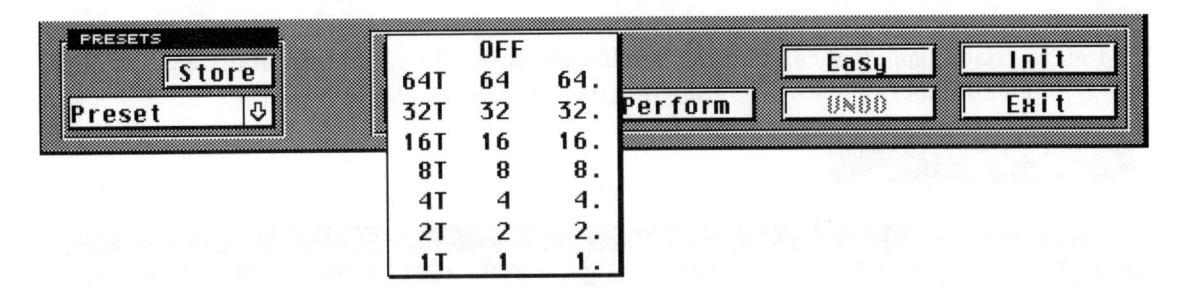

Select the desired quantizing value

The events are processed by the Over Quantize method. This might not mean much to you yet, but we'll return to this subject later. You can, for example, specify conditions where only the events at each bar's downbeat are quantized.
- "Copy" will copy all the events that correspond to the set conditions, to a new Part. Cubase puts this Part in a new track generated at the end of the Track List.
- "Extract" removes all the defined events from the selected Parts and inserts them in a new Part.

You can use this method, for example, to divide a piano passage into two separate Parts, one for each hand. Go to the Key or Score Editor and find out where the split point is. Say it's at C3; go to the Logical Editor from the Arrange window (this is essential) and define the following conditions:

Extracting all notes above C3 and entering them in a new Part

Then activate Extract. The right hand notes are removed and transferred to a new Part. The left hand notes remain in the old Part.

13.10 What you can do

Up until now, we have only defined events, and then deleted, quantized, or copied them. The Logical Editor also enables you to specifically create or edit events, and the "Transform" and "Insert" functions are used to do this. With the aid of these two functions, events specified by the filters are processed using mathematical and other operations.

The Logical Editor

Click the arrow above Value 1 and hold the mouse button down. A selection list appears featuring the four standard mathematical operations (addition, subtraction, multiplication and division), and a number of other options. The following diagram shows these options.

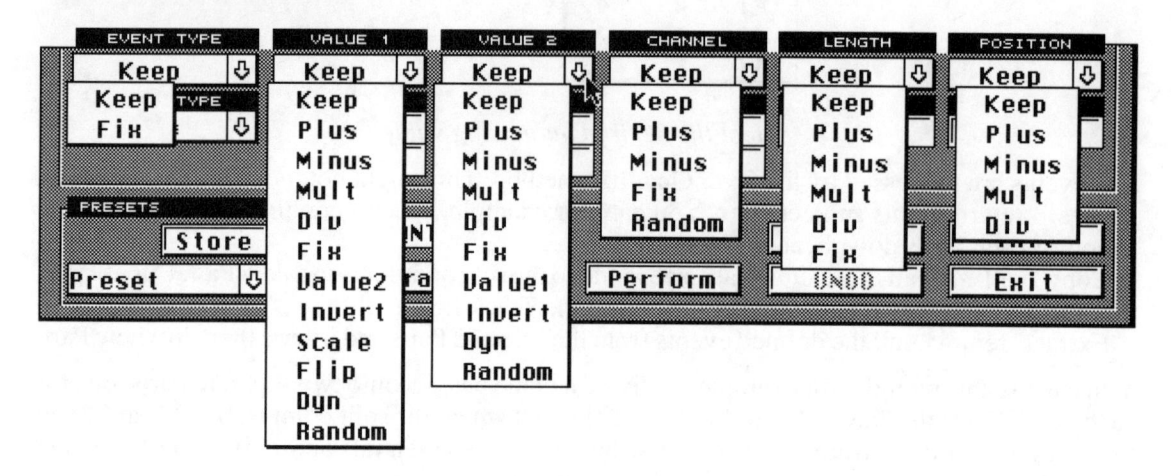

An overview of all the possible processing options

You can assign an operator to each field. Each operator is responsible for a special type of processing.

The exact factor for each edit is entered in the Value field. The operation must be specified in the Operator bar before you can enter values. For multiplication and division, you can input values of up to two decimal places.

Here's a brief summary:
- "Keep" does not execute any actions.
- "Plus" adds the entered values.
- "Minus" subtracts the entered values.
- "Multi" multiplies by the entered values.
- "Div" divides by the entered values.
- "Fix" sets everything to a fixed value.
- "Value 1"/"Value 2" processes Value 1 by the value entered in Value 2, and vice versa.
- "Invert" inverts the values.
- "Scale" scales pitches in the correct key.
- "Flip" turns around values at a designated position.
- "Dyn" continuously changes values for a designated period, and
- "Random" sets random values in a designated period.

Admittedly, all this sounds a bit theoretical. You're probably asking yourself what is to be gained by editing MIDI events with mathematical operations. As always, some examples will help here.

Here too are the two versions, Easy and Expert. As we are now a bit more advanced, let's stay in the Expert mode, and we'll try a standard application for each of the operators.

13.11 Examples of simple mathematical operations

Please use the suggested values for the following exercises. Each of the following is a "Transform" operation.

Example 1: changing a hihat's velocity value
You recorded a drum pattern, but the hihat is too loud. Define the following conditions:

Examples of Simple Mathematical Operations

First use the filter to define what you want to change: notes with a pitch of F#3. The appropriate MIDI note for this example is F#3, but you should enter the appropriate one for your set-up.

We want to change the velocity in the processing range. Value 2 is responsible for velocity in the MIDI transmission. We want to reduce the velocity values for all F#3 notes by 20, i.e. a velocity of 100 becomes 80, 70 becomes 50, and so on.

You could have used division or multiplication to get the same effect. Cubase always rounds off the result of the operation. You can only enter values after the decimal point for multiplication and division, because velocity, note and controller values do not contain fractions.

Example 2: transposition
This simple application relates to notes only. In the processing box, you are transposing notes by a value of 12, i.e. up one octave. Obviously, Minus lets you transpose downwards.

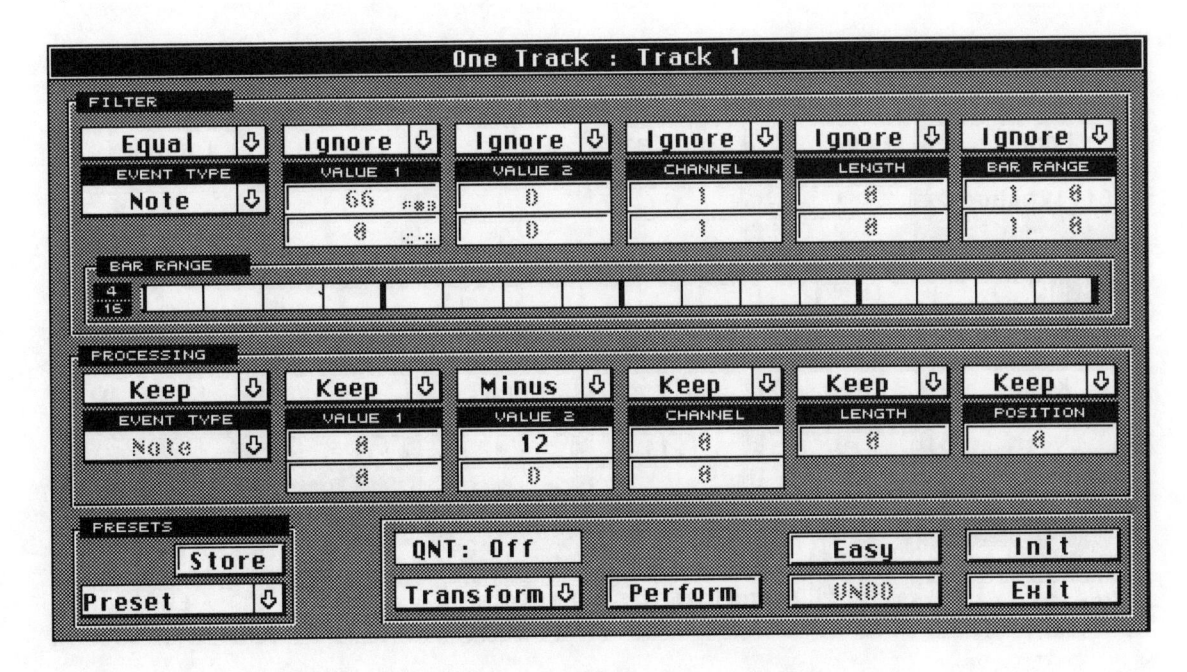

Example 3: adjusting the velocity values for different instruments
Different devices react differently to velocity values. For instance, an old Yamaha DX7 has

The Logical Editor

difficulties with velocity values above 105. The sounds become harsh and shrill, because the Yamaha DX7 only processes values up to 99. In this case, multiply the velocity values by 0.8, or another number lower than 1, and all values are reduced accordingly.

You can, of course, use the same procedure for other devices. The diagram illustrates a sample setting. All notes are affected, regardless of pitch, and Value 2, the velocity, is multiplied by 0.8. Ensure you define just notes, not all MIDI event types, in the filter, otherwise you'll change the non-note MIDI values as well.

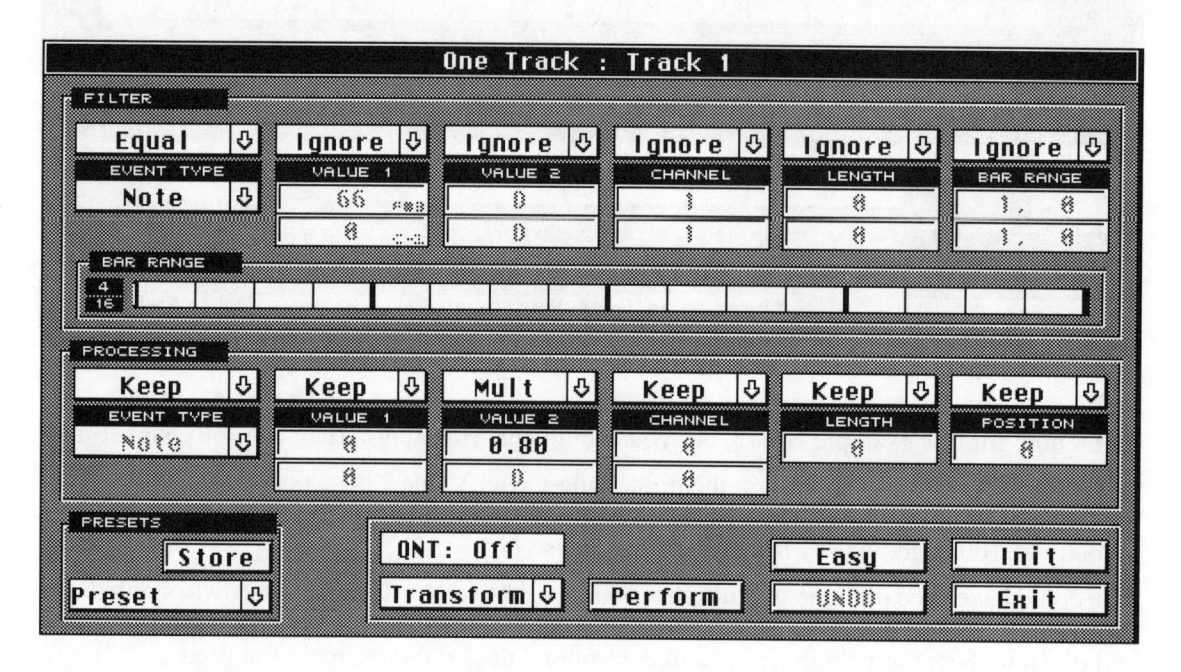

Example 4: scaling controller movements
If the modulation of a controller was a little too intensive, you can scale it back. Enter the following settings:

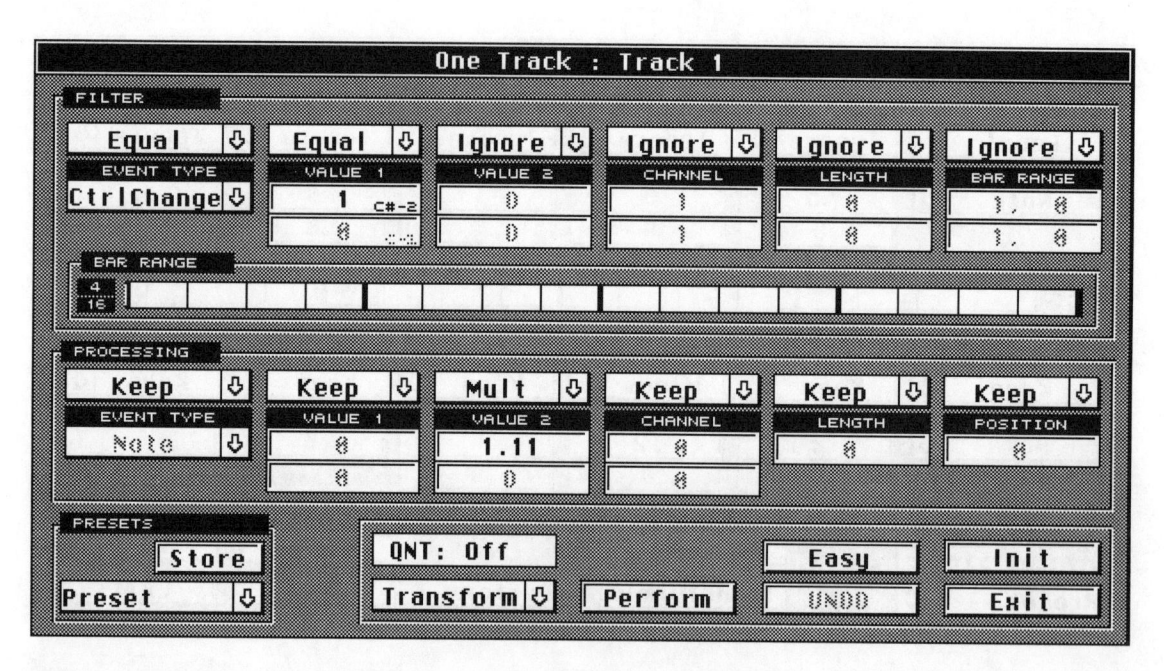

We are editing the modulation Control Change. Enter the appropriate values in Value 1 for other MIDI Control Changes. You can also experiment with Value 2.

Examples of Simple Mathematical Operations

Example 5: re-addressing Control Changes
Say you own a Yamaha FM sound module that can react to breath control values, but you don't have a breath controller available. You can simply re-address another Control Change, such as modulation (Control Change 1).
Record the modulation at the desired positions using the modulation wheel, and convert it in the Logical Editor.

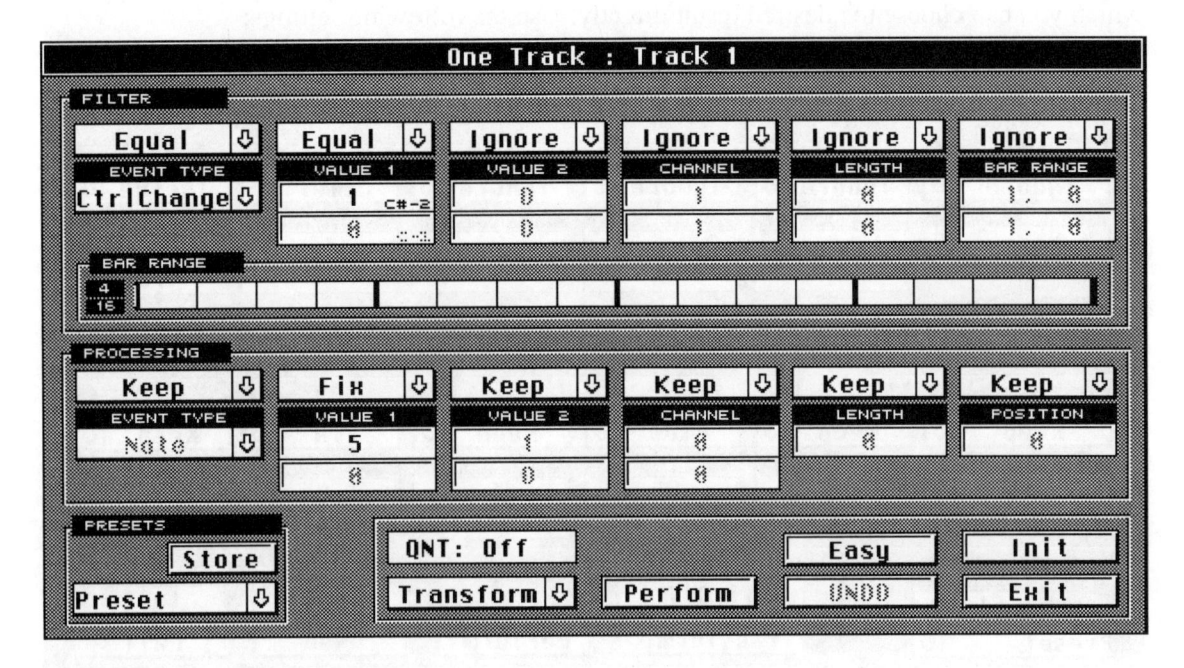

Example 6: playing a "laid-back" snare
You want your snare to be played more "laid-back", i.e. slightly behind the beat. The snare was controlled by MIDI note D1.

The following diagram shows you how to proceed. All D1 notes are moved later by 8 ticks. Obviously you can also move the snare ahead of the beat, or limit the editing to specific bar positions with the Bar Range function.

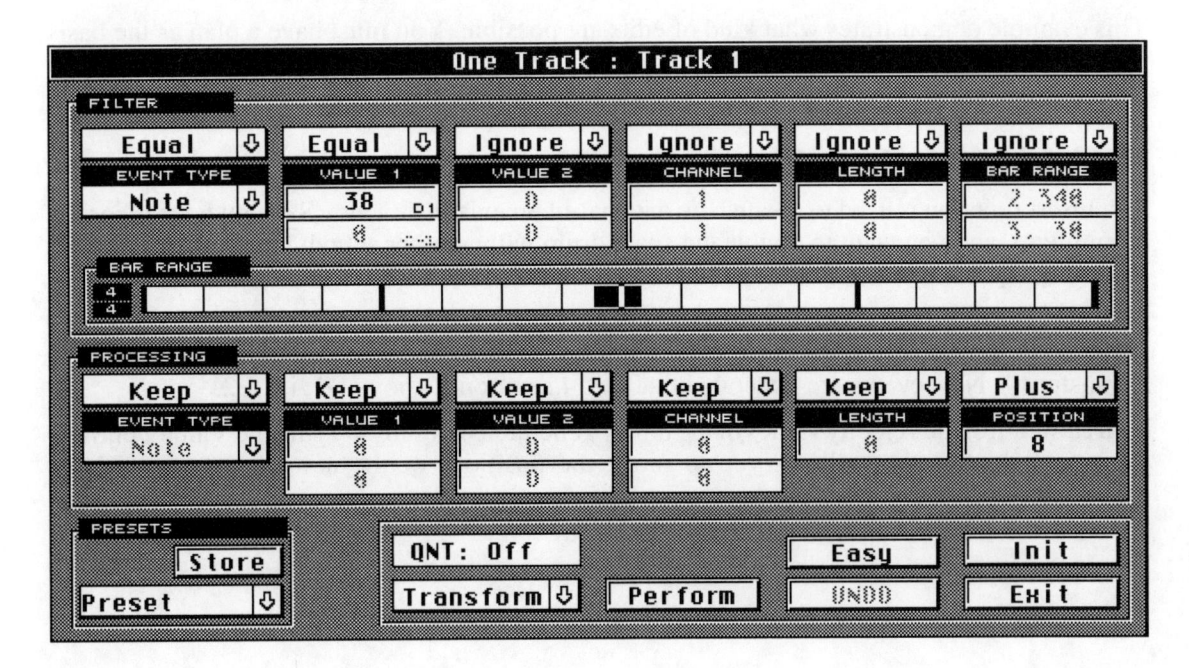

255

The Logical Editor

Example 7: get the funk out
Use this little trick to create a funky bass line. First of all, record the Part as authentically as you can. The slaps can be simulated using notes with a length of 0. For most sounds, all you'll hear is a popping noise.

There's a little effort involved in creating these types of notes. Try to keep the slapped notes as short as possible, Cubase takes care of the rest. The easiest way is to use the FIX operator, in which you can choose the desired result directly. Use the following settings:

```
                    One Track : Track 1
FILTER
  Ignore    Ignore    Ignore    Ignore    Lower     Inside
  EVENT TYPE  VALUE 1   VALUE 2   CHANNEL   LENGTH    BAR RANGE
  Note        0  C-2    0         1         16        1. 18
              0  C-3    0         1         0         4.383
BAR RANGE
  4/4

PROCESSING
  Keep      Keep      Plus      Keep      Fix       Keep
  EVENT TYPE  VALUE 1   VALUE 2   CHANNEL   LENGTH    POSITION
  Note        0         25        0         0         0
              0         0         0

PRESETS
  Store           QNT: Off           Easy      Init
  Preset          Transform    Perform  UNDO   Exit
```

All notes that are shorter than 16 ticks are set to a length of 1. The Bar Range is used to leave each bar's downbeat unchanged.

The velocity values of the brief "slapped" notes are raised, because many sounds are velocity controlled, and switch back and forth between two samples. You can achieve even more precise variations by defining additional pitch and velocity conditions.

This example demonstrates what kind of edits are possible. You must have a plan as the basis for each edit. Establish what you want to do, how you want to go about it, and which events you want to manipulate. Then find the appropriate Logical Editor setting.

13.11.1 The Insert function

The Insert function is used to create new data based on existing events. Say you have recorded a drum Part, and you want to double the snare drum with another sound. No problem, just use the following settings as a guide.

Naturally, you must establish the necessary pitch yourself, for each application; we've chosen D1 as an example. After you have entered all required settings, activate "Insert" instead of "Transform". New events are generated that lie 14 semitones above D1, i.e. E2.

You can control the velocity values of the newly generated notes, by varying the Value 2 entries. Position box operations allows you to move the positions of the new events forwards or backwards.

Examples of Simple Mathematical Operations

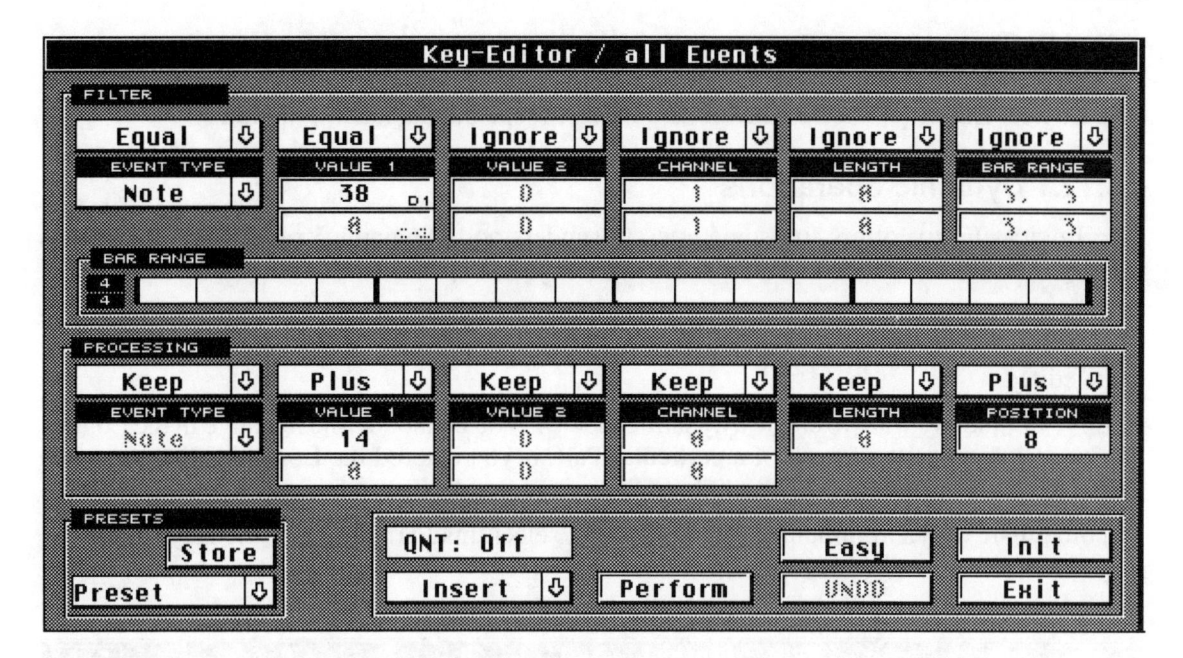

[Key-Editor / all Events screen showing Filter, Bar Range, Processing, and Presets sections]

You can use the Bar Range settings to limit the generation of the new notes to specific bar positions.

Example 8: doubling the bass drum
You've recorded a drum Part, and now you want to place a bass line exactly on the bass drum beats. You can solve the problem with the following settings; the notes in the diagram are again just an example. Cubase generates a new note (E1 in this example) for each bass drum beat (D1 in this example). It creates a new Part on a new track.

You must enter the Logical Editor from the Arrange window, in order for the Extract function to be available.

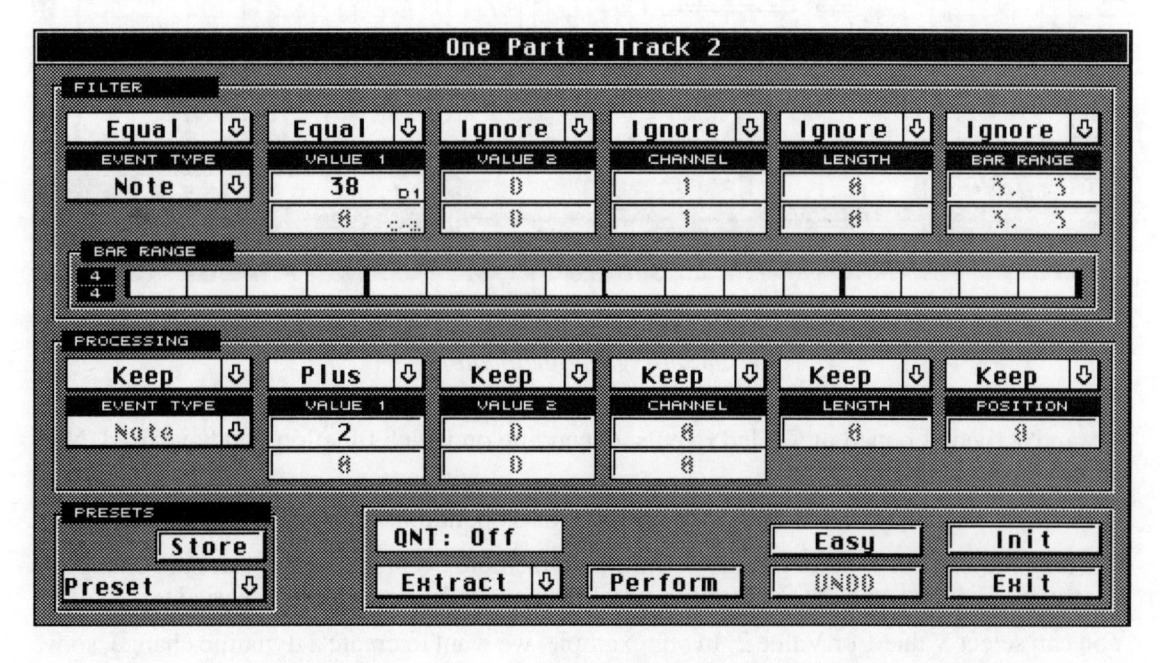

[One Part : Track 2 screen showing Filter, Bar Range, Processing, and Presets sections]

Until now you have only generated notes at the desired positions in a bar. They all have a pitch of E1, but you can change this in one of the other editors. You can also easily add other notes in Overdub mode.

257

The Logical Editor

13.12 Special data manipulations

The Logical Editor features a number of options for special data manipulation.

13.12.1 Dynamic operations

The Logical Editor offers the sometimes misunderstood "Dynamic" option for continuous editing. This allows you to constantly vary values over a specific time interval.

Here's an example that should clarify the function. Each value change operation has three components: the length of the range to be edited, the start and end values, and the type of event to be edited.

In this example, we want to create a dynamic fade-in. You cannot define its range in the Logical Editor. It's equal to the length of a particular Part, if you entered the Logical Editor from the Arrange window, or the cycle or edit loop, if you entered from another editor.

Record a Part with a minimum length of 12 bars, select this Part and go to the Key Editor.

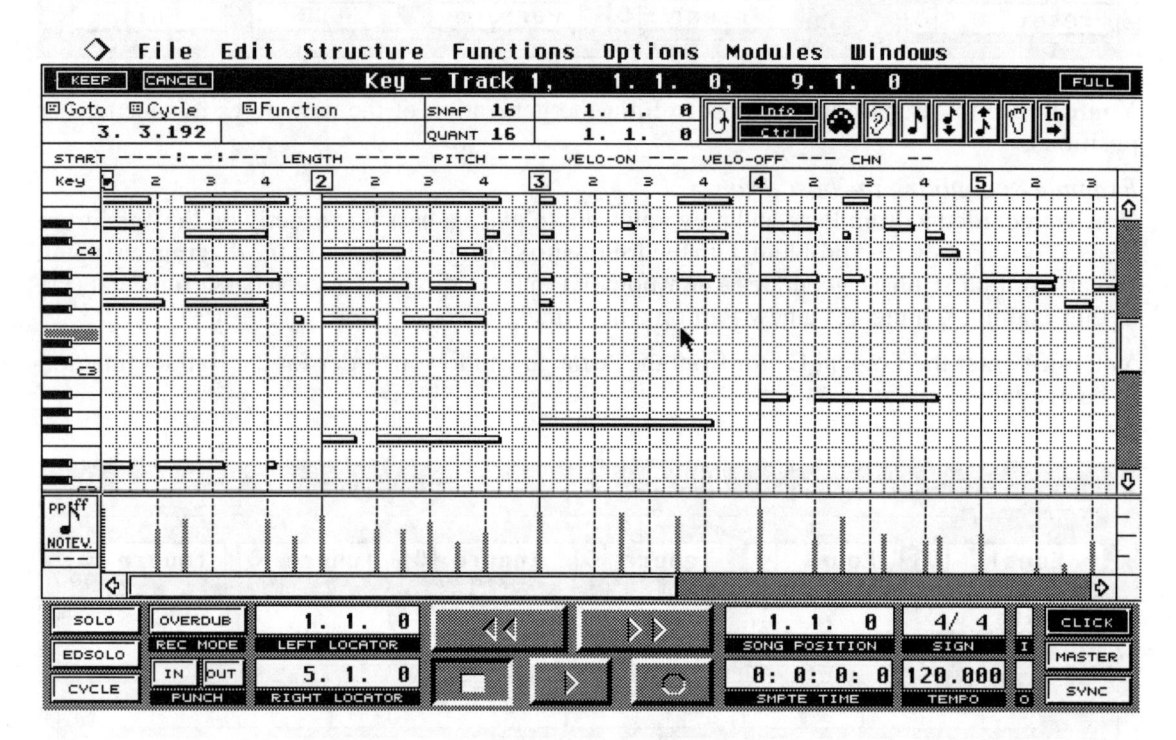

The basis is a piano Part. Note the velocity values in the Controller Display and the settings of the locators

Use the locators to define a four-bar Cycle, or an edit loop of the same length. Go to the Selection box and activate Looped or Cycled Events, depending on which function you have used. Now change to the Logical Editor.

The editor's heading tells you that you have limited its operations to the events in the loop/cycle.

The only required filter setting is the definition of the note event, as we only want to change its dynamics. The next step is to determine which value is to be continuously varied.

You can select Value 1 or Value 2. In our example, we want to create a dynamic change, so we must edit the value responsible for the velocities of the notes, i.e. Value 2.

Special Data Manipulations

The correct Logical Editor settings

For the Value 2 field in the processing range, select the function "Dyn" for dynamic. Click and hold DYN.

Now, all you have to define is the value range in which the change should occur. Enter the desired range, for example from 0 to 127, and activate Transform. The fade-in is finished, and you can listen to the result.

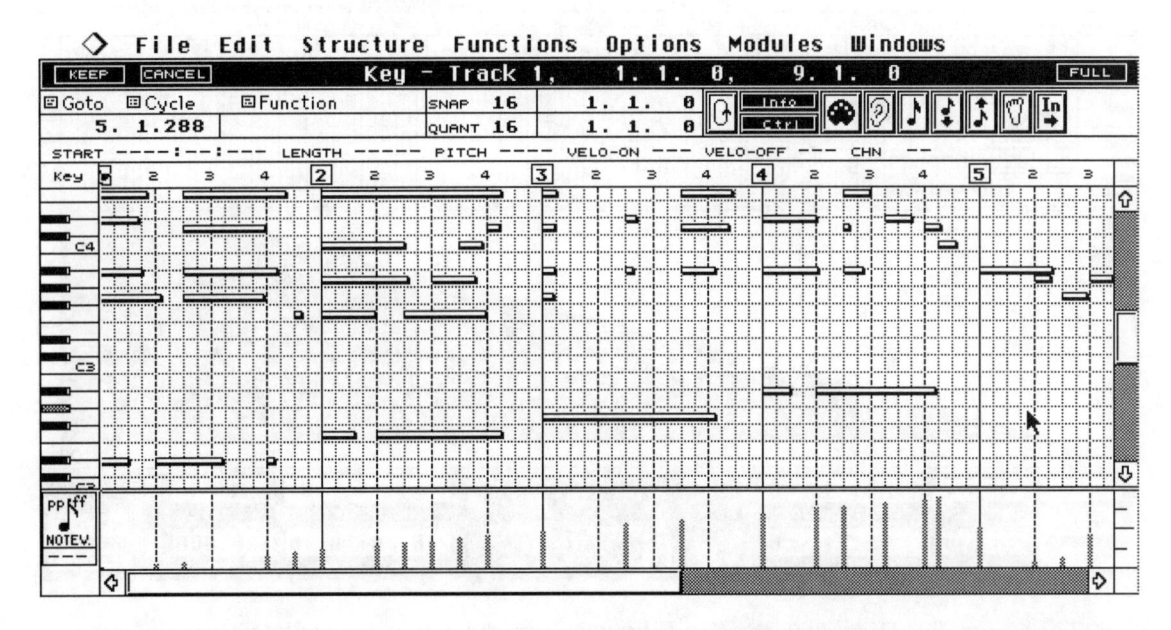

The note velocities are changed to a dynamic fade-in

All velocity values in your Part are changed from bars 1 to 4. This diagram depicts what has happened in the Key Editor's Controller Display. All other velocity values outside the region remain unchanged.

Example 9: creating movements

Although this function is called "Dynamic", it's not restricted to editing notes dynamically. It can also be used in other dynamic applications.

259

The Logical Editor

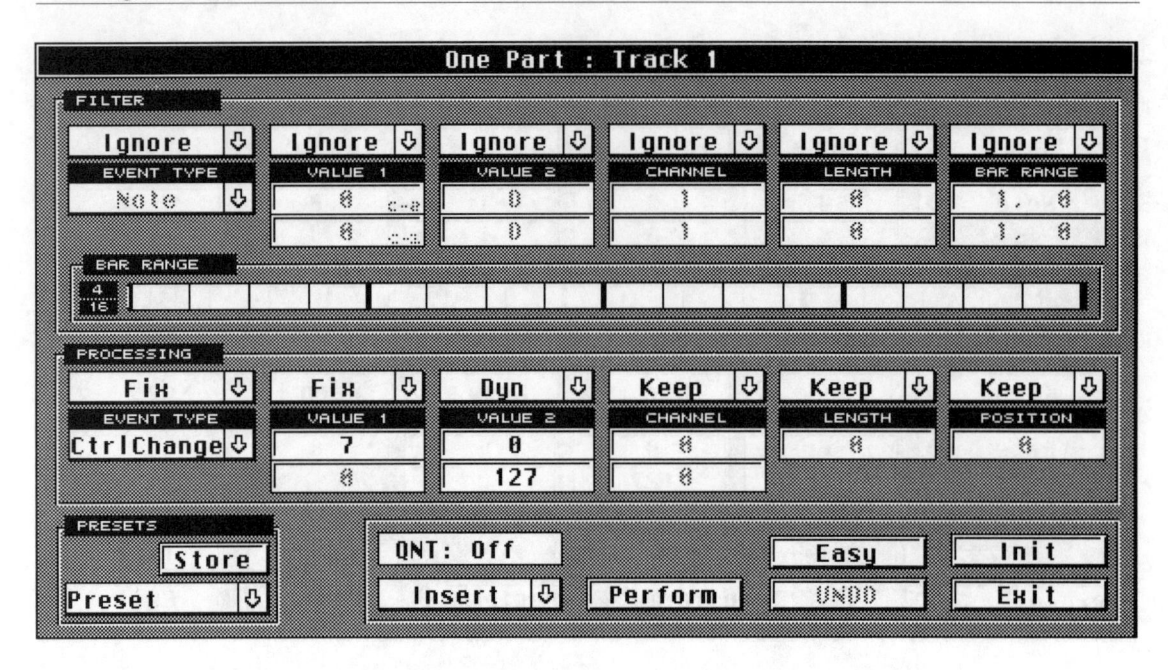

Creating a MIDI fade-in with the Insert function

For instance, you can create or change Control Change movements. Try the following setting, which generates a fade-in for a MIDI volume Control Change.

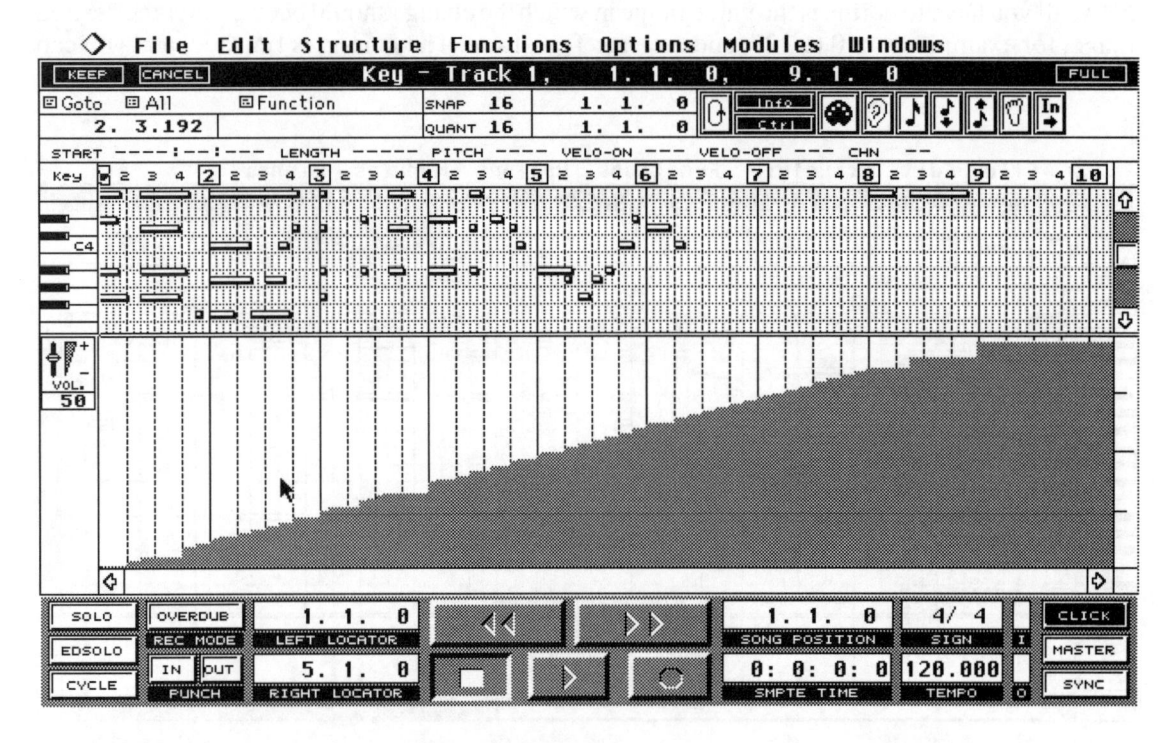

The Controller Display in the Key Editor depicts the newly generated volume events

13.12.2 Invert

Invert reverses the effect of the events. In other words, if you apply Invert to the volume events you have just created, then you create a fade-out. Volume values of 127 become 0, values of 0 become 127, and so on.

You cannot enter values for the Invert function.

Special Data Manipulations

13.12.3 Flip

This operation is similar to the Invert function, except that you can tell Cubase the value from which you want an inversion to start. The value is the axis around which the changes occur. In other words, this value is not changed, but the values above it are flipped around so that they are below it, and vice versa.

13.12.4 Value 1 and Value 2

These parameters are used to apply the "Value 1" result to "Value 2", or vice versa. For instance, a chromatic scale moving upwards can be used to change the velocity values: the higher the note, the higher/lower its velocity value (depending on the setting).

13.12.5 Scale

The Scale function is used to execute transposition in the correct key. Here is an example. Record the following simple chord sequence.

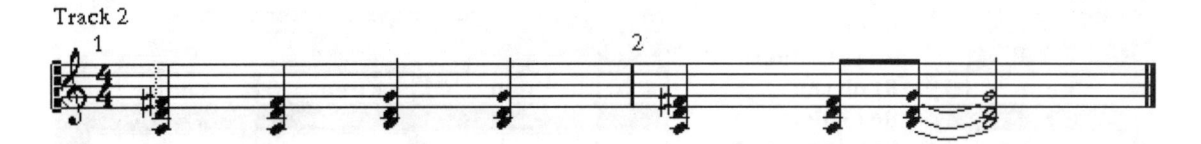

The chord sequence D major - G major...

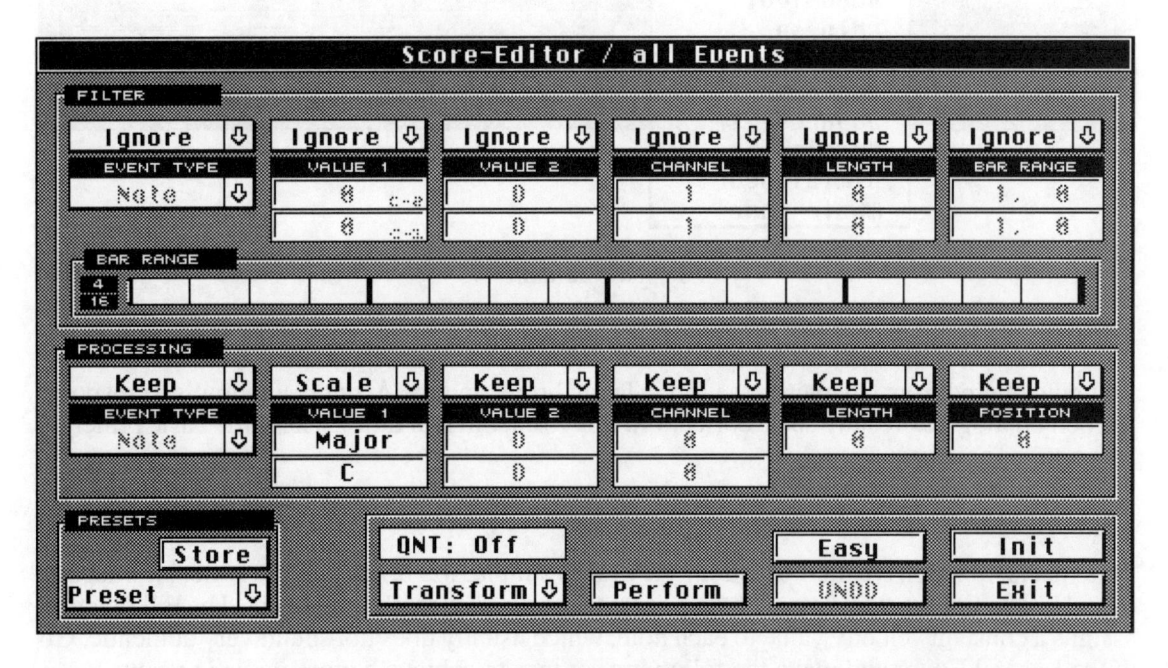

...has these settings applied to it...

Cubase transposes the chord sequence to the key defined by you (C major in our example). Only those notes not contained in the desired key's scale are transposed. In this example, G major remains unchanged because all its notes are contained in the C major scale.

However, the D major chord contains an F#, which is not in the C major scale, therefore it's transposed to conform to this key's scale.

Cubase always transposes to the nearest note below the original, in this case, from F# to F. This applies even if the major chord becomes a minor chord.

The Logical Editor

Track 2

....and is changed to this sequence

When you deal with scale transposition, you designate the root and the scale. Click and hold the field under Value 1 in the processing box. You can now see which scales are available.

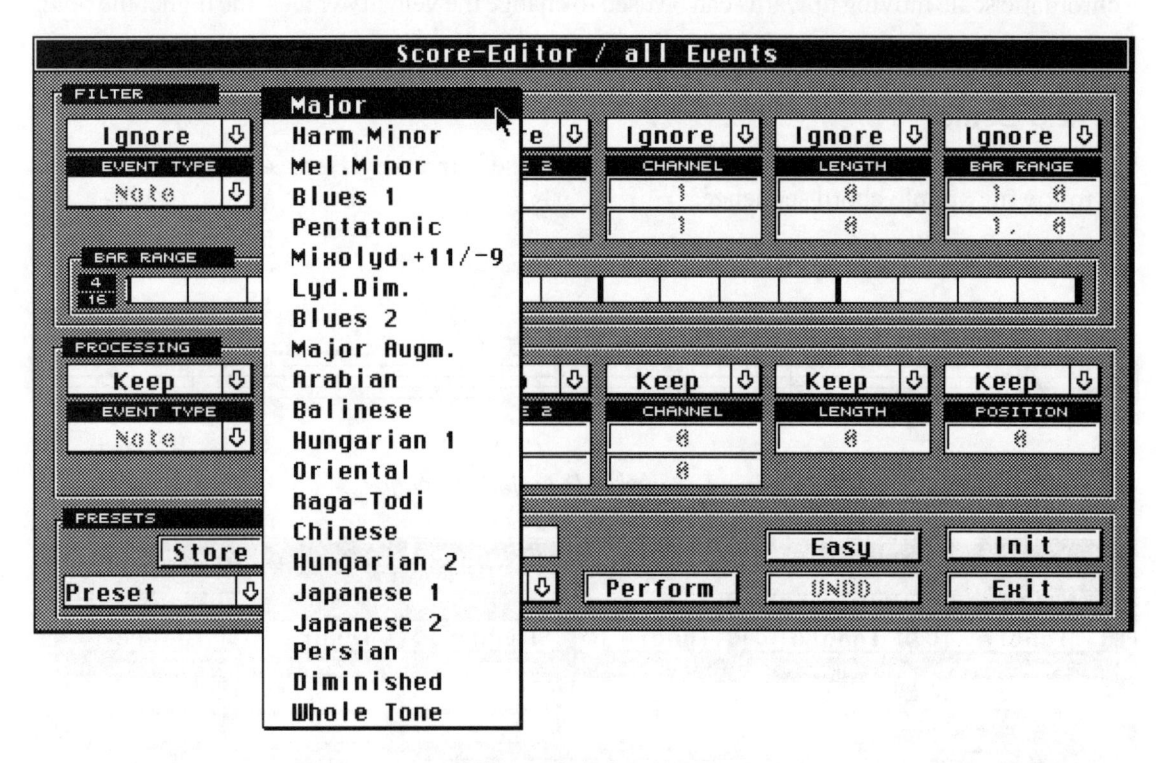

The scale selections

13.12.6 Reference to the Input Transformer

As you gathered from Chapter 7, the Input Transformer and the Arrange window's Transpose/Velocity dialog box feature scale correction, (the former in real time). The same basic principle also applies here.

13.12.7 Random

This special function is called "Random". It's fairly simple, so a brief example is all that's needed here. Use the Fill function in one of the editors to create a sixteenths hihat beat. The Fill function assigns a constant velocity value to each note, which usually does not sound very authentic. Go to the Logical Editor and make the following settings to achieve a more realistic result.

Special Data Manipulations

A Random application

All velocity values are changed at random, but are still limited to the specified range that you have defined, in this case between 75 and 90. The result is a more genuine sounding hihat track.

13.12.8 Using Presets

Steinberg has provided you with 10 Presets for the most common applications. In most cases, the name of the function is self-explanatory. Let's look at two presets to see what they are all about. If the presets aren't currently in the editor, then they probably weren't loaded.

You may have loaded another song or set-up and overwritten the Steinberg presets. You can recall the presets by loading the "DEF.SET" file from your program disk. These presets will now be available in the Logical Editor.

Delete Short Notes (DelShrtNot)
The filter picks out all notes shorter than 15 ticks. You don't need to enter any settings in the processor. For editing purposes, Delete has been set, which removes all notes shorter than 15 ticks. This feature is useful for cleaning up Parts where you accidentally hit a wrong key.

Double Tempo
Let's look at the filter section first. All MIDI events are selected, and only one setting has been entered in the processor section; all position entries are divided by 2. A note at bar position 4.1.0 moves to 2.1.0, a note at position 2.1.0 moves to 1.1.0. The effect is obvious: the bar positioning is halved, which means the tempo is doubled.

Your own presets
You can modify Steinberg's presets at any time. You can either delete the entire preset with "Init", or modify existing presets. The important thing is to remember to save your presets so that they aren't lost.

Select one of the 10 presets. Enter entirely new settings, or modify the existing preset. Click "Store" in the "Presets" field once; the setting is temporarily saved. Click the name twice and the familiar naming box appears. Delete the old name with [Escape] and enter a descriptive name. You can now select and edit the next preset.

The new presets are also available in the Logical Editor's Functions menu. Do not forget to save the presets. You have to do this along with a song or set-up file on a floppy disk or hard disk.

Saving the current arrangement is not enough!

13.13 Final observation

You'll probably agree that the Logical Editor presents an enormous number of possibilities. The many examples in this chapter only represent the tip of the iceberg. You can experiment with all the different options to get a better picture of what the Logical Editor is capable of.

Bear these basic rules in mind:
- Not every possible setting in the Logical Editor makes sense. Try to work to a structured method.
- First think about the problem, picture the solution, and develop a Logical Editing strategy to implement it, and
- the Logical Editor often offers several solutions to the same problem. Experiment and try to discover all the available options.

14 Timing

The basic advantage that sequencers have over tape machines is that they allow simplified post production editing of recorded music. Some good examples of this are:
- the options that you ran through in the Arrange window, which enable you to quickly alter the structure of your songs, and
- the editors, which allow you to correct mistakes and specifically edit individual events.

We're all human, and even the best musicians can run into timing problems by today's exacting recording standards. This is why sequencers have an extensive repertoire of quantizing options, which correct timing inaccuracies in accordance with defined criteria. In the early sequencer days, your only possible remedy for a sequence with some slight mistakes was to remorselessly quantize it to precise machine grooves. Nowadays, quantizing options are available that retain the song's character, and allow you to use quantizing as a creative tool.

The topic of quantizing, i.e. the automatic correction of the time position of notes, is closely related to the whole question of rhythm. Timing problems usually have various causes, and consequently, different solutions.

Apart from normal human error, which we'll look at in detail in the section on quantizing, there are also a few technical shortcomings, which we'll cover first.

14.1 Hardware limitations

You probably know this scenario: you were sure that your timing was impeccable when you recorded a song, but, after listening to the result, it seems you must have been mistaken. Even quantizing is not always a magic wand. Sometimes it can make matters worse.

Unfortunately, the problem is often not the sequencer. You can safely assume that delays in Cubase are not the cause of the problem. Cubase transfers the notes to the MIDI out port fast enough to rule this out. Timing errors, other than the human variety, are usually due to two factors.
1. Less than optimum MIDI transmission, and
2. Delays in generating sounds within your sound modules.

Unfortunately, the second factor has been neglected in the past few years. We'll study this phenomenon towards the end of this section.

Some corners of the music community are quick to criticise perceived faults in the MIDI standard. This is the line musicians with supposedly golden ears will give you. The paradox in this theory is that it was computers and MIDI that redefined the meaning of timing, and now some people claim that the machines cannot meet the stricter timing standards that they actually

Timing

established in the first place. It's hard to see the logic in this argument. On the other hand, manufacturers never tire of extolling the most astounding feats their devices can perform. Timing? No problem!

Let's look at the facts. Actually, there is an element of truth in both arguments.

14.2 MIDI communication

In Chapter 5 we saw that individual events are transferred in series, i.e. one after another. Although our ears perceive some notes to be simultaneous, for example in a chord, they are still transferred one after the other via MIDI. The notes are actually transferred as a super-quick arpeggio.

To use a descriptive cliché, the transmission of a Note on command (three bytes) is as fast as lightning. The precise rate of MIDI data transmission is 31,250 Bauds (31.25 KBauds); this means 31,250 bits per second (1 bit/sec. = 1 Baud).

The three MIDI note bytes contain 24 bits. Six additional bits, the start and stop bits, are added to this number. These two bits proceed and follow each MIDI byte to delimit it from the next byte.

This means that a Note On command contains a total of 30 bits. To get the transfer rate, you simply divide the number of bits by the transfer speed:

30 (bits) ÷ 31,250 (bits/sec.) = 0.00096 sec. = 0.96 milliseconds.

You might think this is quite fast. The human ear can't detect an interval like that, and therefore it's not important. However, a sequencer doesn't just play one note. It plays many at the same time. On top of this you have the synchronization signals such as the MIDI clock, or even more data-intensive loads such as Control Changes and Aftertouch events. Even a chord with eight voices contains a delay of around eight milliseconds between the first and eighth note.

It's often doubtful whether this delay is noticeable. Delay recognition depends on your natural musical hearing skills, and how intensively your ear has been trained. Delays can be perceived from roughly 20 milliseconds upwards, which proves that irritating delays caused by MIDI occur only with very dense note data. Sometimes you can't place the delay, you just feel that the rhythm is halting or slightly jagged. Some musicians become so hypersensitive to this phenomenon they hear delays when, from an objective point of view, delays cannot possibly be heard.

The fact is there is a threshold, albeit fairly high, above which the density of note events means that MIDI delays are unavoidable. Another complication is that these delays are caused by the number of events waiting to be processed. Since the number of parallel notes in a song is seldom constant, the delays are inconsistent as well.

A simple experiment will illustrate this point:
- Record a snare Part in quarter beats on a free track.
- Quantize the recording and go to the List Editor to check that each beat is precisely at the quarter position (1.1.0, 1.2.0, 1.3.0, and so on).
- Copy the Part to another track and assign both tracks to the same MIDI channel as your drum module, and
- mute one of the two tracks and start playback. Then after a few bars, switch the muted track back on.

You'll hear something similar to a phasing effect at each beat. This acoustic effect is caused by a delay, albeit a minimal one, between the two notes. This delay between the notes, which are supposed to be playing simultaneously, is caused by the MIDI transmission and the computer processor in your sound module.

Of course, the professional applications speak for themselves; nowadays very few studio productions are completed without the use of MIDI and sequencing. Noticeable MIDI delays and related problems only occur when you want to (or have to) jam a very large number of events into the MIDI circuit at the same time. Musicians who work solely with Cubase and a few MIDI sound modules probably won't notice such problems.

14.3 Cubase solutions

There are a number of strategies to help avoid such delays. Here are a few tips:
- Whenever possible, avoid unnecessary tone doubling in your arrangement. String passages, for example, often do not need a parallel line an octave down if there is already a bass line playing the same notes. This may also contribute to a more transparent arrangement.
- Try to create more "transparent" drum Parts. You don't need a hihat beat at a position where a splash cymbal plays, and drowns it out anyway. A human drummer only has two hands and two feet, and he can't do five things at once.
- Filter out unnecessary MIDI data as described in Chapter 5, or delete it completely. Aftertouch events are often recorded unintentionally and place an enormous load on the MIDI circuit.
- Thin out Control Change data; this too is described in Chapter 5.
- Use quantizing with care, and try to limit it to those applications where it's needed for technical or stylistic reasons.
- If a track drags, move it earlier with the delay function of the Inspector, by entering a negative value for the delay. This ensures that the notes of the individual tracks aren't all squeezed through the MIDI cable at once, and the data stream is broken up.
- Create doubled sounds by changing your sound module's input channel rather than copying a track and setting the copy to another MIDI channel.
- Instruments where timing is a critical factor, especially drums, should be assigned to the first eight tracks of Cubase. If delays do occur, the information on these eight tracks has priority, and
- assign instruments where timing is less critical, such as strings, to the other tracks.

14.4 Hardware solutions

In addition to the internal Cubase solutions, there are also hardware solutions. You were introduced to one of these at the beginning of the book. If you're using more than three sound modules, employ a MIDI Thru box instead of going via the MIDI Thru ports. Admittedly, with most contemporary devices, the MIDI Thru circuits don't cause delays, but you can't be sure with some of the older ones. Unfortunately, this holds true for poor quality MIDI Thru boxes as well, especially if they include merge functions.

The best and most effective solution is to use additional MIDI outputs for your ST. Steinberg has a number of options on offer. The 19" SMP 24 and the Midex expander are highly recommended. All the details and additional functions are discussed in the chapters on Additional Hardware, M*ROS, and Synchronization.

One special feature of the MIDEX expander is of particular relevance to the issue of timing; it has four additional independent MIDI channels, which can be assigned via Cubase to different addresses. The MIDI circuit's data load is therefore lightened, and you can also access more than 16 MIDI channels. Let's look at a practical exercise to see how this works.

It's essential that you let Cubase know about the additional hardware before you start the program, otherwise the Output column (and later the Input column) will only have the "ATARI" and "M*ROS" selections available. To find out how this is done, read the "M*ROS and Switcher" chapter. This covers Steinberg's M*ROS driver concept, which gives you virtually unlimited hardware extension applications. For instance, you could install the SMP 24 and the MIDEX expander at the same time, and so have even more MIDI channels available.

Place the mouse pointer on the double dividing line between the Part Display and the Track List in the Arrange window. Once it's exactly on the line, the mouse pointer turns into a hand. Keep holding the mouse button down and drag the mouse to the right until the Output column appears. Click and hold any line in this column.

Timing

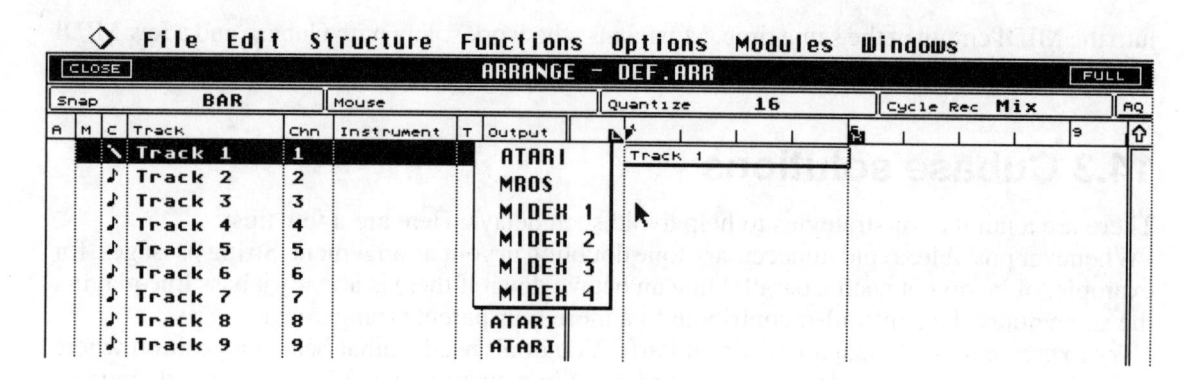

Each track can be assigned a separate output

You can now select a MIDI output for each individual track; its data is sent via this output only, and does not burden the other outputs. Click the first track's Output column with the mouse button and select the desired output from the pop-up menu. Cubase naturally displays the name of each output, and each output has 16 MIDI channels available. This means that if you use Midex, for example, you have a total of five different outputs available (four Midex outputs and the normal Atari output), giving you a total of 80 MIDI channels which you can address independently.

Reserve separate MIDI outputs for rhythmically important instruments or sounds, such as the drum sounds from a sampler or a drum expander.

All settings entered here, including the assignments of tracks to outputs, are saved along with the song/arrangement (the DEF.ARR file as well).

As well as a greater number of outputs, the additional hardware also offers extra inputs. Midex, for example, features two inputs. The data arriving at these inputs is merged with the information from the original Atari MIDI input.

This means you can record several MIDI instruments (for example, a weighted and a plastic keyboard, the drum pads of a MIDI kit, or whatever) without having to go through the hassle of changing your cable configuration from one recording to the next. Select "MIDI Input" from the Options menu. Click and hold the arrow of the "Record from Inputs" entry.

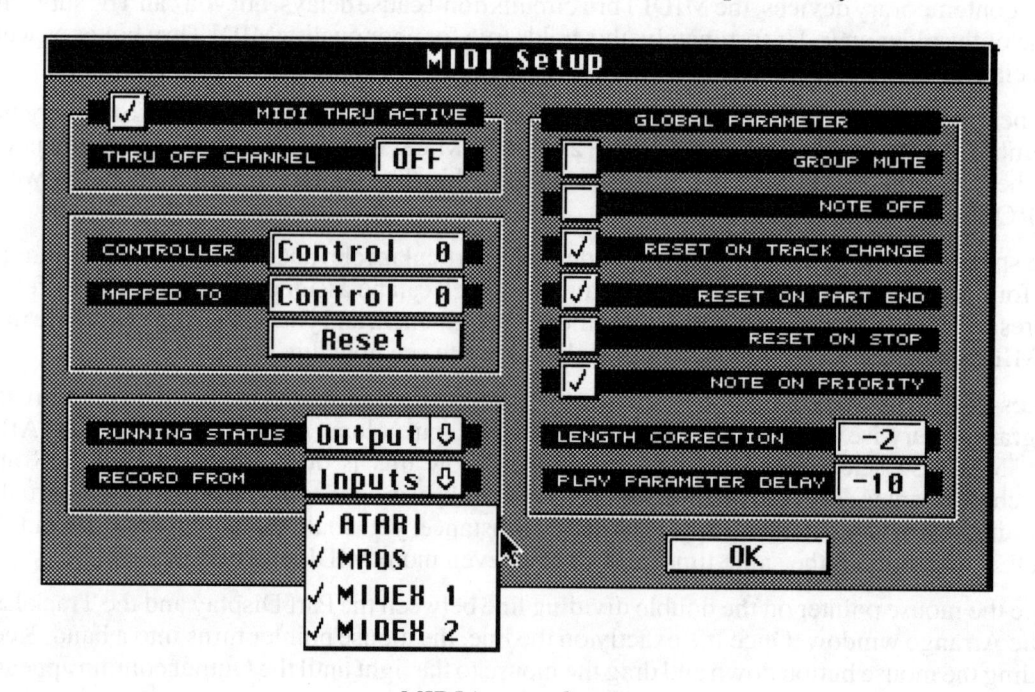

MIDI input selection

268

You can (and must) switch on the required inputs in the menu list which appears. In this case, you don't need to buy a MIDI Thru box with a merge function. The "Multi record" function enables several musicians to record simultaneously. You can choose whether you want the signals to be merged, or distributed over a maximum of four individual tracks. We covered this in Chapter 7.

14.5 Synopsis

With skilful use of the tricks discussed above, and with the help of additional hardware, you can create extensive and complex productions. Those of you who use just a few instruments, or even a single multi-mode instrument, will rarely run into problems caused by MIDI communication.

14.6 The whole truth

Timing problems which occur in smaller systems often have totally different causes, which many musicians fail to identify.

Incorrectly positioned sample starts can cause timing problems before you even get started.

Some instruments are technically below par. The performance standards of MIDI instruments have been improved over the past few years. One of the most important performance features of contemporary devices is the ability to produce several different sounds "multitimbrally" at the same time. However, all instruments have a limited number of voices at their disposal, usually between eight and 16, so the assignment of voices to sounds must be determined, or undertaken by the instrument itself. The latter is referred to as dynamic voice assignment.

Let's look at an instrument operating multitimbrally. Say you recorded four tracks in Cubase, e.g. drums, bass, strings and piano. The voice requirements for each sound vary, depending on the music, as follows:

Track 1 - drums require between 1 and 3 voices

Track 2 - bass only ever requires 1 voice

Track 3 - strings require 3 - 4 voices, and

Track 4 - piano varies between 1 and 8 notes played at a time.

This means your device must offer between a maximum of 16 and a minimum of 6 voices with four different sounds available.

This means some heavy duty computing from your instrument. Its done by the instrument's internal processor, and that's the catch. Some manufacturers don't exactly go to town with their processors, for reasons of cost. Consequently, timing problems are inherent in some instruments. Unfortunately, if you want to alleviate the problem you haven't got many options. You can experiment with the Inspector's delay function by entering negative values for Parts or Tracks to move an instrument's timing forward a bit.

This operation can only be used successfully when your instrument is consistently "too late". The problem with the aforementioned multitimbral instrument is that delays depend on the amount of data being processed, so that sometimes the notes are right on time, and at other times delays occur. Cubase can't cure this problem.

If possible, try to withdraw voices from this instrument, and reassign them to other devices. Some musicians resort to multitimbrality only when there are no other sound modules available, but, of course, this is an expensive luxury. With multi-track recording, it sometimes makes more sense to synchronise the sequencer to tape, and overdub the tracks as you go. In other words, don't record 24 packed MIDI tracks with two modules, or even a single instrument. Play and record the first Cubase track, then the second one, and so on. This lets you reduce the number of simultaneously transmitted notes for each recording, and avoid crude timing problems (don't forget to mute the tracks not being used during a given pass so as to minimise the data load). Refer to the Synchronization chapter for the details of how this works.

14.7 More on voice assignment

Some multitimbral instruments have two options for voice assignment; the dynamic and permanent modes (Voice Reserve). In many cases, permanent voice assignment offers more stable timing, because the internal processor's computing tasks are reduced. If you decide to use this method, you have to know in advance how many voices each sound in your song actually needs, otherwise you might waste valuable voices.

14.7.1 Voice priority

You don't need to figure out the number of voices when you use dynamic voice assignment. Some of the more sophisticated devices use additional strategies in this mode to minimise the unpleasant side effects which can occur.

For example, if the maximum number of voices is exceeded in an instrument, the voices which are still sounding are simply cut off. However, some devices allow you to control what should happen in this situation.

In this case the synthesizer or sampler operates according to "priorities". You determine if the device should:
- hold the last note played, i.e. switch off the previous notes,
- prioritise the notes which were played first, i.e. these are not cut off until they receive a Note Off command,
- hold the lowest note, which is appropriate for bass lines, and
- prioritise the highest note, which may be suitable for a solo.

There are other variations, depending on the instrument, which we won't go into here. Refer to your instrument's manual for details of the relevant options.

14.7.2 The actual number of voices

If you want to (or have to) use the multitimbral mode in your equipment, it's extremely important that you're certain about the actual number of voices your devices have available.

The manufacturer's number is usually limited to a single sound level, i.e. to sounds that are not stacked or generated by several oscillators.

Let's take the popular and fairly clearly structured Roland D-50 as an example. This device is basically 16 voice polyphonic, but many sounds are substantially improved in the dual mode. This stacks two sounds, so the number of polyphonic voices is reduced to eight. The same applies to a number of other synthesizers; although the jargon may vary, the principle remains the same.

The use of stereo samples in a sampler, or of cross fades between several sounds in an instrument may also reduce the number of available voices. Look at the operator's manual to see if this is the case.

14.7.3 Legato

Another reason for "unexplained" voice theft is legato playing. Record a track with strings in chord triads, keeping your playing as legato as possible. Then go to the Key Editor and look at the result. You'll probably notice that some chord notes are still sounding, even after the next chord is played. These brief, unnecessary overlaps waste valuable voices. Even though you thought that your string Part "used" only three voices, you can see that at some points it used several more.

This type of overlap is impossible to avoid while recording, so you must remedy the situation afterwards. You've got two options.

More on Voice Assignments

The first is to trim the appropriate notes in one of the editors. However, Cubase has a much more user-friendly option. The Functions menu contains the "Legato" command, which you can use to create legato playing, and also to avoid unwanted overlapping of notes. Select "Edit Quantize" from the Functions menu.

A selection box appears featuring the entry "Legato". Enter negative values in Overlap to isolate the chords; you can also prevent overlapping notes. Positive values force the legato, so if you want a seamless change from one chord to the next, but you left little "gaps" between the chords during the original recording, you can easily fix it with this function. The Overlap value (in ticks - see Chapter 15 for details) is displayed in the List and Key Editors. Changes are displayed immediately. Note: the legato function only works properly when the number of voices in the track stays the same from one chord to the next. If you start with a chord with four voices, and end with a triad, the extra note from the first chord may drone through the entire track.

14.7.4 Doubled notes

Cubase has a solution for yet another problem. Now and again, you might record double notes by mistake. This tends to happen in the cycle mode, when in the heat of the moment, you don't notice that the first cycle has already finished. Double notes sound slightly flanged, especially drum sounds. Instead of using the familiar method of completely deleting the last cycle, Cubase gives you the option of deleting just the doubled notes. "Doubled" notes are defined as two notes of the same pitch and start time, and on the same MIDI channel in a single Part. First select the Parts, and then use the "Delete Doubles" command in the Functions menu (or press [Control][H]). Cubase takes care of the rest.

When dealing with potential timing problems, remember the information about Control Change data and Cubase's solutions discussed in Chapter 5.

15 Quantizing

In this chapter we'll look at the different options available to improve the precision of the rhythms in your Cubase recordings. Human timing, when you break it down into numeric values, is rather imprecise. Most sequencers, including Cubase naturally, offer a number of options for correcting these human failings. In order to understand exactly what happens during such a process, we will take a look at how sequencers represent time positions.

15.1 The Cubase time grid

As soon as you start recording in Cubase, a digital clock begins to run inside your computer. This notes the time positions at which certain MIDI events occur. Of course the timing is not absolute (it couldn't be read on your wrist watch), but is always measured in relation to the start of your recording.

An example of the internal recording of MIDI events:

Start of the recording	0:00:00
Note played	0:00:01
Note released	0:00:05
Next note played	0:00:08

Recording starts at the zero point, and Cubase "registers" the time at which MIDI messages arrive.

Obviously this time relation also depends on the song's tempo; if you change the tempo afterwards, the start times of your notes are altered accordingly. The recorded values are also translated into time signatures and note lengths by the computer.

Theoretically, time can be subdivided infinitely into an infinite number of smaller units (...years, months,...hours, minutes,....milliseconds,...etc.) but this is not possible with a computer. The computer must be able to assign specific times to MIDI events.

To do this, the computer must be given a fixed subdivision into which it can slot notes. You could picture this as a grid, but it would be more accurate to refer to it as a "resolution". This resolution is already given in part (bars, whole notes, half notes, etc.). However, every musician knows that this kind of subdivision is rather coarse, and can only give a general impression of the actual musical events; otherwise the broad field of interpreting written music would not exist. We need a resolution more accurate than the notation gives us. Sequencer programmers make every effort to come up with the most detailed scanning possible.

In Cubase, every bar is divided into 1536 "ticks". This fine resolution allows the computer to

Quantizing

assign specific time positions to the various bits of musical information, and also allows the musician to record the finest nuances of his or her playing, thereby preserving the groove and feeling of the song.

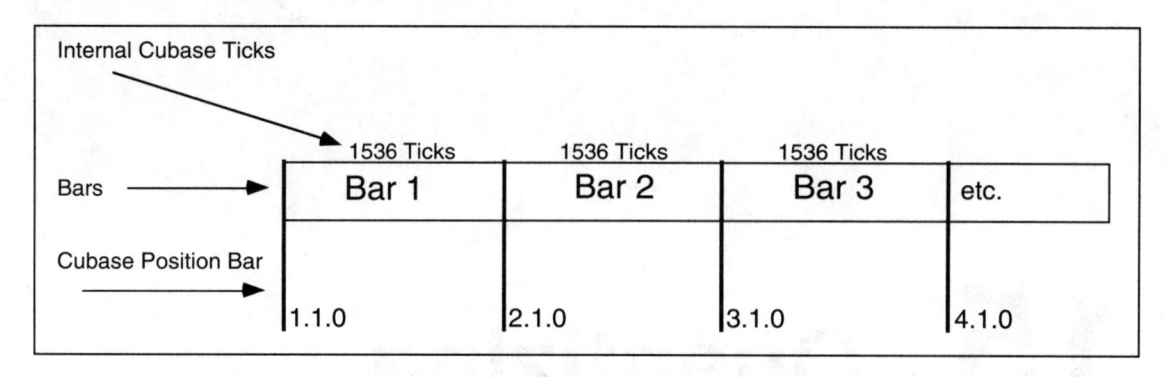

Every bar is divided into 1536 ticks

The length of individual notes can be obtained by dividing these 1536 ticks by the note's value. A whole note is equivalent to 1536 ticks, a half note 768 ticks, a quarter note 384 ticks, and an eighth 192 ticks.

This resolution may be seem rather confusing to computer novices, so Steinberg chose a form of representation which is a mixture of musical comprehensibility and technical necessity. We've already covered these subdivisions in previous chapters.

Event positions, e.g. note start points, are divided into:
- bars
- quarter notes
- 1536nds (ticks)

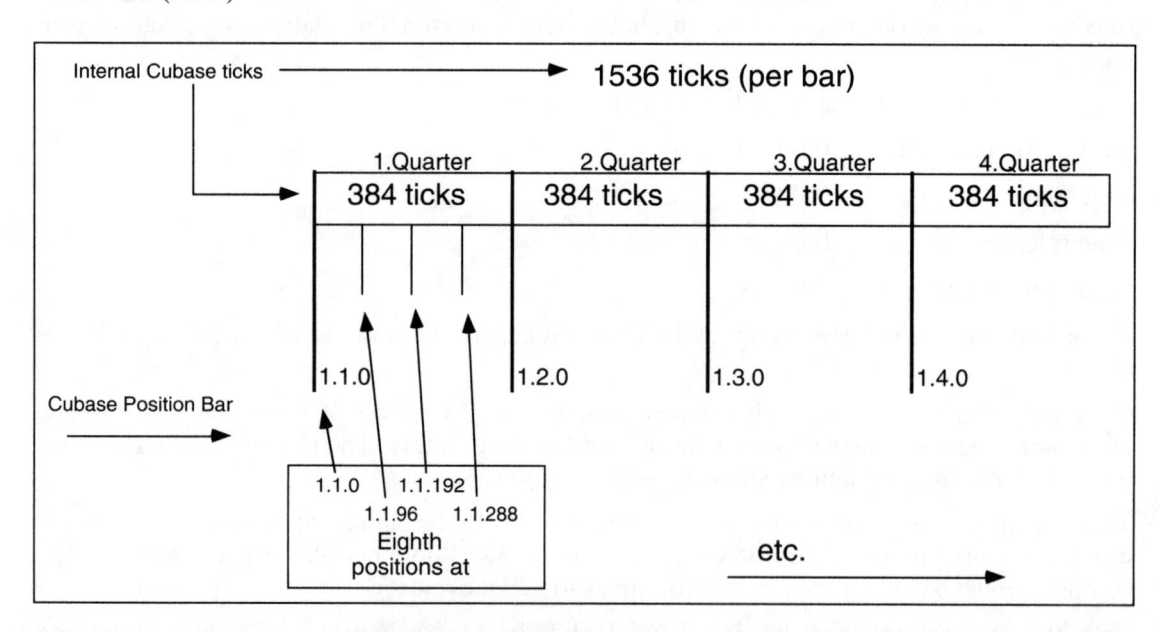

The subdivision of a bar into eighths

Here are a few examples, which have deliberately been kept simple. Obviously, a note can start at any tick or bar position (e.g. 1.2.311).

Notes should have their start points at the following positions in these examples:
- 1.1.0 - The note starts at the first bar, on the first quarter, at tick 0. This is equivalent to the beginning of an arrangement or song.
- 2.3.0 - The note starts at the second bar, on the third quarter, at tick 0. If we use our newly

acquired knowledge to convert this position into ticks, we get the following result: the first number (the bar) is not relevant to the number of ticks, because each bar contains 1536 ticks, and the count begins anew with each bar's downbeat. The note starts at the third quarter, i.e. at tick 769.
- 3.4.192 - The note starts at the third bar, on the last quarter, at tick 192, i.e. the last off beat in the bar.

15.2 Note lengths

A note's length is important as well as its start point. Let's take a look at this in the List Editor.

Note lengths in the List Editor. (All other note values (position, pitch, etc.) are not depicted so you get a clearer view.)

Note lengths are always displayed in ticks. Here is a conversion table of the notes shown in the diagram above.

1536	whole note
768	half note
384	quarter note
192	eighth note
128	eighth triplet
96	sixteenth note
64	sixteenth triplet
48	32nd

The subdivisions go all the way down to the length of a tick, i.e. a 1536th note.

15.3 Challenge Cubase

Let's have a little fun and do an experiment to see what Cubase and your synthesizer can take. You can use this opportunity to see how fast notes can be sent via MIDI. Follow these steps:
- delete all Parts,
- create a four bar, empty Part in the Arrange window, and select it,
- go to the List Editor,
- select "Insert Note" from the menu next to the Mouse position box,
- set Snap to Off and Quantize to "64T",

Quantizing

- activate "Fill" in the small Function menu,
- Cubase computes for a brief moment, and then the following window appears:

Create the notes first...

- go to the Logical Editor,
- select the following setting and activate "Perform".

...and then whip them into shape in the Logical Editor

- Cubase computes for a while. Leave the Logical Editor and go back to the List Editor.
- You have created a Part containing notes with a pitch of C3, a length of one tick, and situated at one tick intervals.
- Every tick in four bars has a note on it, which makes 6144 notes.
- Set Cubase to a tempo of 250 and go to the beginning of the arrangement.
- Make absolutely sure that the cycle mode is not active.
- Select a sound on your sound module with the fastest attack envelope, e.g. a piano.
- Turn the volume on your instrument down to a tolerable level.
- ...and finally, start playback.

Cubase plays the events at an incredible rate. Depending on the sound, you may not be able to hear each individual attack, but only a constant tone. In fact, the computer is so busy with this operation that it cannot react to any input. The situation doesn't return to normal until the four bar Part is completed. Strangely enough, Cubase ends up somewhere in the vicinity of Bar 20. If Cycle mode active after all, you would have had no choice but to hit your computer's reset button. But don't worry, just restart the program.

This little experiment demonstrates Cubase's upper tolerance limit, which is obviously very high. It is recommended that you refrain from this type of operation in future, and remember: never torture Cubase for fun!

15.4 Back to note lengths

Cubase treats note lengths in a special way. You may remember that in Chapter 5 we discussed how Note Off commands (or Note On commands with a velocity of 0) are used to switch notes off in the MIDI standard. Most other sequencers simply record a Note On, and at some point afterwards, a Note Off message, and this combination is simply reeled off during playback. However, this can cause problems. If you cut a Part, for example, you may sometimes loose the Note Off command, resulting in a MIDI drone. Cubase uses a different system. Initially, it does record the Note On and Note Off messages, and then computes the note length from these two values. During playback, the program first sends the Note On command, and then, after the computed time elapses, the Note Off message. However, even if you cut the Part, the Note Off command is not lost because it is bound timewise by the computer to the Note On command. Generally, this is a very practical arrangement, but at times it can lead to difficulties. The following diagram gives you an illustration.

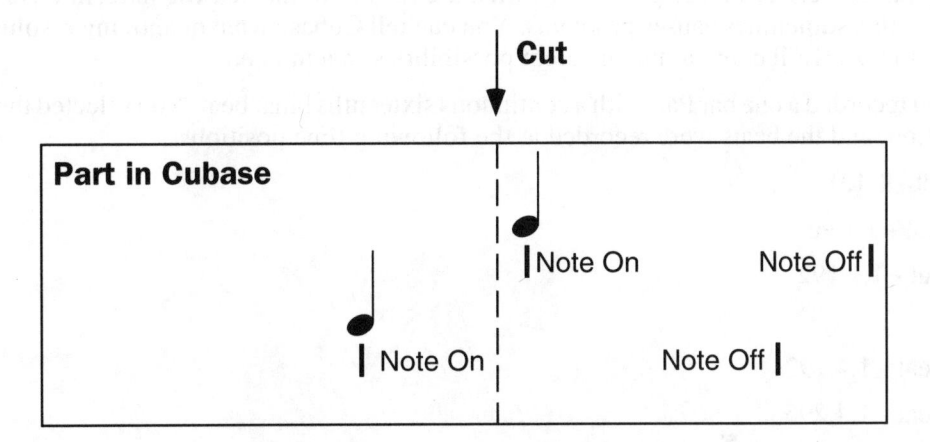

Cutting Parts, and the effect on events

You want to use the Pencil from the Toolbox to cut a Part. Notes that start after the new end of the Part are thereby removed. Notes that start prior to the cut, but end after it, sustain beyond the end of the Part.

To prevent this problem, you use the "Cut Events" command in the Structure menu, which shortens the length of any events that continue after the end of the Part. All you have to do is cut the desired Parts with the appropriate Toolbox implement, select the Parts and then activate the "Cut Events" command.

15.5 How does quantizing work?

Now that we've covered the background, it is fairly easy to explain the basic function of quantizing. A normal quantizing operation simply scans with a coarser resolution than the 1536ths, and the notes are assigned to the nearest point in the selected resolution. If a note lies

Quantizing

between 0 and 49 percent behind a resolution point, then it is pulled earlier. Conversely, if a note lies between 50 and 99 percent behind a resolution point, Cubase will push it later to the following sixteenth position.

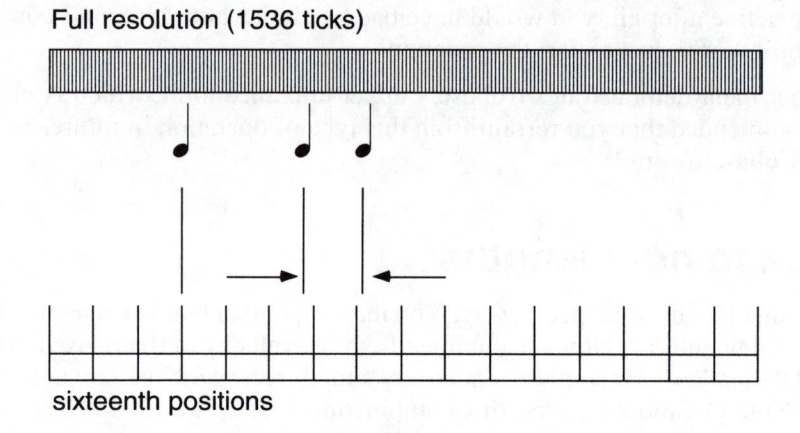

The way quantizing works

In this example, a recording is made at maximum resolution (1536 ticks), and each incoming MIDI message is assigned to its nearest tick position. Quantizing then uses a different resolution. In our example it uses sixteenths, which means that it scans at intervals of 96 ticks per bar instead of 1536 ticks per bar. In other words, events can only be placed every 96 ticks.

If events are already recorded at these positions, they stay there. The only events affected are those situated between these positions, which are moved to the nearest sixteenth. As you can imagine, this sometimes causes problems. You can tell Cubase what quantizing resolution you want it to use; we'll come to the different possibilities in a moment.

Say you recorded a one bar Part with a continuous sixteenths hihat beat. You selected the highest resolution, and the beats were recorded at the following time positions:

1st beat - 1.1.0

2nd beat - 1.1.96

3rd beat - 1.1.192

....

15th beat - 1.4.192

16th beat - 1.4.295

15 beats are at the correct sixteenth positions, but the final beat went astray, being seven ticks too late. You now select sixteenths quantization. The first 15 beats remain at their (correct) positions, but the last one is moved to its proper position of 1.4.288. The quantizing function calculates the nearest correct position according to the value that you entered, and moves the note there. In our example, this worked fine. However, it wouldn't work if the timing of the last note was so bad that it ended up closer to the first beat of the next bar than the last sixteenth position of the bar you recorded. Cubase doesn't know what your intentions are, it just follows the quantization rules.

This means that quantizing can only correct mistakes within a certain range. If the beats are too far off, Cubase's quantizing won't help.

15.6 Selecting the quantizing factor

Before you quantize a recording, you need to ascertain the smallest note value in the piece. Here's an exercise:

Selecting the Quantizing Factor

- Create a Part containing many different note values. You could do this by running your hand along the length of the keyboard.
- Stop Cubase, start playback, and the result sounds like what you originally played. Cubase does not quantize automatically, you must first instruct the program to do it.

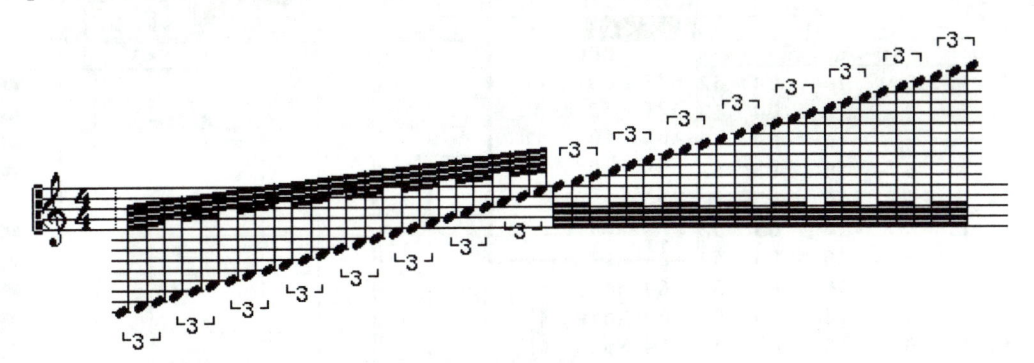

This is what your recording might look like in the Score Editor

Set the quantizing factor to quarters. The quantizing factors are located in the middle of the Info Line (QUANT). Click and hold the number with the mouse pointer, and select the desired factor from the pop-up menu. All useful values are available, from a whole note through various triplets to the "Off" setting.

Move the mouse pointer to "16" with the mouse button still held down, and this number will be highlighted. Now release the mouse button, and 16 will be entered in the Quantizing display. Alternatively, you can use the alphanumeric keypad's numbers (not the numeric keypad on the right) to enter values from 1 to 64 directly. Here are the key assignments:

[1]	whole note
[2]	half
[3]	quarter
[4]	eighth
[5]	sixteenth
[6]	32nd
[7]	64th

The [T] and [.] keys are used for triplets and dotted notes, respectively.

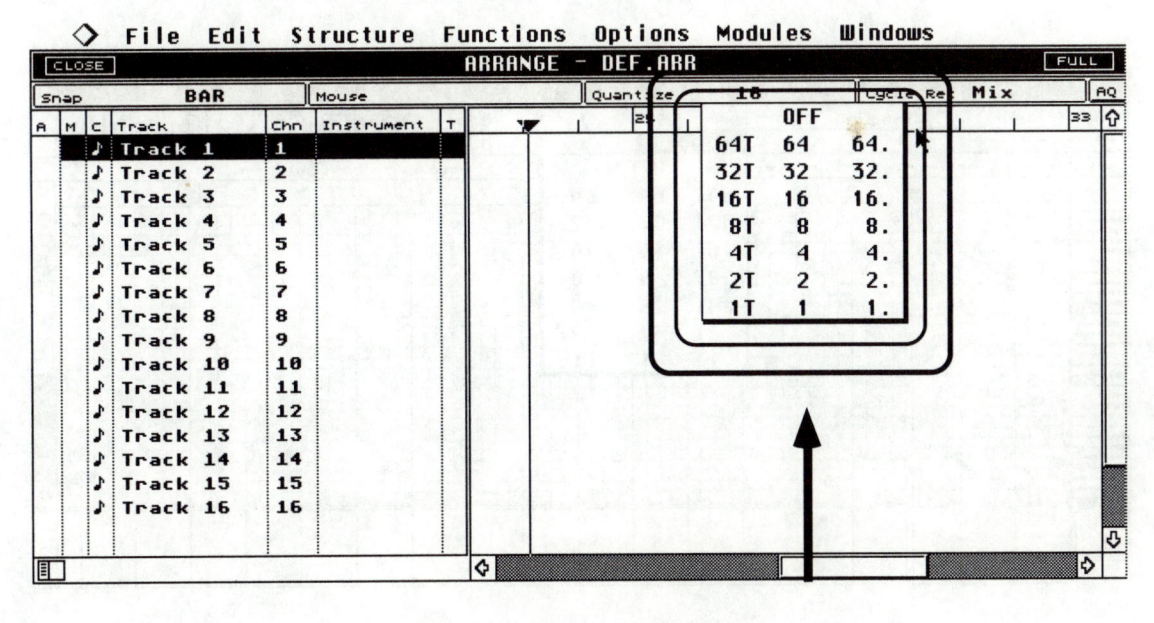

Selecting the quantizing factor

Quantizing

Quantizing is also available in the editors. The procedure is identical.

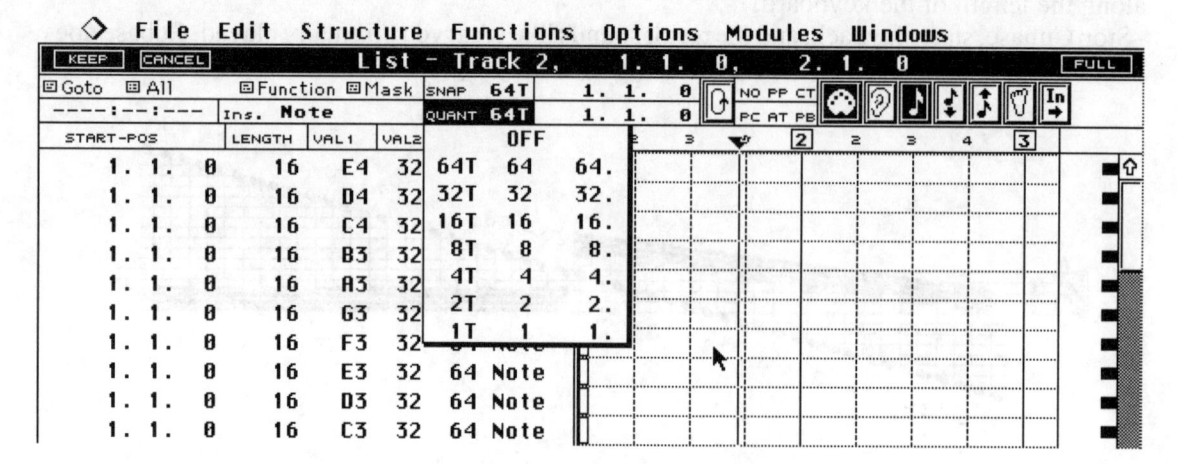

Quantizing factors in the List Editor

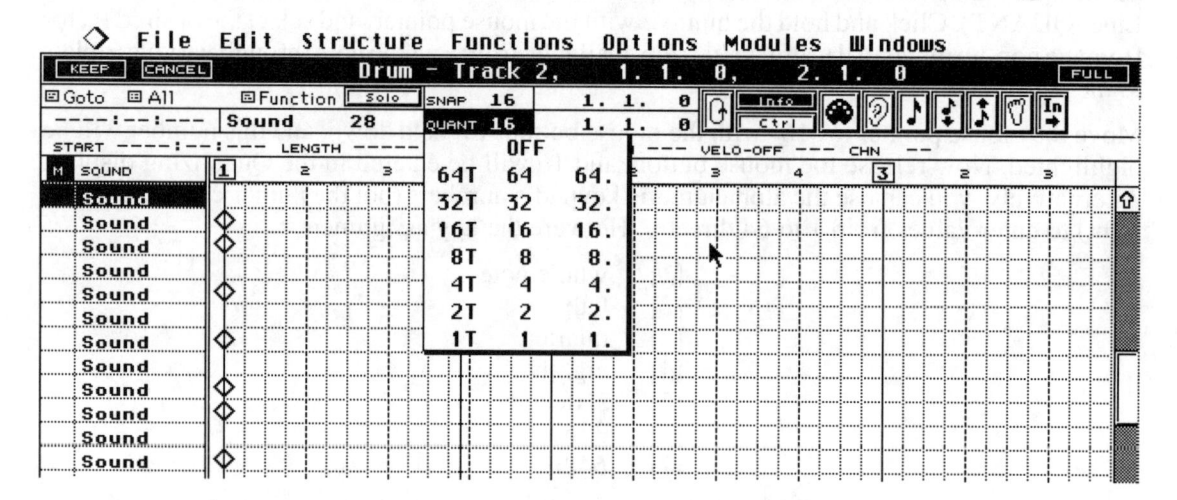

Quantizing factors in the Drum Editor

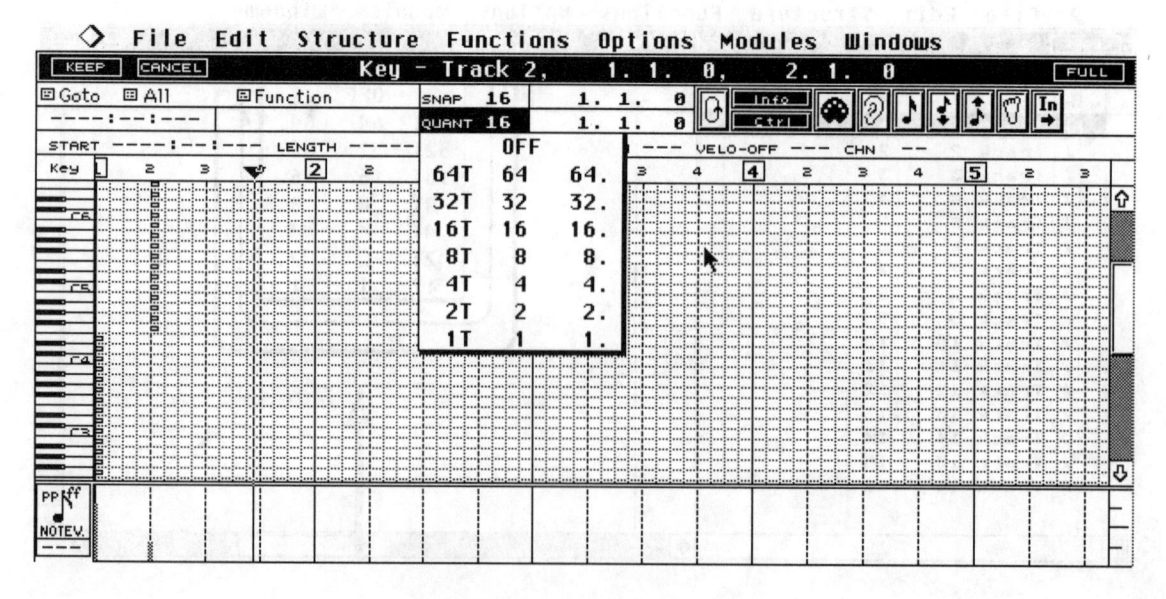

Quantizing factors in the Key Editor

Quantizing is naturally available in the Score Editor as well. However, bear in mind that the Score Editor also uses quantizing when displaying the notes. The visual display is not a true representation of the actual audible result. This applies to the diagrams depicting notes in this chapter as well. Refer to Chapter 16 for more information on this topic.

You may recall that there is another special feature in the Drum Editor which allows you to quantize each drum note individually.

15.7 Quantize ... now!

Simply selecting the value does not activate the quantizing function; we are going to do this now. Ensure your Part is selected and activate "Over Quantize" in the Functions menu (press [Q]).

Listen to the recording, and then try quantizing using other factors. What exactly happens? Cubase assigns the notes to other positions. When set to sixteenths, all notes are moved to 16th positions, when set to quarters, they are moved to the quarter positions, etc. After quantizing to quarters, your glissando could end up looking like this:

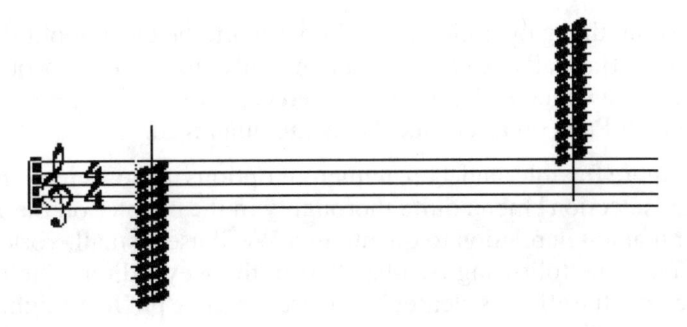

The glissando after quantizing to quarters

You will notice that only certain time positions contain notes, in accordance with the quantizing factor (quarters, eighths, sixteenths). The notes are still there, but they have been moved to the nearest position set by the quantizing factor.

15.8 Two essential rules

Two essential rules can be derived from the preceding example. The quantizing factor you select must take account of the smallest desired note position. For instance, if your Part contains sixteenth notes, you can't quantize to quarters, because the sixteenths will be moved to the quarter positions and you will lose the rhythm.

You can also run into problems if you select a quantizing factor that is too fine for your Part. Say you slightly mis-timed the first beat, and then set a very fine quantizing factor (e.g. 32nds). The relevant note may not be moved all the way to the downbeat, but may just end up at the next 32nd position after it. In a bad case, a chord could be pulled apart.

The important point to remember is that Cubase doesn't move the notes during recording, but during playback, even if the editors seem to indicate that data that has been altered. You can change the quantizing at any time and try out different factors. You can also undo the whole process simply by selecting "Undo Quantize" in the Functions menu.

15.9 Critical observations on quantizing

The increased use of sequencers, and consequently of quantizing, in recent years, has permanently influenced our perception of music. The discussion about "computerized music" as opposed to "handmade music" (whatever that means) has always revolved around a few central issues.

Quantizing

Apart from the sterile sounds produced by poor quality samples, a major criticism is the mechanical precision from which sequencer productions all too often suffer. In most cases, it is undesirable to have the imaginary "musicians" on the sequencer tracks mercilessly pounding away on quarters and sixteenths (apart from when quantization is used deliberately for reasons of style, e.g. in techno productions).

What this means is that if you immediately subject every track you record to drastic quantization, don't be surprised if your recording sounds strangely smooth and sterile and has no "feel".

The rule which emerges is that you must decide with your own ears whether or not a recording meets your timing expectations. Don't automatically quantize everything. If there are just a few notes you are not happy with, it is often preferable to quantize them "manually" in one of the editors, instead of quantizing the entire track or Part. Cubase features these options, so you may as well use them. The program has many different quantizing options, ranging from hard ones, which can have their uses, to "soft" types of quantizing.

15.10 Quantizing with Cubase

Before we try some quantizing operations, it is important to be clear about the material that is going to be quantized. Basically, Cubase quantizes only notes, and no other MIDI events. Quantizing in the Arrange window affects all selected Parts, even if they are on different tracks. If no Part is selected, all Parts on a selected Track are quantized.

The editors are even more flexible, and there numerous options in the "selection" menu. We have already covered the "selection" menu quite thoroughly in the chapter on the Key Editor, but it is worth going over it again in relation to quantizing. We'll use a small, very specific example for this purpose. Create the following two-bar Part in the Key Editor. The pitch of the notes doesn't really matter, but the effect is clearer if you use the same pitch throughout the Part. Enter the following precise positions:

Note 1 - 1.1.0
Note 2 - 1.2.0
Note 3 - 1.3.0
Note 4 - 1.4.46
Note 5 - 2.1.0
Note 6 - 2.2.24
Note 7 - 2.3.0
Note 8 - 2.4.0

All notes should have a length of 96 ticks (sixteenth notes).

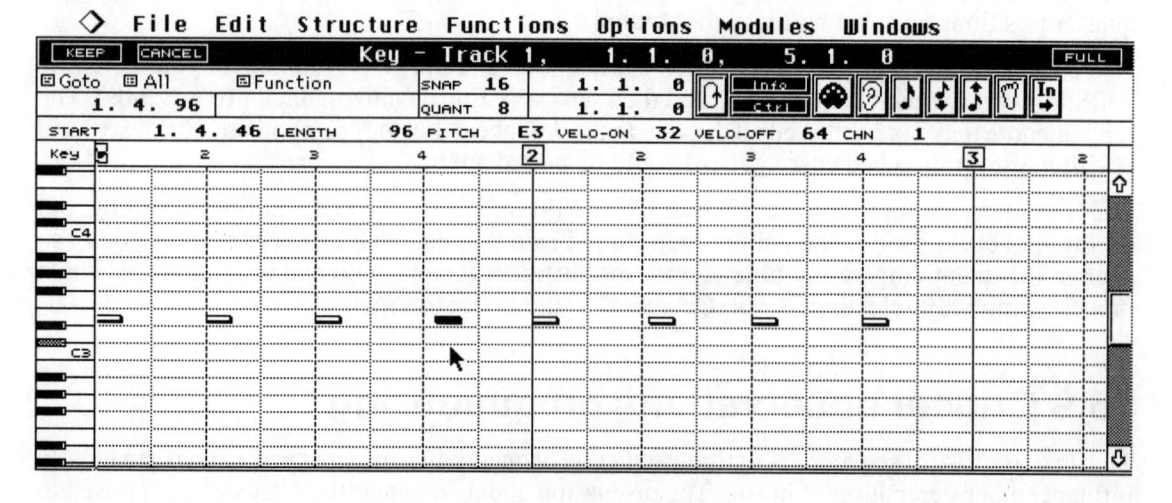

The finished Part looks like this

Sixteenth notes were entered at eighth intervals in the Key Editor. Notes four and six are not precisely at the eighth positions. You can't quantize the entire Part, because it is only note four that you want to quantize. You can do this with the help of the "selection" menu. Select the desired note with the Atari's cursor keys [->] and [<-] (not the mouse pointer!), and choose "Selected Events" from the "selection" menu.

Choose "Selected Events" from the "selection" menu

Select the "eighths" quantizing factor and press [Q]. Watch what happens.

Only the selected note is quantized and pulled forwards to the nearest eighth position. The sixth note remains where it is. Another experiment illustrates the process even better. First activate "Undo Quantize" in the Functions menu. The quantizing is removed, and the note is back at its original position. Now select the "sixteenths" quantizing factor and activate the quantize function.

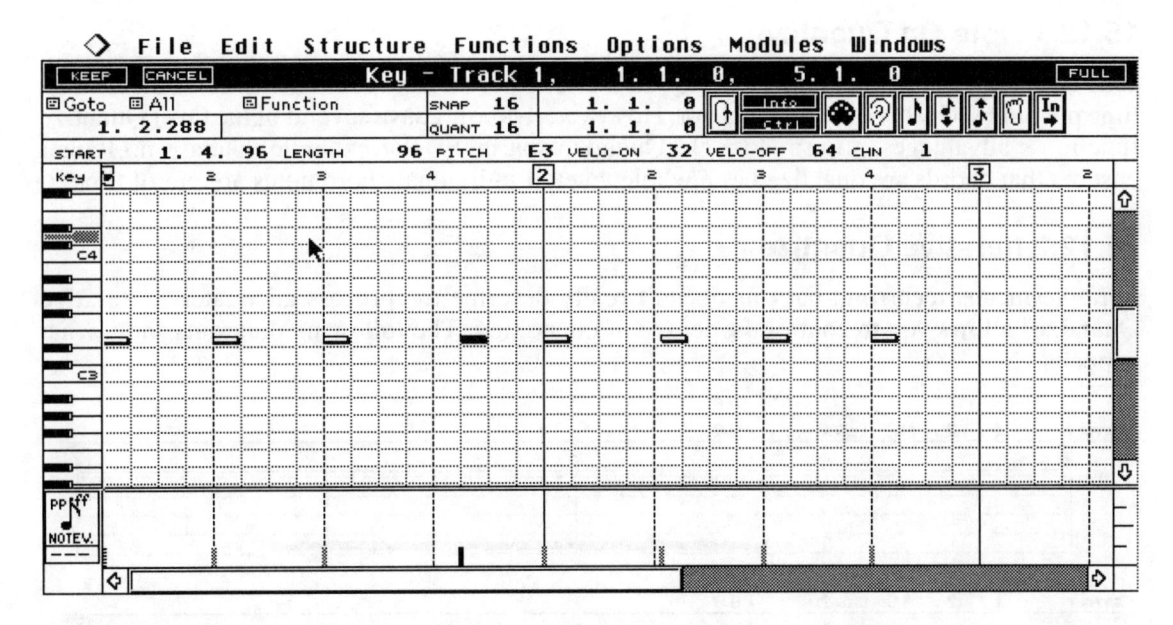

Quantizing to sixteenths

Again, Cubase only quantized one note, but the result is not the desired one. The note was not moved forwards to the eighth position, but backwards to the sixteenth position.

We selected the wrong quantizing factor. The note was closer to the following sixteenth position than the preceding sixteenth position, which is the eighth position that we want. In this case, Cubase had to move the note backwards.

Back to the "selection" menu, where you can define which notes you want to quantize. If you need to remind yourself of the options (All, Selected, Looped, etc.) refer to Chapter 8. Here too you

Quantizing

can modify or remove a quantize operation whenever you want. You also have the option of leaving the editor via "Cancel", which does exactly what it implies; it cancels all changes, including quantizing.

15.11 Manual quantizing

The following method is not strictly a quantize operation, but it can achieve the same effect. Say you have recorded a Part where only one single note is out of time.

In this case, you don't need to quantize. Go to the Key Editor, identify the note and click it. The note is moved to the nearest Snap position.

When you use this method, you set the Snap value to determine where the note is going be moved to. Don't let the grid display put you off, as this relates only to the quantizing factor, which doesn't apply to this operation.

15.12 The different types of quantizing

In the examples so far, we have only used the normal Cubase quantizing function, known as "Over Quantize". In this function, Cubase tries to "analyze" your playing and move notes to their correct positions. Chords are left intact whenever possible. All you have to worry about is entering a sensible quantizing factor, which shouldn't be a problem with the knowledge you've gained so far.

The Functions menu features other types of quantizing operations, which we'll take a look at now.

15.12.1 Note On Quantize

This operation is very similar to Over Quantize. The note's start point is moved to the nearest time position set by the quantizing factor. However, it doesn't have several of the Over Quantize function's advantages, so use Note On Quantize sparingly. For example, Cubase no longer ensures that chords are quantized as a whole, even if individual chord notes are out of time.

15.12.2 Iterative Quantize

Iterative means recurring, but this doesn't really describe the process adequately. "Iterative Quantize" allows you to control the degree of quantizing. The following diagrams show what happens.

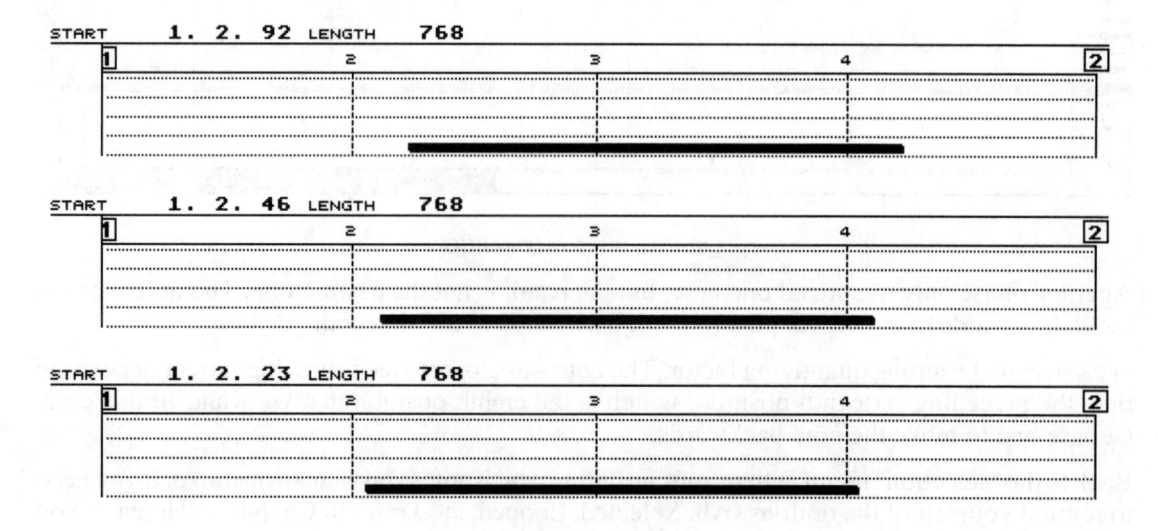

The Different Types of Quantizing

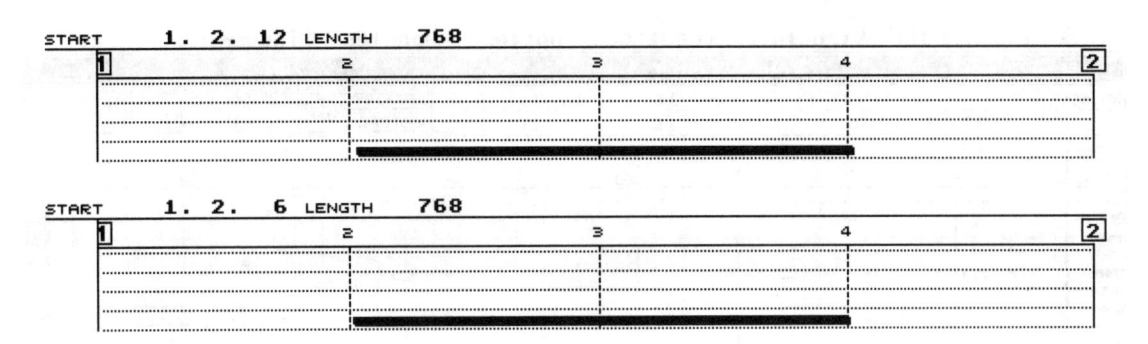

```
START    1. 2. 12  LENGTH  768
```

```
START    1. 2.  6  LENGTH  768
```

Several Iterative Quantize operations

A note is located at position 1.2.92. You select a Quantization factor of 4, i.e. you want to quantize to the nearest quarter note. With the normal Over Quantize function Cubase would move the note to the nearest quarter note position, i.e. 1.2.0.

However, we select the "Iterative Quantize" function from the Functions menu (press [E]) instead. Repeated use of Iterative Quantize moves the note towards the nearest quantizing position, which in this case is the quarter note. You can determine its intensity by selecting "Edit Quantize" from the Functions menu.

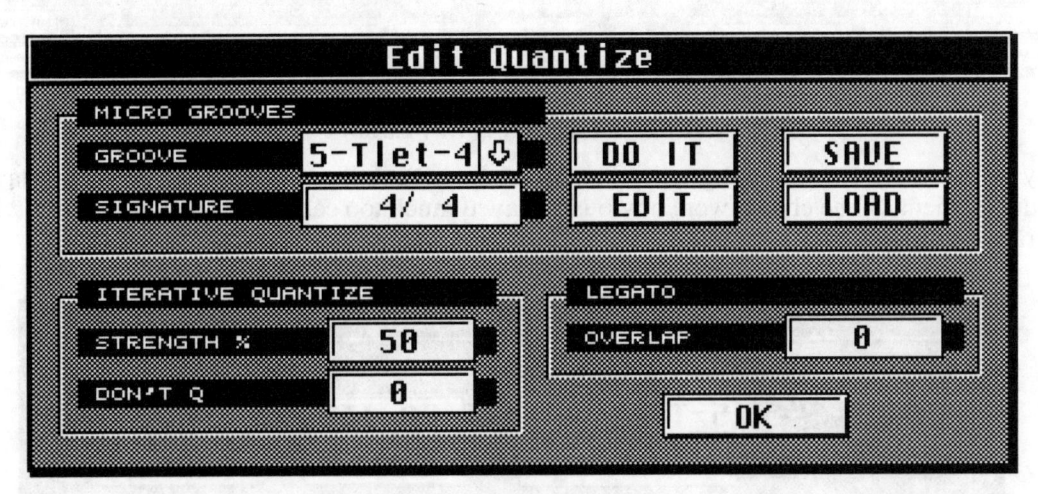

The Edit Quantize dialog box

The Iterative Quantize portion of the box has all the necessary settings. "Strength" controls the amount of influence, 50% in our example.

This means that if Cubase drags the note from 1.2.92 to 1.2.0 in a normal quantize operation, the Iterative function initially drags it only half as far, in this case to 1.2.46, then half this distance the next time (1.2.23), and so on.

The percentage values between 0 and 100 control the Iterative function's intensity. 0 denotes no change, and 100 produces the same effect as Over Quantize. With a little finesse you can "soften" the quantizing effect with these settings.

Don't Quantize
The "Don't Quantize" setting is used to exclude notes from quantizing. Before and after certain positions, you define areas you don't want Cubase to quantize. The unit of measurement is the tick.

The following examples demonstrate exactly how this function works. Let's look at a piano Part first.

Quantizing

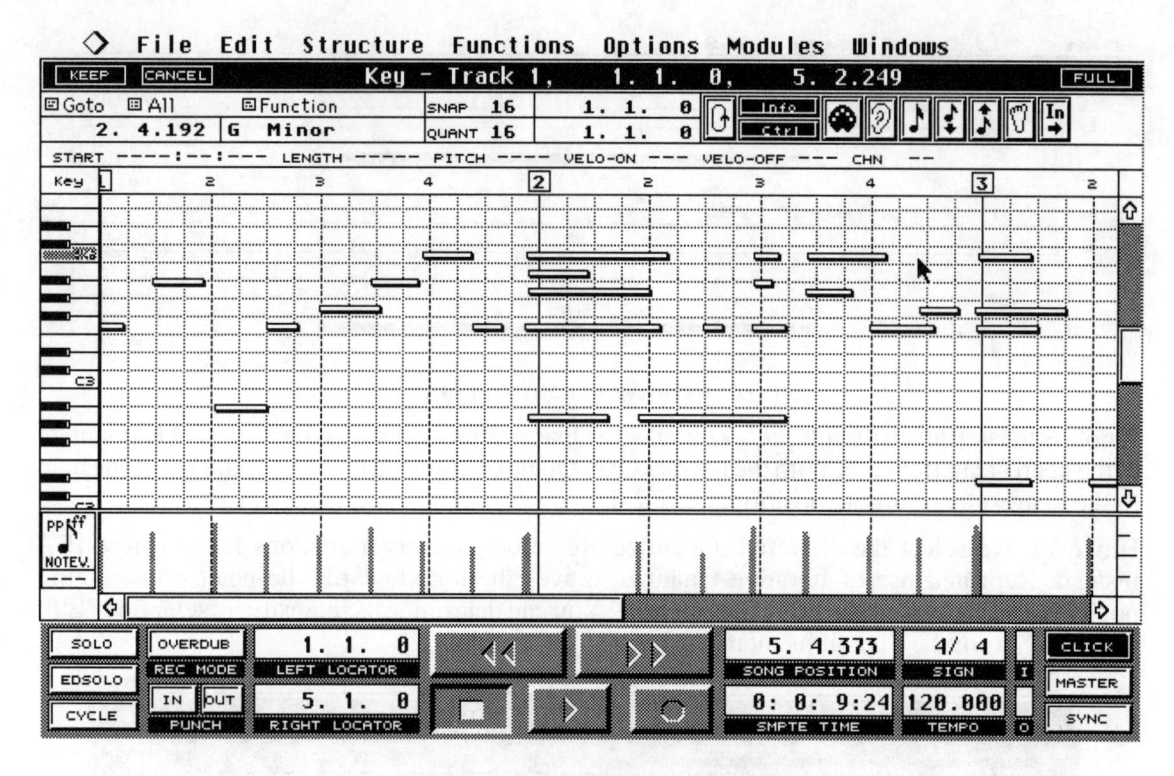

A piano Part in the Key Editor

Say we made a few mistakes at position 2.1.0, and also in the following bars that are not displayed at the moment. Some chords were obviously played much too early, so we enter the following Iterative settings:

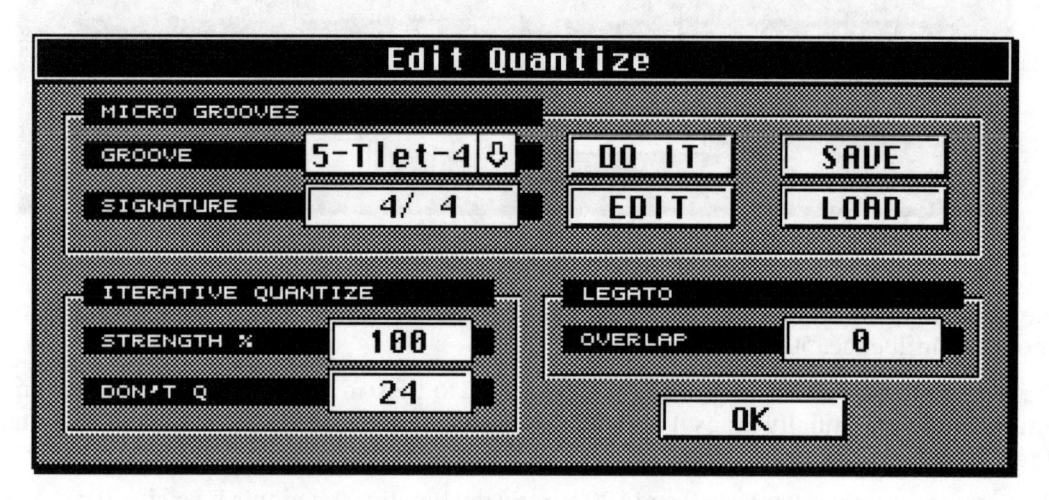

The required Iterative Quantize settings

All notes less than 24 ticks before and after the sixteenth quantizing points are not quantized. All notes outside this area are moved 100%, i.e. to the nearest quantizing point. Let's have a look at the result.

The Different Types of Quantizing

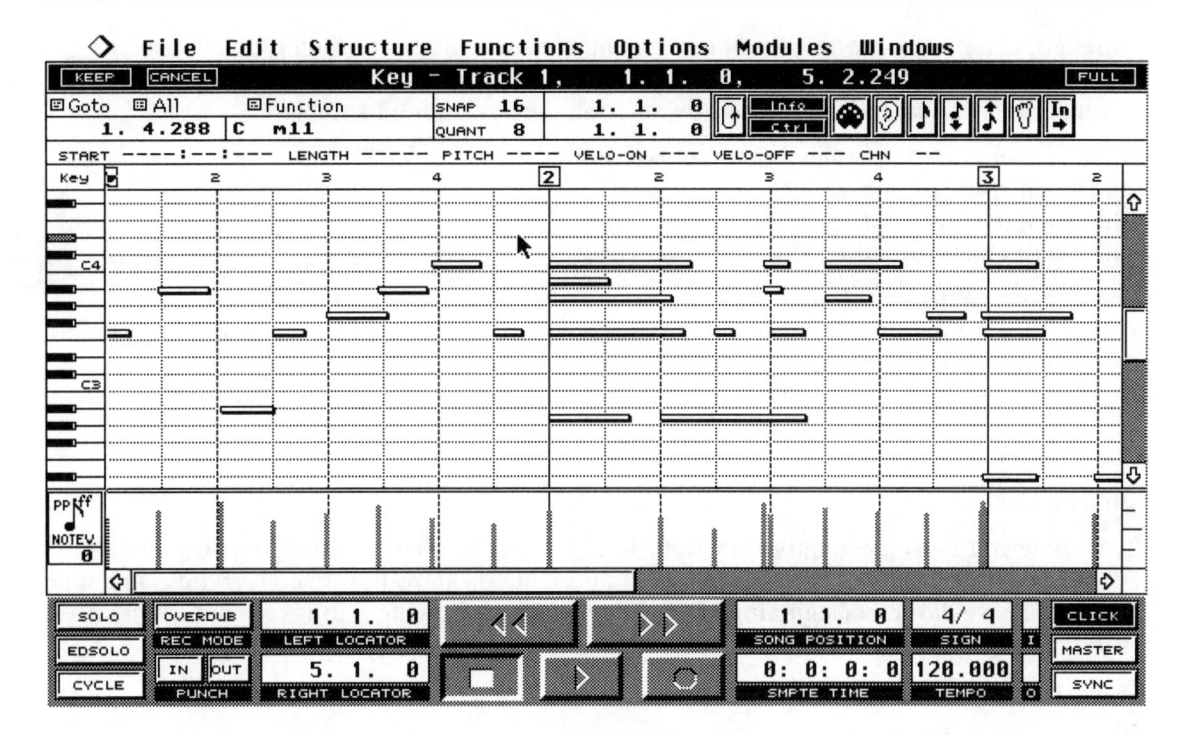

The result

The chord notes are moved to position 2.1.0 exactly, while the other events remain unaltered. Basically no event in a recording is ever going to be at exactly the right position, after all we're not robots. Often it's not a good idea to correct a few notes to their precise positions, because none of the other events are going to be 100 percent exact either.

Iterative Quantize lets you do this. For the above example, you could simply enter a different strength value so that the notes are moved in the right direction, but not precisely on to the quantizing positions.

You can use the Iterative operation several times in a row, and monitor the result each time to see if it sounds good. Each step is half the previous one, so you'll never actually reach 1.2.0. The following diagram shows the relationship:

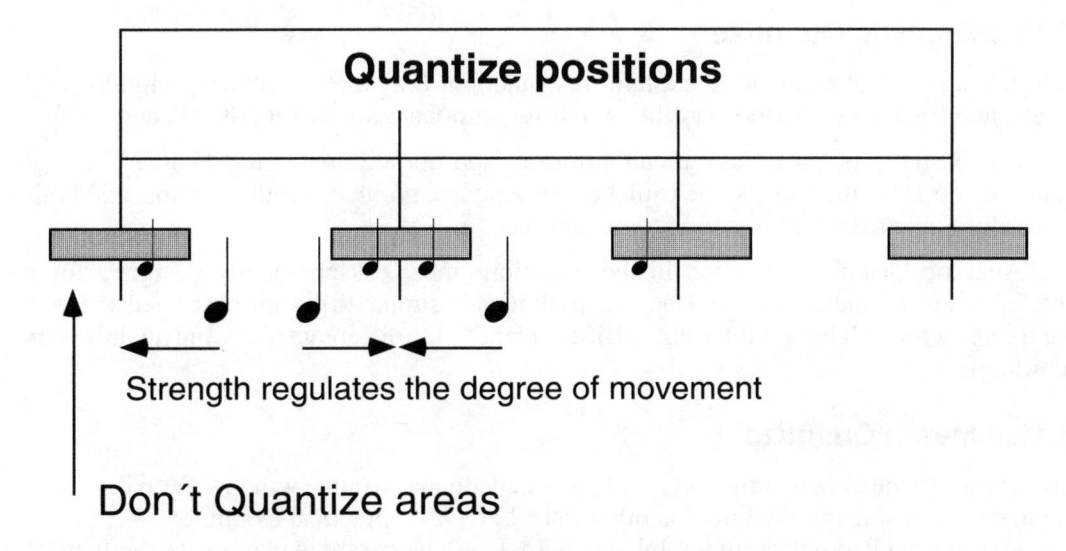

Quantize positions

Strength regulates the degree of movement

Don't Quantize areas

The relationships between moved and unmoved notes

- Notes in the Don't Quantize area are not quantized.
- The size of the area is defined in ticks.

287

- Strength determines the amount of movement of notes outside the Don't Quantize areas.
- All notes outside the areas are moved to the nearest quantizing position.
- You define the quantizing positions by entering the quantizing factor.

Three elements are important in an Iterative setting:
- the quantizing positions,
- the strength value, and
- the Don't Quantize setting.

Creative use of Iterative Quantize:
You can use the Iterative Quantize creatively, as well as for repairs. Record a Part with eighth chords and try the following setting.

Quantize factor   8T

Don't Quantize 0

Strength   10%

Every time you apply the Iterative function, the eighth rhythm is moved towards a triplet rhythm. Try to find similar settings on your own. It's important you know how to convert ticks into note lengths, like we did at the beginning of this chapter. The following settings are not a typical use of Iterative Quantize.

Quantize factor   8

Don't Quantize 192

Strength   100%

You are expanding the Don't Quantize area to the next quantizing position, because 192 ticks are equal to an eighth. This quantizing is the same as the normal quantizing operation, so it doesn't make sense to use Iterative Quantize for this purpose.

Iterative Quantize and Undo
Bear in mind that if you apply Iterative Quantize several times, you're restricting the use of the Undo function. Each quantizing operation is always based on the previous one, but with Undo you can only reverse the last operation.

If you decide to use Iterative Quantize several times, do it in one of the editors. That way, you can Undo all changes made since you switched to the editor if you leave it via Cancel.

15.12.3 Analytic Quantize

We'll use a practical example to explain this function. Play a Part featuring eighths, eighth triplets, and finally a glissando. Try the two different quantizing factors (8, 8T, and so on).

Can you see the problem? Cubase can't find an appropriate quantizing factor. The eighth quantizing destroys the triplets, the triplet quantizing is a problem for the eighths, and both of these values quantize your glissando to extinction.

The "Analytic Quantize" function in the Functions menu is specifically designed for this situation. Use this function for Parts that are rhythmically similar to the one described above. The quantizing factor isn't important. Cubase tries to identify the different values and quantizes them accordingly.

15.12.4 Match Quantize

This very useful quantizing function is only available in the Arrange window. You can use it to quantize a Part using the rhythm of another Part. Let's try a practical example:
- Record a two bar Part with a eighths hihat pattern. Don't worry about playing it exactly in time.
- Record a second Part with a snare and a bass drum (as in the diagram below). Ensure the timing is as exact as possible. Ideally, you should create the Part in the drum editor.

The Different Types of Quantizing

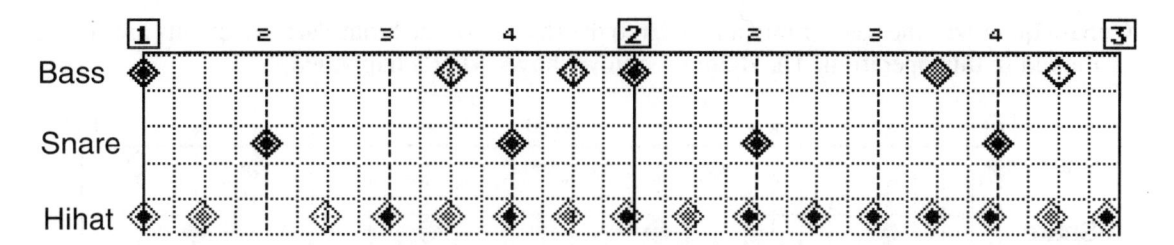

This is how your two drum Parts should look in the drum editor

- Go to the Arrange window and select a quantizing factor of 8.
- Select the Match Quantize tool from the Toolbox.

The Match Quantize tool

- Click the Part containing the hihat pattern with the Match Quantize tool. Drag the Part to the bass drum/snare Part while holding down the mouse button. Then release the mouse button.

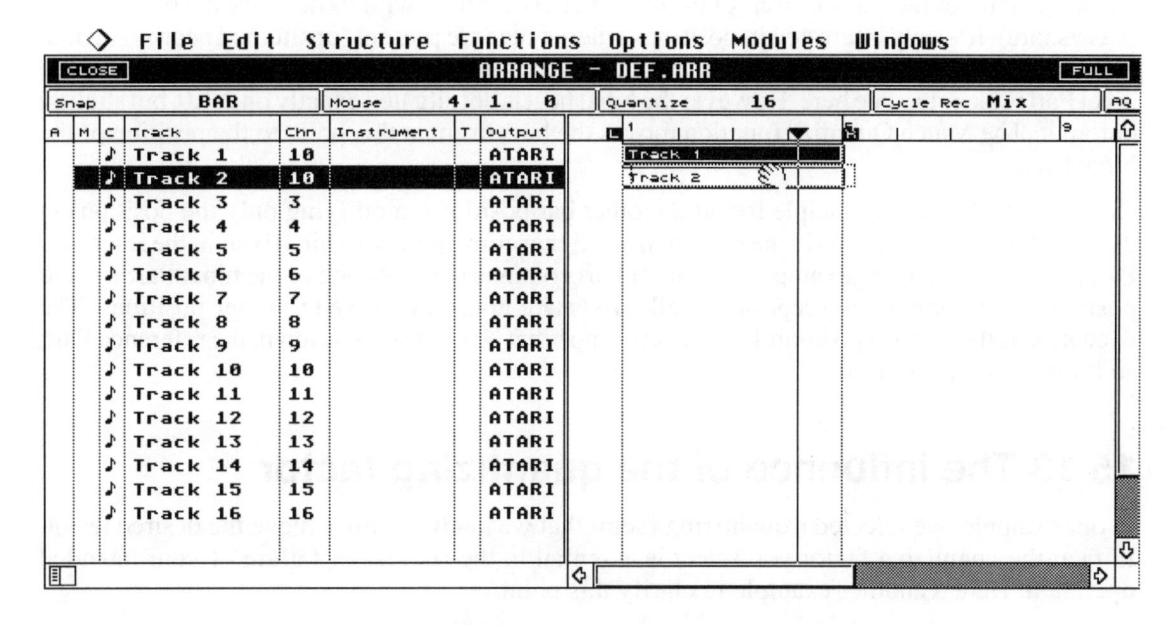

Drag the hihat Part to the other drum Part

Cubase asks you the following question:

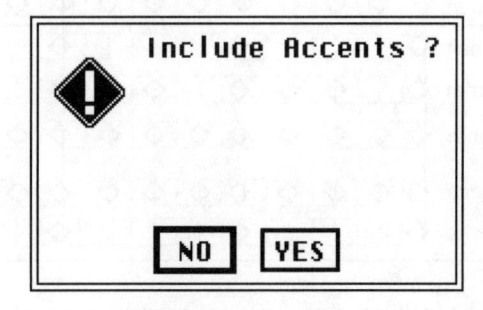

The question

- Quit by pressing [Return] or click "Yes".

289

Quantizing

Cubase quantizes the bass drum/snare Part to the rhythm of the hihat Part. No events are copied or moved in this operation. The diagram below shows what's happened.

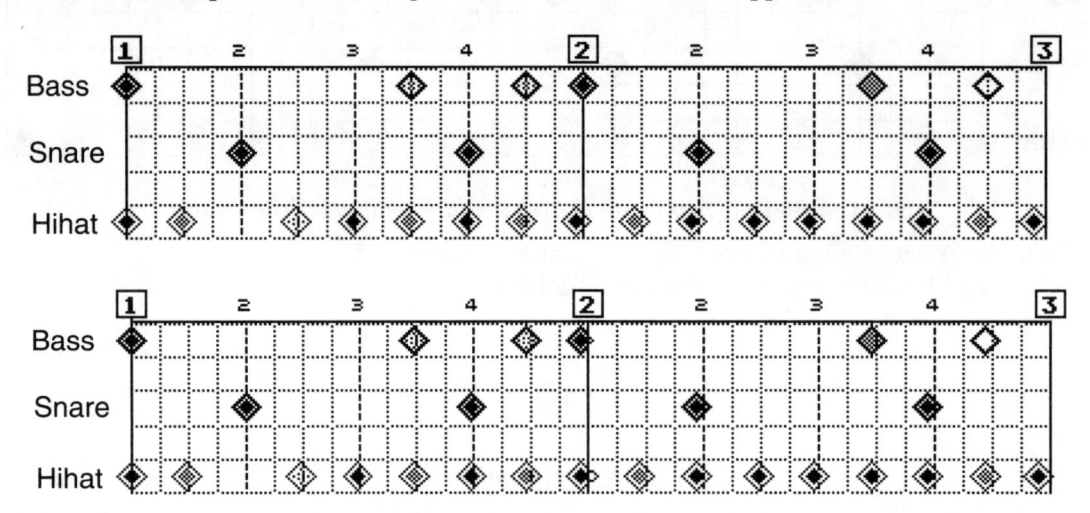

The finished operation

Cubase compares the bar positions of the reference Part (hihat) with those of the destination Part (bass/snare). It's only interested in positions where notes are present (or situated nearby) in both Parts; position 2.1.0 is the best example. Cubase finds notes at this position in both Parts. The hihat Part is the reference here. However the hihat beat is not situated exactly on 2.1.0, but slightly before it. The Match Quantize function moves the bass drum at this point to the position of the hihat beat.

Cubase uses the same principle for all the other bar positions, modifying only the positions in the target Part. All positions in the bass/snare Part that correspond to a hihat beat in the reference Part are modified. In our example, the target Part contains notes at each of the hihat Part's event positions, with only one exception; so all bass/snare notes are moved to other positions. The exception is the snare at position 1.2.0. There's no hihat beat at this position in the reference Part, so it remains unquantized.

15.13 The influence of the quantizing factor

In our example, we selected a quantizing factor that we knew would achieve the desired result. In fact, the quantizing factor you select is essential to the success or failure of your intended operation. Here's another example to clarify this point.

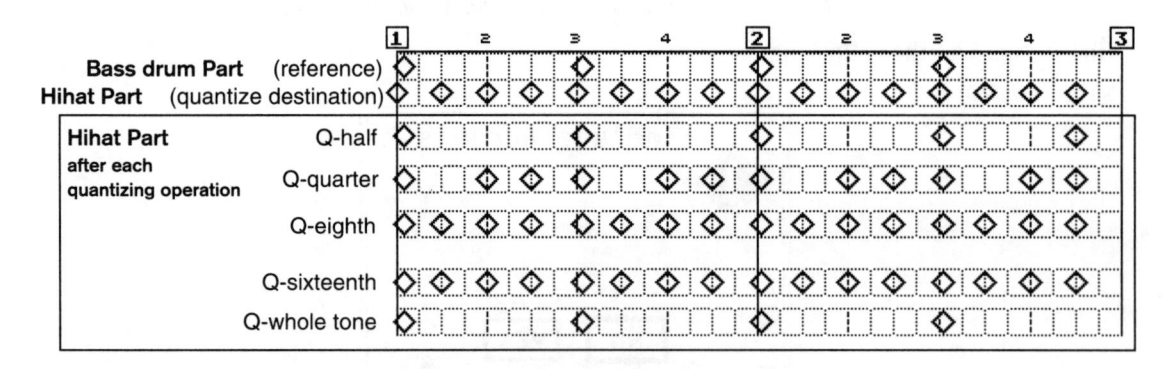

The influence of different quantizing factors

Two Parts were created on different tracks, one containing a hihat quantized exactly to eighths, the other a bass drum played in half notes. The timing of the bass drum is not exact, but lags behind the beat (on purpose). The bass drum Part is the reference to which the hihat Part will be quantized. First, select a quantizing factor. Then, use the Match Quantize tool to drag the bass drum Part over to the hihat Part. The diagram shows how each different Quantize factor influences the result.

15.13.1 First example

The preceding example used quantizing to half beats. Cubase first analyses the half beat bar positions (1.1.0, 1.3.0, 2.1.0...) in both Parts. The half beat positions of the hihat Part are changed according to the values in the reference Part. The events in the hihat Part are moved slightly backwards at the 1.1.0 and the 1.3.0 positions. We've already come across this effect in the first match quantize exercise.

In addition, Cubase checks the areas around the reference notes, using the Quantize factor, and quantizes them if necessary. In this example, we originally selected half note quantizing, which means that the areas within a half note before and after the bass drum reference positions are quantized as well. This results in our eighths hihat pattern being changed into a half beat hihat pattern.

15.13.2 Second example

The second example uses a Quantize factor of 4, i.e. quarter notes. Here too, the notes at the reference positions were initially moved slightly backwards. In addition, the notes at the 1.1.192 / 1.4.192 positions were moved forwards to the next quarter note position. Why? Simply because these notes were within the "catchment area" of one quarter note, which we defined with the selected Quantize factor.

Question: why did Cubase leave the note at the 1.2.0 position where it was?

Answer: because the reference Part does not contain a note at this position, and because this position is not within the predetermined catchment area.

Question: why did Cubase also leave the notes at the 1.2.192/1.4.192 ... positions where they were?

Answer: because the reference notes after them were moved slightly backwards, so that the notes before them were no longer within the catchment area, and were not caught.

15.13.3 Third example

The Quantize factor was 8, and the result should be obvious. Notes at the reference positions were changed, but all other notes in the target Part are outside the catchment area, and remain unchanged, which is what we wanted.

15.13.4 Examples 4 and 5

The knowledge you have gained so far should enable you to see what has happened. Quantize values smaller than 8 show no change, because the notes in the example are on the eighth positions, and there are no more notes within the range of sixteenths.

Using whole notes as a Quantize factor would produce the same results as a half note Quantize factor, because in the reference Part only half note positions are occupied.

Two questions remain unanswered. First: what does "Include Accents" mean? Not only can you quantize the target track with the rhythm of the reference track, but you can also transfer the reference Part's velocity values to the target Part.

The second question refers to the length of the Parts. What happens if the reference Part is shorter or longer than the target Part? This is not a problem, because Cubase simply subtracts or adds the necessary portion. If the destination Part is longer than the reference Part, then Cubase adds on copies of the reference Part (virtually) until it is the correct length, and vice versa.

Quantizing

15.13.5 Creative Groove Quantizing

This type of quantizing is especially useful when you want to match the grooves of two Parts, e.g. a drum Part and a bass Part. You can also save Parts that you think have turned out well rhythmically as reference Parts on a floppy disk, and use them to edit other arrangements.

The whole process is very complex, and not easy to understand. You have two choices: you can decide to forget all the theory and just experiment, but be sure to always make backup copies of Parts on another track, if they are important to you.

On the other hand, any results you get will be the product of random actions, and you will have to rely on luck. If you really want to apply the Match Quantize function (and the Groove Quantize function that we'll look at in a minute) in a really useful and creative way, you need to understand how it works.

Work your way carefully through the Match Quantize section. At least try the simplest exercises to get a better picture of what is involved. This will guarantee predictable results when you are working with more complex musical material later on.

15.13.6 Freeze Quantize

When using Match and Groove Quantize, and sometimes Iterative Quantize as well, it's essential the timing of the destination Parts is correct. Cubase can only usefully apply the different quantizing functions to Parts where the timing is not totally out.

If you edit Parts where the timing is shaky, you can come up with surprising and usually unusable results. It's a definitely an advantage to pre-quantize a track before you start to get into the creative quantizing options.

However, this poses yet another problem: Cubase always refers back to the original data when it quantizes. Quantizing is a play parameter that does not change the notes permanently: they are simply played back according to the set quantizing factor. This might mean that you can't undertake a proper Groove Quantize, even though you pre-quantized the notes and the Part sounded perfectly alright.

In this case, you should first use "Freeze Quantize" to fix the result. Cubase then no longer just plays the quantizing back, but converts the original data to the new values, and your original timing is thereby lost. To "freeze" the quantization, select the desired Parts and activate "Freeze Quantize" in the Functions menu.

Note: You cannot Undo Freeze Quantize.

Prior to a Match Quantize operation, you should quantize only the destination tracks, never the reference track.

15.13.7 Groove Quantize

Groove Quantize works in a similar way to Match Quantize. The only difference is that the reference grooves do not come from another Part, but are programmed by you.

A small experiment will illustrate this:
- Create two bar Parts on two different tracks in the Drum Editor. Track 1 should contain a bass drum in quarter beats, Track 2 a sixteenths hihat pattern.
- Choose a quantizing factor of "16".
- Select the hihat Part.
- Set a loop and start playback.
- Select "Groove Quantize" from the Functions menu.
- Click the first entry in the list, "5-TLET-4".
- Listen closely to the rhythmic changes of the hihat pattern.
- Call up the list again and select the next entry.
- Try all the entries, one after another.

Your Own Grooves

```
✓ 5-Tlet-4
  5-Tlet-8
  Shuffle1
  Shuffle2
  Shuffle3
  Shuffle4
  Random 1
  Random 2
  2+and 4-
  3rd -4
  Pre 2+4
  PreSnare
  Laidback
  Triplet
  Moreback
  Running
```

The basic grooves offered by Steinberg

Let's look in detail at the structure of one of these grooves:
- Select "Edit Quantize" from the Functions menu.
- "Micro Grooves" is what we want to look at.
- Click and hold the downward arrow in the "Groove" line.
- Select "Shuffle 4" from the list which appears.
- Click "Edit".

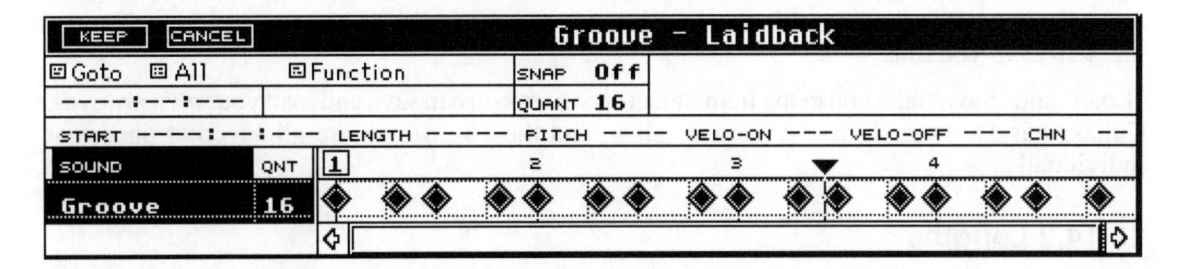

The Groove Edit dialog box

The dialog box that appears, called the "Groove Edit", is a bit like the Drum Editor, and you can program a one-bar groove here. What characterizes the "Shuffle 4" groove is that it uses eighth triplets. If you apply this groove to a track containing eighth notes, the straight eighth beat notes are left unchanged, but offbeats are turned into triplets. The result, as you have already heard, is a shuffle.

In contrast to the Match Quantize function, you can preprogram your own grooves here, as you would in the Drum Editor. The quantizing factor is absolutely essential. Before we get started, you should take a look at the other groove presets.

15.14 Your own grooves

Creating your own grooves is relatively simple. You can either develop existing grooves, or start from scratch. In this case the diamonds do not represent events, but quantizing positions, which serve as reference points. It does not matter whether you create your own grooves as Parts and use Match Quantize, or whether you create and use patterns in Groove Quantize; the results are

Quantizing

the same. Groove Quantize simply allows you to save and call up your grooves when you need them, and so is the more user-friendly option.

15.14.1 Changing reference points

This works the same way as in the Drum Editor, so you should go to the Drum Editor before you start changing reference grooves. This is not absolutely vital, it's just that better tools are available in the Drum Editor. Select "Edit Quantize" from the Functions menu, and then "Edit" from the dialog box which appears.

Make sure that you select the correct time signature in the Signature field. Refer to the chapters on tempo and synchronization for more information. A groove always has a length of one bar in the selected time signature.

Here's a brief review of the rules for editing events :
- Select points by clicking with the mouse.
- You can also use the rubber band.
- Delete points with [Backspace] or [Delete].
- You can also use the Eraser.
- Snap and Quantize work in the same way as in the Drum Editor.
- The Functions menu provides the usual assistance.
- The Goto and "selection" sub-menus do not apply.
- Set the reference points with the drum stick at the desired positions.
- Precise positioning of starting points is done in the Info Line.
- Do not change any of the other values (pitch, length, etc.).
- Use the Kicker tools to "kick" notes backwards or forwards.
- Keep saves the new groove, Cancel deletes all changes.

Any groove you create in this manner can be named, and saved to or loaded from a floppy disk at any time. Naming a groove is done in the Edit Quantize dialog box. Unfortunately, you can't do it in the Groove Edit box; you have to go back to the editor or the Arrange window, and then to the Edit Quantize box. For this reason, it's better to name grooves before you create them, as this will save you time.

"Load" and "Save" take you to the Item Selector, where you can save and load your own grooves. Cubase has 16 internal groove memory slots, and the 16 grooves are all saved at once, not individually.

15.14.2 Lengths

Until now, we've talked only about the starting points of notes, and not their lengths, but this factor has almost the same amount of influence on the audible result. The best example is probably a funky clavinet riff, which thrives on correct note lengths. Cubase doesn't change note lengths during quantizing. Only the start positions are moved, unless you actually want to change the lengths as well.

We've already looked at one of these functions in the section on timing, where we saw how Legato is used to create or avoid overlapping notes. The Functions menu contains two further options.

Fixed Length
"Fixed Length" sets all selected notes, or all notes in the selected Part/track, to the length of the quantize value. If you select a factor of 8, Cubase changes all notes to eighths.

Length Size
This operation quantizes the note lengths. The start position is not modified, but the end point of the note is lengthened, or shortened, to the nearest quantizing factor position. If you use this function skilfully in combination with Note On quantizing, you can simulate the Note On/Off quantizing of a vintage sequencer. Typically, this function is used to edit funk bass or clavinet tracks, even though Cubase's Logical Editor gives you more options in this respect.

16 Notation and Page Layout

Version 3.0 features high-performance notation and page layouting. This chapter shows you how to use them to maximum effect and achieve the best results.

16.1 Notation display difficulties

Generally, translating music into notation is a complex undertaking for any computer. Consider this: if you give three musicians the same sheet music and ask them to play the piece, what happens? You will almost certainly recognize your music, but there will interpretative differences. The pitch will be the same, but the rhythm, articulation and even tempo may differ quite a bit. This all comes under the term "interpretation". The reasons are clear: the notation cannot prescribe exact playing techniques, other than the exact pitch values. Rhythmic nuances especially are going to differ from one interpretation to the next. How else could you explain the differences amongst orchestras and conductors? Notation is a relatively abstract science.

What does this have to do with Cubase? Well, we face a similar problem. Cubase is first and foremost an excellent sequencer program designed to record and playback music to the highest standards of precision. To take this music and produce acceptable notation from it requires that the program also has some form of abstract reasoning. The computer program must decide if rhythmic "pushes and pulls" within the performance are actually little interpretative idiosyncrasies that should be left unannotated, or whether such characteristics should be exactly reflected by what you see in the score, complete with 64th notes and rests, etc.

An additional requirement is the ability to recognize and display notes and their relationships to all the other musical factors in the proper musical context. This may seem trivial to you, but you will see as we proceed in this chapter that programming influences the results in many ways. The bottom line is that the results in terms of layout and precision depend on the standards you set. This is dictated by what purpose you have in mind for the notation. There is substantially less effort involved in producing a lead sheet for the members of your band, than producing a piano score fit for publishing.

16.2 The basic conditions

Your recorded Parts and Tracks serve as the basis for Cubase's music notation. Cubase uses the Score Editor for the display, so you must load this module. It doesn't matter whether you

Notation and Page Layout

recorded the notes you want to print in realtime or produced them with the aid of an Editor. We will run through exercises of varying complexity in this chapter.

Let's get started. Create an Arrangement that resembles the following structure. What you play is not as important as keeping to the structure and instrumental content:
- Track 1 contains the drums. Use a kick drum, snare, closed and open hihat, and a few tom fills.
- Track 2 is for the bass.
- Track 3 is for two-handed piano accompaniment.
- Track 4 is for a melody instrument, saxophone in this case.

Record a relatively short Part about eight bars long. This should be enough for our first experiments.

16.3 The first important rules

Cubase's notation requires that certain rules be followed:
- The rules on presenting Parts and Tracks are the same as those we discussed in the Score Editor (refer to Chapter 10).
- Most Score Editor editing is used to optimize the notation *display*, and does not affect the actual musical MIDI content.
- However, in some cases, you are required to edit MIDI notes.
- *Always* make a backup copy of your original recording before you work on notation in the Score Editor. Disregard this if you want to use the Score Editor purely as a MIDI Editor.
- Start the printing preparations only when you are satisfied with the (rhythmic) display of all the notes in your Parts and Tracks.
- The use of quantization makes both your and Cubase's life that much easier. This is yet another reason to work with a copy of your original piece.

The concept of notation preproduction may not mean much to you as yet, so let's go to the Score Editor and run through the procedure. Our Arrangement has four Tracks, and as we want to print all four of them, select them now. You can, of course, enter a single Part or Track for printing purposes in the Score Editor later. Generally, Cubase prints only those portions of your Arrangement which are in the Score Editor. The order the staves are displayed in is derived from the Track order. Before you start changing things, you should establish the correct Track order on the Arrange window. If you want to print everything, choose Select All ([Control][A]) from the Edit menu and go to the Score Editor. This may take a moment, depending on how complex your recording is.

Select all the Parts...

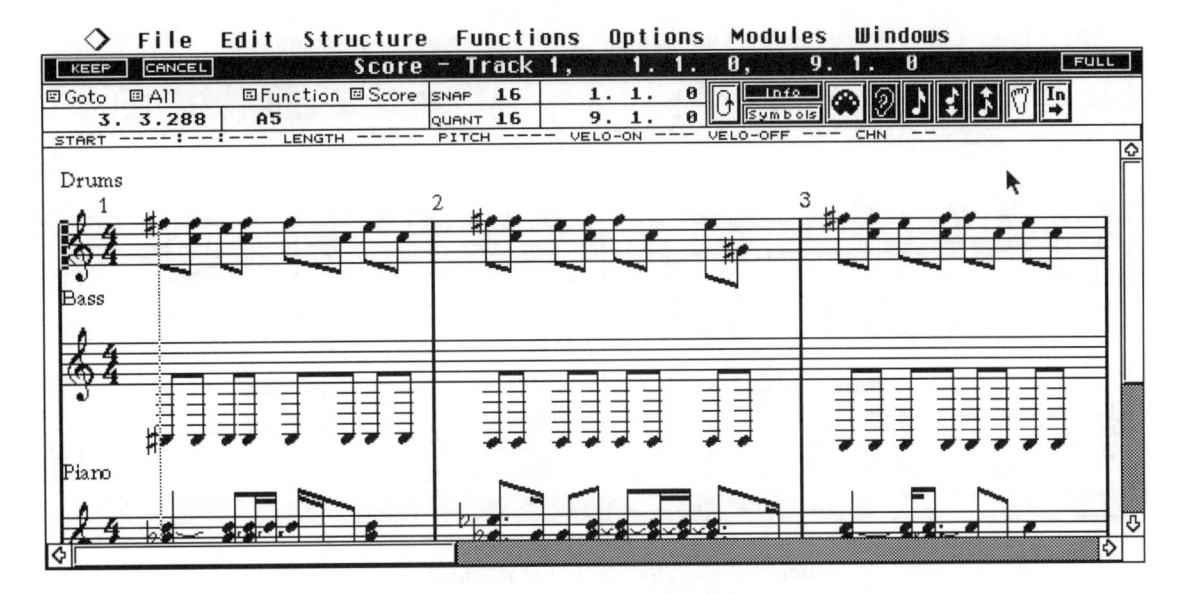

...and go to the Score Editor

Cubase displays a section of score on your screen. Use the scroll bars to move around in the window. Did you stick to the suggested instrument order? If you did, the concept of notation preproduction should be getting clearer.

The drum Track looks rather strange, the bass notes are hanging way too low, and the piano Track could definitely benefit from a split system. In short, the whole lot could do with some improvements.

16.4 The essential corrections

We went through some of the following steps in Chapter 10. So that you don't have to go back and look, we'll review these steps using our example. The order in which they are taken is basically the same every time you prepare for notation.

16.4.1 The correct key and clef

Find the correct key, in this case Bb major, as follows:
- Double-click the clef symbol of the bass Track.
- Select the correct clef and key signature from the dialog box that appears: click the clef with the left/right mouse buttons until the right clef appears. Click in the staff next to the clef to select the key signature. Each left click moves the key down a fifth, the right moves the key up a fifth.
- In our example, you must click twice with the left mouse button to go from C major to Bb major.
- Exit the dialog box.

Your settings are entered in the staff.

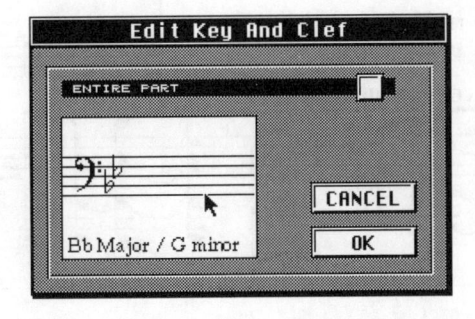

Select the correct key and clef for the bass staff...

Notation and Page Layout

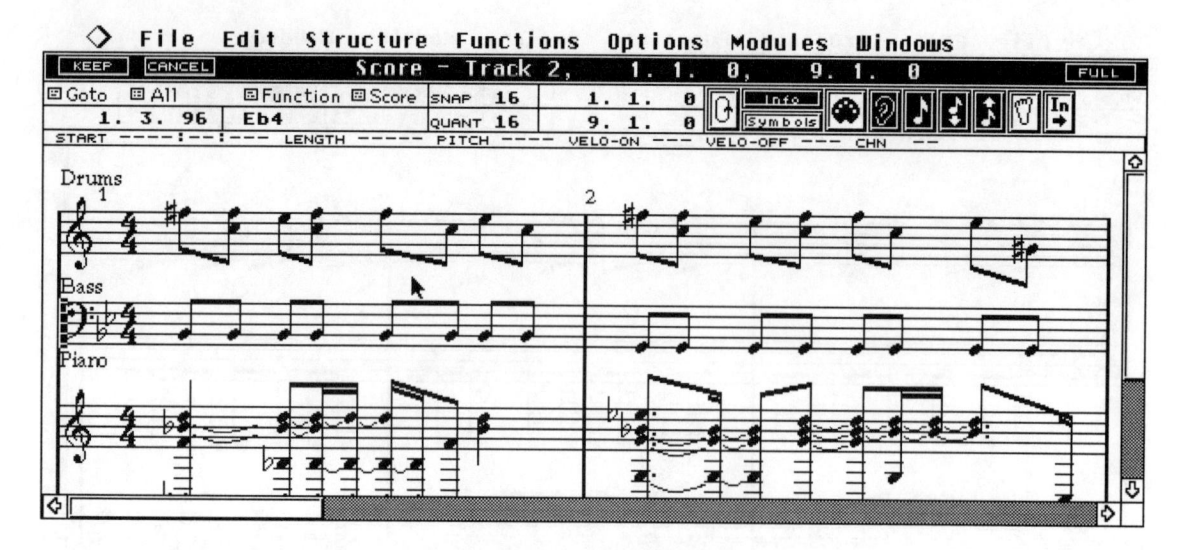

...and the display improves dramatically

The bass Track already looks a lot better. Keep in mind that the steps we ran through above apply to the selected staff only, so you may have to repeat the operation whenever a staff requires it. The sax Track needs to be given the correct key and the other staves represent special cases that we will look at now.

16.4.2 Staff settings

Piano Parts and other keyboard instruments are usually annotated as split staves because of their ranges. Our example is no exception to this rule. Staff Settings in the Score sub-menu is of help here. You can set a range of parameters for *each individual staff* using this dialog box. Before you can work on a staff, it has to be selected by clicking its beginning.

Let's split the piano Track into two staves:
- Select the piano staff,
- choose Staff Settings from the Score sub-menu,
- click the box next to the Split Point inscription so it gets a checkmark,
- leave the split point at C3 for the time being,
- exit the dialog box with [Return].
- Cubase automatically assigns the treble clef to the upper staff, and the bass to the bottom staff.
- You must assign the correct key to each of the staves.

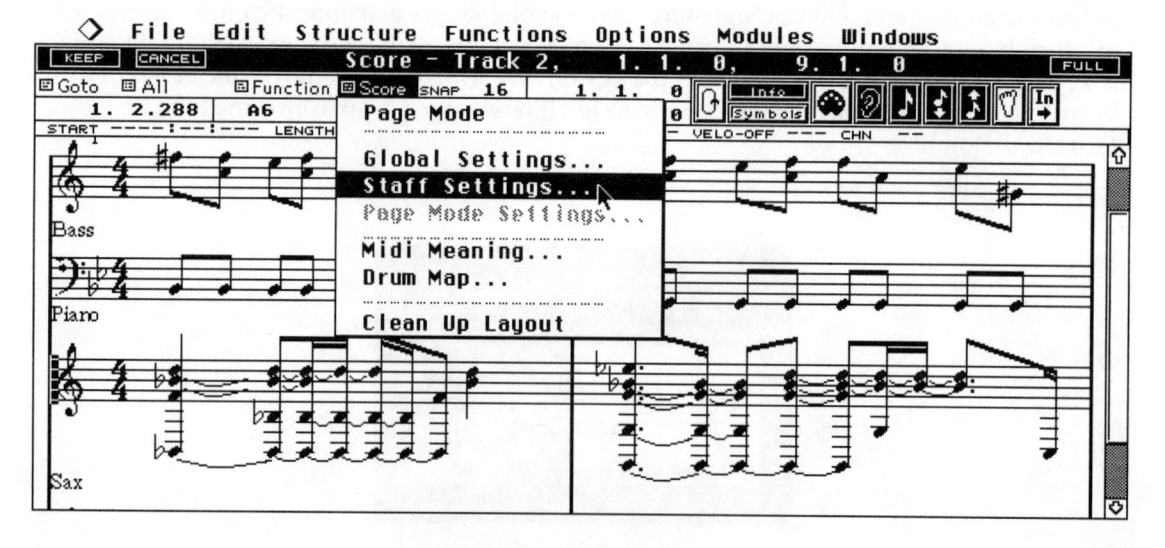

Select the piano system...

298

The Essential Corrections

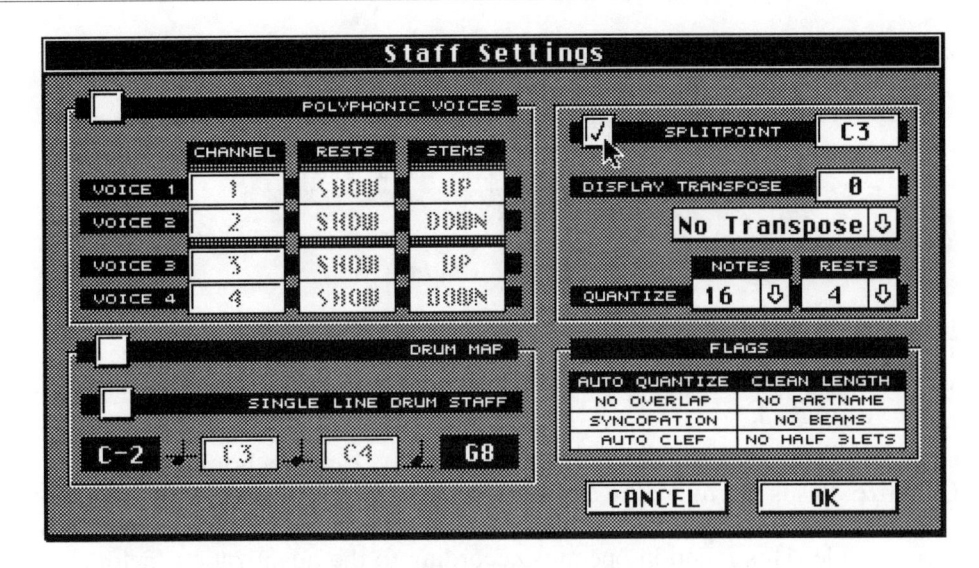

...and choose Staff Settings from the Score sub-menu

The result after you have selected the correct key as well

The display now looks much better. The whole thing is easier to read. Of course you can change the split point to whatever value is necessary for the piece you are dealing with.

These settings always apply to the entire Track, not just individual Parts. If you later move Parts to other Tracks, the destination Track staff settings apply, so you may have to make changes to the Parts.

16.4.3 Flags

Until now, we've been changing the environment the notes are in, and not the display of the notes themselves. Look at the piano system and you can see that its notes are not displayed correctly in a musical sense. The number of tied notes is especially irritating. The Staff Settings box features a number of options used to improve the note display. We'll look at its Flags first. Activate No Overlap for the piano system by clicking it once.

299

Notation and Page Layout

The Flags fields

The display is now tidier: Cubase displays lengthy notes that start at the same positions as short notes without ties. This is not correct in a strict sense, but it does help to clean up the display. We'll look at ways to deal with this display problem later on. For now, use whatever display style that is easiest for you to read.

The other Flag functions are also used to edit the display. Here's a brief review:

- Auto Quantize: this is not related in any way to the usual MIDI quantizing operations. Here Cubase quantizes the notation *display*. Complex algorithms are used to make the display as realistic as possible. This function operates according to the quantization factors in the Staff Settings box (refer to the next section).
- Auto Clef: this function automatically finds the correct clef. Split staves do not require this function.
- No Partname: this removes the Track name from the beginning of each staff in the display.
- Clean Lengths: this tries to recognize chords and quantizes their notes to the correct length (only in the display). This avoids unnecessary and incorrect ties.
- Syncopation: syncopations are displayed in a more readable manner.
- No Beams: all the beams between notes are removed, an important factor in vocal notation.
- No Half Triplets: where notes extend into a tuplet group, the triplet is displayed more clearly.

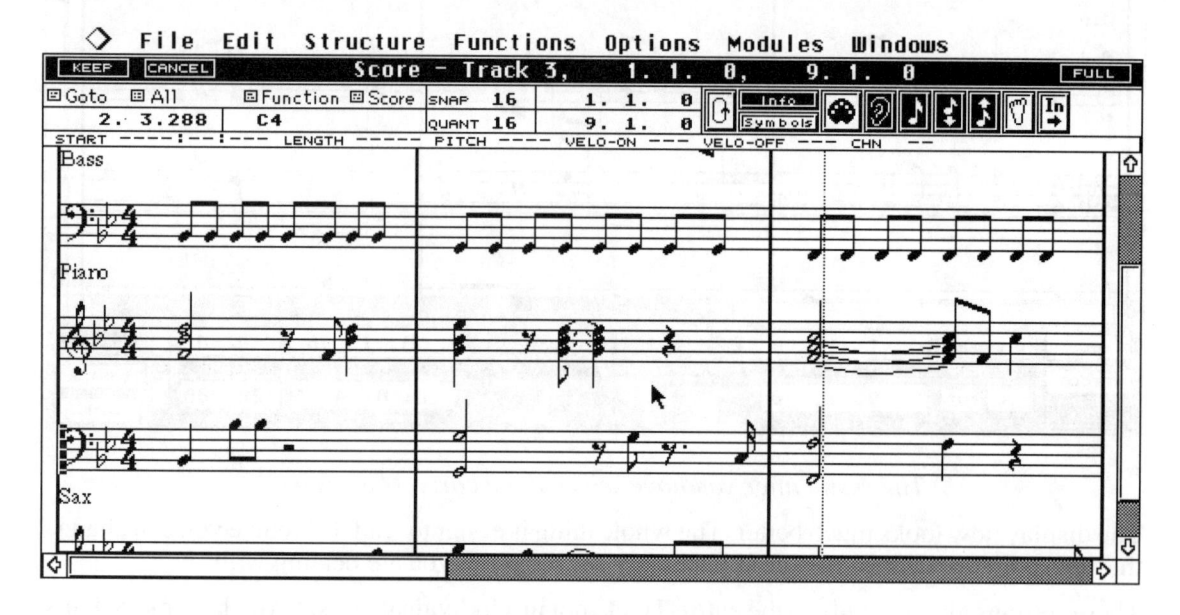

More improvements to the display

Try out all the functions to see how they work.

16.4.4 The display quantization

The Auto Quantize function tries to display notation as accurately as possible. You can also quantize the display of notes and rests manually in the Staff Settings dialog box. This function too applies to the display readability only, not to the actual MIDI notes. Change the quantization factor by clicking and holding the downward arrow under the Notes or Rests entries. Select the desired value or values from the list.

What values are appropriate? There is no standard answer to this question. One thing is certain, do not enter a value coarser than the smallest note in the staff. For instance, if you played sixteenths, don't enter an eighth quantization factor.

Use this quantizing function only if no binary or tertiary note values are in the staff at the same time. This problem can be solved by the Auto Quantize Flag only, which you would need to activate in this case.

16.4.5 Additional guidance

Most of these functions are designed to help you optimize the readability of the notation or simplify the display. You can see that the process towards achieving the ideal-looking notation is something that makes big demands of the program and of you. In many cases, you have to decide what you want the display to look like. Often, there are a number of options that Cubase can't decide for you. If you want the best notation for a specific passage, you must *know* what it should look like. You can work your way up to this ideal, step by step.

Some compromises are necessary, such as the display of grace notes. Although you could use different display quantizations to cope with them, the rest of the notation would not look right. In many cases, you may need to quantize not just the display, but the MIDI notes as well.

Cubase always uses the actual note values in the Track as a basis for the display. If you have played notes slightly later than, and not on, the beat, the notation should not normally reflect this; instead, you would insert a remark such as "laid back".

Minor editing of positions and lengths of the actual MIDI notes can also work miracles. Depending on the note's environment, reducing its length by as little as 1 or 2 ticks, e.g. changing a half note (768 ticks) to 767/766 ticks sometimes does the trick. Cubase might then interpret the relationships between notes differently and give you the desired result.

Even if these type of operations may sound somewhat illogical at first, try them out, whether by using the Editors or the various MIDI quantizing functions. Remember that Cubase allows you to quantize individual sections as well as notes. All in all, you have a wide range of options at your disposal. If you don't remember how to process notes, review the appropriate sections in chapters 10 "The Score Editor" and 15 "Quantizing".

Of course, these operations not only improve the notation display, but they also change your original recording, so always work with copies of the original Tracks.

Tip: create a copy of your song before you begin preparing the notation. Enter an "N" at the end of the copy's name. For example: make a copy of SERENADE.SNG and call it SEREN_N.SNG so you can distinguish between the original and the notation versions.

16.4.6 Polyphony

The operations discussed above should already present you with more or less legible notation. However, we have not yet found an apt solution for keyboard instruments that can play polyphonically or for polyphonic phrasing produced by several instruments within one staff. Take a look at the following diagram.

Extract from a piano Part

Notation and Page Layout

This is a piano Part, already displayed as a split system and assigned the correct clefs and key. The problem is immediately apparent: sustained notes are not displayed correctly, but have a number of ties.

Notes that were sustained with the pedal are annotated as short notes, even though your ears tell you differently. Notes sustained with a pedal must be brought up to the correct length, either individually, or with the aid of the Logical Editor.

The ties are not only musically incorrect, but they are also difficult to read. If you want to get rid of ties as quickly as possible, use the No Overlap Flag in the Staff Settings box.

The effect of the No Overlap Flag

The display is now more legible, but in this case even more incorrect. The only solution is to use Cubase's Polyphonic Voices function.

Go to the Staff Settings box and activate Polyphonic Voices. The Split Point setting is automatically deactivated because it becomes unnecessary. Go back to your notation. Not much has changed, other than there are more rests than are necessary.

16.4.7 The theory behind polyphony

Polyphony is what happens when you have independent voices playing within a staff or split system.

Cubase supports the display of polyphony, up to a maximum of four voices, two each in the upper and lower staves. The program of course can't guess which voices you want where, so you have to tell it. How does Cubase distinguish between different voices? By using different MIDI channels.

As a maximum of four voices is possible, so four different MIDI channels are required. Let's again emphasise the difference between notes' own MIDI channels and their relationship to a Track's MIDI channel.

Cubase distinguishes between the channels of the events it records (which are dictated by the transmit channel of the device sending the events), and the channels you assign to the Tracks in the Arrange window. A Track's MIDI channel always has priority over the actual channels of the events in it, unless it is set to "Any" channel which leaves the events' channels intact as they playback.

For polyphony, Cubase uses the MIDI channels of the actual notes. This means that you can change these around to suit the polyphony and you won't hear any difference, unless the Track channel setting is "Any".

Go back to the Staff Settings box. You must now assign a MIDI channel to each voice for the display. A maximum of four assignments are possible.

Your selection depends on the number of voices you need. Each voice can be assigned to one of the 16 MIDI channels, or to "Off". This controls the number of staves. If you need just two voices of polyphony, set two voices to "Off".

The Essential Corrections

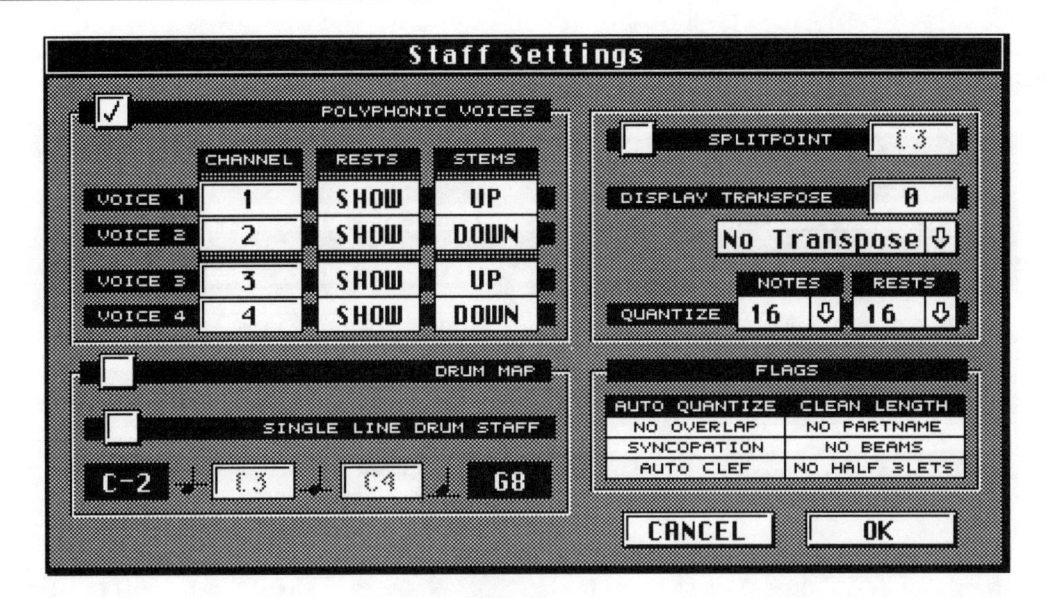

The polyphonic settings

The MIDI channels you use are up to you. Try to select adjoining channels (e.g. 1, 2, 3, 4 or something similar) to simplify operations later on. For the first exercises, it is advisable to use a Track where you recorded on a single MIDI channel as opposed to one that contains several channels (such as might happen if you used a sophisticated mother keyboard). Find out which channel this is. If you're not sure, click any note in the Score Editor: the Info Line displays each clicked note's MIDI channel and other parameters.

Now set Voice 1 in the Staff Settings box to this MIDI channel (channel 1 in our example), and the following voices to the next MIDI channels (2, 3, 4). Select the other display settings (e.g. display quantizing) and return to the Score Editor.

Don't panic!

Don't worry about the wacky notation - we're about to deal with that. As we said earlier, Cubase organizes the display using the MIDI channels as a reference. If we assume that you have recorded on a single MIDI channel, the program can't assign notes yet. The next step is to undertake this note assignment.

You have to decide for each note, which voice you want to assign it to: you do this by selecting its MIDI channel. Click a note that would normally belong to the bottom staff: in its Info Line, change its MIDI channel from 1 to 2, then to 3, and finally to 4. The note moves to the bottom staff and the fourth polyphonic voice. Ensure you don't give a note any MIDI channel that is not assigned to a polyphonic voice.

If you assign a note to a MIDI channel that is not assigned to a polyphonic voice, then the note is removed from the display (though you'll still hear it on playback).

You could now manually assign all the notes individually. However, Cubase has a whole bunch of options that work much more quickly. The Logical Editor is used to start us off. It can be used

303

Notation and Page Layout

to change whole groups of notes to a different MIDI channel. For our example, we want to assign a basic split point. Enter the following settings:

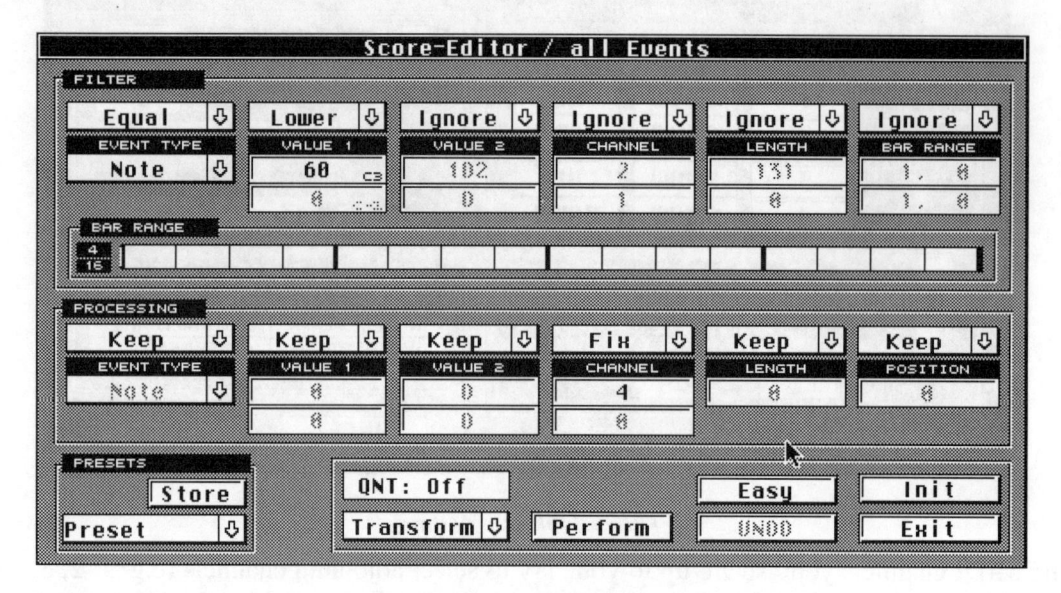

The correct Logical Editor settings

All notes below C3 are assigned to MIDI channel 4, i.e. the fourth voice in the bottom staff. This quickly gives us a coarse assignment of notes to staves according to their pitch. You must of course designate the split point depending on the situation. The result following the above Transform operation is a fairly acceptable split between the two staves.

Note assignments to the staves

Of course, you can only do a rather coarse division in the Logical Editor. Let's start correcting the bottom staff first. Select the notes that you want to be in Voice 3: you can use any of the inputting methods you know already: normal clicking or the rubber band, with simultaneous use of [Shift]. To assign selected notes to the Voice 3, press [Alternate][3].

You could instead use the Logical Editor, depending on the range of the notes' pitches (if the voices' ranges overlap anywhere, don't use the Logical Editor - if they don't, then you're able to give it a clear split point).

The bottom staff's polyphony is nearly finished. Go back to the Staff Settings box for the final settings. "Rests" is used to remove (Hide) rests from the display or allow (Show) them. "Stems" defines the stems' direction (up/down). Select an appropriate setting and check out the results in the Score Editor.

16.4.8 More on assigning notes to voices

Use the same steps for the notes in the upper staff. Click the notes you want to assign and use [Alternate] with [1] and [2] to select Voices 1 and 2.

The Function sub-menu features a dialog box that also does the same job.

The Essential Corrections

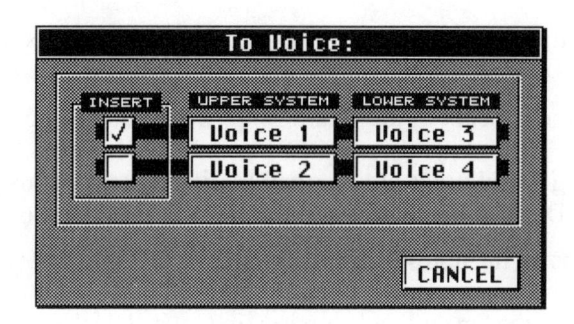

The "To Voice" dialog box

The keystroke method is certainly quicker. However, in some situations, the To Voice dialog box can be simpler:

The To Voice function
Select one or more notes and use the To Voice function to designate which voice, 1/3 or 2/4, you want the selected notes to be put in (click the appropriate Insert box). The box closes and the notes are assigned. Repeat for the other notes. The Staff Setting box must of course have the appropriate settings entered in it. You can use this method to enter a string quartet: it also allows you to playback the four voices on different MIDI channels so that different sounds can be used, by giving the Track the "Any" channel setting. The notes' actual MIDI channels then determine which MIDI devices should be addressed.

Recording four voices
If you want to be able to record your voices in realtime, such as for a string ensemble, record the voices one after the other on the same Track, selecting a different transmit channel each time; set the Track's channel to "Any". To be able to do this, your master synthesizer must be able to send on different channels. You could also record four separate Tracks and then merge them.

As the voice assignments were made as you recorded, you just have to assign the MIDI channels to the voices and carry out the Rest and other parameter settings in the Staff Settings box.

Even after using all these options, you may still encounter minor problems, especially with rests. Don't worry about it as Cubase offers more detailed solutions used during page layout.

16.4.9 Drum notation

Now we'll go back to the example at the beginning of the chapter. The drum staff is still in a sorry state. Select the staff and enter the correct clef. The following diagram depicts the notes of the drum staff without the other Tracks.

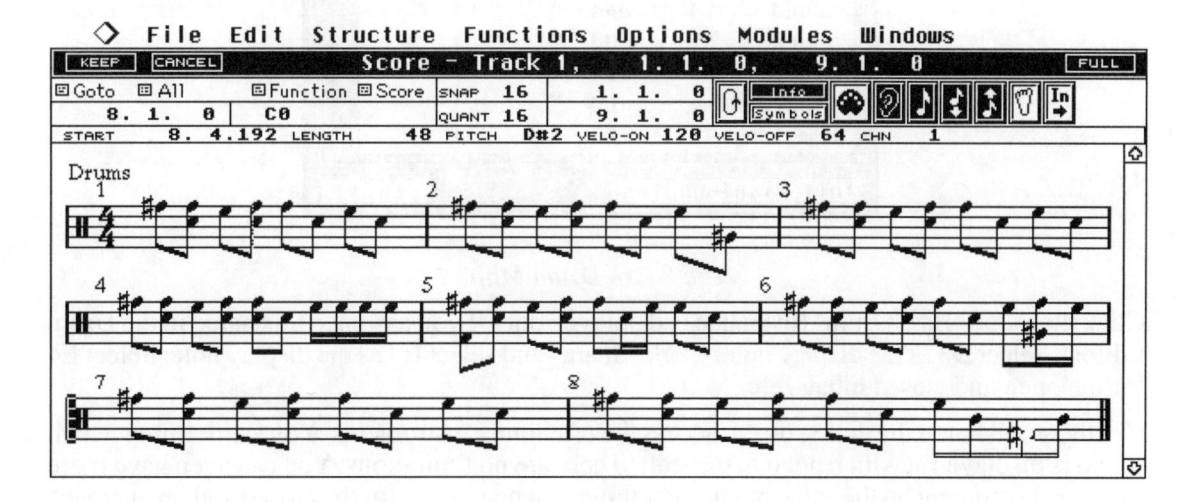

The drum staff

Notation and Page Layout

The clef is correct, but the note display is totally incorrect. Cubase is displaying the recorded MIDI events, not the regular notation using percussion symbols. There is a solution!

Chapter 11 introduced the concept of the Drum Map, where incoming notes are "mapped" to a different outgoing pitch. This is exactly what the Score Editor's Drum Map does to the *display*: The positions of existing MIDI notes are mapped to different positions on the staff. This does not affect the actual MIDI notes themselves, only the way they look on screen or on paper.

The whole thing depends on the notes' original pitches. It is important which way you recorded the drum Parts. You know you have two options, Drum Tracks via the Drum Map, or normal MIDI Tracks. Let's look at the Drum Track version first - we'll deal with the MIDI Track version later. Ensure "Drum Map" is active in the Staff Settings box.

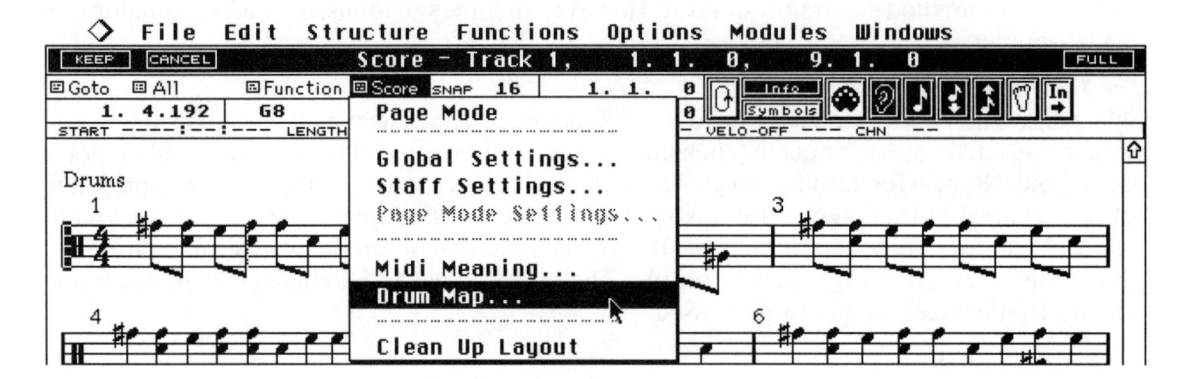

Accessing the Score Drum Map

Choose "Drum Map..." from the Score sub-menu. A dialog box appears containing the instrument names you assigned to the Drum Map in the Drum Editor.

You can now see how important it is to assign names there. The second column ("Display") lists the destination pitch that you want Cubase to display. We'll look at the other columns in a moment. Now enter the correct display pitches. There are all kinds of ways of displaying drum notation, but we'll stick to one of the most common ones.

The Score Drum Map

Click the name "Bass Drum" (the name is displayed only if you assigned this name in the Drum Editor). Select D3 as the display note. Click "Snare" and select B3 as the display note. Select E4 for the open and closed hihats, etc.

Use the scroll bar of the dialog box to access the remaining instruments. You are defining which sound is displayed at which pitch in the staff. There are no limitations. You can even have more than one instrument on the same pitch, something you need to do for the closed and open hihats. Once you have assigned destination pitches for all the instruments, click on Exit.

The Essential Corrections

The initial result (extract)...

The score looks much better, at least so far as the pitches are concerned. The correct symbols are still missing. Go back to the Drum Map. You can assign a display symbol to each sound, using the Head column. The bass drum, snare and toms already have the correct symbols, but the cymbals and the hihat notes are incorrect. Select the desired sound name with a mouse click.

Select the correct symbol in the Head column by clicking it with the left and right mouse buttons. Finish the assignments and go back to the Score Editor. Most of the display criteria have now been fulfilled.

... looks fairly decent

We want to give the drum staff a final coat of polish, so we'll use the polyphonic note display we discussed in the previous section. For this you must assign the hihat and the other notes to different polyphonic voices. You know how this works, i.e. via different MIDI channel assignments. We only have to assign two different pitches, so the Logical Editor is the way to go. First, we'll assign the closed hihat to a different MIDI channel. Find out its pitch (the originally recorded pitch, not the display one). If you are unsure what it is, simply click a closed hihat note, and the Info Line will display its actual pitch. In this case, it is A2. This is what the required settings might look like in the Logical Editor:

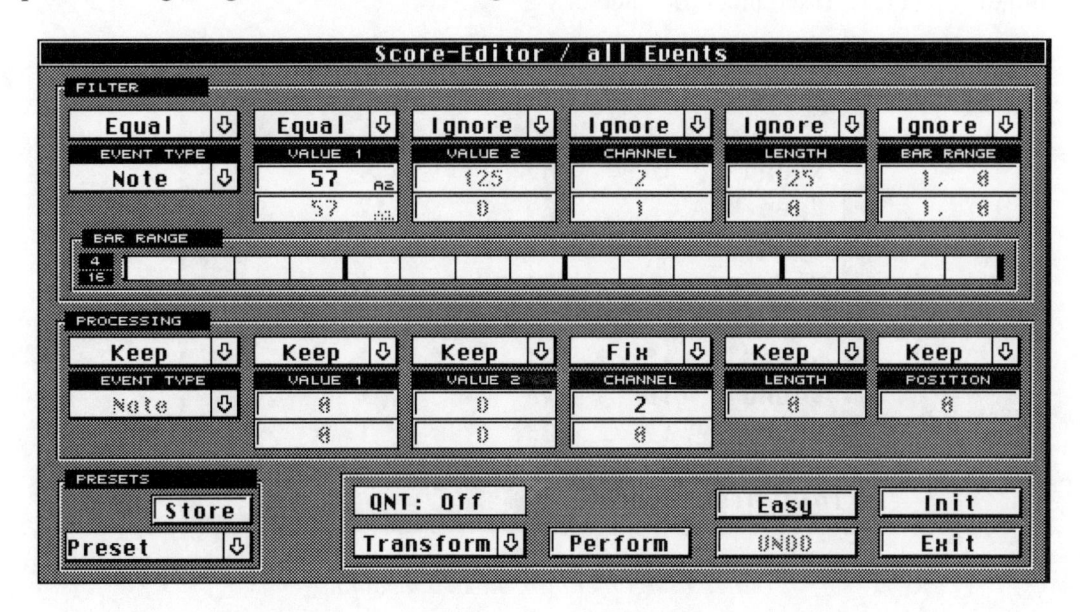

The Logical Editor settings for the correct MIDI channel assignment

307

Notation and Page Layout

All A2 notes are assigned to MIDI Channel 2. The pitch of the open hihat needs to be assigned to the same channel as well. When you've finished, go to the Staff Settings menu.

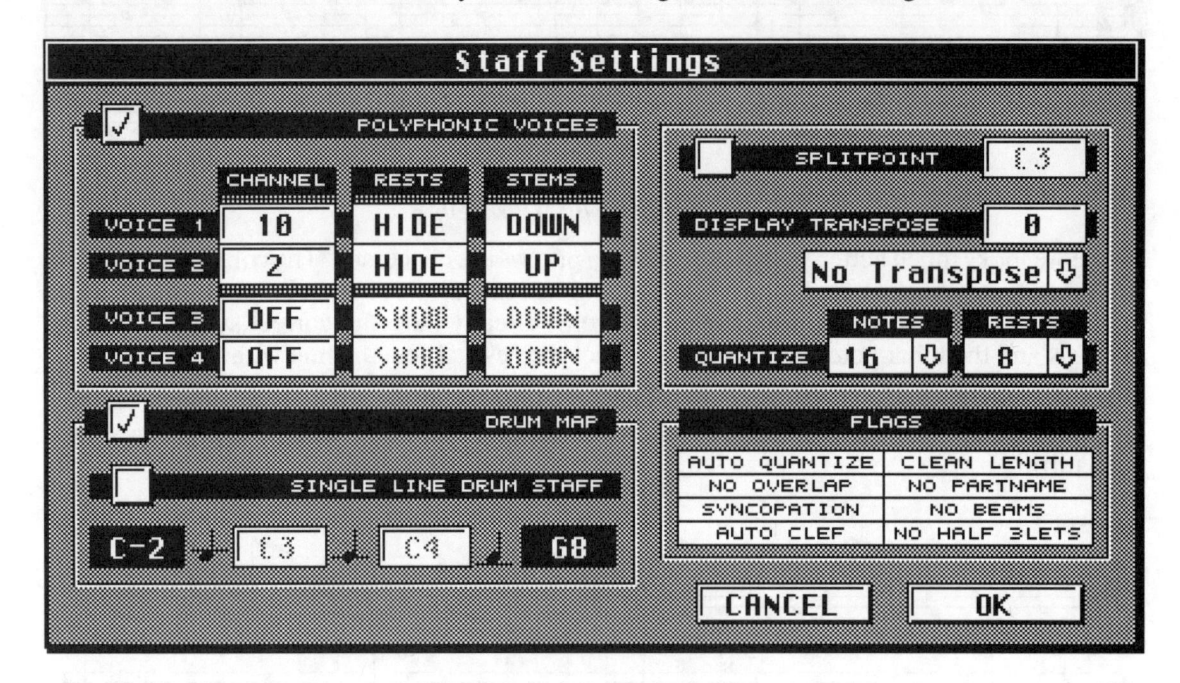

The polyphonic assignments

Activate Polyphonic Voices. Assign the MIDI channel of the open and closed hihat to Voice 2. Keep in mind that this is always the channel of the actual notes, not the current Track channel. The rests can be hidden, the stems should point up.

Assign the MIDI channel of the other notes to Voice 1. If you are not quite sure what it is, go back to the Score Editor and click a bass drum or snare note and the Info Line will give you its MIDI channel. In our example, MIDI Channel 10 is correct. Designate whether or not you want to see the rests, and the stems should point down. Exit the dialog box.

We have entered the polyphonic conditions correctly, but no changes are displayed. You have to go to the Drum Map dialog box. Assign each sound to a polyphonic voice in the Voice column. Assign the open and closed hihat to Voice 2.

Voice assignment for the drum sounds

As soon as you leave the Drum Map, the polyphonic display appears as it should.

The Essential Corrections

The display is now easy to read

16.4.10 Drum notes and MIDI Tracks

At the beginning of this section, I said that a normal MIDI Track can also be assigned drum notation. The operation is almost the same as for the Drum Tracks, with one major difference: the Score Drum Map does not list the sounds' names, but MIDI notes instead.

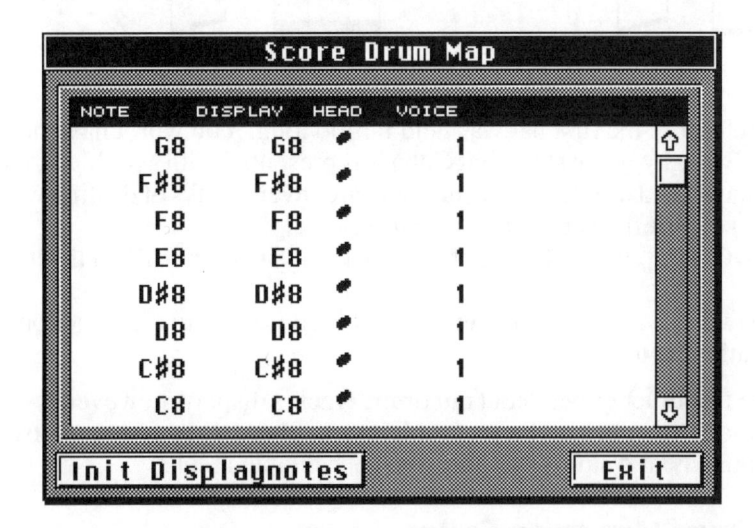

The Score Drum Map for MIDI Tracks

All assignments are done the same way. The difference is that you can't quickly assign the actual pitches to the displayed pitches, but you have to find out what the actual notes pitches are first. For example: what are the actual pitches of the bass drum, snare or hihat? Only then can you assign each of these instruments to a display pitch. Keep in mind that the Score Drum Map is independent of the Drum Editor map. You *must* ensure you activate the Drum Map setting in the Staff Settings box for those MIDI Tracks that contain drum notes, otherwise your display will not be correct.

Generally speaking, it's better to use Drum Tracks for drum notation. If you used a normal MIDI Track to record drum events, or loaded a MIDI file which doesn't contain Track classes, you can easily convert the Track to the Drum Track class: refer to Chapter 11 for all the details.

"Init Display Notes" is used to set the display notes to the Drum Editor map's input values (for Drum Tracks), or the MIDI values (for MIDI Tracks). This means the display values are equal to the input notes set in the Drum Editor for the individual instruments. In other words, the display notes equal the MIDI notes, e.g. C2 = C2.

16.4.11 Facts on drum notes

As with everything in this book: experiment with the settings. For instance, there are no rock-solid guidelines to help you choose the various display quantizing functions - there are just too many variables involved and it all depends on how you recorded the notes, and so on. Study of

Notation and Page Layout

the various relevant sections of this book will at least show you what you have to do to achieve *basically* decent results. Should none of the display quantizations or other options help you achieve the result you're looking for, try to target problem notes by moving them by a few ticks. Cubase then interprets the inter-note relationships differently, and you might get the result you want.

Another phenomenon is of central importance to drum notes. As a rule, drum notes are very short. At times you may be tempted to hold a key down longer than necessary during recording. This doesn't affect what the sound is doing, but it certainly affects Cubase, which doesn't know you are playing drum sounds: it interprets all notes according to their values. Creating longer notes than required may lead to problems with the display. The following diagram illustrates how this might look:

Some drum notes here are unnecessarily long

The second snare beat in the first bar was held far too long. You won't have heard a difference as a snare sample will always be short, but Cubase is presented with a problem: it recognizes that a half note was played and tries to display it. There are several ways of dealing with this problem:
- Play drum notes as briefly as possible during recording.
- Activate the No Overlap Flag. This is not a cure-all, e.g. it will not affect the lengthy hihat note in the first bar.
- Set the drum Tracks' notes to a fixed length via Fixed Length in the Functions menu. Enter a suitable quantization factor.

You are bound to find other gripes about our drum Track's display; however, the section on page layout has solutions to most of these problems. In these first few exercises, we want to concentrate on quickly and simply getting some acceptable results.

16.4.12 The Drum Map as an Editor

The Score Drum Map is not limited to helping with the display. It can also be used to edit notes in the display. Notes can be created and moved. Use the Note from the Toolbox to place a snare beat at any bar position. Once you place the snare note on the staff's middle line, you hear the snare played. This applies to any of the other staff lines. In other words, Cubase uses the Score Drum Map to generate a MIDI note to match the one you position in the score. You can use this method to write drum grooves which are immediately correct notation-wise.

16.4.13 Rhythm notation: the single line drum staff

There is another method used in music to annotate rhythms: the single line drum staff. It can be used for simple rhythms. Record a basic rhythm Part using no more than three instruments. Activate Single Line Drum Staff in the Staff Settings box. This type of staff can represent three instruments, one each above, below, and on the line. You have to tell Cubase which MIDI notes you want, and where in the display. The function does not target specific notes, but note ranges. If you want to convert an existing Part, you still have to know which MIDI notes you recorded. It is another matter entirely if you just want to write a rhythm score without wanting to hear a specific MIDI result. In this case it doesn't matter where you play: simply define three note ranges (we'll look at this in a minute) that are well apart and play something. You can use a Drum Track if you want, but you don't have to.

The range for the note under the staff line always starts with the lowest possible MIDI note, that is C-2. The second field from the left is used to enter that range's *upper* limit. This note is also

The Essential Corrections

the *lower* limit of the note range for the note on the staff line. Next enter the *upper* limit for the center range in the third field from the left, which is also the *lower* limit of the note above the staff line. The third range's upper limit is fixed at G8.

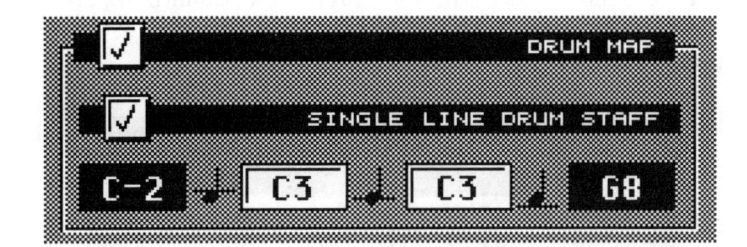

Define the ranges here

Your settings have defined a maximum of three ranges. All notes are now assigned to one of the three staff positions (over, under and on the line). You also have the option of activating the Drum Map. This allows you to use special symbols, such as guitar-type rhythm symbols. Keep in mind that Cubase uses the same Score Drum Map for all the Parts and Tracks; you may have already assigned symbols to drum sounds, so make absolutely sure you use other MIDI notes in the rhythm notation from the ones in the drum notation, otherwise the two staves might interfere with each other. If you proceed carefully, you can quite happily use several different types of notation in a single Arrangement.

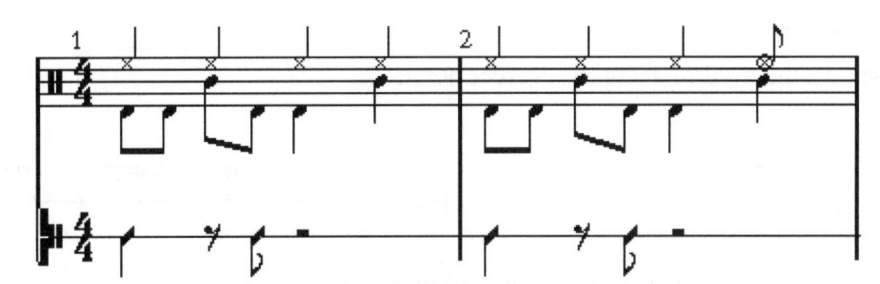

Drum and rhythm notation in a single Arrangement

16.4.14 Rhythm notation for guitarists

If you write guitar notation, you are probably familiar with the rhythmic notation conventions used. These conventions can be automated quickly and simply:
- Define a line in the Drum Editor's Drum Map by naming it "Guitar".
- Set the input and output notes to a value that none of your drum sound are using - say C5.
- "Write" your rhythm in the Drum Editor.

Creating a Drum Map and writing the guitar notes in the Drum Editor

Notation and Page Layout

- Go to the Score Editor and activate Drum Map and Single Line Drum Staff.
- Define only one range for the note on the staff line: choose C-2 in the second box and G8 in the third box.
- You may have to process the display with the polyphonic, quantizing and Flag functions.
- Go to the Score sub-menu's Drum Map settings.
- Find the sound entitled "Guitar" and select the desired note head.

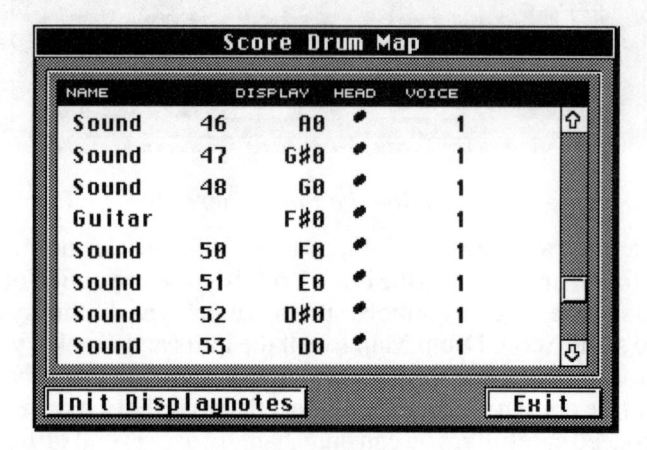

Assign the desired symbol

- Exit the dialog box.

Cubase displays the rhythm using the correct notation.

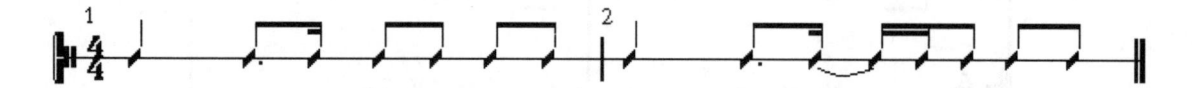

This is what your rhythm might look like

You can "step input" the rhythm in the Drum Editor in the way we just discussed, or record it in realtime. If you do the latter, any notes will be accepted as valid for the defined range - in our example, we use the entire MIDI note range. In other words, it doesn't matter where you play on your keyboard, the notes are always displayed as rhythm on the staff line without any pitches.

This simplifies matters, but there is a catch: you can only play one note at a time, otherwise Cubase places several notes at one position. On the other hand, it is much easier to use only the note for which you entered the correct symbol in the Score Drum Map - C5 in our example. Every time you play a C5, Cubase enters the note at the correct position and adopts the assigned symbol. This explains why you should use a free note for guitar notation. If you use a MIDI drum note such as a hihat, Cubase enters the guitar notes at the right positions but uses the hihat symbol. If you now go to the Score Drum Map and change the symbol assignment for the "guitar Track", you destroy your Drum Track's notation because all Tracks use the same Score Drum Map.

16.5 The layout phase

Cubase distinguishes between two modes for notation: the Edit Mode and Page Mode. We did not need to distinguish between these two modes for the exercises we've been doing so far, since they all had to be done in the Edit Mode. On the other hand, preparing the page layout and detailed notation editing should be done in the Page Mode. Before you go to the Page Mode, follow these basic steps:

In the Arrange window...
- Sort the Tracks in the order they should print.

The Layout Phase

- Select all the required Parts.
- Merge Parts if necessary.
- Make a backup copy.

In the Score Editor...
- Set up the correct staves.
- If necessary, configure the Drum Map.
- Use polyphony or split systems.
- Quantize the display.
- If necessary, edit the lengths and positions of individual events or of larger ranges.
- Attempt to create the best possible display.

Only when you've gone through the above steps does it make sense to carry out more detailed layouting. Go to the Page Mode by choosing it from the Score sub-menu. Choosing it again (it's now called "Page Mode") returns you to Edit Mode.

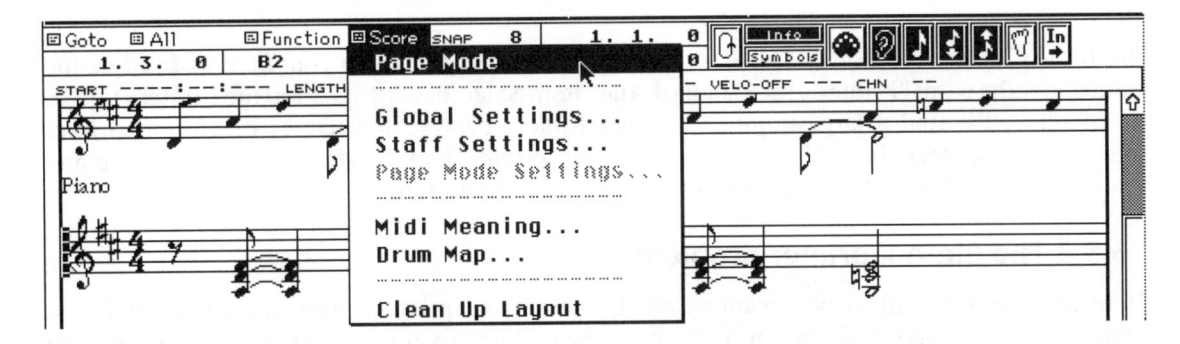

Activating Page Mode

The notation display has changed. Your screen displays what will later be printed.

You can zoom the display in order to get a better picture. Hold the mouse button down on the Zoom field. Select a display factor: 100% is the normal display, 200% enlarges it and 75% or 50% reduce it accordingly.

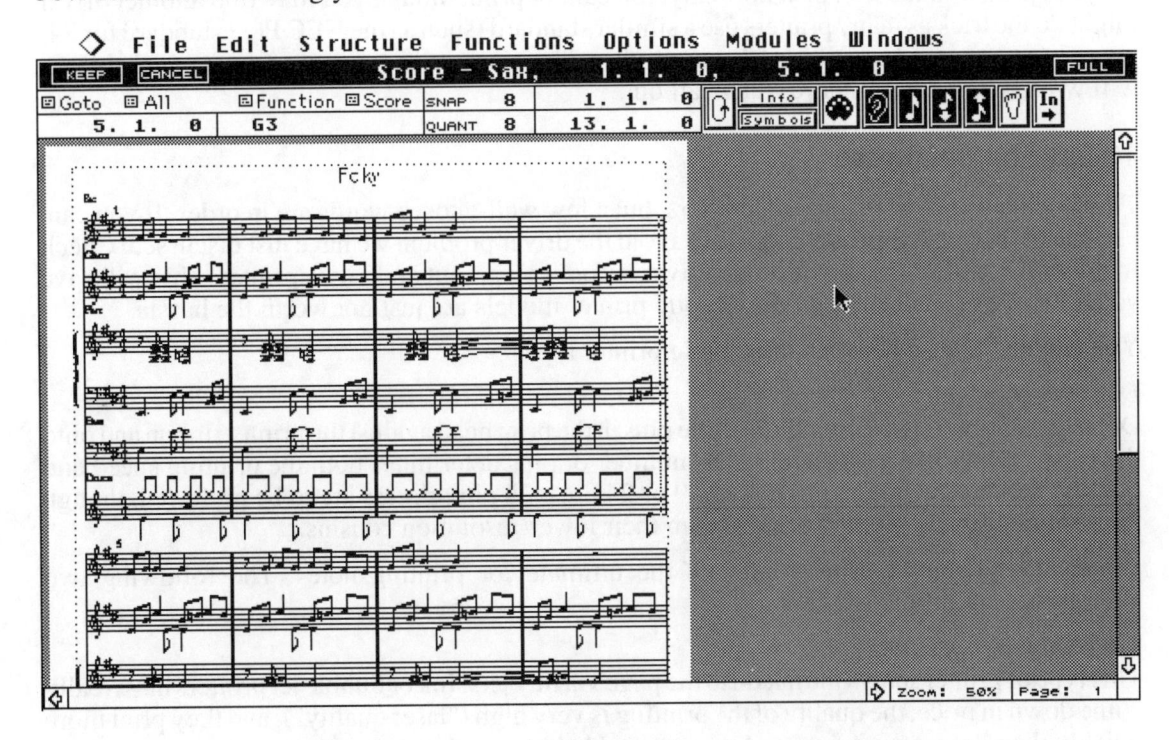

A 50% zoom

313

Cubase attempts to display as much information as possible on your screen. You can hide the Transport Bar and the Info Line to make more space. The best solution is, of course, a larger monitor which shows one or even two pages.

Where your piece is longer than 4 or 8 bars, Cubase carries the notes over to the next "page". Click the page number in the horizontal scroll bar via the right and left mouse buttons to turn the pages. Cubase must structure the page each time, which may take a few moments depending on your computer.

If you want to go to a page that is a greater distance from the one you are on, enter its page number after double-clicking the word "Page".

16.5.1 Choosing the printer

Before we go on, the right printer must be selected. Choose Printer Setup from the File menu. The settings we will enter here ensure that you can print, and that your screen page is the right size.

Insert the Cubase Additionals 1 disk, or make sure its contents are on your hard disk. Click the field under the word "Printer": the standard Atari Item Selector appears. Find the Printers folder, in which you'll find a large number of other folders bearing the names of various printer manufacturers. Open the folder that relates to your printer, look for the exact model name and load the driver. The name is entered in the printer configuration.

16.5.2 The eternal printer problem

Here are a few technical observations on the subject of printers. The printer driver is the communications medium between Atari and Cubase. The driver is responsible for transmitting the graphic information, and insuring that it is correctly interpreted. If you don't have the right driver, you may not be able to print at all, or the printout might be incorrect.

First of all, the driver must be installed in Cubase, something we've just done. If you save the configuration as DEF.SET or DEF.ALL, you will always have the correct driver available. Steinberg provides the most ideally suited drivers for most printer models. If there is no driver for your printer in the file, then normally you cannot print, though you may find another driver might do the trick as many printers use a similar standard (such as the NEC P6/7 standard for 24-pin printers) or are compatible with one another. There's only one way to find out which drivers will work with your printer: try them all out.

16.5.3 The hardware

This is not a technical manual on printers, but a few well-chosen words are in order. If you can, use one of the popular printer models to avoid the driver problem we have just discussed. Check that Steinberg offers the appropriate driver before you go out and buy a printer - this will save you a lot of time and energy. More exotic printer models are just not worth the hassle.

You can distinguish between three basic printer types:

Dot matrix printers
Dot matrix printers work by striking little pins in the print head against the printer ribbon and onto the paper, rather like a typewriter. The number of pins determines both the printing speed and quality: the most common printers use 9 or 24 pins. 24 pin printers are to be preferred, though they are marginally more expensive than their lower-resolution cousins.

However, dot matrix printers are not the ultimate for printing notes. The following two alternatives are infinitely better:

Ink/Bubble Jet printers
This type of printer sprays the ink on to the page via tiny jets. Ink or bubble jet printers have really come down in price; the quality of the printing is very high ("laser quality"), and they print more quickly than dot matrix printers. And, as an added bonus, these printers are silent.

The Layout Phase

Laser printers
Laser printers give the best printing quality and are also the fastest. There are lots to choose from, and they can be basically divided between those that support Postscript and those that don't. Postscript is a page description language developed by a company named Adobe that is used for professional applications and operates without a set resolution. Its advantage is that you always get the best possible results. Cubase doesn't support Postscript, so there's little point in going out and buying a (more expensive) Postscript printer for your musical work. Cubase operates with a maximum resolution of 300 dpi (dots per square inch) so use a less expensive conventional laser printer which will still give you the maximum resolution.

Tip: Atari also produces decent laser printers, and they plug directly into the Atari's DMA port. This guarantees you a relatively fast printout because data transfer via this interface is extremely quick, and also because Atari laser printers do not have RAMs, unlike third-party lasers: they make use of the computer's memory for the page layout. This means that you really need a minimum of 4 MB of RAM when you're operating Cubase with an Atari laser.

Atari laser printers must be switched on whenever they are connected to the computer while you are working, even if you don't intend to print that session; otherwise the printer blocks the DMA bus and can corrupt data you save to disk. You may be tempted to switch off the printer because of its fan noise - don't! If the fan disturbs you while you are working, either prop open the rear panel (for the SLM 804 - this stops the fan), or buy the additional hardware designed to solve this problem. Of course, you could always unplug the printer cable from the DMA port, but if you make a habit of this you may damage the interface. Never unplug the DMA cable while the device is still on.

16.5.4 Page size

Now that you have selected the correct driver, click and hold the arrow beside the Paper Size field in the Printer Configuration box to tell Cubase the size of page you're using. The standard formats are listed here. Printers usually use A4 paper.

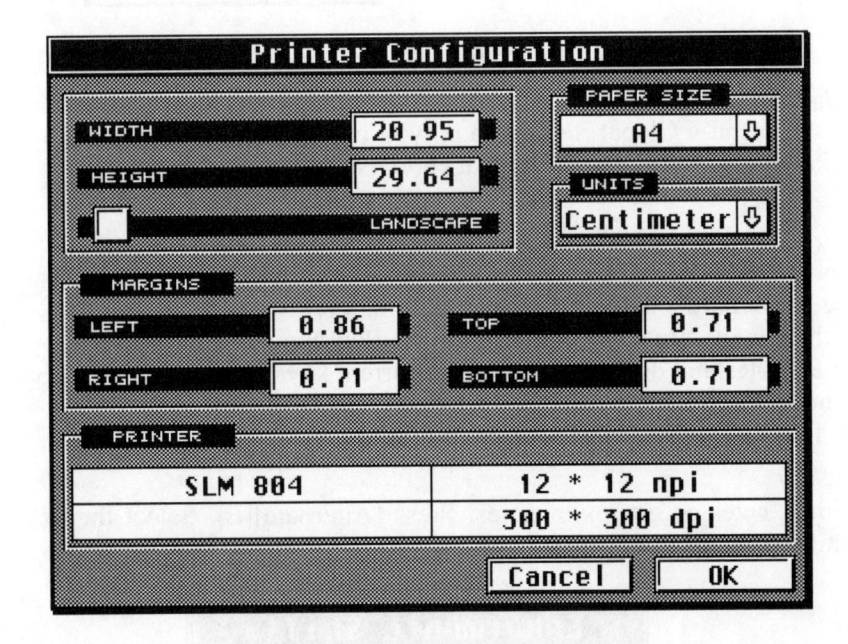

The Printer Configuration box

Your selection automatically designates the printing area (width, height) in the left half of the box. You can change these dimensions if necessary and view them as inches or centimetres. You can also determine if Cubase should print the standard portrait format, or landscape - it depends on your score: if it contains a number of staves, use Portrait. If it's a Part extract, use Landscape because more bars can be displayed across the page.

Notation and Page Layout

The margin values (top, bottom, right and left) are preset. You can change these if you want.

Page Mode shows the paper size (white on a grey background) and shows the margins as dotted lines. Although there are lots of parameters, you generally won't need to change much. Selecting the printer driver, the page format and the Portrait/Landscape orientation is usually enough.

You can play back and edit in Cubase even when you are in Page Mode. The screen does take some time to restructure itself, depending on your computer so you may have to be very patient.

16.5.5 Special functions

Cubase offers a number of special functions for special displays. We are not going to run through each and every one of them because using them is extremely simple. Here is a complete list:

Display transpose
Some instruments (classified as "transposing instruments") are annotated in a different key to the one they are played in. The Display Transpose function in the Staff Settings box lists several of these transposing instruments, or you can manually select the value as you see fit. This function affects the display only.

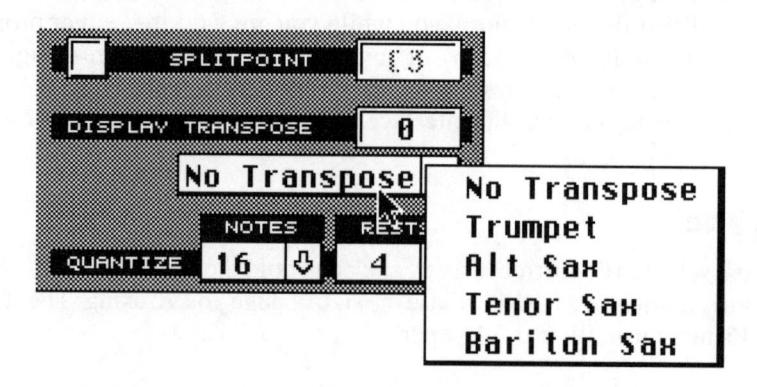

Display Transpose in the Staff Settings box

Displaying chord symbols
In the Score sub-menu's Global Settings box, you can determine how Cubase shows chord symbols. Make your selection - we'll look at chords later.

Handling accidentals
Accidentals are also defined in the Global Settings box. You have four options:
- Regular: a note that is outside the current key receives an accidental. It remains in force until the end of the bar or until a natural is shown.
- Help: this is the same as "Regular", but if a note in the key appears in the next bar, it gets a natural.
- Not in key: all notes that do not belong to the current key are marked with sharps and flats. Naturals are not displayed.
- All: sharps, flats and naturals are shown for all notes.

Enharmonic Shift
Select individual notes or groups of notes. Press [Alternate][E]. Select the desired display enharmonisation from the dialog box.

Enharmonic Shift

16.5.6 Special symbols

Special symbols are all symbols that are not entered in your computer via a MIDI recording. In a strict sense, the rhythm notation falls into this category. However, we have seen how you can enter rhythm by "playing".

The Note Stems
The stem directions are set when you enter the polyphonic settings. However, there are some cases where you must alter the note stems individually. Select the note(s) and choose Flip Stems from the Function sub-menu ([Alternate][X]).

You can also keep beams from being displayed (No Beams in the Staff Settings box), or apply beams to a group of notes. The Subgroups function in the Page Mode Settings box must be checkmarked. If you want to combine several notes under one beam, select the notes and activate Group in the Functions menu. ([Alternate][G]). There is no direct "ungrouping" command to undo this function, so if you want to dissolve the group, select the notes that you still want beamed together and activate Group again.

Designate if you want to display beams horizontally or slanted in the Page Mode Settings box. With horizontal beams, screen refreshing is executed more rapidly and Drum Tracks look more authentic.

The symbol list
Click Symbols in the Functions Bar. A list featuring musical symbols appears at the right border of your screen. With a few exceptions which we'll come to, these symbols are self-explanatory. Use the arrows to scroll the list in order to access other symbols. Symbol positioning is uniform throughout your notation: select the Pencil from the Toolbox. Select the desired symbol and click the position where you want to place the selected symbol. The symbol is inserted. You can move, copy or delete it via the mouse pointer. In this respect, symbols are treated just as you would notes. You can also click a symbol in the list and drag it to the desired position in the score.

The mouse click method is enough for many symbols. However, several symbols require additional manipulation.

Accents, staccato symbols
These articulation symbols are permanently assigned to individual notes. Select the symbol from the list and click the desired note. The symbol remains assigned to the note even if you move the note.

Tempo
The tempo symbol gets its value from the first entry in the Master Track.

Prima, Seconda Volta, Slurs, Crescendi, Diminuendi
There are several operational steps involved when you use these symbols. First select the symbol from the list, click on the position where you want the symbol to start. Hold the mouse button down and drag the pointer to the desired end point. Release the button. You can edit this position later on. A selected symbol has several anchor points with which you can edit it. Drag the anchor points to change the length, height or position of the symbol.

If you are creating text objects, you can change the text.

Key signature/clef
Until now, we've said that the key signature and clef have to be entered in the preparatory phase. This is true, but you can change them at any time. Select the key signature and clef symbols and enter them. The familiar dialog box appears so you can enter the required settings in it. Of course you can enter these changes anywhere within your music.

Text
(See also Lyrics below.) Text is text you can enter anywhere on the page. Simply insert the Text symbol at any position and enter the text in the dialog box that appears. Confirm via OK. Keep in mind that you have no more than 40 characters available per text symbol. If you need more, then use several objects side by side. The size and font can be determined in all dialog boxes that

Notation and Page Layout

relate to text functions. Click and hold the arrow next to the Size number and select the size. Then click and hold the arrow next to the Font box and select the font from the list. "Cubase" and "Chords" are special fonts that cannot be used for normal text. These fonts contain special characters such as the normal Cubase note symbols that you can use anyway.

Lyrics
(See also Text above.) Lyrics consist of normal text, but they are assigned to notes. Select the symbol from the list and click the first note you want to assign lyrics to using the pencil. In the dialog box that appears, enter the text, font and the size. As soon as you press [Return] or click OK, the text is inserted. You can change its vertical position at any time.

Another method enters the lyrics more rapidly: follow the above steps but do not exit the dialog box: instead, use [Tab] to go to the next note. Cubase then opens a new dialog box in which you can enter the desired text. If you don't want to enter lyrics at a note's position, simply press [Tab] again without entering anything.

Special options for text and lyrics
The first syllable or word of the lyrics is entered at the first position you click, so never click the note in the staff, but below it. If you don't, the text is inserted in the staff. If this happens accidentally, select all the text events and reposition them as follows: press and hold [Shift] and double-click the first text entry. All events of the same type, i.e. all text events, are selected and can be moved.
Unfortunately, Cubase does not distinguish between text and lyrics so you may have to de-select text events you don't want to include. Hold [Shift] down when you are doing this so you can select more than one at a time.

If you hold [Alternate] down while changing the font or size, then all currently selected text events in the score are affected. This allows you to quickly process large amounts of text.

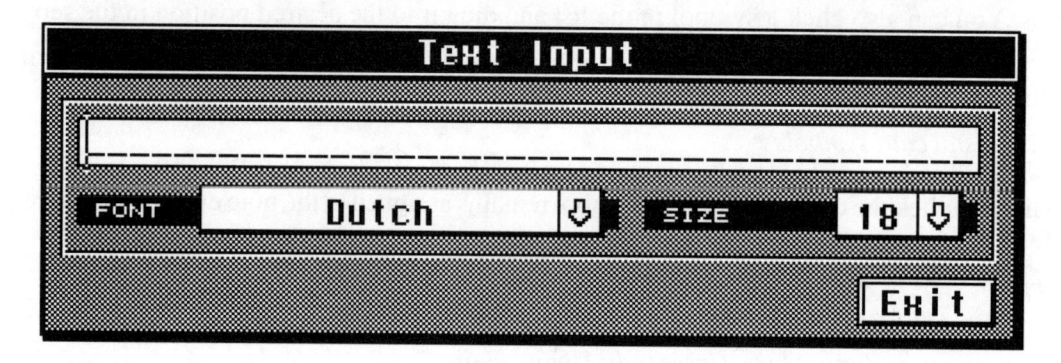

Text input

You can use other fonts than the ones included in Cubase. You just have to install them in the Cubase .DAT folder. Bear in mind that Cubase attempts to access specials fonts in the Fonts folder for the printing. You can print without these special fonts, but they usually produce better results. Cubase asks you during the first printing attempt where the Fonts file is located. Insert the correct disk or find the folder on your hard disk. This operation is optional - you can print without the special fonts.

Guitar fretboard symbols
Positioning guitar fretboard symbols works the same way as with other symbols. You enter the finger positions in the fretboard by double-clicking the desired position with the normal mouse pointer. To be safe, use the highest zoom factor (200%) when you're doing this so you can position them more comfortably.

If you click above the fretboard you can enter crosses for muted strings. Use the text event to enter the fret positions. Create the desired fretboard symbol and show the fret position with a text event. When they are in the correct positions relative to each other, select the two events and choose Group from the Functions menu.

The Layout Phase

The two events now belong to each other. If you select one of the elements and move it, the other is moved right along with it. To separate the two elements, select one of them and again choose Group.

Chord symbols
Cubase offers several simple methods used to insert chord symbols. Let's look at the simplest one first. Select all the chord's notes and choose Make Chords from the Function menu. Cubase analyzes the chord and enters the correct symbol.

This usually works without difficulty. However, you may have to manually enter a chord symbol from time to time by using the chord symbol from the symbol list.

Position it with the pencil or by dragging it to the correct position. Enter all the required settings in the box that then appears. The symbol is inserted as soon as you exit the box. Keep in mind that the Global Settings box defines the basic display.

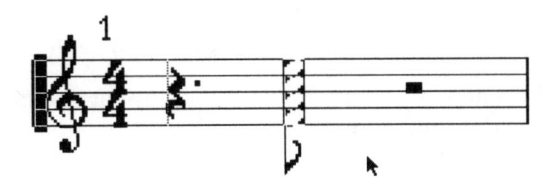

Creating chords: first select the notes...

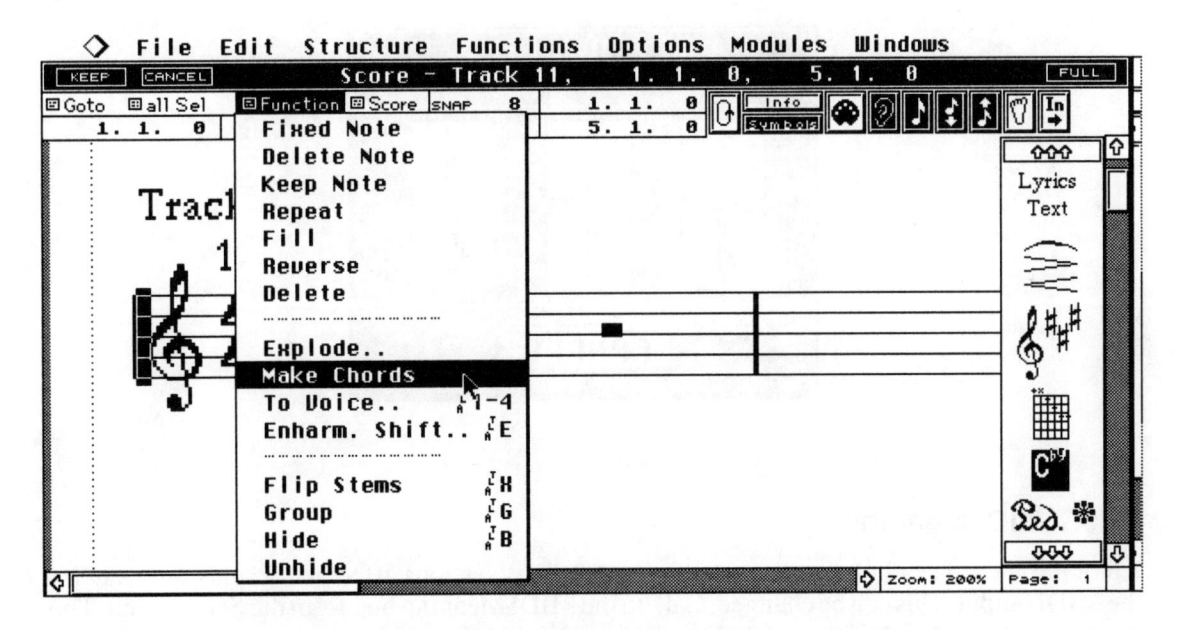

... then choose Make Chords from the Function menu...

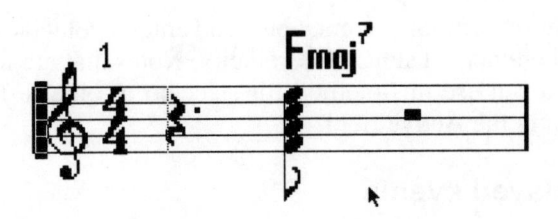

... and the chord symbol is inserted

319

Notation and Page Layout

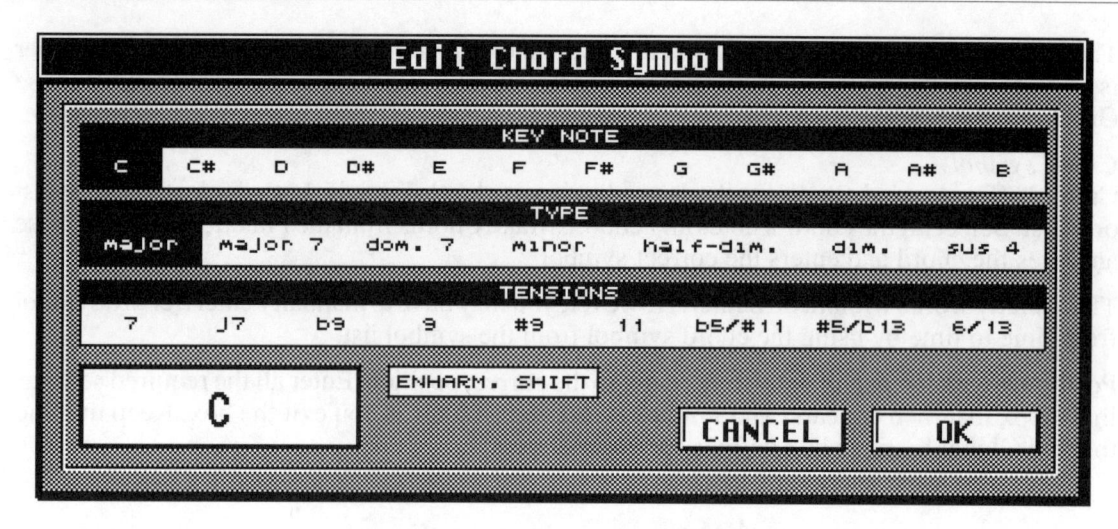

Alternatively, define the chord manually

You can edit chords symbols at any time by double-clicking them and entering the edits in the dialog box that appears (see diagram above).

Bar lines
Double-clicking a bar line calls up another dialog box in which you can designate the type of bar line you want. Selected bar lines apply to all staves at the same bar position.

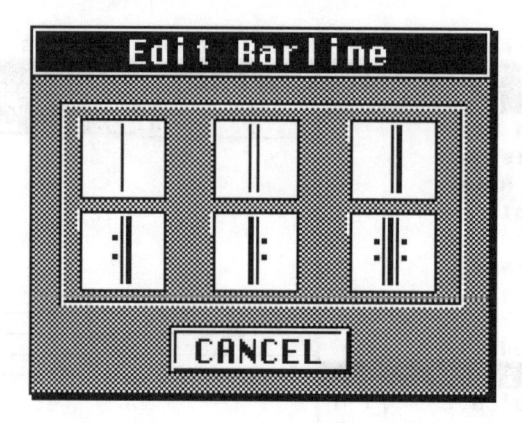

Bar lines

16.5.7 MIDI Meaning

All of the special symbols we discussed in the previous sections affect the display only and not the MIDI output. This can be changed. Call up the MIDI Meaning box from the Score menu. This is where you can decide if the symbols in the box should affect their corresponding MIDI notes' velocity and length values. The settings are entered as percentages.

If you assign an articulation symbol to some notes and enter a velocity factor of 50%, the notes assigned to this symbol are played at half the velocity. Notes that are not assigned to a symbol remain unchanged. You can use this method for staccato or other effects. Ensure that MIDI Meaning is switched on in the Active field.

16.5.8 Hiding displayed events

You can remove notes, bar lines, bars - in short, anything from the display. Select the desired events and choose Hide from the Function sub-menu (Alternate][B]). The symbols are only hidden from the Page Mode display. Call the events back into the display via Unhide. The playback is not affected.

320

The Layout Phase

Try to plan ahead when hiding events. Unhide returns *all* hidden symbols back to the display. For instance, if you have hidden 12 symbols but notice that you made a mistake on the eighth one, you are beyond the point of no return. You have to unhide all the symbols and start over again. If you made the mistake after the last hide operation, activate the Undo function.

The hide function can be used for special purposes such as creating weird scales by hiding bar lines and time signatures or correcting the score by manually removing unnecessary rests from the display.

16.5.9 The song title

The song title is a special text event. The title is displayed at the top of the first page as soon as you activate the Page Mode. The current Arrangement's name is used as a default. A double-click opens a dialog box in which you can enter a new name and other information.

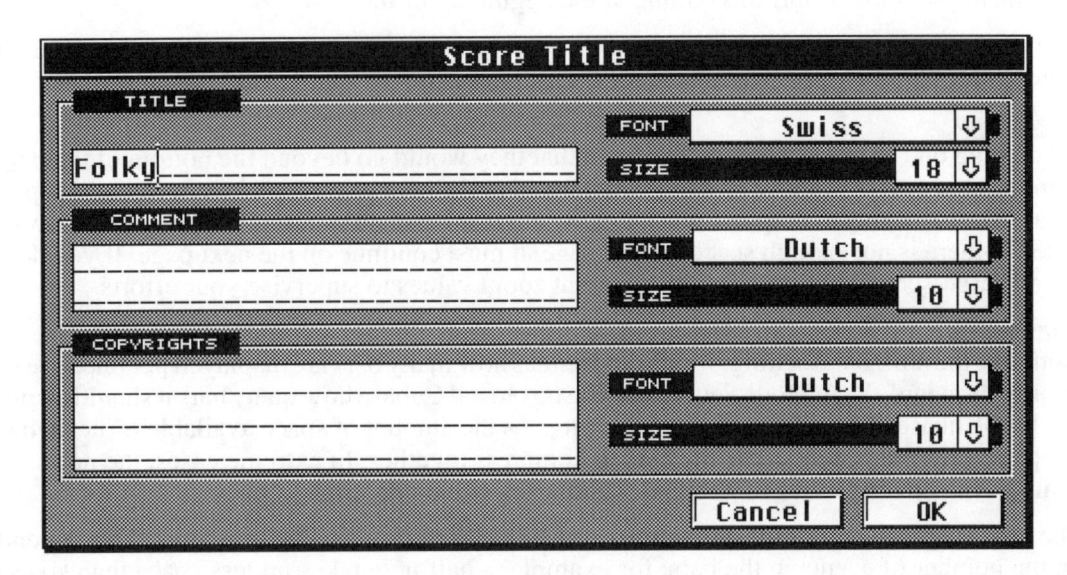

Song title settings

16.5.10 Layout

So far we've worked on the notes and their musical environment i.e. the special symbols. Now that we have the basics out of the way, let's look at layout operations, in other words, how individual bars are positioned on the pages.

Page Mode has lots of ways of laying out a page. You can move complete staves or individual notes without influencing playback. Make sure that you follow the next steps in the order they are written, otherwise your printed material will look wrong:

Let's look at the basic rules first:
- Staves can never go beyond the edge of the page, whether defined by the paper size or the margin settings.
- Cubase stretches the bars from the left to the right margins, leaving no gaps.
- A staff always contains whole bars - a bar is never split between two staves.
- All Tracks and Parts selected in the Arrange window are laid out one below the other. For example, if you recorded 8 Tracks, the first few bars of the 8-staff score are displayed one below the other. Cubase attempts to display the score's next few bars lower down on the same page. If there is not enough room, it uses the next page to print them - in this case, each page will have a fairly big chunk of unused space below each score. In most cases, these can be removed.

Moving staves
Check that the spacing between individual staves is as you want it. To change it, select the Layout tool from the Toolbox.

Notation and Page Layout

The Layout tool

Click a space in front of the staff and drag it to the desired position. The relative spacing between it and its neighbours is maintained, i.e. they are moved too. You can prevent this by pressing [Control] at the same time so that the staff being dragged is moved on its own.

As it is probable that you want to change the inter-staff spacing for the entire score, Cubase can do this as well. If you press [Control][Alternate], all of the staves are moved. For instance, if you move the first bar in the second staff and hold this key combination, every second staff of the score is moved with it. This applies only to the staves that *follow* the staff being dragged. As a rule, then, you should start this editing at the beginning of the score.

Keep in mind that vertical movements of this sort can be used not only to exploit the available page space, but also to provide space for lyrics, chords or fretboard symbols.

Page break

If you drag one or more staves so far down that they would go beyond the bottom of the page, then these and all the following staves are moved to the next page. This is referred to as a page break. The reasoning is simple: Cubase always attempts to display a song's staves one below the other. If there is not enough space on one page, it must continue on the next page. If you don't have a large-screen monitor, use the different zoom values to supervise your efforts.

Bars per line

Optimize the horizontal setting, which determines how many bars are displayed per line. Use the Score sub-menu's Page Mode Settings dialog box to tell Cubase how many bars it should display per line. Cubase always adheres to this setting. As the amount of space available is dictated by the page width, this may cause the bars to compress together. In extreme cases, the notes and symbols may overlap - if this happens, choose fewer bars per line.

The next step is to determine the number of bars per line on a line by line basis. This depends on the number of events in the bars; for example, a half note takes up less space than sixteen 32nds. Use the Scissors tool to move bars onto the next line by clicking the tool on the last bar line that you want to display in the current line: all the bars after this point are moved onto the next line. All the following bars adjust accordingly.

Changing bar widths

In some cases, it may be enough to change the width of individual bars. All Cubase bars are preset so that they have equal widths regardless of the number of events they contain. To change the bar widths for individual bars, select the Layout tool from the Toolbox, click on the desired bar line and drag it to the left or right. In this case, only the widths of the bar before and the bar after the bar line that you just moved will change. You can also move the bar lines all the way to the left or right. In this case, the width of the entire line changes. You can decide if:
- all bars in the line are compressed, or
- just the bar next to the bar you're moving (hold [Control] down during the operation).

There are a number of applications for this operation. For instance, Cubase often stretches the final bar of a piece across the entire page. In this case, simply compress the bar.

16.5.11 Creating upbeats

Record the first bar of your arrangement as an upbeat, then ensure that the bar numbers are correct by choosing Synchronization from the Options menu. A dialog box appears containing the Bar Display field: enter "-1" and confirm via OK. Cubase displays what was bar 2 as bar 1.

The beginning of your upbeat probably contains several unnecessary rests. Select these throughout the score and choose Hide from the Function sub-menu ([Alternate][B]). Then move the left bar line with the Layout tool so that the bar width is corrected.

The Layout Phase

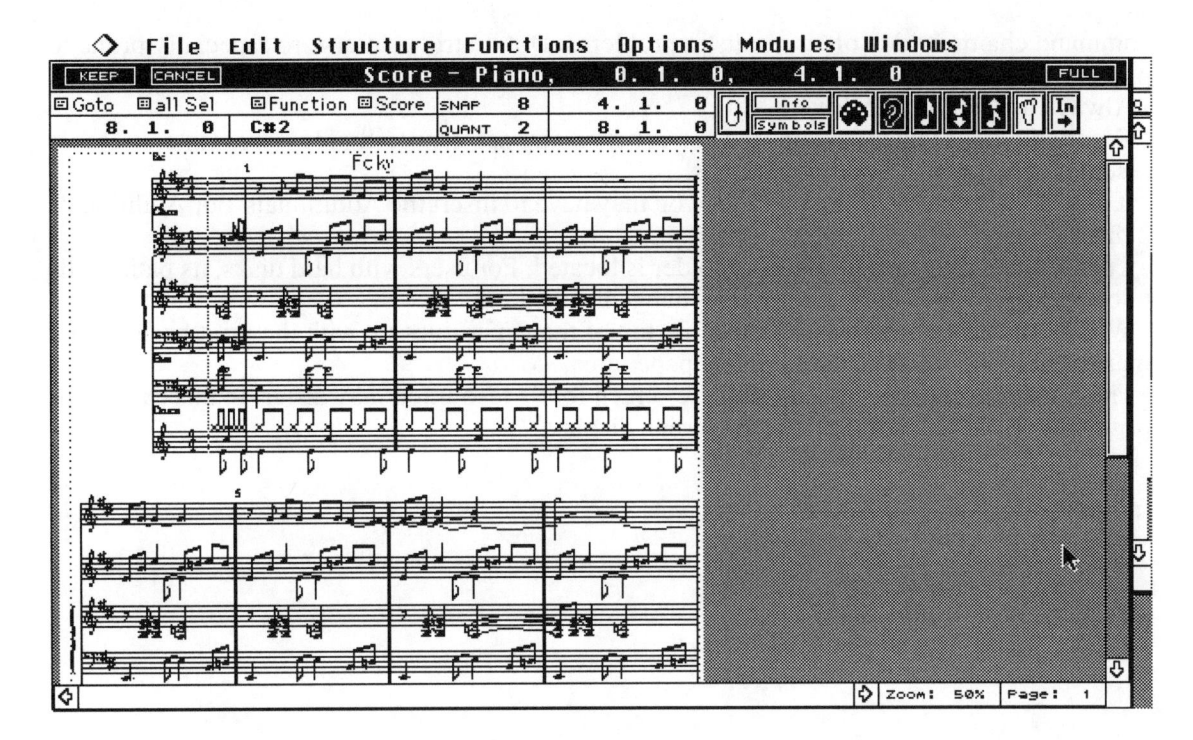

An upbeat in the score

16.5.12 Numbering the staves

You will find the "Bar Numbers every X bar" entry in the Global Settings box. This is where you enter the bar number intervals. "Off" means that Cubase does not show any bar numbers, "1" enters a number of each bar, and "2" in every other bar.

16.5.13 The final polish

There are a few very special Flags in the Page Mode Settings that ought to be mentioned.
- Equal Spacing ensures that two 16ths take up the same amount of space as an 8th. This is usually not desirable as the display looks unusual.
- Real Book ensures that the clefs appear only at the beginning of each page instead of in each line. This does not apply to clef changes within the song.
- No Part Name in the Staff Settings dialog box hides the name at the beginning of the selected staff from the display.

16.5.14 Printing

Now that we've taken care of all of the finer details, we can start printing. Ensure that the printer is correctly connected and that it's switched on. Choose Print from the File menu ([Alternate][D]). You can determine how many pages you want to print. If you just want to print certain pages, de-activate All Pages and select the desired number of pages.

Click OK and printing starts. If you want the printing to be as fast as possible, i.e. for checking, select the Fast Mode. The printing speed is increased but the quality is poorer because the resolution is halved. You do not need this option for a laser printer.

You can abort the printing at any time by pressing [Esc]. The printer finishes the current line; laser printers finish the current page.

16.5.15 Troubleshooting

Printer control is one of the few miracles of our time. Unfortunately, there are few standardized

Notation and Page Layout

command chains, which often results in problems. Dot matrix printers are especially prone to problems. Here are a few standard guidelines:
- Always use the correct driver.
- Ensure the Font folder contains the correct character set, especially for laser printers. This is essential when you use additional fonts.
- If you are working with floppy disks, you may have to insert the Additionals 1 or Additionals 2 disks.
- Cubase remembers where the Font folder is located. For users with hard disks, its path needs to be registered once only, unless you change its position.
- With dot matrix printers, ensure that the top of the paper lines up with the print head so that maximum use is made of the available paper area.
- The printer's resolution and the Cubase screen font's resolution may differ. In this case, your print out will differ slightly from the screen display.

17 Synchronization

You are already familiar with setting the basic tempo and time signature for a piece. You can change both of these in the right half of the Transport Bar. This is fine as long as you don't need tempo and time signature changes within the Song.

Things are different though, if you want to build changes (e.g. ritardandi) into an Arrangement or Song, or if you need to synchronise Cubase to external devices, such as a tape deck or other MIDI device. Cubase offers an large number of options for just such eventualities.

17.1 The Master Track

Picture the Master Track as an additional invisible Track. Its function is to control tempo and time signature changes within an Arrangement. Open the Master Track dialog box in the Edit menu ([Control][M]). Alternatively you can double-click the Master box to the right of the Transport Bar.

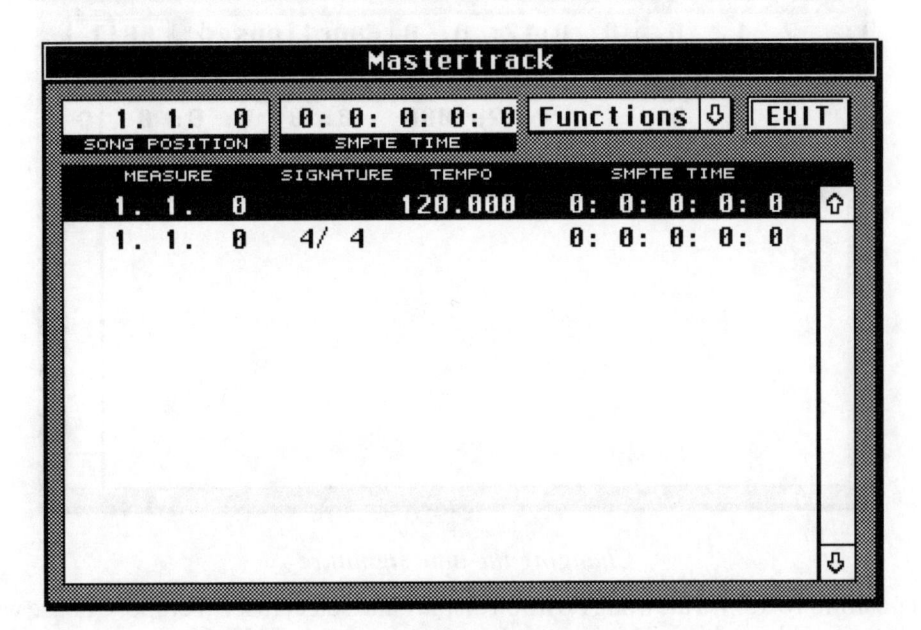

The Master Track

The fields are largely self-explanatory. The Song Position at which you want to make changes is displayed in the top left corner of the box. Don't confuse this position with the current song

Synchronization

position in the Transport Bar. We'll look at the SMPTE Time later, as it is related to the Song Position. The Functions menu allows you to select various commands. More on this in a moment.

Exit is used to leave the Master Track box.

The main field (virtually empty at the moment) is where you will enter your tempo and time signature changes. The Master Track can never be completely empty. Bar position 1.1.0 always contains a time signature and a start tempo.

These settings are not necessarily related to the ones in the two fields in the Transport Bar. If you enter changes there, the values in the Master Track will not be changed at the same time. This is only possible in reverse. If you enter changes in the Master Track, then these changes will be reflected in the two displays.

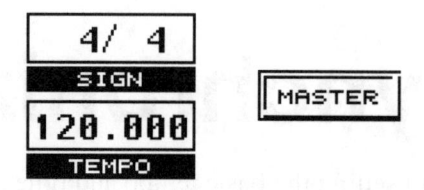

Value changes in the Transport Bar do not influence the Master Track

Let's try an experiment. Call up the Master Track dialog box if you haven't done so already. In the following steps, you must first specify the position in the Master Track where you want to insert changes. Go to position 7.1.0 in the Master Track's Song Position box by clicking with the mouse.

Click the down arrow next to the Functions box and select Insert Signatures from the list. Cubase enters a time signature change at position 7.1.0. This always defaults to 4/4, but this can of course be changed. Click the numerator or the denominator, depending upon which value in the time signature you want to change. 3/4 will be fine for the purpose of our experiment.

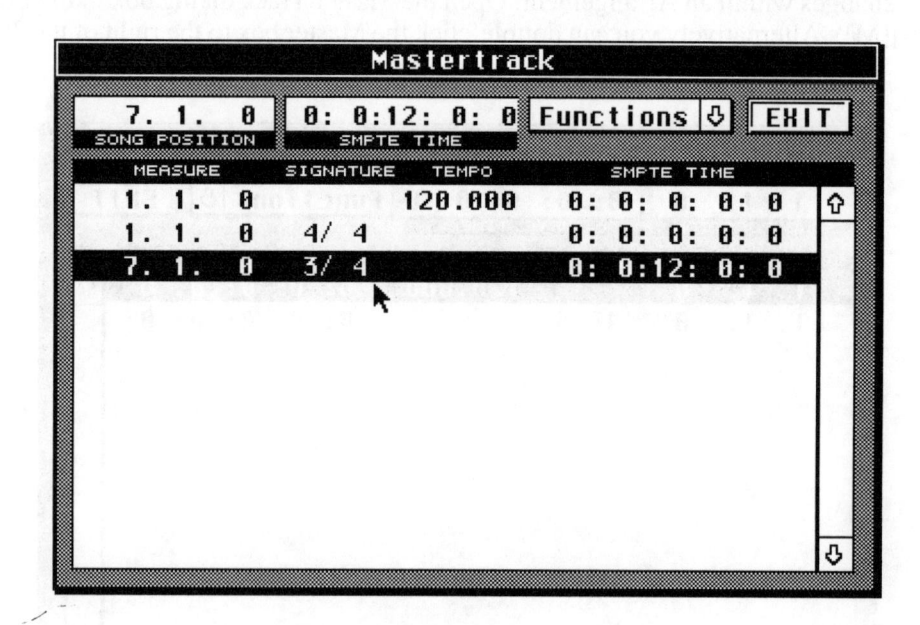

Changing the time signature

Go to bar position 10.1.0 via the Song Position display and select Insert Tempo. Cubase will enter a tempo change at this position. This always defaults to a tempo of 120. You can change this value to suit your needs using the mouse. Set it to 205.

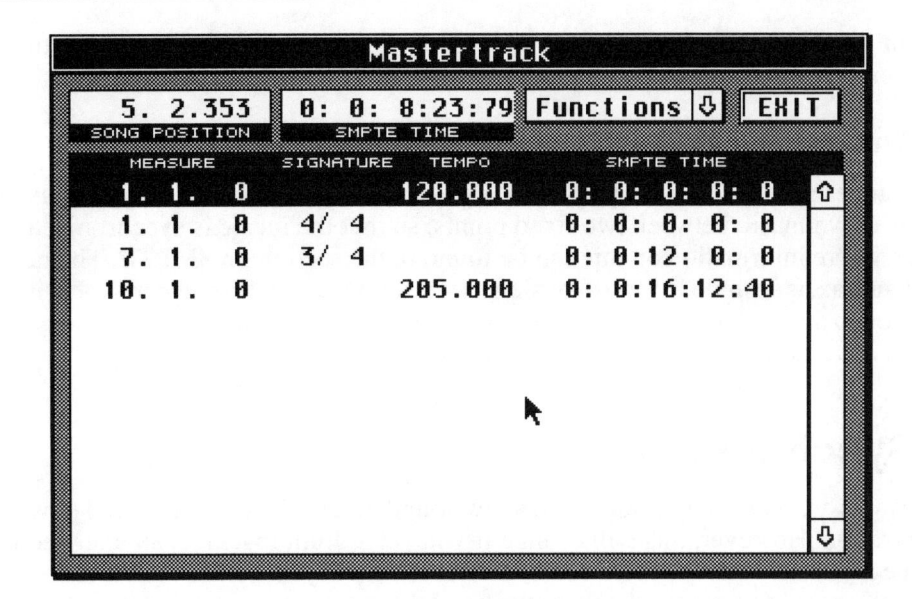

The Master Track

```
              Mastertrack
    5. 2.353   0: 0: 8:23:79  Functions ⇩  EXIT
  SONG POSITION    SMPTE TIME
     MEASURE    SIGNATURE  TEMPO       SMPTE TIME
      1. 1.  0              120.000  0: 0: 0: 0: 0
      1. 1.  0    4/ 4               0: 0: 0: 0: 0
      7. 1.  0    3/ 4               0: 0:12: 0: 0
     10. 1.  0              205.000  0: 0:16:12:40
```

The result

You can change time signatures and tempos already entered in the Master Track at any time. Only the bar positions remain constant. If you want to change one of these positions, you have to enter the change again at the desired position and delete the original entry.

Deleting entries is simple. Select all entries you want to delete by clicking them (you can select several entries by pressing and holding [Shift]). Select Delete Selection ([Delete]) from the Master Track's Functions menu, and all the selected entries are deleted.

Now that we have entered some settings in the Master Track, let's see how they work. Go back to the Arrange window and activate the Master Track by clicking Master in the Transport Bar ([M]). This step is absolutely essential because if you don't activate the Master Track, its settings are not used. Start playback and watch the Transport Bar's bar and tempo boxes. Cubase will make all changes entered in the Master Track at the appropriate points.

17.1.1 Additional information

Time signature changes are automatically entered in your scores, so you don't have to do this manually. The Master Track's Functions menu offers some other useful functions.

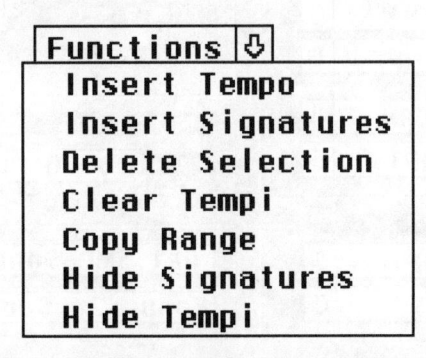

```
Functions ⇩
  Insert Tempo
  Insert Signatures
  Delete Selection
  Clear Tempi
  Copy Range
  Hide Signatures
  Hide Tempi
```

The Functions menu

- Clear Tempi removes all tempo entries except the first one.
- Hide signatures removes time signature changes from the display. This serves to make the display more legible, with the changes being made just the same.
- Hide Tempi does the same for tempo changes. You can only have one of these selected at any one time.
- Copy Range copies all entries between the two locators in the Master Track to the current bar

Synchronization

position in the Arrange window, not to the Master Track. You can use this function to copy complex tempo changes quickly without having to insert them at another position.

17.1.2 The graphic Master Track

Tempo changes are especially important in film scores. Often you find that you have to speed up or slow down music between two fixed points, so that the music is synchronized to picture sequences. More information on this can be found in the section on SMPTE. The new Cubase module, Cuetrax, is designed to assist musicians who compose and arrange in sync with pictures. It allows you to display the Master Track graphically. The module also has some very intelligent options for the automation of tempo computations and changes.

17.2 Synchronization

As long as you are only using Cubase and a few sound modules, you won't need to worry about synchronization. However, this will change if you get a drum machine, another sequencer, or even a tape machine. In any of these cases, Cubase must be synchronized to the external device. Both devices must be started at the same time and the tempo must match precisely at all times. This sounds fairly simple but things can get rather complex.

You might think simultaneously starting two devices at identical tempos would guarantee that they would stay together. This is, unfortunately, not the case. First of all, it is virtually impossible to start the two devices at exactly the same time, and secondly, the machines wouldn't run at exactly the same speed even if the tempos entered are identical. Minimal variations, however tiny, will result in differences in the running time which will build up as the Song goes along.

Different methods have been developed over the years to make synchronization possible. These have often been incompatible and sometimes rather simplistic. However, let's not concern ourselves with these problems. We are only interested in those methods which are available in Cubase. We'll work through these using some practical exercises. All synchronization settings are entered in a dialog box. Select Synchronization from the Options menu.

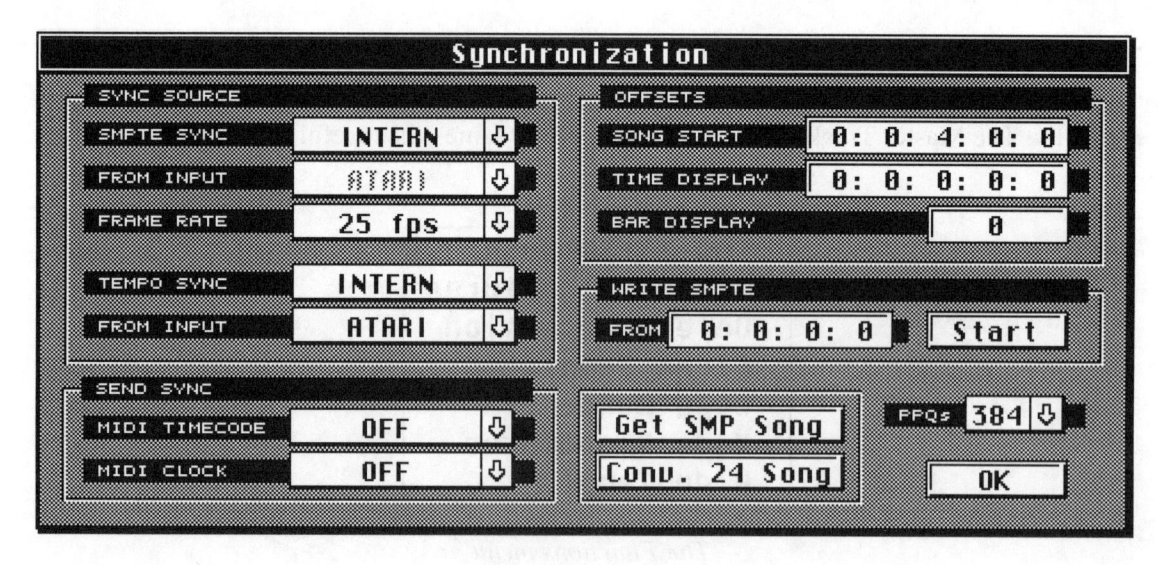

The Sync dialog box

The box is divided into three basic areas. The right half is used primarily for SMPTE and various conversions. The left half is divided into two sections. Send Sync controls the various synchronization signals which can be output. Sync Source defines (among other things) whether Cubase is operating as the sender (master) or the receiver (slave). We'll look at these terms in detail later on in the chapter.

328

17.3 Cubase and simple MIDI synchronization

This subject area is of prime importance when running Cubase with drum machines or other sequencers. At the beginning of the MIDI era, several MIDI commands were specified, of which the two most important are Start and Stop. These simple transport functions were derived from tape recorders. In addition to these, MIDI Clock was defined with a resolution of 96ths steps to control tempo. These commands, together with several others, are jointly referred to as System Real Time messages. In other words, they are transmitted in realtime, in a single MIDI byte. You can find the correct format in the appendix.

In the synchronization process, one device is designated as the master which controls the tempo and the transport commands of one or more slaves. As a rule, the best solution is to use Cubase as a master for pure MIDI synchronization operations, as the program contains wide-ranging control options.

What happens during a simple MIDI synchronization? First of all, the master sends a Start command to the slave. The slave registers this information and waits for the first MIDI Clock message. These MIDI Clocks are sent by the master at regular 96th note intervals, as set by the MIDI Standard. Every time the slave registers a MIDI Clock command, it moves on a 96th interval. The tempo that the master sends dictates how fast these 96th ticks are sent. The whole operation is terminated by the Stop command which is sent as soon as you press the stop button on the master.

If you own a device which can only be synchronized to the MIDI Clock, select Synchronization from the Options menu. Click the arrow next to the MIDI Clock box and select the output through which the MIDI Clock should be sent while holding the mouse button down. This would normally be the Atari output. If you are using additional hardware such as MIDEX, you will have several outputs to choose from. Midex, M*ROS and how to work with several outputs are all covered in Chapter 19 in greater detail.

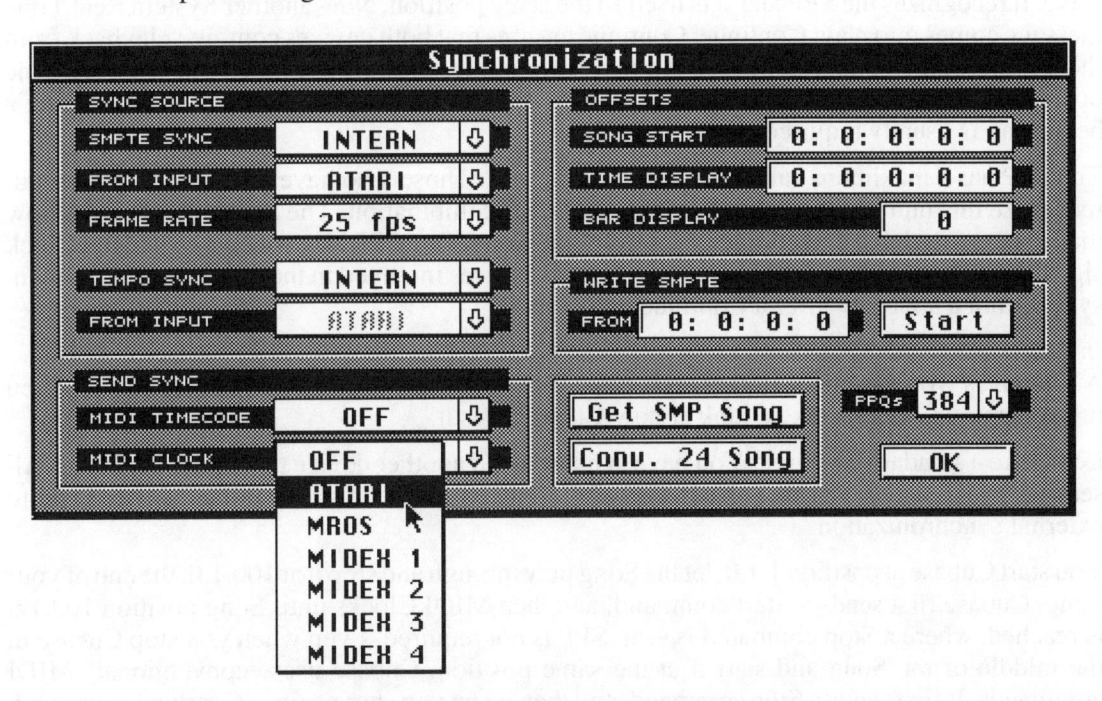

Simple synchronization with MIDI Clock

This is all you need to do within Cubase to set up the synchronization. The only thing left is to make sure that your slave i.e. drum machine or similar device, is in the correct operating mode. Most devices give you the option to set the sync to "external". In this context, external means that the device does not generate the tempo itself, but receives it from an external source, in this case Cubase. It will also follow tempo changes entered in the Master Track.

Synchronization

We have already used the procedure described above in a previous chapter when we were recording across auto-rhythms from a domestic-type keyboard. This method can be used for all sync applications in which MIDI devices are required to run in sync with Cubase. This includes not only drum machines, personal keyboards and sequencers, but also more unusual applications such as the wave sequences on a Korg Wavestation or the echo repeats on an effects processor that can be controlled via MIDI Clock.

17.4 Song Position Pointers

As long as you are dealing with simple overdubs, everything should work fine. You will run into problems however when you want to start synchronized playback from any other position than the beginning of the Song. MIDI Clock contains no positional information, it only serves to transmit tempo. If you fast forward Cubase to a certain Song position and run it from there, although a connected drum machine would also start playing, and at the right tempo, the two devices would not be at the same point in the Song. You could of course avoid this problem by always starting Cubase at position 1.1.0. MIDI's developers realized that in practice this could become really tedious. As a result, there is a solution.

The theory:
The results of their ponderings is called Song Position Pointers, or SPP's for short. In addition to MIDI Clock and the Start/Stop commands, another message is sent giving the current position. This positional information is not transmitted constantly, but only under certain circumstances. It is not classified as a System Real Time message. The MIDI standard groups this message together with a few others under the heading of System Common messages.
According to the MIDI standard, all devices involved in the sync process should only transmit or recognize SPP's when stopped. Any subsequent position change is then sent as an SPP to the slave. It recognizes the SPP and sets itself to the same position. Now another System Real Time message comes into play: Continue. Continue ensures that both devices continue playback from the position they were stopped at. Although Continue is sent in simpler MIDI Clock sync operations as well, some MIDI devices will not continue in sync. A start from the Song's beginning is usually required.

The SPP has a maximum value range of 16,384 steps. Those who have studied computers will recognize this number as the result of an LSB/MSB combination. The SPP value denotes how many sixteenths have passed since the start of the Song. One SPP step is equal to 6 MIDI Clock signals. The sixteenths resolution ensures that all devices involved in the synchronization are in sync within a sixteenth after a Continue command.

In practice:
As soon as you set the MIDI Clock box, Cubase sends a SPP. SPP operation is often misunderstood, so let's take a look at how Cubase uses it.

Let's take a standard case first. You have synchronized another device to Cubase via MIDI. All settings in the Sync menu are correct, the cable connections are in place, and the device is set to external synchronization.

You start Cubase at position 1.1.0, let the Song play through and stop it at 100.1.0, the end of your Song. Cubase first sends a Start command, and then MIDI Clocks until Song position 100.1.0 is reached, where a Stop command is sent. SPP is not required. Even when you stop Cubase in the middle of the Song and start it at the same position, Cubase uses "conventional" MIDI commands. It first sends a Stop command, and then when you start again, a Continue command. You should know that a Start command is only ever used at position 1.1.0. Cubase uses the Continue command for all other positions. SPP only comes into play when you want to start at a position other than 1.1.0 or you have used the rewind/fast forward functions. Cubase sends the new bar position via the SPP after you have released the rewind/fast forward buttons or made any other change. This happens when you fast forward Cubase during playback as well. It doesn't matter whether you use the keys, the mouse or direct input of numeric value.

The locators are an exception in this regard. As soon as you place Cubase at one of the locator positions, the bar position is sent via SPP's. When you press the start button, Cubase sends a Continue command. This is especially important if you are at a location after the left locator. Hitting the stop key twice now will send Cubase to the left locator's position.

It is important for the SPP where the locator is situated. If it is not at 1.1.0, the Song position is sent as an SPP via MIDI. Then when you run the sequence, a Continue command will be sent. If the left locator is at 1.1.0 no SPP is sent. Cubase sends a MIDI Start command instead.

The problem:
Basically, the SPP is a very useful facility, but is not supported by all devices. Drum machines in particular often disregard the SPP. In this case, you have no choice but to run each time from the beginning of the Song.

The best way around this is to record the external device's rhythm data into Cubase via MIDI. Then Cubase can simply trigger the drum machine's sounds. This method is to be recommended, as it removes the need for synchronization once you have recorded the data.

Another problem can be caused when Cubase sends an SPP during playback after repositioning. The MIDI Standard only allows for SPP's to be sent when devices are stopped. As a result, some devices may ignore SPP commands that are sent during playback.

17.5 Older sync formats

A number of analog sync procedures were used prior to the MIDI standard, e.g. DIN FSK. If you want to use one of these to synchronize to Cubase, you need a converter that generates analog sync signals from MIDI Clock signals or vice versa. Cubase cannot generate these sync signals. There are a number of peripheral devices on the market that solve this problem.

17.6 SMPTE

Today's average production involves substantially more complex situations than the relatively simple synchronization of several MIDI devices. One of the biggest problems is synchronizing a MIDI sequencer to a tape machine. This could be either an audio or video tape recorder; in other words, devices that do not usually incorporate a MIDI interface.

Nevertheless, many productions require that MIDI events in a sequencer are in sync with analog signals on a tape Track. This also applies to the synchronization of pictures and music in film dubbing. The entire post production process would not be possible without sync standards.

Sync problems between sound and film haven't just existed since the inception of the MIDI standard. Mechanical solutions used to be applied, and some of them have survived to this day. Video technology forced developers to find a completely new solutions. In 1967, the time code used for most synchronization was developed. In 1972, the American Society of Motion Picture and Television Engineers (SMPTE) accepted this development as the standard. The European Broadcast Union (EBU) followed suit. Today, we refer to it as the SMPTE/EBU standard.

SMPTE/EBU Time Code divides time into its familiar units: hours, minutes and seconds. Of course seconds provide too coarse a resolution for optimum synchronization, which is why it is broken down even further.

The engineers did not use the next standard division, milliseconds, but the number of pictures or frames per second (showing its origins in the film industry). The frames are in turn divided into 80 bits. Different countries use different frame rates. We'll look at this problem in a few moments.

A SMPTE word looks like this:
hours   minutes   seconds   frames   bits

Synchronization

Let's clear up some potential misunderstandings right away: in contrast to MIDI, SMPTE signals are audible analog. Special hardware is required to convert SMPTE code into MIDI signals.

The frames

The SMPTE/EBU standard contains 4 different frame rates. This is a result of the different international film and video standards. 35 mm film has 24 frames per second. The European video PAL norm uses 25 frames, and the American monochrome NTSC norm uses 30 frames per second. American colour video is a special case having its frame rate reduced from 30 to 29.97. This may seem like a minimal reduction, but it leads to problems when using conventional time codes. An agreement was reached where two frames per minute are dropped. This is why this format is called "Drop Frame".

We won't get into details on the different frame rates and the subsequent problems. The standard throughout Europe is 25 frames per second with practically no exceptions.

The actual frame rate is strictly speaking irrelevant when it comes to synchronizing a sequencer to a tape recorder, as it is only a case of somehow synchronizing the music and the sequencer as precisely as possible. However, it is a different story when dubbing films. The correct frame rate is essential for synchronizing acoustic information to film.

In Europe, you should always use the 25 Frame setting, unless another frame rate is absolutely imperative. Never use different frame rates in the course of a single production.

LTC and VITC

There are basically two types of SMPTE codes: LTC and VITC. The more common type of time code is recorded on a multi-track recorder or a video recorder's sound track. Digital information is converted to an audio signal and vice versa. This is usually referred to as LTC (longitudinal time code). LTC is recorded, as the name suggests, along the length of the tape. This is the only possible way of working for tape recorders, and most video recorders.

LTC has a major disadvantage inherent in its design. If the playback rate goes outside a certain range, the audio signal can no longer be read. Extremely expensive synchronizers can process the signal so that the SMPTE code can be read at very high or low speeds, even during fast forward and rewind functions. Normal synchronizers give up at rate changes of 10 - 15%. However, all synchronizers, even expensive ones, have one thing in common: once the tape machine is stopped, no time code can be sent or received.

Film dubbing often requires that acoustic events i.e. dialogue, effects, etc. be precisely placed to picture. A special time code was developed for this purpose, known as VITC (vertical interval time code). This time code is inserted in a video recorder's video track, something which can be done only during copying or recording operations.

VITC code is written like a picture signal in one or more lines; to be more precise, in the upper line that contains no picture. Normally, you cannot see this code. If the picture is not centred on the monitor, you can see the bits race by at the upper screen edge.

The advantages of this type of SMPTE code are that VITC can be read at any speed, even when in the picture pause position. Every video head is always in motion, and thus creates a relative motion. What's more, the signal does not depend on tempo.

VITC does have its disadvantages. The space available for recording data is extremely limited. The beginning and the end of the sync word must be entered exactly at the defined position. Synchronization timing must be absolutely precise - the cheaper VHS or U-Matic recorders have a problem with this. Some bits can be lost due to overly high tolerances when recording a video with sync impulses. The result is that the entire VITC signal is illegible.

For this reason, professional sync applications use time base correctors that process the signal accordingly; in this case, first generation VHS copies can be used. You should always use the highest quality video recorder, preferably U-Matic devices, when using VITC time code. Your nerves and your budget will be eternally grateful. Generating and positioning VITC is technically more complex than the normal LTC, and requires special and expensive interfaces.

If you are not using VITC on a professional basis, then normal LTC will suffice. We'll talk about the required hardware in a moment. In the following section, the term SMPTE will be used, even when LTC is meant.

What does all this have to do with Cubase?
If you want to synchronize Cubase to a tape machine, or a video recorder's audio track, you will need to use SMPTE code. You have several options. First of all you will need some additional hardware that can read and write SMPTE code. Apart from third party manufacturers who offer a broad range of devices, there are 3 hardware options available from Steinberg: the SMP 24, Time Lock and the MIDEX+. We'll use MIDEX+ for the following exercises. Bear in mind that MIDEX+ not only offers SMPTE code for Cubase, but also additional MIDI Ins and Outs and slots for copy protect dongles. We'll look at this later.

17.7 MIDEX+ and practical synchronization

Install MIDEX+ and its associated software driver. Refer to Chapter 19 for this. Connect the MIDEX SMPTE output to your tape machine's audio input. This can also be a video recorder. Connect the tape machine's output to the SMPTE input.

If you are using a video recorder, you must assign an audio track to the sync signal. For the following exercises, you need a stereo video recorder which allows post production synchronization. Otherwise, you have to enter the time code during the copy procedure parallel to the picture. A professional video company's video tape should already come with the correct time code. MIDEX+ generates LTC.

How you decide to record this is up to you. If you absolutely must use VITC, use the required external devices.

17.7.1 Generating a sync track

Now that we've connected the cables, let's record the SMPTE code to tape. The record level is very important.

N.B. Under no circumstances should you set the levels too high or too low, especially on digital machines. It may cause problems in reading the code later on. Leakage to other tracks may also lead to sync problems. Switch off the noise reduction system for the sync track. This also applies when you want to read the track later.

Go to the synchronization menu and select MIDEX against SMPTE Sync in the Sync Source area. Start recording at your tape machine or video recorder. Click Start in the Write SMPTE area of the dialog box. Cubase will now send SMPTE code which will then be recorded to tape. Normally, recording starts from position 0:0:0:0. You can change this in the Write SMPTE area, if necessary. The maximum recording length is 24 hours.

N.B. Record more code than necessary. You cannot change the code later. The professional method is to record code for the entire tape length. Remember which frame rate you have used (normally 25 frames). Recording time code should always be your first task before you start recording music. Protect the time code from potential damage.

After the recording is complete, stop the send process in Cubase by pressing any key.

17.7.2 Starting Cubase

Recording a sync Track is only the first step. Rewind the Track. Activate the Sync button at the right bottom of the Transport Bar. Ensure all audio connections are correctly installed, and start playback.

As soon as the time code starts, Cubase will start to playback (just in this example). It is important to realize that the time code does not control the sequencer tempo, but is only responsible for synchronization between the tape and the sequencer. Cubase continues to draw its tempo

Synchronization

information from the Master Track. Rewind and fast forward the tape. Cubase always starts from the position where you stop the tape. The sequencer and the tape literally "stick" together.

You can freely determine at which SMPTE position Cubase starts. This does not have to be position 0:0:0:0 as in our example. It is actually better not to start the Song from where SMPTE starts on tape, as you need a few seconds of "run-up" tape to ensure there is always code on the tape, even if the tape machine overshoots after rewinding.

So, start Cubase with a little delay, called an "Offset". It is defined in Cubase by the Song Start Offset function. Enter several different offsets in the Sync dialog and see how the program reacts. Your current Arrangement starts when the SMPTE time entered in Offset is reached. The offset you define is up to you.

If you keep an eye on the little problem areas, synchronization between Cubase and MIDEX+ is a very easy to achieve. You can also increase or decrease the tempo of a Song that is already on tape. You can change the tape speed in a margin of around 10 to 15% without running into any time code problems with MIDEX+.

Keep in mind that you are also changing the pitch, so your MIDI sequencer pitches will no longer match. You have one of two choices: either change the pitch at your MIDI sound module, or record the sounds from your MIDI sound module onto tape, and then change the machine's tempo.

17.7.3 Post production synchronization

As a rule, you can let your devices take care of the synchronization if you proceed carefully. However, if you have forgotten the Offset value or the Song tempo, you will have problems when synching up at a later date. This can happen when you are working with other people's compositions. Use a track sheet and keep it up to date by taking precise notes of the Start Offset, tempo, and sync format information.

A damaged time code track is much more difficult to deal with.

Finding the original offset and tempo values for the existing sync track is normally a process of trial and error. First let's find the right offset. If a sync track does exist, feed it to Cubase, but first switch record on. Once the SMPTE signals reach Cubase via MIDEX, Cubase will begin playback. Play a MIDI note on any Cubase Track. Stop the tape deck and go to any Cubase Editor. Click the Mouse position display twice. Cubase will now display the SMPTE format instead of bars. You can read where your note was positioned. Enter this time in the MIDI Offset. Of course this value is only approximate. You have to find the correct value by experimenting. If there was a sync start point, chances are it was a round number.

Once you have discovered the correct start point, you have to figure out the exact tempo. This is substantially more difficult, as absolute precision is required.
- Try to get close to the tempo by experimenting.
- Enter this tempo as the first Master Track entry.
- Ensure that the rest of the Master Track is empty, and the Master button in the Transport Bar is not active.
- Activate Sync in the Transport Bar.
- Cubase must be synchronized to SMPTE time.
- Select an empty Cubase Track.
- Record Tempo in the Options menu must be active.
- Go to the Human Sync dialog box in the Options menu.
- Enter tempo values around the one found in the previous exercise in "Max" and "Min". We used 120, so enter 122 and 118.
- Deactivate the Smooth function.
- Max Increase and Decrease must be set to 30.000, Offset to 1.000.
- Clear the grey areas in the note field of the Human Sync box with the right mouse button.
- Create the following areas:

SMPTE Synchronization Without MIDEX+

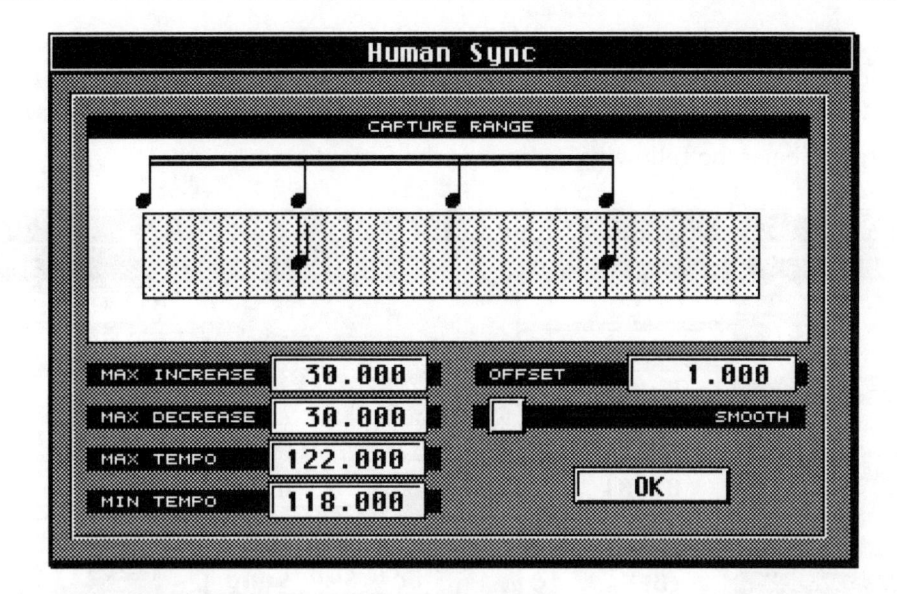

[Human Sync dialog box with Capture Range grid showing quarter notes; fields: MAX INCREASE 30.000, MAX DECREASE 30.000, MAX TEMPO 122.000, MIN TEMPO 118.000, OFFSET 1.000, SMOOTH checkbox, OK button]

- Click the first field in the grid with the left mouse button. You have just defined a range. Click this range's dividing line with the pointer and drag the grey area to the centre of the field (under the third sixteenth) while holding the mouse button down.
- Click the last field in the grid and drag the grey area to the centre of the field until it meets the first field.
- Exit the dialog box.
- Set Cubase to record.
- Start playback of the SMPTE track.
- Cubase will start once the SMPTE offset point is reached.
- Play quarter notes along with the recorded music.
- Try to keep the timing as tight as possible and stop recording once the Song has played through.

Cubase records all tempo changes in the Master Track. The range is minimized by the settings we have just entered, to avoid accidental jumps in the tempo. Cubase uses your crotchets to compute the tempo. If you play faster than the original tempo, then Cubase speeds up. If you played slower, the program applies the brakes. You're playing to the tape, thus adjusting the sequencer to the tempo of the Song. To play it all back later, simply activate the Master button for the playback before you send the SMPTE time code to the computer. Cubase controls the tempo according to the Master Track settings.

By the way, you can use the same method to recreate a "forgotten" sync track. So when you want to work on a track where the sync track has been lost or damaged just record a new sync track on an empty track and do this in exactly the way described above. We will discuss the other possibilities of the Human Sync dialog box later.

17.8 SMPTE synchronization without MIDEX+

Of course you can synchronize Cubase to SMPTE time code without the Midex or SMP 24. In principle there are two options: with and without MIDI Time Code.

Most external sequencers generate a MIDI Clock with Song Position Pointers when they read a SMPTE signal. This is enough to simply play a Song in sync with a film. However, this method has a decisive disadvantage.

You have already found out that SMPTE code contains no information about a connected sequencer's tempo. You can designate any tempo in Cubase. The Master Track offers you a number of options. A synchronizer that generates MIDI Clock signals and SPP's designates the tempo by the intervals at which it sends the MIDI Clock. All synchronizers create a tempo map using the MIDI Clock for this purpose. Basically, this is the counterpart to the Cubase Master

Synchronization

Track. A synchronizer has a limited user interface, and thus offers less clarity and fewer processing capabilities. If you have to use an external synchronizer with MIDI Clock, then Cubase has to be the slave. You cannot use the Master Track. All your tempo settings are invalid.

For this purpose, enter the following settings in the Sync dialog:

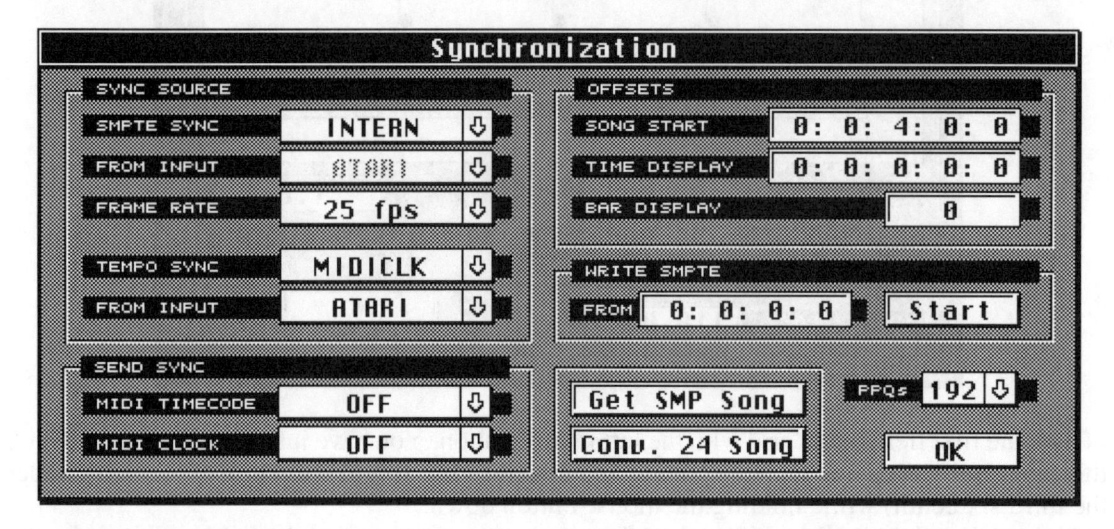

```
                    Synchronization
  SYNC SOURCE                  OFFSETS
  SMPTE SYNC    INTERN         SONG START    0: 0: 4: 0: 0
  FROM INPUT    ATARI          TIME DISPLAY  0: 0: 0: 0: 0
  FRAME RATE    25 fps         BAR DISPLAY        0
  TEMPO SYNC    MIDICLK        WRITE SMPTE
  FROM INPUT    ATARI          FROM  0: 0: 0: 0     Start
  SEND SYNC
  MIDI TIMECODE OFF            Get SMP Song     PPQs 192
  MIDI CLOCK    OFF            Conv. 24 Song        OK
```

The only important entry is the correct Tempo Sync setting; all the others are irrelevant. Your external synchronizer generates all the MIDI Clock, SPP, Start, Stop and Continue commands. Cubase reacts to these accordingly.

You can also use these settings if you want to synchronize Cubase to another device with MIDI Clock (with or without SPP), and you want to use Cubase as the slave. Don't forget to activate the Sync button in the Transport Bar.

17.9 The resolution

The normal MIDI Clock has a resolution of only 96th beats. Older sync devices forced slave sequencers to send this resolution even if they had much higher resolutions. Cubase, however always uses the maximum resolution internally, and interpolates the intermediate steps independently. So it is not limited when operating as a slave to MIDI Clock.

Cubase always attempts to record MIDI notes with the highest priority, and then other MIDI events. If problems do occur during peak input and heavy computer activity, you can re-define the playback resolution in the Sync dialog from 1536ths to 768ths, or 384ths. This affects the playback only, and not the recording. Only use this option when you have no other choice.

17.10 MIDI Time Code

Nowadays, many synchronizers are capable of generating MIDI Time Code (MTC) or deriving it from SMPTE signals. MIDI Time Code is similar in structure to SMPTE. The resolution is not as high, but it actually presents fewer problems than the previous Clock/SPP solution. MTC solves many problems caused by the conversion of SMPTE to MIDI Clock and SPP. MTC was officially integrated into the MIDI standard in 1987. Unfortunately, not many sequencers are capable of generating MTC, or even reading it yet. Cubase can do both.

You must have a device that is capable of converting SMPTE signals to MTC. Some synchronizers can already do this. If you own one of these devices, you don't need MIDEX+. If you own a MIDEX+, then you don't need MTC. MIDEX+ and Cubase can generate MIDI Clock and MTC while operating in the SMPTE mode. You can thus integrate virtually any external device in the system.

MTC is treated in the same way as SMPTE. Enter MTC as the sync source next to the SMPTE Sync entry in the Sync dialog box.

Just like SMPTE, MTC has no tempo information. The advantages are that you can use the Master Track and offsets. You don't have to worry about stop, start, etc. The only problem is the huge amount of data. MTC resolution is extremely high, so there is an enormous amount of data in the MIDI line, which is why you should never send MTC along the same connection you are using for MIDI notes. Use additional hardware that has the necessary Ins and Outs, and reroute the MTC data in the Sync dialog. From Input in the Sync source area, and MIDI Time Code in the Send Sync area are where you enter the information.

17.11 Pros and cons

If you need to use SMPTE in the studio, then the MIDEX+ is certainly the best solution. The ROM port enables extremely rapid data exchange. The SMP 24 and the Time Lock are both recommended, as they are very similar to MIDEX+ in terms of handling and operation. Additionally, they provide more MIDI outputs and dongle ports.

Use MTC only if you have a synchronizer that offers this option. You will still need to come up with extra MIDI Ins and Outs because of the heavy data load.

MTC has a more important role to play on the Macintosh, as the interface/hardware situation is different and you can run several programs simultaneously in sync under Multifinder (or the Finder from Version 7 onwards). Although this is also entirely possible on the Atari, the lack of programs capable of handling MTC makes it less worthwhile.

Some of the MTC protocol's capabilities remain unexploited. This communications standard includes the ability to transmit cue points, which is a capability SMPTE does not have. For this reason, MTC may become a much more comprehensive, and therefore more popular alternative in the future.

A further advantage is the way MTC is transmitted. Standard SMPTE is an audio signal, which can be damaged or even completely destroyed. In contrast, MTC takes the form of digital data (like all MIDI messages), so its communication involves far fewer potential problems. When you consider the strides in development of digital recording, such as hard disk recorders, a digital format such as MTC certainly makes sense.

17.12 Special SMPTE features

Cubase offers numerous special options for film and post production applications. You can display all bars and positions in the SMPTE format. Double-click the Mouse position display in the Arrange window. Cubase will display the mouse position and the bar display in the SMPTE format. You can pin-point positions very precisely. The same holds true in the Editors, where you can place events right on SMPTE frames.

17.12.1 Track Lock

Cubase Version 3.0 also avoids another problem very elegantly. As you know, SMPTE synchronization is independent of the sequencer's tempo. We'll use a special dubbing situation as an example of the problems this can cause. Let's say you have recorded sampler sound effects on the first four Cubase Tracks in sync with the picture. You have recorded music on four other Tracks. After you have finished, you notice that the music ought really to run slightly faster. As you are locked to the video copy via SMPTE, you can speed up the sequencer tempo in the Master Track to the value you think is appropriate. So you increase the tempo. Unfortunately, you thereby also move the sound effects away from their synchronized positions.

Cubase removes this problem with the Track Time Lock function. You can set each Track to

Synchronization

follow the set tempo, or remain locked to SMPTE time, keeping its events in sync. This is set in the T column of the Arrange window. Click it, and a lock symbol will appear for the Track in question. All events on the Track will be locked to their SMPTE time, even if you program tempo changes. This is only the case if the changes are made in the Master Track. You can of course continue to move or copy events in the Editor, but don't forget that the time grid in the Editors and the Arrange window do not correspond to SMPTE time. This means that you should set the Snap function to Off, and that you cannot quantize events to SMPTE times.

You can return a locked Track to the normal mode at any time. If you have changed the tempo in the Master Track, then the event positions must be re-computed. These computations may take a moment, depending on the amount of data and the extent of the tempo change.

17.12.2 Creating polyrhythms

By using the following technique you can come up with an interesting effect. Say you want to place two sections of music with different tempos in such a way that one blends into the other, or they run in parallel.

This is how you go about it:
- Record the two pieces on different Tracks.
- Set the tempo for the first piece, move the parts to the required position, and assign the lock symbol to the Track.
- Copy the parts of the second piece to the desired position on an empty Track.
- Set the tempo in the Master Track.

The first Song's tempo will not change, as it is locked to SMPTE time. You can play two Songs with two different tempos so they overlap or are completely parallel to each other. The important thing to remember is to use different Tracks.

Two Tracks with two different tempos running in one Arrangement

17.12.3 Human Sync

We've already used Human Sync in an earlier example. You can use this feature for substantially more complex tempo mapping in post production. Generally speaking, Human Sync is used to alter sequencer tempos using specific criteria.

Here's an example: set the Tempo Sync option in the Sync dialog box to Human. The Human Clock dialog box settings control the your sequencer's tempo from MIDI note input. Cubase needs some more information from you in order to do this reliably. The most important thing is how often it should expect incoming notes. You must enter these values in the grid of the Human Sync dialog box. You define these by drawing ranges. We have already tried this. Draw quarter notes the same way you did in the synchronization example. Activate Sync in the Transport Bar and play four MIDI notes on your keyboard. Cubase starts playing according to your tempo at the fifth note. The count-in number is equal to the time signature setting. Ensure that the Master Track is inactive.

This was a very simple example of a Human Sync operation. You can also continuously control the tempo, which is what we did in the post production sync example. The settings are used to define the range of the desired changes. Max and Min define the tempo range within which you want to remain. For most applications, it is better to keep this range as narrow as possible. There are few pieces of music where the tempo needs to vary from 30 to 250. You just need to know if you want to increase or decrease the tempo towards the end of the Song. The maximum tempo change is defined by the Max Increase and Max Decrease settings. The less you limit Cubase, the more precise your timing must be.

You can record these changes at any time. Try the following exercises:
- You can dictate the tempo to your sequencer in a live application. You don't have to use crotchets, you can play normally. Ensure the correct settings are entered in the grid in the Human Sync dialog box.
- You can convert a tape machine's click Track signals to MIDI notes via a suitable device (e.g. Aphex "Impulse") and use these to control the tempo via the Human Sync function.
- When recording parts in, you can play difficult passages slowly, and the easy ones faster. When working in this way, do not activate the Record Tempo Mutes option and then the they will all be played back at the same tempo.

17.12.4 Additional functions

The Sync dialog has two very special functions that we should not forget. Get 24 Song is a function used in conjunction with Steinberg's SMP 24/SMP24 II devices. If you activate this command, Cubase will get the tempo from the connected SMP 24. This includes other SMP 24 Song information. This data will replace the current Cubase Master Track settings.

Convert 24 Song converts Song Master Tracks that were recorded with Steinberg's Pro-24 and SMP 24 to the Cubase Master Track format. During the conversion you will be asked to input which mode was used for the original recording.

Synchronization

18 MIDI Processor and IPS

Cubase Version 3.0 is modular. If your computer has enough RAM memory, you can load modules at any time to increase the program's range of capabilities - we had a good look at how this works in Chapter 7. This chapter covers the various functions of the individual modules. In addition to the two you already know, the Score editor and the MIDI Mixer, Steinberg supplies two other modules, the MIDI Processor and the Interactive Phrase Synthesizer.

18.1 The MIDI Processor

This module enables you to generate delay effects by processing MIDI events in real time. We'll try a few practical exercises and then look at the theory. For the following experiments, ensure that Cubase is *not* running, and that the Remote Control is switched off.
- Select Track 1 with MIDI Channel 1.
- Select the MIDI Processor from the Modules menu. The dialog box that will appear contains all the parameters you'll need.

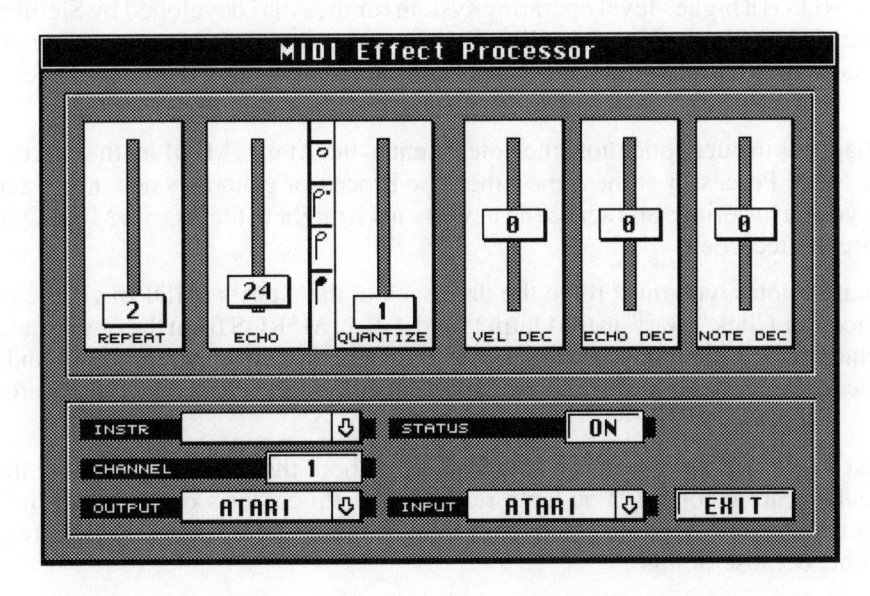

Enter these values in the dialog box

MIDI Processor and IPS

Enter the following fader settings:
- Repeat 2
- Echo   24
- Quantize 1
- Echo Dec 0
- Vel Dec 0
- Note Dec 0

Here values are changed using a slightly different method than previously. The sliders are comparable to faders. Click one of the small value boxes. Move the mouse up and down while holding the mouse button down. The small box will follow your movements, the values within it changing accordingly.

This method is fine for getting roughly the right position. The precise setting is made by clicking above or below the appropriate box so that the value is moved up or down by one unit.

You must also set the Channel to MIDI Channel 1. If you have named the MIDI channels, the name will appear in the Instrument column. For now, leave the Input and Output settings at "Atari". Now you just have to activate the Processor. Click the Status field. The display will change from Off to On. To switch the Processor off again, click the Status field once more.

Play any key on your keyboard. Cubase will generate a second note after the one you just played. Change the Repeat value - this controls the number of repetitions. The input note is included in the number. Repeat 2 generates the original plus one repetition, Repeat 3 the one original plus two repetitions, and so on. The time interval between individual repetitions is controlled by the Echo value. Experiment with different settings.

The MIDI Processor generates a delay effect by copying the input event and displacing the copy by the designated number of ticks relative to the original note. Each value change represents a difference of eight ticks. A delay the length of a quarter of a bar (384 ticks) is equal to an echo value of 48. The maximum delay time is 192, i.e. 1536 ticks, which is equal to the length of an entire bar. The interval between the repetitions is controlled by the sequencer's tempo setting, regardless of whether it is running or stopped.

Try setting Repeat to 4 and Echo to 48, starting to record, and then playing a note on the downbeat of each bar. Cubase will generate three repetitions at quarter note intervals.

Listen to the result of your recording. You will hear your original notes on the one, but no echoes. The reason for this is the Processor's input/output configuration. You must use M*ROS to record the echoes. M*ROS is a higher-level operating system for the Atari developed by Steinberg - see the next chapter for details - and is used to link Cubase with other M*ROS-compatible programs (sequencers, editors) and facilitates internal ST communication and data exchange between them.

This is what happens in our application: the note is sent to the Atari's MIDI In, then recorded and sent on to the MIDI Processor at the same time. The Processor generates new notes according to the criteria you have defined and sends the new events straight to the Atari's MIDI Out, which means they are not recorded.

To record the new notes, you must route the data back to the Atari's MIDI In via the invisible M*ROS connection. Click "Atari" in the Output field. Select M*ROS from the menu that appears by pressing and holding the mouse button. Note: the menu selections in the Input and Output fields differ according to your hardware configuration, although Atari and M*ROS are always listed.

Delete the last Track and record a new one. This time, both the original notes and the MIDI Processor's echoes are recorded. You have rerouted the Processor's output from the Atari's MIDI Out to the internal M*ROS connection and Cubase can now access and record the generated events because of this.

If this exercise was unsuccessful, go to the Options menu and select MIDI Setup. The dialog box contains a field entitled Record From. Click and hold Inputs. Atari and M*ROS must be checked, i.e. active in the selection menu. If not, activate one or both of them by clicking. Leave the dialog box via [Return] and repeat your recording. We won't go into the explanation now as once again, Chapter 19 has all the answers.

18.1.1 Other applications

Now that we know how to activate the MIDI Processor and record the generated data on a Cubase Track, let's look at some of the Processor's other applications. Try out the following parameters in practice.

Vel Dec affects the velocity values of the generated notes. In a normal echo effect, the repetitions are not as loud as the original. Enter negative values, e.g. -12: if your original note has a velocity of 80, the first repetition will have a value of 68, the second echo 56, etc. The note's volume will be reduced and may even take on a different timbre, depending on the sound program. Positive values increase the velocity for each successive echo.

Not Dec is a parameter which may be familiar to harmonizer users. Each echo is transposed up or down by the given interval.

Echo Dec allows you to create other unusual effects. It subtracts the defined time value from each echo. Say you are using a delay value of 48, equal to a quarter note. Set the Echo Dec value to -3 (equal to 24 ticks = 64th note). The first repetition is played at the next quarter note position, minus a 64th, the second one at the next quarter note position minus a 32nd, etc. In a nutshell, the repetitions follow at increasingly shorter intervals.

Cubase subtracts the value prior to the first repetition. Keep this in mind when you are entering the setting.

18.1.2 Quantizing

The repetitions can be quantized. Let's look at what the Processor actually does using some numeric examples. Say a Track contains two notes at positions 1.1.0 and 1.1.40. The delay value is 24 (192 ticks = an eighth). We want two repetitions. What happens?

Original	1.1.0	1.1.40
1st echo	1.1.192	1.1.232
2nd echo	2.1.0	2.1.40

The interval between repetitions is an eighth note (192 ticks). The first note was played on the downbeat, so the repetitions are played at the second and third eighths in the bar. The second note is slightly out of time. The repetitions are played at the correct intervals, but are off the beat. However, if you set the MIDI Processor's Quantize function to eighths (a setting of 24 = 192 ticks), then the original note remains in the same position, but the repetitions are corrected to the next eighth. In our example, this means the repetitions would now happen at the same times, even though the original notes were not played exactly together.

Tip: the Processor's Quantization function is not very precise. You may experience variations of up to +/- 4 ticks. The standard Cubase Quantization function can be used to correct this ([Q]).

When you record the notes generated by the MIDI Processor, you come across the following phenomenon, where the MIDI Processor plays the repetitions but also replays the original note, too. The Track you are recording on therefore contains two identical original notes at the same position. Doubled notes cause the dreaded phasing effect, which is especially noticeable in drum sounds. There are two solutions:

a) Process the Track using the Delete Doubles function in the Functions menu. It will remove these doubled notes.

b) Select MIDI Setup from the Options menu. Click and hold Inputs. A number of entries will appear in the list - what it actually contains depends on your hardware configuration, although

MIDI Processor and IPS

Atari and M*ROS are always listed. Both entries are active. Select the Atari entry and release the mouse button. The Atari entry will be deactivated. Cubase will now only record the data sent via the internal M*ROS circuit, and data sent via the Atari's MIDI In port is not recorded, which means that the doubled note problem is completely cured. However, do not forget to reactivate the Atari's MIDI In after you have finished working with the MIDI Processor (by checkmarking it). Cubase will not record any data if you fail to do this.

18.1.3 Processing previously recorded Tracks

You can use the MIDI Processor to work on previously recorded Tracks. Select the desired Tracks or Parts and activate the Inspector. Switch the Output parameter from Atari to M*ROS. The data contained in the Part is now sent through the internal M*ROS connection, and not to the MIDI Out.

Leave the Inspector and select a Track on which you want to record. Ensure the MIDI channel setting is correct. Go to the MIDI Processor and enter the desired parameter settings. The Processor's input and output must be set to M*ROS. Start recording.

The data on the source Track will be sent to the Processor via M*ROS, processed there, and then recorded on the selected Track again via M*ROS.

You can of course send the data from several Tracks to the Processor at the same time. Simply set the Tracks' outputs to M*ROS in the Play Parameter boxes. The original notes and those generated in the Processor will be merged onto the selected Track. If you set the Processor's MIDI channel to "Any", then the Tracks' MIDI channel assignments will be retained. In this case, set the newly recorded Track's MIDI channel to "Any" as well.

18.2 The IPS module

The Interactive Phrase Synthesizer is one of the most complex sections of Cubase. Its purpose is to generate new musical phrases based on the material you provide, or to alter existing lines. All operations are performed in realtime, but you can of course record and play back the results.

The Interactive Phrase *Synthesizer* is aptly named. The IPS is a synthesizer that takes phrases you have provided and synthesizes new musical material using different modules and parameters. You will recognize LFOs, modulators and many other devices from your experience with other synthesizers. The difference here is that it is notes we are working with instead of sounds.

Unfortunately, the way the IPS works can only be explained using theoretical examples. But before we get into the theory aspect, let's try a few practical experiments. Ensure the IPS module is loaded. If not, refer to the Special Functions chapter for the information on how to load this module.

18.2.1 The first IPS phrase

Record a short Part in the Arrange window featuring a bass riff, say one bar in length. Quantize the Part and process it with the Freeze Quantize function because any of the Inspector's Play Parameter settings are ignored by the IPS. If you want these settings to be retained, activate Freeze PP in the Functions menu.

All IPS operations are based on phrases. Always create a phrase before you initiate any IPS functions. The length of any phrase is limited to 1000 notes. What you decide to do with this phrase is entirely up to you - you can manipulate the rhythm, melody, or whatever else comes to mind. The phrase must first be recorded in the Arrange window and then transferred to the IPS memory.

Select a Part and activate Copy to Phrase from the Options menu. The dialog box which appears allows you to keep Track of all your phrases. Select the arrow and click the slot to which you want to copy the phrase.

The IPS Module

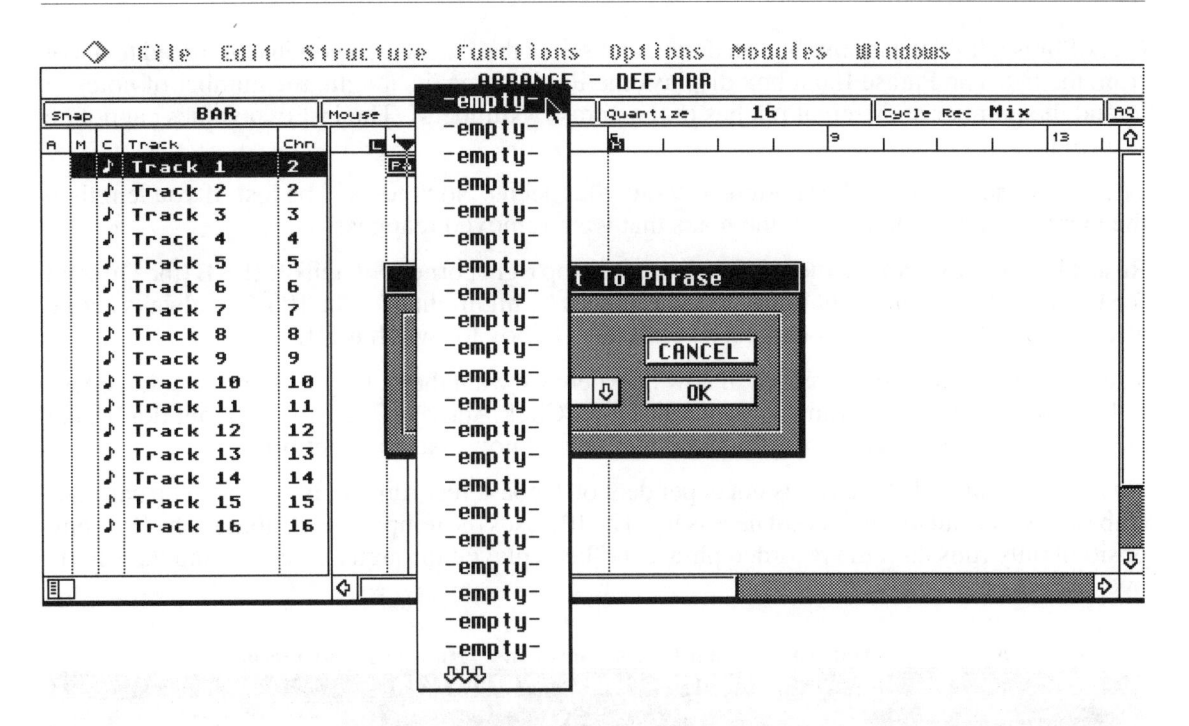

The 32 phrase slots

As soon as you confirm with OK, then the Part's contents are stored in the selected phrase slot. A total of 32 slots are available. The phrase cannot be copied back to a Part. The original Part will not be changed, but you should save it if you think you might need it again.

After you have created your phrase, go to the IPS. Click Phrase Synth in the Modules menu. Your first reaction to the IPS is probably one of complete confusion because of the dozens of function parameters. But don't worry! Everything is laid out very logically. We will work our way through the individual parameters one after another using practical exercises. First we must enter the phrase in the IPS. The Phrase Input field at the screen's top left corner is used for this.

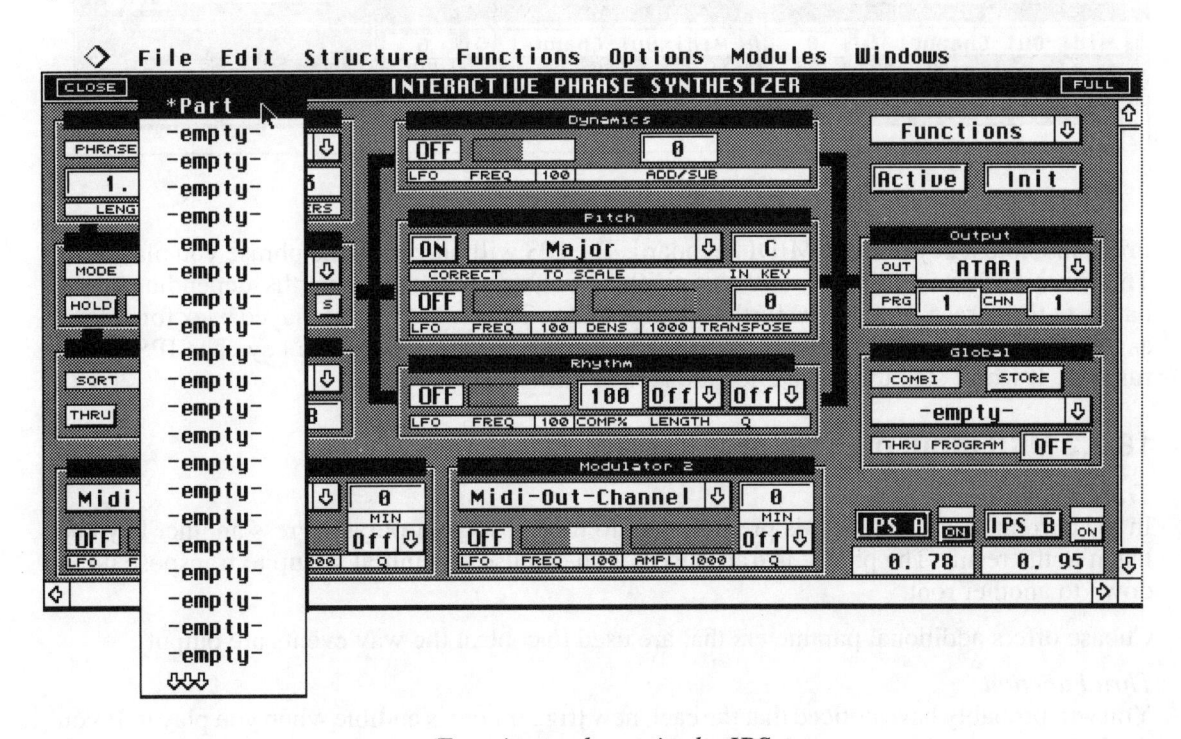

Entering a phrase in the IPS

MIDI Processor and IPS

Click Phrase, hold the mouse button down, and select the Part which you just assigned to a slot from the list. The Phrase Input box displays the Part's name, its length, the number of notes in it, and the number of different pitches in the phrase (Numbers). The last two values cannot be changed.

The length, however, can be shortened to suit your needs. No notes will be lost. If you lengthen the phrase again at some point, the notes that were removed reappear.

Reset all values by clicking the Init function at the top right corner. Switch off IPS B (the On field for IPS B at the bottom right of the IPS should not be highlighted). The IPS B is always active after you execute the Init procedure, so click the On box to switch it off.

The settings for our first exercise will now be where we want them. Play a key on your keyboard to hear the connected instrument's sound timbre. Click Active to start the IPS, but don't play anything yet. The IPS A's Song Position display will now start to count off.

Always remember that the IPS is not dependent on Cubase recording or playback. You can start Cubase if you want to, but it is not necessary. The IPS uses the tempo set in Cubase. The IPS song position only runs until the recorded phrase has been played through to the end, and then starts over again.

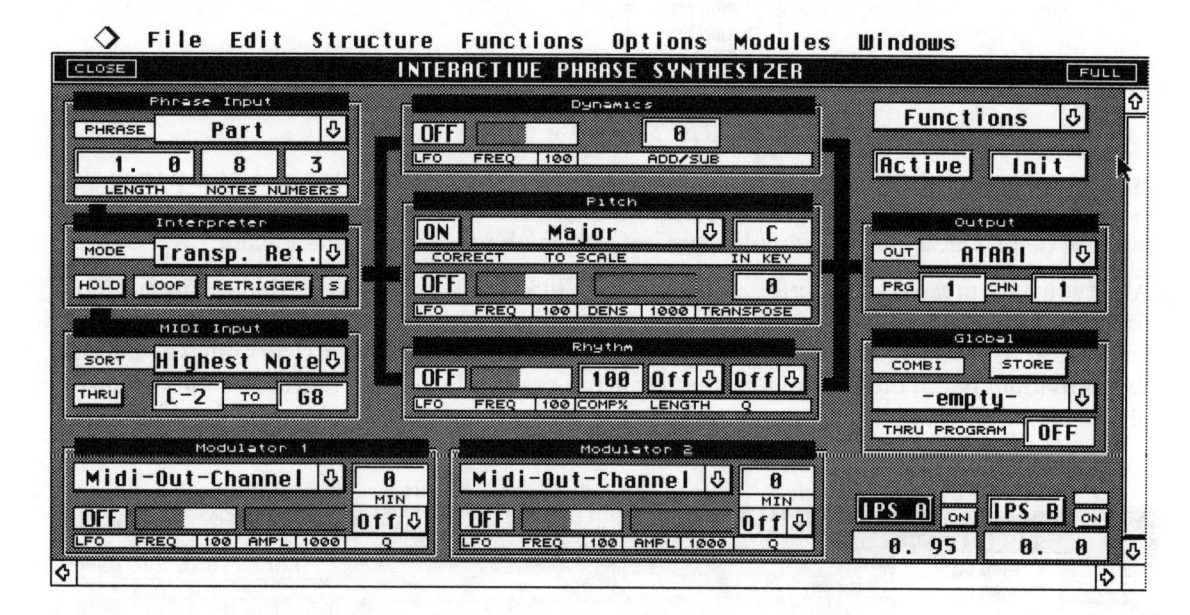

The first exercise

Press and hold a key on your MIDI keyboard. The IPS will play back the phrase you played in. There may be some differences to the original, particularly in the note lengths, depending on the nature of the phrase. This can be further changed later. The phrase will be played back for as long as you hold the key down. Playback will stop as soon as you release the key. The IPS is still running. It won't stop until you click the Active button again.

18.2.2 MIDI input parameters

Transposition
In the current setting, the IPS is programmed to transpose your phrase. Press another key and listen to the result. The phrase is transposed. You can use this initial set-up to transpose up or down to another root.

Cubase offers additional parameters that are used to control the way events are output.

Thru Function
You will probably have noticed that the each new trigger note is audible when you play it. If you don't want to hear this note, click Thru in the Input box. The IPS will then use the MIDI note you

play solely as a reference for transposition, and will not send it to the output.

Channel and Output Assignments

Another important setting defines the output for MIDI events. The IPS has its own output channel. You can define the MIDI channel and the MIDI output (Atari, M*ROS, or other additional hardware) in the Output box. You can also send MIDI Program Change messages. Try sending to your instrument on various MIDI channels.

Note Priorities

Let's look at the MIDI Input section. We have just seen that the MIDI Input determines which MIDI note is used as the basis for changes. The IPS can only use a single MIDI note as a reference in the current setting, even if you play chords. A number of limiting conditions can be entered to define the reference note more precisely and so avoid misinterpretations. Some of these may remind you of monophonic, analogue synthesizer functions. Click and hold the entry next to Sort. Select one of the options which appears to define which note is used as the reference note:
- Lowest Note: a chord's lowest note,
- Highest Note: a chord's highest note,
- Lowest Velocity: the note with the lowest velocity value,
- Highest Velocity: the note with the highest velocity value,
- Last Note: the last note played,
- First Note: the first note played.

These settings are only important in situations where several notes are played at the same time. The program uses these settings to decide between notes. You can try a few simple experiments to see how these functions operate. Select Lowest Note and play any note around the centre of your keyboard. Cubase plays your phrase. Hold the key down and play several other notes in the upper register. The IPS ignores these notes, using the low note as the sole reference point. On the other hand, if you play notes lower then the one you are holding down, Cubase recognises that a lower note has been played and uses the lower note as a reference.

Your phrase is transposed accordingly. Experiment with the other settings to see how they work.

Keyboard Range

You can define a MIDI note range as an additional filter for the input notes. Simply enter an upper and lower limit in the MIDI Input box. The IPS will only accept notes within this defined range.

Tip: if you use the IPS in a live situation, you can use your left hand to play reference notes and your right to play melody lines.

18.2.3 A brief review

The IPS is an extremely complex subject, so let's briefly review the information provided by this first example:
- You can use any Part as an IPS phrase.
- Phrase length is limited to 1000 notes.
- Phrases are stored in one of 32 IPS slots.
- The phrase input box is used to select the phrase in the IPS.
- Phrase length can be altered without irretrievably losing notes.
- The MIDI input is used to produce a reference note that determines how a phrase is processed. For instance, a MIDI note can serve as a transposition reference note.
- You play the reference note on your keyboard.
- Only one reference note at a time is possible or necessary.
- Use the Sort function to define the note that the IPS uses as a reference.
- This is only required when you play several notes at one time.
- The Thru function you can decide whether the note you play is used as a reference only, or is also sent to the MIDI Out.
- You can define a MIDI range from which notes are accepted.
- You can route the signals generated in the IPS to other MIDI channels and Cubase outputs via the IPS output section.

18.2.4 Interpreter settings

One of the IPS's most important components is the Interpreter. It takes the phrase and the notes you play live and combines them to produce new results. This sounds rather mysterious, so let's take a closer look. We'll stick with our first example for the moment.

Hold

Activate the Interpreter's Hold function and press a key on your MIDI keyboard. Cubase will plays the same phrase. Release the key, and the IPS will continue to play. The Hold function holds the last note you have played until you play a new one. The phrase is always played through to the end, even if you press a key before the phrase has finished. However, the Retrigger button can be used to cut the phrase off, so that the phrase will be restarted as soon as you press another key. Loop continuously repeats the phrase. You can see that settings of the Interpreter buttons are inter-dependent. The whole process is further complicated by the inter-relationship with the Interpreter's Mode setting. We'll look at this in a moment.

Transpose Retrigger/Transpose Continue

Until now, we have worked in the Interpreter's Transpose Retrigger mode only. It was used to trigger simple transpositions of a phrase. The phrase is played from the beginning every time you press a key. However, the Interpreter features other operating modes.

Click the field next to Mode and select Transpose Continue from the list which appears. Play a note and observe what happens. At first, there appears to be no change. But the IPS does now work a little differently. Once you release a key and then press it again, the phrase is played from the release point on. This function depends on the Retrigger and Loop button settings. In this setting, the Hold button has no effect.

Repeat

In the setting we have been using till now, the IPS has used the phrase's rhythm *and* relative note positions as a reference, and the note you played as the transposition reference. In the Repeat Mode this is very different. The IPS uses only the phrase's rhythmic structure as a reference, and you control the pitches from the keyboard.

Try this exercise: record a rhythmic Part in the Arrange window and enter it as a phrase (select Part, then choose Copy to Phrase from the Modules menu).

Return to the IPS and select the new phrase in the Phrase Input box. Set the Interpreter Mode to Repeat. Activate the IPS and hold any chord on your keyboard. The IPS plays the chord in the new phrase's rhythm. In this case, the MIDI Input settings are unimportant. You can play any notes or chords you want to. Try the Loop, Hold, and Retrigger functions to hear their effect.

Mute Play

In this mode, Cubase compares the notes in the phrase with the notes you play, and only sends those in common. This is particularly effective for drums. You can bring the various percussion instruments in and out by holding or releasing keys.

Record a drum Part with a number of different instruments. Start the IPS in the Repeat mode. You can turn notes off and on by pressing the keys of particular instruments. For instance, if you recorded a hihat on F#, the hihat is only audible when you hold the F# key down. No events are generated. The F# key is an on/off switch for the hihat. The other instruments are controlled by their respective keys. The original phrase's rhythmic structure is retained. Make sure the Loop function is active for drum Parts. Hold and Retrigger have no effect.

While these functions were all relatively simple to explain and understand, the following three Interpreter modes are a bit more complex. These Interpreter modes work on a logical/mathematical basis rather than on musical criteria. This does not mean you can't achieve excellent musical results. On the other hand, you should view these functions as inspiration for new material rather than realizers of pre-conceived ideas.

Sort Normal

The IPS assigns numbers to events in the Sort Normal mode. The number of notes is irrelevant,

The IPS Module

as it is only the different pitches which are numbered. If you played the following sequence:

C3, D3, E3, D3, C3, C3

Cubase would assign the following numbers:

C3 = 1

D3 = 2

E3 = 3

D3 = 2 (this note was already assigned a value)

C3 = 1 (ditto)

C3 = 1 (ditto)

The number of different pitches is displayed under the Numbers entry in the Phrase Input field. Cubase sorts and orders the notes internally, and uses them for later processing.

The notes you play live are also sorted and ordered in the same way. You can designate the Sort mode in the MIDI Input module. This is how you designate the order: Lowest Note assigns 1 to the lowest note, and increases the numbers as the pitch goes up. Highest Note does exactly the opposite.

What happens when you play live in this mode? The IPS compares the two series of notes and only plays those whose numbers appear in both lists. However this has nothing to do with the pitches that will then be sent. The pitch values are determined by the live notes only. Getting confused? Let's look at a practical application.

You have recorded the following phrase.

        C3   C4   C3   F3

IPS sorts and orders the notes in the internal list:

        C3   C4   C3   F3
        1   2   1   3

Why are these numbers assigned in this order? C3 is the first pitch, so it is assigned the number 1. C4 is the next note Cubase "hears", so it is assigned 2. The next note has already been assigned, so it is also 1. F3 is new to the list, so it has 3 assigned to it.

Let's try the simplest example possible. You activate the IPS and press a key, say D2. What happens? Cubase assigns a number to this note in a separate list. This note is held, so only one number is assigned, i.e. 1. Cubase compares the two lists during IPS activity:

Phrase count: C3   C4   C3   F3
                    1   2   1   3

Input count: D2   D2   D2   D2
                    1   1   1   1

Cubase plays just those notes that have matching numeric assignments. In this case, the note played has a value of 1, because your note input features no other values. The musical result looks like this:

        D2   D2

The other two notes are not played because their numbers are not represented in both lists. Are you starting to get the idea of how this function works?

Let's look at another example. Keep the above phrase and this time play two notes as the input, say D2 and E5. The IPS assigns numbers to the notes again. 1 is assigned to D2, and 2 to E5. This is the musical result:

        D2   E2   D2

MIDI Processor and IPS

In this case, only the final note position is not played. It has a number assignment of 3, and you only played two different input notes.

A final example: you played three notes live, D2, E5, and C6. Which musical sequence would you hear?

> D2   E5   D2   C6

Cubase has distinguished three different pitches, and therefore assigned three different numbers. Cubase compares the two lists, finds three pitches in the IPS phrase, and therefore plays all input notes. If you play any more notes, Cubase would assign them numbers in the list, but would not play them because there are no corresponding number assignments in the IPS phrase.

The Numbers value tells you how many of the notes you played will be heard, and from which point Cubase will ignore further notes.

The examples so far have been based on note assignments beginning with the lowest note. Keep in mind that other criteria (lowest, highest, reversed, according to velocity) will produce very different results.

Sort Replace
So far, we have neglected the phrase's rhythmic components to some extent. This mode attempts to fill the "holes" that list comparison produces. Once the IPS finds a number that is not contained in one of the two lists, it plays the first number/note again (where you would normally expect a rest). The note it enters in the musical sequence depends on the sorting order you defined (lowest, highest, etc).

Sort Skip
This mode attempts to avoid holes in the phrase as well, but uses a different method to do so. If it finds no common entry in the list comparison operation, the IPS goes on to the next phrase note and checks if it has a matching input number. The IPS continues to go to the next note until it finds a match, in real time of course. The musical results are structures similar to the arpeggiators featured on the early synthesizers.

We have just covered about half of the IPS's many secrets. You might want to shut your IPS down and take a tea break before we move on to its other functions.

18.2.5 The IPS modules

Now we'll look at the functions of the remaining three module components. So as to avoid unnecessary confusion caused by complex settings, we'll stick with our previous example, the bass riff. The IPS processes the notes sent by the Interpreter according to pitch, length and velocity. These aspects can themselves be extensively processed.

Pitch Module
This module does not control the pitch of the notes played but rather determines which of the phrase's pitches are accessed. Either the Transpose or Sort mode in the Interpreter must be active. You have three parameters to choose from: LFO, Density, and Transpose. What do they do?

Let's look at the simplest function first, the Density. It will omit certain notes. In this case, experimentation has more value than explanation, so try it out and you'll soon see how this function works. Transpose transposes all phrase notes up or down by the preset semitone amount.

The LFO is definitely more complicated. The term LFO is derived from synthesizer terminology and is short for low frequency oscillator. As far as Cubase is concerned, all we need to know about this LFO is that it generates between 0.1 and 30 repetitions per second. The Cubase LFO is nothing more than a sub-routine.

The LFO effect is defined by two values, the Waveform and the Frequency. The LFO does not actually control and set the pitches, but takes them from the Interpreter list. The LFO's task is to control the way the different pitches are accessed and the speed with which they are accessed.

Click Off in the Pitch LFO box and hold the mouse button down. You can now choose from the

The IPS Module

11 waveforms in the pop-up menu that appears. If you choose the icon top centre, the LFO will use the pitches from the Interpreter list unaltered. Experiment with different frequency values. These determine the time intervals at which the Interpreter's pitch data is read and transferred. 100% is the original rate, 200% is twice as fast. If you enter this frequency value, then the pitch data is read at twice the rate. In practice, what this means is that each pitch is played twice. There are many other waveforms available in the LFO used to process the pitches in the list. The symbols are fairly self-explanatory, but bear in mind that the actual pitch is not changed, only the pitch sequence in the list.

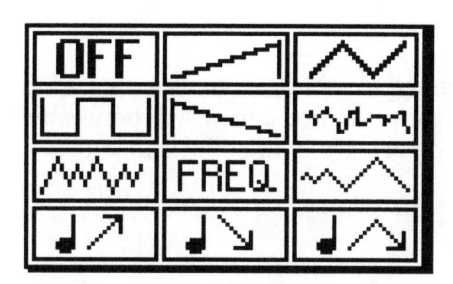

The LFO waveforms

Scale correction is a very important feature. We have already covered this function in the Logical Editor, Input Transformer and other sections of the program. The IPS function works the same way. Select the scale you want to end up with and the root in the box above To Scale. Click On to switch the function off and on.

Rhythm Module

This module is used to influence how a line is phrased. Go to the start of your phrase and set it playing via a MIDI note. Activate the Loop and Hold functions so we can use a continuously repeated string of notes.

Now we'll work with the rhythmic components of the phrase. First try entering different Length values. You will hear the note lengths in your phrase changing. All notes are assigned the same length. Try different "Q" settings. All notes will be quantized equally, with the Q value determining the intervals. The original phrase's rhythmic structure will soon be lost. Comp (compression) increases or decreases the phrase's speed in comparison to Cubase. Here too, an LFO with standard waveforms is available. The LFO uses the length data in the list and sorts the data according to the frequency and waveform settings.

Dynamics Module

This module changes the velocity values of the output notes. The LFO again accesses the list values and generates new values according to the settings. You can also add or subtract a specific number to/from each note's velocity value. These functions are available if you have selected the Transpose mode in the Interpreter.

18.2.6 The modulators

Each of the modulators is used to affect the parameters of the IPS. The LFOs we have already looked at are used as the source. Quantized change is also possible, in which case the changes follow Cubase's timing. Try the following settings:

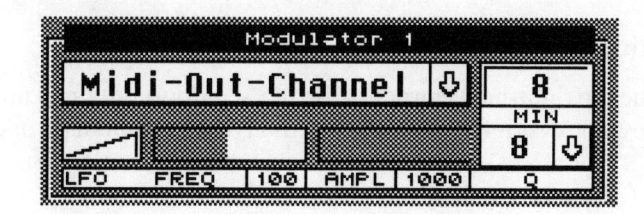

Automatic distribution of phrase notes to different MIDI outputs

MIDI Processor and IPS

Cubase modulates the MIDI output channel via Modulator 1. As a result, the notes in the phrase are sent on different successive MIDI channels.

A Min factor of "8" limits channel assignment to the eight above the original channel. If the original is 1, then channels 2 - 8 are used, one after the other. If you select a different waveform in the modulator's LFO, then the same channels will be accessed, but in a different order.

A Q factor of 8 ensures the move from one channel to the next occurs in time, at eighth note intervals. This is just one of many options. Try your own settings.

18.2.7 IPS B

All the functions we've discussed so far are available twice, as there is IPS B as well as IPS A. Everything in IPS B is identical to A. You can switch between them in the bottom right-hand corner of the IPS window. You can use both at the same time for complex applications. They always run in sync.

18.2.8 Combis

All IPS A and IPS B settings can be saved as a Combi, and called up at any time. A Combi is comparable to a synthesizer's sound program.

Select one of the 32 slots in the Global pop-up menu and click the Store button. Cubase saves the Combi in the ST's temporary memory. You will need to save the Combi on disk before you quit Cubase.

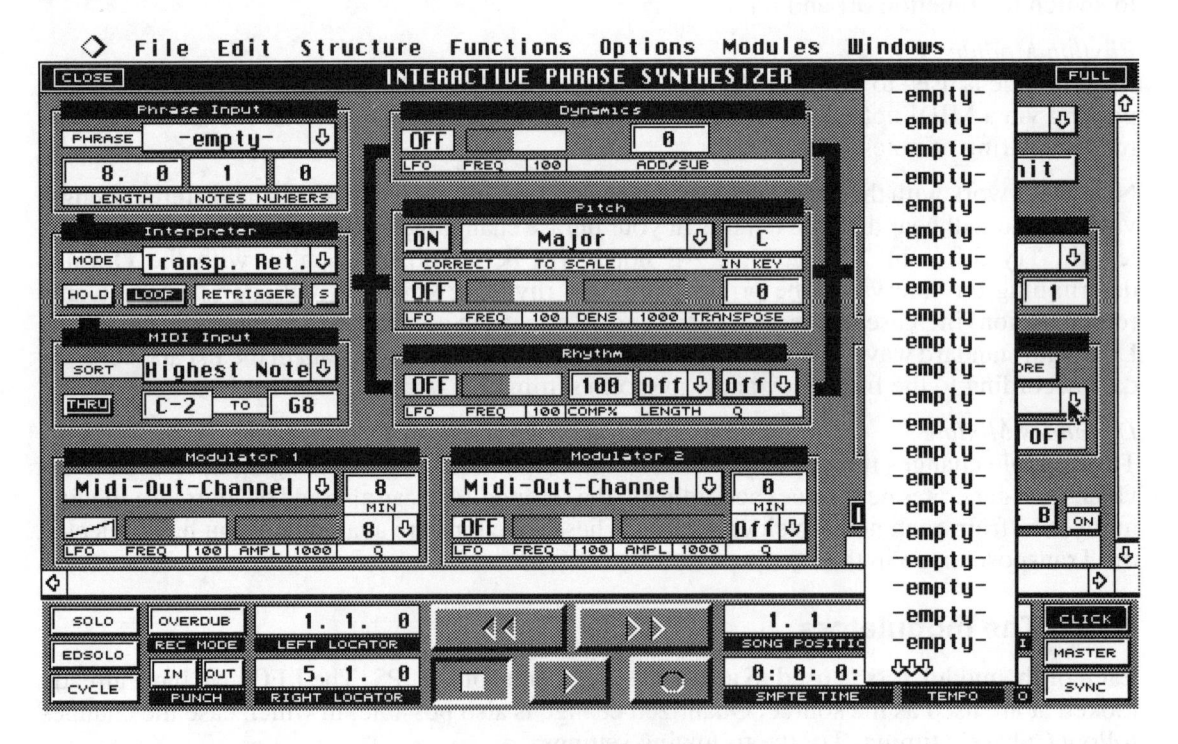

The Combi slots

18.2.9 The Functions menu

The pop-up menu in the top right-hand corner of the IPS window contains a number of additional functions. We'll review these briefly, as you should have no problems working with these.

The IPS Module

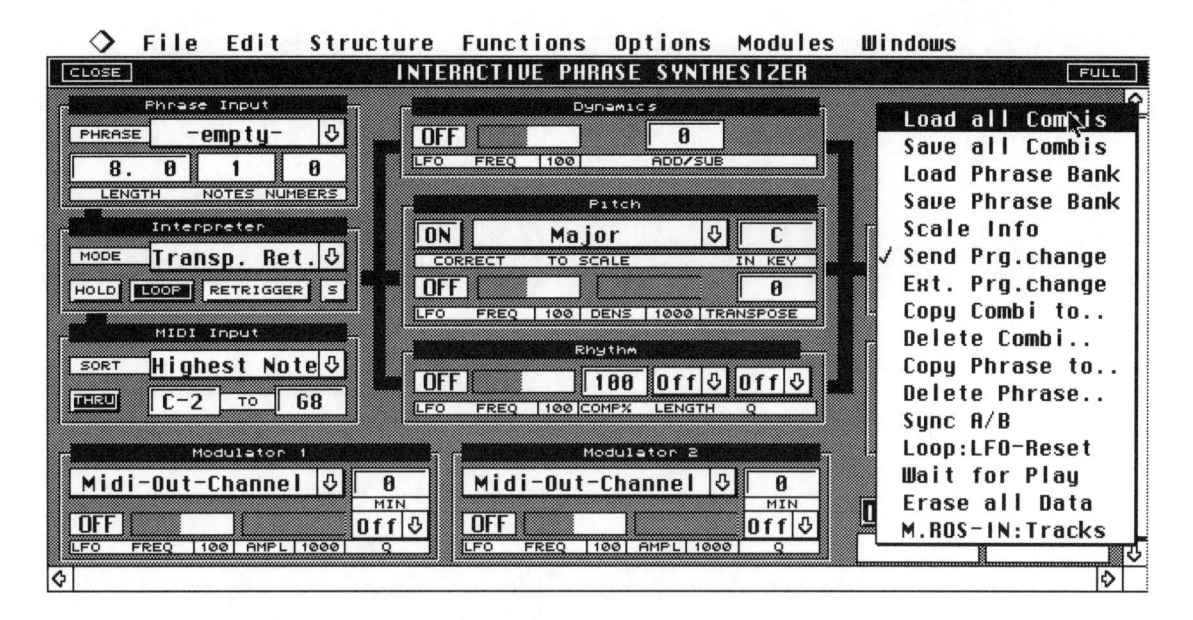

The Functions menu

- Load/Save All Combis loads and saves Combis to and from disk.
- Load/Save Phrase Bank loads and saves individual phrases to and from disk.
- Scale Info displays data on the current scale in the Pitch module.
- Send Prg. Change allows you to send Program Change messages while calling up particular Combis.
- Ext Prg. Change: If this function is active, you can select a Combi via a MIDI Program Change message.
- Copy Combi copies a Combi to another slot.
- Delete Combi deletes a selected Combi.
- Copy Phrase to/Delete Phrase copies and deletes phrases.
- Sync A/B ensures IPS A and B run in sync.
- Loop: LFO Reset: The LFOs are retriggered in sync with the start of each phrase loop.
- Wait for Play: If this function is active, the IPS starts only when Cubase is run.
- Erase all Data: clears all slots.

18.2.10 Recording IPS data in Cubase Tracks

You are sure to want to record IPS data in Cubase. The procedure was described earlier in the chapter. You must assign the IPS output to M*ROS and put Cubase into Record. Cubase must be set to record from M*ROS as well. If you can't remember how to go about doing this, refer back to the beginning of this chapter.

19 M*ROS and Switcher

We've already mentioned M*ROS in several previous chapters, now we're going to examine it in detail. In fact, when working in Cubase you are constantly dealing with M*ROS. M*ROS controls all MIDI communication in your computer, and takes care of communications with external devices such the MIDEX and other hardware peripherals. It also provides an invisible MIDI connection in your computer through which various sections of Cubase and other MIDI programs communicate.

M*ROS is loaded automatically from floppy or hard disk when you run the program and operates continuously in the background. Without M*ROS, Cubase cannot run, so you should never delete the M*ROS directory on your program disk, and never remove an M*ROS file from it. If you are using a hard disk, ensure M*ROS and Cubase are located on the same level of the desktop.

19.1 The M*ROS operating system

19.1.1 The driver concept

M*ROS also takes charge of your computer's various interfaces. On the Atari, this includes not just the MIDI ports, but also the RS-232 interface and the ROM port. Without these, you could not communicate with hardware expanders such as MIDEX, SMP II, etc.

To make the most of such devices, M*ROS uses software drivers to adapt the program to the connected hardware. Steinberg supplies the following drivers: MIDEX, SMP 24, Time Lock, C-Lab Unitor, and drivers for a number of Fostex tape recorders. The first four hardware expanders are not only used for MIDI sync, but offer additional MIDI ports that you can use via Cubase. The Fostex drivers enable you to remote control the transport functions of tape machines.

Installing drivers
Before you can use one or more or the above devices, you have to inform Cubase of the presence of the newly installed hardware. This is dealt with by the drivers. The M*ROS directory on your program disk contains all the drivers. The installation operation is extremely simple, but it can't be done from within the program.
- Quit Cubase, having first saved everything you might need later.
- Insert a copy of your program disk and double-click the appropriate drive's icon to see the contents. Locate the folder labelled M*ROS.

M*ROS and Switcher

- Double-click the folder. As well as the actual M*ROS file, it contains the drivers discussed above. All you have to do now is rename the drivers you want to use.

Let's assume you want the MIDEX driver. Select the file by clicking it. Go to the File menu and select Show Info with the mouse. A new dialog box will appear showing various information on the selected file, including the file name.

- To install the driver, you must change this preset name.

- Remove the disk's write protection. Replace the .DR suffix with .DRV for driver. All you have to do is type [V] on your keyboard, then press [Return] or click OK. The driver is now installed. You can install any further drivers you may need in the same way. The procedure is exactly the same for hard disk owners.

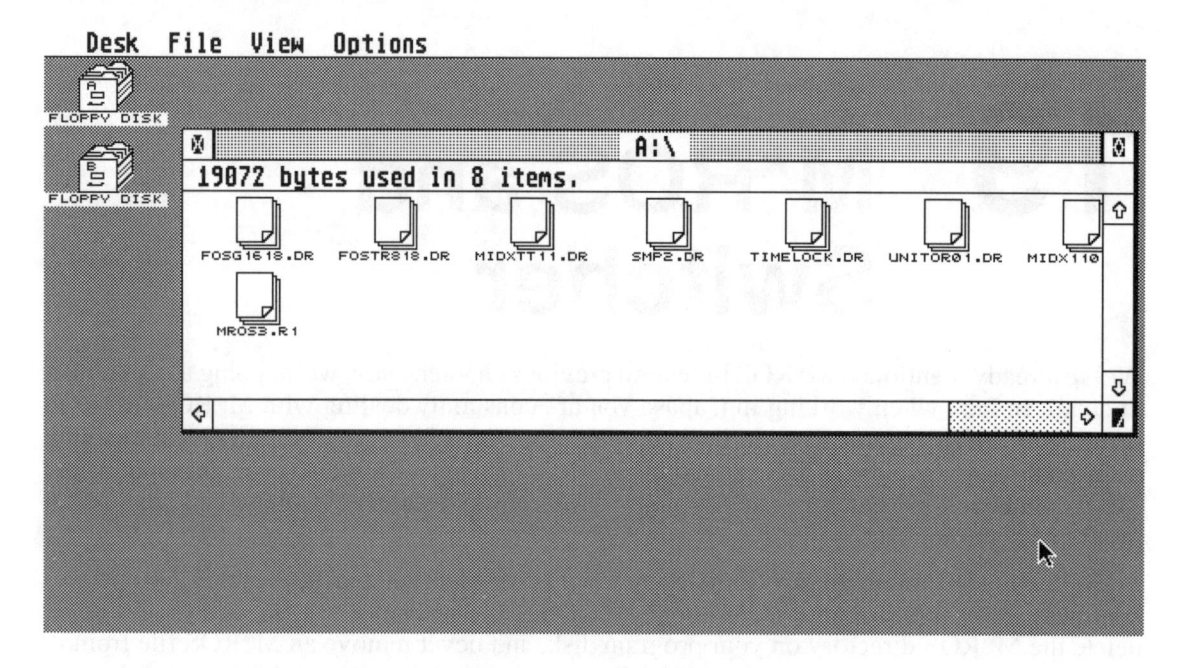

*The M*ROS drivers in the M*ROS directory*

The next time you run the program, the additional hardware options will be available for use, i.e. sync or additional MIDI ports. You can access the additional hardware from many points in the software:

Accessing additional hardware from the Arrange window

The M*ROS Operating System

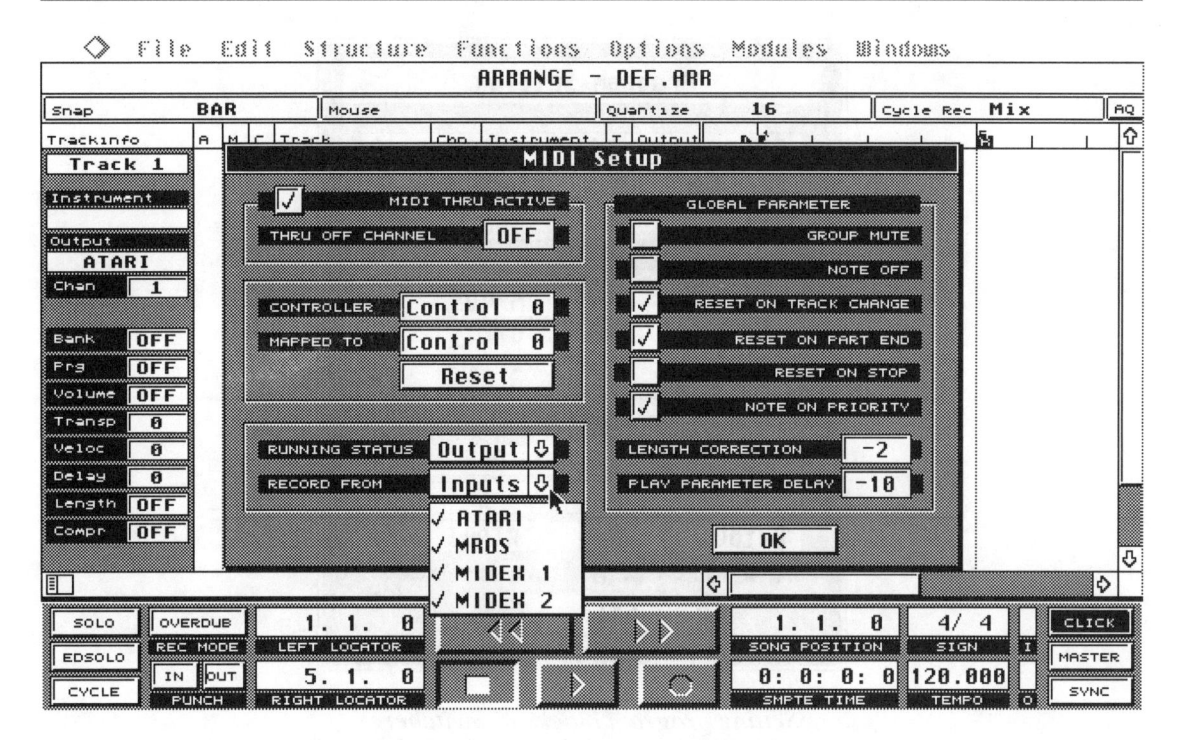

This applies to both inputs and outputs

M*ROS remains resident in memory, i.e. it is re-loaded only after you have switched the computer off completely and then re-booted the program. This may lead to some confusion. For example, when you run Cubase and then you leave the program at some point to install other drivers, the new device names don't seem to be present in the program. This is because of the way M*ROS works.

As long as an old version of M*ROS without the newly installed drivers remains in memory, no changes will be accepted. You will have to turn the computer off, wait a few moments before switching it back and then run Cubase. Now the drivers will be recognized and loaded.

You should be aware that simply pressing the reset switch at the rear of the computer to do this may not be enough in some circumstances. In earlier versions of Cubase, all driver installation was dealt with by a separate little program whose functions were self-explanatory. Evidently, this is no longer necessary as it is not supplied with Cubase Version 3.0.

19.1.2 M*ROS and more

Apart from the obvious exceptions (the MIDI Processor and IPS), you will have relatively little interaction with M*ROS while working in Cubase. However it will become much more useful when you are running several programs in memory at the same time and you want to exchange data between them.

To this end, Steinberg has developed Switcher. Switcher enables you to run several programs in memory simultaneously. As this book went into print, it was unclear whether Steinberg would continue to support Switcher from Version 3.0 onwards. Nevertheless, we should look briefly at its workings. Switcher divides the main memory of your computer into blocks of various sizes, which you can specify.

You can load a program into each of the blocks. Key commands are then used to switch between programs. You can, for instance, run Cubase and one or more editors at the same time. Editor data can then be transferred and recorded in Cubase via M*ROS.

357

M*ROS and Switcher

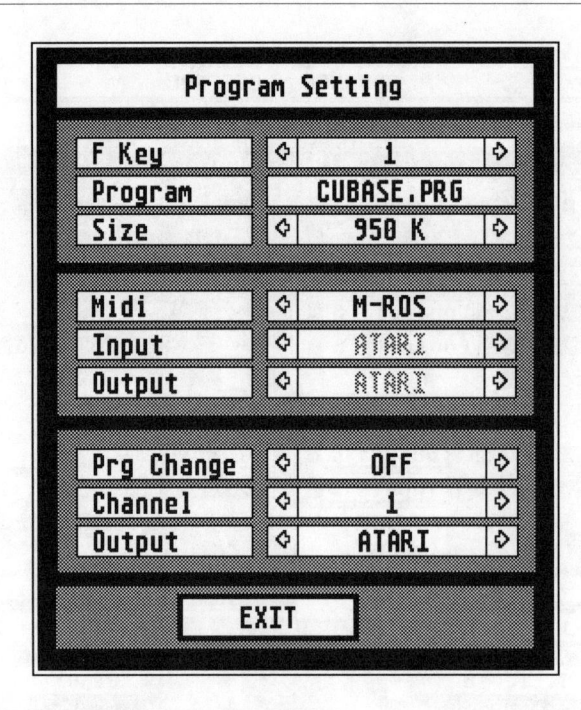

Setting program blocks in Switcher

This sounds good in theory, but in practice there are a few pitfalls. First of all, you need substantially more memory because the programs all have to be held in it at the same time. 1 MB of memory will simply not be enough, 2 MB is an absolute minimum, but 4 MB will give you plenty of room to work. So you would do well to think about memory expansion.

The next potential problem area is compatibility between the programs. M*ROS programs run best, but M*ROS is really only properly supported by Steinberg. Fortunately, Steinberg has a broad selection of editors available for you to choose from. By using M*ROS-compatible programs you can, for example, trigger a device via Cubase and edit its sounds simultaneously.

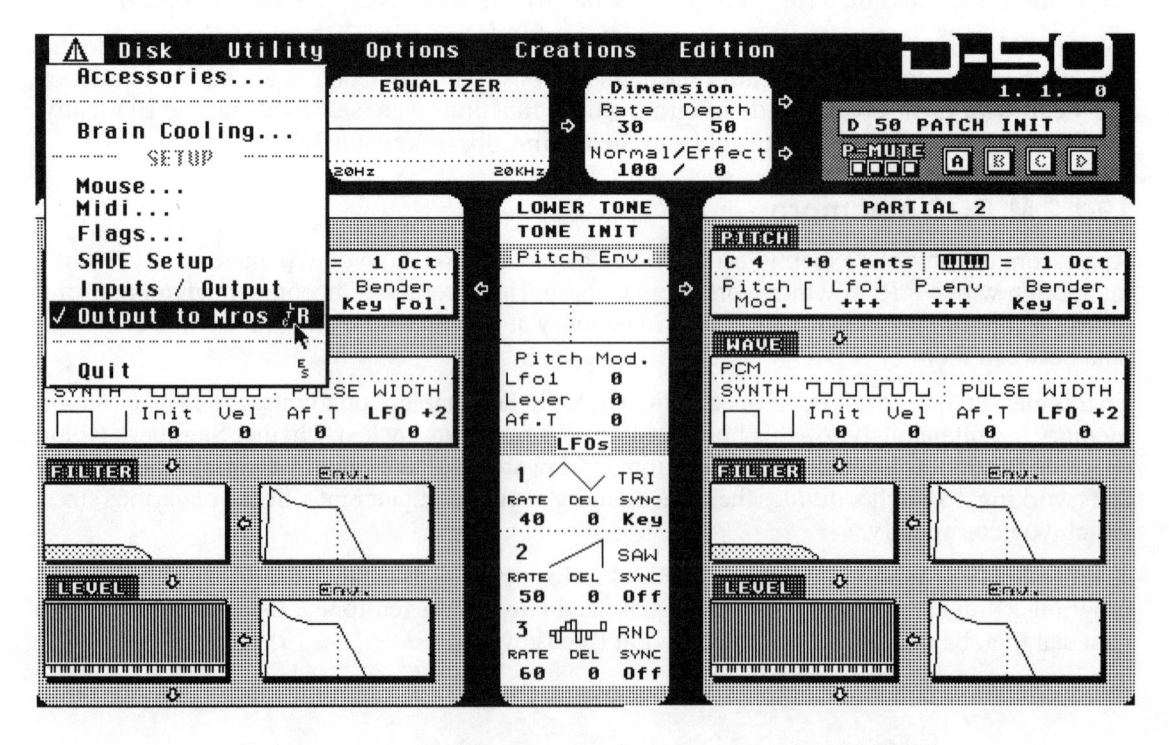

*You can transmit data from Synthworks editors via M*ROS*

The M*ROS Operating System

Programs that are not M*ROS compatible can also be run in conjunction with Cubase. However, it is difficult to generalise about which programs will work, and which ones won't. You have to find this out for yourself. Make sure you have backed up all important files so you won't lose anything if the system crashes.

Another M*ROS problem is RAM memory assignment. Each program must be assigned part of the available RAM, and you have to find out how much each program requires. Again experimentation is really the only way to discover this.

There is another problem which only additional hardware can solve: most programs are copy protected by a piece of hardware (key, dongle). Without these little devices, which are usually inserted in the Atari's ROM port, programs protected in this way will not run. Unfortunately, the Atari only has one ROM port. So the manufacturers came up with the idea of a ROM port expander which holds several dongles. The Steinberg MIDEX is one example of this sort of expander. This device can take up to four keys, offering several advantages even if you want to run several programs simultaneously. You can keep all program keys inserted and avoid all that tedious switching of keys every time you change programs. N.B. make sure you never insert a key in the ROM port while the computer is switched on.

When M*ROS programs access port expanders there is an extra advantage. The program automatically recognizes where the key is inserted, and switches to the correct slot. Non-M*ROS programs cannot do this. You will need to use the Cubase desk accessory program, Keyslot.ACC.

Switcher and accessory operation is explained in detail in the Cubase manual.

20 Cubase on the Macintosh

The Cubase Macintosh version is similar to the Atari version in most respects. This chapter covers the important differences. It is not this book's job to act as a introduction to all the Macintosh's capabilities. Consult the extremely informative Macintosh manuals for all the necessary operation information, especially that of the mouse and mouse button. However, we will touch on some of the Macintosh's important handling and internal design aspects that are not absolutely essential to Cubase operations in this chapter.

20.1 Hardware

Cubase runs on all Macs, starting with the Macintosh Plus through to the IIfx. The latter requires a minor software modification, which you easily carry out yourself.

In the case of different models, there are different requirements you should be aware of. You need at least 2 MB of RAM for the current version of Cubase. Virtually all the newer Macs come with 2 MB of memory and an internal hard disk. Unlike the memory size, the hard disk is not an absolute necessity, but it is definitely recommended for professional applications. Older Macintosh models (SE, Plus, and the early Classic versions) can be easily expanded with both. The additional memory is very inexpensive these days.

20.2 Available memory and the System

When you switch it on, the Macintosh loads various files and system directories to its memory. These include the Finder, the System file and fonts which are absolutely essential to operation, and small additional files containing accessory programs. The entire process is called "starting". After the start is complete, you will find yourself on the desktop (called the Finder on the Mac). It looks very similar to the Atari's.

The System Folder will either be on your hard disk (in which case you don't need to worry about it) or on your system floppy. If you do not have a hard disk, you always have to boot the computer with this disk, not the Cubase disk in the floppy drive.

If you don't have a great deal of memory, the boot procedure is particularly significant. All files loaded during boot-up use up RAM memory. If you find that you don't have enough memory available, you must ensure that only files you really need are loaded. Remove any unnecessary fonts, desk accessories, and Control Panels. The Apple Macintosh manual explains very clearly how to go about doing this.

Those of you whose Macs have 2 or more MB of RAM won't normally run into this problem, although using dozens of small accessory programs can demand a lot of memory. System Version 7.0 requires almost 2 MB for itself, not including room to run programs. If you use your Macintosh for uses other than music, e.g. to publish books, then keep your eye on memory-hungry accessories. Fonts in particular take up a lot of memory. Using an accessory like Master Juggler or Suitcase II will help you deal with this.

Always make sure that you are using the current operating system. The System version and the memory usage can easily be checked: go to the Apple menu at the far left of the menu bar in the Finder. Select the first entry which is "About Macintosh" in some versions and "About the Finder" in others.

The box which appears will list the Finder and System versions. It also tells you how much total memory you have, and how much of it is available. Below these entries, the amount of memory the finder and system files are using is listed, as well as the memory accessed by active programs. This information will be soon be of use.

20.3 For Macintosh IIfx Users only

The Macintosh IIfx interface has a minor compatibility problem whose source and effects we don't want to get into here. The important thing to know is that if you are using this computer, you have to carry out an additional operation.

On the Additionals disk you will find the "Macintosh IIfx" folder. In it, you will find the "Macintosh IIfx Serial Switch" program. It is imperative that you copy this file to your System Folder. The program will be loaded when you Restart the IIfx. The Control Panel will now contain additional settings that allow you to set the Macintosh IIfx hardware to a compatible operating mode. Do this and then restart the computer again. Cubase can now be run without problems. You do not need to repeat this procedure on future boot-ups.

20.4 Installation

After these introductory remarks, let's get on with the installation of Cubase. In contrast to the ST version, the copy protection of the Macintosh version is on the original disk. You can make as many copies as you want on hard disk and floppy, but these copies can be only be used in conjunction, with one exception.

20.4.1 Booting from floppy disk

Make a safety copy of the program disk. Insert this copy of the original disk and open its window. Run Cubase from the copy by double-clicking on the program icon. The disk will be ejected from the drive after a moment and the computer will ask you to insert the original disk. Set the write protection tab on the original disk and then insert it.

Once the disk has been verified as an original disk, it will be ejected and you will be asked to replace your copy. The load procedure will be completed. You can eject this disk, and insert the disk on which you want to save arrangements and songs. Refer to the Macintosh manual on disk operations. Pay close attention to the sections on formatting and disk ejection.

Although it is possible to run Cubase from floppy disk it is not to be recommended. There are hardly any Mac programs which run at an acceptable speed from floppy disk as the computer needs to access data on the program disk at frequent intervals. A hard disk is much faster in this respect. New Macintosh models are not available without one, so this advice only concerns owners of some older Mac SE, Plus, and Classics.

20.4.2 Booting from hard disk

An internal or external hard disk simplifies and speeds up Cubase operations. There are two ways to work:

Copy the Cubase program and all the additional files you need (Mixer Maps, Drum Maps, etc.) from floppy to a folder on the hard disk. Run Cubase by double-clicking on the program icon in this folder. To run, the original program disk must be present in the floppy drive so that Cubase knows you are a registered user, i.e. you own an original program disk. If you forget to insert the disk, Cubase will prompt you. Make sure the disk is write protected, and then insert it. Unfortunately, if you don't have the original disk available, you won't be able to run Cubase.

This procedure is rather tedious, so there is an installation routine for hard disks where the master disk does not need to be inserted. Let's work our way through this procedure. Follow these steps exactly to avoid potential complications.
- Deactivate all virus protection programs you may be using (e.g. Gate Keeper or SAM) for the duration of the procedure, if you use them.
- Create a new folder with a suitable name.
- Insert the original program disk and run Cubase from the floppy by double-clicking on the program icon. For once the disk should not be write-protected. The program will automatically see that your computer has a hard disk.
- A dialog box will appears after a while, containing the Installation menu.
- Click Install. The normal selection window will appear. Open the folder you have just created, which will of course be empty.
- Click Install, and the installation procedure will be completed automatically.
- Once the procedure is completed satisfactorily, Cubase will let you know. Confirm by pressing [Return]. You will now be back in the original dialog box. It tells you that you have used up one of two possible installations. You can only install the program one more time. This will be explained more fully in a moment.
- Exit the box by clicking Quit. Eject the disk, activate the write protection, and keep the disk in a safe place.
- Open the new folder on the hard disk directory and run Cubase by double-clicking it.
- On the Mac, you can move the program icon to the desktop so that you can access your principle programs directly after starting. Programs can also be automatically run on starting. Consult your Macintosh manuals for details.
- Once you have installed the program on the hard disk, the original disk is not required to run the program.

Let's look at this operation in detail to gain a better understanding of it. Cubase looks for a test routine each time the program is run. This is normally only available on the original program disk. This is why this disk must be inserted for the program to be run in the normal way. The installation routine transfers not only the necessary files but also the test routine to your hard disk so that working with a hard disk is as straightforward as possible. This test routine no longer needs to be found on the original floppy disk as it is now located on your hard disk, albeit invisible to the desktop.

The number of available hard disk installations is limited to two, so that the program cannot be installed on a limitless number of hard disks.

20.4.3 The Cubase Key

The copy protection that Steinberg use on the Mac has a distinct advantage over that used on the ST without tying you to a justifiable but burdensome hardware dongle.

However, software installation requires more caution. *Never* undertake any of the following actions without first executing the Remove operation described below.
- Formatting the hard disk.
- Deleting the Cubase program by dragging its icon to the trash basket.
- Using a hard disk defragmentation program such as Disk Express or Speed Disk.

- Changing the invisible "Cubase Key" file as it contains vital information. You can use certain programs, e.g. ResEdit, to make the file visible. Under no circumstances should you make any changes to it.

If you carry out any of the above actions without first following the Remove procedure, the same thing will happen: all Cubase installations on the hard disk will be irretrievably lost. You will have to reinstall the program from the original disk. If you've used up both hard disk installs, you will not be able to install the program again.

20.4.4 Remove

Use the following procedure to remove a Cubase installation from the hard disk. Remove the write protection from your original disk and insert it in the drive. Run Cubase *from the floppy disk* by double-clicking.

Click Remove in the dialog box that will appear. The normal selection window will appear. Locate the Cubase file and double-click it to execute the Remove procedure. Exit the dialog box with Quit once the procedure is completed. You will be returned to the finder. Eject the disk. The Cubase installation has been removed from your hard disk, and placed back on the master disk. Use this disk and the procedure described above to re-install the program at a later date.

20.5 Cubase and the Finder (System 6.0.x)

Cubase works in conjunction with the standard Finder as well as under Multifinder. You can only use one program at a time in the Finder. Cubase automatically makes use of the total amount of memory available. From within Cubase you can find out how much memory is available at any time. Go to the Apple menu and click "About Cubase". A dialog displays how many events, Parts and Groups are still free. The more events are available, the greater the amount of available memory in the Finder mode.

20.6 Cubase in the Multitasking mode

System Version 7.0 and up allow you to load several programs to the Mac's memory and switch between them. System Version 6.0.x enables you to do this via Multifinder. Macintosh multitasking is similar to the Atari ST Switcher mode. However, under the standard Macintosh operating system simultaneous use of several MIDI programs is not possible.

If you switch to another program in the Multifinder during recording or playback, Cubase will cease all activity. Apple developed the "MIDI Manager" to take care of this problem. The MIDI Manager is installed in the System Folder and thereby is automatically loaded at system startup. It not only enables you to switch to other programs while working in Cubase, but also offers other features as well. MIDI Manager's great disadvantage is its operating speed. It has to co-ordinate many MIDI operations in the Finder/Multifinder, to the detriment of the Mac's performance. Only use MIDI Manager if you have to use several MIDI programs on the one Mac.

MIDI Manager comes as part of the Cubase package. Simply copy it to the System Folder if you find you need it.

20.7 Memory requirements

In the Version 7.0 Finder and the Version 6 Multifinder, programs are allocated a fixed amount of memory from the software house. In Cubase's case, this is more than 1 MB. This means you can only start Cubase if there is enough RAM available. If you try to start the program despite the fact that the necessary memory is occupied by other applications, the Macintosh will make you aware of this.

This important function can also cause some confusion. The fixed memory assignment still holds even when more than enough memory is available for the program than Multifinder actually assigns.

For example: your Macintosh has a 4 MB RAM. You start Cubase in the Multifinder mode. Cubase uses 1.2 MB. You need approximately 800 KB (it may be more or less depending on the software) for your system files. That means a total of 2 MB has been used up. In principle, you could use the remaining 2 MB for Cubase applications, such as for more events.

In this case, you can change the memory allocations for yourself. Select the Cubase program symbol in its folder (making sure you don't double-click this time), and select the "Info" entry in the File menu ([Command key][I]) from the File menu. The Information dialog boxnow appears. In the bottom right corner, the memory assignments are displayed. You can change these by entering different values in the Application Memory Size field. Make sure you don't assign too much memory. 2 MB is sufficient for most applications. If you want to undo the changes at a later time, use the same method. Make sure that you do not assign less than the 1200 KB minimum.

20.8 Choosing an interface

If you are toying with the idea of using Cubase on a Mac, you need to choose a MIDI interface. The Macintosh does not come with one of these as standard, so additional hardware is required. Cubase works on any standard MIDI interface for the Mac. The MIDI interface is connected to the modem or printer port.

You can choose any of the numerous devices on the market, from the simple MIDI In/Out versions (Apple, J.L. Cooper, Anatek), to the mid-price options featuring several connections and additional sync options (J.L Cooper, Passport Transport), or sophisticated, upmarket devices which can take the place of entire MIDI patchbays (Mark of the Unicorn's "MIDI Time Piece"). Depending on individual features, you can address several MIDI busses, each with 16 channels via multiple ports, similar to the Atari ST/MIDEX/SMP 24 setup. MOTU's MIDI Time Piece can provide up to 128 channels.

Most interfaces allow you to continue to use the printer and modem via a switch or thru circuit. Refer to the respective interface's manual for the correct installation procedure.

20.9 Differences from the Atari ST

Compared to the Atari ST version, the Macintosh does not limit Cubase operations in any way; all musical examples throughout this book can be applied. The only differences are to be found in those examples based on additional hardware requirements. The additional MIDI outputs and hardware options discussed throughout the book do not apply to the Macintosh version. The decisive factor here is number and type of outputs your MIDI interface has. Use the options that apply to your setup.

One of the major differences is of course the fact that the Macintosh mouse has just one button. This means that all right mouse button operations are not possible with the Macintosh mouse, i.e. entering values, calling the Toolbox, positioning locators, etc. Cubase Macintosh uses key commands instead. Refer to the table in the appendix.

20.10 The Toolbox and value changes

The only really substantial differences are in Toolbox and value change operations. The Toolbox is an option in the Menu Bar. You can click to select any tool in the same way as in the Atari version. Cubase allows you to position the Toolbox anywhere on your screen so don't have to keep returning to the Menu Bar.

Click the Menu Bar and call the Toolbox while holding the mouse button down. Move the mouse pointer down while continuing to hold the mouse button down. As soon as your pointer leaves the Toolbox, its frame tears away from the Menu Bar. You can place the frame anywhere you want within the screen. As soon as you release the mouse button, the Toolbox is positioned at this spot and can be accessed there. Click the small square in the left upper corner to return the Toolbox to the Menu Bar. The Toolbox can be moved about the way you would a normal window.

Value changes are different from the ST in some areas of the program. You can enter the values directly with a double-click on the appropriate field. However, the missing right mouse button requires a different solution: click a value. It is surrounded by a dotted frame. Click the upper edge of the box to raise the values. A click on the lower edge decreases the values.

Those of you accustomed to the ST may find this difficult to deal with at first. There is a hardware solution. Other manufacturers offer mice with two buttons for the Macintosh (e.g. Logitech). You can define the functions for the additional button in any program using the desk accessory supplied with the mouse, thereby allowing you to use the right button on Cubase for the Macintosh.

A tip to close the chapter: there are a vast number of worthwhile desk accessories for the Mac. Detailed information on these can be found in the appropriate technical publications.

Appendix

Appendix 1: Computer tips

Most musicians are not what you might call computer buffs, so here are some tips and tricks, as well as lots of background information. Although there's no substitute for intensive computer training, the following information, which applies to the Atari ST and the Macintosh, is bound to be of some help here and there.

Hardware for the Atari ST

The Atari ST's operating system has undergone several improvements over the years. Many ST computers, especially the 1040 ST models, still have the older TOS 1.2 version. I highly recommend you consider installing the latest version of TOS, especially if you use a hard disk. Later versions speed up hard disk operations amongst other things, plus there's a new Item Selector dialog box which makes it easier to select drives. Another advantage is that floppy disks are written in a format similar to DOS, which means that 3.5" disks written by IBM and compatible PCs can be directly read by the ST, and vice versa, allowing you to exchange text and MIDI files with other PC users, provided the data itself is compatible.

Tip: if you decide to switch from the Atari to the Mac, you can transfer your Cubase songs without losing any data. Cubase Mac accepts all song files that were written on an ST and transferred using a terminal program or floppy disk.

Atari is planning for the future with its new generations of hardware. The 1040 ST and Mega ST model ranges are being added to or replaced by faster computers. The TT, which boasts a 32 MHz processor, has four times the clock pulse frequency of the ST. The 16 MHz Mega STE is twice as fast. These later computers benefit from much improved operating systems with enhanced ease of use.

Cubase, from version 3.0 on, runs on all Atari models although there are substantial differences in speed due to the various processors. Screen-refreshing is much faster on the Mega STE and TT, and this is most noticeable in the notation and page layout applications. The output of MIDI notes, on the other hand, is the same whatever the computer. Screen-refreshing on the more lowly ST's can be accelerated by the use of special drivers. These drivers (e.g. NVDI) are third-party software and are not factory-fitted - you'll find details in the specialist ST computer magazines.

Hardware for the Mac

Apple now offers a broad range of hardware. In principle, Cubase will run on all Macintosh computers: the higher the processor's frequency and performance specifications, the more fun

Appendix

you will have working with the program. A Classic or older Plus/SE model requires you to make some compromises in the ease of use department. From the Classic II, SE/30, LC/LC 30 models onwards, you can work on a professional level. The Mac IIsi, IIci, IIfx and Quadra models are state of the art machines. PowerBooks are the portable alternative, especially suitable for music on the move.

Bear in mind that the IIfx and Quadra's can pose some problems. The IIfx requires that you copy the "FX Serial Switch" Init that it comes with to the system folder. In the future, similar solutions will be available for the Quadra models to take care of the communications problems that arise at the moment. Cubase runs in System 7 without any problems.

Mac users must acquire a MIDI interface to establish communication between their computer and MIDI. Dozens of manufacturers offer suitable devices. Which of these you choose, from a simple device such as the Anatek Mac Interface, or ultra-sophisticated units such as Mark Of The Unicorn's MIDI Time Piece or Anatek's SMP 16, is entirely up to you. Many devices include SMPTE synchronization. One innovation is present in the Yamaha TG100, which has a built-in Mac MIDI interface.

The interfaces are hooked up to the printer or modem ports. Virtually all interfaces allow you to switch between printer/modem operations and the MIDI system, but check this all the same.

Increasing the memory

As we saw in chapter 19 and in chapter 16 when we discussed the Atari laser printer, some uses that you put your computer to require more memory than is provided by the standard models. 1 MB computers such as the 1040 ST or the Mega 1 ST should have their memories increased to at least 2 MB. This is relatively easily done for the older 1040 ST's, and very easily done for the 1040 STE's; all ST's and STE's have a RAM limitation of 4 MB. The cost depends on the current RAM prices. Talk to your computer dealer or have a look at the ads in the specialist magazines.

There are basically two types of upgrade. In later models like the STE's, RAM "SIMM" chips are simply plugged in; for earlier models, there's a bit more work which can involve soldering. It's probably a good idea to have it done professionally.

A RAM upgrade for Macintosh models is very simple. The Mac models are upgraded by plugging in SIMM chips. As a rule, the Mac requires more memory than the ST, especially when using System 7: this, if used with a few little additional programs, can use more than 2 MB of memory. If you intend to run more than one program at a time, such as Cubase and a word processor, you will need at least 4 MB.

Storage media for the Atari ST

If you regularly use Cubase and other programs, a hard disk is to be highly recommended. A hard disk is a sort of super floppy disk but which not only has a far greater storage capacity than its floppy cousin, its access times for loading and saving files are vastly quicker, too.

Hard disks start with a storage capacity of 20 MB (equivalent to approximately 28 3.5" floppies) and are manufactured by a huge number of companies including Atari. If you are buying a hard disk for your Atari, check that the drive has a "DMA" port, since this is what the Atari uses to interface with a hard drive. If the drive has a SCSI (Small Computer Systems Interface - referred to as "scuzzy") interface, you will need an additional "SCSI-to-DMA Converter" box that translates between the two systems. The Atari TT supports SCSI and DMA. Hard disk prices have been dropping for some time, apart from which, once you have worked with a hard disk, you'll never want to go back to floppies!

The hard disk is connected to your Atari's DMA port, and is usually a "stand-alone" device with its own case, power supply, etc. You can also get a hard disk built into your old Mega ST computer. The new Mega STE and TT models come factory-fitted with hard disks, or hard disk-ready.

You should save the contents of your hard disk onto floppy disks from time to time, as a backup.

This is a time-consuming, boring job even if you have the best backup software to do the job. However, as some hard disk owners will testify much to their chagrin, it's time well spent if anything should happen to the hard disk. You can also backup your hard disk contents using a "tape streamer", or another hard disk.

Once a hard disk is full, that's it: you have to delete data so you can carry on using it, or archive the files you use least onto floppies to make way for the fresh data. However, instead of using the fixed hard disks we've been discussing until now, the viable alternative is to use removable hard disk drives, where the disk comes in the form of a cartridge which can be removed from the drive; in all other respects, these devices are identical in performance to a fixed hard disk drive. The big advantage is that the storage capacity is unlimited, since all you have to do is swap cartridges and continue working. A cartridge usually has a 44 MB capacity, but now the 88 MB format is gaining ground. The new 88 MB drives can read 44 MB cartridges, but not write to them.

The thing to watch with fixed hard disks is that the read/write heads should be "parked" away from hard disk when the drive is being transported, or they could be damaged by physical shocks (a very expensive repair) or even damage the disk itself so that data becomes irretrievable. Many drives "auto-park" the heads when you switch them off, but many don't - these have to be user-parked using special commands. This is why many users prefer to leave their hard disk drives in a stationary location, and use floppies when on the move. However, the answer is to use a removable cartridge drive if you move around, since by removing the cartridge you are, by default, separating the hard disk from the heads.

Many professional users have switched over to using magneto-optical disks, where the disk, similar to a CD, is written to with a laser. It is relatively rugged as a medium, it comes in the form of a removable cartridge, and can contain large amounts of data (starting at 600 MB, though the new 128 MB standard is gaining popularity); on the downside, the drives are very expensive, and have slightly slower access times which can restrict the uses to which they are put.

What archiving medium you go for depends on what you do and what you need (and what you can afford!). If you work with lots of songs and programs in a studio, or you work with samples and sample editors, you will need a high-capacity hard disk drive or optical drive. If you use Cubase in your home studio and do not have to manage a massive data load, a smaller hard disk will do the job; either way, floppies are slow and inefficient by comparison.

Storage media for the Macintosh

The Macintosh operating system relies more heavily on external storage media than the Atari does. Although you can operate a Mac (up to System 6.07) without a hard disk, it becomes practically impossible to work without one. Apple no longer produces computers without hard disks. The smaller Apple models are a dream to operate, and the communication with external storage media is excellent.

The standard SCSI interface allows access to all the storage media discussed above. As well as the internal hard disk, up to six additional SCSI devices can be used at the same time. The SCSI protocol has to be handled correctly, and this is very well explained in the excellent Apple operating manuals.

Computers on stage

Computers are increasingly being used live. There are no inherent problems in so doing, but there are things you have to watch out for. Your computer was not designed with this type of application in mind, and many people consider computers to be too fragile for stage use. If you go ahead, provide the computer with a safe, padded location, carry it around yourself (don't leave it to the crew!) and always backup all data in triplicate! Be especially careful if your computer has a built-in hard disk and isolate it from hard knocks and mechanical shocks.

If you regularly use a computer on stage, you can have it dismantled and reassembled in a rugged

Appendix

rack-mounting assembly. If you think you cannot afford it, can you afford the possibility of computer crashes or damaged hard disks?

Voltage stabilizers/mains filters are highly recommended as they help keep the current constant. This reduces the risk of hardware damage and computer crashes during gigs.

The mouse

If your mouse starts to act up, don't take it to the vet. The problem may be a simple one. The mouse's underbelly features a roller ball that relays the mouse movements to your computer. Dust is forced into the mouse's housing as the ball turns, causing the mouse pointer to behave unpredictably: it becomes difficult to manipulate, or may not respond at all.

To clean the mouse, remove the cover that keeps the ball from falling out. Remove the ball. You can now see two or three rollers that are probably filthy. Remove the muck by carefully scratching it off with a match stick (don't use anything metal!), then reassemble the mouse. Some mice can be dismantled which gives improved access to the dusty components.

The other potential problem area with mice are the switches which become worn out: no need to replace the mouse - you can get replacement micro-switches that give the mouse a new lease of life.

Even with meticulous care, your mouse will eventually succumb to wear and tear. If it is on its last legs, you have to get a new one. There are all kinds of mice on the market. Third-party replacement mice for the Atari are almost always better than the original one. As for the Mac, it is rare for the mouse to need replacing, but you might consider a mouse that offers two or three buttons that are programmable.

A tracker ball is an alternative to the mouse. It looks like an upside down mouse, where you directly manipulate the (much larger) ball with your hand. Its big advantage is that it takes up almost no space as the whole thing remains stationary. You could even place the tracker ball on your master keyboard. Users who switch over to tracker balls never go back to using a mouse.

Fan noise

Many devices (e.g. Mega ST, Megafile, SLM 804) have fans that seem to be left-overs from a vacuum cleaner assembly line, judging by the noise they produce. In many cases, you can get replacement fan assemblies or have the device modified to run more quietly. The Atari SLM 804 laser printer poses a more difficult problem. If you turn it off when you don't need it and yet it remains connected to the computer, it blocks your entire system and corrupts data you save to disk. If you leave it disconnected until you need it, you have to power down your whole system, hook it up, then boot the system again - more troublesome than it's worth. There are two ways around this:
- Switch the laser printer on when working with Cubase and open the rear panel. The SLM 804 is then in standby mode, and the fan is off. Simply close the panel when you want to print, and after a few seconds, the printer is fully operational.
- The second solution is a small hardware buffer device. It is installed between the DMA port and the printer, allowing you to operate your computer when the printer is switched off.

Some of the Apple models are also rather noisy. Talk to your dealer about customizing kits that reduce the noise problem.

Large-screen monitors

Cubase is capable of displaying several editors and Arrange windows on your screen at the same time. This feature is very practical, but you can easily run out of space, and your screen will look rather cluttered. A large-screen monitor is the solution. It has approximately four times the display surface of your Atari monitor and allows the editors and Arrange windows to be freely positioned on the screen.

There are numerous monitors available on the market for the Mega ST models. Some are better than others. They come with a video card that you plug into the computer that drives the monitor. Additionally, the Atari requires a software driver, which Steinberg includes in the Cubase package. Consult the READ ME file on the program disk.

Apple owners can rejoice, in that the Mac supports large screens. Here, the video card is installed in the NuBus or PDS slot and should be done by a specialist. The size and quality of the screen depend on your willingness to part with cash.

Useful software

Apart from the "main" programs, i.e. sequencers, editors and word processing, which we won't go into here, there are all sorts of additional small programs for your computer. Even if you are not a computer freak, and have no intention of becoming one, you should still consider getting the following for the Atari:

A good, fast disk-copying program to make backup floppy disks. These make sense if you do a fair amount of copying of your files for backup purposes, and are available either commercially or as Public Domain software.

A replacement Item Selector program, or replacement Desktop program. These are designed to start automatically when you switch the computer on and allow you to do all sorts of clever things which the standard desktop doesn't.

As for the Mac, there are so many useful utilities that it's difficult to single any one out. Your shopping list should include the Norton Utilities program that allows lost data to be retrieved.

Danger! Virus on the rampage!

Let's close on an unpleasant subject: computer viruses. These are little programs, written by clowns who think they're clever, that interfere with normal computer operations, and can cause system crashes and data loss. A virus is designed to duplicate itself. Under certain circumstances, it can transfer itself from an "infected" floppy disk to your computer's RAM, and from there onto others floppies or even onto your hard disk. Unless you have a special program that looks for viruses as you put a floppy in the drive, the virus will replicate itself unnoticed; it's only later that weird things can start to happen to your screen or data. Some viruses are supposed to do "funny" things to your computer, like make the mouse move back-to-front; you may chuckle at the joke now, but as soon as you discover corrupted data on your floppy disks and hard disk, your laughter will soon turn to anger.

There are precautions that help you avoid viruses altogether. Whatever your computer:
- Get yourself a good virus detecting and deleting program and keep it up to date.
- Install an automatic virus detecting program that auto-checks any floppy you insert in the drive. Bear in mind that computer games and other programs have data that looks like a virus but isn't, so don't assume detection of a "virus" is proof that you have one. Check all floppies for viruses, even if they come from a reputable source. Manufacturers can make mistakes.
- Keep all your floppy disks write-protected (tab open): nothing can be written to a disk that is so protected.
- Check your entire stock of floppies every so often.
- Be extra vigilant when using a modem and importing data from bulletin boards, etc.
- On a positive note, viruses are totally deleted from memory when the computer is switched off, so if in doubt, switch off and start again with a floppy you know to be "clean".

Appendix

Appendix 2: Conversion tables

Program Change table

MIDI Program Changes offer 128 possible values, starting with zero.

Manufacturers have a tendency to ignore the straight forward 0, 1, 2, 3... way of counting program locations for their synthesizers and use whatever system one of their engineers dreamed up. The following conversion table covers the commonest systems and should help you find out what Program Change number you need to insert in Cubase to address the equivalent program location in the device.

The first column shows the 0 - 127 numbering system defined by the MIDI standard. Very few instruments actually use this system (the later Oberheim devices do, but only up to 99).

Column 2 shows the system used by a few manufacturers (Steinberg included), which starts with 1, not 0.

The third column is in octal, i.e. eight programs are defined as a bank, as used by the Roland D-50 and others.

The fourth column is also in octal, but the bank is defined by a letter rather than a number. The Kawai K1, for instance, features this system.

The final column also uses banks, but it has 16 programs per bank. The Kawai K4 and Yamaha SY77 use this method.

The complexity of the numbering system depends on the number of program locations available. Systems 3 and 4 are exclusively used for devices with up to 64 locations (up to 8-8 or H-8), although we have carried the counting on to the end so that our table is complete.

Some devices use different storage banks or external storage media (cards, cartridges), e.g. the Kawai K1 (I-i and external E-e) or the Roland D-50 (Internal/Card). You will also encounter the terms "Preset", "User", etc.

As a rule, if there are not more than 128 locations, they can be accessed using MIDI Program Change commands. This partially applies to accessing external cartridge sounds, too.

Internal "mapping" is often used in devices with more than 128 locations. For instance, if a device features 200 locations, all of which cannot be directly addressed via MIDI, then the 128 MIDI Program Change messages must be assigned to the internal sounds using a map. This configuration could look like this:

MIDI Program Change 1 selects the device's Program #45,

MIDI Program Change 45 selects the device's Program #35, etc.

Of course, this a compromise as you can't access all of the available sounds via MIDI.

Do not mistake the banks discussed above for the MIDI Bank Change commands discussed earlier in the book. This command efficiently solves the problem of addressing more than 128 memory locations, but at the time of writing it was supported by the Korg Wavestation only. Older devices cannot interpret this command, and therefore ignore it.

Program Change table

0	1	1-1	A-1	A-1	64	65	9-1	I-1	E-1
1	2	1-2	A-2	A-2	65	66	9-2	I-2	E-2
2	3	1-3	A-3	A-3	66	67	9-3	I-3	E-3
3	4	1-4	A-4	A-4	67	68	9-4	I-4	E-4
4	5	1-5	A-5	A-5	68	69	9-5	I-5	E-5
5	6	1-6	A-6	A-6	69	70	9-6	I-6	E-6
6	7	1-7	A-7	A-7	70	71	9-7	I-7	E-7
7	8	1-8	A-8	A-8	71	72	9-8	I-8	E-8
8	9	2-1	B-1	A-9	72	73	10-1	J-1	E-9
9	10	2-2	B-2	A-10	73	74	10-2	J-2	E-10
10	11	2-3	B-3	A-11	74	75	10-3	J-3	E-11
11	12	2-4	B-4	A-12	75	76	10-4	J-4	E-12
12	13	2-5	B-5	A-13	76	77	10-5	J-5	E-13
13	14	2-6	B-6	A-14	77	78	10-6	J-6	E-14
14	15	2-7	B-7	A-15	78	79	10-7	J-7	E-15
15	16	2-8	B-8	A-16	79	80	10-8	J-8	E-16
16	17	3-1	C-1	B-1	80	81	11-1	K-1	F-1
17	18	3-2	C-2	B-2	81	82	11-2	K-2	F-2
18	19	3-3	C-3	B-3	82	83	11-3	K-3	F-3
19	20	3-4	C-4	B-4	83	84	11-4	K-4	F-4
20	21	3-5	C-5	B-5	84	85	11-5	K-5	F-5
21	22	3-6	C-6	B-6	85	86	11-6	K-6	F-6
22	23	3-7	C-7	B-7	86	87	11-7	K-7	F-7
23	24	3-8	C-8	B-8	87	88	11-8	K-8	F-8
24	25	4-1	D-1	B-9	88	89	12-1	L-1	F-9
25	26	4-2	D-2	B-10	89	90	12-2	L-2	F-10
26	27	4-3	D-3	B-11	90	91	12-3	L-3	F-11
27	28	4-4	D-4	B-12	91	92	12-4	L-4	F-12
28	29	4-5	D-5	B-13	92	93	12-5	L-5	F-13
29	30	4-6	D-6	B-14	93	94	12-6	L-6	F-14
30	31	4-7	D-7	B-15	94	95	12-7	L-7	F-15
31	32	4-6	D-8	B-16	95	96	12-8	L-8	F-16
32	33	5-1	E-1	C-1	96	97	13-1	M-1	G-1
33	34	5-2	E-2	C-2	97	98	13-2	M-2	G-2
34	35	2-3	E-3	C-3	98	99	13-3	M-3	G-3
35	36	5-4	E-4	C-4	99	100	13-4	M-4	G-4
36	37	5-5	E-5	C-5	100	101	13-5	M-5	G-5
37	38	5-6	E-6	C-6	101	102	13-6	M-6	G-6
38	39	5-7	E-7	C-7	102	103	13-7	M-7	G-7
39	40	5-8	E-8	C-8	103	104	13-8	M-8	G-8
40	41	6-1	F-1	C-9	104	105	14-1	N-1	G-9
41	42	6-2	F-2	C-10	105	106	14-2	N-2	G-10
42	43	6-3	F-3	C-11	106	107	14-3	N-3	G-11
43	44	6-4	F-4	C-12	107	108	14-4	N-4	G-12
44	45	6-5	F-5	C-13	108	109	14-5	N-5	G-13
45	46	6-6	F-6	C-14	109	110	14-6	N-6	G-14
46	47	6-7	F-7	C-15	110	111	14-7	N-7	G-15
47	48	6-8	F-8	C-16	111	112	14-8	N-8	G-16
48	49	7-1	G-1	DD-1	112	113	15-1	O-1	HH-1
49	50	7-2	G-2	D-2	113	114	15-2	O-2	H-2
50	51	7-3	G-3	D-3	114	115	15-3	O-3	H-3
51	52	7-4	G-4	D-4	115	116	15-4	O-4	H-4
52	53	7-5	G-5	D-5	116	117	15-5	O-5	H-5
53	54	7-6	G-6	D-6	117	118	15-6	O-6	H-6
54	55	7-7	G-7	D-7	118	119	15-7	O-7	H-7
55	56	7-8	G-8	D-8	119	120	15-8	O-8	H-8
56	57	8-1	H-1	D-9	120	121	16-1	P-1	H-9
57	58	8-2	H-2	D-10	121	122	16-2	P-2	H-10
58	59	8-3	H-3	D-11	122	123	16-3	P-3	H-11
59	60	8-4	H-4	D-12	123	124	16-4	P-4	H-12
60	61	8-5	H-5	D-13	124	125	16-5	P-5	H-13
61	62	8-6	H-6	D-14	125	126	16-6	P-6	H-14
62	63	8-7	H-7	D-15	126	127	16-7	P-7	H-15
63	64	8-8	H-8	D-16	127	128	16-8	P-8	H-16

Appendix

Numbering formats

As some instruments' manuals refer first to one numbering format, then to another for certain tasks, such as creating your own MIDI Manager velocity editor, the following conversion table will be of help. It contains all the values available in the MIDI standard.

0	00	0000 0000	80	50	0101 0000	160	A0	1010 0000
1	01	0000 0001	81	51	0101 0001	161	A1	1010 0001
2	02	0000 0010	82	52	0101 0010	162	A2	1010 0010
3	03	0000 0011	83	53	0101 0011	163	A3	1010 0011
4	04	0000 0100	84	54	0101 0100	164	A4	1010 0100
5	05	0000 0101	85	55	0101 0101	165	A5	1010 0101
6	06	0000 0110	86	56	0101 0110	166	A6	1010 0110
7	07	0000 0111	87	57	0101 0111	167	A7	1010 0111
8	08	0000 1000	88	58	0101 1000	168	A8	1010 1000
9	09	0000 1001	89	59	0101 1001	169	A9	1010 1001
10	0A	0000 1010	90	5A	0101 1010	170	AA	1010 1010
11	0B	0000 1011	91	5B	0101 1011	171	AB	1010 1011
12	0C	0000 1100	92	5C	0101 1100	172	AC	1010 1100
13	0D	0000 1101	93	5D	0101 1101	173	AD	1010 1101
14	0E	0000 1110	94	5E	0101 1110	174	AE	1010 1110
15	0F	0000 1111	95	5F	0101 1111	175	AF	1010 1111
16	10	0001 0000	96	60	0110 0000	176	B0	1011 0000
17	11	0001 0001	97	61	0110 0001	177	B1	1011 0001
18	12	0001 0010	98	62	0110 0010	178	B2	1011 0010
19	13	0001 0011	99	63	0110 0011	179	B3	1011 0011
20	14	0001 0100	100	64	0110 0100	180	B4	1011 0100
21	15	0001 0101	101	65	0110 0101	181	B5	1011 0101
22	16	0001 0110	102	66	0110 0110	182	B6	1011 0110
23	17	0001 0111	103	67	0110 0111	183	B7	1011 0111
24	18	0001 1000	104	68	0110 1000	184	B8	1011 1000
25	19	0001 1001	105	69	0110 1001	185	B9	1011 1001
26	1A	0001 1010	106	6A	0110 1010	186	BA	1011 1010
27	1B	0001 1011	107	6B	0110 1011	187	BB	1011 1011
28	1C	0001 1100	108	6C	0110 1100	188	BC	1011 1100
29	1D	0001 1101	109	6D	0110 1101	189	BD	1011 1101
30	1E	0001 1110	110	6E	0110 1110	190	BE	1011 1110
31	1F	0001 1111	111	6F	0110 1111	191	BF	1011 1111
32	20	0010 0000	112	70	0111 0000	192	C0	1100 0000
33	21	0010 0001	113	71	0111 0001	193	C1	1100 0001
34	22	0010 0010	114	72	0111 0010	194	C2	1100 0010
35	23	0010 0011	115	73	0111 0011	195	C3	1100 0011
36	24	0010 0100	116	74	0111 0100	196	C4	1100 0100
37	25	0010 0101	117	75	0111 0101	197	C5	1100 0101
38	26	0010 0110	118	76	0111 0110	198	C6	1100 0110
39	27	0010 0111	119	77	0111 0111	199	C7	1100 0111
40	28	0010 1000	120	78	0111 1000	220	DC	1101 1100
41	29	0010 1001	121	79	0111 1001	221	DD	1101 1101
42	2A	0010 1010	122	7A	0111 1010	222	DE	1101 1110
43	2B	0010 1011	123	7B	0111 1011	223	DF	1101 1111
44	2C	0010 1100	124	7C	0111 1100	224	E0	1110 0000
45	2D	0010 1101	125	7D	0111 1101	225	E1	1110 0001
46	2E	0010 1110	126	7E	0111 1110	226	E2	1110 0010
47	2F	0010 1111	127	7F	0111 1111	227	E3	1110 0011
48	30	0011 0000	128	80	1000 0000	228	E4	1110 0100
49	31	0011 0001	129	81	1000 0001	229	E5	0110 0101
50	32	0011 0010	130	82	1000 0010	230	E6	1110 0110
51	33	0011 0011	131	83	1000 0011	231	E7	1110 0111
52	34	0011 0100	132	84	1000 0100	232	E8	1110 1000
53	35	0011 0101	133	85	1000 0101	233	E9	1110 1001
54	36	0011 0110	134	86	1000 0110	234	EA	1110 1010
55	37	0011 0111	135	87	1000 0111	235	EB	1110 1011
56	38	0011 1000	136	88	1000 1000	236	EC	1110 1100
57	39	0011 1001	137	89	1000 1001	237	ED	1110 1101
58	3A	0011 1010	138	8A	1000 1010	238	EE	1110 1110
59	3B	0011 1011	139	8B	1000 1011	239	EF	1110 1111
60	3C	0011 1100	140	8C	1000 1100	240	F0	1111 0000
61	3D	0011 1101	141	8D	1000 1101	241	F1	1111 0001
62	3E	0011 1110	142	8E	1000 1110	242	F2	1111 0010
63	3F	0011 1111	143	8F	1000 1111	243	F3	1111 0011
64	40	0100 0000	144	90	1001 0000	244	F4	1111 0100
65	41	0100 0001	145	91	1001 0001	245	F5	1111 0101
66	42	0100 0010	146	92	1001 0010	246	F6	1111 0110
67	43	0100 0011	147	93	1001 0011	247	F7	1111 0111
68	44	0100 0100	148	94	1001 0100	248	F8	1111 1000
69	45	0100 0101	149	95	1001 0101	249	F9	1111 1001
70	46	0100 0110	150	96	1001 0110	250	FA	1111 1010
71	47	0100 0111	151	97	1001 0111	251	FB	1111 1011
72	48	0100 1000	152	98	1001 1000	252	FC	1111 1100
73	49	0100 1001	153	99	1001 1001	253	FD	1111 1101
74	4A	0100 1010	154	9A	1001 1010	254	FE	1111 1110
75	4B	0100 1011	155	9B	1001 1011	255	FF	1111 1111
76	4C	0100 1100	156	9C	1001 1100			
77	4D	0100 1101	157	9D	1001 1101			
78	4E	0100 1110	158	9E	1001 1110			
79	4F	0100 1111	159	9F	1001 1111			

Appendix 3: The MIDI Data format

This section lists all the MIDI messages currently in the protocol, in the numeric order of their status bytes. All values are also expressed in hexadecimal.

1000 KKKK -> 1111 KKKK

KKKK is the variable for a channel.

$8n, 1000 KKK, Note Off

Two data bytes follow. This is a separate Note Off command with two additional data bytes that define the pitch and release velocity.

$9n, 1001 KKKK, Note On

Two data bytes follow.

$An, 1010 KKKK, Polyphonic Key Pressure (Aftertouch)

Two data bytes follow.

$Bn, 1011 KKKK, Control Change

Two data bytes follow.

Control Changes 123 - 127 form a special group known as Channel Mode Messages.

Control Change 122 -0- Local Control On, links the keyboard to the internal sound generator.

Control Change 122 -1- Local Control Off, severs this link.

Control Change 123 -0- All Notes Off, switches all notes off in most synthesizers.

The MIDI standard provides for four receive modes:

Mode 1 = Omni On/Poly

Mode 2 = Omni On/Mono

Mode 3 = Omni Off/Poly

Mode 4 = Omni Off/Mono

Control Changes 124 - 127 switch between these modes:

Control Change 124 -0- Omni Off, Omni Receive mode is switched off.

Control Change 125 -0- Omni On, Omni Receive mode is switched on.

Control Change 126 -1- Mono On, Mono Receive mode is switched on.

Control Change 127 -0- Poly On, Poly Receive mode is switched on.

Additional Channel Messages

$Cn, 1011 KKKK, Program Change

This status has just one data byte.

$Dn, 1101 KKKK, Channel Pressure (Aftertouch)

This status also has just one data byte.

$En, 1110 KKKK, Pitch Bend

The two data bytes can have a maximum resolution of 14 bits via the use of an LSB/MSB combination.

System Messages

Status 1111 is reserved for System Messages. The MIDI standard incorporates numerous

Appendix

commands that apply to all the components in a system. There's no need for channel addressing, so the status byte's final four bits, 1111 NNNN (NNNN being the variable that has become vacant), are used to define additional function addresses. However, should a MIDI channel or device number be required, it is often specially encoded in a longer message. There are three types of System Messages:

System Common: contain messages intended for all units in a system.

System Exclusive: used to communicate between devices of the same manufacturer on the highest level, e.g. to transfer sound or sample data.

System Realtime: used for synchronization in realtime applications.

Let's look at these in detail: 240, $F0, 1111 0000, System Exclusive

A System Exclusive message can be of any length. It is headed by this status, and ended by the status End Of Exclusive (EOX) (see below).

System Common Messages

System Common messages comprise additional status types:

241, $F1, 1111 0001, MIDI Time Code

This message is sent four times per frame. One data byte follows. The first three bits define the type of message, the other four contain counter data.

Status Type of message   Counter

F1   0NNN 0 - 7   ZZZZ 0 - 31

The status and data byte must be sent eight times in succession to form a complete MTC word. The data byte's first nibble goes up one value each time, the on-going 0 - 7 order being maintained each time.

F1 0Z, F1 1Z, F1 2Z, F1 3Z, F1 4Z, F1 5Z, F1 6Z, F1 7Z

The variable Z stands for a counter nibble. A complete pass has a length of two frames. The MTC device uses the 0 - 7 order to decide if it should be rewinding or fast forwarding. The message types are as follows:

0 = frame   counter LS nibble

1 = frame   counter MS nibble

2 = seconds counter LS nibble

3 = seconds counter MS nibble

4 = minutes counter LS nibble

5 = minutes counter MS nibble

6 = hours   counter LS nibble

7 = hours   counter MS nibble

The combination of an LS (least significant) and an MS (most significant) nibble provides 128 different values. The highest values are around 60 (hours, minutes). The remaining bits are reserved for future uses. The frame rate is lodged in the unused portion of the hours counter.

All messages must be read before a position can be precisely determined, which slows down rapid positioning. In this case, the "Full Message" can be sent in a single pass as a System Exclusive message with a specially reserved ID code. Complete data sentences with a high information content can be sent independently of the MTC rate. User bits can be sent via another separate System Exclusive format.

MTC contains all the SMPTE format's essential characteristics. SMPTE time data can be sent via MIDI. Unlike MIDI Clock, the MTC transfer rate does not depend on the tempo. Like SMPTE, MTC is an event-oriented code that greatly simplifies the listing of events in terms of absolute time. For example in post-pro dubbing where lists of cues are used, special events can be numbered (14 bit value) and then called by another device in a System Exclusive format. If it's an MTC event, this could be a sequence or any other message chain. Start and Stop markers for MTC events are possible as well as numerous other commands, e.g. Punch In/Out commands for MTC-controlled tape machines.

242, $F2, 1111 0010, Song Position Pointer

The two data bytes that follow form an LSB/MSB combination featuring 14 bit resolution (16.383 song positions). The 1/16th note intervals give a range of 1024 bars at a time signature of 4/4.

243, $F3, 1111 0011, Song Select

A data byte follows, allowing 128 songs to be addressed.

244, $F4, 1111 0100

Not defined.

245, $F5, 1111 0101

Not defined.

246, $F6, 1111 0110, Tune Request

No data byte follows. This message is accepted by some MIDI synthesizers with analog sound generation and automatically tunes the oscillators.

247, $F7, 1111 0111, End Of Exclusive

Ends a System Exclusive message.

MIDI Realtime Messages

248, $F8, 1111 1000, MIDI Clock

It is sent 24 times per 1/4 note. If no Start byte follows, the MIDI Clock information is ignored.

249, $F9, 1111 1001

Not defined.

250, $FA, 1111 1010, Start

Returns the position to the start of the song and starts playback.

251, $FB, 1111 1011, Continue

Restarts from the current position.

252, $FC, 1111 1100, Stop

Stops at the current position. Remains valid even if MIDI clocks continue to be sent.

253, $FD, 1111 1101

Not defined.

254 $FE, 1111 1110, Active Sensing

This message is sent every 300 milliseconds. If it is no longer sent, the receiving device assumes that communication has been severed. If it is in the middle of playing a note, the device will switch it off. Active Sensing is not mandatory for data transfer. Only if a device recognizes and starts to receive Active Sensing will it expect to continue receiving it at regular intervals.

255, $FF, 1111 1111, System Reset

This status reinitialises the entire system in some devices.

Appendix

Appendix 4: Keyboard commands

The following lists all of Cubase's keyboard commands. The Mac version usually uses the [Command] key instead of [Control].

The numeric keypad

Transport functions

[*]	begin recording
[Enter]	begin/continue playback
[0] or spacebar	1st time: stop
	2nd time: go to the left locator/position 1.1.0
	3rd time: go to position 1.1.0
[(]	rewind
[)]	fast forward
[1]	go to left locator
[2]	go to right locator
[Shift][1]	saves song position as left locator
[Shift][2]	saves song position as right locator
[3] - [8]	go to cue points 3 - 8
[Shift][3] - [8]	saves song position as cue points 3 - 8
[9]	go to the last stop position
[/]	Cycle function on/offTheAlphanumeric keypad

The alphanumeric keypad

In all windows

[Control][0]	open file (select file type via [1] to [7])
[Control][S]	save file (select file type via [1] to [7])
[Control][W]	close active window
[Control][Q]	quit program
[G]	raise horizontal zoom factor
[H]	lower horizontal zoom factor
[Shift][G]	raise vertical zoom factor
[Shift][H]	lower vertical zoom factor
[Undo]	reverse last function
[Control][X]	cut
[Control][C]	copy
[Control][V]	paste
[Delete]	delete all selected events/Parts/objects etc.
[Backspace]	delete all selected events/Parts/objects etc.
[Control][A]	select all
[Control][G]	open List Editor
[Control][D]	open Drum Editor
[Control][E]	open Editor of selected Track's Track Class
[Control][R]	open Score Editor
[Control][F]	open MIDI Mixer
[Control][L]	open Logical Editor
[Control][B]	open Notepad
[Q]	execute Over Quantize
[U]	Undo Quantize
[W]	call Note On Quantize
[E]	execute Iterative Quantize
[Z]	Auto Quantize (Cycle mode) on/off

[Control][H]	call Transpose/Velocity dialog box
[F]	Follow Song on/off
[Y]	Remote on/off
[F1] - [10]	call locator combinations 1 - 10
[Shift][F1] - [10]	save locator combinations 1 - 10
[Alternate][F1] - [10]	call mutes 1 - 10
[Alternate][Shift]+	
[F1] - [10]	save mutes 1 - 10
[P]	select song position
[L]	set left locator
[R]	set right locator
[Alternate][P]	L & R locators to Part start/end
[D]	Record mode Overdub/Replace
[I]	Punch In on/off
[O]	Punch Out on/off
[C]	Click on/off
[M]	Master Track on/off
[S]	Solo on/off
[A]	Ed Solo on/off
[X]	Sync on/off
[1] - [7]	enter quantize value
[T]	activate triplets
[.]	activate dots
[Alternate][N]	change instrument name
[V]	delete last version (only in the Record Cycle mode)
[B]	delete sub-Track (only in the Record Cycle mode)
[N]	quantize last version (only in the Record Cycle mode)
[K]	Key Erase function (only in the Record Cycle mode)
[Return]	exit (in dialog boxes)
[Esc]	cancel (in dialog boxes)

In the Arrangement window

[Control][N]	open new Arrange window
[Control][I]	Part Info
[Control][M]	display Master Track
[Alternate][A]	switch Part appearance
[Alternate][J]	change Instrument name
[Alternate][N]	change Track name
[Control][T]	generate new Track
[Control][P]	generate new Part
[Control][K]	Repeat Part dialog box
[Control][J]	hide/unhide Group list
[Control][U]	enter selected Parts in Group
[Alternate][F]	freeze Play Parameters
[right arrow]	go to next Part
[left arrow]	go to previous Part
[upward arrow]	go to Track above
[downward arrow]	go to Track below

Parts and Tracks can be selected one after the other using [Shift].

In all Editors

[Return]	keep
[Esc]	cancel
[Insert]	insert event

Appendix

[Tab]	next event (Step Input)
[Alternate][O]	Edit Loop on/off
[Alternate][L]	set left loop limit
[Alternate][R]	set right loop limit
[Alternate][I]	Info Bar on/off
[Alternate][C]	Controller Display on/off

In the Key Editor

[right arrow]	go to next note
[left arrow]	go to previous note

Notes can be selected one after the other using [Shift].

In the List Editor

[right arrow]	go to next note
[left arrow]	go to previous note

Notes can be selected one after the other using [Shift].

In the Drum Editor

[right arrow]	go to next note
[left arrow]	go to previous note

Notes can be selected one after the other using [Shift].

[upward arrow]	go to next sound
[downward arrow]	go to previous sound
[Alternate][S]	solo
[Alternate][N]	change sound name

In the Score Editor

[right arrow]	go to next note
[left arrow]	go to previous note

Notes can be selected one after the other using [Shift].

[downward arrow]	go to previous staff
[upward arrow]	go to next staff
[Alternate][D]	print
[Alternate][B]	hide
[Alternate][E]	enharmonic shift
[Alternate][G]	group
[Alternate][X]	flip stem
[Alternate][1]	assign Voice 1
[Alternate][2]	assign Voice 2
[Alternate][3]	assign Voice 3
[Alternate][4]	assign Voice 4

In the MIDI Mixer

[downward arrow]	decrease selected value
[upward arrow]	increase selected value
[Control][I]	open Object dialog box

In the Interactive Phrase Synthesizer

[Alternate][H]	IPS on/off (in other windows too)
[Alternate][A]	switch between IPS A and B

Appendix 5: Index

About Macintosh 362
Accents 317
Accidentals 316
Activity display 37
Aftertouch 94, 65
All Events 150
All Notes Off 99
Analytic Quantize 288
Arrange window 31
Arrangements 76
Auto Clef 300
Auto Quantize 300
Auto Save 113
Autoload 121
Automatic quantization 53

Bank select 68, 89
Bar lines 320
Beep 40
Binary numbers 86
Bits 83
Bytes 83

Cable connections 21
Cancel 138
Channel pressure 165
Chase Events 91
Checkmarks 28
Checksum 235
Chord symbols 316, 319
Clean lengths 300
Clear Tempi 327
Clef 180, 297, 317
Clipboard 71, 151
Combis 352
Compass tool 153
Compression 68
Continue 36
Continuous Redraw 216
Control change 164
   continuous 95
   switch 95
Controller Display 137, 151
Controller Map 100
Controllers 92
Converting 24 Song 339
Converting Drum Maps 207
Converting formats 108
Copy 71
Copy Range 72, 327
Copy to phrase 344
Count-in 36, 39
Counters 214
Crescendi 317
Cubase Key 363
Cubase Lite 19
Cue points 48

Cueing 41
Cut 71
Cycle mode 52
Cycled Events 150
Cycled selected events 150

Data bytes 82
Data formats 86
Delay 69
Delete controller data 99
Delete Doubles 53, 271
Delete Last Version 54
Delete subtrack 54
Desktop 24
Diminuendi 317
Disks 20, 104
Display filter 167
Display note 306
Display quantizing 300
Display transpose 316
Dongle 19
Don't Quantize 285
Drivers 355
Drop-down menu 31
Drum Editor 193
Drum Map 193, 205, 306
Drum notation 305
Drum notes 309
Drum Track 193
Dump request 234
Dynamic module 351

Ear icon 141
Edit Loop 143
Edit Mode 312
Editors 135
Ed Solo 138
Enharmonic Shift 316
Entering values 35
Equal Spacing 323
Eraser 62, 145
Event list 163
Explode 186

Fader 215
File type
   Arrangement (.ARR) 107
   DEF.ARR 106
   Part (.PRT) 108
   Setup (.SET) 108
   Song (.ALL) 107
Fixed Length 3294
Flags 299
Follow Song 37
Frames 332
Freeze play parameter 69
Freeze Quantize 292

Functions Bar 33, 137

Get 24 song 339
Ghost Parts 69
Global Cut 71
Global Insert 71
Global Split 71
Glue tool 65
Goto submenu 139
Grid 168, 273
Groove Quantize 292
Group Track 72, 74
Guitar fretboard symbols 318
Guitarists 311

Hard disks 20
Head 307
Hexandecimal number system 88
Hide signatures 327
Hide Tempi 327
Hide Transport 38
Horizontal fader 225
Human Sync 338

Increase By Left Mouse 114
Info Bar 137, 200
Init display notes 309
INote 195
Input split 117
Input transformer 122
Insert signatures 326
Insert Tempo 326
Inspector 67, 89
Instrument 42
Interactive Phrase Synthesizer 344
Interface 365
Interpreter 348
Iterative Quantize 284

Keep 138
Keep note
Key 180, 297
Key Editor 135
Key erase 54
Key signature 317
Keyslot.ACC 359
Kicking notes 145
Knobs 215

Layer 118
Layout 312, 321
Legato 270
Length 69
Length Correction 85
Length Size 294
Link 231
List Editor 161
Loading files 103

Appendix

Local 214
Locators 45
  progamming 56
Logical Editor 237
Looped events 150
Loop selected events 150
LSB/MSB combination 92
LTC 332
Lyrics 318

M*ROS 342, 355, 357
M*ROS driver 267
Macintosh 19
Macintosh IIfx 362
Macintosh installation 362
Magnifying Glass 63, 145
Mask 171
Master fader 229
Master Track 325
Match Quantize 288
Memory requirement 364
Menu Bar 25, 31
Metronome 39
MIDEX 22, 97, 267
MIDEX+ 333
MIDI
  bank select 89
  channel Any 41
  channel pressure 94
  channels 42, 86
  clock 329
  commands 84
  communication 266
  controllers 92
  filter 99
  GM standard 91
  history 81
  In 27, 81
  Local control 21
  meaning 320
  modes 97
  Mixer 211
  Mixer events 167
  Out 27, 81
  poly key pressure 94
  processor 341
  program change 89
  protocol 82
  thru 23, 28, 81
  time code 336
  Midiclick 40
Mixdown 111
Mixer maps 220
Mix Track 211
Modulators 351
Modules 119, 175
Mono mode 97
Mouse Position Display 140
Mouse Speeder 114
MS-DOS 19

Multifinder 364
Multirecord 115
Muktitimbral 22
Musical range 83
Mute 41
Mute configurations 41
Mute events 167

Nibbles 88
No beams 300
No half triplets 300
No Overlap 299
No Part Name 300, 323
Notation 295
Note assignments 196
Note input 191
Note lengths 275
Note stems 317
Note On Quantize 284
Notepad 119

Objects 225
Offset 334
Omni mode 97
ONote 206
Over Quantize 37, 53, 281
Overdub 44

Page layout 295
Page Mode 312
Page size 315
Paint Brush 147
Part 34
  copy 57
  move 57
  selection 59
Part Appearance 63
Part Display 31
Part Info 70
Parts 51
  delete 60
  merge 60
  mute 64
  naming 51
  repeat 60
Paste 71
Pattern 55
Pencil 65, 145
Phrase Input 346
Phrase slots 345
Pitch bend 92, 165
Pitch Module 350
Play Parameter Delay 90
Poly mode 97
Poly key pressure 165
Polyphonic Voices 308
Polyphony 301, 302
Polyrhythms 338
Position Bar 31
Precount Active 39

Preferences 113
Preroll 46
Presets 123, 240, 263
Prima-Seconda Volta 317
Printer driver 314
Printer setup 314
Printing 323
Program change 68, 89, 165
Proportional 231
Punch In/Out
  automatic 45
  manual 45
Push button 225

Quantization function 37
Quantize Last Version 54
Quantizing 273
Quantize factor 278, 290

Real Book 323
Realtime Groups 79
Record button 35
Record mode 44
Record Tempo/mutes 42
Recording mutes 42
Reduce Controller Data 100
Remix 111
Remote control 118
Remote Controller 231
Replace 44
Reset on Stop 131
Resolution 47, 278, 336
Rests 304
Rhythm Module 351
Rhythm notation 310
ROM port 20
Rubber band 59
Running Status 98

Saving files 103
Scale 261
Scissors 62, 65
Score editor 175
Screen layout 179
Select All 296
Selected events 150
Show events 63
Single line drum staff 310
Slurs 317
SMP 24 22, 267
SMPTE 331
Snap 49
Snapshots 218
Software driver 333
Solo 41
Song position 36
Song Position Pointer 330
Song Position Triangle 36
Song title 321
Sounds 232

382

Index

Special events 166
Special symbols 317
Split point 188
Split systems 182
Spooling buttons 36
Staff settings 298
Staccato symbols 317
Standard MIDI Files 108
Start button 36
Static mixes 218
Status byte 82
Staves 180
Stems 304
Step input 148
Stop button 36
Stop events 167
Switcher 357
Symbol list 317
Sync formats 331
Synchronisation 116, 325, 328
Syncopation 300
SysEx data 232
Sys Ex header 101
System Exclusive data 100
System Exclusive events 165
System folder 361
System functions 43
System Version 7.0 362

Tempo 39, 317
Text 317
Text events 166
Thru Off channel 28
Ticks 47, 273
Tile Windows 78, 135
Timing 265
To Voice 305
Toolbox 61, 144, 169, 198
Track 40
Track Class 74, 193
Track Classes 132
Track column 43
Track Lock 337
Tracks 31
  copy 44
  delete 44
  move 44
Transport Bar 31
Transpose 68, 131

Undo 44, 242
Undo Quantize 281
Upbeats 322
Use Cross Hair Cursor 114

Velocity 68, 131
Version 2.01 19, 48
Version 3.0 19
VITC 332
Voice priority 270

Voices 270
Volume 68

Write 214
Write SMPTE 333
Write-protection 20

Zoom 313
Zooming 37

Appendix